# Literacy Development OF Students IN Urban Schools

## RESEARCH AND POLICY

**James Flood**
San Diego State University
San Diego, California, USA

**Patricia L. Anders**
University of Arizona
Tucson, Arizona, USA

**EDITORS**

INTERNATIONAL
**Reading Association**
800 BARKSDALE ROAD, PO BOX 8139
NEWARK, DE 19714-8139, USA
www.reading.org

**Managing Editor**   Shannon T. Fortner
**Permissions Editor**   Janet S. Parrack
**Acquisitions and Communications Coordinator**   Corinne M. Mooney
**Associate Editor**   Charlene M. Nichols
**Production Editor**   Amy Messick
**Books and Inventory Assistant**   Rebecca A. Zell
**Assistant Permissions Editor**   Tyanna L. Collins
**Production Department Manager**   Iona Muscella
**Supervisor, Electronic Publishing**   Anette Schütz
**Senior Electronic Publishing Specialist**   R. Lynn Harrison
**Electronic Publishing Specialist**   Lisa M. Kochel
**Proofreader**   Elizabeth C. Hunt

**Project Editor**   Shannon T. Fortner

**Cover**   Design, Linda Steere; Photographs (clockwise from top left): Image Productions, Skjold, Image Productions, Image Productions, Image Productions

Web addresses in this book were correct as of the publication date but may have become inactive or otherwise modified since that time. If you notice a deactivated or changed Web address, please e-mail books@reading.org with the words "Website Update" in the subject line. In your message, specify the Web link, the book title, and the page number on which the link appears.

**Library of Congress Cataloging-in-Publication Data**
Literacy development of students in urban schools : research and policy / James Flood, Patricia L. Anders, editors.
     p. cm.
Includes bibliographical references and indexes.
ISBN 0-87207-543-5
1. Literacy--United States. 2. Education, Urban--United States. 3. Poor children--Education--United States. I. Flood, James. II. Anders, Patricia L. III. International Reading Association.
LC151.L48214  2005
302.2'244--dc22
                                                                                    2004024968

# Contents

# Foreword

In the last 20 years there has been a significant increase in diversity in the United States, which is most apparent in many of our cities. The issues surrounding the teaching of reading become extremely complex when dealing with students who come from different cultural and linguistic backgrounds. With this rich diversity also comes a new set of issues to be addressed when teaching reading.

James Flood and Patricia Anders have taken a look at some of these very difficult issues concerning reading and diversity. They organized a conference in the spring of 2003 in San Diego, California, as part of the work of the International Reading Association's Urban Diversity Initiatives Commission. They invited scholars from around the United States to write about their concerns on the teaching of reading in urban disadvantaged settings, and they asked leaders in the field to write responses to the papers. What resulted is a wealth of information dealing with topics, facts, and figures that the reading community has not looked at in the past. Most books written about reading instruction deal with how to teach comprehension or phonics, for example. This book deals with who we are teaching and the ramifications for reading instruction.

The book includes topics such as the role of reading instruction in the overrepresentation of culturally and linguistically diverse students in special education in the United States. Another topic deals with poverty and student achievement, which illustrates the gap between the rich and poor. Another chapter focuses on bidialectical issues in literacy. In urban settings, school reform programs are often imposed on districts to help with their literacy problems. The constant change in curricula that teachers and students deal with is unsettling. School reform is a topic in one of the chapters. Another factor discussed is the effects of heath and social welfare on literacy development in urban schools as well as violence as a factor in the lives of urban youth and its effects on school achievement.

In addition to the many concerns, there are very positive discussions as well. One chapter discusses high performance in high-poverty schools, a second discusses what exemplary reading instruction looks like in elementary school, and a third addresses what exemplary reading instruction looks like in high school.

The important topic of teacher preparation and professional development also is presented in the book. How we prepare our teachers needs to be studied in great depth. The knowledge of different languages and cultures is a crucial part of teacher preparation today. Looking at who we teach must be a major emphasis.

The issues concerning the teaching of reading in diverse disadvantaged communities are important and difficult to deal with. This book is a must-read for anyone teaching in an urban setting or preparing teachers to teach reading in diverse communities. I applaud the editors for selecting the important topics for this volume and the authors for their excellent contributions.

*Lesley Mandel Morrow*
*Past President, International Reading Association*
*(2003–2004)*

# Preface

*James Flood and Patricia L. Anders*

I n spring 2002, the Urban Partnership Committee of the International Reading Association (IRA) Board of Directors, under the direction of Donna Ogle, chair and past president of the Association, was discussing plans for offering IRA-designed inservice programs for urban school districts. During the discussion, it became increasingly apparent that the research base for our proposal was sketchy. We each had slightly different notions of what would be an appropriate program of professional development. For this reason, Flood and Anders proposed collecting research syntheses to inform the professional development effort. After some discussion, it was agreed that such a collection would, indeed, contribute to the advancement of literacy instruction in urban districts. It was also agreed that the authors of the syntheses should convene to share their papers, and that respondents from the field of reading should discuss the syntheses in light of literacy development in urban schools. These papers and the responses to each of them became the 26 chapters of this book.

Members of the Urban Partnership Committee served as advisors for both the miniconference and the book. To plan for both we first selected three themes: (1) contexts for literacy development among students in urban schools; (2) issues related to students, teachers, and curricula; and (3) administrative and social systems. To address these themes, we realized that the expertise from researchers in addition to those knowledgeable about reading and writing would be needed. The point was that literacy development is not only the appropriate teaching of reading and writing, but is also complicated by matters of context such as poverty, violence, and health along with in-school concerns such as curricula, instruction, students, and teachers. The Urban Partnership Committee members then generated a list of possible researchers from whom chapters would be invited both to present at the miniconference and to publish in this volume. Flood and Anders contacted each of the nominated researchers, described the project, and invited each to contribute a paper synthesizing research related to a specific topic in his or her area of expertise. In turn, a knowledgeable reading expert was invited to read and respond to each research synthesis. This was thought to be a meaningful way to link the synthesis papers representing multiple perspectives to literacy instruction and programs. Each author and respondent was also asked to generate possible implications for policy at the local, state, or national level.

The authors of each paper completed a draft and agreed to meet for a miniconference at Hoover High School in San Diego, California, USA. Hoover High is an inner city school that partners with San Diego State University. The researchers met in a large classroom to present and discuss their papers. The miniconference was highly interactive. Each participant had a copy of each paper. Each author summarized the paper he or she had written, it was discussed, the respondent summarized his or her response, and discussion continued. After the conference, each author was invited to rewrite and resubmit his or her paper in light of the discussion. Shortly after the conference, each author's resubmission was submitted for this book.

We intend that this publication be a platform for continuing conversations to advance the work of educators and policymakers. There is not one overarching persuasive perspective among these authors; rather, diverse perspectives are presented from the best minds we could find to interpret and synthesize their knowledge base at this time.

The following chapters are organized into three sections, representing the themes around which the syntheses and responses were written. Each section is introduced by brief summaries of each chapter and a note about the author.

In this collection, the reader will find contradictions and redundancies. This is as it should be. The contradictions are points of departure for further studies. A contradiction—an anomaly—is where good research questions lie. Redundancies are also useful: Perhaps a convergence of ideas is emerging in those areas of redundancy. These contradictions and redundancies will provide sources of inquiry and will generate further research and thoughtfulness among urban educators.

Our reviewers were concerned that this collection might not be coherent. We agree, but we have a different perspective on the issue of coherence. This collection is incoherent in the way that an interesting dinner party or a stimulating discussion at a conference is incoherent. Knowledgeable, experienced, and caring scholars are sharing credible and well-informed ideas and perspectives. As editors, we choose to not impose a shape to these chapters, other than categorizing them; rather, we want to encourage conversation about complicated and unresolved issues, and suggest that each reader construct an understanding based on their purposes, experiences, and needs.

In retrospect and on reflection, we realize some additional topics could have been included. We wish we had thought to invite a chapter from each of the perspectives of administration, technology, materials development, and psychometrics. Alas, however, the dinner party is over, and this book is substantial and deserves to be shared.

We intend that the work of educators and policymakers will be informed and advanced by these thought-provoking chapters and that the important dialogue about educating all of our students in urban schools will continue. We look forward to your reactions and to the continued conversation that this book might invoke. IRA members are committed to playing a role in helping to make all the schools in the United States and world as good as they can be, and urban schools are a high priority.

## Acknowledgments

We thank each of the authors and respondents for their remarkable contributions to this volume and their contributions to the children, parents, teachers, and administrators who develop literacy in urban schools. We further acknowledge and appreciate Hoover High School, which hosted the miniconference. We would like to thank the International Reading Association, the National Urban Alliance, and the City Heights Educational Collaborative for their support during this project. We offer special thanks to Drs. Doug Fisher and Ian Pumpian and the staff of the City Heights Collaborative for inviting us to hold the conference in San Diego and for their tremendous support throughout the entire project. We also want to thank Dean Skip Meno of San Diego State University for encouraging us to undertake the project in San Diego, and University President Stephen Weber for hosting us at his home and for his support throughout this endeavor. Finally, we appreciate the support of the Executive Director of IRA, Alan Farstrup, and the staff members of the IRA Books and Production departments.

# Contributors

**Donna E. Alvermann**
Distinguished Research Professor
  of Language and Literacy
  Education
University of Georgia
Athens, Georgia, USA

**Patricia L. Anders**
Head and Professor, Department of
  Language, Reading and Culture
University of Arizona
Tucson, Arizona, USA

**Arnetha F. Ball**
Associate Professor of Curriculum
  Studies & Teacher Education
Stanford University
Stanford, California, USA

**Rita M. Bean**
Professor
University of Pittsburgh
Pittsburgh, Pennsylvania, USA

**Jack Campana**
Director of Student Services
City Heights Educational
  Collaborative
San Diego, California, USA

**Victoria Chou**
Dean and Professor, College
  of Education
University of Illinois at Chicago
Chicago, Illinois, USA

**Eric J. Cooper**
President
National Urban Alliance
  for Effective Education
Lake Success, New York, USA

**Joy G. Dryfoos**
Independent Researcher
  and Writer
Brookline, Massachusetts, USA

**Joyce L. Epstein**
Director, Center on School, Family,
  and Community Partnerships
Johns Hopkins University
Baltimore, Maryland, USA

**Douglas Fisher**
Director of Professional
  Development
City Heights Educational
  Collaborative
San Diego, California, USA

**James Flood**
Distinguished Research Professor
  of Education
San Diego State University
San Diego, California, USA

**Kris D. Gutiérrez**
Professor, Graduate School
  of Education & Information
  Studies
Center for the Study of Urban
  Literacies
University of California, Los
  Angeles
Los Angeles, California, USA

**Jane Hannaway**
Center Director and Principal
  Research Associate
Education Policy Center,
  The Urban Institute
Washington, DC, USA

**Yvette Jackson**
Executive Director
National Urban Alliance
Lake Success, New York, USA

**Charles Taylor Kerchner**
Hollis P. Allen Professor
  of Education
Claremont Graduate University
Claremont, California, USA

**Elizabeth B. Kozleski**
Associate Dean for Research
University of Colorado at Denver
Denver, Colorado, USA

**Diane Lapp**
Distinguished Research Professor
  of Education
San Diego State University
San Diego, California, USA

**Carol D. Lee**
Associate Professor of Education,
  Social Policy, and African
  American Studies
Northwestern University
Evanston, Illinois, USA

**Esther Mosak**
Assistant to the Dean, College
  of Education
University of Illinois at Chicago
Chicago, Illinois, USA

**Festus E. Obiakor**
Professor
University of Wisconsin–Milwaukee
Milwaukee, Wisconsin, USA

**Jennifer E. Obidah**
Associate Professor of Urban
  Schooling
University of California, Los
  Angeles
Los Angeles, California, USA

**Donna Ogle**
Professor
National-Louis University
Evanston, Illinois, USA

**Jeanne R. Paratore**
Associate Professor of Education
Boston University
Boston, Massachusetts, USA

**Mary Helen Pelton**
Director of Violence Prevention
MacNeil Environmental, Inc.
Burnsville, Minnesota, USA

**Timothy V. Rasinski**
Professor
Kent State University
Kent, Ohio, USA

**Douglas B. Reeves**
Chairman
Center for Performance Assessment
Swampscott, Massachusetts, USA

**Virginia Richardson**
Professor of Education
University of Michigan
Ann Arbor, Michigan, USA

**Victoria J. Risko**
Professor of Language, Literacy
  and Culture
Peabody College of Vanderbilt
  University
Nashville, Tennessee, USA

**Virginia Roach**
Assistant Professor of Educational
  Administration
George Washington University
Washington, DC, USA

**Cathy M. Roller**
Director of Research and Policy
International Reading Association
Washington, DC, USA

**Robert Rueda**
Professor
Rossier School of Education
University of Southern California
Los Angeles, California, USA

**Steven B. Sheldon**
Associate Research Scientist
Johns Hopkins University
Baltimore, Maryland, USA

**Cheryl A. Utley**
Associate Research Professor
Juniper Gardens Children's Project
University of Kansas
Kansas City, Kansas, USA

**Richard T. Vacca**
Professor Emeritus
Kent State University
Kent, Ohio, USA

**MaryEllen Vogt**
Professor
California State University, Long
    Beach
Long Beach, California, USA

**Doris Walker-Dalhouse**
Professor of Reading
Minnesota State University
    Moorhead
Moorhead, Minnesota, USA

# SECTION I

# The Human Contexts of Literacy Development in Urban Schools: Poverty, School Violence, and Health Concerns

Most educators have found themselves in conversations about low-achieving schools and heard comments about how difficult it is to educate children and youth who live in challenging circumstances, such as poverty, unsafe buildings, and unhealthy environments. Also, the news often broadcasts and prints sensational reports about violence and how schools in certain neighborhoods or parts of town are unsafe. These concerns led us to invite chapters on these topics. Indeed, if these circumstances do affect what educators are able to do, it is best to understand them as well as possible.

This section begins by taking on one of the most compelling concerns of urban education: poverty. In chapter 1, Jane Hannaway provides a synthesis of the relationship between poverty and school achievement. Rita M. Bean responds to this in chapter 2 by challenging some of Hannaway's assumptions but affirming others.

In chapter 3, Joy G. Dryfoos carefully outlines what we know about children's physical and mental health as related to literacy achievement. MaryEllen Vogt responds in chapter 4 by discussing critical features of programs for helping children in need.

In chapter 5, Douglas Fisher and his colleagues Jennifer E. Obidah, Mary Helen Pelton, and Jack Campana take on the challenge of analytically presenting the data related to school violence. Victoria Chou and Esther Mosak, in their response in chapter 6, discuss various programs that have helped to mitigate violence in districts across the United States.

Steven B. Sheldon and Joyce L. Epstein address the family and literacy development in chapter 7. Jeanne R. Paratore responds in chapter 8 with a description of her own research related to home–school connections.

These chapters provide a context for the chapters in subsequent sections. This broader context helps us to keep more immediate concerns of instruction, which follow in the next section, in perspective.

CHAPTER 1

# Poverty and Student Achievement: A Hopeful Review

*Jane Hannaway*

This chapter focuses on the relationship between poverty and factors associated with poverty and student academic achievement in urban areas. Researchers and practicing educators have long known of the strong link between family background characteristics, particularly family economic status, and the academic achievement of students. Systematic and strong empirical results along these lines are a major part of the body of social science research evidence in education at least since the Coleman Report (Coleman, 1966) more 35 years ago. So much of the news in this chapter is not really news. At the same time, there is increased concern about "closing the gap" in achievement between the haves and the have-nots. Urban school leaders identified "closing achievement gaps" as second only to "academic achievement" in terms of the 10 most important and pressing needs they face. In earlier years, they ranked it considerably lower (5 in 1999–2000; 9 in 1997–98; 7 in 1995–96) (Council of the Great City Schools, 2002).

This concern is driven by increased recognition that (1) cognitive skills are more important than ever for making it in the U.S. economy, and (2) the social fabric of our society is likely to be threatened if disparities widen, especially if they are racially and ethnically defined. So the purpose of this chapter is to try to take a fresh look at the topic to identify trends and consider the efficacy of possible solutions.

I begin by first providing some demographic data on urban areas that show the extent to which urban America is impacted by poverty and also the various dimensions of urban poverty that changed over the 1990s. We then present some student achievement data over a number of years that, on one hand, demonstrate the stubbornness of the achievement disparity problem and, on the other, suggest some of the factors that likely affect it—giving us possible insight into solutions. The next section draws selectively on the research literature to buttress three classes of explanation for the unequal education outcomes that are related to the social and economic status of students. Then we review both: "macro" solutions that focus on social and economic conditions and "micro" remedies that focus on education policies and practices.

## Who Goes to School in U.S. Cities?

The population characteristics of urban America differ in important ways from the characteristics of the country as a whole. As Figure 1.1 shows, the population of cities is more likely to be language minority, Hispanic, African American, and poor. Some of the differences are substantial. Indeed, about one quarter of urban residents are poor, and about one quarter are language minorities, compared to about 16%–17% nationally.

On some indicators, there was improvement over the decade of the 1990s. For example, the percentage of children from families with income below the poverty line went down even slightly more in urban areas than it did nationally. But other indicators, most notably increases in the percentage of the population who are language minorities, signal greater challenges for urban schools. Racially and ethnically, the white population propor-

## Figure 1.1
## Demographics: National Versus Urban, 2000

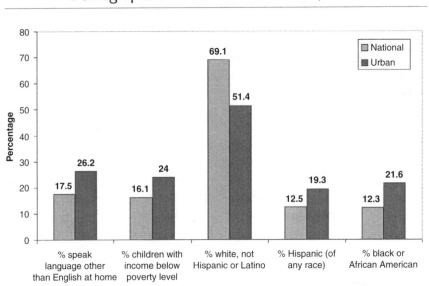

Source: 2000 Census, Summary File 3, Tables GCT-P6, GCT-P11, GCT-P14.

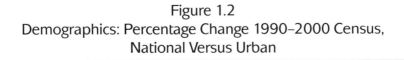

Figure 1.2
Demographics: Percentage Change 1990–2000 Census,
National Versus Urban

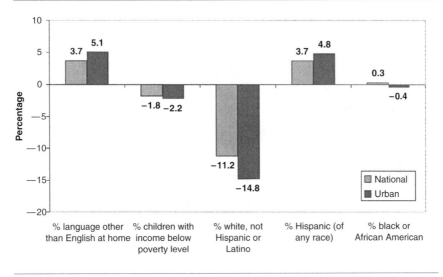

Source: 2000 Census, Summary File 3, Tables GCT-P6, GCT-P11, GCT-P14, & 1990 Census.

tionately shrank more in cities than it did nationally; the Hispanic population grew; and the African American population stayed about the same. (See Figure 1.2.)

The public school population in cities tends to be even more poor and minority than the city population generally. For example, students in districts represented by the Council of Great City Schools are more likely than students nationally to be nonwhite (76.8% vs. 37.9%), eligible for free lunch subsidy (62.3% vs. 37.5%), and English-language learners (18.1% vs. 8.8%) (Lewis, Ceperich, & Jepson, 2003) (see Figure 1.3.). (The Council of Great City Schools is a coalition of 60 of the largest urban school districts in the country; see www.cgcs.org.) Particularly relevant is the fact that urban students are more likely to attend schools with high concentrations of poor students. In fact, a full 40% of urban students attend high-poverty schools.

Not surprisingly, given the characteristics of urban students, they tend not to perform as well academically as other students in the United States. And while there have been times when the gap has widened and narrowed over the last decade, the general picture has been a discouraging one of a

## Figure 1.3
## Student Characteristics: Great City Schools Versus Nationally

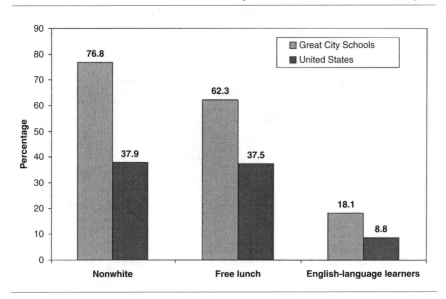

stubborn and large performance disparity. Indeed, compared to their sub-urban counterparts the difference is dramatic. NAEP results show that fourth graders in the suburbs are performing at the level of disadvantaged eighth graders in urban areas. Figure 1.4 shows performance over time by race or ethnicity; differences over time by metro status are unavailable be-cause of changes in definitions.

If we take a longer view, we see something more hopeful. Again we look at differences by race because the NAEP data do not allow us to go back be-yond 1992 with comparisons by metro status. These patterns provide a rea-sonable approximation of performance change in cities given the large concentration of minority students in urban areas. Little change in the black–white gap over the 1990s is again evident, but we also see a large nar-rowing of the gap in the earlier years—from 1971 to 1988 (see Figure 1.5).

Both the persistent gap in student performance and the steep reduction in the performance gap by race over the 1970s and 1980s beg the question of why? What is it about poverty that leads to poor academic performance? Do the explanations offer any insight into possible remedies?

Figure 1.4
Average Fourth-Grade Reading Scale Scores
By Race/Ethnicity, 1992–2000

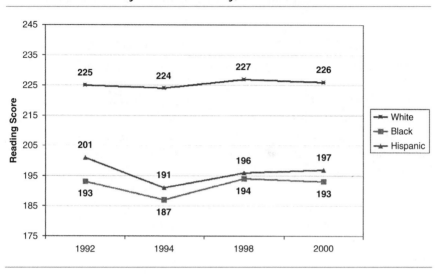

Figure 1.5
Average Score Differences, Black–White Students
Ages 9, 13, and 17

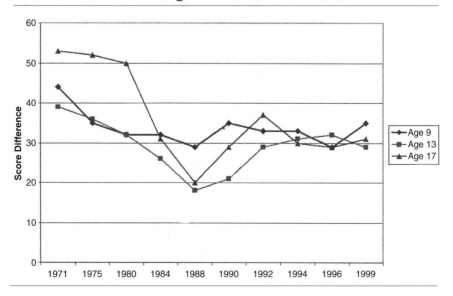

# How Does Poverty Affect Education Outcomes?

I discuss here three different ways in which poverty can affect the academic performance of students and provide supporting evidence for each of them.

## Direct Input of Parents and Families to Student Learning

One argument for the strong association between family background and student performance focuses on the learning that parents direct through their interaction with children at home. Reading with children, conversing with them, and directly teaching them skills all contribute to what students know and how they perform in school. Parents who themselves have more human capital—more education and greater skills—are able to convey more to their children than parents who have limited skills and unsuccessful school experiences. The situation is complicated further when parents are single heads of household—a situation more typical of low socioeconomic status (SES) and minority parents. Although only 15% of white children live with only one parent, 54% of black children and 27% of Hispanic children do so. A similar pattern is evident when we look at economic status. Only 10% of families in the highest income quartile are headed by one parent, but 48% of families in the lowest quintile are headed by a single parent (Lee & Burkam, 2002). There are two convincing bodies of literature that buttress the direct-input argument. The first focuses on the differences in skills that children from different backgrounds bring to formal schooling in kindergarten and first grade, which is discussed in this section. The second focuses on the educationally related experiences that children have outside of school during the school years, which is discussed in the next section. Data on what skills students bring to school in the early years suggest that schools serving lower SES students—and the students themselves—face an uphill battle from the start. Using the recent U.S. Department of Education's Early Childhood Longitudinal Study, Kindergarten Cohort (ECLS-K), Lee and Burkam (2002) found that before even entering kindergarten, the highest SES children had cognitive scores, on average, that were 60% above the scores of the lowest SES children on average. They also found racial differences with blacks scoring 21% lower than whites and Hispanics scoring 19% lower than whites.

Phillips, Crouse, and Ralph (1998) report similar findings with different data. They used the Prospects (1993) and NELS (1988) data and showed that at least one half of the black–white performance gap evident at the end of high school can be attributed to the gap that was evident at the beginning of first grade.

## Out-of-School Experiences

A second area that demonstrates with fairly convincing evidence the advantages that students from more well-to-do families have, apart from any differences in school quality, is their out-of-school experiences. This literature grew out of the observation that disadvantaged youth experience significant learning-loss during the summer months, in comparison to their better-off peers (e.g., Entwisle & Alexander, 1992; Heyns, 1978, 1987). A meta-analysis conducted by Cooper, Nye, Charlton, Lindsay, and Greathouse (1996) examined the effects of summer vacation on achievement test scores and found that summer learning-loss equaled at least one month of instruction. The impact of summer vacation was particularly costly for children from lower socioeconomic backgrounds. Indeed, on some measures middle-class students showed gains in reading achievement over the summer.

The analysis suggests that students' gender, ethnicity, and intelligence are not strongly related to summer learning-loss, but that a family's economic situation, interpreted in terms of the informal educational opportunities likely provided by families, influences how much children regress.

Doris Entwisle and Karl Alexander, Johns Hopkins University sociologists who have followed 800 Baltimore children over the past 20 years, have proposed a "faucet theory" to explain why all children, wealthy and poor, make gains during the academic year, yet the poorest students are those most likely to lose ground during the summer. When school is in session, the resource "faucet" is turned on for all children; during summer vacation, that school resource faucet is turned off (Entwisle, Alexander, & Olson, 2001). During these months, poor families are unable to compensate for the school's resources, so their children's achievement reaches a standstill or even declines. Middle-income families, by contrast, are able to make up for the staunched flow of resources. The authors reason that middle-class parents are more likely to take an active role in their children's learning process than poorer parents, whose own experiences with the educational system have led them to feel intimidated, threatened, or apathetic. In addition, higher family income allows for expenditures on computers, books, travel, camps, and games likely to promote learning during the summer break.

Whatever the explanation, the evidence is consistent and strong enough to suggest that we will be unable to get a good handle on sorting out the relative contributions of families, neighborhoods, and schools on student achievement without a good understanding of what happens to students outside of school and how different sources of learning interact to produce academic learning.

## In-School Experiences

Although the preceding explanation strongly indicates that what goes on out of school has a large and significant impact on student learning, we cannot ignore differences in what happens to students from different backgrounds in school. As we noted earlier, about one half of the performance disparity between blacks and whites can be attributed to what happens before formal schooling; the other half occurs after students have entered school. Here too, there is convincing evidence that schools have different yields in terms of learning for different students. Figure 1.6 shows the predicted gap in performance between a white and black student who entered first grade with the same math and reading skills, suggesting some significant fraction of the discrepancy is related to schooling differences.

A large literature identifies and examines school factors that promote unequal outcomes for students of different backgrounds. These include differences in teacher quality, resources, and support from parents. Next we discuss some of these factors and identify ways in which various interventions, about which we have some evidence, may affect student outcomes by either offsetting or counteracting some of the inequalities that students have at the starting gate or some of the inequalities they face in their schooling process.

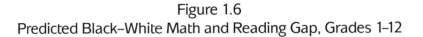

Figure 1.6
Predicted Black–White Math and Reading Gap, Grades 1–12

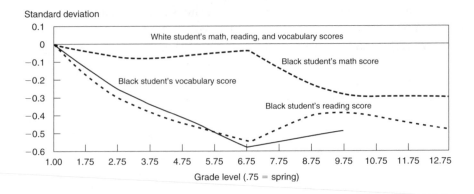

Source: Phillips (2000)

# Closing the Gap: How Can We Counteract Effects of Poverty?

## *Economic and Social Policies*

No doubt the most direct way to counteract disparities in student performance associated with poverty is to reduce poverty. Education practitioners and policymakers, of course, have little control over such conditions; and redistribution policies, in general, are highly contentious and difficult to put into effect. Probably even more difficult to affect in any reliable way is change in norms, values, and family practices. Still, we should not ignore these wider social forces when discussing educational issues. Children are simply better off in many ways when their families are better off.

Grissmer and colleagues (1998) argue that the gains in student achievement shown on the NAEP tests between 1970 and 1990 were substantially a consequence of changes in family factors—in particular, in parents' education and family size. For example, in 1970 only 7% of the parents of 15- to 18-year-olds had a college degree, compared to 16% in 1990. Large changes in family size were also evident. In 1970 about 48% of 15- to 18-year-olds lived in families with at most two children; in 1990, it was 73%. Because family income was unchanged (in real terms), family income per child increased dramatically. The increase in performance for minority students was particularly strong over this period, and change in social class and family structure explains some of the performance gain but leaves a substantial amount unexplained. While Grissmer attributes the unexplained gain to greater societal investments in education, social programs, and equal opportunity programs, other explanations have since emerged, as discussed here next. We turn now to a closer look at changes in the performance gap and specific consideration of education policies and programs.

## *Education Testing and Accountability Policies*

Education accountability policies based on student testing emerged during the 1990s and culminated in the No Child Left Behind (NCLB) legislation of 2001. Schools and school districts are held accountable for the performance of their students. But testing policies have a longer history. In the previous testing policy era of the 1970s and early 1980s, emphasis was placed on minimum competencies and basic skills. Students, rather than schools, tended to be held accountable. If minimum competency tests were not passed, students might not graduate. Such policies—those that focus on more basic skill levels—are likely to have their greatest effect on the bottom of the performance distribution. And analysts have suggested that these earlier policies may have been responsible for the gains by blacks in this period (Lee, 2002). Indeed, closer analysis of the improvement in the test scores of blacks relative to whites shows that it has been predominantly at the lower end of the performance distribution; the top of the distribution has remained unchanged for more than 30 years (Hedges & Nowell, 1999). A reason then suggested for the lack of improvement in the 1990s is the shift to greater concern about higher-order skills (Lee, 2002). In short, different curriculum and testing policies may differentially affect different subgroups of students. While this is hardly a conclusion that can be yet justified, there is additional evidence suggesting at least a related possibility.

It is widely recognized that the TAAS, the test used in the Texas accountability program until very recently, tended to focus on more basic skills. Here, too, on the state tests anyway, we see a narrowing of the gap in reading and math performance between whites and blacks and between whites and Hispanics (Hannaway & McKay, 2001). The increases for minorities were quite dramatic: The pass rate for blacks in reading went from 60% pass rate in 1994 to a 81% pass rate in 2000; the pass rate for Hispanics went from 65% to 81% in the same period. The increase for whites was much smaller (87% to 94%), but their initial rates suggest many whites were already "topping the test" (Hannaway & McKay, 2001).

The Texas performance gains also showed up in the NAEP tests. North Carolina and Texas, both states with annual testing of students as part of their accountability systems, posted the largest average increases in performance on seven assessments between 1990 and 1997 (Grissmer & Flanagan, 1998). The Grissmer and Flanagan analysis (1998) also shows that the scores of disadvantaged students in these two states improved more rapidly than those of advantaged students. So these findings suggest that accountability policies may have a disproportionate beneficial effect on schools serving low SES students. There are at least two reasons to expect this effect (Hannaway, 2003). First, more informal accountability systems (Abelman & Elmore, 1999) that work through parent monitoring may not be as effective in schools serving disadvantaged students as in schools serving middle-class parents. Second, teaching disadvantaged students is particularly challenging, partly because students do not come to school primed in the same way as middle-class children for classroom instruction. Under these circumstances, teachers might jump from strategy to strategy to find effective practices; an accountability system might lead to a more stable instructional focus.

Details of accountability systems can no doubt have different effects on different students. Conducting case studies to get a picture of how the Florida accountability system was affecting schools, we were surprised to learn of the great pressure felt by principals, teachers, and parents in the high-performing "A" schools. The possibility of losing their "A" status, which could occur with small shifts in performance, led these schools to narrow their curriculum, restrict field trips, and focus heavily on test-taking skills (Goldhaber & Hannaway, 2004). While the "tested" performance of these schools might have been maintained, the amount of real learning by students was no doubt curtailed.

The point here is that accountability systems may have real potential for helping to close the gap, but we have to get the details right, and we have to do it in a way that does not impose undue costs on some students.

## Early Childhood Programs

The findings reported in the preceding section showing that disadvantaged students begin school already significantly behind their middle-class counterparts are disturbing. The problem has long been recognized. Indeed, it led to the creation of Head Start nearly 40 years ago. And while nearly 1 million preschoolers from low-income homes are now served by Head Start, the participation of middle-class children in the pre-K program still exceeds the participation of disadvantaged students. (See Figure 1.7.)

Participation alone in early childhood programs, however, is probably insufficient to produce gains for disadvantaged students large enough to result in parity with their more advantaged counterparts. Recent research on kindergarten, for example, shows that reading gains during kindergarten are dependent on the amount of time available for formal instruction. School-level policies about, for example, half-day or full-day programs and the relative emphasis on academics and cultural enrichment activities appear to have a large effect on how much students learn (Borman, Brown, & Hewes, in press). Similarly, there is growing evidence of the significance of focused preschool language and literacy experiences for later reading success (e.g., Dickinson & Tabors, 2001; Smith & Dickinson, 1994; Snow, Burns, & Griffin, 1998). In short, a focus of the curriculum and instruction and the intensity of the effort appear to make a difference.

## School Resources

Much is made in the literature about lower SES schools performing worse because they have lower levels of resources. But when we examine the effect

## Figure 1.7
### Enrollment in Preprimary Education: Percentage of Children Age 3–5 Enrolled in Center-Based Early Childhood Care and Education Programs, By Poverty Level, 1991–2001

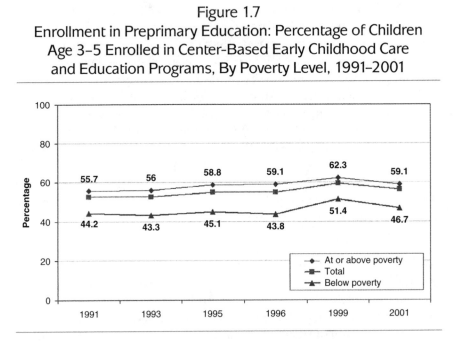

of increased financial resources on student achievement, the results are disappointing (e.g., Burtless, 1996; Hanushek, 1986a, 1986b, 1994a, 1994b, 1996). Although there is debate about this conclusion (Hedges, Laine, & Greenwald, 1994; Krueger, 1999; Ladd & Hansen, 1999), more money alone does not appear to be the easy solution; there is no simple relationship between level of resources expended and student performance. But, when we examine specific resource-related investments, we see more promising results. In the next sections we consider two of these: class size and teacher quality.

**Class Size.** In the last few years, class size has received a great deal of attention from both policymakers and researchers. A number of states have set limits on class size, especially in the early years. And the results of the Student/Teacher Achievement Ratio (STAR) experiment in Tennessee have provided us with important new findings and insights into the effects of reducing class size. Although there are still some technical concerns about the findings (e.g., Hanushek, 1999), a consensus is growing that lower class size promotes student achievement, at least in early grades and at least for disadvantaged students. (See special issue of *Educational Evaluation and Policy Analysis* [Grissmer, 1999]; Krueger, 1999.) So again we see an education policy that appears to have a disproportionately beneficial effect for the most disadvantaged students. In addition, and more important, the beneficial effects persist in higher grades even when class size in these grades is higher (Grissmer, 1999).

**Teacher Quality.** While there is considerable controversy surrounding the identification of characteristics and qualifications that indicate teacher quality, there is agreement that teachers are the most important in-school factor contributing to student achievement (Rivkin, Hanushek, & Kain, 1998). Standard indicators of quality suggest we are in trouble here, especially in the cities. The number of teachers with relatively low academic skills is high (Ballou & Podgursky, 1997; Gitomer, Latham, & Ziomek, 1999); a significant number of secondary teachers have neither a major nor minor in the subject they teach (Darling-Hammond, 1997; Ingersoll, 1999), and especially in urban areas and in schools serving high-poverty students, many teachers lack certification and exhibit other indicators that suggest lower quality (Loeb, 2000). For example, teachers in high-poverty schools tend to have graduated from colleges with lower selectivity than teachers in low-poverty schools (see Figure 1.8) and are also less likely to hold an advanced degree (see Figure 1.9).

## Figure 1.8
## College Selectivity of Teachers by School Poverty

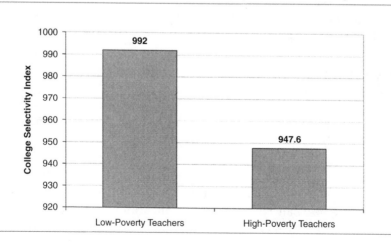

## Figure 1.9
## Percentage of Teachers Without Advanced Degrees
## by School Poverty

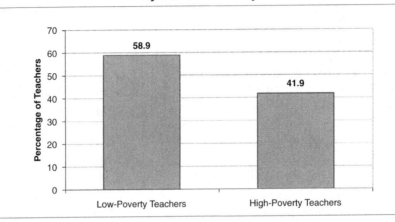

Comparisons of the 1993–1994 and 1999–2000 administrations of the Schools and Staffing Survey (SASS) suggest that the situation may be getting worse in a number of ways (Hannaway, Liu, & Nakib, 2003). For example, although the proportion of teachers without regular certification increased nationally as well as in high-poverty schools, the increase was significantly higher for high-poverty schools (see Figure 1.10). (In high-poverty schools, more than 25% of the students receive free or reduced-price lunch.) When we look just at newly hired teachers, supposedly the vanguard, the discrepancies are even greater (Hannaway et al., 2003).

There is also some hopeful news. Investment in professional development has gone up dramatically, especially in high-poverty schools, no doubt partly driven by requirements in Title I (Hannaway et al., 2003). And there is growing evidence that professional development, if aligned to standards and if intensive, can have significant effects on instructional practice (Balland & Rundquist, 1993; Cohen & Hill, 2001; Corcoran, Shields, & Zucker, 1998; Heaton & Lampert, 1993; McCarthy & Peterson, 1993; Shields, Marsh, & Adelman, 1997; Wiley & Yoon, 1995; Wilson, Miller, & Yerkes, 1993).

The current economy suggests both good news and bad news for the quality of the teaching workforce. On one hand, it is unlikely that teachers' salaries will increase, making it difficult to attract and hire better teachers. But this may be balanced out with less competition in hiring from other industries that are also facing severe financial constraints. And although

Figure 1.10
Percentage of Teachers Without Regular Certification
by School Poverty

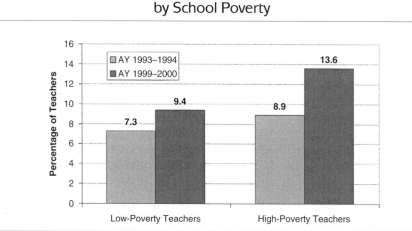

investment in professional development on student achievement is still uncertain, we are increasingly confident it can at least affect teacher behavior.

**After-School Programs.** The findings reported earlier of summer learning-loss point to the need for after-school and summer-school efforts for disadvantaged students to keep pace with their better-off peers. A number of school districts as well as the U.S. federal government have instituted such programs. For example, the Extended Learning Opportunities (ELO) Program, a four-week summer program implemented and evaluated by Montgomery County (Maryland), showed significant academic gains for students (Sunmonu et al., 2002). The U.S. Department of Education has funded 21st Century Learning Communities. Although these and related programs have face validity, we still have relatively little good evidence about their efficacy. The findings of small studies that have found beneficial results are generally not clear-cut, primarily because of selection bias (Jacob & Lefgren, 2002). Most programs are voluntary, and students who sign up for them are often students who are stronger academically, because of unobservable factors such as personal motivation or more motivated parents. Mathematica recently completed an experimental evaluation of 21st Century Learning Communities and found little effect (Dynarski, 2003). The authors, however, do not consider their results the last word. One weakness of the study is the absence of good measures of the "treatment" at the individual student level. That is, we do not know what students were doing while they were in the after-school programs. There is no reason to expect, for example, that students who spent their time simply hanging out with other students would improve their academic performance. And the study team observed large variations both across program sites and across individual students in the extent to which students were involved in academic work.

## Summary and Conclusions

This chapter has attempted to provide a succinct review of the literature on the relationship between poverty and factors associated with poverty, such as race, on student achievement. Although the evidence is strong and clear—performance disparities between students from disadvantaged families and better-off families are large and stubborn—recent research on ways to intervene provides some hope. Well-structured early-childhood education programs, accountability policies, and reductions in class size, for example, all show significant benefits for disadvantaged students that may help to close the performance gap. They appear to have a disproportionate beneficial effect on disadvantaged students. And while we might expect well-designed after-school programs also to have a disproportionate effect on disadvantaged students, the evidence is not yet clear. Improving education for disadvantaged students through hiring and retaining better-qualified teachers is likely to be difficult for a number of reasons beyond the control of education policymakers. But investments in professional development, if done well, may hold some promise.

### Acknowledgments

This chapter was originally prepared for the International Reading Association (IRA) miniconference, San Diego, California, April 10–11, 2003. The assistance of Helen Fu, Erika Germer, and Amy Pandjiris is gratefully acknowledged.

### REFERENCES

Abelman, C., & Elmore, R. (with Even, J., Kenyon, S., & Marshall, J.). (1999). *When accountability knocks, will anyone answer?* (CPRE Research Report Series, RR-42). Philadelphia: Consortium for Policy Research in Education, University of Pennsylvania.

Borman, G., Brown, S., & Hewes, G.M. (in press). Early reading skills and the social composition of schools. In S.M. Ross &

G.W. Bohrnstedt (Eds.), *Instruction and performance consequences of high-poverty schools: Analytic seminars.* Washington, DC: U.S. Department of Education.

Burtless, G. (1996). *Does money matter? The effect of school resources on student achievement and adult success.* Washington, DC: Brookings Institution.

Cohen, D.K., & Hill, H.C. (2001). *Learning policy: When state education reform works.* New Haven, CT: Yale University Press.

Coleman, J.S. (1966). *Equality of educational opportunity.* Washington, DC: U.S. Department of Health, Education, and Welfare, Office of Education.

Cooper, H., Nye, B., Charlton, K., Lindsay, J., & Greathouse, S. (1996). The effects of summer vacation on achievement test scores: A narrative and meta-analytic review. *Review of Educational Research, 66*, 227–268.

Corcoran, T.B., Shields, P.M., & Zucker, A.A. (1998). *The SSIs and professional development for teachers.* Menlo Park, CA: SRI International.

Darling-Hammond, L. (1997). *Doing what matters most: Investing in quality teaching.* New York: National Commission on Teaching and America's Future.

Entwisle, D.R., & Alexander, K.L. (1992). Summer setback: Race, poverty, school composition and mathematics achievement in the first two years of school. *American Educational Research Journal, 29*(2), 405–424.

Entwisle, D.R., Alexander, K.L., & Olson, L.S. (2001, Fall). Keep the faucet flowing: Summer learning and home environment. *American Educator, 25*(3), 10–15, 47.

Dickinson, D.K., & Tabors, P.O. (2001). *Beginning literacy with language: Young children learning at home and school.* Baltimore: Brookes.

Dynarski, M., Moore, M., Mullens, J., Gleason, P., James-Burdumy, S., Rosenberg, L., et al. (2003). *When schools stay open late: The national evaluation of the 21st century community learning centers program: First year findings.* Princeton, NJ: Mathematica Policy Research.

Gitomer, D.H., Latham, A.S., & Ziomek, R. (1999). *The academic quality of prospective teachers: The impact of admission and licensure testing.* Princeton, NJ: Educational Testing Service.

Goldhaber, D., & Hannaway, J. (April, 2004). Accountability with a kicker: Observations on Florida vouchers. *Phi Delta Kappan, 85*(8), 598–605.

Grissmer, D. (Ed.). (1999). Class size: Issues and new findings [Special issue]. *Educational Evaluation and Policy Analysis, 21*(2).

Grissmer, D., & Flanagan, A. (1998). *Exploring rapid achievement gains in North Carolina and Texas. Lessons from the states.* Report commissioned by the National Education Goals Panel (NEGP), Washington, DC. Retrieved October 12, 2004, from http://www.negp.gov/reports/grissmer.pdf

Hannaway, J. (2003). Accountability, assessment, and performance issues: We've come a long way...or have we? In W. Boyd & D. Miretzky (Eds.), *American educational governance on trial: Change and challenges* (2003 Yearbook of the National Society for the Study of Education, pp. 20–36). Chicago: National Society for the Study of Education, University of Chicago, College of Education.

Hannaway, J., Liu, A., & Nakib, Y. (2003, March). *Teacher quality: Current status and outlook: The good, the bad and the uncertain.* Paper presented at the meeting of the American Education Finance Association.

Hannaway, J., & McKay, S. (2001). Taking measure. *Education Next, 1*(3), 8–12.

Hanushek, E.A. (1986a). The economics of schooling: Production and efficiency in public schools. *Journal of Economic Literature, 49*, 1141–1177.

Hanushek, E.A. (1986b). The impact of differential expenditures on school performance. *Educational Researcher, 18*, 45–51.

Hanushek, E.A. (1994a). A jaundiced view of "adequacy" in school finance reform. *Educational Policy, 8*, 460–469.

Hanushek, E.A. (1994b). *Making schools work: Improving performance and controlling costs.* Washington, DC: Brookings Institution.

Hanushek, E.A. (1996). School resources and student performance. In G. Burtless (Ed.), *Does money matter? The effect of school resources on student achievement and adult success* (pp. 43–73). Washington, DC: Brookings Institution.

Hanushek, E.A. (1999). Some findings from an independent investigation of the Tennessee STAR experiment and from other experiments of class size effects. *Educational Evaluation and Policy Analysis, 21*, 143–164.

Heaton, R., & Lampert, M. (1993). Learning to hear voices: Inventing a new pedagogy of teacher education. In D.K. Cohen, M.W. McLaughlin, & J.E. Talbert (Eds.), *Teaching for understanding: Challenges for policy and practice* (pp. 43-83). San Francisco: Jossey-Bass.

Hedges, L.V., Laine, R.D., & Greenwald, R. (1994). Does money matter? A meta-analysis of studies of the effects of differential school inputs on student outcomes. *Educational Researcher, 23*(3), 5–14.

Hedges, L.V., & Nowell, A. (1999). Changes in the Black–White gap in achievement test scores. *Sociology of Education, 72*(2), 111–135.

Heyns, B. (1978). *Summer learning and the effects of schooling.* New York: Academic Press.

Heyns, B. (1987). Schooling and cognitive development: Is there a season for learning? *Child Development, 58*, 1151–1160.

Ingersoll, R. (1999). The problem of under-qualified teachers in American secondary schools. *Educational Researcher, 28*, 26–36.

Jacob, B.A., & Lefgren, L. (2002, May). *Remedial education and student achievement: A regression-discontinuity analysis* (NBER Working Paper 8918). Cambridge, MA: National Bureau of Economic Research.

Krueger, A.B. (1999). Experimental estimates of education production functions. *Quarterly Journal of Economics, 114*, 497–532.

Ladd, H.F., & Hansen, J.S. (Eds.). (1999). *Making money matter: Financing America's schools.* Washington, DC: National Academy Press.

Lee, J. (2002). Racial and ethnic achievement gap trends: Reversing the progress toward equity? *Educational Researcher, 31*(1), 3–12.

Lee, V.E., & Burkam, D.T. (2002). *Inequality at the starting gate: Social background differences in achievement as children begin school.* Washington, DC: Economic Policy Institute.

Lewis, S., Ceperich, J., & Jepson, J. (2002, October). *Critical trends in urban education: Fifth biennial survey of America's great city schools* [Report]. Washington, DC: Council of the Great City Schools.

Loeb, S. (2000). *How teachers' choices affect what a dollar can buy: Wages and quality in K–12 schooling.* Working paper.

McCarthy, S.J., & Peterson, P.L. (1993). Creating classroom practice within the context of a restructured professional development school. In D.K. Cohen, M.W. McLaughlin, & J.E. Talbert (Eds.), *Teaching for understanding: Challenges for policy and practice* (pp. 130–166). San Francisco: Jossey-Bass.

Phillips, M. (2000). Understanding ethnic differences in academic achievement: Empirical lessons from national data. In D.W. Grissmer & J.M. Ross (Eds.), *Analytic issues in the assessment of student achievement* (Proceedings from a research seminar, Washington, DC, November 1998, pp. 103–132). Santa Monica, CA: RAND.

Phillips, M., Crouse, J., & Ralph, J. (1998). Does the Black–White test score gap widen after children enter school? In C. Jencks & M. Phillips (Eds.), *The Black–White test score gap* (pp. 229–272). Washington, DC: Brookings Institution.

Rivkin, S.G., Hanushek, E.A., & Kain, J.F. (1998). *Teachers, schools and academic achievement* (NBER Working Paper

6691). Cambridge, MA: National Bureau of Economic Research.

Shields, A.C., Marsh, J., & Adelman, M. (1997). *The SSIs impact on classroom practice* (SRI Project 3612). Menlo Park, CA: SRI International.

Smith, M.W., & Dickinson, D.K. (1994). Describing oral language opportunities and environments in Head Start and other preschool classrooms. *Early Childhood Research Quarterly, 9*(3&4), 345–366.

Snow, C.E., Burns, M.S., & Griffin, P. (Eds.). (1998). *Preventing reading difficulties in young children.* Washington, DC: National Academy Press.

Sunmonu, K., Larson, J., Van Horn, Y., Cooper-Martin, E., & Nielsen, J. (2002, October). *Evaluation of the Extended Learning Opportunities summer program.* Rockville, MD: Office of Shared Accountability, Montgomery County Public Schools.

Wiley, D.E., & Yoon, B. (1995). Teacher reports on opportunity to learn: Analyses of the 1993 California Learning Assessment System (CLAS). *Educational Evaluation and Policy Analysis, 17*(3), 355–370.

Wilson, S.M., Miller, C., & Yerkes, C. (1993). Deeply rooted change: A tale of teaching adventurously. In D.K. Cohen, M.W. McLaughlin, & J.E. Talbert (Eds.), *Teaching for understanding: Challenges for policy and practice* (pp. 84–129). San Francisco: Jossey-Bass.

# CHAPTER 2

# Poverty and Achievement: A Response to Jane Hannaway

*Rita M. Bean*

For more than 25 years, I have worked as an educator, serving as a teacher, reading specialist, and university faculty member preparing reading specialists. Throughout this time, I have directed projects in schools in which the focus has been to increase teachers' knowledge and competence so that they can provide excellent literacy instruction for their students. Much of my work has been in urban schools with high proportions of low socioeconomic status (SES) students and low achievement overall. Therefore, Jane Hannaway's chapter, especially her suggestions for closing the gap between "the haves and the have-nots," is of great interest to me.

Currently, I am working with librarians who go into classrooms in urban schools to read multicultural books to students. As we talked about these classrooms and students in them, one of the librarians asked, "Is it true that city schools get teachers who are poorly prepared or less competent?" The question was asked not to demean teachers with whom she was familiar but because of a curiosity of why it was so difficult to improve literacy performance of students in these schools. At the same time, as I work with teachers in these same schools, I hear them express their reasons for students' academic difficulties: little exposure to books or other experiences that develop literacy skills, lack of parental involvement in students' education, single-parent homes, and the like. Yet, as expressed so eloquently in Hannaway's chapter, the causes of the achievement disparity between the haves and the have-nots is extremely complex; indeed, as H.L. Mencken stated, "There is always an easy solution to every human problem—neat, plausible, and wrong" (as cited in Merriam-Webster, 2000).

One of the complexities deals with the issue addressed first in Hannaway's chapter, that of the demographics of those who reside and go to school in urban areas. Not only are a large proportion of the urban population poor but they also come from backgrounds that may produce other social and learning difficulties. Hannaway indicates that "the population of cities is more likely to be language minority, Hispanic, African American, and poor." Moreover, urban schools are likely to serve populations that are even more poor and minority than city populations generally. And indeed, the "difficulty of the educational task" becomes greater for schools whose population is poor, whose parents do not have high school diplomas, and where there is a large percentage of single-parent homes (Cooley, 1993).

Hannaway describes three different ways in which poverty can affect students' achievement: direct input of parents and families to student learning, out-of-school experiences, and in-school experiences. She then discusses ways of counteracting the effects of poverty. In this response, I elaborate on each of those three contexts, highlighting findings that are specific to literacy instruction. Also, within each section, I discuss various attempts to close the achievement gap, and I raise issues about these various solutions and why they may or may not be sufficient. I conclude with a discussion of the implications for policy and practice.

# Families and Their Influence on the Learning of Children

## Family Involvement in Schooling

Research on family and community involvement is clear: Students whose families are involved in their learning are more likely to be successful in school (Henderson & Berla, 1995). We also know that children who come from homes with books, where children are read to and there are high expectations for children and achievement, have a greater likelihood for success in school. Many schools, especially urban schools, have made good-faith efforts to develop various types of programs that increase family involvement, from hosting various family activities in which children come to school with family members to developing materials that provide parents with ideas and activities that they can use to increase children's literacy performance. However, school personnel are often disappointed with the results of those efforts, indicating that those students who most need the support of their families are not receiving it. It is critical for educators to understand the many factors that may affect parent involvement, including limited amount of time because of work requirements, unsuccessful or unpleasant experiences with schooling, messages from educators that they are not welcome in schools, or inability to understand how to help the child (Hecht & Dwyer, 2001). Two broad approaches to increasing family involvement follow:

1. Provide teachers (preservice and inservice) with the professional development they need to gain an understanding and an appreciation of the cultural background of the students they teach. Urban families may indeed be "hard-to-reach" (Epstein, 1992), but until more emphasis is placed on the value and need for including parents in the education of their children, we may have limited success.

2. Think outside the box. Traditional approaches to family involvement, such as letters sent home or invitations to an open house at school, may not be enough. Rather, there is a need for a concerted effort that involves not only parents but also the entire family and community agencies that can support the efforts of those families (Neuman, Caperelli, & Kee, 1998). We must enlist the aid of organizations such as the Urban League, churches, and other agencies that are working to improve social and educational conditions for urban families.

## Early Childhood Experiences

As Hannaway indicates, putting an emphasis on family involvement in children's learning when they enter school does not address the issue that children of poverty often come to school less well prepared than their wealthier counterparts. And as Hannaway states, this is not news. Certainly, the development of Head Start in the 1960s was a clear indicator of the belief of those associated with the War on Poverty that education was the means of escaping socioeconomic disadvantage, and that providing young children with health care, nutrition, social support services, and education would prepare them to enter "school on a more equal footing" (Zigler & Styfco, 2000). Head Start has had great expectations placed on it: to improve the performance of low SES children in future grades. Indeed, Zigler, a psychologist involved with the early development of Head Start, stated that it was expected that "Head Start and other early interventions could inoculate children against the harmful effects of growing up in poverty" (Zigler & Styfco, 2000, p. 68). Although there has been some evidence that Head Start and its companion program for grades K–3, Follow Through, has made a difference in the long-term performance of students, effects have not been as great as expected. Zigler and Styfco identify several reasons for this, including the lack of clear goals and a feasible evaluation plan (with well-designed instruments) and the difficulty in monitoring program quality.

Currently, given the research on the brain development of the young child as well as the desire to prepare students to be ready to learn, there is much emphasis across the United States on maximizing the effects of early childhood programs and promoting all-day kindergartens, especially for students of poverty. One would hope that the lessons learned from the past will be taken into consideration as we encourage states and school districts to implement these new endeavors. Issues that must be addressed include program quality, teacher quality, communication, and funding.

**Program Quality.** We will have high-quality programs only if the goals are clear and are based on what we know about children and their growth. The current emphasis on more academic learning in Head Start programs may be necessary, but learning should not occur at the expense of the social and health needs of children of poverty. At the same time, it is critical that we provide programs that build on what we know about developing literacy skills of young children (Snow, Burns, & Griffin, 1998). Standards for such programs must be developed. Further, we must have the assessment tools that enable us to monitor and then assess the extent to which we are achieving our goals.

**Teacher Quality.** Certainly teacher preparation institutions must be responsible for training highly competent teachers who are ready to teach in early childhood programs. But we face another dilemma. We must develop the policies and practices that encourage competent teachers to work in early childhood programs in urban settings. The salaries of those who work in early childhood programs are so dismal that very few graduates of early childhood programs go on to teach in such programs, and if they do, they stay only until they can obtain a position in a public school setting.

**Communication.** We must also ensure that there is clear communication between school districts and early childhood programs so that teachers in early childhood settings understand what is expected of children entering schools, and those in school settings gain a better appreciation and understanding of the instructional emphasis in early childhood settings. The Reading Excellence Act (REA), which emphasized literacy from birth through grade 3, had some important effects on this relationship in an urban district in which I worked. Prior to the REA implementation, there was little communication between the school personnel and the Head Start teachers, even though programs were located within the schools. Given the REA emphasis and the current awareness of the importance of early childhood programs, this is no longer true; in fact, principals in district schools are now responsible for hiring and supervising Head Start teachers.

**Funding.** If we believe that early childhood education can alleviate some of the difficulties that children of poverty face as they enter school, it is critical that we develop an awareness of the importance of a good beginning with many different groups—governmental agencies, foundations, corporate America, and citizens—so that there is a willingness to support early childhood education efforts. Recent figures indicate that the cost per child of providing a year-round early childhood program is $13,000 (not an unreasonable figure given the number of hours per day spent in these classrooms). Until we convince taxpayers and corporate America of the high cost to society associated with poverty and low achievement, and the positive effect that their support may have on a well-educated workforce, we will be hard-pressed to fund quality programs. There are many reasons for lack of support for preschool education. The average citizen may not be aware of the benefits of preschool education. Members of a community may expect the family to assume responsibility for early learning or may resent governmental interference in the education of young children.

## Out-of-School Experiences

As indicated in Hannaway's chapter, students who live in poverty have fewer experiences in their homes and communities that support them and help them develop the skills essential for school success. The work of Alexander, Entwisle, and Olson (2001); Cooper, Nye, Charlton, Lindsay, and Greathouse (1996); and Heyns (1987) indicates the importance of out-of-school experiences of students, especially summer experiences. Indeed, according to Alexander et al. (2001), "practically the entire gap increase across socioeconomic lines traces to summer learning differentials" (p. 174). What is frightening about findings relative to the summer slide is that as students move through school, the cumulative effect of summer losses results in a lag of two or more years of reading achievement by the end of sixth grade.

So, what does this mean for educators? First, the positive news is that schools are making a difference; most students from low SES backgrounds are learning during the school year. Such information needs to be shared with educators, especially those in high-poverty schools, to reinforce their efforts. Second, the data indicate that students of poverty are indeed capable of learning; they learn during the school year but do not have access to the resources during the summer that support and build on their achievement. Third, it appears evident that much has to be done to provide summer experiences for students to reduce the summer slide. It is here that much more work needs to be done.

What sorts of programs are most beneficial? As Hannaway indicates, the evidence on summer programs and their effects is not yet clear. As stated in Alexander et al. (2001), the traditional summer program may not be enough. They suggest that in addition to a focus on the academics, that programs include physical and enrichment activities. It may also be necessary to increase family and community involvement in these programs and activities. Ideas for promoting summer and after-school programs include the following.

*Keep students reading*! McGill-Franzen and Allington (2000) make several recommendations for minimizing summer reading loss, highlighting the importance of summer reading. They suggest that children need access to books and encouragement to read. It seems apparent that school personnel need to work more closely with community librarians, who are eager to collaborate with schools in promoting reading during the school year and summer recess.

*Develop guidelines for out-of-school programs*. Given the increase in summer and after-school programming by schools and community agencies, standards or guidelines to assist program developers must be established so that such programs have connections to schools, their goals, and curricular programming.

In summary, out-of-school programs may be valuable, especially if there are meaningful literacy and other experiences, and if they are connected with the goals and instruction of the schools. There is a need for more systematic research about such programs to determine the relationship between activities and outcomes.

# In-School Experiences

Hannaway makes it clear: Although family input and out-of-school experiences are factors that may contribute to student achievement, a large fraction of the achievement gap can be attributed to what happens in the schools. In this response, I elaborate on three possible solutions mentioned in Hannaway's chapter: teachers, instruction (specifically Title I), and accountability.

## The Teacher Factor

Hannaway discusses the fact that teachers in urban schools may not be prepared to meet the needs of the students with whom they work and, indeed, may be less qualified. Certainly this is an issue that needs to be addressed by both teacher preparation institutions and school districts that employ teachers.

The very best teachers must be encouraged to work in schools with large numbers of children who struggle to learn. Too often, teachers in urban schools become frustrated and disappointed with what they see as their inability to make a difference, the continuing demands to do more to raise test scores, and the lack of support. To hire and then keep competent teachers may mean developing incentives for encouraging teachers to accept and then stay in positions in urban, high-poverty schools. As Hannaway indicates, we must also provide the professional development that assists teachers in learning strategies and techniques to work with children who may need additional support and instruction. Such professional development must be ongoing and job-embedded; it must put the focus on students and what they need to be successful learners. Guskey (1986) concludes that teachers will make changes in their practices if they see that the changes have a positive effect on students' learning. Moreover, this means hiring teachers who believe in their minds and their hearts that the students with whom they work can learn. Teachers who do not have high expectations do not provide students with adequate opportunities for success, resulting in lower, often inadequate, achievement. Several issues relative to teacher quality are described here:

*Teacher-preparation institutions and school districts must work together to prepare teachers.* Although novice teachers may acquire much in the way of knowledge, skills, and attitudes about teaching from their teacher preparation experiences, it is in the classroom that these attributes are expanded on and refined. It is in the classroom that beginning teachers need support, reassurance, and ongoing professional development.

*Schools must identify teachers who are highly qualified to teach children of poverty.* Although teachers must know their content and have up-to-date knowledge about instructional strategies, there are other qualities that are valued and appreciated by students and by their parents. In an evaluation of several effective urban elementary schools, Bean, Eichelberger, and Turner (2002) found that one of the major reasons that parents sent their children to these schools was because there were "teachers who cared." One of the most interesting areas of study relative to achievement of high-poverty students has to do with "resilient" students, those who succeed despite adverse conditions (Waxman, Gray, & Padron, 2002). Teachers who build resiliency in students are caring, have high expectations, and provide opportunities for students to participate and contribute in class. In what ways can we be certain that we are recruiting and preparing teachers who can establish classrooms in which such resiliency is encouraged?

*Schools need to establish incentives and rewards that encourage teachers to stay in urban schools.* Urban schools often lose their highly talented teachers who, when given the opportunity, leave to take positions in schools in which there are fewer challenges and demands. In order to keep these teachers, we not only need to reward them for their efforts, but we should give them opportunities beyond their work in the classroom that may encourage them to stay. They may serve as mentors to novice teachers; they may take positions as literacy coaches. Such responsibility recognizes their efforts and may provide an incentive for them to stay in their schools.

## The Instructional Factor

Closely related to the teacher factor is, of course, the instructional factor. What do we know about effective instruction, especially literacy instruction, for students in urban settings who tend to be poor and minority, and who often speak a second language? Because other chapters in this book address specific instructional issues, especially those related to literacy instruction, I focus only on Title I, which, like Head Start, was developed to address the disparity between the economically disadvantaged and their wealthier counterparts. The goal of Title I, in existence since 1965 (as either Chapter 1 or Title I), has been an ambitious one; the program presently costs over $8 billion a year and serves more than 10 million students (Borman, 2002). Because this heavily funded program began as a funding source and not as a specific programmatic initiative, it has been difficult to determine its effects. According to Borman and D'Agostine (2001) in their meta-analysis of Title I across its years of operation, there has been a positive trend for its educational effectiveness. Yet, it is difficult to generalize across schools and programs given the variation in how Title I programs are implemented, for example, schoolwide versus targeted assistance, emphasis at various grade levels, and subject-matter focus. Although Title I has not met the great expectations for which it was designed, that is, closing the achievement gap between poor students and their more advantaged peers, results from research do suggest that "without the program, children served over the last 35 years would have fallen farther behind academically" (Borman, 2002, p. 241). Moreover, as with Head Start, we have learned the importance of focusing on program quality and using research-based instruction for working with students.

Further, there appear to be some essential elements that are related to successful Title I programs: the need for congruence between what students are learning as part of the core curriculum and what they are receiving as part of the Title I services, and to the degree possible, an attempt to effect instruction in the school as a whole. A well-designed, coherent instructional program, well understood and accepted by teachers, is an important factor in improving student achievement (Marzano, 2003).

## Accountability

Hannaway cites several analyses that indicate that the focus on accountability has had a positive effect on the performance of disadvantaged students (Grissmer & Flanagan, 1998; Hannaway & McKay, 2001; Lee, 2002). At the same time, she discusses the reactions of principals, teachers, and parents to the accountability system in the Florida schools. These educators indicated that they felt enormous pressure, causing them to "narrow their curriculum, restrict field trips, and focus heavily on test-taking skills." There are many issues related to accountability, from procedural and statistical issues to issues of fairness, and ultimately to the long-range effect of accountability for schools, especially schools in which the educational task is a difficult one (Linn, Baker, & Beletenner, 2002). I identify next some of the questions that need to be asked—and answered—as we move toward more accountability as one solution for reducing the achievement gap.

*What effect has the accountability movement had on the curriculum of the schools?* Sadker and Zittleman (2004) raise a number of issues about the emphasis on standardization and testing. First, they wonder whether this focus has created a narrowing of the curriculum, encouraging teachers to teach to the test and creating a system that focuses less on creative and critical thinking and more on factual information that is easier to assess. Likewise, there has been concern that schools will de-emphasize subjects like social studies, music, and foreign language because they are not tested. Finally, there may be too much time given to teaching test-taking skills rather than helping students to gain real understanding of what they are learning.

*In what ways can we recognize the efforts of schools and teachers in urban areas where the educational task is a difficult one and where test scores may be slow to improve?* Berliner, Biddle, and Bell (1995) indicate that one of the problems of accountability programs is that there is not a level playing field for all schools, and thus accountability programs are unfair. And it is in these schools that accountability programs tend to generate the three As of Anger, Anxiety, and Alienation (Berliner et al., 1995).

*What are the long-range effects of accountability on schools, teachers, and students?* For example, recent data about high school graduation rates indicate that fewer students are graduating from high school by the traditional path, and more are leaving high school and pursuing alternative educational paths. Rates have been dropping at an accelerated pace since 1993. Are educational standards and the accompanying accountability measures tracking students from different economic and social strata into different forms of education and reducing their career opportunities (Postsecondary Education Opportunity, 1999)?

Reeves (this volume) discusses high performance in high-poverty schools as assessed by standardized measures. He makes an important point relative to controlling for high mobility or low attendance. How valid or useful is the research when students are not in school for the curriculum and teaching that are being measured? Such adjustments may need to be made to (a) more realistically determine the success of schools and (b) provide evidence to educators and to the general public that poverty is a problem that needs to be addressed by more than the schools. As Hannaway states, there must be more recognition of the fact that "children are better off in many ways when their families are better off."

## Implications

One of the greatest concerns in U.S. education today is urban education, specifically the provision of education for students who live in urban settings who tend to be poor, minority, and second-language speakers. Hannaway's chapter and this response lead to the following implications for practice and policy.

*Educators will need to partner with and gain the support of community agencies, businesses, the government, and foundations to address the issue of early childhood education.* There is indeed much potential in providing students with the resources they need at an early age as a means of preventing future difficulties with learning. However, unless there is a concerted effort, the resources will not be there to develop the programs needed by these students.

*For all programs, early childhood, in school or out of school, we must focus on issues related to high quality.* How do we define it, how can it be implemented, and what measures can we use to assure and assess its effectiveness?

*There is a need to address the issue of accountability in ways that ac-knowledge the "difficulty of the educational task" faced by teachers in schools where there are low numbers of high-poverty students.* Certainly, there is a need for accountability, but to expect the same results at schools with large numbers of high-poverty students—*without* the commitment of resources that are needed to support students' needs, a focus on highly com-petent teachers, and a recognition of the improvement that schools have made—is to ignore the demands placed on urban and other high-poverty schools.

*We must do a better job of implementing the large-scale programs that are currently available to us, such as Head Start and Title I.* As much effort as possible needs to be placed on issues related to implementation, assess-ment, and improvement. This means professional development for those in-volved in the program and accountability relative to implementation efforts and student outcomes. Likewise, the government has a responsibility to fund studies of these large-scale programs to enable developers to make ad-justments that will lead to program improvements.

*There is certainly a need for more and better research relative to the ef-fectiveness of the many different programs that are available to urban chil-dren (summer or after school) so that we have more knowledge about the complexities that exist and elements that matter.* Likewise, we need to con-tinue to study those schools or programs that have been successful. Such studies of schools that have beat the odds and programs that have made a dif-ference are important sources of information for those working in urban schools. Such information should be shared and included in professional de-velopment for teachers in similar schools. At the same time, we must re-member that there may be a need for modifications or variations across settings (Berman & McLaughlin, 1978).

*More effort must be placed on helping teachers work with the families of the children in our urban schools.* Most parents want the very best for their children, and, indeed, there are many urban children of poverty who are suc-cessful. We must employ teachers who care, who recognize the desires and dreams that urban parents have for their children, and who are willing to go the extra mile to make a difference in the lives of the students they teach.

Hugh Price (2002), in his book *Achievement Matters*, says that Masai warriors in Africa greet one another with the words "Eserian Nakera," meaning "How are the children?" The traditional response is "All the children are well" (p. 207). It will take the collective wisdom of all of us—educators, community leaders, parents, and those in government and business—to solve this complex problem so that we too can respond, "All the children are well."

## Acknowledgments

Many thanks to Drs. R. Tony Eichelberger and Gregory A. Morris for reading and responding to this chapter. Their insights are much appreciated.

## REFERENCES

Alexander, K.L., Entwisle, D.R., & Olson, L.S. (2001). Schools, achievement, and inequality: A seasonal perspective. *Educational Evaluation and Policy Analysis, 23*(2), 171–191.

Bean, R.M., Eichelberger, R.T., & Turner, G. (2002). *Evaluation of four inner city extra mile schools.* Unpublished manuscript, University of Pittsburgh, Pittsburgh, PA.

Berliner, D.C., Biddle, B.J., & Bell, J. (1995). *The manufactured crisis: Myths, fraud, and the attack on America's public schools.* Reading, MA: Addison-Wesley.

Berman, P., & McLaughlin, M.W. (1978). *Federal programs supporting educational change, Vol. VIII: Implementing and sustaining innovations.* Santa Monica, CA: Rand.

Borman, G.D. (2002). Title I: The evolution and effectiveness of compensatory education. In S. Stringfield & D. Land (Eds.), *Educating at-risk students* (Yearbook of the National Society for the Study of Education, Vol. 101, pp. 231–247). Chicago: University of Chicago Press.

Borman, G.D., & D'Agostino, J.V. (2001). Title I and student achievement: A quantitative synthesis. In G.D. Borman, S.C. Stringfield, & R.E. Slavin (Eds.), *Title I: Compensatory education at the crossroads* (pp. 25–58). Mahwah, NJ: Erlbaum.

Cooley, W.W. (1993, July). *The difficulty of the educational task* (Pennsylvania Educational Policy Studies Report No. 16). Pittsburgh, PA: University of Pittsburgh.

Cooper H., Nye, B., Charlton, K., Lindsay, J., & Greathouse, S. (1996). The effects of summer vacation on achievement test scores: A narrative and meta-analytic review. *Review of Educational Research, 66,* 227–268.

Epstein, J. (1992). School and family partnerships. In M.C. Alkin (Ed.), *Encyclopedia of educational research* (6th ed., pp. 1139–1151). New York: Macmillan.

Grissmer, D., & Flanagan, A. (1998). *Exploring rapid achievement gains in North Carolina and Texas. Lessons from the states* [Report commissioned by the National Education Goals Panel (NEGP), Washington, DC]. Retrieved October 12, 2004, from http://www.negp.gov/reports/grissmer.pdf

Guskey, T.R. (1986, May). Staff development and the process of teacher change. *Educational Researcher, 15*(5), 5–12.

Hannaway, J., & McKay, S. (2001, Fall). Taking measure. *Education Next, 1*(3), 8–12.

Hecht, J., & Dwyer, D. (2001). Minimal parent involvement. In S. Redding & L. Thomas (Eds.), *The community of the school* (pp. 275–290). Lincoln, IL: Academic Development Institute.

Henderson, A., & Berla, N. (1995). *The family is critical to students' achievement* (2nd ed.). Washington, DC: Center for Law and Education.

Heyns, B. (1987). Schooling and cognitive development: Is there a season for learning? *Child Development, 58,* 1151–1160.

Lee, J. (2002). Racial and ethnic achievement gap trends: Reversing the progress toward equity? *Educational Researcher, 31*(1), 3–12.

Linn, R.L., Baker, E.L., & Beletenner, D. (2002, June). *Accountability systems: Implications of requirements of the No Child Left Behind Act of 2001.* Los Angeles: Center for Research on Evaluation, Standards, and Student Testing (CRESST).

Marzano, R.J. (2003). *What works in schools: Translating research into action.* Alexandria, VA: Association for Supervision and Curriculum Development.

McGill-Franzen, A., & Allington, R. (2001, August). Lost summers: For some children, few books and few opportunities to read. *Classroom Leadership, 4*(9). Retrieved August 21, 2004, from http://www.ascd.org/publications/class_lead/200108/mcgillfranzen_2.html

Merriam-Webster. (2000). *Webster's new explorer dictionary of quotations.* Springfield, MA: Author.

Neuman, S.B., Caperelli, B.J., & Kee, C. (1998). Literacy learning, a family matter. *The Reading Teacher, 52,* 244–252.

Postsecondary Education Opportunity. (1999, September). *Tracking high school graduation 1970 to 1998* (No. 87). Oskaloosa, IA: Postsecondary Opportunity.

Price, H. (2002). *Achievement matters: Getting your child the best education possible.* New York: Kensington.

Sadler, D., & Zittleman, K. (2004, June). Test anxiety: Are students failing tests—or are tests failing students? *Phi Delta Kappan, 85*(10), 740–744, 751.

Snow, C., Burns, M.S., & Griffin, P. (Eds.). (1998). *Preventing reading difficulties in young children.* Washington, DC: National Academy Press.

Waxman, H.C., Gray, J.P., & Padron, Y.N. (2002). Resiliency among students at risk of academic failure. In S. Stringfield & D. Land (Eds.), *Educating at-risk students* (Yearbook of the National Society for the Study of Education, Vol. 101, Part 2, pp. 29–48). Chicago: University of Chicago Press.

Zigler, E., & Styfco, S.J. (2000, Summer). Pioneering steps (and fumbles) in developing a federal preschool intervention. *Topics in Early Childhood Special Education, 20*(2), 67–70, 78.

# CHAPTER 3

# The Effects of Health and Social Welfare Factors on Literacy Development in Urban Schools

*Joy G. Dryfoos*

In my view, educators and policymakers have access to a large amount of research that shows how disadvantaged children in urban schools cannot succeed in school if their health problems get in their way. Obviously, a child with frequent asthma attacks is weakened and loses time in the classroom. Those children with learning disabilities rapidly fall behind their classmates. Stressed-out young people cannot concentrate in school. Clearly, we need a better understanding of the situation, and we need to map out approaches to overcoming barriers and achieving success.

Thus, a first hypothesis is that children confront significant barriers to literacy development if they are sick, hungry, stressed, homeless, or otherwise disadvantaged. A second hypothesis is that those barriers can be overcome with the appropriate interventions at the appropriate time.

Proving these hypotheses requires some outcome measures. How do we know that health and social welfare factors affect literacy development? In this chapter, achievement scores will be used as the indicator of an effect on literacy development. The assumption is that most children should be able to read at grade level, attend school regularly, and get promoted at the end of the year.

How many children are held back because of unaddressed health and social problems? Howard Adelman and Linda Taylor, codirectors of the Center for Mental Health in Schools, have contributed many useful concepts and papers on the subject of addressing barriers to learning (Center for Mental Health in Schools, 1999):

> Ask any teacher: On most days, how many of your students come to class motivationally ready and able to learn? The consistency of response is surprising. In urban and rural schools serving economically disadvantaged families, teachers tell us they're lucky if 10%–15% of their students fall into this group. Suburban public school teachers usually say 75% fit this profile. (p. 1)

The Center for Demographic Policy estimates that 40% of young people are in bad educational shape (Center for Mental Health in Schools, 1999).

We start with the knowledge that most children do not read well (National Center for Education Statistics, 2001). In 2000, only 40% of fourth graders read at or above the proficiency level, 33% of males and 46% of females. Only 6% of males and 10% of females were advanced, and 42% of males and 33% of females scored "below basic." Factors related to lower scores in addition to gender were race (African American, Hispanic, and Indian), school located in central city, and high percentage of students eligible for free lunch (poverty).

The U.S. Census collects data on the age of youths and their years in school (U.S. Census Bureau, 2001). For each grade, there is a "modal" age, for example, 9-year-olds are typically in fourth grade. However, in 2000, 26% of fourth graders were one or more years older than their classmates, and 3% were two or more years older. This situation creates psychological and emotional problems for the misfits. In many cases, being behind in school is an indicator of failure and a useful diagnostic for identifying those who need extra help.

Among almost 33 million students in grades 1–8, 7.9 million, or 24%, were one or more years older, and almost 1 million (3%) were two or more years older. As would be expected, the higher the grade, the larger the proportion of students behind modal grade. Among 15- to 17-year-olds, 31% were behind modal grade. Males were much more likely to have been left back or had a late start in school (36% male vs. 25% female), as were African American (35%) and Hispanic (37%) teens compared to white non-Hispanics (29%).

## Health and Social Welfare Factors

The range of health and social factors that can influence development of literacy is very broad. As shown in Table 3.1, barriers to learning are grouped under health, psychological and behavioral, learning disabilities, and family. It should be acknowledged that many of these factors are interrelated and that poverty status is significantly related to almost all the other factors (see chapter 21 of this volume).

The National Center for Education Statistics (NCES) Kindergarten Study looked at child health status related to the risk status of the child's family (NCES, 1998). The four risk indicators were low maternal education, family on welfare, one parent in the home, and parents speaking a language other than English at home. Those children in families with no risk factors were much more likely to be in excellent health (59%) than those

### Table 3.1
### Health and Social Welfare Factors
### That Influence Literacy Development

| Health Barriers | Psychological and Behavioral Barriers |
|---|---|
| asthma | stress |
| overweight | lack of motivation |
| dental problems | impact of abuse |
| nutritional deficiency/hunger | attention deficit disorder |
| chronic diseases | substance abuse |
|    juvenile diabetes | unprotected sexual activity |
|    cerebral palsy | |
| lead poisoning | Family Problems |
| | poverty |
| Learning Disabilities | lack of health insurance |
| mental retardation | homelessness |
| speech, hearing problems | conflict/violence |
| dyslexia | parental substance abuse |

with one (44%) or two or more risk factors (37%). Some 29% of the children from high-risk families were in fair or poor health compared to 10% of those in no-risk families.

Children from lower-risk families were more likely to engage in positive social behaviors such as making friendships and helping their classmates. Children from high-risk families were less likely to have a positive attitude toward classroom activities, pay attention, and show eagerness to learn, and they were more likely to display antisocial behaviors such as arguing and fighting.

Nicholas Zill of Westat Research Corp's view is that

> it's common to attribute the achievement difficulties that educationally disadvantaged children experience to the inferior schools that they have to attend. What (the Kindergarten Study) shows is that these difficulties cannot be attributed solely to bad schools, because these children are already behind when they reach the classroom door. (Vail, 2000)

# Health Barriers

## Asthma

Asthma is the most serious chronic illness among children in the United States, resulting in numerous visits to emergency rooms and multiple hospitalizations. Asthma accounts for 10 million lost school days annually and is the leading cause of school absenteeism attributed to chronic conditions. It is estimated that 7.7 million children have asthma.

## Overweight

In 1999, 13% of children ages 6–11 and 14% of adolescents ages 12–19 were overweight (Office of the Surgeon General, 2003). More than one in seven children in the United States are overweight, and the percentage of children who are overweight has more than tripled in the past 30 years. Being overweight puts children at risk of many physical problems, such as diabetes, high blood pressure, high cholesterol, and cardiovascular disease, and it is likely to lead to poor social and psychological development. Overweight children experience social discrimination, which is associated with poor self-esteem and depression.

## Dental Problems

David Satcher, former Surgeon General of the United States, reported that more than one third of poor children have untreated dental cavities (Office of the Surgeon General, 2000). Students taking tests with toothaches are unlikely to score as well on tests as those undistracted by pain. Satcher noted,

> Those who suffer the worst oral health include poor Americans, especially children and the elderly...members of racial and ethnic groups. And those with disabilities and complex health conditions are at greater risk for oral diseases that...further complicate their health. Serious oral disorders may undermine self-image and self esteem, discourage social interaction, and lead to chronic stress and depression. Such functions as breathing, eating, swallowing, and speaking are affected, often leading to restricted activity in school. (Office of the Surgeon General, 2000)

Uninsured children are 2.5 times less likely to receive dental care than insured children, and children from families without dental insurance are three times as likely to have dental needs as compared to their insured peers.

## Nutrition and Hunger

Richard Rothstein, former education writer for *The New York Times*, recently suggested that giving children vitamin and mineral supplements, and feeding poor children, might be more effective ways to raise achievement scores than social promotion, increased accountability, or more testing (Rothstein, 2001). His article was based on Michael Murphy and Ronald

Kleinman's evaluation of a universal free breakfast pilot program in 16 Boston schools (Project Bread, 2001). Prior to the start of the program, one fourth of the students were classified as hungry and one third as lacking nutrients in their diets. These students were found to have poorer grades and more symptoms of emotional and behavioral problems.

Six months after the program started, participating students were shown to have increased their math grades, decreased their school absence and tardiness rates, and decreased emotional or behavioral problems. School staff reported positive changes in student behavior and attentiveness.

The Department of Agriculture reported that in 2000, approximately 18% of all children were in "food-insecure" households, its euphemism for hunger. Among families in poverty, almost half of the children were in such homes, compared to about 12% of nonpoverty households (Federal Interagency Forum on Child and Family Statistics, 2002). Using a Healthy Eating Index, 6% of 2- to 5-year-olds had a poor diet, 67% needed improvement, and only 27% had a good diet. For those ages 6–9, 8% had a poor diet, 79% needed improvement, and 13% had a good diet.

Data from the National Health and Nutrition Examination Survey show that 5- to 11-year-old children classified as "food insufficient" (i.e., do not get enough food to eat) had significantly lower arithmetic scores, were more likely to have repeated a grade and seen a psychologist, and had difficulty getting along with other children (Alaimo, Olson, & Frongillo, 2001). In addition, among teenagers, food-insufficient students were more likely to have been suspended from school.

## Lead Poisoning

Eating flakes from lead-based paint or breathing its dust leads to impaired cognitive abilities. The General Accounting Office (1999) reported that about 10% of poor children have dangerous levels of lead in their blood, which can cause reductions in IQ and attention span, reading and learning disabilities, hyperactivity, and behavioral problems. Fewer than one in five children in low-income families are screened for lead.

# Psychological and Behavioral Barriers

## Emotional and Behavioral Disorders

Many mental health experts estimate that 7%–8% of all school-age students have emotional or behavioral disorders (EBD) that require some special intervention in school or in the mental health system, and 3% have severe emotional disturbances (SED) (McLaughlin, Leone, Warren, & Schofield, 1994). Three fourths of SED children are male, and one fourth are African American, and they are more likely to come from low-income single-parent families. Students with EBD are more frequently left back than other students with disabilities, and they are less likely to go on to college.

### Learning Disabilities

Learning disabilities (LDs) affect 10% of boys and 6% of girls ages 3–17, as identified by school or health professionals (Child Trends Data Bank, 2002). The most prevalent problems are speech and language disorders, such as difficulty understanding certain aspects of speech, and academic skill disorders, such as dyslexia.

Although attention-deficit disorder (ADD) is not a learning disability, it interferes with learning and is connected to academic skills disorders. Almost half of all children ages 6–11 with learning disabilities also have ADD (Pastor & Rueben, 2002). The *National Health Interview Survey, 1997–1998*, found that among 6- to 11-year-old children nearly 7% were reported to have a diagnosis of ADD and 8% have a diagnosis of LD, but there was an overlap. Specifically, 3% had been diagnosed ADD/no LD, 4% LD/no ADD, and 4% had both. Among children with neither ADD nor LD, another 1% were reported to be mentally retarded or to have developmental delays.

The Center for Mental Health in Schools points out that school-caused learning problems ought to be differentiated from those caused by central nervous system dysfunctioning (Center for Mental Health in Schools, 2002). Persons with learning disabilities can learn as long as they have the necessary supports and medical treatments. Learning disabilities do influence educational achievement in many ways and can lead to high dropout rates and behavioral problems. Motivation begins to decrease as the demands increase in higher grades, and the child cannot keep up with the standards.

## Family Problems

### Poverty

In 2001, 15% of all children ages 5–17 lived in households where the annual income in the previous year was below poverty level. The poverty rate in public school districts ranged from 29% in central cities to 13% in suburbs. A report from the Maryland State Department of Education on minority achievement put the effects of poverty succinctly: "Poverty undermines achievement" (Maryland Department of Education, 1998). Not only do children fail more frequently in high-poverty schools, poor students perform better when they attend middle-class schools and when they attend effective schools in poor neighborhoods.

## High-Risk Families

Data from the study of kindergarten children previously mentioned yielded a clear relationship between being in a high-risk family and poor health among the children. The National Survey of America's Families provides an overview of the well-being of children according to whether they were in the child welfare system (foster care or placements with relatives) or lived with their parents (Kortenkamp & Ehrle, 2002). A subgroup of the parent care group was identified as high risk: living with a single parent with a low income. Some 27% of the children ages 6–17 involved with the child welfare system had high levels of behavioral and emotional problems, compared to 7% in the parent group and 13% in the high-risk group. Among 12- to 17-year-olds, 32% of those on child welfare had been suspended or expelled from school in the past year, compared to 13% in the parent group and 26% in the high-risk group. Being involved with child welfare and having high-risk parents was related to low levels of engagement in school and lack of involvement in extracurricular activities.

Children in the child welfare system were much more likely to have health problems. Some 28% reported limiting physical, learning, or mental health conditions, compared to only 8% in parent care and 14% with high-risk parents. However, children in the welfare system were more likely than the others to have health insurance, to have a usual source of health care other than the emergency room, and to have received health care in the past year.

## Lack of Health Insurance

A high proportion of children under 18 were covered by health insurance in 2001, including 93% of white children, 89% of African American children, and 76% of Hispanic children. White children are much less likely to be covered by government health insurance (16%), compared to 43% of African American children and 35% of Hispanic children (Ni & Cohen, 2002).

Carolyn Schwarz and Earl Lui reviewed the research on the link between enrollment in health insurance and better school performance (Schwarz & Lui, 2000). They found no studies that looked directly at the question but found data backing up two intermediate steps: (1) Good health is connected with improved school performance, and (2) having health insurance is linked to better health.

Regarding the first step, the researchers quoted Nicholas Zill on school readiness, who pointed out that "the state of a child's physical and mental health can have substantial impact on the child's initial adjustment to school on subsequent performance in school, and on demands that the child makes on school resources" (Zill, 1990). They cited research that shows how poor health can affect school performance in many ways, including contributing to absenteeism, affecting concentration in the classroom, producing disruptive behavior, and affecting students' abilities to participate in extracurricular activities. One study showed that missing more than 10 days in a 90-day semester can result in being left back, especially among those with chronic diseases (asthma, ear infections, arthritis, and seizures). In 1988, U.S. children ages 5–17 lost a total of 222 million days from school because of illness, injury, or chronic health conditions. Teachers in urban areas estimated that 18% of students have health problems that affect their ability to learn (American Academy of Pediatrics, 1992).

Regarding the second step, uninsured children were eight times less likely to have a regular source of care and six times more likely to have gone without needed medical, dental, or other health care. One study found that access to health care improved dramatically within 12 months of health insurance enrollment (Lave et al., 1998). Of particular interest here, after receiving insurance, parents reported feeling less stress, more leeway in allowing children to participate in activities, and improvement in their children's school performance after they were able to obtain glasses.

## Summary of Health and Social Factors Affecting Literacy Development

As we have seen, a wide range of factors influence the lives of children. The prevalence rates for all of these diverse problems cannot be aggregated because many of the children experience multiple risk factors; if they are poor, nonwhite, or in high-risk families, they are particularly vulnerable. Those who experience ill health and chronic diseases are at high risk of being unable to spend adequate time in school, and those with learning disabilities cannot succeed without special attention. Children from high-risk families come to school hungry and less prepared to cope with the demands of the classroom and the social milieu of the school. Students who start out as "losers" because they have been left back rarely make up the deficits and gradually slip further and further behind until they drop out.

## Interventions

Many practitioners in and out of schools have addressed these health and social welfare factors in the design of interventions that try to remove barriers to learning. Our interest here is in the experience of urban schools in coping with these problems. Very few schools have been able to undertake the necessary actions without assistance from outside agencies. Partnerships are established to give the children and their families access to the services they need.

The Coalition for Community Schools has recently published *Making the Difference* (Blank, Melaville, & Shah, 2003), a synthesis of the research on the outcomes of programs based in schools that address health and social factors. That monograph is built on a review of evaluation findings from 49 of my previous research reports (Dryfoos, 2001). I have selected a few examples from the many that are now available in the sources just cited.

### *Children's Aid Society Model Community School*

I start here with the work of the Children's Aid Society in creating full-service community schools because their model encompasses strong interventions at every level to ameliorate the conditions of disadvantaged families and their children. In 1990, the Children's Aid Society (CAS) of New York entered into a partnership with the local School District #6 to develop community schools. The two initial sites, Intermediate School 218 and Elementary School 5, have been the subject of a six-year process and outcome evaluation conducted by researchers from Fordham University (Dryfoos, Quinn, & Barkin, in press). CAS has also developed 11 additional community schools locally and worked with a wide variety of public schools, community-based organizations, and funders to help sites around the country.

CAS's approach to community schools is to provide a "seamless" learning and developmental experience for children, families, and communities. Intermediate School 218 is located in a new building in the Washington Heights community of New York City, where it offers the "Turning Points" approach to middle school reform, including a core curriculum and a choice of four self-contained academies. The school opens at 7:00 a.m. and stays open after school for educational enrichment, mentoring, sports, computer lab, music, arts, trips, and entrepreneurial workshops. In the evening, teenagers use the sports and arts facilities and take classes along with adults who come for English, computer work, parenting skills, and other workshops.

A Family Resource Center provides social services to parents including immigration, employment, and housing consultations and provides them with the opportunity to work as family advocates. In addition, a primary health, vision, and dental clinic is on site. School-supported and CAS-supported social workers and mental health counselors work together to serve students and families. The school stays open weekends and summers, offering the Dominican community many opportunities for cultural enrichment and family participation. Other partners include Mercy College, Hope for Kids, the American Ballet Theatre, and Columbia-Presbyterian Hospital.

The pilot elementary school offers a different array of services in a new building designed to be a community school. It also houses a complete medical and dental clinic as well as a Parent Resource Center, an extended-day program, summer camp, Head Start and Early Head Start, parent involvement, and mental health and social services. Partners include the Manhattan Theatre Institute and Boy and Girl Scouts.

The Fordham University evaluation focused primarily on formative issues during the first three years and selected outcomes in the subsequent three years. The earliest evaluation of IS 218 in 1993 showed encouraging results: highest attendance rates in the district, improved reading and math scores, and no serious incidence of violence (despite the school's location within the highest crime rate area in the city; see Robeson, 1993).

An evaluation of PS 5 conducted in 1995 by Ellen Brickman of Fordham University documents significant improvements in both reading and math achievement (Brickman, 1996). Tracking the class that entered in third grade in 1993, 10% were reading at grade level then, 16% by grade 4, and 35% in grade 5. Scores for math increased from 23% to 56% during the same three-year period.

A three-year evaluation report of both schools was issued in 1999 by Anthony Cancelli and colleagues from Fordham University, contrasting the CAS schools with matched schools in the neighborhood (Cancelli, Brickman, Sanchez, & Rivera, 1999). Three sets of outcomes were examined: psychosocial, parent involvement, and academic for students in grades 3 and 6 when the research started. In regard to psychosocial findings, students in the community schools appeared to have a more positive sense of self-worth and to like their teachers and schools more than the students in the comparison schools. Regarding parental involvement, the research found high, consistent, and meaningful involvement in the community schools, more so than in the other schools. Parents felt welcome in the schools and that they were partners.

Academic achievement over the years improved in both sites, although the rate of increase leveled off or decreased after the initial major gains were recorded. At PS 5, the percentage of children reading at grade level rose from 28% when they were in grade 4 to 42% by the time they reached grade 6. The same cohort math scores moved from 43% at grade level in grade 4 up to 50% by grade 6. The progress matched the improvement rate at comparison schools, although the PS 5 children had lower scores at baseline. The researchers also found a significant positive correlation between attendance at extended-day programs and reading scores.

At IS 218, the research team found a clear pattern of steady though less dramatic improvement over time. Some 39% of students performed at grade level in reading at grade 6, rising to 45% by the time they were in grade 8. For math, the levels went from 49% to 52%.

Finally, the research concluded that seven years after the establishment of the community schools, many of the goals had been reached. The buildings were full of people throughout the day and evening engaged in a wide array of activities. Children were receiving high-quality medical and dental care, and had access to on-site mental health services. Parents were involved in the schools and felt a strong sense of responsibility for their children's education, particularly new immigrants. In regard to psychosocial development, the students had more positive attitudes toward school experiences.

## Stevenson-YMCA Community School Program

The Stevenson Elementary School in Long Beach, California, in collaboration with the local YMCA and the California State University Department of Social Work is an adaptation site for the CAS model. The goal of this community school is to enhance the academic, social, and career development of youth through the active partnerships of youth, parents, school, and community resources in providing an array of school-site activities.

A preliminary evaluation was conducted by Julie O'Donnell at California State University, Long Beach (O'Donnell, 2000). Report card data were collected for a sample of the students, comparing the semester prior to involvement to the end of the first year. First- through third-grade students showed significant progress in their academic achievement in the initial year of the program. The percentage of students who were considered below average declined from 49% to 30%, while the students receiving above average grades went from 19% to 34%. Few changes were noted in work or study habits or personal growth. Fourth and fifth graders also significantly improved their effort, study habits, and homework, and they showed improved academic progress and attendance. The percentage of students with "above average" grades went from 15% to 30%. O'Donnell observed that these preliminary findings support the idea that the community school approach used here (extensive child and parent programming and integration of academic standards in extended-day activities) may be a promising way to enhance academic achievement among students living in low-income areas. However, as she points out, the lack of a control group precludes determining to what degree the community school model contributed to the change.

## Hampton Elementary School

Hampton Elementary School in Greensboro, North Carolina, operates on a year-round calendar (Coalition for Community Schools, 2000). If offers a full menu of services and supports through its Bridges to Success United Way Program. In this model, the United Way forms a consortium with other community agencies to bring an array of services into the school. A full-time nurse arranges dental, health, and vision screening and transportation to outside services. Many outside agencies contribute to enrichment, after-school, and Saturday activities. A unique program is sponsored by the Greensboro Symphony to introduce third graders to classical music and offer musical instruction.

The school reports that attendance rates have increased to 94% and that reading, writing, and math proficiency for grades 3–5 went from 45% to 63% from 1997 to 1999. Parent participation has improved.

## Francis Scott Key Elementary School

Three years ago, in the Francis Scott Key School in Indianapolis, Indiana, over one third of kindergartners showed up for school without adequate immunizations (Blank et al., 2003). Their families did not have either insurance, access to health clinics, or the time and information needed to ensure this basic protection. Children were not able to return to school until they received their shots, and many lost valuable school time as a result. In the 2001–2002 school year, a partnership between the Indianapolis Public School District, United Way's Bridges to Success program, and the local health clinic made it possible for children to receive their immunizations right at the school. One hundred percent of fifth graders and kindergartners received their shots before the school year began, and no school days were missed because of immunizations.

## Stanley Elementary School

Stanley Elementary School in Wichita, Kansas, is open from 7 a.m. to midnight every day (Coalition for Community Schools, 2000). This is a site for Communities in Schools (CIS) in collaboration with the Departments of Health, Human Resources, Parks and Recreation, a branch library, and a senior service center. The CIS model relies on forming a nonprofit governing board to bring case management services into schools. At Stanley, 23 repositioned staff members provide services to student and families on site. Evenings and weekends, the school uses Vista Volunteers to help host college classes, community programs, and recreation for adults. Partnerships with Washburn University and the Yamaha Corporation enhance the curriculum, and many other volunteers provide extended-day tutoring and mentoring.

The program reports that those students who were involved in CIS activities improved their reading scores by 21 percentile rank points from the previous year, and 95% of students were promoted to the next grade.

## Communities in Schools of Passaic

CIS initiated a program in 1994 at the William B. Cruise Elementary School in Passaic, New Jersey, with the goal of reducing the retention rate among kindergarten students, from 21% in the preceding year (Communities in Schools of New Jersey, 2000). Partnered with the United Passaic Organization, CIS provided after-school tutoring of kindergarten students and a strong parent outreach and education component. After one year, the number of students retained in kindergarten was reduced by half, and the remaining students were promoted to first grade after a summer academic program. Based on the success of this program, CIS now serves students in three schools and the new Early Childhood Center. In addition, CIS operates a VISTA program, recruiting parents to work in outreach.

## Excels, Boston

Boston Children's Services/Home for Little Wanderers is the lead agency that works in collaboration with the Boston Public Schools and other agencies to operate Boston Excels, a community school model in five elementary schools (Dryfoos, 2000). Supported by local foundations since 1991, this program's primary goal is to improve academic achievement in high-risk students through a long-term commitment to partnerships with schools. Each school has its own package of interventions, including individual counseling, mentors, academic support, after-school programs, and the development of parent centers. The Efficacy Institute has trained both teachers and parents in values and skills related to enhancing the school climate. Each school has a full-time coordinator and senior-level clinician along with social work interns from university partners.

Several evaluations have been conducted (Boston Children's Institute, 2000). The Educational Development Center did a major study of McKay School, tracking changes from 1990 to 1993. The first report showed an increase in promotion from 95% to 98%, increases in reading and math scores, and teacher reports of improved classroom behavior and parent involvement.

A study in 1996–1997 tracked the replication process in the two new schools. According to the researcher, Sarah Uhl, the replication of Project Excel "exceeded expectations"and generated requests from other schools to begin the process. Looking at the aggregate for the three schools where 1,916 students were enrolled, some 650 had received counseling, 417 families had received support services, 296 crisis intervention services were provided, and hundreds of parents were involved in an array of activities.

A program update in late 1997 reported that the Boston Children's Services worked with 44 public schools and community centers through their partnership with Family Services of Greater Boston, called Solutions for Children and Families. This new arrangement would offer a team of professionals with the training and capacity to "transform schools into effective centers of learning." Project Excel would be the model for these transformations.

McKay's seven years of experience provided a laboratory for learning about this program. The report states that in the three previous years, reading scores had improved 200% and math scores, 50%. More than 100 parents are actively engaged in the school. Ellis and Lee schools are developing rapidly with the addition of fathers' events, special education events, literacy activities for children and their families, improved teacher morale, improved behavior, and other gains.

## Polk Brothers Foundation Community Schools, Chicago

The Polk Foundation in Chicago Full Service Schools Initiative is designed to improve the physical and psychological well-being of children in high-risk communities (Blank et al., 2003). The three schools and their partners selected out of 65 applicants are Brentano Elementary/Logan Square Neighborhood Association, Marquette Elementary/Metropolitan Family Services, and Riis Elementary/Youth Guidance. The schools are open after school and in the evening. Each has a different set of programs including parent involvement, recreation, school remediation, and tutoring. Each partnership was required to set up a governance body and to hire a full-time coordinator to oversee the operations.

Samuel Whalen has conducted documentation and evaluation since the program began in 1997 (Whalen, 1999). The evaluation is designed around tracking successes in four areas: increasing access to services, including a wide range of community stakeholders, improving the school climate, and creating a shared enterprise between the school staff and community service providers. The long-range goal is to improve academic achievement and psychological well-being of the children. These goals were translated into four specific forms of social capital that the partnerships expected to improve: sense of safety and security, places to socialize, availability of help for difficult problems, and availability of adults to act as role models and mentors.

A first report presents data from surveys of students, parents, and teachers in 1997 and 1998, showing the changes that took place one year after the initiation of the program. As would be expected, only small changes were reported in test scores (all positive), although there was some evidence of improvement in the coverage of children by caring adults. Student mobility decreased 2%–5% in the three schools, suggesting that the initiative helped the school hold on to the students.

A second report, tracking change between 1995 and 1999, showed that reading scores improved at rates exceeding citywide averages in all three schools, and at two schools, math scores increased significantly more than citywide. By 1999, all the schools were actively involved with over 25 organizations that enhanced the full-service concepts. Both parents and teachers increasingly perceived the schools as places open after school that contained adults who could help their children with serious problems.

## Pinelands Regional Schools

The Pinelands Regional Middle and High Schools in Tuckerton, New Jersey, are located in a rural, coastal area of the state (Blank et al., 2003). The New Jersey School Based Youth Services Program funded by the New Jersey State Department of Health and Human Services to foster partnerships between schools and community agencies has been operating at Pinelands for 14 years. These partnerships offer primary and preventive health care, mental health and social services, employment assistance, family-planning education, substance abuse counseling, pregnant-teen and teen-parent support services, transportation, a 24-hour Teen Crisis Hotline, and recreational programs and activities to all students in the regional district. Teen pregnancy rates have dropped among young teens from about 20 each year to about 3. The "Pinelands Model" has been recognized as effective by Rutgers University's School of Social Work and has been replicated in others areas of the state. Since 1993, the percentage of students passing the state high school proficiency test has climbed from 74% to 90%.

## Linkages to Learning

Linkages to Learning was initiated in 1993 by Montgomery County (Maryland) to provide services to students and their families to improve the students' performance in the school, home, and community (Dryfoos, 2000). This is a collaboration among the Montgomery County Schools, County Department of Health and Human Services, and several private agencies. By 2000, the program was operating in nine elementary and secondary schools in the county. The program provides social, health, and mental health services and educational support through interagency collaborations.

A formative evaluation was conducted in 1995 by the College of Education, University of Maryland, to find out whether the program met the needs of its potential clients in the first three sites (Leone, Lane, Chapin, & Mayer, 1995). Families were very satisfied with the program. Staff reported that the demand for mental health services could not be met. In the early stages of the program, certain structural problems were identified, such as lack of central decision making, duplication of bureaucratic efforts (multiple forms), no formal agreements on how agencies should interrelate, and lack of communication between school and agency staffs. This evaluation was used to strengthen the program by adding administrative support and getting more resources for mental health services.

With support from the U.S. Department of Education, an evaluation of Linkages was conducted at the Broad Acres Elementary School, using another school as a control over a three-year period (Fox et al., 1999). Broad Acres serves 500 children in grades K–5 from 40 countries, speaking 10 languages; 90% qualify for free and reduced-price meals. In addition to Linkages of Learning mental health, social services, and education services, a health center was added to this site with support from the Robert Wood Johnson Foundation. Analysis of utilization data for a cohort of kindergarten through second graders showed that 61% used Linkages services at some time.

The evaluation was designed to look at the achievement of three out-reach and eight direct service objectives. Many activities were reported that helped families and children deal with their problems. Access to health care was greatly increased, reducing the percentage of families who re-ported no health care access for their children from 53% to 10%, and those with no insurance coverage from 38% to 10%. An outcome evaluation col-lected data on social or emotional and academic functioning over four years from Broad Acres and a (poorly) matched school. Some 119 children, 69 par-ents, and a few teachers were included in the longitudinal sample, reflecting high loss from both schools because of mobility problems (in one year, 40% in the experimental school and 32% in the control). A detailed protocol made up of various research instruments was followed, requiring intensive interviews of respondents conducted by a cadre of university students.

Findings from the parents in the experimental school show a signifi-cant decrease in reported children's negative behaviors at the same time that such behaviors were reported by parents as increased in the control school. Children who had received direct services from Linkages (such as case man-agement or counseling) showed the greatest improvement. Teachers had similar reactions about classroom behavior. The children in the experi-mental school reported no changes in their emotional distress levels, while the children in the control school reported significant increases.

Regarding academic outcomes, children at both schools had higher math achievement at the end of the study than at baseline. However, chil-dren who received educational services through the Linkages program im-proved significantly more than those who did not receive services. Parents at the experimental schools reported being relatively less depressed over time, reported an increase in family cohesion, and demonstrated greater gains in consistency in parenting styles. The data suggest that those children and families who used Linkages services showed significant improvements in outcomes, which was not experienced by those families in the experimen-tal school who did not use the services. The program had an effect on the individuals but not necessarily on the total school climate.

## Summary of the Impact of Comprehensive Health and Social Welfare Programs on Outcomes for Children

In *Making the Difference*, the authors reviewed evaluations from 20 major initiatives such as the Children's Aid Society, United Way, and Communities in Schools, cited previously here (Blank et al., 2003). In 15 of these initiatives, evidence was presented of an improvement in individual academic achievement:

> findings that speak to the power of creating environments and opportunities in the school and community that satisfy all the conditions for learning ...underscore our understanding that academic achievement is intertwined with physical, social and emotional well-being, the development of personal competencies in many areas of life and the engagement of a strong family and community. (p. 41)

Specific findings from the 20 studies showed the following results for young people attending a community school:

- Improved grades in school courses and/or scores in proficiency testing
- Improved attendance
- Reduced behavioral or discipline problems and/or suspensions/ expulsions
- Greater classroom cooperation, completion of homework and assignments, adherence to school rules, and positive attitude
- Increased access to physical and mental health services and preventive care
- Greater contact with supportive adults
- Improvements in personal or family situation, less abuse or neglect
- Increased promotions and on-time graduations
- Increased sense of students' personal control over their academic success
- Decrease in self-destructive behaviors including irresponsible sexual activity and drug use
- Reduced dropping out of school
- Increased sense of attachment and responsibility to the community
- Increased sense of school connectedness
- Positive effects on educational aspirations and credit accumulation

This list of outcomes should be encouraging to those who are trying to create a climate for improving literacy development. This demonstrates that attending to the physical and emotional health of children and involving their families in the process can go a long way toward overcoming the barriers to learning.

# Implications

## Schools Cannot Do It Alone

Given the problems that children present as they enter school and continue to present as they get older and fall further and further behind in school, it seems unlikely that many urban schools have the capacity to cure all the ills (Dryfoos & Maguire, 2002). Other community agencies have to be tapped to provide the necessary resources. Experience with the development of full-service community schools has shown that community health and social agencies are eager to bring their services into the schools. Many agencies can bring their own resources by relocating existing personnel into school buildings. The educational system should not bear the financial burden of curing all the social ills that are presented to them.

## Components of Successful Interventions

What do the successful school-based initiatives have in common? The most comprehensive programs include the following:

- Services that are responsive to the needs of the children and families in that community
- Building open extended hours—afternoons, evenings, weekends, all year
- Services provided through partnership agreements between the school and community agencies
- Access on site to health and mental health care, dental health, group and individual counseling, and case management
- Parent involvement
- Parent resource center
- After-school programs
- Integration of extended services with classroom curricula
- Full-time coordinator

## Different Treatments for Different Problems

The barriers shown in Table 3.1 are not necessarily treated with the same interventions. In Table 3.2, we can see that health barriers are treated largely through medical avenues and health education, whereas psychological barriers may require more intensive treatment such as case management and

## Table 3.2
### Barriers and Interventions

| Barriers to Learning | Interventions |
| --- | --- |
| Health Barriers | School-based clinic, health education, counseling, testing and screening, immunizations |
| Psychological and Behavioral Barriers | Mental health services, case management, group counseling, social skills training, crisis intervention |
| Learning Disabilities | Early identification, intensive treatment, family support programs |
| Family Problems | Case management, counseling, welfare, employment services, educational opportunities, parenting education |

crisis intervention. The response to family problems is much broader, requiring social programs that may deal with education and employment as well as housing and immigration.

## *Is This Feasible?*

We have sketched out an approach to overcoming the many barriers to learning that relies on a model called "full-service community schools." The concepts of community schooling are not new. In some sense, they derive from the century-old teachings of John Dewey and Jane Addams, reformulating educational institutions in terms of community betterment. But the new wave of community schools is relatively young, springing up within the past two decades and emerging from a whole array of independent sources and far-flung places. What they all have in common is the recognition that failing schools must be transformed into successful institutions if the children in that community are going to achieve.

The idea is catching on rapidly. Recently the newly elected Mayor Cicilline of Providence, Rhode Island, announced that developing community schools is a number one priority for his administration (Coalition for Community Schools, 2003). He plans to create community schools that partner with local community organizations to focus on the whole child, the family, and the community. He said, "If the children and youth of Providence are to emerge as the successful scholars, workers, citizens and leaders of the future, school buildings must become centers for learning and youth development, across the city." Mayor Cicilline is interested in providing after-school programs, mentoring, and tutoring for children as well as mental health services, family literacy, parent education, and prevention and health programming through community schools. Under his administration, public school buildings will be open to the community—in the afternoons, evenings, and weekends.

In Boston, the newly organized Full-Services Schools Roundtable is working to expand the number of full-service schools (M. LiPuma, personal communication, January 10, 2003). They plan to convene conferences to bring school and community-based agency officials together, deliver technical assistance, and offer professional development workshops. Chicago is on the way to developing 100 community schools in the next five years, based on the work of the Polk foundation, cited previously here.

The Coalition for Community Schools in Washington, D.C., has 170 partner organizations, including major public and nonprofit educational, youth, and health and mental health agencies and foundations. State chapters are being formed, and the media are beginning to show interest. The funding situation is as unsettled as with other humane causes. Because the field is so broad, many categorical sources can be tapped and fed into collaborative programs.

The route to literacy development is, of course, very complex. Partnerships can help solve some of the personal problems of the students and their families (and even of some of the staff), but the bottom line has to be in the classroom. Even healthy children cannot develop cognitively if they are subjected to unqualified teachers. Bringing all these outsiders into schools can expose youth workers and health professionals to some ineffective teachers and ill-prepared administrators. They are rapidly transformed into advocates for better schools. Together, advocates, professionals, parents, and stakeholders hope to put the two worlds of educational quality and youth development together. We must believe that this effort will result in stronger schools and stronger children.

## REFERENCES

Alaimo, K., Olson, C., & Frongillo, E. (2001). Food insufficiency and American school-aged children's cognitive, academic, and psychosocial development. *Pediatrics, 108*(1), 44–53.

American Academy of Pediatrics. (1992).

*Health care and a child's ability to learn: A survey of elementary school teachers.* Chicago: Porter Novelli.

Blank, M., Melaville, T., & Shah, B. (2003). *Making the difference: Research and practice in community schools.*

Washington, DC: Coalition of Community Schools.

Boston Children's Institute. (2000, March 31). *Boston Excels full service schools: Partnering with public schools to ensure that all students achieve.* Boston: Author. Retrieved August 30, 2004, from http://www.thehome.org/site/pdf/excels_briefing.pdf

Brickman, E. (1996). *A formative evaluation of PS 5: A Children's Aid Society/Board of Education Community School.* New York: Fordham University.

Cancelli, A., Brickman, E., Sanchez, A., & Rivera, G. (1999, Fall). *The Children's Aid Society/Board of Education Community Schools: Third-year evaluation report.* New York: Fordham University.

Center for Mental Health in Schools at UCLA. (1999, October). *Expanding educational reform to address barriers to learning: Restructuring student support services and enhancing school-community partnerships.* Los Angeles, CA: Author.

Center for Mental Health in Schools at UCLA. (2002). *Addressing barriers to learning, 7*(3). Los Angeles, CA: Author. Retrieved August 30, 2004, from http://smhp.psych.ucla.edu/pdfdocs/Reports/Expand.pdf

Child Trends Data Bank. (2002). *Learning disabilities.* Retrieved August 30, 2004, from http://www.childtrendsdatabank.org/indicators/65LearningDisabilities.cfm

Coalition for Community Schools. (2000, April). *Community schools: Partnerships for excellence.* Retrieved August 4, 2004, from http://www.communityschools.org

Coalition for Community Schools. (2003, January 21). *Community Schools Online, 2*(16). Retrieved August 4, 2004, from http://www.communityschools.org

Communities in Schools of New Jersey, Inc. (2000). Handout at Collaboratives for Integrating School Services meeting. Harvard School of Education, Cambridge, MA.

Dryfoos, J. (2000). *Evaluation of community schools: Findings to date.* Washington, DC: Coalition of Community Schools. Retrieved August 4, 2004, from http://www.communityschools.org/evaluation/evalbrieffinal.html

Dryfoos, J., & Maguire, S. (2002). *Inside full-service community schools.* Thousand Oaks, CA: Corwin Press.

Dryfoos, J., Quinn, J., & Barkin, C. (in press). *Community schools in action: Lessons from a decade of practice.* New York: Oxford University Press.

Federal Interagency Forum on Child and Family Statistics. (2002). *America's children: Key national indicators of well-being, 2002* (pp. 84–91). Washington, DC: U.S. Government Printing Office.

Fox, N., Leone, P., Rubin, K., Oppenheim, J., Miller, M., & Friedman, K. (1999). *Final report on the Linkages to Learning program and evaluation at Broad Acres Elementary School.* College Park: University of Maryland.

General Accounting Office. (1999, January 15). *Lead poisoning: Federal health care programs are not effectively reaching at risk children.* Retrieved August 30, 2004, from http://frwebgate.access.gpo.gov

Kortenkamp, K., & Ehrle, J. (2002). *The well-being of children involved with the child welfare system: A national overview. New federalism: National survey of America's families, Series B, No. B-43. Assessing the new federalism: An Urban Institute program to assess changing social policies.* Washington, DC: The Urban Institute.

Lave, J., Kean, C., Lin, J., Ricci, E., Amersback, G., & LaVallee, C. (1998). Impact of children's health insurance program on newly enrolled children. *JAMA: The Journal of the American Medical Association, 279,* 1820.

Leone, P., Lane, S., Chapin, M., & Mayer, M. (1995). *A formative evaluation of Linkages to Learning at Highland Elementary School, Montgomery County, Maryland.* College Park: University of Maryland.

Maryland State Department of Education. (1998). *Minority achievements in Maryland: The state of the state* [Report of Multicultural Task Force]. Baltimore, MD: Author.

McLaughlin, M., Leone, P., Warren, S., & Schofield, P. (1994, June). *Doing things differently: Issues and options for creating comprehensive school linked services for children and youth with emotional or behavioral disorders.* College Park: University of Maryland; Rockville, MD: Westat.

National Center for Education Statistics. (1998). *Early childhood longitudinal study kindergarten class of 1998–1999.* Washington, DC: Department of Education.

National Center for Education Statistics. (2001). *The Nation's Report Card: Fourth-grade reading 2000* (NCES 2001-499). Washington, DC: Department of Education. Retrieved May 6, 2004, from http://nces.ed.gov/nationsreportcard/pdf/main2000/2001499.pdf

Ni, H., & Cohen, R. (2002). *Trends in health insurance coverage by race/ethnicity among persons under 65 years of age: United States, 1997–2001.* Retrieved August 30, 2004, from http://www.cdc.gov/nchs/products/pubs/pubd/hestats/healthinsur.htm

O'Donnell, J. (2000). *Report card results from the Stevenson-YMCA Community School Program, academic year 1998–1999.* Long Beach: California State University.

Office of the Surgeon General. (2000, May 25). *News release.* Retrieved August 30, 2004, from http://www.nih.gov/news/pr/may2000/nidcr-25.htm

Office of the Surgeon General. (2003). *Call to action to prevent and decrease overweight and obesity* [Fact sheet]. Retrieved February 10, 2004, from http://www.surgeongeneral.gov/topics/obesity calltoaction/fact_adolescents.htm

Pastor, P.N., & Reuben, C.A. (2002). *Attention deficit disorder and learning disability: United States 1997–98,*

National Center for Health Statistics, Vital Health Statistics, 10/206 Hyattsville, MD: National Center for Health Statistics.

Project Bread. (2001). *Study shows link between school breakfast and academic achievement.* Retrieved February 10, 2004, from http://www.projectbread.org/MCHI/mghbreakfaststudy.htm

Robison, E. (1993). *An interim evaluative report concerning a collaboration between the Children's Aid Society, New York City Board of Education, Community School District 6, and the I.S. 218 Salome Urena de Henriquez School [and] The Community Schools P.S. 5 and I.S. 218.* New York: Fordham University.

Rothstein, R. (2001, August 1). Food for thought: In many cases, no. *New York Times,* p. B8.

Schwarz, C., & Lui, E. (2000, October). *The link between school performance and health insurance.* Consumers Union. Retrieved August 30, 2004, from http://www.healthykidsproject.org

U.S. Census Bureau. (2001). *School enrollment—Social and economic characteristics of students, October 2000 (PPL-148) Table 2.* Retrieved August 31, 2004, from http://www.census.gov/population/socdemo/school/ppl148/tab02.txt

Vail, K. (2000). *Status of children: A mixed report on early childhood.* Retrieved April 10, 2004, from http://www.asbj.com/evs/00/children.html

Whalen, S. (1999). *Full service school initiative: 1998 evaluation report.* Chicago: Center for Talent Development, Northwestern University.

Zill, N. (1990). *Child health and school readiness: Background paper on a national educational goal.* Washington, DC: Department of Education.

# CHAPTER 4

# The Effects of Health and Social Welfare Factors on Literacy Development: Implications for Teachers and Teacher Preparation: A Response to Joy Dryfoos

*MaryEllen Vogt*

I n her chapter, Joy Dryfoos presents a sobering, depressing, yet realistic depiction of many children who enter the U.S. public school system without the necessary healthy and literate environments to prepare them to become educated and capable adults. These are the children who are underfed and malnourished, unfit and ill, disadvantaged and impoverished. Many of these children and adolescents finish school as functional illiterates who can barely navigate through today's print-rich, literacy-dependent, and technologically savvy world. Sadly, as these students grow into adulthood, many become part of the labyrinth of the U.S. social welfare system or serve as residents of the U.S. penal system (Haigler, Harlow, O'Connor, & Campbell, 1992). Perhaps, not surprisingly, these are many of the same children and adolescents who are born into U.S. urban settings.

As I read and reflected on Dryfoos's informative chapter, which included statistics about children's health issues, social welfare quandaries, and the emotional and psychological barriers to successful educational experiences, as well as how effective interventions (described primarily as school and community-based programs) can overcome some of these formidable problems, several questions came to mind. These questions are not intended to contest any of Dryfoos's hypotheses or recommendations. I cannot argue with anything she has recommended nor dispute the several effective programs that she described.

Instead, these questions are posed to further challenge our thinking about how we may better prepare urban children and adolescents to become literate adults, given the realities of the health and social welfare factors that confront them. At the end of her chapter, Dryfoos suggests that "the route to literacy development is, of course, very complex. Partnerships can help solve some of the personal problems of the students and their families. . .[but] the bottom line has to be in the classroom." Therefore, in this chapter I will focus on teachers and teacher preparation for the urban school. In addition to the questions I pose, I offer instructional implications and recommendations for urban classrooms that are related to the health and social welfare factors suggested by Dryfoos.

# How Do We Avoid Blaming the Victims?

At all grade levels, today's children outperform academically the children from earlier eras of U.S. schooling (Bracey, 1997). However, as Dick Allington (2000) points out, even with this positive indicator, there is a disturbing trend. It appears that U.S. schools work better for some students than for others. Those who come from homes in which parents have lower levels of family income, education, and health care consistently perform below students with families of higher income and educational levels.

As I work with urban teachers, administrators, and teacher educators, we often engage in conversations about topics related to today's students and the belief that many lack experiences and background that enable them to engage successfully in academic kindergarten and first-grade programs. Comments are often made about the children of disadvantaged and impoverished families, and at times, these educators overtly blame family circumstances for students' poor performance and lack of literacy development. For example, within "high-risk" urban families, as defined by Dryfoos, children often live with a single parent, are poor, and do not have health insurance; nearly a third are involved in the social welfare system. Teachers' frustrations about these circumstances are manifested in comments such as "If they'd just get jobs. . . ," "If they'd just stay married and have fewer children. . . ," "If they'd just stay in school. . .," "If they'd just learn English. . .," "If they'd just read to their kids. . .," "If they'd just get off welfare. . . ," "If they'd just support the school. . . ," and so forth.

How can we help teachers to not throw up their hands, even if metaphorically, and declare these children as lost to our educational system? Ascribing blame to the children or their parents serves little purpose. Rather, determining how to effectively reach urban children and their parents must be the focus of our collective efforts.

# How Can We Provide Urban Schools With the Most Prepared and Highly Dedicated Teachers?

The disparity in the teaching force in higher-income suburban schools and lower-income urban schools is glaring. For example, in the Los Angeles Unified School District (LAUSD) in 2001–2002, 73.4% of teachers held a full credential, and 19.1% of teachers were serving on an "emergency credential," meaning that the holder had not received any professional teacher preparation other than occasional district-provided inservice. Another 12.4% of teachers were enrolled in a university or district internship program or a preintern program, in which they were learning to teach while on the job. In comparison, in Irvine Unified School District in Orange County (in affluent Irvine, approximately 50 miles south of Los Angeles), during the same time period, 96.6% of teachers held a full credential, 2.8% were teaching with emergency credentials, and 0.03% were in internship programs (California Department of Education, 2003). The difference in teacher preparedness is reflected in student achievement in these two districts, although many other differences also exist, such as per capita income, educational level of parents, percentage of residents on welfare, percentage of families with medical insurance, and so forth. Not surprisingly the transience in teacher population found in inner-city LAUSD also greatly exceeds teacher mobility in Irvine.

So, how do we entice expert suburban teachers into urban schools and encourage new teachers to work in Los Angeles, rather than Irvine? A differential pay scale, along with teacher preparation and professional development that are unique to the needs of urban children and families, might help provide a more effective teaching force for these schools. The preparation of new urban teachers should not just be more intensive, it must be different, with attention to not only the academic but also the emotional, social, medical, and psychological needs of the student population. Therefore, the commitment to improving the teaching in these schools, even if it is provided by inexperienced teachers, must be shared among district administrators, community leaders, and state and federal policymakers. With a high degree of commitment by all stakeholders to improve teaching while reducing the "blame game," we may be able to discontinue the current practice of placing new, inexperienced, often underprepared teachers in the classrooms that most need pedagogical expertise and an understanding of the particular needs of the children and families who reside in these urban communities.

# Why Does the Medical Model Still Exist When Discussing Urban Literacy Education? Is There a Better Alternative?

Years ago, when I was in graduate school preparing to become a reading specialist, I learned about a series of steps for assessing and teaching "reading *disabled*" students that included the following: (1) give a battery of *tests*, (2) determine a *diagnosis*, (3) write a *prescriptive* plan, and (4) implement a *course of treatment*. My advanced fieldwork took place in a reading *clinic* on campus. We were called reading *clinicians*, and the only thing missing was a white lab coat and stethoscope. For many years, the medical model has had a stronghold in the field of reading, and our job has been, ostensibly, to *cure* students of their reading deficiencies. In today's world, however, with the complex medical, social, and psychological challenges that many students are facing, a medical model in literacy is antiquated at best and potentially damaging at worst. Martha Ruddell (2004) describes three deficit, medical models of instruction that have been prevalent in reading education, special education, and Title I programs. These include

- The Defect Model: Something is wrong with the child. The teacher's role is to find what's wrong and repair it.
- The Deficit Model: Something is missing in the child's development. The teacher's role is to discover what's missing and teach it.
- The Disruption Model: A trauma is interfering with learning; the teacher's role is to identify the trauma and remove it or reduce its impact.

Notice how within these medical models, there is an implied pathology and a search for a cure—something is "wrong" with the student and the teacher has the responsibility to fix it. However, Ruddell (2004) suggests that there is another model that does not focus on what's wrong or deficient with the student. Instead, in this model, the focal point is on the student's achievement potential. Ruddell calls this model

- The Difference Model: There is a difference between a student's performance and expected achievement. The teacher's role is to locate and lessen the difference by providing appropriate instruction to achieve a closer match.

When educators adopt this model of instruction, especially for children in urban settings, the question isn't what needs to be fixed or replaced or removed. Instead, the question becomes, "How do I adjust instruction so that the difference between this student's performance and capability is less-ened?" What's important is that the onus is on the teacher, not just the child. Note that the Difference Model is appropriate for all learners, in-cluding gifted underachievers, struggling readers, and those with learning problems. Teachers must grasp this notion of establishing a match between students' assessed needs and instruction (Lipson & Wixson, 2002), while at-tending at the same time to children's interaction with their family, back-ground, culture, language, life experiences, communities of involvement, and classroom contexts (Vogt & Shearer, 2003). Clearly, this requires that teacher educators prepare new teachers to understand and teach within the Difference Model.

# Are There Other Social or Psychological Factors That May Be Related to the Low Literacy Performance of Urban Students?

The research of Michael Bernard (2002) suggests that we should be exam-ining some psychological and social–emotional factors that have been over-looked previously in the literature on reading and literacy. He describes two domains of children's and adults' psychological function: (1) The Optimist has an internal locus of control with accompanying positive atti-tudes and emotions; (2) The Pessimist relies on an external locus of control with accompanying negative attitudes and emotions. Bernard's findings in-dicate that young people within the first domain usually possess five key foundational characteristics: confidence, persistence, organization, getting along skills, and emotional resilience. These are supported by 11 "Habits of the Mind" (such as self-acceptance, risk taking, high tolerance for frus-tration, tolerance of others, and goal setting). Students who possess these characteristics have been found to achieve to their potential and have a healthier mental outlook. In contrast, students who are angry and unhappy (the Pessimists) have not acquired these capacities; they have higher degrees of anxiety and lower self-esteem; and they demonstrate general work avoid-ance, disorganization, and rebelliousness.

Although researchers (Brenner & Salovey, 1997) in the field of emo-tional intelligence, emotional regulation, and child development have ex-amined the social–emotional competence of young people's success and happiness, Bernard believes it is of equal importance to investigate a stu-dent's negative mind-set and the resulting blocks that impede the develop-ment of confidence, persistence, organization, getting along skills, and emotional resilience (described as "emotional regulation"). Without these life skills, students are at risk for poor mental health, including serious underachievement.

Bernard (2004) states that the development of emotional resilience and regulation determines whether students generate boosters (attitudes and practices that lead to success and achievement, such as healthy self-esteem, organization, confidence) or blockers (attitudes and practices that impede success and achievement, such as anxiety, work avoidance, disorganization, and anger or rebelliousness). Low emotional-regulation skills lead to more blockers, whereas high regulation leads to fewer blockers and more boosters. Bernard has developed an assessment that students, teachers, and parents complete to determine a student's profile for the five foundational skills, as well as the boosters and blockers that enhance or impede an individual's academic achievement (see The Mindset for Academic Achievement and Poor Social-Emotional-Behavioral Development Scale, Bernard, 2001). Bernard's research indicates that when teachers are taught how to assess and develop the five foundational skills, along with the 11 Habits of the Mind, in a comprehensive program for psychological, social, and emotional development, student achievement is increased. He has also found that these foundational characteristics appear to either positively or negatively impact the success of intervention in a remedial setting.

For children who grow up in an urban environment with accompanying deleterious health and social welfare factors, it may be important to examine more closely Bernard's work, as well as the psychological services alluded to in Dryfoos's description of the Polk Brothers Foundation Community Schools. I have often wondered why some children and adolescents who come from disadvantaged environments are able to "beat the odds" and become successful, fully literate adults. Bernard might suggest that these are the students who have early on developed an optimistic attitude, along with the requisite confidence, persistence, organization, getting along skills, and emotional resilience. These positive characteristics may have provided these students the foundation for becoming successful despite sometimes overwhelming challenges.

At present, widely used remediation approaches for improving reading do not include activities or intervention methods that focus specifically on the psychological and emotional characteristics that could be impeding student progress. For at-risk students in urban and other environments, this may be a necessary addition to the current array of reading interventions being implemented in schools.

# How Can Teachers Learn to Partner With Medical and Social Welfare Professionals to Meet Students' Needs?

Dryfoos's chapter focuses on effective community and school partnership programs that have been shown to make a difference for urban students' and their families' lives. She makes the important point that schools cannot carry out by themselves the task of meeting all the diverse needs of urban students. Partnerships and collaborations are necessary, and they enhance the possibility that parents gain access to critical community and school resources and services.

This type of collaborative experience at the preservice level can be very valuable for new teachers. In a project at California State University, Long Beach, funded by the Fordham Foundation, Julie O'Donnell (Department of Social Work), Bonnie Kellogg (Department of Nursing), and I (Department of Teacher Education) created a training program for preservice social workers, school nurses, and secondary teachers. Our purpose was to bring the university students together to learn about how they could work as a team of professionals on behalf of students and families. Their field experiences during two semesters were held at a middle school in a lower socioeconomic area of Long Beach, a large urban community in Los Angeles County. One morning a week before school, the social work, nursing, and education students met with us as their professors to discuss issues, concerns, successes, and ways in which they could provide more appropriate services to the adolescents and families with whom they were working each day in the middle school.

Throughout this project, the university students developed better understandings about the work of their new colleagues through simulations and role-playing activities. Most of the school nursing and social work students had not been in a middle school since their own middle school days, and their field work experiences helped them learn to work closely with students, teachers, administrators, and parents. The preservice teachers valued their collaboration with the social workers and school nurses, and in the end, they expressed strong feelings of support and admiration for their colleagues. All participants ended the project believing that collaboration with other professionals in the school setting is the most effective way to work with students and families in an urban setting. It is important to note that the focus of this collaborative effort was on providing preservice nurses, social workers, and teachers with the skills and experiences to assist them in working in urban schools within the Difference Model (Ruddell, 2004). It was *not* about teaching these professionals how to "fix" adolescents and their families. (For information about another similar university–school project involving social work and Julie O'Donnell, see the Stevenson–YMCA Community School Program discussed in chapter 3.)

## What Is the Role of Family Literacy Programs in Urban Public Schools?

In her chapter, Dryfoos describes a number of "community school" projects, in which the school and community worked together to provide urban families with access to resources and information. Within the field of reading, the concept of family literacy has its roots in similar types of projects. According to the International Reading Association's Family Literacy Committee, "Family literacy encompasses the ways parents, children, and extended family members use literacy at home and in their community. Sometimes, family literacy occurs naturally during the routines of daily living and helps adults and children 'get things done'" (Morrow, 1995, p. 8).

Rather than viewing the home as a "deficit environment," successful family literacy programs engage parents as partners in the process of educating their children (Vogt & Shearer, 2003). The purpose of these programs is not to "train the parents" but to portray the school as a place where parents can comfortably discuss school-related and community concerns. The hope is that parents will then want to become more involved in their children's education. In effective family literacy projects, the school honors and validates home languages and cultures; provides assistance in accessing medical, legal, and other community services; and supports families as they gain proficiency in language and literacy (Vogt & Shearer, 2003).

Through these kinds of family literacy programs, it is hoped, we can put an end to the blame game. In fact, Dorsey-Gaines and Taylor (1988), in their study of literacy contexts of families in poverty, found that children's delayed academic achievement was not necessarily caused by a lack of parental support for literacy development. Instead, what put children at risk was that their parents did not have social, political, and economic support for dealing with real-life challenges such as housing, health, financial, and social needs.

An example of an effective family literacy program is provided by the Claremore (Oklahoma) Public Schools (Vogt & Shearer, 2003). This began as an open house for the Hispanic families in the community. Invitations in Spanish were sent home with children, but they also were posted in the local grocery stores, public laundries, filling stations, and check-cashing establishments. On the evening of the event, in addition to teachers and administrators, representatives from most of the city services were present. The mayor welcomed the families through an interpreter, and an elementary school principal presented an orientation to ESL services in the district. Booths were set up in the cafeteria to provide information on various city and community organizations, including the Fire Department, Red Cross, local university, the Health Department, Civil Defense (with information in Spanish about tornado safety), Police Department, and the Super Recreation Center (a public fitness facility). Information about health and safety issues was provided by the Red Cross and Health Department, and enrollment forms for adult education and General Educational Development (GED) courses were available from the university. The librarian had a "book fair" with many children's books written in Spanish, a local supermarket provided refreshments, and students performed songs and recitations throughout the evening. Children received plastic fire hats, pencils, magnets, stickers, and other trinkets from the booths they visited.

A primary goal of this event was to encourage parents to view the school as a community resource and a comfortable place. Although Claremore isn't exactly an urban district (it's more a suburb of Oklahoma City), lessons can be learned from this school–community effort about how collaboration can foster a positive educational environment for all students.

Additional information about other successful family literacy programs is available on the National Center for Family Literacy (www.famlit.org) and Barbara Bush Foundation for Family Literacy (www.barbarabushfoundation.com) websites.

## Concluding Thoughts

If, as Joy Dryfoos suggests, teachers are ultimately what makes a difference in urban schools, then we need to consider preparing them differently. As with reading instruction, a one-size-fits-all approach to teacher education may no longer be appropriate. Instead, preservice teacher preparation and professional development programs should include information about and on-site experiences related to the health and social welfare factors that affect urban children and their families. With more appropriate education in these areas and ongoing support for teachers, along with pay commensurate with their responsibilities, we may find that current teacher shortages in urban schools are lessened. In addition, we may discover that families, community members, and policymakers afford these teachers the respect they deserve for assuming the challenges and rewards of teaching in urban settings. Appropriately prepared and appreciated teachers, along with adequate community resources for parents and families, may overcome some of the social welfare and even medical challenges facing today's urban schools.

## REFERENCES

Allington, R.L. (2000). *What really matters for struggling readers: Designing research-based programs.* New York: Longman.

Bernard, M.E. (2001). *Program Achieve: A curriculum of lessons for teaching students how to achieve and develop social-emotional-behavioral well-being* (Vols. 1–6, Grades 1&2–11&12). Oakleigh, VIC: Australian Scholarships Group; Laguna Beach, CA: You Can Do It! Education.

Bernard, M.E. (2002). *Providing all children with the foundations for achievement and social-emotional-behavioral well-being* (2nd ed.). Oakleigh, VIC: Australian Scholarships Group.

Bernard, M.E. (2004). *Building the foundations for success and social-emotional well-being in young people: A consultant's guide for working with parents and teachers.* Laguna Beach, CA: You Can Do It! Education.

Bracey, G.W. (1997). *Setting the record straight: Responses to misconceptions about public education in the United States.* Alexandria, VA: Association for Supervision and Curriculum Development.

Brenner, E.M., & Salovey, P. (1997). Emotion regulation during childhood: Developmental, interpersonal, and individual considerations. In P. Salovey & D.J. Sluyter (Eds.), *Emotional development and emotional intelligence:*

*Educational implications* (pp. 168–192). New York: Basic Books.

California Department of Education. (2003). *Demographics unit* (p. 3). Sacramento, CA: Author.

Dorsey-Gaines, C., & Taylor, D. (1988). *Growing up literate: Learning from inner city families.* Portsmouth, NH: Heinemann.

Haigler, C., Harlow, C., O'Connor, P., & Campbell, A. (1992). *Executive summary of literacy behind walls: Profiles of the prison population from the national adult literacy survey.* Retrieved October 11, 2004, from http://www.nces.ed.gov/naal/resources/execsunnprison.asp

Lipson, M.Y., & Wixson, K.K. (2002). *Assessment and instruction of reading and writing difficulties: An interactive approach* (3rd ed.). Boston: Allyn & Bacon.

Morrow, L.M. (1995). Family literacy: New perspectives, new practices. In L.M. Morrow (Ed.), *Family literacy connections in schools and communities* (pp. 5–10). Newark, DE: International Reading Association.

Ruddell, M.R. (2004). *Teaching content reading and writing* (4th ed.). New York: Wiley.

Vogt, M.E., & Shearer, B.A. (2003). *Reading specialists in the real world: A sociocultural view.* Boston: Allyn & Bacon.

# CHAPTER 5

# Violence as a Factor in the Lives of Urban Youth

*Douglas Fisher, Jennifer E. Obidah, Mary Helen Pelton, and Jack Campana*

DEATH

Death is a sin a
Crime of horror
You lose the one
You love so
You go insane
But then you think
Everybody goes
Someday

Briana Hampton, seventh grade

Ask Briana about the poem she wrote, and she will tell you about her experiences growing up in the inner city. She indicates that violence and death are part of her life—part of the experiences that make her who she is. Given these experiences, we wonder how teachers react when students report their experience with violence during class discussions or in their writing. We also wonder if students disengage from school because they are required to talk about and write about things that they either don't care about or don't have experience with. Or for those students who unfortunately experience violence in their lives, do they disengage as a result of a lack of opportunities in school in which to make sense of these circumstances? We believe that Anderson's (2003) question is most relevant: "What happens to the aggression and violence if we don't allow children to express it in healthy ways such as writing?" (p. 228). We also wonder if teachers and administrators are aware of the incidence and prevalence in the lives of the students who attend urban schools and how students are coping with violence in their lives. In this chapter, we provide readers with a review of research on violence as well as the available statistics on this topic. We close the chapter with a set of policy recommendations that schools and districts can use to address the issues of violence.

# The Context of Violence

The Oxford English dictionary (compact edition, 1971) defines *violence* as "the exercise of physical force so as to inflict injury on, or cause damage to, persons or property" (p. 3635). But we acknowledge that violence is more than that—we submit that poverty is a form of violence. We also understand that there are more subtle forms of violence that are not physical, such as verbal abuse and neglect. We focus in this chapter on the type of violence that is consistent with the more formal definition of violence, specifically because research indicates that when children experience violence—whether as a victim, perpetrator, or witness—their experience usually results in adverse effects on their future lives.

Violence plagues U.S. society—to most people it is omnipresent and omnipotent. However, the emotional costs of violence are difficult to ascertain. According to the Archives of Pediatric Medicine (California Attorney General's Office, 2002), "children who have witnessed violence are more likely to miss days of school, get poor grades and exhibit emotional problems. Children with higher exposure to violence exhibit more depression and anxiety than children with lower exposure" (p. 69). Unfortunately, violence at home and at school is a reality in the lives of many students. In the following paragraphs, we outline the types of violence that children, particularly those who live in concentrated areas of urban poverty, are likely to experience in their lifetime.

# Assumptions About Youth and Violence

The contexts of most violence experienced by youth are urban communities overcome with poverty and its associated dysfunctions: on the political level, a dwindling tax base and low voter turnout; on the economic level, high unemployment rates, limited employment opportunities, limited or no access to upwardly mobile jobs, low educational attainment among residents; and consequently, on the social level, high rates of substance abuse, crime, and violence (Jencks & Peterson, 1991; Kozol, 1991). By 1991, central cities were home to 43% of the total U.S. poverty population and 80% of the African American poor (Kasarda, 1993). From these adverse circumstances come the children who attend urban schools. For the most part, especially pertaining to violence, these social problems have garnered these students negative school attention. Consequently, a number of common assumptions exist with regard to violence and its effect on the lives of urban schoolchildren. Among these assumptions are the following:

- In the 1990s, school violence affected mostly white students.
- A new violent breed of young superpredators threatens the United States.
- African American and Hispanic youth are more likely to become involved in violence than other racial or ethnic groups.
- Getting tough with juvenile offenders by trying them in adult criminal court reduced the likelihood that they will commit more crimes. (adapted from U.S. Department of Health and Human Services, 2001)

In ascertaining how best to address violence in the lives of youth, these assumptions warrant closer examination.

## Assumption 1: In the 1990s, School Violence Affected Mostly White Students

Despite the increasing number of violent incidents in suburban and rural schools in the last decade, children who were frequently exposed to violence primarily resided in the urban inner cities of the United States. In the 1990s, as in decades past, violence in schools primarily occurred in schools located in cities or urban areas. These schools were populated with minority (mostly African American and Latino) and low-income student bodies. A 1997 study published by the National Center for Education Statistics noted that among the principals surveyed about the level of violent occurrences at their schools, 17% of city principals reported at least one serious crime, as compared to 8% of rural schools and 5% of suburban town schools (as citied in Donohue, Schiraldi, & Ziedenberg, 1998).

However, a number of incidents of school violence in suburban and rural areas populated by primarily white students have occurred. These incidents were given a high level of media attention because of the unexpectedness of violent occurrences in these schools and the fact that more than one student or adult in each incident (as high as 16 people in one of the incidents) was killed. Nonetheless, suburban and rural schools are far less likely to experience violence among students in the magnitude experienced by urban schools.

## Assumption 2: A New Violent Breed of Young Superpredators Threatens the United States

Donohue et al. (1998), among others, assert that many more juvenile homicide victims are killed by adults than by other juveniles. These authors note that in 1997–1998, 90% of homicide victims under age 12 and 75% of homicide victims between age 12 and 17 were killed by adults. Dohrn (1997) also offers a number of other realities of youth violence, including "if all the youth violence were eliminated, 86% of the violent crimes would still exist; and, the majority of children in detention and correctional facilities are there for nonviolent offenses" (p. 46). Additionally, the Children's Defense Fund reported that

> despite a steady growth in the juvenile population over the past decade, there has been a 23% drop in juvenile violent crime arrests since 1996. In 2000, juveniles accounted for 12.2% arrests for serious violent crime, down 4.4% from 1999. (as cited in National Institute on Out-of-School Time, 2003, p. 1)

Yet, the perception that a new violent breed of superpredators threatens the United States is held by many members of mainstream society and, unfortunately, serves as an indictment of the majority of today's youth, especially youth of color.

This perception of the youth is consistently fueled by media reports. As discussed in the previous section, prolonged and sensationalized media attention resulted in the misconception that school violence was occurring at all types of schools at the same rate. This is an incorrect assumption. To put the exaggerated media attention in a relative perspective, Donohue et al. (1998) wrote that homicides in the United States dropped 13% between 1990 and 1995, according to the FBI, but coverage of homicides on the major television networks' news programs increased by 240% during that time (p. 4). These authors note that media misrepresentation of violence among the youth as being consistently on the rise has resulted in "misdirected public policy being generated to safeguard the schools, even though the real threat may lie elsewhere" (p. 2). Clearly, prolonged media attention to the few major incidents of violence among the youth sustains a particularly derogatory perspective of youth even during periods when violence among the youth has declined.

Another counterargument to the assumption of a new breed of superpredators is the proven link between increased violence among youth and greater access to guns (Gorski & Pilotto, 1993). According to the Centers for Disease Control, children in the United States are 12 times more likely to die from guns than children in 25 other industrialized countries, including Israel and Northern Ireland. In addition, the Office of Juvenile Justice and Delinquency Programs (Torbet, 1997) reported that although killings by juveniles with guns quadrupled from 1984 to 1994, the number of handgun homicides committed by youth remained the same. In short, the entire increase in juvenile homicide during this decade was gun related (Donohue et al., 1998).

Ironically, study findings show that access to firearms is linked to crime because individuals often perceive that possessing a gun will enable them to protect themselves and their material possessions (Kleck & Gertz, 1998). Although most national studies that reach this conclusion are conducted among adults, the findings resonate with reports about youth who carry guns (Canada, 1995; Kellerman, Fuqua-Whitley, Rivara, & Mercy, 1998). Rather than consigning labels to children who commit crimes, more attention should be paid to the facts that much fewer youth than adults commit acts of violence on each other, access to handguns strongly correlates with the increased rate of violence among youth, and, sadly, youth carrying guns may be trying to protect themselves in a society and in schools in which they do not feel safe.

## Assumption 3: African American and Hispanic Youth Are More Likely to Become Involved in Violence Than Other Racial or Ethnic Groups

Although African American and Latino youth outnumber all other groups in reported juvenile crimes, the assumption that these two groups are more likely to become involved in violence begs examination. As mentioned earlier, research shows that gun access, more than any other factor, accounted for the rise in rates of violence among youth in the last two decades. Moreover, racist and discriminatory residential policies have resulted in African Americans and Latinos being the two groups in the United States most likely to live in areas of concentrated poverty. We reiterate that higher rates of violence occur in areas of concentrated poverty as a result of the political and economic disenfranchisement of the residents. Thus, the fact that these groups outnumber other groups in the reported rates of violence has more to do with the disproportionate number of African Americans and Latinos living in poverty and isolation from mainstream America than their racial composition.

Another insidious outcome of this type of reasoning regarding these two racial groups is the disproportionate number of punitive measures directed toward their children in schools. Many schools suspend and expel significant numbers of African American and Latino students (males in particular) yearly (Hunter & Williams, 2003; Skiba, Michael, Nardo, & Peterson, 2002). In their study of race and gender bias in the punishment of schoolchildren, McFadden, Marsh, Price, and Hwang (1992) found that even though African American students accounted for only 36.7% of the disciplinary referrals at the school they studied, these students received 54.1% of the corporeal punishment and 43.9% of the school suspensions. In addition, even though more white students committed the acts for which students received corporeal punishment, black students still received more punishments. The authors then investigated whether the severity of the acts perpetrated by black students was the reason why they received more punishment. Their investigation revealed no evidence in the school's disciplinary files to support such a claim. Such research highlights society's propensity to perceive African Americans and Latinos as more likely to commit crimes without taking into consideration how these groups are treated in society. Making African American and Latino students the focus of anti-youth violence policies obscures the institutional and organizational factor that may contribute to school violence (Hyman & Perone, 1998). Similarly, McFadden et al. (1992) assert that "the more autocratic and punishing the school environment, the more all children, but particularly minority and poor children, are more likely to be alienated from the learning environment" (p. 145). They urge that as the school population becomes more black, Hispanic, and poor, schools must develop more effective and humane methods of controlling children, or an inordinate and ultimately self-defeating amount of time will be spent suspending and expelling children instead of educating them.

## Assumption 4: Getting Tough With Juvenile Offenders by Trying Them as Adults Will Reduce the Likelihood That They Will Commit More Crimes

A number of policy changes in recent years represent the "get tough" approach to addressing youth violence. These policy changes include stricter punishment for drugs and gang-related offenses, a proliferation of discipline-focused interventions such as "boot camps" for juvenile offenders, and lowering the age at which juveniles can be tried as adults (Jones, 1996; Singer, 1996; Torbet, 1996). Many states, including Michigan, Florida, and West Virginia, have passed laws that make it easier for children to be tried as adults (Redding, 1999). However, in 1996 more than half of the cases waived to criminal court were nonviolent drug or property offenses. Moreover, the increased rate of juvenile transfers to adult court has "set the upper age of juvenile court jurisdiction at 15 or 16 rather than 18" (Young & Gainsborough, 2000, p. 3). On the school level, similar punitive measures have been instituted, the most prevalent of which are the zero tolerance policies.

Zero tolerance policies, defined as "a school or district policy that mandates predetermined consequences/punishments for specific offenses" (Drodge, 1997, p. 312), have come under harsh scrutiny in recent years (Burke & Herbert, 1996; Heller, 1996). On the school level, similar to the general institution of punitive measures against the youth, research has shown that such measures are not effective in reducing the number of juveniles who commit acts of violence (Forst & Blomquist, 1991; Morrison, Furlong, & Morrison, 1997; Schneider & Schramm, 1986), and, ironically, studies have shown that schools that have adopted sweeping zero tolerance policies are less safe than schools that have implemented fewer components of such policies (Mayer & Leone, 1999; Pipho, 1998). However, these get-tough policies continue to be pushed despite their often detrimental effects on the lives of children of color who, because of their political, economic, and social status in society, already face a future of limited possibilities.

In summary, a number of assumptions exist about today's youth that often lead to perceptions of these youth as harder to reach, less educable, and more violent than young people in past generations. However, research clearly shows that even though rates of violence among youth have increased in recent decades, youth violence is a complex issue that warrants investigation from myriad perspectives. Clearly, young people need help to combat the often-devastating effects of violence in their lives. Given the social and economic situation experienced by people living in concentrated areas of urban poverty and who are especially vulnerable to violence in their lives, how can practitioners best serve the students who reside in these areas and bring their life circumstances with them to school? In the concluding section of this chapter, we present some strategies that have been used to address violence in the lives of youth.

## Types of Violence That Students Experience

Children and youth in our public schools, especially those in our urban schools, are likely to have experienced violence by the time they enter our classrooms. Some estimates suggest that every student in an urban school has experienced violence either as a victim, perpetrator, or witness by the time he or she reaches high school. Several types of violence are common, including domestic violence, homicide, and suicide. In addition, we will discuss the types of violence that occur on our school campuses.

## Domestic or Relationship Violence

Domestic violence includes acts of violence against a person living in the household, especially a member of one's immediate family. The range of domestic violence that children may witness includes (1) rape (completed or attempted forced vaginal, oral, or anal sex); (2) physical assault (from slapping and hitting to using a gun); and (3) stalking (repeated acts of harassment and intimidation with the victim reporting a high level of fear). In addition, young adults may experience relationship violence with someone they are dating but not residing with.

Table 5.1 contains an overview of the reported rates of domestic violence in the United States. The data from this table are based on telephone calls and self-report. Thus, the actual rates of domestic violence may be much higher. For example, the American Bar Association (ABA) Commission on Domestic Violence suggests that between 1 and 4 million women are assaulted by an intimate partner during a typical 12-month period, and nearly one in three women will experience domestic violence in their lifetime (American Psychological Association, 1996; Bureau of Justice Statistics, 1995). It is important to note that the ABA Commission on Domestic Violence reported that domestic violence is statistically consistent across race but not gender, age, or sexual orientation (e.g., Bureau of Justice Statistics, 1995).

In fact, women between the ages of 19 and 29 are at the highest risk, whereas women ages 46 and older are at the least risk. Similarly, between 90% and 95% of the victims are women. That is not to suggest that domestic violence against men does not occur; it does. But research evidence

Table 5.1
Rates of Domestic Violence in the United States

| Type of Victimization (Over Lifetime) | | | |
|---|---|---|---|
| Percentage | | Number | |
| Women | Men | Women | Men |
| Rape | 7.7 | 0.3 | 7,753,669 | 278,244 |
| Physical assault | 22.1 | 7.4 | 22,254,037 | 6,863,352 |
| Rape and/or physical assault | 24.8 | 7.6 | 24,972,856 | 7,048,848 |
| Stalking | 4.8 | 0.6 | 4,833,456 | 556,488 |
| Total victimized | 25.5 | 7.9 | 25,677,735 | 7,327,092 |

Source: National Institute for Justice and the Centers for Disease Control (2000)

suggests that much of the domestic violence directed toward men is the result of self-defense (Chalk et al., 1998). In terms of sexual orientation, estimates of domestic violence in same-sex couples range from 25% to 33% (e.g., Barnes, 1998), but these figures may be especially low, given the risk of reporting when gay or lesbian couples must "come out" to identify the crime (Island & Letellier, 1991).

The effect on children and youth of witnessing domestic violence varies. Some children emerge from their experiences relatively unaffected. Others experience aggressive behaviors, poor social skills, anxiety, impaired athletic ability, and learning difficulties (e.g., Margolin, 1998). Factors such as social support, conflict resolution training, and youth involvement programs mediate how children will respond to this type of violence.

## Homicide

Another type of violence that children and youth experience is homicide, the killing of one human being by another. According to the National Center for Health Statistics (2001), the homicide rate for urban areas is about double that of smaller communities. More specifically, in large metropolitan counties the homicide rate is 11.5 deaths for every 100,000 people. This compares with small, nonmetropolitan counties in which the homicide rate is 5.4 deaths per 100,000 population. These rates also vary by gender and race, with males and African Americans most at risk.

Homicide is the fourth leading cause of death for children ages 5–9 and youth ages 10–14 (Anderson, 2002). The leading causes of death for children in these age groups are unintentional injuries, malignant neoplasms, and suicide. More children ages 10–14 die from homicide than heart disease, pneumonia, or congenital abnormalities. For youth ages 15–19, homicide has taken over as the second leading cause of death. Only unintentional injuries claim more lives than homicide for this group of young people.

Not only do children and youth die from homicides but they also are unfortunately too often the perpetrators of this crime. The number of homicides committed by children and youth increased during the mid-1980s and early 1990s. The increase in homicides committed by youth has been related to their use of guns as a weapon. Researchers suggest that youth access to guns increased in the 1990s (e.g., U.S. Department of Education, 1998). Between 1980 and 1987, guns were used in 54% of homicides committed by a juvenile. By 1994, most homicides committed by youth (82%) involved guns. The relative decline in homicides by youth between 1994 and 1997 was attributable entirely to a decline in homicides by firearms (H.N. Snyder & Sickmund, 1999).

One approach to reducing the rate of youth who commit homicide is to ensure that they do not have access to firearms. However, as Schiraldi (1998) points out,

> The gun lobby frequently points to Switzerland and Israel, both of which have high gun ownership and lower homicide rates than the United States, as an argument against gun control. However, America has three times as many children in poverty per capita as Switzerland and twice as many as Israel. (¶10)

As with domestic violence, children who witness a homicide respond in diverse ways. The support system that is in place for the child seems to be the major factor in the trajectory of response. Unfortunately for some students, their experience with homicide changes the trajectory of their life, and they begin to perform poorly in school, increasingly become absent, and isolate themselves from their peers.

## Violence to Self and Suicide

Self-directed violence takes many forms. For example, some teens are "cutters," which means that they cut into their skin and create scars. It is interesting that most cutters become addicted to this behavior and rarely, if ever, attempt suicide. Other students mutilate themselves, stick safety pins through their fingertips or other body parts, or scratch an area until it bleeds and scars. However, the most extreme form of self-directed violence is suicide.

As previously noted, suicide is the fourth leading cause of death for children and youth ages 10–14 and the second leading cause of death for young adults ages 15–19. Each year, approximately 500,000 young adults, ages 15 to 25, attempt suicide, and 5,000 young adults succeed (see www.teen-depression.info). Although the teen suicide rates in the United States have declined in the last decade, it is important to note that they remain double those of the 1950s.

Table 5.2 contains data on suicides by age. Rates differ for males and females, with males being approximately four times more likely to commit suicide (National Center for Health Statistics, 2001). However, women are more likely than men to report a history of attempted suicide, with a gender ratio of 3:1 (National Institute for Mental Health, 2002).

However, suicide is not more prevalent in urban communities. In fact, the rate of suicide in large metropolitan counties is 13.2 deaths per 100,000

Table 5.2
Death Rates for Suicide, 1950–2000
(deaths per 100,000 population)

| Characteristic | | 1950 | 1960 | 1970 | 1980 | 1985 | 1990 | 1996 | 1997 | 1998 | 1999 | 2000 |
|---|---|---|---|---|---|---|---|---|---|---|---|---|
| **All ages** | | **13.6** | **12.5** | **13.1** | **12.2** | **12.5** | **12.0** | **11.7** | **11.4** | **11.3** | **10.7** | **10.6** |
| 5 to 14 years | 0.2 | 0.3 | 0.3 | 0.4 | 0.8 | 0.8 | 0.8 | 0.8 | 0.8 | 0.6 | 0.8 | |
| 15 to 24 years | 4.5 | 5.2 | 8.8 | 12.3 | 12.8 | 13.2 | 12.0 | 11.4 | 11.1 | 10.3 | 10.4 | |
| 25 to 34 years | 9.1 | 10.0 | 14.1 | 16.0 | 15.2 | 15.4 | 14.5 | 14.3 | 13.8 | 13.5 | 12.8 | |
| 35 to 44 years | 14.3 | 14.2 | 16.9 | 15.4 | 15.3 | 15.2 | 15.5 | 15.3 | 15.4 | 14.4 | 14.6 | |
| 45 to 54 years | 20.9 | 20.7 | 20.0 | 15.9 | 14.8 | 14.6 | 14.9 | 14.7 | 14.8 | 14.2 | 14.6 | |
| 55 to 64 years | 26.8 | 23.7 | 21.4 | 15.9 | 16.0 | 13.3 | 13.7 | 13.5 | 13.1 | 12.4 | 12.3 | |
| 65 to 74 years | 29.6 | 23.0 | 20.8 | 16.9 | 17.9 | 15.8 | 15.0 | 14.4 | 14.1 | 13.6 | 12.6 | |
| 75 to 84 years | 28.8 | 26.0 | 19.0 | 19.2 | 22.2 | 21.6 | 20.2 | 20.8 | 21.0 | 19.2 | 19.4 | |
| **Male** | | **21.2** | **20.0** | **19.8** | **19.9** | **21.5** | **20.6** | **20.0** | **19.4** | **19.2** | **18.2** | **18.1** |
| **Female** | | **5.6** | **5.6** | **7.4** | **5.7** | **4.8** | **4.4** | **4.3** | **4.4** | **4.3** | **4.1** | **4.0** |

Source: National Center for Health Statistics (2002)

people, compared with 18.0 deaths per 100,000 people in nonmetropolitan counties (National Center for Health Statistics, 2001).

Suicide is one of the more preventable violent deaths. Approximately 80% of the people who attempt or commit suicide demonstrated advanced warning signs. According to the American Association of Suicidology (see www.suicidology.org), some of the signs of potential suicide in teens include the following:

- Talks about committing suicide
- Has trouble eating or sleeping
- Experiences drastic changes in behavior
- Withdraws from friends and/or social activities
- Gives away prized possessions
- Has attempted suicide before
- Takes unnecessary risks
- Is preoccupied with death and dying
- Loses interest in their personal appearance
- Increases their use of alcohol or drugs

According to the National Institute for Mental Health (2002), "The strongest risk factors for attempted suicide in youth are depression, alcohol, or other drug use disorder, and aggressive or disruptive behaviors." Other researchers have suggested that sexual orientation and adjustment to feelings of attraction to members of the same sex have resulted in increased suicide attempts (Remafedi, Farrow, & Deisher, 1991). Some estimates are as high as 46% of gay youth have attempted suicide. Dr. Robert Garofalo and his colleagues (Garofalo, Wolf, Wissow, Woods, & Goodman, 1999) of the Children's Hospital, Boston, reported in the American Medical Association's Archives of Pediatric & Adolescent Medicine that students who are gay, lesbian, bisexual, or not sure of their sexual orientation are 3.41 times more likely to report a suicide attempt.

It goes without saying that thoughts of suicide and suicide attempts interfere with student learning. In addition to the missed learning time, students who are focused on suicide are not paying attention to reading, writing, or learning. Further, when teachers notice these behaviors, they can be among the first responders and possibly save a student's life.

Table 5.3
Student-Reported Episodes of Violence on School Property

|  | Total | White | Black | Hispanic |
|---|---|---|---|---|
| Carried a weapon | 8.5% | 7.8% | 9.2% | 10.4% |
| Male | 12.5 | 12.3 | 10.7 | 15.6 |
| Female | 3.7 | 2.1 | 7.8 | 4.3 |
| Threatened or injured with a weapon | 7.4 | 6.2 | 9.9 | 9.0 |
| Male | 10.2 | 8.2 | 14.0 | 12.7 |
| Female | 4.0 | 3.7 | 5.8 | 4.6 |
| In a physical fight | 14.8 | 13.3 | 20.7 | 19.0 |
| Male | 20.0 | 19.1 | 24.6 | 24.7 |
| Female | 8.6 | 5.9 | 17.0 | 12.3 |
| Property stolen or deliberately damaged | 32.9 | 32.6 | 34.0 | 32.1 |
| Male | 36.1 | 35.7 | 37.5 | 33.4 |
| Female | 29.0 | 28.6 | 30.6 | 30.6 |

Source: T.D. Snyder, Hoffman, and Geddes (1998)

## School Violence

Although students face violence in their communities, the U.S. Department of Justice Bureau of Justice Statistics (2002) reports that students and faculty encounter violence within and adjacent to the school as well. For example, Table 5.3 provides an overview of high school students' reports of violence at school. In addition, according to DeVoe and colleagues (2002),

- In 2000, students ages 12 through 18 were victims of about 1.9 million total crimes of violence or theft at school, which is equivalent to one victim every two seconds school is in session.

- In the same year, students in this age range were victims of 128,000 serious crimes at school (i.e., rape, sexual assault, robbery, and aggravated assault), which is equivalent to one victim every 30 seconds school is in session.

- In 2001, 17% of students in grades 9 through 12 reported carrying a weapon such as a gun, knife, or club in the past 30 days. About 6% reported they had carried a weapon on school property.

- From July 1, 1992, through June 30, 1999, there were 358 school-associated violent deaths in the United States, including 255 deaths of school-age children (ages 5 to 19). In the 1999–2000 school year, 9% of teachers were threatened with injury, and 4% were physically attacked by a student.

- Over a five-year period from 1996 through 2000, teachers were the victims of approximately 1,603,000 nonfatal crimes at school. On average, this translates into 321,000 nonfatal crimes per year, or 74 crimes per 1,000 teachers.

- Over the same five-year period teachers were the victims of 69,000 serious crimes, including rape or sexual assault, and robbery or aggravated assault while at school, averaging 14,000 per year.

Safety is near the bottom of Maslow's Hierarchy of Need (1954). Teachers can't teach and students can't learn when they are afraid. Good teachers leave the profession and good students drop out of school when they fear for their personal safety. Yet the violence just described is at the top of the so-called violence continuum. At the bottom of the violence continuum are putdowns, bullying, and harassment. To stop school violence from escalating to the top, schools have to stop the violence at the bottom of the continuum. The right to a free public education isn't enough. Inherent in the right to an education is also the right of every child to come to school and be physically, psychologically, and academically safe.

Kevin Dwyer, former president of National Association of School Psychologists, estimates that 160,000 students miss school every day in the United States because they fear being bullied. Ronald Stephens (1997) reflects the opinion of many educators today: "School yard bullying is a significant and pervasive problem, and is perhaps one of the most severely underrated problems within our educational system" (p. 72). Some researchers report that between 15% and 30% of the children in school today are involved in bullying episodes as victims or as bullies or as both (Nansel et al., 2001; Olweus, 1994; Rigby, 1994, 1998). Other researchers find the rates of such incidents much higher. A recent study by the National Crime Prevention Council (2002) revealed that 61% of students ages 12 to 17 who were surveyed reported seeing bullying one or more times a day. In another study in the midwestern United States, Hoover, Oliver, and Hazler (1992) reported that in their sample of students from grades 8 to 12, roughly 80% of students reported that they had been bullied at some point in their school careers, and 90% of a younger sample (grades 4–8) also said they were victims.

These figures may just be the tip of the iceberg. Bullying tends to be underreported by students. Hoover and Oliver (1996) and Olweus (1994) found that victims and bullies agree teachers do little or nothing to stop bullying. Because nothing will be done, students reach the logical conclusion: Why should we report it? Even for the vigilant teacher, some of the most devastating forms of subtle bullying behavior (social exclusion; humiliation; vicious rumors; intimidation; extortion; sexual and racial taunting; and threats of violence against family, friends, or self) pass "below the radar" of teachers.

Bullying has consequences for the victim, the bully, and the bystanders. Victims are at risk for academic failure, poor self-esteem, anxiety, depression, unhappiness, health problems, and suicide. Bullies are at risk for lifetime antisocial and criminal behavior. Olweus (1994) reported that individuals with a history of bullying had a fourfold increase in criminal behavior by the time they reached their 20s. The majority of former bullies had at least one conviction, and more than a third had multiple convictions. As witnesses to violence, bystanders suffer as well. The U.S. Department of Education's (1998) Bullying Prevention Manual documents the damage caused to witnesses to bullying. Witnesses to bullying may

- Be afraid to associate with the victim for fear of lowering their own status or of retribution from the bully and becoming victims themselves;
- Fear reporting bullying incidents because they don't want to be labeled a snitch, a tattler, or informer;
- Experience feelings of guilt or helplessness for not standing up to the bully on behalf of their classmates;
- Be drawn into bullying behavior by group pressure; and
- Feel unsafe, unable to take action, or a loss of control.

To read of the devastating effects of bullying, written in children's own words, see www.bullying.org.

No longer can we as educators say "bullying is just part of growing up; it happened to me, and I'm stronger for it. The kids will survive." Schools will be found guilty in both the court of law and the court of public opinion when staff members know about bullying and do nothing to stop it.

The U.S. Secret Service and U.S. Department of Education (Vossekuil, Fein, Reddy, Borum, & Modzeleski, 2002) in their study of 37 school shootings documented that almost three quarters of the attackers felt persecuted, bullied, threatened, attacked, or injured by others prior to the incident. Prior to most incidents, other people knew about the attacker's idea or plan to attack. In nearly two thirds of the incidents, more than one person had information about the attack before it occurred. Yet no one reported this important information to school authorities.

The courts also have affirmed the rights of victims of harassment and bullying. In 1999 the U.S. Supreme Court, in the case of *Davis v. Monroe*

*County Board of Education* (1999), ruled that schools could be held liable if school staff members were deliberately indifferent to student-on-student harassment. The court points out that the harassment must be so severe and pervasive that it undermines and detracts from the victim's educational experience. Under such circumstances, the victim is effectively denied equal access to the school's resources and opportunities, and the school can be held liable. *Nabozny v. Podlesny* (1996) is another important case in the area of antiharassment, intimidation, and bullying. The plaintiff, Michael Nabozny (a gay student), suffered years of verbal and physical abuse at the hands of other students. Although the administration knew about the harassment, they did nothing to stop it. The student twice attempted suicide and had poor grades because he had missed so much school. The Seventh Circuit supported a claim of discrimination under Title IX and a Fourteenth Amendment Equal Protection claim. When the case was remanded, the jury awarded the student $900,000 in damages.

Federal statutes also direct the schools to deal with school violence. In the General Provisions of the reauthorized Elementary and Secondary Education Act (ESEA), *No Child Left Behind* (Title IX, Part E, Subpart 2, Sec.9532 Unsafe School Choice Option) requires that schools deemed to be "persistently dangerous" under the federal definition notify the parents of the designation and offer students the opportunity to transfer to another public school within the district. The district will be required to provide transportation for the students. To implement the law, state departments of education will direct the schools to follow certain procedures. For example, schools in Minnesota must (a) collect and report data on suspensions and expulsions twice each year, (b) develop prevention education and intervention services to maximize safe and caring environments for all students and staff, (c) review the school's crisis plan to ensure that it is up to date and that the community partners in emergency safety have been consulted, (d) consider alternatives to suspension and expulsions, and (e) review school policy and crisis and safety plan with community parents. In Minnesota, which has liberal open-enrollment and home-school statutes, parents will home-school their children or move their children to another district that they perceive as safer. The third author (Pelton) reviewed the requests of parents to open-enroll their students elsewhere. The analysis revealed that 95% of the parents cited "school safety" as the reason for requesting the transfer to a different district.

In some schools, the specter of fear, intimidation, and violence is so much a part of the school that to address these issues would require a change in the culture of the educational environment. Although this might seem

like a daunting task, the good news is that it is indeed possible to create a
school culture that says "no" to violence of any kind. The Learning First
Alliance, a partnership of 12 national educational groups, recently determined that

> the creation of a safe and support learning community must be compre-
> hensive, school wide and woven into the curriculum and the culture of the
> school. It can not be an add-on effort, satisfied by special programs to ad-
> dress specific topics such as bullying, character education or dispute reso-
> lution. (Learning First Alliance, 2001, p. 1)

# Changing the Culture of Violence at School

How does a school bring about a cultural change?

## Step 1: The School Board, the Administrators and the Staff Must Believe That They Can and Should Change the Culture of the School

Unless you have broad acceptance of your vision and have a consistent message being delivered by everyone from the superintendent to the custo-
dian, a cultural change is difficult. Ask yourself and your colleagues these
important questions:

> What is your motivation for the change?
>
> What are the data and the stories that suggest the need for a new culture?
>
> What is your vision for how your school will look with the new culture?
>
> How can you create the vision with your stories and your data so that
> students, staff and community will "buy into" the change?

## Step 2: Assess the Areas of Risk

To develop a comprehensive schoolwide plan, your education team needs
data upon which to make decisions. What are the school's or the district's areas of risk? Clarksean and Pelton (2002) suggest that the site assessment
should address topics related to the physical, educational, behavioral, procedural, and perceptual aspects of school safety. These assessments can be
conducted by school personnel or by consultants hired to provide an outside view of the current situation.

Schools need to analyze their discipline referral data. Where are safety-
related discipline referrals coming from? Are there areas of the building,

times of the day, or types of circumstances that seem to "produce" more discipline referrals? What is the level of adult supervision during those times and in those places? Because perception is reality, it is important to conduct surveys or focus groups to determine how students, staff, and parents feel about school safety issues.

Students should be asked questions such as these:

Are there places in the building where you are afraid to go?

When and where do such things as bullying and drug sales take place?

Do the students seek out help? Why or why not?

What is the level of bullying, illegal drugs, weapons, and so forth, in your school?

Do teachers, staff, and administration follow up on complaints regarding bullying?

Have you seen a gun or a dangerous weapon on school property?

In reviewing student responses to a recent survey, the third author (Pelton) noted that one anonymous student wrote, "Please help me." When staff followed up with the students and asked the anonymous student to identify himself if the student wanted assistance, three students responded they had written the comment and wanted help. In another district a student wrote, "Thanks for trying to make our school a better place. I've lived in hell all my school years."

The staff should be queried regarding issues such as the following:

Are there locations on the school grounds and times during the school day or after school where you are concerned about your safety?

How comfortable are you in disciplining students?

What types of interventions have you used with bullies?

How have you supported victims and empowered bystanders?

Has the school crisis plan been shared with you and do you know your role in that plan?

Have you experienced violence on or adjacent to school property or at school-sponsored activities? Please tell us about it.

Parents should be asked about issues such as the following:

Do you know how to proceed with a complaint if you feel your child has been threatened or bullied?

What safety concerns do you have about the school your children attend?

Has the school told you what to do if a crisis occurs at school?

Are you part of any community effort to help make the school and community safer for children? If not, how would you like to help?

Do you think your school is doing enough to address school safety? If yes, what activities do you find particularly helpful? If no, what would you like for the school to do regarding safety issues?

The analysis of the assessment and the perceptional surveys can then guide the development of your safe school plan.

## Step 3: Develop a Safe School Plan

A safe school plan is different from a crisis plan. By having a safe school plan, you are "planning" to prevent problems; it is proactive. It is critical to have both school personnel and outside agencies involved in your planning process. Once you have the plan, put it into action. No plan, no matter how good, will make a change if you don't act on the strategies and tasks outlined. A good plan is a road map that should be able to show you where you have been, where you want to go, and describe how you'll know when you have arrived.

## Step 4: Examine Your School Board Policies and Procedures

Your policies and procedures must support your vision of a violence-free culture. Does your mission statement address the commitment to a safe school? Do you have policies on guns and weapons, hazing, illegal substances, harassment and bullying, crisis plan, civility policy, student conduct and discipline, and bus safety? Do the policies reflect federal, state, county, and local statutes or ordinances? Are these policies clear and well publicized? The school board should review the policies each year because legal issues and school needs change with time.

## Step 5: Based on the Policies and Procedures, Schools Must Establish Clear, Well-Publicized Rules

The rules against violence must be enforced fairly and consistently. In cases of violations of rules, nonhostile, nonphysical sanctions must be applied consistently. Most students, particularly those living in the chaos of violent communities, appreciate structure. Review the student handbook to ensure that expectations of student behavior are clearly communicated. If students know that the staff will deal consistently and fairly with those who make the school unsafe, they are more likely to take a stand and support victims and report dangerous situations to staff before violence erupts. Students play a critical role in school safety and they must know that the adults in their buildings can be counted on. The staff must buy into the vision, understand the policies and procedures, and *must* consistently intervene, giving the clear message that violence, bullying, and harassment are absolutely not acceptable in the class or the school. Staff members who excuse student behavior undermine the vision of a safe school for all and will be viewed by students as weak. Expect referrals for assaults, bullying, and harassment to go up at first as students test the boundaries of staff members' commitment to the vision.

## Step 6: Train the Staff in the Basics of Violence Prevention

All staff members need to be trained on the basics of violence prevention. The assessment and the survey also will point to areas that may need additional training. For example, on one recent survey of staff, a safe school team discovered that 18% of the staff members were afraid to discipline students. The safe school team included positive discipline as part of their next staff training. Other questions may naturally arise out of the assessment; for example,

> Do all of your staff members know what to do when a visitor is seen in the building without a badge?
>
> What should staff members do if they felt threatened by a parent?
>
> Does everyone know the procedure for releasing a student during the school day?
>
> Does the staff understand the procedure they should follow if they suspect or if a child reports abuse?

## Step 7: Involve the Community, Particularly Parents, in Your Vision

Remember school safety is everyone's business. Educators can't have too many partners. As noted, "Violence is everyone's problem and every member of the community must be enlisted to reinforce lessons learned at school.... And work to reduce violence in the community as well as the school" (Kadel, Watkins, Follman, & Hammond, 1999, p. 32).

No parent or community member would say, "I support violence in schools"; however, when their child is involved in a violent episode, parents may waffle. Make parents and community members your partners. Include them on the safe school team. Share your plan with them. Provide them information on how they can contribute to their children's safety. Follow up promptly on their safety concerns. Empower parents by providing them with training that parallels the prosocial training that their children are receiving.

## Step 8: Institute Prosocial Violence Prevention Curricula for All Students in Grades K–12

Emotional intelligence may be just as important, or perhaps more important, than Intelligence Quotient (IQ) in children's success beyond school. It may be tempting to identify the troubled children and only provide training for them; however, research shows that violence-prevention programs are much more effective when they involve the whole student body rather than singling out the chief offenders (Clarksean & Pelton, 2002; Dwyer, Osher, & Warger, 1998). The prosocial curriculum should include an emphasis on anger management, empathy training, impulse control, problem solving, and antibullying behavior. Staff should be given an opportunity to be trained on the best use of the curriculum so that they can successfully institute the program.

## Step 9: Provide Opportunities for Staff to Study the Issues of School Safety

Teachers and paraprofessionals need time to study the issues of school safety, violence prevention, and bullying in greater depth. Some universities (such as the University of North Dakota) provide graduate courses in violence prevention that are Web-based and therefore accessible to educators throughout the world. Noncredit certificate programs in issues related to school safety, crisis intervention, and violence prevention are also available. Check with your neighboring college or university to find out if they offer similar courses. The more knowledgeable the staff, the more they will provide the leadership and support in directing the efforts to create a cultural change.

## Step 10: Track Your Results and Adjust Your Safe Plan Each Year

Data should be analyzed each year and used to celebrate your successes and revise the plan. As Clarksean and Pelton (2002) write, "safe school planning is not a one-time activity" (p. 35). It must be a living and changing document. Plans should be reviewed, updated, and broadly disseminated annually to students, parents, and staff members. Knowing that you are making a difference reinforces your vision and will help sustain your cultural change. Let everyone know the actions being taken and the positive results being achieved, and celebrate the cultural change.

### Step 11: Staff Members Must Believe
### That the School Can Make a Difference

This is the most important step of all. To bring about cultural change, staff members must believe they can and should make a difference in the lives of their children. As the former director of the FBI, Louis J. Freeh, said,

> I know I speak for every parent and every educator in the nation when I say that violence in our schools is not acceptable, not at all, not ever.... We must find the ways to protect our children and secure for them the safe places they need to learn the hard business of growing up, to learn right from wrong, to learn to be good citizens. (as cited in O'Tool, 1999, p. iv)

Although educators can't control the external forces on their students, they can control the school environment and make a positive, violence-free environment where all are welcome and all are safe.

# Strategies to Address Youth Violence and Their Effectiveness

In the U.S. Surgeon General's report on youth violence (2001), effective and ineffective strategies were identified for addressing the issue of youth violence. To be effective, the approach had to have been studied using a rigorous experimental design. The effects from these studies were evaluated to determine if the approach resulted in significant reductions in violence, and if the approach had been replicated by other studies and could be sustained over time. To be classified ineffective, the approach also had to have been studied using a rigorous experimental design that resulted in data suggesting that there were either no effects or the effects were negative. Naturally, there are a number of approaches that have not been studied or that have been studied using research methods other than experimental designs. Having said that, the effective approaches deserve note. Table 5.4 provides a list of approaches evaluated by the Surgeon General to be effective or not. Note that the approaches are grouped by their level of intervention: all students (primary prevention), selected students at increased risk of violence (secondary prevention), and students who have been violent or seriously delinquent (tertiary prevention). These effective and ineffective strategies

Table 5.4
Effectiveness of Intervention Strategies

| Effective Strategies | Ineffective Strategies |
|---|---|
| **Primary Prevention: Universal** | **Primary Prevention: Universal** |
| Skills training | Peer counseling, peer mediation, peer |
| Behavior monitoring and | leaders |
| reinforcement | Nonpromotion to succeeding grades |
| Behavioral techniques for classroom | |
| management | |
| Building school capacity | |
| Continuous progress programs | |
| Cooperative learning | |
| Positive youth development programs | |
| | |
| **Secondary Prevention: Selected** | **Secondary Prevention: Selected** |
| Parent training | Gun buyback programs |
| Home visitations | Firearm training |
| Compensatory education | Mandatory gun ownership |
| Moral reasoning | Redirecting youth behavior |
| Social problem solving | Shifting peer group norms |
| Thinking skills | |
| | |
| **Tertiary Prevention: Indicated** | **Tertiary Prevention: Indicated** |
| Social perspective taking, role taking | Boot camps |
| Multimodal interventions | Residential programs |
| Behavioral interventions | Milieu treatment |
| Skills training | Behavioral token programs |
| Marital and family therapy by clinical | Waivers to adult court |
| staff | Social casework |
| Wraparound services | Individual counseling |

Source: U.S. Department of Health and Human Services (2001)

can be used to guide policy development at the state and district levels. In addition, this list should be used to fund model demonstration projects and new research initiatives. For more information about these interventions, see Youth Violence: A Report of the Surgeon General (U.S. Department of Health and Human Services, 2001).

## Primary Prevention

The first group includes approaches that can be used with the general population of youth. In general, these strategies focus on individual risk or environmental factors. For example, the use of cooperative groups allows students structured time to interact with peers, which has increased attitudes toward school, improved race and human relations, and facilitated academic achievement (e.g., Slavin, 1990). Further, implementing sound classroom management plans that include behavior monitoring and reinforcement can reduce delinquency up to five years later (e.g., Bry, 1982). Naturally, each of these capacity-building factors has an impact on students and whether or not they engage in violent behaviors.

Two strategies aimed at addressing the issue of violence for all students have been demonstrated as ineffective: peer mediation and grade-level retention (e.g., Gottfredson, 1997). These are important to note as they are frequently used strategies in schools. In terms of literacy achievement, increasing numbers of school districts are using nonpromotion or grade-level retention when students do not achieve specific, measurable goals (e.g., Frey, 2003). The evidence to date suggests that nonpromotion results in negative attitudes toward school and has a negative effect on achievement, attendance, and behavior. Thus, our policies on retention for literacy achievement may result in increased levels of violence. It seems reasonable to suggest, then, that literacy educators focus on providing students access to reading specialists and spend funds in that way rather than expending additional dollars on additional years of schooling that may be counterproductive in terms of reducing youth violence.

## Secondary Prevention

The second group of strategies focuses on specific students who have been identified as at risk of youth violence. Among these, many of the effective strategies are family based, such as parent training and home visits (e.g., Dumas, 1989). The research evidence also suggests that compensatory educational programs such as cross-age tutoring and individualized instruction are effective in improving academic achievement and in reducing problem behaviors (Cohen, Kulik, & Kulik, 1982; Jacobson et al., 2001). In addition, problem-solving, thinking-skills, and moral-reasoning training programs have been found to be effective ways to address specific students (e.g., Kazdin, Bass, Siegel, & Thomas, 1989).

It is interesting to note that the strategies that have not been found to be effective focus on firearms and peer group norms. In the first case, programs that either buy back guns or train youth to operate guns safely have not been effective. In addition, programs that attempt to shift peer group norms by grouping troubled students together have either had no effect or, even worse, have facilitated deviancy and have actually increased gang-related behaviors (e.g., Dishion, Andrews, & Crosby, 1995; Elliott & Menard, 1996). The important note for literacy educators here centers on grouping practices. Remedial reading classes in which significant numbers of students who are at enhanced risk for youth violence may result in greater problematic behavior. Thankfully, there are a number of professional resources on flexible grouping strategies that literacy educators can use (e.g., Nagel, 2000).

## Tertiary Prevention

The final types of strategies are based on implementation for youth who have already demonstrated violent behavior. The goal of tertiary prevention is to reduce the likelihood of further violence by individuals who have already engaged in the behavior. The effective strategies require a multimodal, behavioral, and skills-orientated approach rather than a counseling or less-structured approach (e.g., Lipsey & Wilson, 1998). Family clinical interventions are also an effective way of preventing further violence (e.g., Tremblay & Craig, 1995). Wraparound services in which a social service agency serves as the lead agency and coordinates all the services (school, behavioral therapy, health services, etc.) on an individual basis have also been effective in reducing future arrests. In some cases, specially trained foster care families are required to prevent further violent episodes.

As with the previous levels of intervention, there are a number of ineffective strategies at the tertiary level. More specifically, boot camps and residential programs have not resulted in decreased violent behavior (e.g., Dishion, Patterson, & Griesler, 1994). In fact, in a number of studies, boot camps have increased recidivism and have had a harmful effect on youth. Similarly, sending youth to adult court and incarcerating youth in adult criminal institutions has had seriously negative effects. For example, Bishop (2000) demonstrated that youth sent to adult prisons, compared with those sent to youth correctional facilities, were eight times more likely to commit suicide, five times more likely to be sexually assaulted, and twice as likely to be beaten by staff.

In terms of implications for literacy educators, these data suggest that we must focus our efforts on students who have engaged in violent behavior. We must partner with social service agencies and law enforcement if we are to support these children and youth. Our goal should be to ensure that children who have been violent have access to behavioral interventions, that their families have access to therapy, and that they are educated with students who have not been violent to the greatest extent possible (and legal).

As educators and policymakers, we should understand that boot camps and residential programs are not effective, and that waivers to adult court are counterproductive. Our advocacy at this level must be on ensuring that these students have access to the supports and services they need.

## The Time Is Now

All children in the United States have a right to a free public education, and inherent in that guarantee is the right of every child to be physically, emotionally, and psychologically safe in our schools. As educators and as parents, we will stand for nothing less. The 11 steps for school safety have made a difference in school districts and changed the lives of some students forever. The fourth author (Campana) was discussing some statistics with a friend regarding school violence and bullying. This friend's teenage son overheard the adults' conversation, and after a few minutes, he added, "If even one child is being bullied or is afraid to come to school, that is one too many." Yes, as long as there is one child in a school who does not feel safe physically, psychologically, or academically, our work is not done. The time for change is now.

## REFERENCES

American Psychological Association. (1996). *Violence and the family: Report of the American Psychological Association Presidential Task Force on Violence and the Family*. Washington, DC: Author.

Anderson, M. (2003). Reading violence in boys' writing. *Language Arts, 80*, 223–230.

Anderson, R.N. (2002). Deaths: Leading causes for 2000. *National Vital Statistics Reports, 50*(16), 1–86.

Barnes, P.G. (1998). It's just a quarrel. *American Bar Association Journal, 84*(2), 24–25.

Bishop, D. (2000). Juvenile offenders in the adult criminal system. *Crime and Justice: A Review of Research, 27*, 81–168.

Bry, B.H. (1982). Reducing the incidence of adolescent problems through preventive intervention: One- and five-year follow-up. *American Journal of Community Psychology, 10*, 265–276.

Bureau of Justice Statistics. (1995). *Violence against women: Estimates from the redesigned survey* (Special Report NCJ-154348). Washington, DC: Author.

Bureau of Justice Statistics. (2002). *At a glance*. Washington, DC: Author.

Burke, E., & Herbert, D. (1996). Zero tolerance policy: Combating violence in schools. *NASSP Bulletin, 80*(579), 49–54.

California Attorney General's Office. (2002). *Safe from the start: Reducing children's exposure to violence*. Sacramento, CA: Crime and Violence Prevention Center.

Canada, G. (1995). *Fist, stick, knife, gun: A personal history of violence in America*. Boston: Beacon Press.

Chalk, R., Cordray, D., English, D., Fagan, J., Gelles, R., & King, P. (Eds.). (1998). *Violence in families: Assessing prevention and treatment programs*. Washington, DC: National Academy Press.

Clarksean L., & Pelton, M.H. (2002). Safe schools: A reality check. *Leadership, 32*(1), 32–36.

Cohen, P.A., Kulik, J.A., & Kulik, C.L. (1982). Educational outcomes of tutoring: A meta-analysis of findings. *American Educational Research Journal, 19*, 237–248.

*Compact edition of the Oxford English dictionary.* (1971). Oxford, UK: Oxford University Press.

*Davis v. Monroe County Bd. of Educ.* (1999). No. 97-843, Supreme Court of the United States, 526 U.S. 629; 119 S. Ct. 1661; 143 L. Ed. 2d 839.

DeVoe, J.F., Peter, K., Kaufman, P., Ruddy, S.A., Miller, A.K., Planty, M., et al. (2002). *Indicators of school crime and safety: 2002* (Report No. NCJ-196753; NCES-2003-009). Jessup, MD: ED Pubs.

Dishion, T.J., Andrews, D.W., & Crosby, L. (1995). Adolescent boys and their friends in adolescence: Relationship characteristics, quality and interactional process. *Child Development, 66,* 139–151.

Dishion, T.J., Patterson, G.R., & Griesler, P.C. (1994). Peer adaptation in the development of anti-social behavior: A confluence model. In L.R. Huesmann (Ed.), *Aggressive behavior: Current perspectives* (Plenum Series in Social/Clinical Psychology, pp. 61–95). New York: Plenum.

Dohrn, B. (1997, October). Youth violence: False fears and hard truths. *Educational Leadership, 55*(2), 45–47.

Donohue, E., Schiraldi, V., & Ziedenberg, J. (1998). *School house hype: School shootings and the real risks kids face in America.* Washington, DC: Justice Policy Institute.

Drodge, E. (1997). Confidentiality and the duty to protect: A balancing act for school personnel. *Canadian Journal of Education, 22,* 312–322.

Dumas, J.E. (1989). Treating antisocial behavior in children: Child and family approaches. *Clinical Psychology Review, 9,* 197–222.

Dwyer, K., Osher, D., & Warger, C. (1998). *Early warning, timely response: A guide to safe schools.* Washington, DC: U.S. Department of Education.

Elliott, D.S., & Menard, S. (1996). Delinquent friends and delinquent behavior: Temporal and developmental patterns. In J.D. Hawkins (Ed.), *Current theories of crime and deviance* (pp. 28–67). Newbury, CA: Sage.

Forst, M.L., & Blomquist, M.E. (1991). The changing ideology of youth corrections. *Notre Dame Journal of Law, Ethics, and Public Policy, 5,* 323–375.

Frey, N. (2003). *The gift of time: Providing literacy support to first-grade struggling readers in an urban professional development school.* Unpublished doctoral dissertation, San Diego State University, San Diego, CA.

Garofalo, R., Wolf, R.C., Wissow, L.S., Woods, E.R., & Goodman, E. (1999). Sexual orientation and risk of suicide attempts among a representative sample of youth. *Archives of Pediatric and Adolescent Medicine, 153,* 487–493.

Gorski, J.D., & Pilotto, L. (1993). Interpersonal violence among youth: A challenge for school personnel. *Educational Psychology Review, 5,* 35–61.

Gottfredson, D.C. (1997). School-based crime prevention. In L.W. Sherman, D.C. Gottfredson, D. Mackenzie, J. Eck, P. Reuter, & S. Bushway (Eds.), *Preventing crime: What works, what doesn't, what's promising: A report to the United States Congress* (Report No. NCJ 171676, pp. 125–182). Washington, DC: U.S. Department of Justice.

Heller, G.S. (1996). Changing the school to reduce student violence: What works? *NASSP Bulletin, 80*(579), 1–10.

Hoover, J.H., & Oliver, R.L. (1996). *The bullying prevention handbook: A guide for principals, teachers, and counselors.* Bloomington, IN: National Educational Service.

Hoover, J.H., Oliver, R.L., & Hazler, R.J. (1992). Bullying: Perception of adolescent victims in the Midwestern USA. *School Psychology International, 12*(1), 5–16.

Hunter, R.C., & Williams, D.G. (2003). Zero-tolerance policies: Are they effective? *School Business Affairs, 69*(7), 6–10.

Hyman, I., & Perone, D. (1998). The other side of school violence: Educator policies and practices that may contribute to student misbehavior. *Journal of School Psychology, 36*(1), 7–27.

Island, D., & Letellier, P. (1991). *Men who beat the men who love them: Battered gay men and domestic violence.* Binghamton, NY: Haworth Press.

Jacobson, J., Thrope, L., Fisher, D., Lapp, D., Frey, N., & Flood, J. (2001). Cross-age tutoring: A literacy improvement approach for struggling adolescent readers. *Journal of Adolescent & Adult Literacy*, *44*, 528–536.

Jencks, C., & Peterson, P.E. (Eds.). (1991). *The urban underclass*. Washington, DC: Brookings Institution.

Jones, M. (1996). Do boot camp graduates make better probationers? *Journal of Crime and Justice, 19*, 1–14.

Kadel, S., Watkins, J., Follman, J., & Hammond, C. (1999). *Reducing school violence: Building a framework for school safety* (3rd ed.). Greenboro, NC: The Regional Educational Lab at SERVE.

Kasarda, J.D. (1993). Cities as places where people live and work: Urban change and neighborhood distress. In H.G. Cisneros (Ed.), *Interwoven destinies: Cites and the nation* (pp. 81–124). New York: Norton.

Kazdin, A.E., Bass, D., Siegel, T., & Thomas, C. (1989). Cognitive-behavioral therapy and relationship therapy in the treatment of children referred for antisocial behavior. *Journal of Consulting and Clinical Psychology*, *57*, 522–535.

Kellerman, A.L., Fuqua-Whitley, D.S., Rivara, F.P., & Mercy, J. (1998). Preventing youth violence: What works? *Annual Review of Public Health, 19*, 271–292.

Kleck, G., & Gertz, M. (1998). Carry guns for protection: Results from the national self-defense survey. *Journal of Research in Crime and Delinquency, 35*, 193–224.

Kozol, J. (1991). *Savage inequalities: Children in America's schools*. New York: Crown.

Learning First Alliance. (2001). *Every child learning: Safe and supportive schools: A summary*. Alexandria, VA: Association for Supervision and Curriculum Development.

Lipsey, M.W., & Wilson, D.B. (1998). Effective intervention for serious juvenile offenders: A synthesis of research. In D.P. Farrington & R. Loeber (Eds.), *Serious and violent juvenile offenders: Risk factors and successful interventions* (pp. 313–345). Thousand Oaks, CA: Sage.

Margolin, G. (1998). Effects of domestic violence on children. In P.K. Trickett & C.D. Schellenbach (Eds.), *Violence against children in the family and the community* (pp. 57–101). Washington, DC: American Psychological Association.

Maslow, A.H. (1954). *Motivation and personality*. New York: HarperCollins.

Mayer, M.J., & Leone, P.E. (1999). A structural analysis of school violence and disruption: Implications for creating safer schools. *Education and Treatment of Children, 22*(3), 333–356.

McFadden, A.C., Marsh, G.E., Price, B.J., & Hwang, Y.A. (1992, May 15). A study of race and gender bias in the punishment of school children: Education and the treatment of children. *Family Services of Western Pennsylvania: US, 2*, 140–146.

Morrison, G.M., Furlong, M.J., & Morrison, R.L. (1997). School violence to school safety: Reframing the issue for school psychologists. *School Psychology Review, 23*, 236–256.

*Nabozny v. Podlesny*, No. 95-3634, United States Court of Appeals for the Seventh Circuit, 92 F.3d 446; 1996 U.S. App.

Nagel, G.K. (2000). *Effective grouping for literacy instruction*. Boston: Allyn & Bacon.

Nansel, T.R., Overpeck, M., Pilla, R.S., Ruan, W.J., Simons-Morton, B., & Scheidt, P. (2001). Bullying behaviors among U.S. youth: Prevalence and association with psychosocial adjustment. *Journal of American Medical Association, 285*, 2094–2100.

National Center for Health Statistics. (2001). *Health United States, 2001: With urban and rural health chartbook*. Baton Rouge, LA: Claitor's Law Books.

National Center for Health Statistics. (2002). *Health United States, 2002: With chartbook on trends in the health of Americans*. Lanham, MD: Bernan Associates.

National Crime Prevention Council. (2002). *Are we safe?* Retrieved February 23, 2003, from http://www.ncpc.org

National Institute for Justice and the Centers for Disease Control. (2000). *Extent, nature, and consequences of intimate partner violence: Findings from the National Violence Against Women survey*. Washington, DC: Authors.

National Institute for Mental Health. (2002). *Suicide facts.* Retrieved February 23, 2003, from http://www.nimh.nih.gov/research/suifact.htm

National Institute on Out-of-School Time. (2003). *Making the case: A fact sheet on children and youth in out-of-school time.* Wellesley, MA: Center for Research on Women.

Olweus, D. (1994). *Bullying at school: What we know and what we can do (understanding children's worlds).* Oxford, UK: Blackwell.

O'Tool, M.E. (1999). *The school shooter: A threat assessment perspective.* Quantico, VA: Critical Incident Response Group, National Center for the Analysis of Violent Crime.

Pipho, C. (1998). Living with zero tolerance. *Phi Delta Kaplan, 79,* 725–726.

Redding, R.E. (1999). Juvenile offenders in criminal court and adult prison: Legal, psychological and behavioral outcomes. *Juvenile and Family Court, 50,* 1–19.

Remafedi, G., Farrow, J., & Deisher, R. (1991). Risk factors for attempted suicide in gay and bisexual youth. *Pediatrics, 87,* 869–875.

Rigby, K. (1994). Psychosocial functioning in families of Australian adolescent schoolchildren involved in bully/victim problems. *Journal of Family Therapy, 16,* 173–187.

Rigby, K. (1998). The relationship between reported health and involvement in bully/victim problems among male and female secondary schoolchildren. *Journal of Health Psychology, 3,* 465–476.

Schiraldi, V. (1998). *Making sense of juvenile homicides in America.* Retrieved February 23, 2003, from http://www.abanet.org/crimjust/juvjus/13–2msj.html

Schneider, A., & Schramm, D. (1986). The Washington state of juvenile justice reform: A review of findings. *Criminal Justice and Policy Review, 211,* 231–232.

Singer, S.I. (1996). *Recriminalizing delinquency: Violent juvenile crime and juvenile justice reform.* New York: Cambridge University Press.

Skiba, R.J., Michael, R.S., Nardo, A.C., & Peterson, R.L. (2002). The color of discipline: Sources of racial and gender disproportionality in school punishment. *Urban Review, 34,* 317–342.

Slavin, R.E. (1990). Achievement effects of ability grouping in secondary schools: A best-evidence synthesis. *Review of Educational Research, 60,* 471–499.

Snyder, H.N., & Sickmund, M. (1999). *Juvenile offenders and victims: 1999 national report.* Collingdale, PA: Diane Publishing.

Snyder, T.D., Hoffman, C.M., & Geddes, C.M. (1998). *Digest of education statistics, 1998.* Jessup, MD: ED Pubs.

Stephens, R. (1997). National trends in school violence statistics and prevention strategies. In A.P. Goldstein & J.C. Conoley (Eds.), *School violence intervention: A practical handbook* (pp. 72–90). New York: Guilford.

Torbet, P. (1996). *State responses to serious and violent juvenile crime: Research report.* Washington, DC: Office of Juvenile Justice and Delinquency Prevention.

Tremblay, R., & Craig, W. (1995). Developmental crime prevention. In M. Tonry & D.P. Farrington (Eds.), *Crime and justice: Vol. 19. Building a safer society: Strategic approaches to crime prevention* (pp. 151–236). Chicago: University of Chicago Press.

U.S. Department of Education. (1998). *Preventing bullying: A manual for schools and communities.* Washington, DC: Author.

U.S. Department of Health and Human Services. (2001). *Youth violence: A report of the surgeon general.* Washington, DC: U.S. Public Health Service.

Vossekuil, B., Fein, R.A., Reddy, M., Borum, R., & Modzeleski, W. (2002). *The final report and findings of the "safe school initiative": Implications for the prevention of school attacks in the United States.* Jessup, MD: ED Pubs.

Young, M.C., & Gainsborough, J. (2000). *Prosecuting juveniles in adult court: An assessment of trends and consequences* (Briefing/Fact Sheet). Washington, DC: The Sentencing Project. Retrieved October 13, 2004, from http://tgsrm.org/pdfdocs/Juveniles%20in%20Adult%20Courts.pdf

# Violence in the Lives of Urban Youth: A Response to Douglas Fisher, Jennifer Obidah, Mary Helen Pelton, and Jack Campana

*Victoria Chou and Esther Mosak*

My Constant Fear is Being Shot

After school walking to the L with my cousin
I have fear of being shot
Getting off the L and walking to his house
I have fear of being shot
Leaving out his house and going to practice
I have fear of being shot
Walking back to my cousin house
I have fear of being shot
Playing basketball in an alley
I have fear of being shot
After the last game and I start to walk home
I have fear of being shot
Just being an African American
I have fear of being shot

*–Perspectives Charter School student*

In their synthesis in chapter 5 of the literature on violence as a factor in the lives of urban youth, Douglas Fisher, Jennifer Obidah, Mary Helen Pelton, and Jack Campana first outline and then debunk common assumptions about youth violence. They next describe types of violence experienced by students, following which they enumerate 11 steps for changing a school's culture. They close their chapter by identifying promising strategies for addressing youth violence.

In our response, we briefly review the interrelationships among violence, poverty, and race and ethnicity, a central theme in the authors' analysis. We then explore the authors' recommendation that students who experience violence require a space at school in which to make sense of these circumstances. We examine several kinds of "spaces" that reflect issues of school design and literacy instruction—one created by the formation of intimate learning communities, or small schools; one created by students' expression of the experience of their daily lives; and one created by the inclusion of community members' voices. Taken together, these spaces highlight the indispensable role of adults—educators, parents, and community members—in working together to create a safer school environment. We do circle back, however, and caution that logical, straightforward recommendations like these are not always easy to implement in complex bureaucracies.

In chapter 5, Fisher and his colleagues do not shy away from underlining institutional racism as a root cause of youth problems with violence. Nor do they hesitate to highlight the influence of the media on perpetuating particular portrayals of violence. They present heartbreaking data about acts of violence perpetrated on youths and perpetrated by youths on others and on themselves. Students' fear of violent acts ranging from bullying and harassment to injury and even death can make learning impossible. Nansel, Overpeck, Haynie, Ruan, and Scheidt (2003) studied a U.S. cross-sectional sample of over 15,000 students in grades 6 through 10 and learned that both bullying others and being bullied were markers for more serious violent behaviors that included frequent fighting and fighting-related injuries, as well as weapon carrying.

Teachers are not immune from falling victim to acts of violent behavior while at school. Principals regularly report teacher attrition because of teachers' fears for their own safety and their inability to manage unruly student behavior. It is fear for their own safety that prevents scores of prospective teachers from venturing into classrooms in the *inner city*, a term as laden with racial overtones as Joseph Conrad's "heart of darkness."

Certainly, students are not imagining things when they perceive schools as unsafe places. A survey sponsored by the Consortium on Chicago School Research (Sebring, Bryk, Roderick, & Camburn, 1996) demonstrated significant differences between schools students rated as safest and those they rated as the least safe. Neighborhoods surrounding schools students perceived to be safe experienced 4.6 robberies, 21.9 assaults, and 2.5 drug arrests per thousand residents, compared with 27.2 robberies, 95.9 assaults, and 49.8 drug arrests per thousand residents for neighborhoods surrounding schools students perceived to be unsafe. The researchers point out that, unlike school conditions, neighborhood conditions are much harder to control, and they affect students' sense of safety while in school.

In 2001 a Consortium survey revealed that only 53% of over 57,000 sixth, seventh, and eighth graders felt "mostly safe" or "very safe" outside around the school. With over 26,000 ninth and tenth graders reporting, only 39% felt "mostly safe" or "very safe" outside around the school. Conversely, 89% of sixth, seventh, and eighth graders felt safe in their class, and 80% of ninth and tenth graders felt similarly.

In many of today's neighborhoods, schools are fortresses of metal detectors and high-tech security, despite research suggesting that security measures are insufficient to make schools safe (Gladden, 2002). Indeed, Fisher et al. note in chapter 5 that "studies have shown that schools that have adopted sweeping zero tolerance policies are less safe than schools that have implemented fewer components of such policies." Ayers and Dohrn (1999) write, "As schools become more militarized, they become less safe, in large part because the first casualty is the central, critical relationship between teacher and student, a relationship that is now being damaged or broken in favor of tough-sounding, impersonal, uniform procedures." Such policies are apparently affecting schools in areas of greatest economic need and poorest academic performance. While recent, highly publicized student violence took place in mainly white suburban schools, the external security measures are largely being imposed on urban schools attended primarily by poor students of color (Klonsky, 2000). Heaviside, Rowand, Williams, and Farris (1998), who surveyed 1,200 school principals, confirmed that poor and minority students are more likely to encounter random metal detector searches than other students, and that the use of security officers takes place at a higher rate in large schools and in schools with high minority enrollments.

## The Interplay of Race and Violence

Despite data to the contrary, Fisher et al. demonstrate that many people erroneously conceive of violence as crimes perpetuated against white youths by black and Latino "superpredators." The authors identify "racist and discriminatory residential policies" that have resulted in poor, segregated communities of color and implicate "institutional and organizational factors" in school violence. We concur with the authors' analysis and indeed suggest that a fuller treatment of the insidious interplay of race, racism, and the potential for violent consequences may be warranted:

> Living in a culture of inequality, poverty, discrimination, racism, unemployment, and debasement of values is humanly demeaning especially for blacks, a culture in which the very condition of being black is in some ways

treated as a crime, a crime which leads to crime, because the only outlet for the resulting emotional frustration is its effect, namely violence. In the culture of racism, where so many are scarred and criminalized, the victims are euphemistically called "the race problem," implying that the victims are the cause of it. The latest solution to the problem by government is the threatened enlistment of thousands more police, and the building of more overcrowded prisons. (Montagu, 1942/1997)

Hawkins (2003), who recently assembled nationally regarded researchers to examine the interplay between violent crime and race and ethnicity, asserts that constructs like "crime" and "criminal violence" cannot be viewed as unambiguous and uncontested; rather, the concepts are continually influenced by the "political economy and power differentials found in a given society" (p. xvii).

Furthermore, even if one accepts the idea that definitions of criminal conduct flow from widely agreed-on norms and values, work conducted within the conflict perspective also reminds us of the considerable bias and exercise of discretion that are frequently observed in law enforcement and in the administration of justice. For researchers in this tradition, questions of whether racial differences in crime and violence exist, and the offering of reasons for any observed differences, often cannot be fully disentangled from questions of bias, power, privilege, and protection of group interest.

## Safe Spaces: Fostering Small Learning Communities

Given the need to look beyond externally imposed security measures for elements of climate that reduce violence, we build on the authors' recommendation that students who experience violence in their daily lives require a space at school in which to make sense of these circumstances. We focus here on structures that support networks of trusting relationships among adults in schools and between adults and students. Fisher et al. assert that "the support system that is in place for the child seems to be the major factor in the trajectory of (students') response." Students' connection and attachment to school, for example, predict decreased involvement in violence (Jenkins, 1995; Resnick et al., 1997), and efforts to improve relationships among and between teachers and students can reduce the occurrence of school violence (Gottfredson, 2000).

How best to create safe spaces to learn? A point of departure is *Youth Violence: A Report of the Surgeon General* (Office of the Surgeon General, 2001), which finds that school interventions that address change in a social context seem more effective than attempts to change individual attitudes and behaviors. This seems to be exactly what Fisher et al. in chapter 5 propose by way of an 11-step process for changing school culture. We concur that essential to the change process is the buy-in of every staff member, from the school board to the administrators and the staff, and we would underline from experience that without the commitment of school leadership the process is doomed to failure. Nevertheless, we would also recommend expanding the process to looking at the way entire schools are organized, and at the relationships of teachers to students and schools to communities.

Here we have a substantial body of research about school design, namely the efficacy of smaller learning communities that foster personalization, high student visibility, and close collaboration among teachers. In the Charting Reform study cited earlier, researchers stated, "Safety is a school community problem that cannot be solved without the sustained engagement of adults, both inside and outside the school" (Sebring et al., 1996, p. 23). The advantage of small schools for such engagement has been a stable finding across the Charting Reform series of reports.

Klonsky (2002) sets out the following attributes of small schools:

• School enrollment is no more than 400 students.

• Teachers know students well, and students know teachers well.

• Teachers work collaboratively in a professional community, engage in reflective teaching practices, and look at student work as part of interdisciplinary teams.

• A group of teachers stays together with a cohort of students for several years.

• The school has a high degree of autonomy and teacher leadership.

• The school has a curricular focus or a clear sense of purpose.

In her executive summary of *Small Schools: Great Strides*, a 2000 study of small schools in Chicago conducted by the Bank Street College of Education in collaboration with the Consortium, Patricia Wasley (2001) lists decreased violence among the most important findings.

> Violence occurs less frequently in small schools. Small schools provide a remedy for much of the isolation and alienation, often associated with incidents of teen violence.... Students in small schools are known by teachers and peers. This increased sense of identity and community has led to fewer incidences of violence. (n.p.)

# Safe Spaces: Literacy as a Tool for Self-Expression

Fisher et al. open chapter 5 wondering

> if students disengage from school because they are required to talk about and write about things that they either don't care about or don't have experience with. Or for those students who unfortunately experience violence in their lives, do they disengage as a result of a lack of opportunities in school in which to make sense of these circumstances?

Smaller learning communities, with a shared commitment to creating spaces for student expression, are promising settings for authentic reading and writing. Such reading and writing are a means for students to incorporate their reality into their work at school; they can also serve as the basis on which to build literacy skills. Hal Adams of the University of Illinois at Chicago asserts students can be engaged by allowing the reality of their lives to be a reason for writing. As students are given opportunities to name and give voice to their legitimate anger and fears, writing may serve as the basis of discussion, for the telling of students' stories, and for the start of building literacy communities. Here we are reminded of Sylvia Ashton-Warner's (1986) work in New Zealand in the 1960s. She found that Maori children who were given their choice of which vocabulary to learn to read chose terms that had strong emotional value. For the boys especially, words expressing their fears—like *tiger* and *ghost*—were often chosen and readily learned.

In this perspective on literacy, addressing real-life issues becomes the stuff of reading and writing, rather than more add-on programs targeting topics such as character education or dispute resolution. The Learning First Alliance (2001) found such add-ons less effective than measures to change whole-school climate. Moreover, critical social–emotional skills believed to defuse potential violence and enhance academic achievement are easily integrated into authentic reading and writing activities.

A curriculum that creates spaces and opportunities for self-expression can draw from diverse resources that reinforce students' sense of empathy and responsibility. The language arts experiences we create for students can reinforce values of compassion as well as the critical thinking skills needed to make ethical choices, both in their own situations in school and in reaction to the wider world. Alfie Kohn (2001) writes that schools

> should help children locate themselves in widening circles of care that extend beyond self, beyond country, to all humanity.... The standard by which to measure our schools is the extent to which the next generation comes to

understand–and fully embrace–this simple truth: The life of someone who
lives in Kabul or Baghdad is worth no less than the life of someone in New
York or from our neighborhood. (n.p.)

Parents and guardians, too, can participate in modeling literacy for their
children by making reading and writing a part of their own lives. Hal Adams's
work with parent groups in Chicago school communities helps parents name
the issues in their lives, raise them for discussion, and put them in writing.
Each school publishes its own edition of the journal *Real Conditions*, which
features writings that reflect many forms of violence in the parents' lives, from
random shootings to systematic harassment of undocumented workers. In
addition to being published, the writings are shared at public readings involving parents, students, educators, and community members.

The following example from *Real Conditions* illustrates both the effect
of violence on community members' lives, and those individuals' effectiveness in communicating their life experience in ways that contribute to literacy efforts in schools.

Front Yard
I was born in Kosciusko, Mississippi. When I tell people where I was born,
they also say, "Kosciusko who?" and in turn I always smile. I chose to write
about my front yard in Kosciusko because it was a magical place for me.
The yard was surrounded by fruit trees and right in the middle of the yard
was a big dogwood tree. You were always sure to find big, black, and yellow
bumblebees going in and out of the pink and white blossoms.

My front yard was where my cousins Dixter, Ida Faye, Robert (whom we
called Boottail. To this day I don't know why we gave Robert that nickname),
and I would crawl around on our hands and knees looking for four-leaf
clovers, playing tag, and hide and go seek. My front yard is where I shared secrets, and when the evening fell, it's where I would lie with my hands folded
behind my head in the damp cool grass and watch for falling stars. My front
yard is where Ida Faye's mother fell into my mother's arms screaming and
crying because she had just found out that her husband had been shot and
killed. It's also where we all stood in our Sunday clothes like strangers waiting for a bus, not saying one word to each other, but waiting on the hearse to
take us to Ida Faye's father's going home service.

It's where I would sit and watch my mother hang the laundry to dry. If you
listened to the snow-white sheets that my mother had washed in homemade
lye soap pop and snap in the wind long enough, it would put you to sleep.

It's also where I cried and waved good-bye to my cousin because we were
moving to Chicago. As the car moved down the red dirt road leaving a cloud
of dust, my cousins and my front yard got smaller and smaller until all I could
see was dust.

–Cassie M. Pounds, parent

The involvement of family and community members in schools, whether through literacy programs or other forms of participation, can make the difference in students' perception of school as a safe place. In the 1996 *Charting Reform in Chicago* survey, researchers compared pairs of schools in geographic and socioeconomic proximity, but with different reports of safety by students, and concluded that "Positive school climate is less a matter of community characteristics and much more dependent on how adults in the school community relate to one another" (Sebring et al., 1996, p. 30).

## Easier Said Than Done: Some Challenges

It goes without saying that creating safe havens where students are known and are free to express their thoughts and feelings is much easier said than done. Two intertwined sets of challenges come to mind.

One set of challenges relates to the difficulty of setting up small school or school-within-school structures based on coherence of purpose and on trusting relationships, two essential school supports identified by the Consortium on Chicago School Research. First, trust is difficult to obtain in school communities suffering from neighborhood violence; such schools are also characterized by high student mobility and student truancy, high teacher attrition and turnover, and weak leadership. Second, coherence is difficult to achieve in a time of the widespread standards movement. Some school structures are better suited to addressing student learning standards, that is, traditional departments, than others, namely, small schools that are founded on learner-centered themes. Marrying the two priorities of personalism and standards-based teaching and learning—in a districtwide context where accountability for raising student achievement is the order of the day—requires staff and resources that a struggling school may ill afford.

A second set of challenges relates to teachers and school leaders' cultural and pedagogical competence. School personnel whose cultures may be quite different from those of their students may not know how to work thoughtfully and sensitively with students whose issues may be unfamiliar to them. Here, educators might well draw from the rich "knowledge-giving" resources of intermediary individuals or organizations familiar with our students' communities or, better yet, on the students themselves (e.g., Johnson, 1995).

## Implications

In chapter 5, Fisher et al. outline violence-prevention programs that have been found to have some salutary effect. We believe such programs may obtain greater effect as part of a whole-school change process. We believe that safe, good neighborhood schools are possible and worth working for. We agree with the report's focus on prevention rather than rehabilitation. In schools, real improvements in the relatively short term can be made by forming smaller learning communities, building in time and space for teachers to plan and reflect together, involving parents and community groups in the work of the school, and incorporating meaningful literacy experiences into the curriculum. Both individual learning and culture change must be targeted. We believe the first order of business is organizing schools such that students are known by name and they are given the support necessary to develop the social and literacy skills they need to voice their concerns.

Violence and literacy are broad topics, but the literature indicates there are specific, feasible policy changes that can make schools safer and, at the same time, enhance learning. Although our modest proposals by no means exhaust the possibilities (see, e.g., Noguera, 1996), they offer a beginning. The first step, we reiterate, is a move toward more intimate learning environments, in which both personalism and high expectations for student performance can come to the fore. As mentioned, such a move is more easily proposed than implemented; nevertheless, done well, such environments make it possible for teachers to plan, collaborate, and reflect on their practice. They also make it possible for teachers and parents to work more closely together as they help students articulate their concerns, both in and out of schools, and create spaces for those concerns to be expressed. We recommend that authentic writing should be an essential feature of language arts programs, and that such programs include experiences of literature and writing opportunities that explicitly address issues of race and culture. Raising cultural awareness as part of professional development for teachers and staff may also be expected to diminish violence. Such efforts, we believe, will prove more effective than externally imposed security measures.

## REFERENCES

Ashton-Warner, S. (1986). *Teacher* (Reissued ed.). Rockford, IL: Touchstone Books.

Ayers, W., & Dohrn, B. (1999). *Resisting zero tolerance.* Tempe, Arizona: Education Policy Research Unit, Arizona State University. Retrieved September 3, 2004, from http://www.asu.edu/educ/eps1EPRU/point_of_view_essays/cerai-00-01.htm

Gladden, R. (2002). Reducing school violence: Strengthening student programs and addressing the role of school organizations. *Review of Research in Education, 26,* 263–299.

Gottfredson, D.C. (2000). *Schools and delinquency.* New York: Cambridge University Press.

Hawkins, D.F. (2003). *Violent crime: Assessing race and ethnic differences.* Cambridge, UK: Cambridge University Press.

Heaviside, S., Rowand, C., Williams, C., Farris, E. (1998). *Violence and discipline* problems in U.S. public schools: 1996–97. Washington, DC: U.S. Government Printing Office.

Jenkins, P.H. (1995). School delinquency and school commitment. *Sociology of Education*, 68(3), 221–239.

Johnson, J.A. (1995). Life after death: Critical pedagogy in an urban classroom. *Harvard Educational Review*, 65(2), 213–230.

Klonsky, M. (2000). *Remembering Port Huron. A simple justice: The challenge of small schools*. New York: Teachers College Press.

Klonsky, M. (2002, February). How smaller schools prevent school violence. *Educational Leadership*, 59(5), 65–69.

Kohn, A. (2001). Teaching about September 11. *Rethinking Schools* (Special Report), 5. Retrieved September 3, 2004, from http://www.rethinkingschools.org

Learning First Alliance. (2001). *Every child learning: Safe and supportive schools*. Alexandria, VA: Association for Supervision and Curriculum Development.

Montagu, A. (1997). *Man's most dangerous myth: The fallacy of race* (6th ed.). Walnut Creek, CA: AltaMira Press. (Original work published 1942)

Nansel, R.R., Overpeck, M.D., Haynie, D.L., Ruan, W.J., & Scheidt, P.C. (2003). Relationships between bullying and violence among U.S. youth. *Archives of Pediatrics and Adolescent Medicine, 157*, 348–353.

Noguera, P. (1996, April 28). Reducing and preventing youth violence: An analysis of causes and an assessment of successful programs. *In Motion Magazine*. Retrieved September 3, 2004, from http://www.inmotionmagazine.com/pedro3.html

Office of the Surgeon General. (2001). *Youth violence: A report of the surgeon general*. Washington, DC: U.S. Department of Health and Human Services.

Resnick, M., Bearman, P., Blum, R., Bauman, K., Harris, K., Jones, J., et al. (1997). Protecting adolescents from harm: Findings from the National Longitudinal Study on Adolescent Health. *Journal of the American Medical Association, 278*, 823–832.

Sebring, P., Bryk, A., Roderick, M., & Camburn, E. (1996). *Charting reform in Chicago: The students speak*. Chicago: Consortium on Chicago School Research.

Wasley, P.A. (2001). *Small schools and the issue of scale: Executive summary*. Retrieved September 3, 2004, from http://www.newhorizons.org/trans/wasley.htm

# School Programs of Family and Community Involvement to Support Children's Reading and Literacy Development Across the Grades

*Steven B. Sheldon and Joyce L. Epstein*

C hildren's literacy development is the foundation on which the rest of their education is built (Moats, 2000). Without mastery of early literacy skills and the ability to read, students will not succeed in school. Studies show that children's early literacy skills predict achievement in secondary school (Lyon, 1998). Recognizing the importance of early literacy development, major U.S. federal and state policies and initiatives focus extensively on projects and programs to improve student readiness and the ability to read by third grade (e.g., No Child Left Behind Act, Reading Excellence Act, Reading First Initiative).

Yet, early reading skills are not enough to guarantee student success. Students must develop and extend reading, writing, and other literacy skills across the grades to meet their full potential and to prepare for college and work (Donahue, Finnegan, Lutkus, Allen, & Campbell, 2001). When students read better, they write better, and the chain continues as good writing contributes to achievement in reading and in other subjects (Calkins, 1994; Reeves, 2002).

At all grade levels, students' learning and achievement in reading and language arts are influenced by their experiences inside and outside the classroom. Without question, the quality of teaching in reading and other literacy skills is the main factor in increasing children's reading achievement and literacy skills from year to year (Darling-Hammond, 1997; Haycock, 2001). In addition, decades of studies indicate that, from infancy on, the family environment is an important influence on children's readiness for school, literacy development, and success in school across the grades.

All children are expected to begin formal instruction in their lifelong journey in reading when they are in the first grade. However, it is estimated that 60% of all students find learning to read a challenge (Lyon, 1998). It is, then, important that all students have the best teaching in school *and* the best support at home to help them practice, master, and enjoy reading in preschool, first grade, and at every grade level (Snow, Barnes, Chandler, Goodman, & Hemphill, 1991).

Other chapters in this volume address approaches to reading instruction and teacher quality. Here, we review the results of research on schools' programs of family and community involvement in children's reading and language arts development at different grade levels, and we discuss the implications of that research for policy and practice. We focus particularly on what schools can do to enable all families to support children's reading and literacy skills.

## Families' Influence on Children's Literacy Learning

Research on children's literacy development provides overwhelming evidence of the connections between literacy resources at home and children's literacy development. A report from the U.S. Department of Education (2001) sustains the historic finding that children from homes with more books and more reading by parents tended to perform higher on reading achievement tests than did children from less reading-rich environments. International studies of reading achievement also conclude that home characteristics, including parents' education, books at home, daily newspaper at home, speaking the language of the school's reading test at home, the child reading aloud, listening to stories, and other reading-related conditions, are linked to students' reading achievement across grade levels and across countries (Binkley, Rust, & Williams, 1996).

Information on reading resources at home reflects the socioeconomic advantages of some families but reveals little about the family processes that may improve children's reading skills. Knowing only that some families have literacy-rich environments makes it seem as if other families cannot or will not support reading, and establishes beliefs in the public and among some educators that children's reading skills are formed and fixed in early childhood.

There are, of course, family health, education, and economic factors that help explain why some families have fewer reading resources at home than others. Nevertheless, it is clear that major inequities in family interest, support, interactions, and encouragement for children's reading and literacy skills are a consequence, in large part, of the fact that many schools neither assist families to understand their children's reading programs nor guide them to remain productively involved in their children's literacy learning across the grades.

## School Programs to Involve Families and Communities

Research is accumulating that indicates that school programs to involve families make a difference in *whether* and *which* families become involved in their children's education and how they become involved. A recent review of research on family involvement interventions in schools reported that these programs have mixed results on student achievement in reading and other subjects (Mattingly, Prislin, McKenzie, Rodriguez, & Kayzar, 2002). That review, however, examined diverse programs with varied goals, without attention to whether or how parents or other family members were encouraged or guided to support their children's learning in ways connected to the schools' specific reading or other curricula.

Our inspection of a subset of the studies reviewed suggests a different conclusion about the influence of parent involvement on students' reading skills. Of the 41 studies reviewed by Mattingly et al. (2002), 16 (with a sample size of more than two students) guided parents to become involved with their children on reading and language arts activities. Of the targeted "reading" programs, 15 were reported to produce significant gains on students' reading or language achievement test scores and, where measured, differences between intervention versus comparison groups on reading or language arts skills and scores. The studies were conducted across decades with diverse populations of parents and students. In the Mattingly et al. review, no gains in students' reading or language arts skills were reported if the parent involvement intervention program focused on other kinds of home–school connections such as increasing parent–teacher communications, helping students improve attendance, increasing students' skills at asking questions, or giving parents information about school. These results support other studies that suggest that if parent involvement programs were designed to involve families with reading or language arts skills, then students' achievement would improve in those subjects.

Mattingly et al.'s (2002) review included selected studies conducted through 1999. Another review of research conducted from 1997 to about 2000 adds additional evidence to the subject-specific pattern of results (Henderson & Mapp, 2002). Of 51 studies, 7 examined the impact of family involvement interventions that guided parents to participate in reading-related activities. All seven studies indicated that targeted, reading-related family involvement was associated with increased students' reading and language arts skills in case and control groups or as participants in the interventions over time. Other reviews of research on parent involvement in reading conducted from the mid-1960s to the mid-1980s in the United States and in England revealed the same pattern of results (Miller, 1986; Silvern, 1985). When family involvement was focused on reading activities at home, including reading aloud and discussing stories, students' reading achievement increased (Tizard, Schofield, & Hewison, 1982).

We should not expect too much from family and community involvement as an influence on students' reading achievement across the grades. Children's reading skills are most affected by high-quality instruction from skilled teachers (Snow, Burns, & Griffin, 1998). Nor should we minimize the potential of the "value added" to good teaching of family and community involvement as an influence on students' literacy skills and reading achievement. In a review of 25 studies of family involvement effects on student achievement conducted in the 1990s, Fan and Chen (2001) estimated an effect size of about 0.30—a medium but meaningful effect. They interpreted the effect size as indicating that students from highly involved families (above the median in parent involvement) had achievements measured by tests, GPA, and other ratings that were 30% higher than students from less involved families. If schools conduct well-designed partnership programs and activities at each grade level, small annual effects will accumulate for a sizable total effect of family involvement on student reading, writing, and other literacy skills.

These and other reviewers agree that more and better research is needed to learn, specifically, *which* parental involvement activities contribute measurably to specific reading and other literacy skills (A.J.L. Baker & Soden, 1997; Downey, 2002; Epstein & Sanders, 2000; C. Jordan, Orozco, & Averett, 2001). Among the studies reviewed, many were technical reports not published in peer-reviewed journals, and many were conducted with relatively small and select samples. There also were, however, several large, longitudinal, comparative, and experimental studies that should not be dismissed. The accumulated studies were conducted across decades, across grade levels, in different parts of the country and other nations, and with families with diverse social, economic, cultural, and linguistic backgrounds. The results point parent involvement research and practice in a new and better direction by showing that subject-specific family-involvement activities, not just any involvement activity, have more consistent and stronger effects on students' skills and advances in those subjects.

The next section spotlights selected studies that illustrate the new direction of designing subject-specific family involvement in reading and language arts to maximize the probability of helping students increase skills in those subjects.

## *Family Involvement in the Preschool Years*

Family influences on literacy and reading achievement begin before children enter formal schooling. It has long been recognized that families provide "environments for literacy" at home where children are engaged in literacy activities daily from infancy on (Dorsey-Gaines & Taylor, 1988; Edwards, 1999; Leichter, 1984; Taylor, 1983). Many studies indicate that children's early literacy experiences (e.g., hearing words spoken, being encouraged to talk and sing, reading books together, writing letters) are associated with students' higher scores on school tasks and tests in vocabulary, print knowledge, and letter-sound knowledge. In a comprehensive review of this research, Purcell-Gates (2000) concluded, "Home literacy practices...are facilitative of later literacy achievement in school" (p. 858).

Children between 3 and 5 years old, from low-, middle-, and upper-income families, are exposed to a variety of literacy experiences at home, such as being read to, seeing others reading, and having instruction in letter naming and letter writing (Heibert, 1980; Teale, 1986). The different emphases parents place on print and literacy activities may affect children's understanding of the nature and function of language and writing (Heath, 1983; Purcell-Gates, 1996). Although stories, signs, and labels convey to children that words have a communicative function, these experiences provide different understandings of the richness and meanings of words. On average, by the time they enter school, children from families with low income tend to have more limited perceptions of language usage and literacy skills.

Most preschools provide reading and language experiences to help all students become "ready" for school, and most preschool programs involve families with children in literacy activities. Two experimental studies conducted with families of preschool children in Early Head Start (a federal program for infants and toddlers in families with very low incomes) and Project EASE (Early Access to Success in Education) in Minnesota found that parents could be assisted to work with their children on literacy skills and book-related activities. Both intervention projects found that children in the treatment groups improved their prereading language skills compared to students in the control groups (Mathematica, 2001). The programs increased parents' reading of stories to children, reading at bedtime, and other reading- and language-related activities. One of two studies of the HIPPY (Home Instruction Program of Preschool Youngsters) intervention to increase mothers' reading aloud and working with children on literacy skills came to the same conclusion (A.J.L. Baker, Piotrkowski, & Brooks-Gunn, 1998).

Parent–child storybook reading is one of the most studied types of parent involvement in literacy. Storybook reading is also one of the most commonly encouraged forms of parent involvement by teachers and schools. In their review of 30 years of research on the impact of reading to preschool students, Scarborough and Dobrich (1994) concluded that there is a modest impact of shared storybook reading on students' literacy development, mainly a result of the *quality* of that interaction.

Parent-training workshops are one of the main strategies that educators use to help parents improve the quality of their storybook reading with children in preschool, kindergarten, and the early elementary grades. Studies have examined the effects on students of parent participation in reading workshops. For example, G.E. Jordan, Snow, and Porche (2000) compared the early literacy skills of about 250 kindergarten students from mostly white, middle-class families whose parents received training or not. Parents were taught ways to increase the frequency and quality of parent–child verbal interactions and how to conduct structured activities provided by their child's teacher. Students whose parents were in the training group showed significantly greater improvement on early literacy tests of vocabulary, comprehension, story sequencing, and sound awareness.

Other interventions also have helped parents with low income and limited formal education to learn more effective practices to help children increase their literacy skills. Lonigan and Whitehurst (1998) compared the effects of a shared-reading intervention on preschool children's early literacy skills. Teachers and parents were trained to use dialogic reading approaches. Students were randomly assigned to the following groups: (1) teachers reading to a small group of children, (2) parents reading to their children at home, (3) combined teachers and parents reading to children, and (4) a control group of children who received no special intervention. In this study, students who had either shared reading with a parent, small-group reading with a teacher, or a combination of the two performed better on reading assessments than students who had no shared reading experiences. In addition, including parents in shared-reading activities (either solely or in combination with teachers' use of small-group dialogic reading) was associated with higher levels of vocabulary and use of oral language in children, compared to children in the teacher-only group.

The results of studies of parent-training workshops are important because they show that parents who are assisted to be effectively involved in reading-related activities conduct more and better interactions about reading with their children, and that the students improve their reading and literacy skills (Faires, Nichols, & Rickelman, 2000; Leslie & Allen, 1999; Phillips, Norris, & Mason, 1996). In particular, Lonigan and Whitehurst's study, with its random sample study design, provides strong evidence that parents with low income and less formal education, who may have weaker reading skills than more economically advantaged parents, can effectively support their children's reading and education.

## Family Involvement in the Primary Grades

Children's entry to formal schooling marks an important transition in learning and development. The transition to elementary school also has important consequences for parents' roles in their children's literacy development. Schools and teachers become major influences on children's learning to read. Teachers may work separately from or in concert with parents and other family and community members.

Purcell-Gates (1996) found that parent involvement in reading actually *increased* when children from low-income families began formal schooling. Thus, the transition to elementary school does not necessarily mean that parents retreat from influencing their children's reading and literacy development. For many parents with less formal education, the child's entry to school and communications with helpful teachers may be their first opportunity to understand how they can help and encourage their children learn to read and write.

Storybook reading continues to be an important activity for children in school and at home in the primary grades. Studies suggest there are long-term, multifaceted effects of parent–child storybook reading on children's language development (Sénéchal & LeFevre, 2002; Sénéchal, LeFevre, Thomas, & Daley, 1998). In one study of middle- and upper-income students, first-grade children whose parents read more storybooks to them in the preschool years (*informal* literacy activities) tended to score higher on receptive language skills (i.e., vocabulary and listening comprehension). First-grade children whose parents taught them letters and words using storybooks (*formal* literacy activities) tended to score higher on emergent literacy skills (e.g., alphabet knowledge, decoding, and invented spelling). The research showed that, over time, emergent literacy skills predicted children's reading achievement in first grade, whereas receptive language skills predicted reading achievement in the third grade. These complex results are consistent with other studies that indicate that parental involvement with children on varied reading-related activities helped students develop a number of literacy skills that were important for their later reading achievement. The findings suggest that parents should be guided to engage young children in various literacy activities including listening to stories and learning letters and words to prepare them to learn to read in school.

The results of the Sénéchal et al. (1998) study of economically advantaged and mainly white participants may not apply to students from racial minority groups or to families with low income, which may not offer children the same amount or types of literacy experiences (L. Baker, Serpell, & Sonnenschein, 1995). There is a great need to determine whether similar interventions would have positive effects for all students. Recent reports indicate that, by the fourth grade, students from black and Hispanic families perform poorly in reading compared to white and Asian students (Donahue et al., 2001). More research is needed on the effects of parent involvement in early reading activities for diverse student populations to ensure that interventions are applicable, or that different designs are used to help reduce the persistent racial gaps in reading achievement.

Literacy activities experienced at home by children from middle- and upper-income families may more closely match the school culture than do activities experienced by students from low-income or minority families (Cairney & Rouge, 1997; Heath, 1983). The lack of congruence between home and school activities may be a source of misunderstanding and discomfort for some students and may be linked to students' lower reading achievement. Based on research on literacy classroom practices with low-income children, McCarthey (1999) suggested that teachers establish and maintain frequent and reciprocal communications with families. She argued that by developing a better understanding of children's families and by helping them understand and use reading resources with their children, teachers could increase home–school congruence and continuity for all students.

**Family and Community Connections With Students on Literacy.** In addition to training workshops to improve parents' skills, other interventions help teachers incorporate families and the broader community in their classrooms to make school more meaningful for students. In particular,

Moll (1992) argued that minority and low-income families and communities possess significant "funds of knowledge" that, typically, are not valued by schools but may be rich intellectual and social resources for students. By incorporating culturally relevant resources in their instruction, educators may increase the congruency between the school and family life and help students develop and improve their literacy skills (Durán, Durán, Perry-Romero, & Sanchez, 2001; González, Andrade, Civil, & Moll, 2001).

A limited number of interventions have drawn on the funds of knowledge approach to teaching literacy skills. Among them, Paratore, Hindin, Krol-Sinclair, and Duran (1999) trained parents with low income, who had immigrated to the United States, to observe and become involved in their elementary schoolchildren's literacy activities at home and to construct portfolios of their children's literacy activities to enjoy at home and to bring to parent–teacher conferences. In addition, the researchers trained teachers to understand family literacy, how to collaborate with families, and how to use a family literacy portfolio to communicate with their students' parents.

The family portfolio intervention helped families and teachers better understand family literacy activities and improved the parent–teacher relationships. Discourse analyses showed that, during conferences with their children's teachers, parents who developed literacy portfolios with their children at home talked more and provided teachers with more information about their children's literacy activities at home. Interview data also suggested that the portfolios provided parents and teachers opportunities to share home and school literacy experiences. Teachers became more aware of and sensitive to the home literacy activities of their students, and parents gained a better understanding of how literacy is taught and valued in their children's school (Paratore et al., 1999).

Although this study involved only a small number of immigrant families, the results suggest that parent-training workshops and literacy portfolios may help bridge the traditional divide between minority families and schools. The study did not assess the influence of the intervention on student achievement. Thus, more research is needed on the effects of teacher–parent communications using literacy portfolios on students' early literacy skills.

**Reading Volunteers.** Other interventions have been designed to bring community resources into elementary schools to help children develop literacy skills. Wasik (1998) reviewed empirical research on more than 10 adult volunteer programs focused on helping students learn to read. Most of these programs used community members rather than parents as volunteer reading tutors. There were four common characteristics in these programs: a coordinator with knowledge about reading and reading instruction; structured activities for volunteer tutors to use with students; training for the volunteer tutors; and, unexpectedly, poor coordination between the tutoring activities and the classroom curriculum. Few programs evaluated the effects of the volunteer tutors on students' reading achievement. Wasik concluded that there was potential in community volunteer programs to help improve student reading, but better research was needed to determine actual results.

Building on Wasik's review, S. Baker, Gersten, and Keating (2000) evaluated longitudinal effects on students of a low-cost community volunteer program. After randomly assigning first-grade students to either two years of one-on-one tutoring or to a control group, the researchers compared differences in students' reading achievement at the end of the first and second grades. Students in the tutoring program at the end of second grade had significantly higher oral reading and word comprehension skills and improved their reading skills more than did peers who were not in the tutoring program. The study suggests that, with minimal training, community involvement strategies, such as the use of reading tutors, can have a positive impact on students' reading achievement.

## School Programs to Involve Families in Upper Elementary and Secondary Grades

Most research on parent involvement and students' reading and literacy skills has been conducted with families of young children in preschool and the primary grades. Fewer studies explore the design and effects of family and community involvement beyond the third grade. Yet, educators continue to encourage parent involvement in students' reading, writing, spelling, and other literacy skills in the later grades.

After the third grade, parents report less involvement in their children's education (Dauber & Epstein, 1993; Eccles & Harold, 1996), and educators report fewer efforts to include parents in their children's schooling (Chen, 2001; Donahue et al., 2001; Epstein & Dauber, 1991). It is often assumed that as students get older, they need less supervision on learning activities at home, yet studies are accumulating that indicate that family and community involvement has a positive influence on student achievement and other measures of success through high school (Catsambis, 1998; S. Lee, 1994; Simon, 2001). Studies suggest that family and community involvement can boost students' reading and writing skills and English GPA in the middle and high school grades. It is still rare, however, for secondary schools to have well-designed interventions to assist all families to interact with their teens on homework or coursework in specific subjects (Sanders & Epstein, 2000).

The lack of research on parent involvement in reading with older students may reflect a belief that families' influence will not be strong or useful when students' tasks turn from *learning to read* to *reading to learn*. It may be easier for teachers to ask parents to read aloud or go over letters and words with their young children than for teachers to develop ways for families to interact with older students on reading comprehension and writing skills. Thus, researchers may not study family involvement in the upper grades because it is rare, and educators may not create interventions to increase this kind of involvement unless they are aware of new ways to engage families in discussions with older children about their schoolwork and homework.

The research that does exist on family and community involvement with students in the upper elementary grades suggests that parent–child interactions continue to contribute to increased reading achievement. Intervention programs have been shown to help parents increase their abilities and confidence to interact with their children on reading and other literacy skills. Diverse populations have been assisted to become engaged with their children on reading, writing, and/or spelling, including teen mothers with preschool-age children (Neuman & Gallagher, 1994); Latino parents of kindergarten students (Goldenberg, Reese, & Gallimore, 1992); Mexican American families, students, and schools (Delgado-Gaitan, 1990); families of elementary-age students in Portugal (Villas-Boas, 1998) and Scotland (Topping, 1995); families of adolescents in middle and junior high schools (Davidson & Koppenhaver, 1988); and others.

The success or failure of interventions to involve families with their children in reading, language arts, or other literacy skills rests on the *design* and *quality of implementation* of the parent involvement programs, and their connections to students' class work and assessments. Most intervention studies report increases in the nature and extent of parents' involvement, but not all studies measured effects on student achievement over time.

One study provides some information about these effects. A study of third- and fifth-grade students from families with low income in inner-city schools found that, controlling for prior reading achievement, students in classrooms with teachers who more frequently involved families in learning activities at home had higher gains in reading achievement from one year to the next than did students in other teachers' classrooms (Epstein, 1991). The data did not identify the specific practices teachers used to involve parents in children's reading, but follow-up interviews with teachers, parents, and administrators in the schools indicated that most involvement activities focused on reading and reading-related activities. The effects of parent involvement were associated with students' reading gains and not math gains, reinforcing the likelihood that the parents' involvement in reading activities at home was connected to students' reading gains. The subject-specific connections in this study prompted researchers and educators to develop new designs for "interactive homework" to help educators design assignments that enable students to share interesting things they are learning in class with family partners (Epstein, Salinas, & Jackson, 1995; Van Voorhis & Epstein, 2002).

Other intervention studies reinforce the importance of parental involvement in reading activities to influence students' reading skills. Shaver and Walls (1998) report that workshops for parents of students from second through eighth grade promoted involvement of parents with children on learning packets for reading at home and how to use them. Students increased their reading comprehension skills and total reading scores. Also, a study of 71 Title I schools in 18 school districts found that outreach to parents on several types of involvement, including materials on how to help students at home, improved reading achievement over time as students moved from third to fifth grade (U.S. Department of Education, Office of the Deputy Secretary, 2001). The authors reported that gains in test scores between grades 3 and 5 were 50% higher for students whose teachers and schools reported high levels of parent outreach in the early grades.

## Parent Involvement and Adolescents' School Achievement

Research on literacy learning in adolescence has been overshadowed by efforts to understand the development of reading skills in young children (Moje, Young, Readence, & Moore, 2000). Adolescents' reading skills are more complicated than the decoding and comprehension skills taught to elementary school students (Greenleaf, Schoenbach, Cziko, & Mueller, 2001). For that reason, varied resources, including family and community involvement and support, may help older students who have not mastered the metacognitive strategies needed to comprehend and analyze the complex content in middle and high school texts and other course materials.

Family and community involvement is largely absent from discussions about adolescent literacy and how to teach reading to middle and high school students. Older students with weak reading skills often are given remedial instruction in vocabulary, comprehension, and writing skills, but little attention is given to the role that family or community reinforcement, interaction, and support might play in encouraging students to put forth effort to master reading competencies and to achieve ultimate success (Greenleaf et al., 2001).

The absence of family and community involvement in adolescent literacy is striking because several studies have shown that, in addition to excellent teaching in school, both contexts—home and community—may help increase students' reading achievement at the secondary level. Research on a nationally representative sample of secondary students show that, after controlling for prior levels of achievement, students tend to score higher on reading achievement tests and/or earn higher grades in English if their parents have discussions with them about school and about their future plans, check their homework, and maintain high educational expectations (Desimone, 1999; Ho & Willms, 1996; Keith, 1991; S. Lee, 1994; V.E. Lee & Croninger, 1994; Simon, 2001). These studies suggest that parents' interest in and support for reading and other subjects may play an important role in adolescents' academic development.

Other studies report that high schools' communications with families are associated with higher levels of students' reading achievement. Controlling for prior achievement, schools that communicated more often with students' families tended to have students who gained more on their reading achievement tests than did schools that did not maintain strong communication practices (Parcel & Dufur, 2001). Parcel and Dufur's work suggests that if schools establish frequent, positive, and purposeful communications, more parents may be able to provide their children with support for learning that is more closely coordinated with the teachers' goals and that will translate into improved student learning. Clear and helpful communications may be essential in secondary schools, where parents often feel less confident about their abilities to help adolescents with more advanced curricular activities.

Studies of secondary schools that are working to develop effective programs of family and community involvement indicate that if essential program elements are implemented, middle and high schools can have partnership programs that are equal in quality to elementary schools (Sanders, 1999; Sanders & Simon, 2002). And, as noted earlier, parents' involvement can help secondary students increase their preparedness for class, attendance, achievement, report card grades, and aspirations for higher education.

These studies offer clues about the potential importance of family and community involvement in the upper grades. They point out how important it is to develop and evaluate specific strategies to increase partnerships. Without interventions designed to involve family and community members with students on English and language arts in middle school and high school, we will not know which practices are more or less likely to improve student achievement in reading and literacy skills at these grade levels.

One intervention has been designed to increase family involvement with students on language arts homework in middle school. A study of Teachers Involve Parents in Schoolwork (TIPS)–Language Arts included 683 students in grades 6 and 8 in two central city middle schools where over 70% of the students qualified for free- or reduced-price lunch (Epstein, Simon, & Salinas, 1997). The students shared writing prompts, ideas, and drafts of stories or essays, and they conducted "family surveys" to discuss their family partners' experiences that related to their own. Students' writing samples were collected in the fall, winter, and spring of the school year. Analyses statistically controlled for parent education, student grade level, attendance, fall report card grades, and fall writing sample scores to identify the effects of TIPS interactive homework on students' skills in the winter and spring, and on student and family attitudes about school and homework at the end of the school year. After accounting for their initial skills, students who completed more TIPS homework assignments had higher language arts report card grades. When parents participated, students improved their writing scores from fall to winter and from winter to spring, regardless of their initial abilities. Parents overwhelmingly agreed that TIPS gave them information about what their children were learning in class. The study demonstrated that TIPS interactive homework could be successfully implemented in the middle grades, parents with little formal education could become productively involved with their children on homework, and students' writing skills improved. This and other TIPS studies indicate that families may be an underused resource in adolescents' learning.

## Summary

We draw four main conclusions from this overview of research on schools' programs of family and community involvement for students' reading and literacy learning:

1. *Programs of school, family, and community partnerships can correct the historic pattern that only some families become involved with their children's reading and literacy learning.* Historically, most parents have been left on their own to create a supportive home environment for reading and literacy skills, even in their children's infancy and earliest grades. This has produced inequities, because only some parents are familiar enough with schools and educational programs to support, guide, and encourage their children's reading, writing, and other literacy skills across the grades. Most parents, even those with years of formal education, say that they need information and guidance from their children's schools to know how to remain involved in their children's education at all grades levels. Research is accumulating that indicates that schools' programs of family and community involvement can be designed to help all parents support their children's work and progress in reading and literacy, regardless of the parents' education or socioeconomic status.

2. *Subject-specific family and community involvement activities are likely to improve students' reading, writing, and other literacy skills.* Across the grades, studies indicate that subject-specific involvement activities affect student achievement in the targeted subjects. This is important because many researchers have expected any and every measure of involvement to positively influence student achievement in reading and other subjects. The subject-specific connection of family involvement and results for students also is important in practice. Educators can design age-appropriate, family-friendly activities that encourage and enable all parents to help their children master and enjoy reading, writing, storytelling, talking, and listening.

In reading, if teachers communicate clearly in forms and languages that parents understand, all parents can help their children recognize sounds and letters; write letters, numbers, and words; read aloud; listen to and tell nursery rhymes and stories in any language; read for understanding; become accurate and fluid in reading; improve spelling and vocabulary; read for pleasure and enjoyment; and continue to improve reading and writing skills in the older grades. Helping children practice and celebrate the mastery of skills at home can be accomplished without parents having to be experts themselves in the rhetoric of reading.

In writing, if teachers design focused and engaging interactive homework assignments, the students themselves will be able to work with family partners to practice spelling, vocabulary, and related language arts skills, and read aloud the letters, narratives, essays, poems, and stories that they write.

*3. The quality of programs of school, family, and community partnerships counts.* Studies indicate that, in addition to the subject-specific design of involvement activities, the quality of implementation, extent of outreach to all families, continuity of programs, and the frequency and consistency of participation make a difference in whether parents become and remain productively involved with their children on reading, language arts, and other literacy skills, and whether students improve these skills (Izzo, Weissberg, Kasprow, & Fendrich, 1999; Sheldon, 2003). These factors also make a difference in whether community programs such as reading tutors have their intended effects (Invernizzi, Rosemary, Juel, & Richards, 1997; see also Dryfoos, chapter 3, in this volume). Several studies have identified "essential elements" of excellent programs of family and community involvement, as well as the elements necessary to organize high-quality programs (Epstein, 2001; Sanders, 1999; Sanders & Simon, 2002; Sheldon & Van Voorhis, 2004).

*4. Researchers need to improve the breadth and depth of studies on family and community involvement for students' reading, writing, and other literacy skills.* Intervention studies of family and community involvement with children on reading have focused on a rather narrow range of involvement activities, with many studies of workshops for parents of young children. The nature of traditional workshops makes it relatively easy to examine whether parents attend the training sessions or not, follow up with activities with their children, and determine whether students' achievement improves. It is important to expand the research agenda to study a wider range of family and community involvement activities related to students' reading and other literacy skills across the grades.

One way to extend the agenda is to study the effects of different kinds of involvement activities. A framework of six types of involvement (Epstein, 1995, 2001) guides the design of comprehensive programs of school, family, and community partnerships focused on school improvement goals, including improving students' reading skills. Each type of involvement may be represented by many different activities, as suggested by the following examples:

*Type 1—Parenting.* Provide parenting workshops on how to read aloud with young children at home and how to establish a literacy-rich home environment to support reading at home across the grades. Activities may include home visits to meet with parents to discuss their children's reading programs and reading-related activities that parents would feel comfortable conducting at home. Workshops may be offered in various languages in preschools, libraries, and other community locations to help parents of young children learn how to read aloud with toddlers, guide early language development, and support prereading skills.

*Type 2—Communicating.* Conduct parent–teacher–student conferences specifically about reading goals and students' reading progress, and communicate effectively with parents and students about actions for improving or sustaining reading and other literacy skills. Communicate with all parents to clarify the school's goals for reading and language arts and how progress in these subjects is measured, monitored, and reported to students and to parents on report cards and in annual school reports on test scores.

*Type 3—Volunteering.* Organize reading volunteers, spelling buddies, tutors, and other well-trained literacy helpers to work with individual children or small groups who need extra help before, during, or after school on reading, writing, and other literacy skills.

*Type 4—Learning at Home.* Assign weekly interactive reading and writing homework assignments for all students to share their work and ideas with family partners. These assignments guide students to demonstrate, discuss, and celebrate reading skills, writing, speeches, and other literacy activities at home.

*Type 5—Decision Making.* Have the PTA or PTO conduct book fairs, family reading night, and other reading- and literacy-related programs.

*Type 6—Collaborating With the Community.* Work with business partners to provide books for students to help establish a literacy-rich home environment and to increase students' reading for pleasure. Conduct adult literacy programs with community agencies for parents and family literacy programs for parents and children to attend together.

There are, of course, many other activities for each type of involvement that schools may choose in order to establish a comprehensive partnership program that will increase students' motivation and skills in reading, writing, and other literacy skills. For many examples, see Epstein, Sanders, et al. (2002), Jansorn and Salinas (2004), and annual collections of ideas of promising partnership practices at www.partnershipschools.org.

The research reviewed indicates that subject-specific family and community involvement activities are most likely to produce subject-specific results for students. Research is needed to provide better empirical evidence of the effects of particular interventions and specific practices of family involvement on children's reading and other literacy skills. We need to know *which* practices with *which* families at *which* grade levels will produce *which* results in reading, writing, and other literacy skills for *which* students. These unknowns establish a broad and exciting research agenda. The results of such studies will be of immediate interest in practice.

## Implications for Policy and Practice

Researchers and educators concur that the optimal environment for children's learning is where the school, home, and community work together to support children's literacy development. Everyone agrees that high-quality teachers are needed for all children to learn and continually improve reading, writing, and other literacy skills. But it also is necessary for all teachers to know how to communicate effectively with all students' families and to tap useful community resources to support students' reading and literacy skills. Although more and better studies are needed to advance knowledge and the surety of conclusions, the available research has several immediate policy and practical implications.

Parents at all grade levels and in all socioeconomic and cultural groups can support and encourage their children's reading, writing, and other literacy learning. Students' families and communities are important influences on reading, literacy, and overall school success through high school. It is important for educators to understand that parents and community partners are untapped, ready resources who can support, encourage, and guide children's reading and literacy skills across the grades.

All preschools, elementary schools, middle schools, and high schools can develop comprehensive programs of partnership, which include activities to help all families support and encourage their children's reading, writing, and other literacy skills. It is particularly important for educators to continue to emphasize family involvement with children on reading and literacy skills beyond the early grades. This will require teachers to plan and implement age-appropriate, family-friendly, and culturally sensitive activities that will promote positive conversations and exchanges of parents with children about reading, writing, and language arts. As students mature and as the school curriculum becomes more complex, family involvement activities for the six types of involvement for middle school and high school students will differ from those conducted with elementary schoolchildren. For example, preschools and elementary schools may emphasize parent–child shared reading, whereas middle and high schools may guide students to read their writing activities aloud with family members and conduct oral history interviews with parents and other adults in the community. Although the guidelines may differ for families with older and younger students, it seems that students at all grade levels benefit from family discussions about schoolwork, tutoring that is consistent with the classroom curricula, and homework that is designed for students to show and share what they are learning in class without expecting parents to "teach" school subjects.

District and state reading and language arts leaders can help all elementary, middle, and high schools establish and continually improve their programs of family and community involvement, and increase the effectiveness of activities to involve families with students on reading, writing, and other literacy skills. This can be done if districts and states support facilitators who help schools improve family and community involvement plans and activities, just as district and state leaders help schools continually improve the quality of curriculum and instruction (Epstein, Williams, & Lewis, 2002; Epstein, Sanders, et al., 2002).

Educators need inservice education and ongoing technical assistance to develop, implement, and continually improve their programs and practices of school, family, and community partnerships linked to reading, writing, and other literacy skills. This includes information on how to develop or select activities linked to reading and language arts goals for the six types of involvement and how to meet key challenges to involve all families so that all students benefit from that support (National Institute for Literacy, 2001; National Institute of Child Health and Human Development, 2000). Educators must be helped to understand how to recognize and draw from the knowledge, skills, and talents of students' parents and how to use the strengths of families' diverse cultures, languages, literatures, and experiences to engage families with students in reading, writing, and other literacy activities. This kind of professional development may be provided by district and state leaders for partnerships, informed curriculum consultants, and other local and national resources.

There are many resources that can help schools, districts, and states develop partnership programs based on the best research to date. For example, practical programs such as Family Reading (Handel, 1999) and Reading Starts With Us (in Spanish and English) (Goldsmith & Tevlin, 2000) offer well-developed workshops for parents of young children to learn to read with children in grades pre-K to 2. The Teachers Involve Parents in Schoolwork (TIPS) process includes several hundred interactive homework assignment prototypes for family involvement in writing, reading, and other language arts skills in the middle grades (Association of Supervision and Curriculum Development, 2001; Epstein et al., 1995; Van Voorhis & Epstein, 2002). For overall program planning, the National

Network of Partnership Schools (NNPS) at Johns Hopkins University assists educators in elementary, middle, and high schools, and state and district leaders to use research-based approaches to develop, evaluate, and sustain programs of school, family, and community partnerships (www. partnershipschools.org). Some schools in NNPS, including schools in urban areas, have designed and implemented activities to involve family and community partners with students on reading, writing, and other literacy skills (see chapter Appendix).

Preservice and advanced education is needed in colleges and universities to prepare teachers and administrators to understand school, family, and community partnerships and to develop effective programs of family and community involvement linked to improving reading and other school improvement goals. In particular, courses that prepare educators to teach reading, language arts, and English need to include information on the ways that family and community involvement can assist teachers to help students reach learning goals in these subjects. Resources are available to assist professors of education and educational administration with this new approach (Edwards, 2004; Epstein, 2001; see also the Family Involvement Network of Educators of the Harvard Family Research Group, www.finenetwork.org).

## REFERENCES

Association of Supervision and Curriculum Development. (2001). *How to make homework more meaningful* [Video]. Alexandria, VA: Author.

Baker, A.J.L., Piotrkowski, C.S., & Brooks-Gunn, J. (1998). The effects of the Home Instruction Program for Preschool Youngsters (HIPPY) on children's school performance at the end of the program and one year later. *Early Childhood Research Quarterly, 13*(4), 571–588.

Baker, A.J.L., & Soden, L.M. (1997, March). *Parent involvement in children's education: A critical assessment of the knowledge base.* Paper presented at the annual meeting of the American Education Research Association, Chicago.

Baker, L., Serpell, R., & Sonnenschein, S. (1995). Opportunities for literacy learning in the homes of urban preschoolers. In L.M. Morrow (Ed.), *Family literacy connections in schools and communities* (pp. 236–252). Newark, DE: International Reading Association.

Baker, S., Gersten, R., & Keating, T. (2000). When less may be more: A 2-year longitudinal evaluation of a volunteer tutoring program requiring minimal training. *Reading Research Quarterly, 35,* 494–519.

Binkley, M., Rust, K., & Williams, T. (1996). Reading literacy in an international perspective: Collected papers from the IEA reading literacy study (Report No. NCES-97-875). Washington, DC: U.S. Government Printing Office.

Cairney, T.H., & Ruge, J. (1997). *Community literacy practices and schooling: Towards effective support for students.* Department of Employment, Education, Training and Youth Affairs: Australia.

Calkins, L.M. (1994). *The art of teaching writing.* Portsmouth, NH: Heinemann.

Cairney, T.H. & Ruge, J. (1997, December). *Clash of discourses: Examining the literacy practices of home, school and community*. Paper presented at the annual meeting of the National Reading Conference, Scottsdale, AZ.

Catsambis, S. (1998). *Expanding the knowledge of parental involvement in secondary education: Effects on high school academic success* (Report No. 27). Baltimore: Center for Research on the Education of Students Placed at Risk.

Chen, X. (2001). Efforts by public K-8 schools to involve parents in children's education: Do school and parent reports agree? *Education Statistics Quarterly*, *3*(4), 7–14.

Darling-Hammond, L. (1997). *The right to learn: A blueprint for creating schools that work*. San Francisco: Jossey-Bass.

Dauber, S.L., & Epstein, J.L. (1993). Parents' attitudes and practices of involvement in inner-city elementary and middle schools. In N.F. Chavkin (Ed.), *Families and schools in a pluralistic society* (pp. 53–71). Albany: State University of New York Press.

Davidson, J., & Koppenhaver, D. (1988). *Adolescent literacy: What works and why*. New York: Garland.

Delgado-Gaitan, C. (1990). *Literacy for empowerment: The role of parents in children's education*. London: Falmer.

Desimone, L. (1999). Linking parent involvement with student achievement: Do race and income matter? *Journal of Educational Research*, *93*(1), 11–30.

Donahue, P.L., Finnegan, R.J., Lutkus, A.D., Allen, N.L., & Campbell, J.R. (2001). *The nation's report card: Fourth-grade reading 2002* (NCES 2001–499). Washington, DC: Office of Educational Research and Improvement, National Center for Education Statistics.

Dorsey-Gaines, C., & Taylor, D. (1988). *Growing up literate: Learning from inner-city families*. Portsmouth, NH: Heinemann.

Downey, D.B. (2002). Parent and family involvement in education. In A. Molner (Ed.), *School reform proposals: The research evidence (Research in educational productivity)*. Greenwich, CT: Information Age.

Durán, R., Durán, J., Perry-Romero, D., & Sanchez, E. (2001). Latino immigrant parents and children learning and publishing together in an after-school setting. *Journal of Education of Students Placed at Risk*, *6*(1–2), 95-113.

Eccles, J.S., & Harold, R.D. (1996). Family involvement in children's and adolescents' schooling. In A. Booth & J.F. Dunn (Eds.), *Family-school links: How do they affect educational outcomes?* (pp. 3–34). Hillside, NJ: Erlbaum.

Edwards, P.A. (1999). *A path to follow: Learning to listen to parents*. Portsmouth, NH: Heinemann.

Edwards, P.A. (2004). *Children's literacy development: Making it happen through school, family, and community involvement*. Boston: Allyn & Bacon.

Epstein, J.L. (1991). Effects of teacher practices of parent involvement on change in student achievement in reading and math. In S.B. Silvern (Ed.), *Advances in reading/language research: Literacy through family, community, and school interaction* (pp. 261–276). London: JAI Press.

Epstein, J.L. (1995). School/family/community partnerships: Caring for the children we share. *Phi Delta Kappan*, *76*(9), 701–712.

Epstein, J.L. (2001). *School, family, and community partnerships: Preparing educators and improving schools*. Boulder, CO: Westview.

Epstein, J.L., & Dauber, S.L. (1991). School programs and teacher practices of parent involvement in inner-city elementary and middle schools. *The Elementary School Journal*, *91*(3), 289–305.

Epstein, J.L., Salinas, K.C., & Jackson, V.E. (1995). *Manual for teachers and prototype activities: Teachers involve parents in schoolwork (TIPS) language arts, science/health, and math interactive homework in the middle grades*. Baltimore: Center on School, Family, and Community Partnerships.

Epstein, J.L., & Sanders, M.G. (2000). Connecting home, school, and community:

New directions for social research. In M. Hallinan (Ed.), *Handbook of the sociology of education* (pp. 285–306). London: Kluwer Academic/Plenum.

Epstein, J.L., Sanders, M.G., Simon, B.S., Salinas, K.C., Jansorn, N.R., & Van Voorhis, F.L. (2002). *School, family, and community partnerships: Your handbook for action* (2nd ed.). Thousand Oaks, CA: Corwin.

Epstein, J.L., Simon, B.S., & Salinas, K.C. (1997, September). Effects of Teachers Involve Parents in Schoolwork (TIPS) language arts interactive homework in the middle grades. *Research Bulletin, 18.* Bloomington, IN: Phi Delta Kappa.

Epstein, J.L., Williams, K.J., & Lewis, K.C. (2002, April). *Five-year study: Key components of effective partnership programs in states and school districts.* Paper presented at the annual meeting of the American Educational Research Association, New Orleans, LA.

Faires, J., Nichols, W.D., & Rickelman, R.J. (2000). Effects of parental involvement in developing competent readers in first grade. *Reading Psychology, 21*(3), 195–215.

Fan, X., & Chen, M. (2001). Parental involvement and students' academic achievement: A meta-analysis. *Educational Psychology Review, 13*, 1–22.

Goldenberg, C., Reese, L., & Gallimore, R. (1992). Effects of literacy materials from school on Latino children's home experiences and early reading achievement. *American Journal of Education, 100*(4), 497–536.

Goldsmith, E., & Tevlin, A.M. (2000). *Reading starts with us.* New York: Scholastic.

González, N., Andrade, R., Civil, M., & Moll, L. (2001). Bridging funds of distributed knowledge: Creating zones of practice in mathematics. *Journal of Education of Students Placed at Risk, 6*(1–2), 115–132.

Greenleaf, C.L., Schoenbach, R., Cziko, C., & Mueller, F.L. (2001). Apprenticing adolescent readers to academic literacy. *Harvard Educational Review, 71*(1), 79–129.

Handel, R.D. (1999). *Building family literacy in an urban community.* New York: Teachers College Press.

Haycock, K. (2002). *Dispelling the myth, revisited: Additional tables.* Washington, DC: The Education Trust.

Heath, S.B. (1983). *Ways with words: Language, life, and work in communities and classrooms.* New York: Cambridge University Press.

Heibert, E.H. (1980). The relationship of logical reasoning ability, oral language comprehension, and home experiences to preschool children's print awareness. *Journal of Reading Behavior, 12*(4), 313–324.

Henderson, A.T., & Mapp, K.L. (2002). *A new wave of evidence: The impact of school, family, and community connections on student achievement: Annual synthesis, 2002.* Austin, TX: National Center for Family & Community Connections with Schools.

Ho, E.S-C., & Willms, J.D. (1996). Effects of parental involvement on eighth-grade achievement, *Sociology of Education, 69*(2), 126–141.

Invernizzi, M., Rosemary, C., Juel, C., & Richards, H.C. (1997). At-risk readers and community volunteers: A three-year perspective. *Scientific Studies of Reading, 1*(3), 277–300.

Izzo, C.V., Weissberg, R.P., Kasprow, W.J., & Fendrich, M. (1999). A longitudinal assessment of teacher perceptions of parent involvement in children's education and school performance. *American Journal of Community Psychology, 27*, 817–839.

Jansorn, N.R., & Salinas, K.C. (Eds.). (2004). *Promising partnership practices: The 7th annual collection from members of the National Network of Partnership Schools.* Baltimore: National Network of Partnership Schools, Johns Hopkins University.

Jordan, C., Orozco, E., & Averett, A. (2001). *Emerging issues in school, family, & community connections: Annual synthesis, 2001.* Austin, TX: Southwest Educational Development Laboratory.

Jordan, G.E., Snow, C.E., & Porche, M.V. (2000). Project EASE: The effect of a family literacy project on kindergarten students' early literacy skills, *Reading Research Quarterly, 35*, 524–546.

Keith, T.Z. (1991). Parent involvement and achievement in high school. In S. Silvern (Ed.), *Advances in reading/language research: Literacy through family, community, and school interaction* (pp. 125–141). London: JAI Press.

Lee, S. (1994). *Family-school connections and students' education: Continuity and change of family involvement from the middle grades to high school.* Unpublished doctoral dissertation, Johns Hopkins University, Baltimore.

Lee, V.E., & Croninger, R.G. (1994). The relative importance of home and school in the development of literacy skills for middle-grade students. *American Journal of Education, 102*(3), 286–329.

Leichter, H.J. (1984). Families as environments for literacy. In A. Oberg, H. Goelman, & F. Smith (Eds.), *Awakening to literacy* (pp. 38–50). London: Heinemann.

Leslie, L., & Allen, L. (1999). Factors that predict success in an early literacy intervention project. *Reading Research Quarterly, 34*, 404–424.

Lonigan, C.J., & Whitehurst, G.J. (1998). Relative efficacy of parent and teacher involvement in a shared-reading intervention for preschool children from low-income backgrounds. *Early Childhood Research Quarterly, 13*(2), 263–290.

Lyon, G.R. (1998, April). *Overview of reading and literacy initiatives.* Statement before the Committee on Labor and Human Resources. Retrieved May 22, 2003, from http://www.nichd.nih.gov/publications/pubs/jeffords.htm

Mathematica Policy Research Inc. & Center for Children and Families at Teachers College, Columbia University. (2001). *Building their futures: How early Head Start programs are changing the lives of infants and toddlers in low-income families.* Retrieved May 22, 2003, from http://www.acf.dhhs.gov/policyand planning/researchreports

Mattingly, D.J., Prislin, R., McKenzie, T.L., Rodriguez, J.L., & Kayzar, B. (2002). Evaluating evaluations: The case of parent involvement programs. *Review of Educational Research, 72*, 549–576.

McCarthey, S. (1999). Identifying teacher practices that connect home and school. *Education and Urban Society, 32*(1), 83–107.

Miller, B.I. (1986). *Parental involvement effects on reading achievement of first, second, and third graders.* East Lansing, MI: National Center for Research on Teacher Learning. (ERIC Document Reproduction Service No. ED279997)

Moats, L.C. (2000). *Speech to print: Language essential for teachers.* Baltimore: Brookes.

Moje, E.B., Young, J.P., Readence, J.E., & Moore, D.W. (2000). Reinventing adolescent literacy for new times: Perennial and millennial issues. *Journal of Adolescent Adult Literacy, 43*, 400–410.

Moll, L.C. (1992). Bilingual classroom studies and community analysis: Some recent trends. *Educational Researcher, 21*(2), 20–24.

National Institute for Literacy. (2001). *Put reading first: Helping your child learn to read (A parent guide: Preschool through grade 3).* Washington, DC: National Institute for Literacy, National Institute of Child Health and Human Development, U.S. Department of Education.

Neuman, S.B., & Gallagher, P. (1994). Joining together in literacy learning: Teenage mothers and children. *Reading Research Quarterly, 29*, 382–401.

Paratore, J.R., Hindin, A., Krol-Sinclair, B., & Duran, P. (1999). Discourse between teachers and Latino parents during conferences based on home literacy portfolios. *Education and Urban Society, 32*(1), 58–82.

Parcel, T.L., & Dufur, M.J. (2001). Capital at home and at school: Effects on student achievement. *Social Forces, 79*(3), 881–911.

Phillips, L.M., Norris, S.P., & Mason, J.M. (1996). Longitudinal effects of early literacy concepts on reading achievement:

A kindergarten intervention and five-year follow-up. *Journal of Literacy Research, 28*, 173–195.

Purcell-Gates, V. (1996). Stories, coupons, and the "TV guide": Relationships between home literacy experiences and emergent literacy knowledge. *Reading Research Quarterly, 31*, 406–428.

Purcell-Gates, V. (2000). Family literacy. In M.L. Kamil, P.B. Mosenthal, P.D. Pearson, & R. Barr (Eds.), *Handbook of reading research* (Vol. 3, pp. 853–870). Mahwah, NJ: Erlbaum.

Reeves, D. (2002). *Reason to write handbook: Elementary school edition.* New York: Kaplan.

Sanders, M.G. (1999). Schools' programs and progress in the national network of partnership schools. *Journal of Educational Research, 92*(4), 220–229.

Sanders, M.G., & Epstein, J.L. (2000). Building school-family-community partnerships in middle and high schools. In M.G. Sanders (Ed.), *Schooling students placed at risk: Research, policy, and practice in the education of poor and minority adolescents.* Mahwah, NJ: Erlbaum.

Sanders, M.G., & Simon, B.S. (2002). A comparison of program development at elementary, middle, and high schools in the national network of partnership schools. *The School Community Journal, 12*, 7–27.

Scarborough, H.S., & Dobrich, W. (1994). On the efficacy of reading to preschoolers. *Developmental Review, 14*(3), 245–302.

Sénéchal, M., & LeFevre, J. (2002). Parental involvement in the development of children's reading skill: A five-year longitudinal study, *Child Development, 73*, 455–460.

Sénéchal, M., LeFevre, J., Thomas, E.M., & Daley, K.E. (1998). Differential effects of home literacy experiences on the development of oral and written language. *Reading Research Quarterly, 33*, 96–116.

Shaver, A.V., & Walls, R.T. (1998). Effect of Title I parent involvement on student reading and mathematics achievement.

*Journal of Research and Development in Education, 31*(2), 90–97.

Sheldon, S.B. (2003). Linking school–family–community partnerships in urban elementary schools to student achievement on state tests. *Urban Review, 35*(2), 149–165.

Sheldon, S.B., & Van Voorhis, F.L. (2004). Partnership programs in U.S. schools: Their development and relationship to family involvement outcomes. *School Effectiveness and School Improvement, 15*, 125–148.

Silvern, S. (1985). Parent involvement and reading achievement: A review of research and implications for practice. *Childhood Education, 62*(1), 44, 46, 48–49.

Simon, B.S. (2001). Family involvement in high school: Predictors and effects. *NASSP Bulletin, 85*(2), 8–19.

Snow, C.E., Barnes, W.S., Chandler, J., Goodman, I.F., & Hemphill, L. (1991). *Unfulfilled expectations: Home and school influences on literacy.* Cambridge, MA: Harvard University Press.

Snow, C.E., Burns, S., & Griffin, P. (Eds.). (1998). *Preventing reading difficulties in young children.* Washington, DC: National Academy Press.

Taylor, D. (1983). *Family literacy: Young children learning to read and write.* Portsmouth, NH: Heinemann.

Teale, W.H. (1986). Home background and young children's literacy development. In W.H. Teale & E. Sulzby (Eds.), *Emergent literacy: Writing and reading* (pp. 173–206). Westport, CT: Ablex.

Tizard, J., Schofield, W.N., & Hewison, J. (1982). Collaboration between teachers and parents in assisting children's reading. *British Journal of Educational Psychology, 52*(Part 1), 1–15.

Topping, K. (1995). *Paired reading, spelling, and writing: The handbook for teachers and parents.* London: Cassell.

National Institute of Child Health and Human Development. (2000). *Report of the National Reading Panel. Teaching children to read: An evidence-based assessment of the scientific research literature on reading and its implications for reading instruction* (NIH Publication

No. 00-4769). Washington, DC: U.S. Government Printing Office.

Van Voorhis, F.L., & Epstein, J.L. (2002). *TIPS interactive homework CD for the elementary and middle grades*. Baltimore: Center on School, Family, and Community Partnerships, Johns Hopkins University.

Villas-Boas, A. (1998). Effects of parental involvement in homework on student achievement in Portugal and Luxembourg. *Childhood Education, 74*(6), 367–371.

Wasik, B.A. (1998). Volunteer tutoring programs in reading: A review. *Reading Research Quarterly, 33*, 266–291.

U.S. Department of Education, Office of the Deputy Secretary. (2001). *The longitudinal evaluation of school change and performance in Title I Schools, Volume 1* (Executive summary). Retrieved October 13, 2004, from http://www.ed.gov/offices/OUS/PES/esed/lescp_vol1.pdf

# Appendix

## *Examples of Reading, Writing, and Language Arts Activities in Programs of School, Family, and Community Partnerships*

Schools in the National Network of Partnership Schools (NNPS) at Johns Hopkins University are invited to share information on their promising partnership practices each year. In addition, NNPS guides each school to form an Action Teams for Partnerships (including teachers, parents, administrators, and community partners) to plan and implement family and community involvement activities that support student learning and success. Many schools are working to involve families and community partners with students in reading, writing, and other language arts.

The examples that follow illustrate a wide range of reading activities that schools are implementing to address all six types of involvement: parenting, communicating, volunteering, learning at home, decision making, and collaborating with the community. Components of these activities aim to increase and improve (a) parents' understanding of the school's reading program and how to support their children's reading and writing at home; (b) communication between teachers and parents about reading, including formal exchanges of information in workshops and materials that are sent home, and informal contacts at school events; (c) parent and community volunteers to assist students who need help in reading; (d) opportunities for students to read at home, practice new skills, and share their reading and writing with family members; (e) strategies to involve all families in reading-related activities, regardless of the parents' education, culture, or home language; and (f) ways for community businesses and organizations to help schools emphasize the importance of reading. Some activities include components for more than one type of involvement, such as combining communications with parents and reading activities for children to conduct at home.

Some family and community involvement activities celebrate books with guest readers, professional storytellers, or published authors; spotlight students who read aloud stories and poems that they wrote; and organize family–child interactions such as writing and illustrating family stories or family books. As schools develop their programs of school, family, and community partnerships, they design or adapt activities to fit the needs and interests of the parents and students they serve. There are, for example, many variations of Family Reading Nights for parents, students, and educators.

Schools often link reading-related events to National Children's Book Week, American Education Week, Read Across America Week, and a Dr. Seuss Birthday or Cat in the Hat Day. Some schools schedule reading events one day a week or once a month for different grade levels throughout the school year, such as Thursday Reading Nights or First Fridays. Others schedule activities occasionally, according to teacher availability and other school schedules.

To customize reading events for their students and families, some schools have guest readers who read stories aloud in English, Spanish, or other languages. Some schedule the activities with breakfast, lunch, or dinner. Others use after-school or evening hours. The activities may be adapted for different grade levels. For example, a student poetry reading for student, teacher, parent, and community audiences may be conducted in elementary, middle, or high schools to spotlight and celebrate student work. The organization and format of the activity may differ at each school level, based on the developmental characteristics of the students, challenges to invite all families, and other local factors. All the activities aim to demonstrate that reading is taken seriously in the school and that the educators recognize the importance of school, family, and community partnerships for helping students to improve reading habits, attitudes, skills, and test scores.

The examples not only illustrate practical approaches to school, family, and community partnerships in reading but also provide ideas for researchers to study the nature and effects of specific reading-related family and community involvement activities on teacher–parent connections, parents' knowledge and actions, and students' reading attitudes and skills.

## Selected Activities

### Workshops and Meetings for Parents

*P.A.I.R.S–Parents Actively Involved in Reading Strategies.* Storyteller sessions and demonstrations are conducted to show parents how students learn to read, how to help students with reading skills, and how to select books for students. The activity includes a trip to the school library to select books to bring home to read with children. Other schools call similar workshops Breakfast and a Book or Parents as Reading Partners. They add strategies to encourage parents to read with their children and ways parents may improve their own reading skills. Breakfast is provided, along with reading-related gifts for parents to bring home.

*Latino Literacy Program.* Spanish-speaking parents gain information and share ideas on how to become more involved with their children's literacy learning at home. Parents conduct various art and language activities, learn about bilingual books to read at home, and create a family album and story to share with other parents at the workshop and with their children at home. Attendees are introduced to and visit the school's lending library for parents.

*Open Court Parent Workshops.* Educators and experienced parents introduce parents of students from kindergarten through grade 5 to the school's reading program and the Open Court textbook series that the children will use. Sessions are conducted in Spanish and English to familiarize parents with students' spelling cards, sight words, sample stories, and how to help children at home in positive ways. The activity may be adapted to any reading curriculum.

*Equity Book Club.* Parents are invited to attend a dinner to discuss high-quality children's literature on issues of equity. The discussions increase understanding in a school that serves a diverse population of students and families. The evening, conducted three times a year, includes a reading, potluck dinner, guided discussions, and copies of a selected book.

## Activities for Parents and Students Together

*Jumpstart to Reading.* Kindergarten and first-grade students and their parents come together to hear a story. Parents also receive information on how students learn to read and ways to encourage reading at home. Parent–child pairs receive a new book to take home. Other schools call similar parent–child activities Parent/Family Book Club, Storytelling Night, Family Reading Night, and D.R.E.A.M. (Do Read Every Available Minute) Night. These include parents and children at all grade levels or different grade levels each month. The activities may involve a professional storyteller, help families meet other families, provide parents with ideas from their children's teachers of activities to conduct at home about specific stories, and strengthen parent–teacher interactions about reading.

*Open Library Night.* Parents and students have access to the school library one evening a week to check out books together.

*Family Center Learning Nights.* Parents and children are invited to reading and literacy gatherings on selected Thursday evenings throughout the year. They are guided by teachers and curriculum leaders to make a family book with family photos. Parents may attend sessions on how children learn to read and how to help at home. Some sessions are organized to meet an author of books for children or on parenting.

*Bridges to Literacy.* Parents and children are invited to various reading-related events that strengthen multicultural understanding. They may read selected books together, visit the school library, complete a crafts activity related to reading about different cultures, complete a cooking activity by reading recipes, and participate in storytelling and drama activities to improve speaking skills. Parents and educators also share ideas on how to support literacy development at home with several kinds of activities. Other schools conduct similar activities on different themes. The Makowski Marketplace links the multicultural books and related activities and games to the backgrounds of the students at the school. At Family Right to Read Night, parents and students are invited to read books on a particular topic. For example, one evening featured books about bears along with related reading, art, writing, and other activities.

*Camp Read-A-Lot.* Parents and students listen to stories read aloud in English and Spanish at a "camp night" at school and conduct various activities with books. The event is conducted by parent and community volunteers, in collaboration with community groups and organizations. Students and parents take home books in English and Spanish and reading-related activities to conduct and enjoy at home to increase students' reading for pleasure.

*Families Who Write and Read Succeed Night.* Parents and students with diverse cultural backgrounds are invited to write and illustrate a book together on a theme that is important to all families (e.g., friendship, celebrations, learning). Translations are made for families who write in different languages. Families read their books, share them at the event, and take them home. New and used books also are donated to the school for distribution at this event.

*Family Literacy Nights.* As a result of collaborative planning between the school and community organizations, parents are offered courses to learn English; parents, students, and teachers are offered courses to learn Spanish and computer skills; and students are given opportunities to obtain help with homework.

*Book Swap.* Students and parents exchange gently used books periodically throughout the school year. The events include reading stations to read books, art activities, and storytelling, as well as locations for books for parents and students at different grade levels. Parents and students may pick up reading lists of books recommended for students at different grade levels.

### Information and Materials for Parents

*Family Reading Resource Center.* Parents may pick up materials to take home to help students practice reading, vocabulary, and other skills. Workshops for parents are conducted periodically that explain how to use various materials with their children.

### Spotlight on Student Work

*Keep Books.* First graders bring home books called Keep Books, which the students may read, write in, and share with their family partners. The students may collect and keep up to 48 books during the school year. The school works with the Early Literacy Learning Initiative at Ohio State University to conduct this activity.

*Story Bags.* Students take home a different Story Bag each week to share with a family partner. The bag contains a book, guidelines for parents with suggested questions to discuss with their children, and an activity to conduct related to the story. Students and parents write a short comment or reaction to the book and return it with the bag to the teacher.

*Reading BINGO.* BINGO lists different reading and writing activities in the boxes on the game card. Students who complete five activities in a row during a month (such as reading a recipe, writing a thank-you note, drawing a map, writing directions, listing products at a grocery store from A to Z, or other reading and word activities that are listed) win the game and are awarded a book to take home.

*Get Caught Reading.* Students are asked to pledge to read at least 20 minutes per night for five nights per week, with parent's approval of the child's promise. During one randomly selected week, teachers and other staff call students at home between 7:00 and 7:30 p.m. If the students are "caught reading," they are recognized in school the next day. Parents verify that their child is reading as part of their homework.

*Authors in Training.* Students in grades 4 and 5 read their poetry to parents and other community members at a Poetry Picnic. Students also read their poetry on a local radio show and some of their work also is printed in the community newspaper.

*Dad's Day Breakfast and Writing Showcase.* Students read essays and other written work for their dads or other family members. Students also share writing portfolios. Everyone has breakfast.

*A Reading Partnership.* Students who are incarcerated in a school within a detention center and their parents read *And Still We Rise* or other selected books. Students and parents are given a copy of the book and discuss its messages in their phone conversations or regular visits. They also discuss the book with the school staff. This book club is helping to connect parents, students, and staff in new ways.

*Reading Goals and Challenges.* Many schools set goals for students, collectively, to read a large number of books during a school year (e.g., one school may set a goal for students to read 51,000 books in all; another school's goal may be 100,000, depending on the size of the student population). Some schools supplement the reading goal with activities such as parent, grandparent, community, and child reading nights; pancake suppers with stories and books to read; breakfasts and books; and other reading-related events.

## Gala Events and Celebrations

*Read Across America Week.* Many schools celebrate this week with reading-related activities scheduled at various times during the day and evening and on different days, so that all parents can find time to attend at least one reading event. Activities include listening to guests read aloud children's books and listening to students read their writings. Local celebrities may be invited to participate, and local bookstores and businesses are asked to sponsor events and provide books for children.

*A Birthday Party for Dr. Seuss* (sometimes called Cat-in-the-Hat Day). Many schools organize programs in honor of Dr. Seuss each February. They may conduct activities all week or on one day to celebrate and feature books by Dr. Seuss. Activities include an evening of celebrity readers (e.g., teachers, community business people, elected officials, and others) of Dr. Seuss books. Some people wear costumes. Children and families listen to stories, conduct art activities, have snacks (sometimes called Seuss-snacks), swap Dr. Seuss or other books, and receive books that are donated.

*Salute to National Book Week.* Students, teachers, and parents demonstrate a love of literature on each day of the week. Activities include trivia games on favorite books; parent, staff, student, community, and celebrity readers for each class; and related school library activities.

## Reading Volunteers

*Books to Go.* This activity aims to increase parent awareness of reading skills that children learn at each grade level, improve students' skills and test scores, increase students' interest in reading, and increase the number of books that students have at home. Volunteers collect donations of new and gently used books and sell them to students for 50 cents each. Different carts of age-appropriate books serve different grade levels. In one school, more than 5,000 books were exchanged in this way for students in pre-K to grade 2 over two years.

*B.E.A.R (Be Excited About Reading).* Community members, including parents, elected officials, organizations, and businesses come to the school to read books aloud in different languages. Translators also are present. The reading volunteers visit with all students in the school's 50 classrooms. Reading bears are prominent symbols.

*Lunch Bunch.* Students in grades 1–5 who have not completed the school's requirement to read for 20 minutes at home as part of each night's homework complete the assignment by reading during the lunch period with a parent, community partner, or student volunteer.

*Partners in Literacy.* Teachers train volunteers to listen to children read a book at a listening center and to work with each student on a designated sight vocabulary reading list during language arts classes. Volunteers include parents, grandparents, senior citizens, other community partners, school board members, and businesses.

*Book Talks.* Parents and other volunteers in a junior high school select a book for early adolescents from a list provided by the school library director, read it, and present a 5–10 minute talk to share their reactions with students. Teachers work with the library director to select books linked to particular units of work in different school subjects and then schedule the volunteers to come to those classes at a convenient time. The presenters discuss the books with up to four classes on a given day. The program aims to show students that adults enjoy books and to help students identify good books in the media center that are linked to their class lessons.

### Community Partners

*Reading Book Bags 'N' Buddies.* The school trains community volunteers to read books, tutor, conduct activities, and talk with students about reading in grades pre-K to 3.

*Buddy Reading Program.* This program pairs future teachers in an education college with fourth- and fifth-grade students in a local school to talk about a specific novel or biography via the Internet.

*Ozzie's Reading Club.* A city's minor league baseball team works with students in a local school in several ways. The players read stories at a Reading Club Night. The teachers and team design a baseball reading game. Over eight weeks, students read a set number of books or pages to reach first base, second base, and so on. Those who make a "home run" by completing the reading program receive a free ticket to one of the team's Reading Club Night games. The readers march in a parade at the ballpark and receive other prizes from the team.

*Paws for Reading.* The mascot of the Detroit Tigers baseball team partners with an elementary school to read and discuss the poem "Casey at the Bat." The teachers also set up a reading raffle for children to enter a drawing for a monthly reading prize. Prizes for the raffle and other school accomplishments include ballgame tickets.

The above activities were conducted by schools in the National Network of Partnership Schools in Los Angeles and Saugus, California; Danbury and Meriden, Connecticut; Valdosta, Georgia; Naperville, Illinois; Wichita, Kansas; Baltimore, Maryland; Detroit, Grand Blanc, and Ypsilanti, Michigan; Carver, Minnesota; Angier and Clayton, North Carolina; Brooklyn and Buffalo, New York; Bucyrus, Canton, Cleveland, Cuyahoga Falls, Grove City, Wapakoneta, and Zanesville, Ohio; Providence, Rhode Island; Eau Claire, Kaukauna, Stevens Point, Viroqua, and Winneconne, Wisconsin; and Winnipeg, Canada. For more information on these and other family and community involvement activities, see the annual collections of Promising Partnership Practices on the website of the National Network of Partnership Schools at Johns Hopkins University (www.partnershipschools.org) in the "In the Spotlight" section.

CHAPTER 8

# Family and Community Involvement in Children's Reading and Literacy Development: A Response to Steven Sheldon and Joyce Epstein

*Jeanne R. Paratore*

teven Sheldon and Joyce Epstein review and summarize evidence of the effects of schools' programs of family and community involvement on children's reading and language arts development. Unlike the majority of work on this topic that focuses on the characteristics of parents who become involved in their children's learning, Sheldon and Epstein maintain a determined and continued focus on the characteristics of schools and teachers who "enable all families to support children's reading and literacy skills." In so doing, they avoid the tendency to fix the blame for low levels of parent involvement on parents, and they remind us one more time that in matters of schooling, the actions of individual teachers may be the most critical in making a difference in children's learning lives.

I have organized my remarks by returning to the three main conclusions Sheldon and Epstein draw from their overview of research. Briefly stated, these conclusions are that (1) programs of school, family, and community partnerships can be effective in engaging all families in children's academic success; (2) subject-specific family and community activities are more likely to improve children's academic success; and (3) we need better research to fully understand how to design and implement effective home–school partnership programs.

In response to their work, I hope to make two central points. First, to be effective, home, school, and community efforts must be conceptualized as multilevel, long-term efforts that cohere from year to year. Second, to be effective, home, school, and community partnerships must transform

(Swap, 1993) the ways teachers and parents think about literacy in particular, and teaching and learning in general.

## Home–School Partnership Programs Work

Sheldon and Epstein report substantial evidence to sustain a conclusion that school programs that support home, school, and community involvement can make a positive difference in children's school achievement. But of perhaps greater importance than the general finding that such programs improve children's school success is their statement that existing research "indicates that school programs to involve families make a difference in *whether* and *which* families become involved in their children's education and how they become involved." In considering this statement, I am reminded of the work of some of our colleagues in literacy education. For example, Michalove, Shockley, and Allen (1995) note that the language we use makes a difference in the ways we conceptualize and position home–school partnerships and, thus, in whether or not such efforts are successful in engaging all parents. They explain,

> Programs are implemented; partnerships are developed. Programs are adopted; partnerships are constructed. Parent involvement programs as America's schools have implemented them have serious problems. By their very nature, most programs have steps, elements, or procedures that become static. A program cannot constantly reinvent itself, change with each year, be different in every classroom, and for every teacher–family–child relationship. Yet schools and parents have a shared and vested interest in children that almost demands some kind of collaboration. (p. 91)

Michalove et al. argue that if we wish to develop genuine partnerships with parents, we need to understand and engage practices that will enable learning between parents and teachers to be reciprocal. This point of view is consistent with Sheldon and Epstein's comment that studies that tell us how few reading resources economically poor students have at home may "reveal little about the family processes that may improve children's reading skills." Indeed, our field is rich with studies that tell us what families do not know or have or do. But there is also work—although far less voluminous—that can help us meet our obligation to learn about the processes that make a difference.

As Sheldon and Epstein note, the work of Luis Moll and his colleagues (Diaz, Moll, & Mehan, 1986; Gonzalez et al., 1995; Moll, 1992; Moll, Amanti, Neff, & Gonzalez, 1992; Moll & Greenberg, 1990) and that of Concha Delgado-Gaitan (1990, 1992, 1994, 1995) are important examples. The work of these researchers is noteworthy because it departs from what some have called the "compliance model" of parent involvement (e.g., Lareau, 1989; Taylor, 1991), employing instead a model of learning reciprocity in which parents and teachers are both givers and receivers of important information. Other examples of home–school partnerships that recognize the importance of reciprocal learning between parents and teachers can be found in the work of Auerbach (1997); Baumann and Thomas, (1997); Cairney and Munsie (1995); Compton-Lilly and Comber (2003); DeBruin-Parecki and Krol-Sinclair (2003); Handel (1999); McCarthey (1997, 1999); Paratore, Hindin, Krol-Sinclair, and Durán (1999); Quintero and Huerta-Macias (1990); and Rodriguez-Brown (2001). Of particular importance in each of these works is that these researchers make no attempt to suggest a "program" that might work; rather, each describes and explains the practices that they used to build a partnership.

These studies are also important in furthering our understanding of the factors that do not influence parents' interest, motivation, or ability to support their children's reading success. They add to the evidence cited by Sheldon and Epstein that "parents with low income and less formal education, who may have weaker reading skills than more economically advantaged parents, can effectively support their children's reading and education." In addition, although absent from this particular list, several studies (Paratore, Melzi, & Krol-Sinclair, 1999; Shanahan, Mulhern, & Rodriguez-Brown, 1995; Valdés, 1996; Vasquez, Pease-Alvarez, & Shannon, 1994) indicate that parents' ability to effectively support their children's reading success is not dependent on their level of English language proficiency. Rather, evidence suggests that there are literacy universals, including, for example, concepts about print, motivation and interest in reading, and response to literature, that can be effectively shared and developed in any language.

As noted by Goldenberg (2002), even the most effective parent-training programs may be likely to draw from the population of parents who are already motivated to help their children in school. Developing a better understanding of what parents already know and do, and learning to build on family literacies as a bridge to school literacies, may be an integral step is broadening the pool of participants.

## The Content of Effective Programs

In their second main conclusion, Sheldon and Epstein shift their focus from the effectiveness of home–school partnership programs in general to an examination of what, in particular, accounts for program effectiveness. This focus is, at least in part, a response to the research synthesis by Mattingly, Prislin, McKenzie, Rodriguez, and Kayzar (2002) in which they report that their analysis of 41 parent involvement programs provided "little support for the widespread belief that parent involvement programs are an effective means of either improving student academic achievement or changing parent, teacher, and student behavior" (p. 571). Sheldon and Epstein challenge that finding on the basis that the review aggregated the results of studies that were diverse in program types, goals, and practices. They report that their own reexamination of the cluster of 16 programs that provided parents specific instruction on how to assist their children on reading and language arts activities indicated that children made significant achievement gains in such programs. Based on this and other evidence, they conclude that "across the grades, studies indicate that subject-specific involvement activities affect student achievement in the targeted subjects." This conclusion is consistent with that of St. Pierre, Gamse, Alamprese, Rimdzius, and Tao (1998), whose examination of data from the National Even Start Evaluation revealed conflicting findings from earlier to later years of project implementation related to the projects' effects on children's reading and language achievement. Their analysis of the data led them to suggest that the different outcomes may be attributable to a change in the content of the parenting education component of Even Start's programs, from a focus in early years on literacy education (during which time there was evidence of positive effects on children's literacy and language outcomes) to more diffuse objectives in later years, including child nutrition, health, and life skills (during which time there were no significant effects on children's literacy and language outcomes).

Evidence of the superiority of subject-specific interventions is important because it suggests the critical need to look beneath the surface of parent involvement programs and cause teachers, administrators, and researchers to work together to unpack what makes (or might potentially make) a difference in the effectiveness of home–school interventions. To fully understand the importance of content, it is likely that we need to engage in a more fine-grained analysis—examining not just whether or not interventions are subject specific but also analyzing the types (and lengths) of interventions and the types of school and teacher actions that make a difference in parents' and children's behaviors and in children's learning outcomes.

One example of research that might guide us in understanding the specific actions that underlie successful home–school partnerships is the work of Hart and Risley (1995) on the everyday experiences of young children. Their evidence led them to conclude that there is less need for programs to teach parents *how* to talk or interact with their children and more need for programs to teach parents the importance of *how much* to talk and interact with their children. Hart and Risley reported that the differences in the amount of talk among parents was so consistent month to month that by the time children reached 3 years of age, the differences in amount of language heard by children were enormous. The more parents talked to their children, the larger their vocabularies grew; and the larger their vocabularies, the higher their performance on IQ tests. Hart and Risley suggest that their findings should not only influence how we intervene with parents, but should also influence how we assess the effectiveness of intervention programs. To understand children's outcomes, we need to understand the ways in which program activities have helped parents to implement focal practices, and the extent to which parents have, in fact, embedded such practices in their daily routines.

I cite Hart and Risley's study as only one example of the importance of analyzing what may seem to be very tiny details in discerning the type of information that may be helpful to parents. There are many other examples of research that can and should guide us in planning (and subsequently evaluating) the content of programs intended to support parents' efforts to help their children succeed in school. There is a large and continually growing body of research that informs the particular types of early literacy experiences that provide the foundation for success in early literacy (e.g., Arnold & Whitehurst, 1994; Beals, DeTemple, & Dickinson, 1994; DeBaryshe, 1995; Dickinson, & Sprague, 2001; Edwards, 1991; Evans, Shaw, & Bell, 2000; Leslie & Allen, 1999; Purcell-Gates, 1996; Reese & Cox, 1999; Sénéchal & LeFevre, 2002; Sénéchal, LeFevre, Thomas, & Daley, 1998; Sénéchal, Thomas, & Monker, 1995).

We might also consider the grades or ages at which parents are invited to participate in parent involvement programs within the context of the content of such programs. As Sheldon and Epstein note, educators have primarily conceptualized home, school, and community partnerships as primary-grade interventions, perhaps based on an assumption that, thereafter, parents and children will be grounded in the strategies and routines we have sought to teach. Evidence, though, suggests otherwise. For example, Barnett, Young, and Schweinhart (1998) found that early cognitive gains resulting from early intervention programs that include a parent intervention component quickly fade out, at least for some learners. They suggested that the "chief effect of preschool education was on subject-matter knowledge and skills" (p. 181) rather than on general intellectual ability. Similar findings of short-term academic gains are reported by White, Taylor, and Moss (1992) and by St. Pierre et al. (1998). When we join the evidence that early learning gains are often not maintained with the evidence that Sheldon and Epstein provide related to the effectiveness of home–school interventions in later grades, a strong argument can be made for increasing attention to home–school partnership efforts across age and grade levels, with focal content shifting as children advance in reading and writing abilities.

## Quality of Research

A third major conclusion reached by Sheldon and Epstein is that we need to improve the breadth and depth of studies that examine the relationships between family and community involvement and children's learning outcomes. Especially noteworthy is their claim that "we need to know *which* practices with *which* families at *which* grade levels will produce *which* results in reading, writing, and other literacy skills for *which* students." Implicit in this statement is the understanding that different practices are likely to work with different families at different age levels, in collaboration with different teachers—an understanding that we cannot seek a "one-size fits all" curriculum for either parents or children. Given what is known about the diversity among children, their parents, and their teachers, this seems a wise and necessary direction for research that will yield evidence worthy of influencing practice.

## Conclusions and Policy Implications

My reading of Sheldon and Epstein's research summary and my own work in this area lead me to suggest two major policy implications. First, home, school, and community partnerships should be reconceptualized as long-term, multiyear efforts. Second, future investigations must be designed in ways that allow us to study and understand the effects of transmission and transformation models.

## Multiyear, Long-Term Home, School, and Community Partnerships

The evidence related to parent involvement programs indicates that when outcomes are considered in relation to literacy-related goals and objectives for children, interventions are successful in achieving short-term, higher levels of performance for children on literacy-related measures. However, as has been noted, there is also evidence that, for many children, these early gains diminish over a relatively short period of time. This finding may speak to the importance and persistence of the factors that put children at risk for school failure in the first place—in particular, the effects of economic, language, and cultural differences on school-based learning. The evidence underscores the need for serious and determined examination of ways to extend the effects of home–school interventions beyond the preschool and primary-grade years.

In pursuing this line of study, I do not believe the issue is as simple as increasing the frequency of occurrence of home, school, and community involvement efforts across age and grade levels. Rather, it may be that successfully extending home–school partnerships beyond the early grades will require deeper understanding of the types of partnerships that help parents to sustain early forms of literacy support; of the ways that early literacy interventions should evolve into new and different forms of parental support as children advance through school; and of the ways that family needs differ from each other, how needs change over time as children grow and learn, and how forms of home–school partnerships must evolve to meet different and changing family needs.

Reconceptualizing home, community, and school interventions as multiyear efforts that cohere from one year to the next will require not only a greater economic commitment by schools and funding agencies. It will also require a deeper understanding of the types and timing of activities that parents can realistically make a long-term commitment to while they continue to maintain their family, community, and employment responsibilities.

## Transmission and Transformation

As noted by Lareau (1989) and Taylor (1991), home–school interventions are commonly marked by an expectation by the school or teacher that parents will comply with the requests of the school, providing information or assisting with completion of various assignments. Such programs have been shown to be successful—at least when short-term gains are measured. But few parent intervention programs have been found to have long-term, sustained effects on children's school success. It may be that the lack of long-term gains is related to the expectation for compliance—that for parents and children alike, behaviors motivated by compliance may be fleeting, ending when the program ends. In contrast, behaviors motivated by changes in beliefs and understandings by all participants in an effort—what Swap (1993) called transformation—may be more likely to be sustained beyond the life of a particular intervention. These statements are not claims—they are rather hypotheses. Is it the case that programs that primarily emphasize transmission of information to parents yield different outcomes from those that emphasize reciprocity of learning between parents and teachers? If so, what types of events or activities lead to transformation in parents' and teachers' understandings of home and school literacies and of teaching and learning? Would the so-called hard-to-reach parents be more (or less) likely to participate in a partnership that was characterized by the exchange rather than the transmission of information? Does it matter whether such events or activities take place during children's early school years or later school years? Do the two program models—transmission and transformation— yield different results with different families? It seems to me that investigations that yield answers to some of these questions might help us to more effectively conceptualize and implement home, school, and community partnerships that having lasting effects on children, parents, and teachers.

## Conclusion

Discussions of home–school partnerships as they relate to children's academic success often come around eventually to the issue of responsibility— what should we expect of teachers and what should we expect of parents in relation to promoting children's school success? Early in their chapter, Sheldon and Epstein help us to place the importance of family involvement in perspective with this comment:

> We should not expect too much from family and community involvement as an influence on students' reading achievement across the grades. Children's reading skills are most affected by high-quality instruction from skilled teachers (Snow, Burns, & Griffin, 1998). Nor should we minimize the potential of the "value added" to good teaching of family and community involvement as an influence on students' literacy skills and reading achievement.

Snow, Barnes, Chandler, Goodman, and Hemphill's (1991) investigation of the home and school influences on children's literacy led them to conclude that excellent teachers can override what they characterized as "less than ideal" home conditions. In chapter 21 of this volume, the successful schools described by Douglas Reeves seem to lend support to this conclusion—parent involvement is absent from the list of factors he identified as characteristic of the successful schools he studied.

However, although we would like it to be otherwise, many students attend classrooms where teachers are not exemplary but rather, as Snow and her colleagues described them, merely "intermediate." In these cases, Snow et al. found that the actions of parents and teachers had a complementary effect—together, they provided students enough guidance and support to succeed. They concluded that "in the absence of excellence in the classroom, the role of the home becomes much more important" (p. 161).

In the context of today's urban classrooms, this may be a critical observation. We must work to provide students the best classroom instruction possible. But we must also acknowledge that, as yet, we are a long way from universal teaching excellence. That acknowledgment may raise the stakes for increasing our understanding of home, school, and community efforts that are not dependent on a single exemplary teacher. We should instead prepare parents to sustain over long periods of time the types of literacy support they learn to provide their children.

## REFERENCES

Arnold, D.S., & Whitehurst, G.J. (1994). Accelerating language development through picture book reading: A summary of dialogic reading and its effects. In D.K. Dickinson (Ed.), *Bridges to literacy: Children, families, and schools* (pp. 103–128). Cambridge, MA: Blackwell.

Auerbach, E.R. (1997). *Making meaning, making change: Guide to participatory curriculum development for adult ESL literacy*. Washington, DC: Center for Applied Linguistics.

Barnett, W.S., Young, J.W., & Schweinhart, L.J. (1998). How preschool education influences long-term cognitive development and school success: A causal model. In W.S. Barnett & S.S. Boocock (Eds.), *Early care and education for children in poverty: Promises, programs, and long-term results* (pp. 167–184). Albany: State University of New York Press.

Baumann, J.F., & Thomas, D. (1997). If you can pass Momma's tests, then she knows you're getting your education. A case study of support for literacy learning within an African-American family. *The Reading Teacher, 51*, 108–120.

Beals, D.E., De Temple, J.H., & Dickinson, D.K. (1994). Talking and listening that support early literacy development of children from low-income families. In D.K. Dickinson (Ed.), *Bridges to literacy: Children, families, and schools*. Cambridge, MA: Blackwell.

Cairney, T., & Munsie, L. (1995). *Beyond tokenism: Parents as partners in literacy*. Portsmouth, NH: Heinemann.

Compton-Lilly, C., & Comber, B. (2003). *Reading families: The literate lives of urban children*. New York: Teachers College Press.

DeBaryshe, B. (1995). Maternal belief systems: Linchpin in the home reading process. *Journal of Applied Developmental Psychology, 16*, 1–20.

DeBruin-Parecki, A., & Krol-Sinclair, B. (Eds.). (2003). *Family literacy: From theory to practice*. Newark, DE: International Reading Association.

Delgado-Gaitan, C. (1990). *Literacy for empowerment: The role of parents in children's education*. London: Taylor & Francis.

Delgado-Gaitan, C. (1992). School matters in the Mexican-American home:

Socializing children to education. *American Educational Research Journal*, *29*(3), 495–513.

Delgado-Gaitan, C. (1994). Spanish speaking families' involvement in schools. In C.L. Fagnano & B.Z. Werber (Eds.), *School, family and community interaction: A view from the firing lines* (pp. 85–98). Boulder, CO: Westview.

Delgado-Gaitan, C. (1995). *Protean literacy: Extending the discourse on empowerment*. London: Falmer.

Diaz, S., Moll, L.C., & Mehan, H. (1986). Sociocultural resources in instruction: A context-specific approach. In *Beyond language: Social and cultural factors in schooling language minority students* (pp. 187–230). San Mateo, CA: Asian American Curriculum Project.

Dickinson, D.K., & Sprague, K.E. (2001). The nature and impact of early childhood care environments on the language and early literacy development of children from low-income families. In S.B. Neuman & D.K. Dickinson (Eds.), *Handbook of early literacy research* (pp. 263–280). New York: Guilford.

Edwards, P.A. (1991). Fostering early literacy through parent coaching. In E.H. Hiebert (Ed.), *Literacy for a diverse society: Perspectives, practices, and policies* (pp. 199–213). New York: Teachers College Press.

Evans, M.A., Shaw, D., & Bell, M. (2000). Home literacy activities and their influence on early literacy skills. *Canadian Journal of Experimental Psychology*, 54, 65–75.

Goldenberg, C. (2002). Making schools work for low-income families in the 21st century. In S.B. Neumann & D.K. Dickinson (Eds.), *Handbook of early literacy research* (pp. 211–231). New York: Guilford.

Gonzalez, N., Moll, L.C., Tenery, M.F., Rivera, A., Rendon, P., Gonzales, R., et al. (1995). Funds of knowledge for teaching in Latino households. *Urban Education*, *29*(4), 443–470.

Handel, R.D. (1999). *Building family literacy in an urban community*. New York: Teachers College Press.

Hart, B., & Risley, T.R. (1995). *Meaningful differences in the everyday experiences of young American children*. Baltimore: Brookes.

Lareau, A. (1989). *Home advantage: Social class and parental intervention*. London: Falmer.

Leslie, L., & Allen, L. (1999). Factors that predict success in an early literacy intervention project. *Reading Research Quarterly*, *34*, 404–424.

Mattingly, D.J., Prislan, R.A., McKenzie, T.L., Rodriguez, J.L., & Kayzar, B. (2002). Evaluating evaluations: The case of parent involvement programs. *Review of Educational Research*, *72*(4), 549–576.

McCarthey, S. (1999). Identifying teacher practices that connect home and school. *Education and Urban Society*, *32*(1), 83–107.

McCarthey, S.J. (1997). Connecting home and school literacy practices in classrooms with diverse populations. *Journal of Literacy Research*, *29*(2), 145–182.

Michalove, B., Shockley, B., & Allen, J. (1995). *Engaging families: Connecting home and school literacy communities*. Portsmouth, NH: Heinemann.

Moll, L.C. (1992). Literacy research in community and classrooms: A sociocultural approach. In R. Beach, J.L. Green, M.L. Kamil, & T. Shanahan (Eds.), *Multidisciplinary perspectives in literacy research* (pp. 211–244). Urbana, IL: National Council of Teachers of English.

Moll, L.C., Amanti, C., Neff, D., & Gonzalez, N. (1992). Funds of knowledge for teaching: Using a qualitative approach to connect homes and classrooms. *Theory Into Practice*, *31*(1), 132–141.

Moll, L.C., & Greenberg, J.B. (1990). Creating zones of possibilities: Combining social contexts for instruction. In L.C. Moll (Ed.), *Vygotsky and education: Instructional implications and applications of sociohistorical psychology* (pp. 319–348). New York: Cambridge University Press.

Paratore, J.R., Hindin, A., Krol-Sinclair, B., & Durán, P. (1999). Discourse between teachers and Latino parents during conferences based on home literacy portfolios. *Education and Urban Society*, *32*(1), 58–82.

Paratore, J.R., Melzi, G., & Krol-Sinclair, B. (1999). *What should we expect of family literacy? Experiences of Latino children whose parents participate in an intergenerational literacy program*. Newark, DE: International Reading Association; Chicago: National Reading Conference.

Purcell-Gates, V. (1996). Stories, coupons, and the "TV Guide": Relationships between home literacy experiences and emergent literacy knowledge. *Reading Research Quarterly*, *31*, 406–428.

Quintero, E., & Huerta-Macias, A. (1990). All in the family: Bilingualism and biliteracy. *The Reading Teacher*, *44*, 306–312.

Reese, E., & Cox, A. (1999). Quality of adult book reading affects children's emergent literacy. *Developmental Psychology*, *35*(1), 20–28.

Rodriguez-Brown, F.V. (2001). Home-school collaboration: Successful models in the Hispanic community. In P.R. Schmidt & P.B. Mosenthal (Eds.), *Reconceptualizing literacy in the new age of multiculturalism and pluralism* (pp. 273–288). Greenwich, CT: Information Age.

Sénéchal, M., & LeFevre, J. (2002). Parental involvement in the development of children's reading skill: A five-year longitudinal study. *Child Development*, *73*(2), 445–460.

Sénéchal, M., LeFevre, J.A., Thomas, E.M., & Daley, K.E. (1998). Differential effects of home literacy experiences on the development of oral and written language. *Reading Research Quarterly*, *33*, 96–116.

Sénéchal, M., Thomas, E., & Monker, J.A. (1995). Individual differences in vocabulary acquisition. *Journal of Educational Psychology*, *87*, 218–229.

Shanahan, T., Mulhern, M., & Rodriguez-Brown, F. (1995). Project FLAME: Lessons learned from a family literacy program for minority families. *The Reading Teacher*, *48*, 586.

Snow, C.E., Barnes, W.S., Chandler, J., Goodman, I.F., & Hemphill, L. (1991). *Unfulfilled expectations: Home and school influences on literacy*. Cambridge, MA: Harvard University Press.

Snow, C.E., Burns, S., & Griffin, P. (Eds.). (1998). *Preventing reading difficulties in young children*. Washington, DC: National Academy Press.

St. Pierre, R., Gamse, B., Alamprese, J., Rimdzius, T., & Tao, F. (1998). *Even Start: Evidence from the past and a look to the future (National evaluation of the Even Start family literacy program)*. Washington, DC: U.S. Department of Education, Planning and Evaluation Service.

Swap, S.M. (1993). *Developing home-school partnerships: From concepts to practice*. New York: Teachers College Press.

Taylor, D. (1991). *Learning denied*. Portsmouth, NH: Heinemann.

Valdés, G. (1996). *Con respeto: Bridging the differences between culturally diverse families and schools*. New York: Teachers College Press.

Vasquez, O., Pease-Alvarez, L., & Shannon, S.M. (1994). *Pushing boundaries: Language and culture in a Mexicano community*. New York: Cambridge University Press.

White, K.R., Taylor, M.J., & Moss, V.M. (1992). Does research support claims about the benefits of involving parents in early intervention programs? *Review of Educational Research*, *62*(1), 91–125.

# School Contexts of Literacy Development in Urban Settings: Curriculum, Students, and Teachers

I n this section, authors address issues close to the substance of schooling: reading curriculum and instructional practices, linguistic and learning characteristics of students, and the professional preparation of teachers. Taken as a whole, readers will find this section brimming with theories and practices basic to the consideration of urban literacy development, programs, and research, all of which should richly inform administrators and policymakers.

Diane Lapp and James Flood begin this section by describing the curriculum and organization of instruction in an urban first-grade classroom. One remarkable attribute of chapter 9 is the coherent link between theory and practice. The first part of the chapter explains the theoretical knowledge about reading that a teacher needs to successfully instruct students. Doris Walker-Dalhouse's response in chapter 10 confirms Lapp and Flood's assertions and foregrounds the linguistic and cultural knowledge needed by a reading teacher.

In chapter 11, Donna E. Alvermann provides a synthesis of exemplary literacy instruction in grades 7–12. She describes the complexities inherent in adolescent lives and the multiple literacies needed to navigate those complex lives. She pleas for educators to recognize, value, and take advantage of these complexities and to provide critical, empowering, and motivating curricular and literacy opportunities. Richard T. Vacca confirms Alvermann's suggestions and extends them in chapter 12 by denouncing the narrow view many hold of adolescent literacy.

Virginia Richardson and Patricia L. Anders provide a synthesis of the professional preparation and development of teachers in chapter 13. They touch on preservice education but devote most of their chapter to continued professional education. The synthesis is concluded with implications for practice, policy, and research. In chapter 14, Eric J. Cooper and Yvette Jackson confirm and extend Richardson and Anders's points by providing examples from the professional development experiences available through the National Urban Alliance.

Each of these chapters foregrounds the principles and assertions made by Carol D. Lee in chapter 15. Lee first presents folk beliefs about language, then interrogates those assumptions, drawing on the nature of language, and concludes with implications for teachers, researchers, leaders in professional organizations, and policymakers. Arnetha F. Ball, in chapter 16, extends Lee's discussion by highlighting the valuable research that exists about African American Vernacular English (AAVE). She then argues that educators need to better inform themselves about the linguistic resources students bring to the classroom.

Kris D. Gutiérrez's contribution, chapter 17, addresses the issues of learners challenged to learn English, and points out that inequalities exist affecting children's and youths' opportunities to learn. From this chapter and in Robert Rueda's response in chapter 18, readers are challenged to consider the linguistic and class backgrounds of the teaching force and the overly simplistic model of learning to read and write that is privileged by those in power.

The assumptions, principles, and issues raised in chapters 7 through 16 are poignantly brought to bear in chapter 19 by Cheryl A. Utley, Festus E. Obiakor, and Elizabeth B. Kozleski. This chapter is a rich resource: It discusses confusions and misinformation around definitions of categories in special education, provides statistics that document issues of overrepresentation of minority students in special education, decries the lack of information in research studies about the cultural and linguistic backgrounds of students and their teachers, and calls for richer, more complex theories of disability informed by sociocultural theories. Victoria J. Risko thoughtfully responds in chapter 20, theorizing that it is important to distinguish cultural and linguistic differences from disability. Her chapter concludes with powerful implications for researchers, teacher educators, and policymakers.

Section II addresses reading educators directly. It provides syntheses and reflections about classroom instruction, teacher education, language, and students. Each chapter raises issues and offers implications that should provide for rich discussion and, we hope, the advancement of policy and the conduct of future research.

CHAPTER 9

# Exemplary Reading Instruction in the Elementary School: How Reading Develops—How Students Learn and How Teachers Teach

*Diane Lapp and James Flood*

Recently when we bumped into a friend of ours, Pat Marsh, a masterful first-grade teacher in an urban school in southeast San Diego, we asked her about her new first-grade class. She replied, "I have my work cut out for me this year. This is probably the most academically diverse class I've ever had." She explained that two of her students, Anthony and Kaila, knew some but not all the letters of the alphabet, and one boy, Cedric, the class scientist, wouldn't be satisfied with her explanation about duck feathers floating on water (after a shared reading of *The Chick and the Duckling*) until she worked on the duck feather experiment with him as the rest of the class watched in amazement.

Ms. Marsh told us that three of her students seemed to understand the notion of rhyming but hadn't quite mastered it, and one girl, Teresa, was already reading chapter books on her own. As we probed further, she told us that 11 of her 20 students were English-language learners with a wide variety of levels of English proficiency, and four were African American Vernacular English (AAVE) speakers. She also not-so-secretly shared her delight with her students' progress in the two short weeks that they had been together.

We kept in touch with Ms. Marsh throughout the year, visiting her classroom on numerous occasions; we were constantly in awe of what we saw. In June, it came as no surprise to us that all her students were being promoted to second grade as on-grade (or above-grade) readers. When we asked about her students' success, she told us the same thing that she told us last year and the year before and the year before that. "Individualize; get to know your students' strengths and build on them. Get to know exactly what they need and give it to them, and work really hard, too."

Ms. Marsh was fully equipped to teach her students to read: She understood how reading develops over time; she used the best instructional strategies available to help her students make sense of texts; she continuously assessed and diagnosed their needs and matched their developing skills with appropriate books; and she devised a learning environment where every child had the opportunity to become a skillful, motivated reader. At her school, teachers and administrators continually discussed policy documents from the Council of Great City Schools, which guided their thinking about the instruction that should occur in urban schools (Lewis, Ceperich, & Jepson, 2002; Snipes, Doolittle, & Herlihy, 2002), and they also relied on ideas from two websites (www.urbanteacher.com and www.ed.gov/pubs/urbanhope/index.html) that included recommendations for urban schoolteachers and students to kept them apprised of new research and instructional insights that enabled them to provide engaging leaning experiences for all of their students. We will discuss Ms. Marsh's secrets of success in greater detail later in this chapter.

# How Reading Develops Over Time

## *The Development of Word Identification Skills*

Students' growing sensitivity to the English language develops from birth and is the basis for word identification skills, the prerequisites for learning to read. Word knowledge occurs as students play with words; it occurs as they listen, speak, read, and write. It also happens as they are taught the skills that they will need to become proficient, independent readers and writers. Many children who enter urban schools come to their classrooms with a more limited repertoire of linguistic skills than are needed to succeed in many classrooms, and this slows down their progress (Lapp et al., 2004).

Students acquire word identification skills through their discovery of the patterns of the English language (Salus & Flood, 2003); this is an extremely complex task because the English language is not entirely regular (Bus & van IJzendoorn, 1999). Most of the difficulty in identifying English words stems from the nature of the English language itself, because it is both phonetic and morphophonemic in its structure (Byrne, 1999). An example of this occurs in the ways in which English words are pluralized: The regular plural sound can be /s/ or /z/ or /ez/, but each of these is encoded with the same letter: *s*. This phenomenon preserves the morphology of the language but violates its phonological properties.

English is also difficult for students to master because of the way in which it encodes phonological relations, for example, the "long a" can be encoded as *ai, aigh, eigh, ay*, or *a_e*. Students need specific word knowledge beyond sound and symbol knowledge to recognize words. The task of learning to read words is huge because students have the seemingly overwhelming task of learning to interactively use three different sources of knowledge to make meaning: morphological, phonological, and orthographic.

## The Importance of Learning to Decode

By the end of the elementary school years, most students have learned to read words by using a wide array of information about letter-sound patterns, clusters of letters, and syllables. When students have acquired these skills, they usually can identify words automatically with little effort (LaBerge & Samuels, 1974), and this enables them to focus more directly on comprehension than on word identification. For those who have not quickly mastered the code, life is filled with literacy problems. Many researchers have found that students with inadequate word identification skills who continue to rely on context cues are almost always identified as poor readers throughout their school years (Booth, Perfetti, & MacWhinney, 1999; Bruck & Waters, 1990; McConkie & Zola, 1987; Perfetti, 1984; Snowling & Olson, 1994; Stanovich 1994; Velluntino et al., 1995).

## Stages of Word Identification

Ehri (1998) and Stahl and Murray (1994) maintain that students pass through a series of stages as they learn to recognize words: prealphabetic, phonetic cue reading, and full alphabetic.

**Prealphabetic: Development of Print Awareness.** In the prealphabetic stage, students recognize words holistically as single logographs. Many researchers have found that young children do not automatically attend to the letters in words or to the words themselves. A child might recognize the word *monkey* because there is a tail on the *y* (Gates & Bocker, 1923) or the word *look* because it has two "eyes" in the middle. In their study of the ways in which young children learn words, Gough, Juel, and Griffith (1992) found that young students were more likely to rely on a thumbprint on a word card than any letter information included on the card. They concluded that students do not intuitively make use of letter–sound information to recognize words.

Students' knowledge of word identification can be invariably traced back to their early literacy experiences. Becoming literate builds on a child's understanding of speech, and it requires awareness that words in books and on signs in the general environment convey meaningful messages (Au & Kawakami, 1994; Hiebert, 1999; Mason, 1980). Children first become aware that written language can be observed and analyzed in words and letters as they see written language in familiar contexts. For example, children grow in their understanding that letters that are pointed out to them have a relation to the spoken and written word that is being shown and spoken to them as in the case where a proficient reader says to the child, "This is a *K*" (on the Special K cereal box) or "these are *M*s" (on the bag on M&Ms). Doake (1985) found that these early experiences with environmental print make children aware of the purposes of print and motivate them to attend more closely to print as a means to making meaning.

Peterman and Mason's work (1984) clearly demonstrates that word identification has its roots in children's basic understanding of the purposes of print. In their studies, they found that kindergarten children could point to words when they were asked where there was something to read, but they would then ignore the print when they were asked what the words said. As a result of these studies, they argued that students knew that reading involved print, but they did not realize that they could not "read" without using letter information. Over time, Peterman and Mason found that children realized that they should attend to both pictures and print when trying to recall a page of text, but they were uncertain about where words began and ended. Some children at this stage were not able to distinguish letters from words.

To become literate in English, students must be taught about the regularity of sound-to-spelling correspondences (Ehri, 1995, 1998, 1999). Initial learning about the relationships between sounds and letters often begins through home literacy activities such as hearing nursery rhymes, stories, and interesting words, and through discussing words pointed at in these contexts (Bissex, 1980). Taylor (1998) found that knowledge of nursery rhymes at 3 years of age strongly related to later reading performance. Yaden, Smolkin, and MacGillivray (1993) studied children's reading of alphabet books and found that statements such as "*B* is for bear" made no sense to the children until they had a basic understanding that words consisted of sounds.

However, when students did not use sound-to-spelling regularities in English words, they tended to rely on other types of information to make meaning. Context clues provided by pictures and sentences in books make it easier for beginning readers to identify words, and when these cues are not available, beginning readers experience great difficulty. As proof of this, Stanovich, Cunningham, and Freeman (1984) found that beginning readers are likely to make oral reading errors that are consistent with sentence context but inconsistent with sound-to-spelling information.

**Phonetic Cue Reading: Development of Phonemic Awareness.** In the second stage of word identification development, the *phonetic cue reading* stage, students develop phonological awareness as they begin to use some partial sound information in the word, such as the initial or final sound. Students in this stage frequently substitute a word that begins with the same letter as the actual word they are trying to read: for example, *door* for *deer*. As students learn more words, phonetic cue reading becomes more and more inefficient, and students realize that they need more strategies to unlock meaning.

Many researchers have found that the ability to segment the sounds of words into phonemes, which is known as phonemic awareness, is the initial step in reducing overreliance on context. Phonemes are the sounds of letters and letter groups in words, for example, *c-a-t*, *s-ea-t*, *sh-a-p-es*. Children are not initially aware of phonemes; at first, they seem to recognize the syllable as a unit and then notice that the syllable has two major subunits, the onset and the rime (Treiman & Weatherston, 1992). The *onset* is the initial portion of the syllable, *c* in *cat*, *s* in *seat*, and *sh* in *shapes*. The *rime* includes the vowel and the ending consonants, for example *at* in *cat*, *eat* in *seat*, and *apes* in *shapes*. Treiman and Weatherston (1992) found that young children could analyze spoken syllables into onsets and rimes before they could identify phonemes. This suggests that children could be helped to hear syllables in words, then onset and rimes, and then individual phonemes.

After children can distinguish onset and rimes in words, they will be able to separate and manipulate phonemes in words. For example, students will discover that they can remove the final *r* from *Peter* to make the word *Pete*. With these discoveries, students begin to understand the regularities of sound-to-spelling patterns. Based on this knowledge, they begin to figure out words that they have not previously seen (Calhoon & Leslie, 2002).

Stanovich, Cunningham, and Cramer (1984) and Yopp (1988) have shown that word and letter-sound analysis ability are highly correlated with each other and with the ability to analyze words into letter sounds, which allows students to discover the alphabetic principle of sound-to-spelling regularities (Calfee, Lindamood, & Lindamood, 1973). Liberman and Shankweiler (1985) maintain that understanding this aspect of written language structure provides "a basis for constructing a large and expandable set of words—all the words that ever were, are, and will be—out of two or three dozen signal elements (phonemes)" (p. 9).

Several studies have shown that phonemic awareness in kindergarten benefits children's later reading achievement (Bradley & Bryant, 1983; Lundberg, Frost, & Peterson 1988). The training that teachers provided in these studies included rhyming, segmenting sentences into words, segmenting words into syllables, segmenting initial letters of words from the remaining letters, and segmenting two-letter words into phonemes. Two recent meta-analyses of the effects of phonemic awareness training found that the training transferred significantly to beginning reading (Bus & van IJzendoorn, 1999; Ehri, 1999).

Ehri (1999) also found that phonological awareness training with letters created effective sizes nearly twice as large as training without letters on both reading and spelling tasks. Even the training without letters had significant effects on the reading and spelling measures. She found that the training was most effective with small groups for small amounts of time. This research led her to believe that phonological awareness is an insight that is learned in an all-or-nothing manner; therefore, elongated periods of training are counterproductive.

**Full Alphabetic: Using All Letters and Sounds.** In the third stage, *the cipher* or *full alphabetic* stage (Ehri, 1995), children use all the letters and sounds to make meaning. In this stage, a child's reading can be labored because it relies so heavily on sounding out words and other less efficient strategies. During this time children learn that sounds can be represented by letters, and that they can map graphemes onto phonemes. Many researchers have found that students profit from phonics instruction in this third stage of word recognition (Ehri, Nunes, Stahl, Steven, & Willows, 2001; Powell & Hornsby, 1995). (For a detailed review of phonics instruction, see P. Cunningham, 2000; Heilman, 1998; Hull & Fox, 1998; Lapp, 1991; Lapp, Flood, Brock, & Fisher, 2005.)

Teachers can assist students in developing the skill of decoding through systematic instruction that teaches them to examine the letters and letter patterns of each new word encountered in their reading. They go through a period when they need to analyze and segment each sound in a word—for example, c/a/t—and then they learn to synthesize by blending the sounds together, and, finally, they use analogues to help them decode (these are frequently referred to as word families *c-at, r-at, s-at*). Throughout this process, students are also acquiring sight words, that is, words that defy phonics analysis like *the* and *through*.

# Helping Students Make Sense of Texts: Developing Reading Comprehension

Although comprehension of texts is the overall goal of all reading instruction from the very beginning of a child's literacy development, it becomes an even greater focus of instruction as students become fluent at automatically decoding almost all words they encounter in their texts.

*Reading comprehension* is a term that has been used for decades, but it is a construct that has never been defined in a consistent way. In fact, it has frequently been defined in contradictory ways. For example, some educators have argued that reading comprehension is a set of skills (identifying main idea, recognizing cause and effect relationships, inferring) that readers use to unlock the literal meaning of a text, whereas others have argued that it is a process by which readers interpret textual messages at many different levels (literal, inferential, aesthetic). Both definitions contain important elements of reading comprehension, but neither is inclusive enough to be useful to us as we attempt to develop efficient and effective instruction for our urban students.

We argue for a more comprehensive definition of reading comprehension, like the one that was developed by the panelists of the RAND Reading Study Group (2002): "Reading comprehension (is) the process of simultaneously extracting and constructing meaning through interaction and involvement with written language." The words *extracting* and *constructing* emphasize both the importance and the insufficiency of relying on the text as the sole determinant of reading comprehension. Certainly, the text is critical in the process, but equally critical are the *reader* who is processing the text; the mental *activity* in which the reader is engaged, for example, skimming, reading for a fact, and reading for pleasure; and the larger sociocultural *context* in which the reading takes place (classroom, home, community center; alone, in a group, with a teacher).

## *Word-Level Decoding Skills and Reading Comprehension*

Many researchers have argued that skilled readers are competent decoders who use their decoding abilities to comprehend texts. Gough and Tunmer (1986) argue that students who can decode words in texts will be able to comprehend them. Other researchers argue the connection from the opposite side—word-level decoding is a critical bottleneck in comprehending a text; if readers cannot decode words, they will not be able to comprehend texts (Adams, 1990; Ehri, 1998; Pressley, 1998). Ehri (1995) and Goswami

(2000) have argued that readers need to use "chunk" analysis such as common blends, prefixes, suffixes, Latin and Greek roots, and rimes like *ight*, *ite*, and *ipe*, because recognition and comprehension of words occur within short-term memory and actually compete with one another for space in the reader's brain.

## Vocabulary and Reading Comprehension

Readers' knowledge of word meanings greatly affects their comprehension (Brassell & Flood, 2004; Freebody & Anderson, 1993; McKeown, Beck, Omanson, & Pople, 1985). This explains the phenomenon that students who read extensively also possess the greatest vocabularies (A. Cunningham & Stanovich, 2002). Reading and knowledge of information are mutually interdependent—the more one reads, the greater one's knowledge store; and the greater the knowledge store, the greater the comprehension.

The relationship between vocabulary knowledge and comprehension is extremely complex because it is confounded by the relationships among the following variables: vocabulary knowledge, cultural knowledge, conceptual knowledge, and instruction. When the National Reading Panel (National Institute of Child Health and Human Development [NICHD], 2000) examined the question of whether the actual teaching of vocabulary improved comprehension, they did not find compelling evidence that explicit teaching increased students' independent reading abilities or that it promoted vocabulary growth. But A. Cunningham and Stanovich (2002) did report that powerful correlational relationships existed between the amount of reading that students were doing and their measured vocabulary growth.

Although many researchers who examined vocabulary instruction have looked at the effectiveness of teaching individual words, few have carefully examined the relationship between vocabulary instruction that highlights individual words and reading comprehension. The strongest evidence to date about the effects of vocabulary and reading comprehension comes from the work of Isabel Beck and her colleagues (Beck, McKeown, & Kucan, 2002; Beck, Perfetti, & McKeown, 1982).

The question of the selection of which words to teach explicitly as vocabulary items has been a thorny issue for reading comprehension theorists and educators for many years. Graves (1999) and others have suggested that the selection of words to be taught should be taken into consideration, as well as the differences between teaching new concepts and teaching new labels for familiar concepts. Laufer and Nation (1999) offer an additional instructionally relevant way to categorize words: high-frequency words (*car*, *driver*);

domain-specific technical vocabulary (*raceway*); low-frequency words (*carburetor*); and high-utility words (*gas*). These distinctions are important because they enable teachers to prioritize the words that they want to give the most time and attention to during their lessons (Anders & Bos, 1986).

Teaching individual words assumes detailed explanations of their meanings, which are often delivered through instructional definitions. Although Scott and Nagy (1997) have explored different ways to teach definitions, very little is known in this area, even though there is no question that a major component of a well-developed comprehender's repertoire is the ability to cope with unfamiliar words that they encounter in reading. In order for readers to effectively cope with unfamiliar words, they must be able to use context skills, morphology skills, and dictionary skills. Fukkink and de Glopper (1998) found that instruction in the use of context clues improved both vocabulary knowledge and comprehension ability, but the jury is still out on the use of context clues to improve comprehension because Kuhn and Stahl (1998) have argued that this kind of instruction is not demonstrably better than sustained practice.

## Sentence- and Text-Level Processing and Reading Comprehension

Competent readers have a vast storehouse of knowledge about many topics, which they access when they are reading. This knowledge is organized in their minds in such a way that readers can "get at" it to help them make sense of print—this knowledge, sometimes called *schema knowledge*—serves as a structure for organizing relations between and among ideas (Anderson & Pearson, 1984; Langer, 1984). For example, competent readers may have schema knowledge for a restaurant: They know its purpose (eating), where its purpose is done (a building) and by whom (customers), and when it's done (certain hours of the day). Specific customs are embedded within the schemata, for example, waiting to be seated, ordering from the menu, paying the bill, and tipping the server.

Schema knowledge helps people understand the relationships among events easily as soon as one small piece of the schema is identified (readers know to access their restaurant schema as soon as the word *waitress* is used in the text). Bauer and Fivush (1992) have shown that very young students have schemata for events in their own lives (bedtime rituals, dinnertime, games) that help them make inferences as they hear and read stories with events that match their schemata. Thus, the wider the child's experiences, the greater his or her ability will be to comprehend texts.

## Controlling and Monitoring Comprehension

Good comprehenders monitor their own comprehension as they construct meaning from texts (Paris & Winograd, 2003). They establish a purpose for reading and they continually check themselves to make sure that this purpose is being met. They notice when things go awry. When their background knowledge is insufficient for dealing with the information in the text, they fix the problem by rereading, reading ahead, seeking help from a knowledgeable person (teacher, peer), or consulting alternative resources. Teachers like Ms. Marsh realize that developing reading proficiency is a complex phenomenon with direct connections to the learner's culture, language, experience, and previous knowledge (Lyons, 2003; Ramirez, Yuen, & Ramey, 1991).

## Reading Fluency

*Reading fluency* is defined as "the freedom from word identification problems that might hinder comprehension in silent reading or the expression of ideas in oral reading" (Harris & Hodges, 1995, p. 85). Although acquiring fluency in reading has been traditionally associated with younger readers as an effective practice for developing comprehension, there is also evidence that suggests that the practice of developing students' fluency is also effective for older students (Berninger, Abbott, Billingsley, & Nagy, 2001; NICHD, 2000). Being a fluent reader involves effortless, automatic word recognition with appropriate phrasing and expression. This ability is usually lacking in readers who are struggling with comprehension (Allington, 1983b; Fleischer, Jenkins, & Pany, 1979; Thurlow & van den Broek, 1997). In 1966, Heckelman reported on the beneficial effects of the neurological impress method (NIM) as a way to develop reading fluency. Echo reading, repeated readings of texts, and Readers Theatre, in which readers practice their comprehension skills by reading and rereading scripts, have also been shown to be very effective practices for all students—novice, intermediate, and proficient. All of these practices have been found to be particularly effective for second-language learners who are in the process of mastering English (Dixon-Krauss, 1995) and for students struggling with their reading (Allington, 1983a).

Tan and Nicolson (1997) have also reported that students can develop fluency and subsequent comprehension skills by reading and rereading isolated lists of isolated words. However, this practice is still considered controversial by many educators, but the evidence continues to support it as a part of fluency development.

## Retaining, Organizing, and Evaluating Information

Good comprehenders also use strategies to help them retain, organize, and evaluate information that is contained in a text. They use a set of well-defined, highly researched strategies as they read. The National Reading Panel Report (NICHD, 2000) recommends six key strategies that all readers should use on a regular basis with narrative and information texts:

1. *Question generating.* Readers ask questions of the author and themselves as they read.

2. *Question answering.* Readers attempt to answer the questions they have asked as well as the questions that may have been generated by the author.

3. *Paraphrasing.* Readers try to reword sentences to make them more comprehensible to themselves.

4. *Summarizing.* Readers try to synthesize and briefly recompose the text in their own words.

5. *Knowledge activation of ideas and vocabulary words.* Readers bring knowledge "stores" to their consciousness (including declarative knowledge and procedural knowledge).

6. *Visualizing.* Readers generate visual pictures or iconic representations of the information contained in the text.

## Explicit Teaching of Strategies

Students need to be taught strategies in a very direct, visible way because explicit instruction provides a clear explanation of the tasks involved in comprehending. It also helps students pay careful attention to each of the tasks as well as encourages them to activate their prior knowledge. Explicit teaching invites the student to break the task into small pieces, and it also provides direct, continual feedback from the teacher.

Wong and Jones (1982) found that explicit instruction in comprehension strategies is especially helpful for struggling readers, but it is not as necessary for competent readers who have already mastered and internalized these strategies. They argue that good readers need to be engaged with quality texts that will trigger the use of the interactive strategies that they possess. This finding is often overlooked in our efforts to ensure that every student is given the benefit of instruction, but it needs to be especially considered when teaching proficient readers—"too much of a good thing" can lead to disastrous results. If we insist on teaching strategies that students already know and use wisely on their own, we may be courting boredom or even frustration.

## Interactive Strategy Instruction

Brown (1997) argues that strategies need to be closely linked to knowledge and understanding in a content area to learn them fully and to perceive them as valuable tools for learning. Integrated strategy instruction requires a balance of teaching the content itself as well as teaching reading comprehension strategies. If comprehension strategies are taught with an array of content and a range of texts that are too wide, then students will not fully learn the strategies. However, if strategies are taught in too narrow a base of content material, then students will not have a chance to know how to transfer the strategies (Rosenshine & Meister, 1994).

The most important aspect of strategy development is to focus on enabling students to become self-initiating users of the strategies (Alexander & Murphy, 1998), because students who spontaneously apply a strategy in the correct situation, such as questioning, will improve their comprehension.

# Choosing Appropriate Texts

In recent years, there has been a great deal of research on the appropriateness of specific texts for individual readers. The proliferation of trade books has made multicultural literature available to students on an extremely wide array of topics (Willette & Harris, 1997). There has also been a proliferation of leveled readers that have been written to match the developing skills of students. Although this is not a new idea (Gates & Bocker, 1923), contemporary reading texts include a wider array of factors in their design than reading texts of the past. The point of these leveled readers is to provide practice materials for students who are in the process of acquiring literacy skills. Although the jury is still out on many issues concerning the justification of these leveled texts on the basis of their decodability, they are in wide use throughout urban schools in the United States (Hoffman, Roser, Salas, Patterson, & Pennington, 2001; Hoffman, Sailors, & Patterson, 2002; Roser, Hoffman, & Sailors, 2003). As students acquire basic literacy skills, the question of just-right books also becomes increasingly more complex because writers who appeal to children's tastes often make no attempts to control their sentence length, syntactic difficulty, or semantic choices. Having said this, it is still important to match students with texts that they can comfortably read with fluency and comprehension (Menon & Hiebert,

1999); therefore, we maintain that books should be leveled for developing readers using an array of instruments that examine many factors, for example, visual and pictorial context clues, size of print, numbers of words per page, font and format, sentence length, sentence difficulty, repetition of words, engaging content, and many others.

Many researchers have studied the issue of special materials for students in urban schools as a possible source of help in their literacy development, but most studies have found that materials like the dialectic readers of the 1970s were inefficient and actually counterproductive in developing literacy skills. As far as the content of stories and information texts are concerned, it seems appropriate and necessary to include multicultural literature that reflects the full ranges of students' cultures and experiences within our urban classrooms. Researchers have found that urban students' tastes are developmentally similar to students of their age who do not attend schools in urban environments; for example, young children enjoy stories about animals, and adolescents enjoy high adventure (Sebesta & Monson, 2003). Although this finding is factual, Sipe (1998) found that urban students frequently interpret texts in ways that are dissimilar to students in more affluent suburban schools. Sipe (1998), using Rosenblatt's transactional response theory to interpret children's retellings, cites an example of a young urban child's retelling of *Little Red Riding Hood* as a story about a girl from "the 'hood."

## Learning About Genres and Text Structures

Knowledge of genres and text structures is an important component of reading comprehension, and students who possess knowledge of a variety of text structures understand that texts unfold in different ways. As most children enter school, they have a rudimentary sense of narrative structure, which allows for an easy transition from oral to written language (Lapp, Flood, Brock, & Fisher, 2005). However, some urban children's cultural experiences with narratives do not match the narrative structure of school texts, and this can become a source of continuing frustration for them if they are not instructed in the narrative form of the books used in their classrooms.

Throughout their school career, children are introduced to a variety of other genres including poetry, drama, and information texts, which are more challenging to them because they have not yet acquired the strategies they need to process these texts. They often process them in seemingly random ways that do not help them to recognize or retain the texts' most critical information (Duke, 2000). Explicit teaching of expository structures has been shown to help students identify the information in a text in a coherent, organized way (Armbruster & Armstrong, 1993); this is accomplished through a variety of instructional techniques including mapping, questioning, and summarizing (Boyle & Weishaar, 1997; Moss, 2003).

## Assessing, Diagnosing, and Instructing

Silliman and Wilkinson (1994) maintain that teachers are faced with the challenge of variability among students in language and literacy skills and the question of how best to promote the development of these skills. Lapp, Flood, and Goss (2001); Lapp and Flood (2003); and Lapp, Flood, Brock, and Fisher (2005) have reported on the effectiveness of one model of instruction, *assessment, diagnosis, and instruction*, or ADI, which calls for teachers to first assess their students' abilities and their needs and then carefully analyze the results of the assessments to generate a diagnosis of what needs to be done. The model shown in Figure 9.1 is one means of organizing knowledge regarding the ways in which children develop their language and literacy skills. We divide literacy learning into oral and written processes.

In section A of Figure 9.1, we list the early literacy development of children before coming to school if they have been exposed to school-related literacy experiences. Differences in the literacy achievement of children with greater and fewer home literacy experiences often continues throughout their school careers (Anderson, Hiebert, Scott, & Wilkinson, 1985). In section B, we identify how literacy continues to develop throughout a child's school life. Because of the range of literacy that will exist among students at any grade in an urban school, it is important for teachers to continuously observe and assess student performance, identify strengths, diagnose needs, and plan instruction. Once the diagnosis is complete, teachers can plan appropriate instruction that meets the needs that were discovered in the diagnosis (Morrow, 2005; Strickland, Ganske, & Monroe, 2001). The diagnosis is based on sound assessment and the teacher's understanding of literacy development.

### Explicit Teaching of Skills and Strategies: Guided Practice and Independent Practice

The literature on teaching reading and writing consistently suggests the inclusion of explicit teaching and modeling by the teacher and guided practice with opportunities for independent practice with feedback from the teacher (Flood, Lapp, & Fisher, 2005; Pressley et al., 2001). It also calls for careful scaffolding by the teacher to enable students to refocus and reengage their ef-

## Figure 9.1
## Language in the World of the Child

**Section A: Before School--The Foundation**

**Oral Language** ———————— **Written Language**

| **Communication-Early** | **Conversation** | **Writing** | **Reading** |
|---|---|---|---|
| Crying<br>Cooing<br>Babbling<br>Experimenting with sounds<br>Experimenting with words<br>Generating sentences<br>Learning syntax<br>Learning semantics | Socializing through Language<br>turn taking<br>language rituals<br>listening<br>Phonemic awareness<br>rhyming<br>segmenting<br>substituting | Scribbling<br>Drawing<br>Copy environ-mental print<br>Random letters<br>Early invented spelling<br>Transitional spelling | Emergent Stage<br>*Pre-alphabetic phase*<br>looking at pictures<br>pretend reading<br>attending to words & letters<br>development of concepts of print<br>(Functions of print) |

**Section B: During School--Developing Concepts/Vocabulary (More Formal Instruction)**

| | | | |
|---|---|---|---|
| Vocabulary Development<br>Complex Syntactic Structures<br>Complex Semantic Development | Expanded voices<br>Registers | Alphabetic Writing<br>Standard Orthography<br>Composition<br>words -------><br>phrases ------><br>sentences ----><br>paragraphs --><br>full texts ------><br>Audience and purpose<br>Organization<br>Coherence | Early Stage<br>*Phonetic cue reading phase*<br>Learning the alphabetic code<br>Alphabetic Synthetic phonics<br>c/a/t/<br>Developing Stage<br>*Cipher or full alphabetic phase*<br>Onset and rime<br>Analytic phonics<br>Chunking<br>1. one syllable words<br>2. two syllable words<br>3. three syllable words<br>Fluent Stage<br>Strategies<br>rereading<br>fixing/crosschecking cues<br>inferring<br>visualizing<br>summarizing<br>(Sight Word Development ↓) |

Source: Lapp and Flood (2003)

forts during reading (Chan & Cole, 1986; Risko & Bromley, 2000). Allington and Woodside-Jiron (1999) maintain that classroom teachers are in the best position to assess and diagnosis their own students. Because of their personal knowledge of each student, teachers are also in the best position to implement highly individualized instructional plans that are effective.

## *Grouping and Management*

Teachers who are skilled at diagnosing a child's needs both before and during reading are more capable of planning subsequent instruction using flexible grouping patterns than teachers who are not well trained in diagnosis (P.M. Cunningham, Hall, & Defee, 1998). Designing effective groups is an extremely complex task for students; some researchers have argued that it is the single most valuable management tool that teachers have to effect excellent instruction for every child within their classrooms.

The use of flexible grouping patterns provides a structure that accommodates multiple interactive learning configurations. A major rationale for implementing flexible grouping is that no single type of classroom arrangement can be entirely conducive for meeting the needs of every student. This has recently been documented by many teachers who have witnessed the ill effects of long-term ability grouping on students that did not allow time for focused teacher-directed interactions with individuals and with small groups of students with similar needs or strengths (Allington, 1983a; Hiebert, 1983; Pallas, Entwisle, Alexander, & Stluka, 1994). Continuous evaluation of each student's instructional needs supports a classroom with flexible learning formats such as whole group, small group (homogeneous and heterogeneous), partners (homogeneous and heterogeneous), one to one (student and teacher), and peer tutoring (older and younger students), where explicit, direct, and indirect instruction can occur.

Flexible grouping formats provide the means through which teachers can provide the most effective teaching and learning experiences for every child. Students who grasp a concept that is introduced through a whole-group format may become bored and unchallenged as the information is retaught in a different manner in an attempt to ensure mastery for those who did not totally understand it during the first presentation. The next steps in their instruction should accommodate such variability (Roller, 1996).

This differentiation is essential in an urban classroom because the findings from many researchers suggest that when urban and suburban students are given equal resources, those from urban poverty settings can overcome their achievement difficulties (Minority Student Achievement Network Survey, in press). These data are extremely important because several other researchers have suggested that even when adequate resources are available, some urban poor students disengage because of social and cultural factors that have not been addressed in the school (Ogbu, 2002).

Pressley et al. (2001) note that effective teachers of reading comprehension engage in a diverse array of instructional practices within a complex environment that fosters the development of comprehension abilities. Effective teachers establish a complex set of management routines that they use to ensure minimal disruption in their classrooms and maximal amounts of time on task. In the classrooms of effective teachers, almost all the time is spent on instruction in an atmosphere of support and encouragement where developing readers feel comfortable taking risks.

Effective teachers use a wide variety of instructional practices as they work with their students to develop comprehension skills. They continually ask high-level comprehension questions that require their students to draw inferences and think beyond the text. Effective teachers help their students make connections from many different reading materials at their appropriate reading levels, and they use small-group instruction to meet the individual needs of each of their students. For many decades it has been well documented that numerous institutional factors within U.S. urban communities, schools, and classrooms have operated against minority children's adjustment and academic performance (Delpit & Dowdy, 2002; Lapp, Fisher, Flood, & Moore, 2003; Nieto, 2001, 2003; Ogbu, 1987; Valdes, 1996; Valenzuela, 1999; Vernez & Abrahamse, 1996). Effective teachers, however, take the high road; they believe that all children can succeed if differentiated instruction is a part of their school plan.

## Creating a Successful Literacy Learning Environment in One Classroom

As promised in the beginning of this chapter, we will share Ms. Marsh's secrets of success, which she calls her "beehive of activities," that ensure that each child has ample time for personalized instruction and independent practice. Her organization and management system emphasizes the principles of good instruction that have been noted earlier, and her instruction brings these well-researched principles of good instruction to life.

As you enter her classroom, you're immediately struck by the orderliness of her routines and rituals. If you stay the entire day, you will see her students engaging in nonstop literacy activities, but we will focus our remarks on her 90-minute literacy block, which occurs as soon as her "housekeeping" chores are completed (e.g., taking attendance). Ms. Marsh begins the literacy instructional block with a read-aloud or shared reading of a wonderful piece of literature that is chosen to motivate her students' overall interest in reading. The text she chooses is also selected because it enables her to focus on a particular skill, which she discusses in a 10-minute minilesson following the read-aloud or shared reading. Occasionally, Ms. Marsh does both a read-aloud and a shared reading with a minilesson to reinforce a particular skill that she believes her students need to master.

After the read-aloud or shared reading and minilesson, Ms. Marsh asks her students to complete an independent practice session. During this time, she confers with individual students to make sure that they have understood the skill that she introduced in the minilesson. When this is finished, she begins the independent reading time, in which students read texts at their own levels. She alternates between assigned leveled texts, which contain information that extends the topic of the read-aloud or shared reading and permits the students to practice the skills of the minilesson, and self-selected texts that they enjoy. These texts also match their reading levels.

During independent reading, Ms. Marsh begins the individualized (guided) reading groups at her teacher table. These small groups, ranging from one to four students, work with Ms. Marsh on specific skills and strategies that they still need to practice. This is also the time when Ms. Marsh conducts a small-group book club for students who are working on literacy discussion strategies.

This is the schedule for her literacy program:

| Activity | Number of Minutes |
| --- | --- |
| Read-aloud or shared reading | 10 |
| Minilesson | 10 |
| Independent practice of minilesson skill | 15 |
| Independent reading or guided reading | 30 |
| Centers or guided reading groups | 25 |
| Total | 90 |

After independent reading, the students participate in center work. Ms. Marsh uses Lapp and Flood's "Center Activity Rotation System" (or CARS; see Lapp, Flood, & Goss, 2001) for 25 minutes, in which the students usually work in two centers per day. The centers provide opportunities for students to extend their knowledge about a topic, practice their skills, or construct responses to the topics that they have been reading about during the literacy block. The centers include listening, writing, library, resource, computer, and conference centers.

Ms. Marsh uses CARS to address the needs of each of her students. This model allows her the flexibility to group students heterogeneously for work on a specified task while she concurrently addresses the individual needs of a homogeneous group at a teacher center. As shown in the diagram in Figure 9.2, students are heterogeneously grouped (A–E) at learning centers during a multiday rotation while Ms. Marsh meets with a small homogeneous group (A) of students to address a specific area.

## Figure 9.2
## Center Activity Rotation System (CARS)

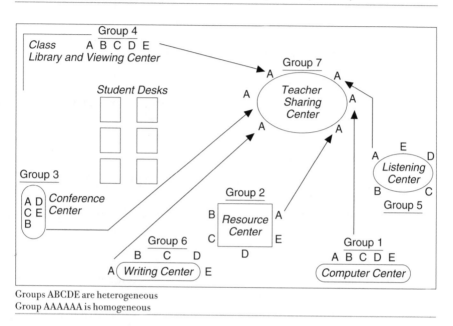

Groups ABCDE are heterogeneous
Group AAAAAA is homogeneous

During the 90 minutes, Ms. Marsh's students have had opportunities for direct, explicit instruction and modeled lessons (read-aloud or shared reading with minilessons; guided, small-group instruction; conferencing); and independent practice (independent practice of minilesson skills; independent reading time; center work). They also have had opportunities for individualized instruction from their teacher (conferencing; guided, small-group instruction) and collaboration and discussion with their peers (guided, small-group instruction and center work) as well as ample opportunity for sustained silent reading during their independent reading time.

It is no wonder that Ms. Marsh's students continue to beat the odds in her urban classroom in a school that traditionally reflects the underachievement of most urban schools in the United States.

## Policy Implications

In this chapter we focused specifically on exemplary literacy instruction for urban elementary schools. Policy implications for students and teachers abound from the existing research data that have been included in this synthesis. The two most overarching implications are (1) elementary-age students in urban schools learn best when their instruction is individualized for them by their teachers; and (2) they learn best when their instruction occurs in a well-managed, organized classroom environment. These two guiding principles lead to a set of policy guidelines that we will divide into four categories: Policy Guidelines for Teachers; Policy Guidelines for Students; Policy Guidelines for Classroom Organization and Management; and Policy Guidelines for Instruction.

### Policy Guidelines for Teachers

- Teachers must be provided with opportunities to become knowledgeable about the ways in which literacy develops, and they must be knowledgeable about the most sound pedagogical approaches to teaching literacy skills and strategies to urban students.
- Teachers must become familiar with the backgrounds of each of their students through assessments, observations, home visits, and frequent teacher development sessions, in which they are continually informed about new ways of learning more about their student's lives.

### Policy Guidelines for Students

- Student's individual needs must be assessed, diagnosed, and taken into consideration when instruction is planned for them by their classroom teachers and other professionals who are instructing them.
- Students must be provided with opportunities for some choices in their reading and writing activities. This will help them develop their independence as readers and writers.

### Policy Guidelines for Classroom Organization and Management

- Classrooms must be well-organized, inviting, safe environments where learning can take place efficiently and effectively.
- Reading materials must be diverse and must include quality literature (narrative fiction texts as well as expository, information texts and poetry and drama texts).
- Reading materials must include leveled, practice texts; just-right books; and grade-level and above-grade-level classics.
- Each classroom must contain a well-stocked classroom library where students can select books that interest them.

### Policy Guidelines for Instruction

- Teachers must assess and diagnose each student's strengths and needs before designing their instruction. Once the diagnosis of student needs is determined, then appropriate instruction and instructional materials can be selected to meet their needs.

• Teachers must provide explicit instruction in literacy skills and strategies through modeling and guiding.

• Ample opportunities for independent practice as well as opportunities for independent reading and writing must be provided for students.

• Continuous assessment must be conducted to provide instruction that matches students' current needs.

# Conclusion

We have deliberately chosen not to make distinctions by methodology about the studies we have cited in this chapter. Although many of the citations referenced in this chapter also appear in the National Reading Report and the RAND Study Group Report, many citations do not appear in those works primarily because of the methodological choices made by the researchers. We believe that the studies cited in this chapter best represent what we know about the reading development of elementary students as well as the best instructional practices for elementary-age students.

We also realize that we have not explicitly discussed home and community relations and linguistic and cultural issues related to literacy achievement, which are critical components of literacy development for elementary-age students. Space limitations prohibited such a discussion in this chapter, but these topics are comprehensively discussed in other chapters in this volume.

## REFERENCES

Adams, M.J. (1990). *Beginning to read: Thinking and learning about print.* Cambridge, MA: MIT Press.

Alexander, P.A., & Murphy, P.K. (1998). Profiling the differences in students' knowledge, interest, and strategic processing. *Journal of Educational Psychology, 90*(3), 435–447.

Allington, R.L. (1983a). Fluency: The neglected reading goal. *The Reading Teacher, 36*, 556–561.

Allington, R.L. (1983b). The reading instruction provided readers of differing reading abilities. *The Elementary School Journal, 83*(5), 548–559.

Allington, R.L., & Woodside-Jiron, H. (1999). The politics of literacy teaching: How research shaped educational policy. *Educational Researcher, 28*(8), 4–13.

Anders, P.L., & Bos, C.S. (1986). Semantic feature analysis: An interactive strategy for vocabulary development for language-minority students. *Journal of Reading, 96*, 295–309.

Anderson, R.C., Hiebert, E.H., Scott, J.A., & Wilkinson, I.A.G. (1985). *Becoming a nation of readers: The report of the Commission on Reading.* Washington, DC: National Institute of Education.

Anderson, R.C., & Pearson, P.D. (1984). A schema-theoretic view of basic processes in reading. In P.D. Pearson, R. Barr, M.L. Kamil, & P. Mosenthal (Eds.), *Handbook of reading research* (pp. 255–292). New York: Longman.

Armbruster, B.B., & Armstrong, J.O. (1993). Locating information in text: A focus on students in the elementary grades. *Contemporary Educational Psychology*, *18*(2), 139–161.

Au, K.H., & Kawakami, A.J. (1994). Cultural congruence in instruction. In E.R. Hollins, J.E. King, & W. Hayman (Eds.), *Teaching diverse populations: Formulating a knowledge base* (pp. 5–23). Albany: State University of New York Press.

Bauer, P.J., & Fivush, R. (1992). Constructing event representations: Building on a foundation of variation and enabling relations. *Cognitive Development*, 7, 381–401.

Beck, I.L, McKeown, M.G., & Kucan, L. (2002). *Bringing words to life: Robust vocabulary instruction*. New York: Guilford.

Beck, I.L., Perfetti, C.A., & McKeown, M.G. (1982). Effects of long-term vocabulary instruction on lexical access and reading comprehension. *Journal of Educational Psychology*, *74*(4), 506–521.

Berninger, V., Abbott, R., Billingsley, F., & Nagy, W. (2001). Processes underlying timing and fluency of reading: Efficiency, automaticity, coordination and morphological awareness. In M. Wolf (Ed.), *Dyslexia, fluency, and the brain.* Timonium, MD: York Press.

Bissex, G.L. (1980). *GNYS at work: A child learns to write and read.* Cambridge, MA: Harvard University Press.

Booth, J., Perfetti, C., & MacWhinney, B. (1999). Quick, automatic, and general activation of orthographic and phonological representations in young readers. *Developmental Psychology*, *35*(1), 3–19.

Boyle, J.R., & Weishaar, M. (1997, Fall). The effects of expert-generated versus student-generated cognitive organizers on the reading comprehension of students with learning disabilities. *Learning Disabilities Research and Practice*, *12*(4), 228–235.

Bradley, L., & Bryant, P.E. (1983). Categorizing sounds and learning to read—a causal connection. *Nature*, *301*, 419–421.

Brassell, D., & Flood, J. (2004). *Vocabulary strategies every teacher needs to know*. San Diego, CA: Academic Professional Development.

Brown, A.L. (1997). Transforming schools into communities of thinking and learning about serious matters. *American Psychologist*, *52*(4), 399–414.

Bruck, M., & Waters, G. (1990). Effects of reading skill on component spelling skills. *Applied Psycholinguistics*, *11*(4), 425–437.

Bus, A.G., & van IJzendoorn, M.H. (1999). Phonological awareness and early reading: A meta-analysis of experimental training studies. *Journal of Educational Psychology*, *91*, 403–414.

Byrne, B. (1999). *The foundation of literacy: The child's acquisition of the alphabetic principle*. East Sussex, UK: Psychology Press.

Calfee, R.C., Lindamood, P., & Lindamood, C. (1973). Acoustic-phonetic skills and reading: Kindergarten through twelfth grade. *Journal of Educational Psychology*, *64*(3), 293–298.

Calhoon, J.A., & Leslie, L. (2002). A longitudinal study of the effects of word frequency and rime-neighborhood size on beginning readers' rime reading accuracy in words and nonwords. *Journal of Literacy Research*, *34*(1), 39–58.

Chan, L.K., & Cole, P.G. (1986). The effects of comprehension monitoring training on the reading competence of learning disabled and regular class students. *Remedial & Special Education (RASE)*, *7*(4), 33–40.

Cunningham, A., & Stanovich, R. (2002). Reading matters: How reading engagement influences cognition. In J. Flood, D. Lapp, J.R. Squire, & J.M. Jensen (Eds.), *Handbook of research on teaching English language arts* (2nd ed.). Mahwah, NJ: Erlbaum.

Cunningham, P. (2000). *Phonics they use: Words for reading and writing.* New York: Longman.

Cunningham, P.M., Hall, D.P., & Defee, M. (1998). Nonability grouped, multilevel instruction: Eight years later. *The Reading Teacher, 51,* 652–664.

Delpit, L., & Dowdy, J.K. (2002). *The skin that we speak: Thoughts on language and culture in the classroom.* New York: New Press.

Dixon-Krauss, L.A. (1995). Partner reading and writing: Peer social dialogue and the zone of proximal development. *Journal of Reading Behavior, 27*(1), 45–63.

Doake, D. (1985). Reading-like behavior: Its role in learning to read. In A. Jaggar & M.T. Smith-Burke (Eds.), *Observing the language learner* (pp. 82–98). Newark, DE: International Reading Association.

Duke, N.K. (2000). For the rich it's richer: Print experiences and environments offered to children in very low- and very high-socioeconomic status first-grade classrooms. *American Educational Research Journal, 37*(2), 441–478.

Ehri, L.C. (1995). Phases of development in learning to read words by sight. *Journal of Research in Reading, 18*(2), 116–125.

Ehri, L.C. (1998). Grapheme-phoneme knowledge is essential for learning to read words in English. In J.L. Metsala & L.C. Ehri (Eds.), *Word recognition in beginning literacy* (pp. 3–40). Mahwah, NJ: Erlbaum.

Ehri, L.C. (1999). Phases of development in learning to read words. In J. Oakhill, R. Beard, & D. Vincent (Eds.), *Reading development and the teaching of reading: A psychological perspective* (pp. 79–108). Oxford, UK: Blackwell.

Ehri, L.C., Nunes, S.R., Stahl, S.A., Steven A., & Willows, D.M. (2001). Systematic phonics instruction helps students learn to read: Evidence from the national reading panel's meta-analysis. *Review of Educational Research, 71*(3), 393–447.

Fleischer, L.S., Jenkins, J., & Pany, D. (1979). Effects on poor readers' comprehension of training in rapid decoding. *Reading Research Quarterly, 15,* 30–48.

Flood, J., Lapp, D., & Fisher, D. (2005). *Teaching writing.* San Diego, CA: Academic Professional Development.

Freebody, P., & Anderson, R.C. (1983). Effects of vocabulary difficulty, text cohesion, and schema availability on reading comprehension. *Reading Research Quarterly, 18,* 277–294.

Fukkink, R.G., & de Glopper, K. (1998). Effects of instruction in deriving word meaning from context: A meta-analysis. *Review of Educational Research, 68*(4), 450–469.

Gates, A., & Bocker, E. (1923). A study of initial stages in reading by preschool students. *Teacher's College Record, 24,* 469–688.

Goswami, U. (2000). Phonological and lexical processes. In M.L. Kamil, P.B. Mosenthal, P.D. Pearson, & R. Barr. (Eds.), *Handbook of reading research* (Vol. 3, pp. 251–267). Mahwah, NJ: Erlbaum.

Gough, P., Juel, C., & Griffith, P. (1992). The effect of phonemic awareness on the literacy development of first grade students in a traditional or a whole language classroom. *Journal of Research in Childhood Education, 6*(2), 85–92.

Gough, P.B., & Tunmer, W.E. (1986). Decoding, reading, and reading stability. *Remedial and Special Education, 7,* 6–10.

Graves, M.F. (1999). A vocabulary program to complement and bolster a middle-grade comprehension program. In B. Taylor, M.F. Graves, & P. van den Broek (Eds.), *Reading for meaning: Fostering comprehension in the middle grades* (pp. 116–135). New York: Teachers College Press; Newark, DE: International Reading Association.

Harris, T.L., & Hodges, R.E. (Eds.). (1995). *The literacy dictionary: The vocabulary of reading and writing.* Newark, DE: International Reading Association.

Heckelman, R.G. (1966). Using the neurological impress remedial technique. *Academic Therapy Quarterly, 1,* 235–239.

Heilman, A.W. (1998). *Phonics in proper perspective* (8th ed.). Columbus, OH: Prentice Hall.

Hiebert, E.H. (1983). An examination of ability grouping for instruction. *Reading Research Quarterly, 18*, 231–235.

Hiebert, E.H. (1999). Text matters in learning to read. *The Reading Teacher, 52*, 552–566.

Hoffman, J.V., Roser, N.L., Salas, R., Patterson, E., & Pennington, J. (2001). Text leveling and "little books" in first-grade reading. *Journal of Literacy Research, 3*(3), 507–528.

Hoffman, J.V., Sailors, M., & Patterson, E.U. (2002). Decodable texts for beginning reading instruction: The year 2000 basals. *Journal of Literacy Research, 34*(3), 269–298.

Hull, M.A., & Fox, B.J. (1998). *Phonics for the reading teacher* (7th ed.). Columbus, OH: Merrill/Prentice Hall.

Kuhn, M., & Stahl, S. (1998). Teaching students to learn word meanings from context: A synthesis and some questions. *Journal of Literacy Research, 30*, 119–138.

LaBerge, D., & Samuels, S.J. (1974). Toward a theory of automatic information processing in reading. *Cognitive Psychology, 6*, 293–323.

Langer, J.A. (1984). Examining background knowledge and text comprehension. *Reading Research Quarterly, 19*, 468–481.

Lapp, D., Block, C.C., Cooper, E.J., Flood, J., Roser, N., & Tinajero, J.V. (2004). *Teaching all the children: Strategies for developing literacy in an urban setting.* New York: Guilford.

Lapp, D., Fisher, D., Flood, J., & Moore, K. (2003). "I don't want to teach it wrong": An investigation of the role families believe they should play in the early literacy development of their children. In D.L. Schallert, C.M. Fairbanks, J. Worthy, B. Maloch, & J.V. Hoffman (Eds.), *51st yearbook of the National Reading Conference* (pp. 275–286). Oak Creek, WI: National Reading Conference.

Lapp, D., & Flood, J. (2003). Understanding the learner: Using portable assessment. In R.L. McCormack & J.R. Paratore (Eds.), *After early intervention, then what? Teaching struggling readers in grades 3 and beyond* (pp. 10–24). Newark, DE: International Reading Association.

Lapp, D., Flood, J., Brock, C., & Fisher, D. (2005). *Teaching reading to every child* (4th ed.). Mahwah, NJ: Erlbaum.

Lapp, D., Flood, J., & Goss, K. (2001). Desks don't move—Students do: In effective classroom environments. *The Reading Teacher, 54*, 31–36.

Laufer, B., & Nation, P. (1999). A vocabulary-size test of controlled productive ability. *Language Testing, 16*(1), 33–51.

Lewis, S., Ceperich, J., & Jepson, J. (2002). *Critical trends in urban education: Fifth biennial survey of America's great city schools.* Washington, DC: Council of the Great City Schools.

Liberman, I.Y., & Shankweiler, D. (1985). Phonology and the problems of learning to read. *Remedial and Special Education (RASE), 6*(6), 8–17.

Lundberg, I., Frost, J., & Peterson, O.-P. (1988). Effects of an extensive program for stimulating phonological awareness in preschool students. *Reading Research Quarterly, 23*, 263–284.

Lyons, C. (2003). *Teaching struggling readers: How to use brain-based research to maximize learning.* Portsmouth, NH: Heinemann.

Mason, J. (1980). When do students begin to read? *Reading Research Quarterly, 15*, 203–227.

McConkie, G., & Zola, D. (1987). Visual attention during eye fixations while reading. In M. Coltheart (Ed.), *Attention and performance XII: The psychology of reading* (pp. 385–400). London: Erlbaum.

McKeown, M.G., Beck, I.L., Omanson, R.C., & Pople, M.T. (1985). Some effects of the nature and frequency of vocabulary instruction on the knowledge and use of words. *Reading Research Quarterly, 20*, 522–535.

Menon, S., & Hiebert, E.H. (1999). *Literature anthologies: The task for first-grade readers* (CIERA Report #1-009). Ann Arbor, MI: Center for the Improvement of Early Reading Achievement, University of Michigan.

Minority Student Achievement Network Survey on Student Attitudes Towards School. (in press). Retrieved October 11, 2004, from http://www.msanetwork.org

Morrow, L.M. (2005). *Literacy development in the early years: Helping children read and write* (5th ed.). Boston: Allyn & Bacon.

Moss, B. (2003). *Twenty-five strategies for guiding readers through information texts.* San Diego, CA: Academic Professional Development.

National Institute of Child Health and Human Development. (2000). *Report of the National Reading Panel. Teaching children to read: An evidence-based assessment of the scientific research literature on reading and its implications for reading instruction* (NIH Publication No. 00-4769). Washington, DC: U.S. Government Printing Office.

Ogbu, J.U. (1987). Variability in minority school performance: A problem in search of an explanation. *Anthropology and Education Quarterly, 18*(4), 312–334.

Ogbu, J.U. (2002). *Black American students in an affluent suburb: A study of academic disengagement.* New York: Free Press.

Pallas, A.M., Entwisle, D.R., Alexander, K.L., & Stluka, M.F. (1994). Ability-group effects: Instructional, social, or institutional? *Sociology of Education, 67*(1), 27–46.

Paris, S., & Winograd, P. (2003). *The role of self-regulated learning in contextual teaching: Principals and practices for teacher preparation.* Ann Arbor, MI: Center for the Improvement of Early Reading Achievement.

Perfetti, C. (1984). Reading acquisition and beyond: Decoding includes cognition. *American Journal of Education, 93*(1), 40–60.

Peterman, C., & Mason, J. (1984, December). *Kindergarten students' perceptions of the forms of print in labelled pictures and stories.* Paper presented at the annual meeting of the National Reading Conference, St. Petersburg, FL.

Powell, D., & Hornsby, D. (1995). *Learning phonics and spelling in a whole language classroom.* New York: Scholastic.

Pressley, M., Wharton-McDonald, R., Allington, R., Block, C.C., Morrow, L., Tracey, D., et al. (2001). A study of effective first-grade literacy instruction. *Scientific Studies of Reading, 5*(1), 35–58.

Ramirez, J.D., Yuen, S.D., & Ramey, E. (1991). *Executive summary of the final report: Longitudinal study of structured English immersion strategy, early-exit and late-exit transitional bilingual education programs for language-minority children* (U.S. Department of Education, Contract No. 300-87-0156). San Mateo, CA: Aguirre International.

RAND Reading Study Group. (2002). *Reading for understanding: Toward an R & D program in reading comprehension.* Santa Monica, CA: RAND.

Risko, V.J., & Bromley, K. (Eds.). (2000). *Collaboration for diverse learners. Viewpoints and practices.* Newark, DE: International Reading Association.

Roller, C.M. (1996). *Variability not disability: Struggling readers in a workshop classroom.* Newark, DE: International Reading Association.

Rosenshine, B., & Meister, C. (1994). Reciprocal teaching: A review of the research. *Review of Educational Research, 64*(4), 479–530.

Roser, N.L., Hoffman, J.V., & Sailors, M. (2003). Leveled texts in beginning reading instruction. In J.V. Hoffman & D.L. Schallert (Eds.), *Read this room: The texts in beginning reading instruction* (pp. 21–20). Mahwah, NJ: Erlbaum.

Salus, P., & Flood, J. (2003). *Language: A user's guide.* San Diego, CA: Academic Professional Development.

Scott, J.A., & Nagy, W.E. (1997). Understanding the definitions of unfamiliar verbs. *Reading Research Quarterly, 32*, 184–200.

Sebesta, S., & Monson, D. (2003). Reading preferences. In J. Flood, D. Lapp, J. Squire, & J. Jensen (Eds.), *Handbook of research on teaching the English language arts* (pp. 835–847). Mahwah, NJ: Erlbaum.

Silliman, E.R., & Wilkinson, L.C. (1994). Observation is more than looking: Assessing progress in classroom language. In. G.P. Wallach & K.G. Butler (Eds.), *Language learning disabilities in school-age children and adolescents: Some principles and applications* (pp. 145-173). Boston: Allyn & Bacon.

Sipe, L.R. (1998). First-and second-grade literary critics: Understanding students' rich responses to literature. In T.E. Raphael & K.H. Au (Eds.), *Literature-based instruction: Reshaping the curriculum* (pp. 39-69) Norwood, MA: Christopher-Gordon.

Snipes, J., Doolittle, F., & Herlihy, C. (2002). *Foundations for success: Case studies of how urban school systems improve student achievement.* Washington, DC: Council of Great City Schools.

Snowling, M., & Olson, J. (1994). The effects of phonetic similarity and list length on students' sound categorization performance. *Journal of Experimental Child Psychology, 58*(1), 160-180.

Stahl, S.A., & Murray, B.A. (1994). Defining phonological awareness and its relationship to early reading. *Journal of Educational Psychology, 86*(2), 221-234.

Stanovich, K.E. (1994). Romance and reality. *The Reading Teacher, 47*, 280-291.

Stanovich, K.E., Cunningham, A., & Cramer, B. (1984). Assessing phonological awareness in kindergarten students: Issues of task compatibility. *Journal of Experimental Child Psychology, 38*, 175-190.

Stanovich, K.E., Cunningham, A., & Freeman, D. (1984). Relation between early reading acquisition and word decoding with and without context: A longitudinal study of first-grade students. *Journal of Educational Psychology, 76*(4), 668-677.

Strickland, D.S., Ganske, K., & Monroe, J.K. (2001). *Supporting struggling readers and writers: Strategies for classroom intervention.* York, ME: Stenhouse; Newark, DE: International Reading Association.

Tan, A., & Nicholson, T. (1997). Flash cards revisited: Training poor readers to read words faster improves their comprehension of text. *Journal of Educational Psychology, 89,* 276-288.

Taylor, D. (1998). *Family literacy: Young children learning to read and write.* Portsmouth, NH: Heinemann.

Thurlow, R., & van den Broek, P. (1997). Automaticity and inference generation during reading comprehension. *Reading and Writing Quarterly: Overcoming Learning Difficulties, 13*(2), 165-181.

Treiman, R., & Weatherston, S. (1992). Effects of linguistic structure on students' ability to isolate initial consonants. *Journal of Educational Psychology, 84*(2), 174-181.

Valdes, G. (1996). *Con respeto: Bridging the distances between culturally diverse families and schools.* New York: Teachers College Press.

Valenzuela, A. (1999). *Subtractive schooling: U.S. Mexican youth and the politics of caring.* Albany: State University of New York Press.

Velluntino, F., Scanlon, D.M., & Spearing, D. (1995). Semantic and phonological coding in poor and normal readers. *Journal of Experimental Child Psychology, 59*(1), 76-123.

Vernez, G., & Abrahamse, A. (1996). *How immigrants fare in U.S. education.* Santa Monica, CA: RAND.

Willette, A.I., & Harris, V.J. (1997). Preparing preservice teachers to teach multicultural literature. In J. Flood, S.B. Heath, & D. Lapp (Ed.), *Handbook of research on teaching literacy through the communicative and visual arts* (pp. 460–469). New York: Macmillan.

Wong, B.Y.L., & Jones, W. (1982). Increasing metacomprehension in learning disabled and normally achieving students through self-questioning training. *Learning Disability Quarterly, 5*(3), 228–240.

Yaden, D.B., Smolkin, L.B., & MacGillivray, L. (1993). A psychogenetic perspective on students' understanding about letter associations during alphabet book readers. *Journal of Reading Behavior, 25*, 43–68.

Yopp, H.K. (1988). The validity and reliability of phonemic awareness tests. *Reading Research Quarterly, 23*, 159–177.

# CHAPTER 10

# Examining Exemplary Reading Instruction in Urban Settings: Implications for Teachers and the Students They Teach: A Response to Diane Lapp and James Flood

*Doris Walker-Dalhouse*

A major challenge to education in urban settings is improving the quality of instruction for students at risk for failure (Waxman & Padron, 1995). Academic underachievement has been attributed to both ineffective teaching practices (Cazden, 1986) and low teacher expectations (Evertson & Weade, 1991). These findings and the work of teachers who have been found to be effective in urban settings can inform us about how to help teachers to foster students' learning through better instruction.

In their chapter, Diane Lapp and James Flood review critical research and dimensions of effective literacy instruction in urban elementary schools. Their analysis focuses on (1) reading development over time; (2) helping students make sense of text; (3) choosing appropriate books; (4) assessing, diagnosing, and instructing; and (5) creating successful literacy learning environments. Based on their review of the research, they provide a model for effective literacy instruction in urban schools. Foremost is the recognition that effective reading instruction requires a teacher who is knowledgeable about the reading and writing processes. Their research synthesis supports an instructional plan that includes attention to phonemic awareness, phonics, vocabulary, comprehension, and reading fluency. These aspects of reading are developed within large instructional time blocks and in learning environments that are well organized, well managed, and characterized by a variety of flexible grouping options. However, I have chosen to focus my attention on additional teacher knowledge, instructional considerations, materials, and learning environment factors needed for effective literacy instruction of urban learners.

# Teacher Background Knowledge

Lapp and Flood explain clearly and succinctly the development of reading over time. Their review of the literature establishes a body of knowledge of the reading process on which the instruction of students in urban schools should be based. At the core of the knowledge needed by teachers is an understanding of word identification and comprehension processes, the relationship between word identification and comprehension, and the connection between comprehension and reading fluency. This is essential for developing skills in decoding, phonemic awareness, phonics, understanding word meanings in text, and communicating the meaning of text orally and in writing.

Language minority and African American students compose approximately 31% (Antunez, 2003) and 24.8% (National Center for Education Statistics, 2002), respectively, of the students enrolled in urban or public schools. This suggests that the knowledge base of teachers should also include an understanding of the language development of English-language learners (ELLs) (see Cummins, 2001) and the dialect of urban African American students. Teachers need to understand the three dimensions of language proficiency that affect language development and reading: (1) conversational fluency, (2) discrete language skills, and (3) academic language proficiency. Conversational fluency focuses on the facility in engaging in face-to-face conversations in familiar settings. Discrete language skills reveal knowledge of phonics, grammar, and literacy, which are learned in direct instructional context and formal and informal learning opportunities, whereas academic language proficiency focuses on subject-specific vocabulary or low-frequency vocabulary and the production of complex oral and written language forms (Cummins, 2003). Teachers need to understand that ELLs acquire phonological awareness and decoding skills when they are explicitly taught in the primary grades, but that difficulties exist in students' ability to transfer this knowledge as they develop academic proficiency (Kwan & Willows, 1998).

Teachers also need to understand the complexity of the linguistic and cultural backgrounds of urban students and the socioeconomic dimensions of language use. Linguistic and cultural variations in language use, particularly that of speakers of African American Vernacular English (AAVE) (Brock, Boyd, & Moore, 2003; Perry & Delpit, 1998), impact teachers' understanding of urban children's literacy development and provide information about the strategies and materials needed for successful literacy instruction. Understanding these dimensions implies a valuing of linguistic diversity, but does not preclude teaching students Standard American

English. Students need to be biliterate to function more effectively in the larger society (Au, 1998).

## Instructional Considerations

Motivation to read is another variable that needs to be addressed because self-concept in reading is related to reading achievement. Although emergent and beginning readers generally have positive feelings about learning to read, there is a decline in reading motivation over the elementary years especially for less proficient readers (McKenna, Kear, & Ellsworth, 1995). Less proficient readers have also been found to have lower self-concepts when compared to more proficient readers (Chapman, Tunmer, & Prochnow, 2000; Henk & Melnick, 1995; Gambrell, Palmer, Codling, & Mazzoni, 1996). The instructional practices, materials, and grouping procedures used in urban classrooms need to motivate students to learn, develop positive self-concepts, and achieve high levels of reading achievement (Haberman, 1991; Waxman & Padron, 1995). Teachers need to be both committed to changing traditional instructional methods and supported in their efforts by school administrators who value strong professional development for teachers (Waxman, Padron, & Stringfield, 1999).

Cultural considerations should also play a more prominent role in making personal connections to urban readers. Culturally responsive teaching involves using the cultural characteristics, experiences, and perspectives of diverse learners as tools for teaching them. According to Gay (2000), teachers need to know the cultural values, traditions, communication and learning styles, contributions, and relational patterns of students. Teachers who demonstrate cultural caring and build cultural learning communities in their classrooms foster positive student–teacher relations and create classroom environments reported to be essential for student achievement (Compton-Lilly, 2000; Gay & Howard, 2000).

## Print Resources

Lapp and Flood emphasize the importance of matching books to readers. However, they cite the need for more research on the assessments and factors used in leveling texts. This is important in motivating students to read and in developing their reading skills. Students need to be exposed to a range of books containing a variety of complex language patterns, structures, and genres of literature.

Dialectal readers have resurfaced as alternative instructional materials. After reviewing the literature on the effect of students' ethnic and cultural backgrounds on their engagement with oral and written text, Brock et al. (2003) recommend that there should be further research to determine the value of using dialectal readers with speakers of AAVE. Children in urban settings are often expected to read materials that are not relevant to their lives and that do not reflect the reality of their world (Inabinette, 1993). The use of dialectal readers with these children might make the reading materials more relevant to their lives and more reflective of the reality of their world, which will motivate them to read. However, there are still obstacles to the inclusion of multicultural literature in the school curriculum that emanate from a lack of appreciation of multiculturalism (Bloom, 1998; Harris & Willis, 2003). There is, however, some support for the use of multicultural literature in improving students' recall and comprehension of text (Bell & Clark, 1998) and overall reading performance (Au, 1998; Strickland, 1994).

Traditionally, urban students have been taught with programs that emphasize word attack or word identification skills rather than comprehension and critical thinking (Inabinette, 1993). As a result, cognitively guided instruction and critical or responsive teaching have been identified as potentially successful in helping students who are at risk for failure, and many urban children fall into this category. Cognitively guided instruction focuses on students' cognitive learning strategies, direct teaching and modeling of cognitive learning strategies, and using and modeling approaches to help students develop metacognitive and cognitive techniques for monitoring their learning (Linn & Songert, 1991; Waxman & Padron, 1995; Waxman, Padron, & Knight, 1991).

Comprehension strategies specified in the National Reading Panel report (National Institute of Child Health and Human Development, 2000) support this type of instruction and will actively engage urban students in comprehending text.

## Learning Environment

Teachers are key figures in creating the classroom environment. All students need teachers who believe in their ability to learn and to become literate. Positive feelings about school are fundamental to academic achievement. Interesting, challenging, and caring teachers will teach students to achieve. I believe that the degree of student progress observed by Pat Marsh, the first-grade teacher described by Lapp and Flood, was influenced by her high expectations for students, and this was ultimately one of the secrets to her success.

## Conclusions and Policy Implications

The research synthesis by Lapp and Flood provides valuable insight into what exemplary instruction at the elementary level should include. The snapshot they provided of a real urban teacher and her literacy instruction reinforces their key points. The policy implications they have generated have the potential to create similar successful classrooms in other urban school settings. Some policy implications that might be added to their list are as follows:

1. Teachers should have ongoing preparation in using culturally relevant teaching practices if they are to be effective literacy teachers in urban schools (Lazar, 2004).

2. Teachers should participate in planned workshops about the effect of race, socioeconomic status, gender, attitudes, and behaviors of students (e.g., African American) on teacher expectations for academic success (Ogbu, 2003).

3. Teachers should become knowledgeable about the effect of AAVE on the acquisition of Standard American English.

4. Teachers should be provided with opportunities to become knowledgeable about literacy instruction for ELLs.

5. Teachers must develop an awareness of the impact of culture on language use and development.

6. Teachers need to increase their understanding of the value and use of multicultural literature in classroom instruction. Specific instruction should also be provided at the preservice and inservice levels to assist teachers in reflecting about their cultural identities, responding to multicultural literature, and integrating multicultural literature in their curriculum (Willis & Harris, 1997).

### REFERENCES

Antunez, B. (2003). *English language learners in the great city schools: Survey results on students, languages, and programs.* Washington, DC: Council of the Great City Schools.

Au, K.H. (1998). Social constructivism and the school literacy learning of students of diverse backgrounds. *Journal of Literacy Research, 30*(2), 297–319.

Bell, Y.R., & Clark, T.R. (1998). Culturally relevant reading material as related to comprehension and recall in African American children. *Journal of Black Psychology, 24*(4), 455–475.

Bloom, A. (1998). *The closing of the American mind: How higher education has failed democracy and impoverished the souls of today's students.* New York: Simon & Schuster.

Brock, C., Boyd, F., & Moore, J. (2003). Variations in language and the use of language across contexts: Implications for literacy learning. In J. Flood, D. Lapp, J.R. Squire, & J.M. Jensen (Eds.), *Handbook of research on teaching the English language arts* (2nd ed., pp. 446–458). Mahwah, NJ: Erlbaum.

Cazden, C. (1986). Classroom discourse. In M.C. Wittrock (Ed.), *Handbook of research on teaching* (3rd ed., pp. 432–463). New York: Macmillan

Chapman, J.W., Tunmer, W.E., & Prochnow, J.E. (2000). Early reading-related skills and performance, reading self-concept, and the development of academic self-concept: A longitudinal study. *Journal of Educational Psychology, 92*(4), 703–708.

Compton-Lilly, C. (2000). "Staying on children": Challenging stereotypes about urban parents. *Language Arts, 77*(5), 420–427.

Cummins, J. (2001). *Negotiating identities: Education for empowerment in a diverse society* (2nd ed.). Los Angeles: California Association for Bilingual Education.

Cummins, J. (2003). Reading and the bilingual student: Fact and friction. In G.G. Garcia (Ed.), *English learners: Reaching the highest level of English literacy* (pp. 2–33). Newark, DE: International Reading Association.

Evertson, C.M., & Weade, R. (1991). The social construction of classroom lessons. In H.C. Waxman & H.J. Walberg (Eds.), *Effective teaching: Current research* (pp. 135–159). Berkeley, CA: McCutchan.

Gambrell, L.B., Palmer, B.M., Codling, R.M., & Mazzoni, S.A. (1996). Assessing motivation to read. *The Reading Teacher, 49*, 518–533.

Gay, G., & Howard, T.C. (2000). Multicultural teacher education for the 21st century. *Teacher Educator, 36*(1), 1–16.

Haberman, M. (1991). The pedagogy of poverty versus good teaching. *Phi Delta Kappan, 73*(4), 290–294.

Harris, V.J., & Willis, A. (2003). Multiculturalism, literature, and curriculum issues. In J. Flood, D. Lapp, J.R. Squire, & J.M. Jensen (Eds.), *Handbook of research on teaching the English language arts* (2nd ed., pp. 825–834). Mahwah, NJ: Erlbaum.

Henk, W., & Melnick, S.A. (1995). The reader self-perception scale (RSPS): A new tool for measuring how children feel about themselves as readers. *The Reading Teacher, 48*, 470–482.

Inabinette, N. (1993). Reading in the urban environment. In S.W. Rothstein (Ed.), *Handbook of schooling in urban America* (pp. 365–378). Westport, CT: Greenwood.

Kwan, A.B., & Willows, D.M. (1998, December). *Impact of early phonics instruction on children learning English as a second language.* Paper presented at the 48th annual meeting of the National Reading Conference, Austin, TX.

Lazar, A.M. (2004). *Learning to be literacy teachers in urban schools: Stories of growth and change.* Newark, DE: International Reading Association.

Linn, M.C., & Songert, N.B. (1991). Cognitive and conceptual change in adolescence. *American Journal of Education, 99*, 379–417.

McKenna, M., Kear, D.I., & Ellsworth, R.A. (1995). Children's attitudes toward reading: A national survey. *Reading Research Quarterly, 30*, 934–955.

National Center for Education Statistics. (2002). State nonfiscal survey of public elementary and secondary education: School year 2000–2001 [Data file]. Retrieved April 12, 2004, from http://nces.ed.gov/NCES/ccd/data/txt/stnfis00lay.txt

Ogbu, J. (2003). *Black American students in an affluent suburb: A study of academic disengagement.* Mahwah, NJ: Erlbaum.

Perry, T., & Delpit, L. (Eds.). (1998). *The real Ebonics debate: Power, language, and the education of African-American children.* Boston: Beacon Press.

Strickland, D.S. (1994). Educating African American learners at risk: Finding a better way. *Language Arts, 71*(5), 328–336.

Waxman, H.C., & Padron, Y.N. (1995). Improving the quality of classroom instruction for students at risk of failure in urban schools. *Peabody Journal of Education, 70*(2), 44–65.

Waxman, H.C., Padron, Y.N., & Knight, S.L. (1991). Risks associated with students' limited cognitive mastery. In M.C. Wang, M.C. Reynolds, & H.J. Walberg (Eds.), *Handbook of special education: Emerging programs* (Vol. 4, pp. 235–254). Oxford, UK: Pergamon.

Waxman, H.C., Padron, Y.N, & Stringfield, S. (1999). Teaching and change in urban contexts. *Teaching and Change*, 7(1), 3–16.

Willis, A., & Harris, V.J. (1997). Preparing preservice teachers to teach multicultural literature. In J. Flood, S.B. Heath, & D. Lapp (Eds.), *Handbook of research on teaching literacy through the communicative and visual arts* (pp. 460–469). New York: Macmillan.

# CHAPTER 11

# Exemplary Literacy Instruction in Grades 7–12: What Counts and Who's Counting?

*Donna E. Alvermann*

This chapter reports on the status of research into exemplary literacy instruction in grades 7–12, thus partially covering what is commonly referred to as the middle years (typically grades 6–8) and high school. Its focus is on research that pertains to urban education, though in some instances, as in the *Report of the National Reading Panel* (NRP) (National Institute of Child Health and Human Development [NICHD], 2000), findings were not disaggregated according to geographic locale. Unlike earlier reviews of adolescent literacy instruction (e.g., Alvermann, 2001, 2002b; Bean, 2000), this chapter takes into account research that has relevance for U.S. urban educators but was conducted in the larger international community. Finally, this chapter views cultural and linguistic diversity not as markers of marginal differences but rather as factors central to interpreting the research on adolescent literacy and its implications for instructional leaders and policymakers in urban school districts.

As McDermott and Varenne (1995) have noted, all cultures (including urban schools) are historically evolved ways of "doing" life. They teach people about what is worth working for, how to succeed, and who will fall short. To be concise, one might say cultures are about what counts. Yet I would argue it's not as simple as that. In addition to teaching about what counts as exemplary adolescent literacy instruction, for example, various subcultures working within urban schools and the general population are going about their counting in different ways. Thus, it is important to ask not only what counts but also who is doing the counting—for example, is it those interested in closing the achievement gap? In exploring culturally responsive teaching strategies? In redefining exemplary instruction from a "new literacies" perspective? I believe these are neither inclusive nor separate constituencies, but for efficiency and the purpose of organizing this chapter, I will address them as if they were.

## Closing the Achievement Gap

Although recent administrations of the National Assessment of Educational Progress (NAEP) find that a majority of students at the eighth- and twelfth-grade levels are reading at or above the basic level, far fewer students have reached the proficient or advanced levels, which require competency over challenging subject matter, applications of subject matter knowledge to real-world situations, and analytical skills appropriate to the subject matter (U.S. Department of Health and Human Services, 2000). For example, data reported in *The Nation's Report Card: U.S. History 2001* revealed that less than 20% of students comprehend at the proficient level, with significant achievement differences favoring nonminority over minority students, students in rural and suburban schools over those in urban schools, and students from higher-income over lower-income homes (Lapp, Grigg, & Tay-Lim, 2002). This has led educators and policymakers to intensify their efforts to close the persistent gap in academic achievement between minority and nonminority students (Institute for Urban and Minority Education, n.d.).

The research literature that addresses the perceived gap between basic and more advanced levels of reading development among adolescents is largely focused on comprehension of text and vocabulary development. Another body of research looks at students' motivation and self-efficacy in learning from text. A third research area focuses on contexts of literacy instruction. Each of these areas is discussed next with particular attention given to research that has been compiled and published in the *Handbook of Reading Research: Volume 2* (Barr, Kamil, Mosenthal, & Pearson, 1990), *Handbook of Reading Research: Volume 3* (Kamil, Mosenthal, Pearson, & Barr, 2000), the *Report of the National Reading Panel* (NICHD, 2000), the National Reading Conference's position paper titled *Effective Literacy Instruction for Adolescents* (Alvermann, 2001), and the RAND Reading Study Group's *Reading for Understanding* (2002).

## Comprehension of Text and Vocabulary Development

According to the RAND Reading Study Group (2002), a great deal is known about the prerequisites for successful reading comprehension, including comprehension at the more advanced levels. For example, drawing from the work of numerous literacy researchers and the *Report of the National Reading Panel* (NICHD, 2000), which was commissioned by the U.S.

Congress to assess the availability of evidence-based research on reading instruction for classroom application, the authors concluded that

- Effective reading instruction provides students with a repertoire of strategies for fostering comprehension.
- Strategy instruction that is embedded within subject-matter learning, such as history or science, improves students' reading comprehension.
- Effective strategies for teaching students to comprehend complex materials include self-questioning, answering a teacher's questions, cooperative learning, comprehension monitoring, representing information using graphic organizers, making use of different text structures, and summarizing.
- The more explicit teachers are in their strategy instruction, the more successful low-achieving students are in their reading and learning.
- Vocabulary knowledge is strongly related to successful text comprehension, and it is especially important in teaching English-language learners.
- Exposing students to various genres of text (e.g., informational, narrative, poetry) ensures that they do not approach all reading tasks with the same purpose in mind.

In interpreting these conclusions, it is important to recall that the database that informed them is not without its limitations. For example, the NRP report was based solely on experimental and quasi-experimental research studies, which were designed primarily to test the effectiveness of certain cognitive processes in comprehending printed texts, often within controlled conditions that did not represent typical classroom learning environments. Studies that took into account the sociocultural and situation-specific aspects of reading in content area classrooms (e.g., Dillon & Moje, 1998; Guzzetti & Hynd, 1998; Obidah, 1998; Sturtevant, 1996) were excluded from consideration because they did not fit the criteria that the panel had specified as evidence of highly rigorous and "scientific" research. This resulted in a report that reflects a rather narrow and restrictive view of the reading process. In fact, six of the seven categories of text comprehension that the panel found effective—self-questioning, answering a teacher's questions, comprehension monitoring, representing information using graphic organizers, making use of different text structures, and summarizing—point to strategies content area teachers might use if their view of the reading process is one in which students work by themselves to extract information from printed texts. As pointed out elsewhere (Wade & Moje, 2000), this rather narrow view of the reading process risks disenfranchising large groups of students for whom printed texts are not the primary means through which they learn.

A further limitation of the NRP's database is its omission of studies that focused on English-language learners or attended to the social organization of learning and instruction in large urban schools serving children who live in poverty. Before jumping to conclusions about what this might mean in terms of implementing the NRP's findings, however, a caveat is in order. Along with Gee (1999) and Moll and Ruiz (2002), Gutierrez et al. (2002) argue that "the issue is not poverty but rather how being a poor child becomes a debilitating condition in schools" (p. 329). Thus, the larger issue is how schools treat poor children, many of whom speak a language other than English as their first language. Considering these limitations, then, one is left to wonder about the generalizability of the NRP's findings for teaching adolescents in urban schools, though granted it would be unwise to assume that urban youth would benefit any less from such teaching than their more economically advantaged peers.

## Motivation and Self-Efficacy

During adolescence, as well as later in life, it is the belief in the self (or lack of such belief) that makes a difference in how competent a person feels. Perceptions of self-efficacy are central to most theories of motivation, and the research on exemplary literacy instruction bears out the hypothesized connections. For example, providing clear goals for a comprehension task to students who are experiencing reading difficulties and then giving feedback on the progress they are making can lead to increased self-efficacy and greater use of comprehension strategies (Schunk & Rice, 1993). Similarly, creating technology environments that heighten students' motivation to become independent readers and writers can increase their sense of competency (Kamil, Intrator, & Kim, 2000). The research is less clear, however, on the shifts that occur in students' motivation to read over time. Although decreases in intrinsic reading motivation have been noted as children move from the elementary grades to middle school, explanations vary as to the cause, with a number of researchers attributing the decline to differences in instructional practices (Eccles, Wigfield, & Schiefele, 2000; Oldfather & McLaughlin, 1993).

In an extensive review of how instruction influences students' reading engagement and academic performance, Guthrie and Wigfield (2000) concluded that various instructional practices, while important, do not directly impact student outcomes (e.g., time spent reading independently, achievement on standardized tests, performance assessments, and beliefs about reading). Instead, the level of student engagement (including its sustainability over time) is the mediating factor, or avenue, through which classroom instruction influences student outcomes. What this means is that teachers must take into account the degree to which students engage (or disengage) over time in a learning task. Guthrie and Wigfield's conception of the engagement model of reading calls for instruction that fosters student motivation (including self-efficacy and goal setting), strategy use (e.g., self-monitoring for breaks in comprehension and analyzing new vocabulary), growth in conceptual knowledge (e.g., reading trade books to supplement textbook information, viewing videos, and hands-on experiences), and social interaction (e.g., collaborating with peers on a science project or discussing an Internet search with the teacher).

## Contexts for Literacy Instruction

The research literature on school reform shows that when urban districts make a concerted effort to involve teachers, students, parents, and community leaders, the context for the schooling process can change dramatically and, with it, students' achievement levels. For example, data from work conducted as part of the Coalition of Essential Schools (Levine, Sizer, Washor, & Peters, 2001), as well as case studies of urban high schools engaged in reform efforts that personalize literacy instruction, actively engage students in subject matter learning, and make use of multiple forms of assessment (Darling-Hammond, Ancess, & Falk, 1995; Greenleaf, Schoenbach, Cziko, & Mueller, 2001; Meier, 1995), suggest that it is possible to begin to close the achievement gap by changing the contexts for learning. Other successful U.S. reform efforts, such as the national teacher-researcher network of English and social studies teachers and university faculty (Freedman, Simons, Kalnin, & The M-Class Teams, 1999), have focused on optimizing the context for literacy instruction by focusing on issues of diversity, bias, and inequality.

The contexts for literacy instruction are undeniably important, as Moore (1996) demonstrated in an in-depth synthesis of the qualitative research on strategy instruction. Specifically, he found that (1) the type of strategy taught is less important than the nature of the context in which it is taught, and (2) engaging students in cooperative learning activities is conducive to subject-matter learning. Not surprisingly, the RAND Reading Study Group (2002) found similar support for these practices in the experimental and quasi-experimental research literature on comprehension instruction. Teachers working within contexts that are conducive to learning provide students with adequate background information and relevant hands-on experience as a means of preparing them to read a textbook, view a video, listen to an audiotape, or search the Web for related content (Alexander & Jetton, 2000). Teachers also look for ways to integrate reading and writing because they know that each of these processes reinforces the other and can lead to improved comprehension and retention of course content (Tierney & Shanahan, 1991). In sum, teachers create exemplary contexts for literacy instruction when they provide students with opportunities to use what they already know as a basis for learning new content in mutually supportive classrooms that celebrate diversity rather than view it as a problem to be overcome or "normalized."

## Exploring Culturally Relevant Teaching Strategies

Urban schools in the United States with large numbers of minority students have on occasion sparked some of the most creative teaching to be found anywhere, especially among teachers who have both a deep understanding of a particular subject's domain structure and a desire to make teaching that subject more responsive to students' cultural knowledge. For example, Lee (1997, 2001) used signifying, which is a form of talk widely practiced within the African American Vernacular English (AAVE) speech community, to scaffold or facilitate her underachieving high school students' literary responses to the mainstream canon. In writing about her experiences as a teacher in the Cultural Modeling Project that she developed, Lee (2001) explained,

> Signifying...involves innuendo, double entendre, satire, and irony, and is dense in figurative language. It often involves forms of ritual insult, but is not limited to insult. An example of signifying might be "Yo mama so skinny she can do the hula hoop in a cheerio." (p. 122)

Although signifying is valued for language play in its own right, Lee used her ninth graders' tacit knowledge of this discourse to help them hypothesize the meanings of various canonical texts (especially the tropes, ironies, and satires associated with these texts) and to change their hypotheses as evidence warranted. Lee took on the role of more knowledgeable other (Vygotsky, 1986) as a means of guiding and supporting her class of underachievers as they learned to bridge differences in home and school cultural practices.

The Cultural Modeling Project, although designed especially to assist adolescents who struggle to read in literature classes, has applications across subject areas. For example, Ballenger (1997) used a similar instructional strategy in her work with a multigrade (grades 5–8) Haitian bilingual science classroom. Briefly, Ballenger used a form of Haitian discourse known as argumentative discussion to facilitate her students' entry into a formalized way of "talking" science. Because argumentative discussion figures prominently into everyday adult interactions in Haitian society, her students were familiar with its various forms, including give-and-take talk about politics, sports, religion, and the like. Although often engaged in purely for entertainment purposes, much like signifying, argumentative discussion also contains elements of scientific discourse—the very same elements, in fact, that scientists use to construct relationships between evidences and claims. It is a discourse acquired by younger members of Haitian society as they first observe (and later participate in) this storytelling genre. In the inquiry-based bilingual science classroom that Ballenger described, underachieving youth were encouraged to express themselves in both Creole and English as they used culturally familiar rhetorical skills to present their arguments and defend their personal opinions about a variety of topics, including the conditions necessary for mold to grow.

Although these two examples of culturally relevant teaching using students' oral language skills are valued for what they bring to the research literature on exemplary literacy practices, it is the case that such teaching is often less favored among educators and policymakers who view literacy teaching and learning as being concerned exclusively with written language. For example, Meacham (2001), in his review of the literature on literacy and cultural diversity, writes

> Historically and into the present, dominant political interests within discussions of literacy policy have had a narrowing impact on what constitutes legitimate literacy practice. Dominant political interests that affirm prevailing relations of power promote what Royer (1994) refers to as "strong text" literacy characteristics. "Strong-text" literacy conceives of literacy as a structurally singular, exclusively written language practice. When mentioned at all, cultural and linguistic diversity are taken up as threats to conceptual coherence. In other words, in the realm of mainstream literacy politics and policy, cultural diversity is seen as marginal, and even detrimental, to effective literacy conception and practice. (p. 181)

What constitutes legitimate literacy practice and why it is the case that "strong-text" literacy, or Literacy spelled with a big *L* and singular in nature (Street, 1995), typically trumps other forms of literacy is best explained by examining the relations of power in everyday literacy practices. Such relations are often not apparent, at least not to those who view reading and writing as neutral processes largely defined through either psychological models or holistic approaches to literacy acquisition. This view of literacy—what Street (1995) has called the autonomous model of literacy—has dominated Western thinking up to the present. Viewing literacy practices as ideologically embedded does not require giving up on the cognitive aspects of reading and writing. Rather, according to Street (1995), the ideological model subsumes the autonomous model of literacy in its attempt to understand reading and writing processes "as they are encapsulated within...structures of power" (p. 161).

## Redefining Exemplary Instruction From a New Literacies Perspective

By emphasizing the ideological nature of literacy practices, Street (1995) opened the way for seeing them as socially constructed within seemingly absent but always present power relations, a view that is prevalent among individuals who subscribe to a new literacies perspective (Luke & Carrington, 2002; Luke & Elkins, 1998; New London Group, 1996; Willinsky, 1990)—one that takes into account how globalization, new information communication technologies, and multimedia are transforming our ways of knowing and making meaning in a digital world (Alvermann, 2002a; Flood & Lapp, 1995; Lankshear & Knobel, 2003). These changes are not lost on adolescents or their teachers, and they have significant implications for teaching and learning in content area classrooms.

The term *adolescent literacy*, broader in scope than secondary reading, is also more inclusive of what young people currently count as texts (e.g., textbooks, music lyrics, magazines, graphic novels, weblog digital texts, and hypertexts). In fact, it is the case that many adolescents of the Net Generation are finding their own reasons for becoming literate—reasons that go beyond reading to acquire school knowledge of academic texts (Bean & Readence, 2002; Hagood, 2002; Ivey & Broaddus, 2001; Moje, 2000, 2002; Moore, Bean, Birdyshaw, & Rycik, 1999; Nixon, 1998; O'Brien, 2003). This is not to say that academic literacy is unimportant; rather, it is to emphasize the need to address the implications of youth's multiple literacies for classroom instruction. For as Vacca (1998) observed, and it is still the case today, "we know very little about what counts as literacy from adolescent perspectives or the literacies that adolescents engage in outside of an academic context" (p. xvi).

A small but growing body of research on youth's out-of-school literacy practices provides empirical evidence of the dynamic and permeable boundaries between age categories that were once thought separate and hierarchically in opposition to one another. Whether in homeschooling environments (Young, 2000), community-based after-school programs (Alvermann, Young, Green, & Wisenbaker, 1999; Garner, 2002; Hull & Schultz, 2001, 2002), youth organizations (Heath & McLaughlin, 1993; Kelly, 2001), or digitally manipulated environments where youth are free to exchange information through anonymous networks (Duncan & Leander, 2000; Lewis & Fabos, 1999), age differences appear to have little influence over the ways in which adults and adolescents alike make use of various literacy practices. In fact, the research on youth's out-of-school literacies complicates the very notion of adolescence—a term Appleman (2001) refers to as a status category, or "a kind of purgatory between childhood and adulthood" (p. 1). This research disrupts certain assumptions about what counts (or should count) as valued literacy practices among people of all ages, while not falling prey to an overly simplistic celebration of youth culture (Hagood, 2000; Hinchman, Bourcy, & Thomas, 2002; Hull & Schultz, 2001; Lewis & Finders, 2002; Sefton-Green, 1998).

What this body of research does not provide, however, is an in-depth look at how young people go about developing a sense of critical awareness of the ways in which they are implicated in the production and consumption of popular media texts that do not privilege print. With few exceptions (e.g., Dillon & O'Brien, 2001; Chandler-Olcott & Mahar, 2001; Kamberelis & Dimitriadis, 1999; Moje, 2000; Myers, Hammett, & McKillop, 2000), researchers interested in adolescents' critical awareness have worked in classrooms where the curriculum is primarily print driven and necessarily constrained by school-based norms for teaching and learning. Thus, it remains unclear as to whether teaching youth to be critically aware using largely conventional print texts within the confines of a school curriculum can sufficiently prepare them to do the same with symbol systems other than print in out-of-school contexts. This concern is not trivial for it marks a very real tension in a posttypographic world (Reinking, Labbo, McKenna, & Kieffer, 1998). Consider, for example, the tension created when teachers subscribe to the notion that "speech makes us human and literacy makes us civilized" (Olson, 1988, p. 175). In using this saying to make his point, Olson was referring to written language and the bias it imparts both to the way we think about knowledge—how we organize it, store it for reuse—and the cognitive consequences of schooling and literacy. Luke and Luke (2001) refer to this same bias as resulting from our "inoculation by print" (p. 110).

Yet the ability to analyze media messages presumes that one is at least visually (if not sound) literate. The Alliance for a Media Literate America

(AMLA; 2000)—a national, grassroots membership organization committed to bringing media literacy education to all 60 million students in the United States—defines media literacy in terms of what it accomplishes: "the ability to...communicate, as well as to understand media messages, and media makers, both professional and community based" (n.p.). Becoming visually literate, then, involves expanding print literacy skills by developing a greater awareness of how things come to have the meaning that they have and why those meanings vary from one individual to the next. As Muffoletto (2001) explains, "Being 'visually literate' means more than having the ability to produce/encode and read/decode constructed visual experiences; it...is to be actively engaged in asking questions and seeking answers about the multiple meanings of a visual experience" (n.p.).

## Implications for Instruction and Policy

Although much is known about exemplary literacy instruction for adolescents, the challenge lies in implementing this research in ways that make sense to teachers whose plates are already full and overflowing. This is no small matter. In fact, remarking on the gravity of the challenge, members of the RAND Reading Study Group (2002) noted that despite a fairly well-articulated knowledge base on the value of strategy instruction that fosters reading comprehension, such instruction continues to receive too little time and attention in most content area classrooms. Important as strategy instruction is, there are larger needs not being met, perhaps due in part to a general reluctance among U.S. teachers to move beyond older programs and methods (Anders, 2003) in search of newer and more comprehensive ways of ensuring that youth's literacies in and out of school work together. For that to happen, as well as for the achievement gap to narrow, I propose the following:

• Instruction that is exemplary should take into account adolescents' personal and everyday literacies in ways that enable them to use those literacies as springboards for engaging actively in academic tasks that are both challenging and worthwhile. To accomplish this presumes an openness on educators' and policymakers' parts to think of adolescence as something other than "a kind of purgatory between childhood and adulthood" (Appleman, 2001, p. 1). It also presumes a willingness to view literacy teaching at the middle and high school levels differently. For as Lesko (2000) has so aptly stated, "if we want to see adolescence differently, we must first understand the ways we currently see, feel, think, and act toward youth, or we will merely tinker with the reigning practices" (p. 10).

• Instruction that is exemplary should be embedded in the regular curriculum and make use of the new literacies (Lankshear & Knobel, 2003), including multiple forms of texts (print, visual, and digital) that can be read critically for multiple purposes in a variety of contexts. For this to become a reality, it will be important to teach students how to use relevant background knowledge and strategies for reading, discussing, and writing about a variety of texts. It will require the support of administrators and policymakers who buy into the idea that all students, including those who struggle to read in subject area classrooms, deserve instruction that is developmentally, culturally, and linguistically responsive to their needs.

• Instruction that is exemplary should address issues of self-efficacy and engagement. It will need to involve youth in higher-level thinking as they read, write, and share orally. It will mean avoiding, as Wade and Moje (2000) recommend, a transmission model of teaching with its emphasis on skill and drill, teacher-centered instruction, and passive learning, but substituting instead a participatory model of instruction that actively engages students in their own learning (individually and in small groups) and that treats texts as tools for learning rather than as repositories of information to be memorized and then all too quickly forgotten.

• Instruction that is exemplary will need to draw from a knowledge base built on both experimental and qualitative research. To continue current U.S. policies for funding and reporting research that largely ignore rigorous and systematically designed qualitative research, in effect, relegating it to the status of a pseudoscience (Gutiérrez et al., 2002), will produce at best only a partially informed knowledge base. At worst, such policies will be detrimental to discovering what counts as literacy from adolescents' perspectives. These policies will also deter researchers from exploring ways to integrate "what counts" into instructional practices that hold promise for closing the achievement gap. A broadening, rather than a narrowing, of what counts as research on adolescent literacy instruction will produce a knowledge base on which to make instructional decisions that take into account both the "what works" and "for whom" questions of experimental designs and the "who's counting and why" questions of qualitative research.

## REFERENCES

Alexander, P.A., & Jetton, T.L. (2000). Learning from text: A multidimensional and developmental perspective. In M.L. Kamil, P.B. Mosenthal, P.D. Pearson, & R. Barr (Eds.), *Handbook of reading research* (Vol. 3, pp. 285–310). Mahwah, NJ: Erlbaum.

Alliance for a Media Literate America. (2001). *Foundation declaration*. Retrieved August 21, 2004, from http://www.medialit.org/readingroom/article390.html

Alvermann, D.E. (2001, September). *Effective literacy instruction for adolescents*. Executive summary and paper commissioned by the National Reading Conference. Retrieved March 17, 2003, from http://nrconline.org

Alvermann, D.E. (Ed.). (2002a). *Adolescents and literacies in a digital world*. New York: Peter Lang.

Alvermann, D.E. (2002b). Effective literacy instruction for adolescents. *Journal of Literacy Research, 34*(2), 189–208.

Alvermann, D.E., Young, J.P., Green, C., & Wisenbaker, J.M. (1999). Adolescents' perceptions and negotiations of literacy practices in after-school read and talk clubs. *American Educational Research Journal, 36*(2), 221–264.

Anders, P.L. (2003). Secondary reading programs: A story of what was. In D.L. Schallert, C.M. Fairbanks, J. Worthy, B. Maloch, & J.V. Hoffman (Eds.), *51st yearbook of the National Reading Conference* (pp. 82–93). Oak Creek, WI: National Reading Conference.

Appleman, D. (2001, April). *Unintended betrayal: Dilemmas of representation and power in research with youth*. Paper presented at the annual meeting of the American Educational Research Association, Seattle, WA.

Ballenger, C. (1997). Social identities, moral narratives, scientific argumentation: Science talk in a bilingual classroom. *Language and Education, 11*(1), 1–14.

Barr, R., Kamil, M.L., Mosenthal, P.B., & Pearson, P.D. (Eds.). (1990). *Handbook of reading research* (Vol. 2). White Plains, NY: Longman.

Bean, T.W. (2000). Reading in the content areas: Social constructivist dimensions. In M.L. Kamil, P.B. Mosenthal, P.D. Pearson, & R. Barr (Eds.), *Handbook of reading research* (Vol. 3, pp. 629–644). Mahwah, NJ: Erlbaum.

Bean, T.W., & Readence, J.E. (2002). Adolescent literacy: Charting a course for successful futures as lifelong learners. *Reading Research and Instruction, 41*(3), 203–210.

Chandler-Olcott, K., & Mahar, D. (2001, November). Considering genre in the digital literacy classroom. *Reading Online, 5*(4). Retrieved March 10, 2003, from http://www.readingonline.org/electronic/elec_index.asp?HREF=hillinger/index.html

Darling-Hammond, L., Ancess, J., & Falk, B. (1995). *Authentic assessment in action: Studies of schools and students at work*. New York: Teachers College Press.

Dillon, D.R., & Moje, E.B. (1998). Listening to the talk of adolescent girls: Lessons about literacy, school, and life. In D.E. Alvermann, K.A. Hinchman, D.W. Moore, S.F. Phelps, & D.R. Waff (Eds.), *Reconceptualizing the literacies in adolescents' lives* (pp. 193–223). Mahwah, NJ: Erlbaum.

Dillon, D.R., & O'Brien, D.G. (2001, April). *Reconceptualizing "at-risk" adolescent readers as literate intellectuals*. Paper presented at the meeting of the American Educational Research Association, Seattle, WA.

Duncan, B., & Leander, K. (2000, November). Girls just wanna have fun: Literacy, consumerism, and paradoxes of position on gURL.com. *Reading Online, 4*(5). Retrieved March 2, 2001, from http://www.readingonline.org/electronic/elec_index.asp?HREF=/electronic/duncan/index.html

Eccles, J.S., Wigfield, A., & Schiefele, U. (2000). Motivation to succeed. In W. Damon & N. Eisenberg (Eds.), *Handbook of child psychology: Vol. 3: Social, emotional, and personality development* (5th ed., pp. 1017–1095). New York: Wiley.

Flood, J., & Lapp, D. (1995). Broadening the lens: Toward an expanded conceptualization of literacy. In K.A. Hinchman, D.J. Leu, & C.K. Kinzer (Eds.), *Perspective on literacy research and practice* (44th yearbook of the National Reading Conference, pp. 1–16). Chicago: National Reading Conference.

Freedman, S.W., Simons, E.R., Kalnin, J.S., & The M-Class Teams. (1999). *Inside city schools: Investigating literacy in multicultural classrooms*. New York: Teachers College Press.

Garner, R. (Ed.). (2002). *Hanging out: Community-based after-school programs for children*. Westport, CT: Bergin & Garvey.

Gee, J.P. (1999). Reading and the new literacy studies: Reframing the National Academy of Sciences Report on Reading. *Journal of Literacy Research, 31*(3), 355–374.

Greenleaf, C.L., Schoenbach, R., Cziko, C., & Mueller, F.L. (2001). Apprenticing adolescent readers to academic literacy. *Harvard Educational Review, 71*(1), 79–129.

Guthrie, J.T., & Wigfield, A. (2000). Engagement and motivation in reading. In M.L. Kamil, P.B. Mosenthal, P.D. Pearson, & R. Barr (Eds.), *Handbook of reading research* (Vol. 3, pp. 403–422). Mahwah, NJ: Erlbaum.

Gutiérrez, K.D., Asato, J., Pacheco, M., Moll, L.C., Olson, K., Horng, E.L., et al. (2002). "Sounding American": The consequences of new reforms on English language learners. *Reading Research Quarterly, 37*, 328–343.

Guzzetti, B., & Hynd, C. (Eds.). (1998). *Perspectives on conceptual change: Multiple ways to understand knowing and learning in a complex world.* Mahwah, NJ: Erlbaum.

Hagood, M.C. (2000). New times, new millennium, new literacies. *Reading Research and Instruction, 39*(4), 311–328.

Hagood, M.C. (2002). Critical literacy for whom? *Reading Research and Instruction, 41*(3), 247–266.

Heath, S.B., & McLaughlin, M.W. (Eds.). (1993). *Identity and inner-city youth: Beyond ethnicity and gender.* New York: Teachers College Press.

Hinchman, K.A., Bourcy, L.P., Thomas, H., & Olcott, K.C. (2002). Representing adolescents' literacies: Case studies of three white males. *Reading Research and Instruction, 41*(3), 229–246.

Hull, G., & Schultz, K. (2001). Literacy and learning out of school: A review of theory and research. *Review of Educational Research, 71*(4), 575–611.

Hull, G., & Schultz, K. (Eds.). (2002). *School's out! Bridging out-of-school literacies with classroom practice.* New York: Teachers College Press.

Institute for Urban and Minority Education. (n.d.). Cognitive development, school readiness, and academic motivation. Retrieved August 21, 2004, from http://iume.tc.columbia.edu/pathways/achieve3/study.asp

Ivey, G., & Broaddus, K. (2001). "Just plain reading": A survey of what makes kids want to read in middle school classrooms. *Reading Research Quarterly, 36*, 350–377.

Kamberelis, G., & Dimitriadis, G. (1999). Talkin' Tupac: Speech genres and the mediation of cultural knowledge. In C. McCarthy, G. Hudak, S. Miklaucic, & P. Saukko (Eds.), *Sound identities: Popular music and the cultural politics of education* (pp. 119–150). New York: Peter Lang.

Kamil, M.L., Intrator, S.M., & Kim, H.S. (2000). The effects of other technologies on literacy and literacy learning. In M.L. Kamil, P.B. Mosenthal, P.D. Pearson, & R. Barr (Eds.), *Handbook of reading research* (Vol. 3, pp. 771–788). Mahwah, NJ: Erlbaum.

Kamil, M.L., Mosenthal, P.B., Pearson, P.D., & Barr, R. (Eds.). (2000). *Handbook of reading research* (Vol. 3). Mahwah, NJ: Erlbaum.

Kelly, M.M. (2001). The education of African-American youth: Literacy practices and identity representation in church and school. In E.B. Moje & D.G. O'Brien (Eds.), *Constructions of literacy: Studies of teaching and learning in and out of secondary school* (pp. 239–259). Mahwah, NJ: Erlbaum.

Lankshear, C., & Knobel, M. (2003). *New literacies: Changing knowledge and classroom learning.* Buckingham, UK: Open University Press.

Lapp, M., & Grigg, W.S., & Tay-Lim, B.S.H. (2002). *The nation's report card: U.S. history 2001* (National Center for Education Statistics Publication No. NCES-2002-483). Jessup, MD: ED Pubs.

Lee, C.D. (1997). Bridging home and school literacies: Models for culturally responsive teaching, a case for African-American English. In J. Flood, S.B. Heath, & D. Lapp (Eds.), *Handbook of* research on teaching literacy through the communicative and visual arts (pp. 334–345). New York: Macmillan.

Lee, C.D. (2001). Is October Brown Chinese? A cultural modeling activity system for underachieving students. *American Educational Research Journal, 38*(1), 97–141.

Lesko, N. (2000). *Act your age! A cultural construction of adolescence.* New York: Routledge.

Levine, E., Sizer, T., Washor, E., & Peters, T. (2001). *One kid at a time: Big lessons from a small school.* New York: Teachers College Press.

Lewis, C., & Fabos, B. (1999, December). *Chatting online: Uses of instant message communication among adolescent girls.* Paper presented at the 49th annual meeting of the National Reading Conference, Orlando, FL.

Lewis, C., & Finders, M. (2002). Implied adolescents and implied teachers: A generation gap for new times. In D.E. Alvermann (Ed.), *Adolescents and literacies in a digital world* (pp. 101–113). New York: Peter Lang.

Luke, A., & Carrington, V. (2002). Globalisation, literacy, curriculum practice. In R. Fisher, M. Lewis, & G. Brooks (Eds.), *Language and literacy in action* (pp. 231–250). London: Routledge/Falmer.

Luke, A., & Elkins, J. (1998). Reinventing literacy in "New Times." *Journal of Adolescent & Adult Literacy, 42*, 4–7.

Luke, A., & Luke, C. (2001). Adolescence lost/childhood regained: On early intervention and the emergence of the techno-subject. *Journal of Early Childhood Literacy, 1*, 91–120.

McDermott, R., & Varenne, H. (1995). Culture as disability. *Anthropology and Education Quarterly, 26*(3), 324–348.

Meacham, S.J. (2001). Literacy at the crossroads: Movement, connection, and communication within the research literature on literacy and cultural diversity. *Review of Research in Education, 25*, 181–208.

Meier, D. (1995). *The power of their ideas: Lessons for America from a small school in Harlem.* Boston: Beacon Press.

Moje, E.B. (2000). "To be part of the story": The literacy practices of gangsta adolescents. *Teachers College Record, 102*, 651–690.

Moje, E.B. (2002). Re-framing adolescent literacy research for new times: Studying youth as a resource. *Reading Research and Instruction, 41*(3), 211–228.

Moll, L.C., & Ruiz, R. (2002). The schooling of Latino students. In M.M. Suarez-Orozco & M. Paez (Eds.), *Latinos: Remaking America* (pp. 362–374). Berkeley: University of California Press.

Moore, D.W. (1996). Contexts for literacy in secondary schools. In D.J. Leu, C.K. Kinzer, & K.A. Hinchman (Eds.), *Literacy for the 21st century: Research and practice* (45th yearbook of the National Reading Conference, pp. 15–46). Chicago: National Reading Conference.

Moore, D.W., Bean, T.W., Birdyshaw, D., & Rycik, J.A. (1999). Adolescent literacy: A position statement. *Journal of Adolescent & Adult Literacy, 43*, 97–112.

Muffoletto, R. (2001, March). An inquiry into the nature of Uncle Joe's representation and meaning. *Reading Online, 4*(8). Retrieved February 25, 2003, from http://www.readingonline.org/new literacies/lit_index.asp?HREF= muffoletto/index.html

Myers, J., Hammett, R., & McKillop, A.M. (2000). Connecting, exploring, and exposing the self in hypermedia projects. In M.A. Gallego & S. Hollingsworth (Eds.), *What counts as literacy: Challenging the school standard* (pp. 85–105). New York: Teachers College Press.

National Institute of Child Health and Human Development. (2000). *Report of the National Reading Panel. Teaching children to read: An evidence-based assessment of the scientific research literature on reading and its implications for reading instruction* (NIH Publication No. 00-4769). Washington, DC: U.S. Government Printing Office.

New London Group. (1996). A pedagogy of multiliteracies: Designing social futures. *Harvard Educational Review, 66*(1), p. 60–92.

Nixon, H. (1998). Fun and games are serious business. In J. Sefton-Green (Ed.), *Digital diversions: Youth culture in the age of multi-media* (pp. 21–42). London: University College London Press.

Obidah, J.E. (1998). Black-mystory: Literate currency in everyday schooling. In D.E. Alvermann, K.A. Hinchman, D.W. Moore, S.F. Phelps, & D.R. Waff (Eds.), *Reconceptualizing the literacies in adolescents' lives* (pp. 51–71). Mahwah, NJ: Erlbaum.

O'Brien, D. (2003, March). Juxtaposing traditional and intermedial literacies to redefine the competence of struggling adolescents. *Reading Online, 6*(7). Retrieved March 15, 2003, from http://www.readingonline.org/newliteracies/lit_index.asp?HREF=obrien2/

Oldfather, P., & McLaughlin, H.J. (1993). Gaining and losing voice: A longitudinal study of students' continuing impulse to learn across elementary and middle school contexts. *Research in Middle Level Education, 3*, 1–25.

Olson, D.R. (1988). From utterance to text: The bias of language in speech and writing. In E.R. Kintgen, B.M. Kroll, & M. Rose (Eds.), *Perspectives on literacy* (pp. 175–189). Carbondale: Southern Illinois University Press.

Reinking, D., Labbo, L., McKenna, M.C., & Kieffer, R.D. (Eds.). (1998). *Handbook of literacy and technology: Transformations in a post-typographic world*. Mahwah, NJ: Erlbaum.

Royer, D. (1994). The process of literacy as communal involvement in the narratives of Frederick Douglass. *African American Review, 28*, 363–373.

Schunk, D.H., & Rice, J.M. (1993). Strategy fading and progress feedback: Effects on self-efficacy and comprehension among students receiving remedial reading services. *Journal of Special Education, 27*(3), 257–276.

Sefton-Green, J. (1998). Introduction: Being young in the digital age. In J. Sefton-Green (Ed.), *Digital diversions Youth culture in the age of multimedia* (pp. 1–20). London: University College London Press.

RAND Reading Study Group. (2002). *Reading for understanding: Toward an R & D program in reading comprehension*. Santa Monica, CA: RAND.

Street, B.V. (1995). *Social literacies: Critical approaches to literacy in development, ethnography, and education*. Reading, MA: Addison Wesley.

Sturtevant, E.G. (1996). Lifetime influences on the literacy-related instructional beliefs of experienced high school history teachers: Two comparative case studies. *Journal of Literacy Research, 28*(2), 227–257.

Tierney, R.J., & Shanahan, T. (1991). Research on the reading-writing relationship: Interactions, transactions, and outcomes. In R. Barr, M.L. Kamil, P.B. Mosenthal, & P.D. Pearson (Eds.), *Handbook of reading research* (Vol. 2, pp. 246–280). White Plains, NY: Longman.

Vacca, R.T. (1998). Foreword. In D.E. Alvermann, K.A. Hinchman, D.W. Moore, S.F. Phelps, & D.R. Waff (Eds.), *Reconceptualizing the literacies in adolescents' lives* (pp. xv–xvi). Mahwah, NJ: Erlbaum.

Vygotsky, L.S. (1986). *Thought and language* (Rev. ed.). (A. Kozulin, Ed. & Trans.). Cambridge, MA: MIT Press.

Wade, S.E., & Moje, E.B. (2000). The role of text in classroom learning. In M.L. Kamil, P.B. Mosenthal, P.D. Pearson, & R. Barr (Eds.), *Handbook of reading research* (Vol. 3, pp. 609–627). Mahwah, NJ: Erlbaum.

Willinsky, J. (1990). *The new literacy: Redefining reading and writing in the schools*. New York: Routledge.

Young, J.P. (2000). Boy talk: Critical literacy and masculinities. *Reading Research Quarterly, 35*, 312–323.

# CHAPTER 12

# Let's Not Minimize the "Big L" in Adolescent Literacy: A Response to Donna Alvermann

*Richard T. Vacca*

onna Alvermann reports on the status of research into exemplary literacy instruction in grades 7–12. According to Alvermann, the research has relevance for U.S. urban educators, but the vast body of research has been conducted in the larger educational community. To date, there isn't a substantial body of research centered on exemplary literacy instruction for adolescents in urban settings. As a result, Alvermann's organizing principle in the paper is twofold: (1) to identify generally what has counted as exemplary literacy instruction for adolescent learners and (2) to explore who's doing the counting, namely, those interested in closing the achievement gap, redefining exemplary instruction from a "new literacies" perspective, and exploring culturally responsive teaching strategies.

Historically, literacy instruction for students in grades 7–12 has received marginal attention by policymakers, curriculum planners, and school administrators. Such instruction has been piecemeal at best, often limited to "remedial readers" in junior high and high school settings. The public debate over literacy has focused on the literacy learning of young children. Vacca and Alvermann (1998) argued that in the United States the lack of policy and schoolwide commitment for the ongoing literacy development of older students has resulted in a national crisis. Few policy initiatives have worked their way into the public consciousness beyond early literacy development. Moreover, it is difficult to find comprehensive literacy programs for all students throughout middle and high schools. The crisis in adolescent literacy, according to Vacca and Alvermann (1998), is born of a "benign" neglect for the literacy needs of adolescents, misconceptions about literacy development, and a general disregard for the "hidden" or personal literacies in adolescents' lives.

# The Adolescent Literacy Construct

The crisis in adolescent literacy has resulted in a paradigmatic shift in the way the literacy field conceptualizes literacy learning and teaching for students in middle and high school settings. In the past decade there has been a concerted effort to move away from what has traditionally been called *secondary reading* to what is currently identified as *adolescent literacy*. Secondary reading instructional practices often were associated with the "skill and drill" of reading labs in junior and senior high schools or "remedial" classes for students who struggled with reading. Adolescent literacy, however, conveys a broader, more powerful construct to describe literacy learning and instruction among young adolescents in middle and junior high schools and teenagers in high school settings.

The adolescent literacy construct acknowledges the powerful language bonds that exist among reading, writing, talk, listening, and viewing. Yet it also acknowledges the multiple literacies that adolescents develop in and out of school and the multiple texts that they are likely to encounter in their lives. Readence (2002) refers to adolescent literacy as the effort to reconceptualize the literacy of adolescents by going beyond school and textbook-based definitions of literacy. Such a reconceptualization suggests that the literacies of adolescents and their interactions with a wide range of texts, including but not limited to CD-ROMs, popular music, television, film, magazines, and the Internet, impact their emerging individual and social identities. If this is the case, then to what extent should schools in urban and nonurban settings provide the time and space for students to learn with multiple texts and to use the "new literacies" that are associated with them? To what extent can the hidden literacies that adolescents bring to school be used as bridges to learning as they engage in school-related instructional activities?

Alvermann alludes to the tension that exists between "Literacy with a big L" and the multiple or hidden literacies that exist in the lives of adolescents. All too often the literacies that adolescents value the most are nonacademic. These literacies may involve computer games, MTV, teen magazines, or popular TV shows. Although these nonacademic literacies appear to be less valuable than school-based *Literacy*, it is these very nonacademic literacies that are likely to motivate students' interest in further schooling throughout life (Vacca & Alvermann, 1998).

Unfortunately "Literacy with a big L" often gets a bad rap by overzealous advocates of adolescents' multiple literacies. There is a tendency to view school-based Literacy as a way of doing school—reading to find the correct answer or writing to answer homework questions. In an era of accountability, school-based Literacy achievement may be interpreted narrowly as the ability to read and write to answer test questions. However, this need not be the case. The relationship between academic achievement and literacy is a powerful one. The research literature on exemplary literacy instruction for students in grades 7–12, by and large, focuses on the development of academic or content literacy (Vacca, 2002).

Content literacy reflects the ability to use language processes such as reading, writing, and talking to learn in various subject areas in a comprehensive, school-based curriculum. It is the level of skill that students need in an academic subject to comprehend and respond to ideas in texts used for instructional purposes. Content literacy is of critical importance in the academic lives of students because it helps to shape the strategies by which they learn with texts. Cognitive and metacognitive principles, engaged learning, and strategy-based instruction undergird content literacy practices as students put literacy to use to develop vocabulary and comprehend texts. Numerous reading research studies related to prior knowledge, text structure, and strategic learning have had a major impact on content literacy and have resulted in constructs that, when put into practice, can transform teaching and learning in grades 7–12.

- Literacy learners use prior knowledge *before*, *during*, and *after* reading to construct meaning.

- Exemplary literacy instruction can develop engaged readers and writers who are knowledgeable, strategic, motivated, and socially interactive.

- Modeling is an important form of classroom support for literacy learning.

- Students who engage in daily discussion about what they read are more likely to become critical readers and learners.

- Skill readers know how and when to use strategies to construct meaning.

- Reading and writing abilities develop together.

## REFERENCES

Readence, J.E. (2002). Adolescent literacy. In B.J. Guzzetti, D.E. Alvermann, & J.L. Johns (Eds.), *Literacy in America: An encyclopedia of history, theory, and practice* (pp. 13–15). Santa Barbara, CA: ABC-CLIO.

Vacca, R.T. (2002). Content literacy. In B.J. Guzzetti, D.E. Alvermann, & J.L. Johns (Eds.), *Literacy in America: An encyclopedia of history, theory, and practice* (pp. 101–104). Santa Barbara, CA: ABC-CLIO.

Vacca, R.T., & Alvermann, D.E. (1998, October). The crisis in adolescent literacy: Is it real or imagined? *NASSP Bulletin, 82*, 4–9.

# CHAPTER 13

# Professional Preparation and Development of Teachers in Literacy Instruction for Urban Settings

*Virginia Richardson and Patricia L. Anders*

The various calls for quality teachers who will ensure that "no child is left behind" are often justified by a deep concern for what is happening (or not happening) in urban schools. There are few who would argue with descriptions of the often dismal conditions in urban schooling and the relative poor literacy performance of children and youth, but there is considerable disagreement around the solutions to these problems.

It is interesting that the solutions being pressed for and experimented with today focus on the teacher as being instrumental in a child's education and the key figure in educational reform. Although this may seem obvious to us today, the teacher has often been ignored in past reform efforts. The solutions have focused on curriculum reform, various input factors such as funding, and commercial instructional programs and materials sold as "teacher-proof" or easily implemented with short inservice programs. Although curriculum, standards, instructional programs, and funding are all critical elements in the reform of education, the teacher is the one who must orchestrate all these elements in the classroom, within a school and community that provide both unique and generalized opportunities and challenges.

The focus on reform involves many elements that are thought to increase teacher quality. These include preservice teacher education programs that are designed to teach the skills, abilities, knowledge, and habits of mind with which new teachers enter the profession; licensing and certification processes; recruitment and retention policies; organizational development such as schoolwide reform efforts; new instructional programs; and professional development. Our focus in this chapter will be on teacher education and professional development. All the elements should work together, however, and so they will be addressed in terms of the way they impact or are impacted on by the need for and practice of professional development.

We begin by defining professional development and the various approaches taken in the field. Next, we briefly summarize the literature related to the professional preparation of teachers; highlight issues that are specific to urban education; and conclude with implications for research, practice, and policy.

## Views of Professional Development

There are two approaches to the definition of professional development. Professional development may be defined as any action taken by practicing teachers to develop their knowledge, skills, or habits of mind toward the purpose of improving instruction. It may also be defined in relation to a purposeful educational program designed to engage teachers in developing their knowledge, skills, or habits of mind. Most literature on professional development uses the second definition, as we will in this chapter. This definition of professional development includes more traditional programs such as workshops and inservice training around a specific curriculum, as well as newer conceptions such as inquiry approaches, study groups, and book clubs.

In sorting through the various forms of professional development, one has to consider four factors: (1) the goals, (2) the agency of the participants, (3) the nature of the process, and (4) what teachers will learn in the programs. The first two factors are interrelated. For example, a school district may determine that it is implementing a new reading program in grades K–3. The staff development is an implementation workshop in which someone from outside the school tells the teachers about the new reading program, how to use the materials, and what is expected of them and their students. This reduces if not eliminates teachers' agency in selecting the goal and the particular reading program to be implemented. However, these are not completely overlapping factors. For example, a school district may decide on a set of goals related to the improvement of reading instruction and allow teachers to determine processes and programs through a long-term inquiry process. In the case of the implementation workshop, the opportunity is determined and presented by someone other than the participating teachers, whereas the longer-term, inquiry-oriented professional development program involves the participants in setting goals and determining processes.

The third factor, the nature of the process of staff development, varies depending, in part, on the form. Examples of forms are a one-day workshop, a graduate course at a local university, a workshop in combination with additional elements such as follow-up coaching, expert help that involves classroom observation and follow-up discussions concerning improvement, observation of other teachers in their classrooms, and inquiry approaches to professional development (Richardson, 1994b). The various processes include lecture, small-group discussion, two-way observation of classroom action followed by a discussion, observation of videotape followed by a group discussion, and others.

The fourth factor to be considered in looking at differences among programs focuses on what teachers actually learn from the program. This is the area of differentiation that has received the least attention and is the most complex. It is the case that traditional workshops and short-term inservice programs have received considerable negative attention in the literature as well as in school lunchrooms. Smylie (1989) found that a sample of teachers ranked district-operated workshops the lowest among a set of opportunities to learn. It is difficult to determine whether teachers learn anything from these activities because the assessment device generally is a survey-type instrument that asks teachers about the degree to which the material was enjoyable. At the same time, traditional longer term professional development programs that introduce teachers to process–product effective-teaching results do, in fact, affect teachers' practices and student learning (Brophy & Good, 1986). Process–product studies examine the relationship between teacher behaviors and student learning. The results of these studies suggest the behaviors that more effective teachers use in their classrooms. The degree of teacher effectiveness is determined by the student gains on standardized achievement tests. For example, one such behavior that was found to be important in effective teaching is time on task (Fisher et al., 1980).

The highest-ranked activity in Smylie's (1989) survey concerning opportunity to learn was learning by experience in the classroom. Many teachers also appear to enjoy and value action research and inquiry opportunities for examining their practice. However, much of the research on these inquiry professional development programs focuses on in-depth descriptions of the processes themselves. It is assumed, and there is some evidence for this, that the deep, long-term inquiry processes lead to changes in ways of thinking, habits of mind, and instructional practices (Richardson & Placier, 2001). These are very different learning outcomes than the behaviors observed in process–product forms of professional development that focus, for example, on length of wait time or on the fidelity and efficacy of particular instructional strategies. These two different approaches also call for differences in program design and research approaches.

The next section presents a brief history of attention to and research on professional development. This history is important because our understanding of effective professional development strategies is drawn from all forms of the research on professional development that has been conducted over the last 20 years.

# Professional Development and Its Research

There was little attention paid to conducting research on professional development until the last 10–12 years. Prior to that, professional development was examined within implementation strategies and as treatments in experimental studies of effective teaching behaviors. If the occasional short-term workshops were assessed, the evaluations consisted mostly of short surveys asking the participating teachers if they liked the workshop and found it useful. On the average, teachers found the workshops neither enjoyable nor particularly useful (Smylie, 1989).

## Implementation and Effective Teacher Behaviors

In the early program implementation process in which programs such as MACOS (Man a Course of Study) were developed at a national level and then implemented in schools across the United States (Shaver, 1987), the dissemination of effective instructional programs was initially handled through very limited inservice training of the one-time workshop variety. Research on the implementation process uncovered the importance of professional development to success in the implementation process, with *success* being defined as the degree to which the new practices adopted by the teachers matched the original practice being promoted (Berman & McLaughlin, 1975, 1976). These large-scale implementation studies revealed that where there was successful implementation of new programs, there was also a good chance that a strong emphasis was placed on professional development. An understanding also emerged that the professional development involved in such a process would be longer term than that of an initial workshop. For example, the procedure of coaching teachers who were implementing a new program was developed at that time (Joyce & Showers, 1981).

Concurrently, a number of experimental studies tested causally the results of correlation process–product studies. The initial correlational studies identified teacher behaviors that were present in the classrooms of teachers whose students had higher achievement gain scores than the students of other teachers on standardized reading and mathematics measures (Brophy & Good, 1986; Gage, 1978). The experimental studies were designed to determine whether changes in teachers' behaviors affected the achievement of their students. These experiments required the researchers to work with the teachers in staff development settings. It was at this point that what are considered some of the effective staff development practices today were developed and used. For example, Jane Stallings and her colleagues worked closely with the subject teachers in her sample to help them understand, with a different lens, their existing practices in teaching reading. Through close observation, descriptions of each teacher's instructional behaviors, using constructs that matched the behaviors found to be effective in the correlational studies, were developed and presented to the teachers. These assessments were then used as diagnostic instruments, and individual teachers were asked to adjust some of their behaviors that fell short of those identified in the studies. This was a longer term professional development process in which individual teachers and their contexts were taken into account; classroom observation was an integral element of the process (Stallings, Needels, & Stayrook, 1980). This literature led to the professional development work that centered on increasing direct instruction and time on task (Fisher et al., 1980). Process–product research is still being conducted. For example, Taylor, Pearson, Clark, and Walpole (1999) conducted a study of the teaching of reading in 14 schools to identify the school and instructional practices that related to students doing well in reading. Floden (2001) suggests that a reemphasis on effects studies in research on teaching is called for.

## Cognition and Subject Matter Emphasis

Two intertwined trends, beginning in the 1980s, strongly affected the approaches to and research on professional development. The first was a shift from behaviorism to cognitive processes, and the second was a shift from generic teaching skills to instructional approaches within subject matter.

The cognitive revolution entered the field of research on teaching in the mid-1970s during a conference funded by the National Institute of Education that was designed to plan the future of research on teaching in 10 areas. One of the 10 conference papers was titled *Teaching as Clinical Information Processing* (Gage, 1975). This paper strongly influenced the field of research on teaching, which then began to move with some rapidity toward a cognitive orientation during the 1980s. This movement expanded even further as the sense of cognition moved from the somewhat behaviorist orientation of information processing and rational planning toward a more constructivist set of inner ways of thinking such as theories, beliefs, and epistemology. Accompanying this was an understanding of the importance of what individual participants bring into the professional development process and therefore the importance of considering individuals and the context in which they work.

At the same time, the work was shifting from a search for generic teaching behaviors toward an examination of instruction within the different subject-matter areas. Most of the process–product work that led to the notions of time-on-task focused on elementary school reading and mathematics, because the purpose of the studies was to identify teacher behaviors that would be effective across all subject matter areas. It became clear in these studies, however, that context made a difference in the results. Context factors included grade level, subject matter, and the particular group of students in a class. It turned out that an elementary schoolteacher, using the same methods, could be effective in teaching reading but not mathematics. And the studies began to uncover differences in effective teaching behaviors depending on whether the subject matter was reading or mathematics (Good & Grouws, 1979). Thus, it was suggested that the research ought to focus on teaching within the subject matter area (L.S. Shulman, 1974).

The newer view of effective teaching strongly influenced the nature of the professional development programs. No longer were behaviors of singular interest in these processes. A shift to pedagogy that was grounded in constructivist learning theory became both the content and process of the professional development programs. Direct instruction was no longer the favored mode of teaching, although it was later recognized as one possible component of a constructivist classroom (Richardson, 2003).

The goals of constructivist professional development relate to the need for thoughtful teachers, whose autonomy, commitment, and knowledge allow them to make the necessary instructional decisions within their context and in relation to each child's needs. Professional development began to look quite different, and although the one-shot workshop continued to be the norm in many school districts, the research and literature began to focus on new forms of professional development and characteristics of the process that would lead to dramatic changes in teachers' beliefs that, in turn, would lead to more constructivist practices in the classrooms. And these studies are conducted within specific subject matter areas such as reading, rather than across subject matter areas.

## Effective Professional Development

There are many summaries of research on staff development that suggest program characteristics thought to be effective (Anders, Hoffman, & Duffy, 2000; Little, 1989). These characteristics have emerged from various studies, and as a set, they appear to have been accepted by many as paradigms of effective practice (Wilson & Berne, 1999). Independent of each other, we have, over the last couple years, summarized these characteristics and come up with very similar lists. Richardson's (2003) list includes the following:

- Schoolwide: The reform should involve everyone in the school to develop a school culture of improvement and adjust to the specific context.
- Long-term process with follow-up.
- Agreement among participants on goals and vision.
- A supportive administration.
- Adequate funds for materials, outside speakers, substitute teachers, and the like.
- Buy-in from participants.
- Encouragement of collegiality: learning communities and dialogue within group.
- A focus on subject matter content rather than generic teaching methods.
- Acknowledgment of participants' existing beliefs and practices.
- Involvement of an outside facilitator/staff developer.

We have known about the first six characteristics for some time, but the last four are more current and are of particular interest to us. It should also be pointed out that many of these are overlapping, and the involvement of one may imply the incorporation of another.

The studies that contributed to this list include small-scale studies that focus on the nature of the teacher change process and on the development of an understanding of the elements of professional development processes that may be used by others and large-scale studies that attempt to determine, describe, or test the factors, elements, aspects, or characteristics of effective professional development programs. These four characteristics are those that might be overlooked or ignored in large-scale attempts at school reform because of the difficulty in implementing them and the possibility of loss of control by those administering the reform process.

# Dialogue

Dialogue among participants and between a participant and a facilitator or staff developer has been an important element of recent long-term constructivist professional development programs. In a summary of recent programs with goals related to the acquisition of professional knowledge, Wilson and Berne (1999) categorized them in terms of the topics of the discourse: opportunities to talk about subject matter, opportunities to talk about students and learning, and opportunities to talk about teaching. Au (1990), for example, worked with teachers one-on-one as the duo observed videotapes of classroom teaching and discussed the tape for 45 minutes following the lesson. The goal was to work toward instruction that incorporated four dimensions that frame Au's (1985) model of effective reading instruction. These included "(1) an emphasis on higher-level thinking, (2) active, systematic instruction, (3) responsiveness, and (4) theme development" (Au, 1990, p. 275).

Context for dialogue is an important dimension. For example, Flood, Lapp, Ranck-Buhr, and Moore (1995) created book clubs (see also Bealor, 1992) as a context for dialogue (and professional development). The researchers and the elementary teachers and their principal read multicultural literature as a means of discovering beliefs, attitudes, and practices related to children of diverse backgrounds. The books served as a mediating tool for discovering these powerful insights, which also led to changes in practice.

Kathy Short (e.g., Matlin & Short, 1996) used a different context: the study group. For the past 10 years, Short has worked with groups of teachers and groups of principals to address their issues, questions, and needs. The study groups are organized around a particular theme or topic. Short provides resources, which the participants read or view, but most important, they talk. The talk is not random; Short has an agenda, but it is an agenda that is responsive to the interests, needs, and questions of the participants.

The question of what use dialogue is to professional teacher learning is responded to by Cazden (2001), who summarizes five hypotheses developed by John Bruer (1994) concerning the importance of intensive discourse in reform programs:

> Social interaction...allow[s] skilled thinkers to demonstrate expert strategies to the naïve. [It] makes hidden through processes public and shared.
>
> Communal interactions allow students to share and distribute the cognitive burdens of thinking. A group provides a more informationally rich context for learning.... There are greater varieties of cues to trigger recall of information from individual memories.
>
> Dialogue requires both language comprehension and language production. [Because] production is cognitively more demanding, dialogue might then result in deeper processing of information.
>
> Social settings send the message that thinking and intelligence are socially valued.
>
> Thought, learning, and knowledge are not just influenced by social factors, but are irreducibly social phenomena. Discourse doesn't make thought visible, rather thought is internalized discourse. (p. 75)

However, as Wilson and Berne (1999) point out, dialogue by itself may or may not be effective. They suggest that teachers should be gaining knowledge of both subject matter and students. Kennedy (1998) examined research on inservice programs and concluded that projects that focused on subject matter and knowledge of students have a greater impact on student learning than those that focus on teaching behaviors.

Garet, Porter, Desimone, Birman, and Yoon (2001) conducted a review of the literature and identified a set of elements in staff development programs that appear to lead to reform in math and science instruction. The elements included the following: a focus on content knowledge; opportunities for active learning; coherence with other learning activities; activities that take account of the context in which the teacher participants work; collective participation of teachers in the same school, grade, or subject; and a process that extends over a period of time.

A survey of over 1,000 teachers assessed their sense of the degree to which the professional development led them to learning and then changing their classroom practice. Most of the professional development experiences of the teachers did not meet the criteria for high quality listed previously; however, the high-quality professional development experiences were positively correlated with teachers' learning and change. The authors concluded that it is through the core features that the following structural features significantly affect teacher learning: (a) the form of the activity (e.g., workshop versus study group); (b) collective participation of teachers from the same school, grade, or subject; and (c) the duration of the activity.

# Community

As suggested in the Garet et al. (2001) study, what has been labeled as community, collective, or collegial activity is also an important element of what has been identified as successful professional development programs (Palincsar, Magnusson, Marano, Ford, & Brown, 1998). Obviously, community is closely related to dialogue, in that a community has the opportunity to establish a trusting and collegial norm that allows teachers to express their questions and reflect on their failures and successes. An example of the importance of community is presented in a study by Raphael, Florio-Ruane, and George (2001). The Teachers' Learning Collaborative is a group of teachers who work and live in a diverse set of communities across Michigan. In their work, they used an activity cycle for inquiry and change that relied on their community sense of problem formulation and change. This cycle included the following steps:

1. Frame a common problem.
2. Engage in authentic reading, writing, speaking, and listening to address it.
3. Take from these activities insights for action to solve the problem.
4. Investigate the adequacy of your solution to solve the common problem.
5. Share what is learned with others who have conducted similar inquiry.
6. Recycle the common problem with new insight and additional possible solutions.

The collective focused on the problem of working with students who, because of reading difficulties, were alienated from classroom literacy. They brought into their classrooms many of the elements of the activity cycle in which they engaged in inquiring into the question.

Again, however, communities of practice are not effective simply because they exist. They need to move the group to a place where teacher participants are allowed or pushed toward deep investigations and critiques of their own and each other's practices. Nor has it been adequately demonstrated that such "strong" community activity leads to changes in practice more quickly or effectively than "weak" communities (Little, 1990b). For example, Placier and Hamilton (1994) found that in two schools in which an inquiry-based professional development program was being implemented the sense of community and collegiality was quite weak. And although the community sense strengthened in one school over the course of the program, the teachers in both schools made considerable changes.

Little (2002) has recently analyzed the issue of determining teacher learning and opportunities to learn in community processes, using a study of community dialogue in a high school Academic Literacy Group as an example. She highlights the dilemmas of determining teacher learning in these community discussions and suggests ways of determining whether the strong sense of community is present in a community of practice, whether opportunities to learn are present, and whether the teachers are learning.

## Consideration of Beliefs

In moving toward a more constructivist sense of teacher learning and professional development, we now recognize that beliefs that the teacher participants bring into the program with them can block or enable learning. An example of a professional development program based on the importance of beliefs is the Reading Instruction Study (Anders & Richardson, 1991; Richardson, 1994a). The project was designed to examine the use of research in the teaching of reading comprehension and the collaborative staff development process, using practical arguments (Fenstermacher, 1994) that involved videotaping of teachers' classrooms and discussions with individual teachers around the videotapes. This process was designed to help teachers, both in groups and individually, inquire into their beliefs and practices (in relation to current research on reading and practices described by other teachers) and to support their attempts at change. We found that over the three-year period the teachers changed their beliefs and practices in directions that related to dialogues about practices in the teaching of reading, including those in the individual practical argument sessions and the group discussions. Bos and Anders (1994) conducted a substudy and found that the students of the teachers who participated in the staff development process achieved more in certain aspects of reading comprehension than did the students in a contrast school. In a follow-up study, Anders and Evans (1994) found that the teachers continued to elaborate on and develop their beliefs after the formal professional development program was concluded. The teachers reported, through interview, that their practices had also changed to be commensurate with these newly elaborated on—and continuously developing and changing—beliefs.

In contrast, Peck (2003) investigated a professional development program that did not take into account teachers' beliefs and experiences. The professional development was top-down and involved the imposition of a reading program and methods on the teachers. Peck reports that the teachers responded to the professional development in confused ways: They felt discouraged, devalued, and misunderstood. As a result, they had difficulty learning how to implement the desired program. Peck points out that these teachers were not resistant because they did not want to change; they evidenced resistance because they were disregarded in the professional development process.

Ortiz (2001) conducted a yearlong professional development program with primary-level teachers. The teachers were each interviewed about their teaching of reading beliefs and were videotaped when they were teaching reading. These two "texts" became the primary resources for the professional development process. As teachers viewed each other's videotapes and discussed each other's interviews, they elaborated on the relationship of their beliefs and practices. Ortiz provided additional research-based literature, which the teachers and Ortiz used to mediate their developing understanding of teaching reading. The changes in these teachers' beliefs and instructional practices were remarkable. The participants formed a community of critical friends who examined each other's beliefs and practices and helped each other to change.

## Facilitators in the School

In most of the school-level reform programs (e.g., Accelerated Schools, Paideia, Success for All), facilitators are considered a critical element of the process. Facilitation is a quite newly developed process and requires that an individual work with a group of teachers over a long period of time to help them change their practices. (See American Institutes of Research [1999] for a comprehensive description of current reform programs.)

In programs such as Success for All, facilitators are asked to ensure that teachers are changing their practices. The role goes beyond the restricted sense of "staff developer," in which someone presents a workshop and then leaves. The facilitator often works full- or part-time within a school or with a group of teachers and engages in such activities as consulting closely with teachers, observing in classes, modeling practices by working with students, videotaping the classrooms, and engaging in extensive dialogue with the teachers.

Most of the small-scale studies described in this chapter involve a facilitator who is also the researcher. For example, in a study of engaging teachers with subject matter through the use of a form of a book club, Grossman, Wineburg, and Woolworth (2001) met with a group of English and Social Studies teachers monthly for three years. Anders and Richardson (1991) acted as facilitators and researchers in their study of the practical argument staff development process, and Ortiz was a teacher in the school where she was also a researcher. Short, a professor, developed relationships with the principals and teachers with whom she worked over several years; she also analyzed the study groups with the participants and has published with them.

Unfortunately, it is difficult to determine whether the facilitator's presence makes a critical difference to the outcome of the process primarily because processes that are completely teacher led are seldom formally studied and therefore do not enter the literature (Le Fevre & Richardson, 2002). At the same time, these projects work with volunteer schools and teachers. As we begin to explore urban reform projects in the next sections, the sense of the need for a facilitator may become more critical.

# Urban Schools and Issues That Impact on Professional Development in Urban Schools

The professional development work already described responds to the need for individual and groups of teachers to develop an improvement orientation that leads to teacher learning in improved instruction while maintaining a sense of autonomy, competence, and worth. This is a difficult goal to pursue, although the literature indicates that it is possible. However, the difficulties are exacerbated within urban areas. In the first place, there are specific context conditions in urban schools and classrooms that call for preservice preparation that contains elements specific to urban settings. There are also serious problems related to recruitment and retention of teachers. These four issues or elements—teacher preparation, recruitment, retention, and professional development—interact and must be considered together in a reform process. Thus, efforts at affecting the literacy instruction in urban schools require that attention be paid to teacher preparation, recruitment, and retention practices in combination with professional development and partnerships among school districts and teacher preparation institutions.

## *Teacher Preparation*

This section is both shorter and longer than it should be for the following reasons: First, the inclusion of a preservice teacher education literature review causes us to exceed the space allotted for this chapter. Second, even though this chapter is primarily about professional development, preservice teacher education is an important component of teacher learning and change and thus needs to be included. And third, we expect that our readers are more interested in teacher professional development than in preparation. We know, however, that teachers need to be hired, and we have some evidence that might be of help to those who are doing the hiring.

The preparation of teachers to teach reading has not been a high priority of the research community. We propose two fundamental reasons for this lack of research interest. First, throughout the 1950s, 1960s, and 1970s, teacher educators were highly reliant on helping future teachers to learn about using published materials for the teaching of reading. In addition, there were only a few methods, such as Language Experience Approach and the Directed Reading–Thinking Activity, that most future teachers were encouraged to learn. This rather simple view changed, however, when teachers were expected to be less reliant on materials and more responsible for understanding the reading process in relationship to the students who were their charges. Teacher educators did not conceptualize the requisite knowledge of language and psychology, which is needed by a teacher to be the decision maker in the classroom, in curricular ways. This is in no way an indictment of changing theories of the reading process; it is, however, an indictment of systems and resources that were not capable of responding to the needs of preparing professional teachers. Second, there are almost no published articles that cite a major funding source for teacher education research. Researchers need support to conduct their research, and those funding sources have been few and far between. Teacher educators and others are now (re)conceptualizing their programs to better prepare teachers to teach reading and the language arts, and they are doing so in a climate rife with diminishing resources and criticism.

The good news is that preservice teachers learn what they are taught, and the literature on teacher education in reading is beginning to suggest some potentially positive trends. One such trend is the nature of preservice teacher field experiences. Worthy and Patterson (2001) report that the perspective for studying field experiences has shifted from "practicing" to "engaging" in observing, studying, and reflecting on interpersonal relationships, problem solving, and the unique encounters teachers have with students in the classroom.

Teacher educators ask their students to write in reflective journals (Bean & Zulich, 1992) and, as in the inservice programs, to engage in critical dialogue in communities of practice (Mosenthal, 1987). These methods contribute to future teachers being more sophisticated about the relationship of their theories or beliefs and the practices they choose to employ. Grossman, Valencia, et al. (2001) explored the use of these types of methods with preservice teachers of writing. They conducted a longitudinal study of these teachers in their classrooms and developed 10 case studies. From their report, we gain confidence that constructivist and reflective teacher education is a powerful influence on the preparation of teachers.

Maloch et al. (2003) followed 101 preservice teachers through their first year of teaching in urban, suburban, and rural school districts in different regions of the United States. Their purpose was to explore differences in the understandings, beliefs, and decision making of beginning teachers from teacher preparation programs: programs identified as excellent by the International Reading Association's National Commission on Excellence in Elementary Teacher Preparation (Hoffman & Roller, 2001), which included specific and concentrated experiences and courses in reading, and general education programs with less emphasis on reading. Data, which were collected from structured telephone interviews conducted during September, January, and June, were analyzed using inductive data-driven analyses and yielded three themes: instructional decision making, negotiations, and community. The teachers in the specialized programs were articulate when discussing their teaching and were much more confident than the teachers from the general programs. Reading specialization graduates assumed a responsive instructional stance. They were less concerned about "covering" material or getting their kids to "pass a test" and more concerned about offering instruction appropriate for their students. Furthermore, these teachers understood that they were just at the beginning of their professional development. They sought more experienced mentors, they reported "hearing their professors in their head," and they sought out colleagues with whom to solve problems. Their strong sense of community provided a context for reading specialization teachers to assume leadership roles: More experienced teachers sought them out for advice, and the beginning but knowledgeable teachers were able to affect the school climate and the professional development of the school.

Maloch et al. (2003) concluded their report by emphasizing that we must remember "teacher preparation is a complex and intricate venture that encompasses much more than following a prescribed list of content objectives" (p. 56). It must include preparation in how teachers continue to develop professionally and how to negotiate challenges within the culture of teaching. Their findings suggest that reading teacher preparation programs should strategically prepare teachers through the provision of purposeful course work, apprenticeship opportunities, and a clear vision and focus on reading that cross all of the preservice teachers' experiences.

## Recruitment

Problems of teacher recruitment are particularly prevalent in urban areas. The difficulty in recruiting quality teachers leads to teachers hired out of subject matter, teachers not prepared for the multicultural context of urban schools, and teachers who are, in fact, not prepared in pedagogy but have gone through short-term alternative programs or become long-term substitute teachers with no pedagogical preparation. For example, in the Houston, Texas, public schools, of the 333 new teachers hired for grades 4–8 in 2000, only 65% held B.A. or B.S. degrees (Raymond, Fletcher, & Luque, 2002).

This is a particular problem in the reading field. One could consider that teachers who had majored in history would have some of the appropriate content knowledge if they were teaching history in a secondary school. However, reading is not a content major in most undergraduate schools. Thus teachers who have not attended a typical elementary teacher education program will generally not have any knowledge or skills on teaching reading.

It is also the case that the demand for teachers of color has increased dramatically, given the demographic characteristics of the student population and the smaller number of teachers of color entering the profession (Lewis, 1996). The majority of teachers who enter the teaching profession within an urban setting often do not have the skills, knowledge, or background experience to work effectively with populations of students different from themselves.

## Retention

The National Commission on America's Future (NCTAF) stated that more than 30% of beginning teachers leave within the first five years. As Ingersoll (2001) points out, the turnover rate of teachers is remarkably high compared to other professions. The problems are particularly severe in the large urban areas with high percentages of high-poverty schools. With high turnover each year, school districts have to recruit large numbers of teachers, and, as already mentioned, many of these teachers may not be certified, may have content knowledge deficiencies, or may not have B.A. or B.S. degrees.

## Professional Development

The sheer size of urban districts—large number of schools and many, many teachers, students, and administrators—leads to great difficulties in implementing professional development with the characteristics listed previously. Retaining teacher autonomy, ensuring school and teacher buy-in, and providing opportunities for dialogue around teaching practices are difficult features to develop and support at the school district level. Further, these approaches to professional development, particularly inquiry approaches, lead to outcomes over which the school districts have little control, and they may differ from school to school and classroom to classroom.

This problem of size often leads to attempts to standardize the teaching and instructional approaches across the school district. For example, the Detroit School District recently mandated Open Court as the reading approach required in all elementary school classrooms. All teachers in the school district are receiving inservice training in the use of Open Court. These kinds of mandates lead to a reduction in the sense of teacher agency and to burnout and retention problems. Although such programs may be stopgaps, particularly for teachers who have not received a solid teacher preparation in the teaching of reading, they are not long-term solutions, and indeed, they may lead to unintended negative consequences.

The question then becomes how a large urban area can plan and implement staff development programs that have embedded within them the principles and practices already described with goals of building knowledge and skills in reading instruction, retaining autonomy for teachers to adapt their instruction to their context and student needs, and building commitment to reaching all students. This is difficult to do, because the programs described here have involved teachers and schools in voluntary programs; they are time-consuming and, at least in the short run, relatively expensive; and the results will not lead to a standard program across classrooms and schools. It is easier to mandate a specific program or curriculum, even with extensive evidence that such programs do not work in the long run.

All of these issues will be approached from a policy standpoint in the next section.

# Bringing It All Together: Implications for Policy

While this is a chapter that focuses on professional development, conditions in urban schooling suggest that professional development alone will not make the difference necessary for extensive reform of literacy instruction in these school districts. The following themes underlie the recommendations that follow:

- Teacher learning is considered across teachers' preparation and professional life.

- A number of elements of the reform process should be considered simultaneously.

In this section, we are focusing on partnerships, teacher recruitment and retention, teacher preparation, and professional development.

## Partnerships

In a survey of 2,413 superintendents in the midwestern United States, several strategies for recruitment and retention were identified as features of the more successful programs. Partnerships between school districts and higher education teacher education programs were described as highly effective recruitment strategies, which also have the potential to improve the quality of teacher preparation programs (Hare & Heap, 2001). Other strategies that were identified as effective included support programs for new teachers, more collaboration and involvement of teachers, flexible use of salary schedule, and "growing your own" teachers.

One way in which partnerships aid in the preparation of teachers is that they increase the probability of "conceptual coherence" (Grossman, 2000) between the ideas they learn as students and the values of the school in which they teach. Nonetheless, partnerships are difficult to sustain and develop. They require a trusting relationship, motivation on the part of all partners, and appropriate training and support for all those involved in the process (Griffin, 2002; Tushnett et al., 1995).

## Recruitment and Retention

Of all the potential strategies for recruitment and retention of teachers, the one that appears to be of most interest and has received the greatest attention in the literature is an induction program for beginning teachers. These programs support new teachers through mentoring by experienced teachers. A number of studies point to the importance and effects of induction programs on the retention of high-quality teachers. For example, research on California's Beginning Teacher Support and Assessment system suggests teacher attrition in districts in which this program is operating has dropped to less than 10% (Wood, 1999). This compares to a statewide trend of 50% in the first three years of teaching.

However, induction programs vary widely, with some being more effective than others. A number of descriptive studies indicate that different approaches to mentoring can strongly affect the outcomes. For example,

Feiman-Nemser and Parker (1993) compared two beginning teacher programs and found striking differences in the ways in which the mentors approached their work. These differences were attributed to a number of factors including mentor preparation.

Mentoring programs should provide both psychological and instruction-related support (Stansbury, 2000), be reasonably long term (Conyers, Ewy, & Vass, 1999), and be developmentally appropriate for the beginning teacher (Feiman-Nemser, Carver, Schwille, & Yusko, 1999; Reiman & Thies-Sprinthall, 1997). The analysis of cases in small groups is a particularly appropriate approach to working with new teachers (Carter & Richardson, 1989; Odell & Huling, 2000; J.H. Shulman & Colbert, 1988). Hare and Heap (2001) also suggest that one-on-one mentoring and mandatory participation of all new teachers are important features of successful programs. Ladson-Billings (2001) has prepared a set of cases that are particularly helpful for new teachers in urban schools.

It is also clear that mentors themselves and the administrators of buildings in which new teachers are present should receive support and education in new teacher needs and programs and in ways of supporting the mentor teachers (Little, 1990a; J.H. Shulman & Colbert, 1988). Ingersoll (2001) suggested that school culture is an important element of support for new teachers. On the basis of a study of reasons teachers gave for leaving the profession, he suggests four organizational solutions that could reduce turnover: increased support from the school administration, enhanced faculty input into school decision making, reduction in student discipline problems, and increased salaries. These factors would undoubtedly affect all teachers in a school, including mentors and new teachers. In sum, the National Center for Research on Teacher Learning (2000) listed the following five elements that lead to successful mentoring programs: (1) Mentoring must be connected to a vision of good teaching if it is to contribute to educational reform. (2) Mentoring must be informed by an understanding of how one learns to teach. (3) Mentoring must be viewed as a professional practice not merely a new role for experienced teachers. (4) Mentors need time to mentor and opportunities to learn to mentor. (5) Mentoring is affected by the professional culture of the school and broader policies and values.

Another program of interest today, one that should be implemented in combination with the induction programs, is providing bonuses for teacher education students who have practice taught in the school district and are hired to teach. These bonuses are given after the first and second year of teaching in the district.

## Teacher Preparation

Teacher preparation programs, as described above, are in the midst of revival. The best programs recognize the complexity of teacher education and are incorporating extensive field experiences that are linked to extant theories of teaching and learning and the construction of future teachers' theories and understanding of practice. They incorporate habits of mind that promote problem solving, community building, critical inquiry, and an attitude of lifelong learning.

In addition, one must consider the structural elements of effective teacher preparation programs for urban schools whether they are alternative programs (such as one-year programs for career changers) or traditional programs. Two recent reviews of the literature provide us with important information about elements of successful alternative teacher education programs. Humphrey et al. (2000) and Wilson, Floden, and Ferrini-Mundy (2002) suggest that alternative routes attract a more diverse pool of prospective teachers in terms of age and ethnicity, and that alternative routes attract career changers and others who might not have become teachers. Further, these programs prepare teachers who have a higher probability of teaching in urban settings than students in regular programs. However, evaluations of alternative route programs produce mixed results, indicating a need to examine the specific features of successful alternative programs.

The features that contribute to successful programs are those that (a) specifically prepare students for urban settings and teaching minority children and (b) include professional development for teachers and administrators in the schools in which students are interning. Ladson-Billings (2000) describes the difficulty and promise of preparing teacher education students for teaching African American students. She has a number of recommendations that are very useful in working with preservice and inservice teachers in urban areas. In addition, the field experiences for the teacher interns should be extensive, focused, and well structured; and cooperating teachers, who exert great influence on the student interns, should be well prepared for their role, as should the receiving school (Wilson et al., 2002).

## Professional Development

The urban issues raise the problems of the difficulties of implementing the professional development programs that lead to successful change in large urban settings. One way of considering how this could be accomplished is by examining those successful programs that have attempted to scale up from small, very labor intensive projects with world-renowned experts working extensively with the teachers in a given school to engaging a larger number of schools in the process in a way that provides the expertise to the teacher in a somewhat more efficient way. Such projects place the expertise in the hands of the teachers and facilitators as they begin to work more extensively with the Internet.

An example of such a project is one in which one of the authors has been involved at the Center for the Improvement of Early Reading Achievement (CIERA) at the University of Michigan, with Barbara Taylor and David Pearson and funded by the U.S. Department of Education. (Information on this and other projects within CIERA may be found on the CIERA website: www.ciera.org.) Called the Instructional Change Study, this project is working in a number of schools across the United States, trying, in a sense, to "scale up" the inquiry approach, but to ensure that the whole school is engaged in the effort. There are a number of elements in this framework:

1. Seventy-five percent of the teachers in a given school must agree to participate.
2. A school facilitator is hired to help teachers in the change process.
3. The facilitator receives considerable training and support from the project.
4. A change team within the school is appointed by the principal or selected by the other teachers.
5. Much of the planning goes on in grade-level meetings, and a member of each grade-level team is a member of the change team.
6. There are no specific "answers." Teachers themselves determine what the changes will be in the schoolwide reading program.

However, they are given some expert help and a number of choices to select among. These choices of research-based programs and considerable additional help in relation to the change process are provided on a website devoted to this process.

The project is data rich. Student test scores and results of classroom observations are meant to be used by the teachers in developing their plans and by the researchers in assessing the success of the project.

This framework is based on an examination of the school organizational and teacher change research literature, and an initial process–product study of effective teaching behaviors in schools with low-income student populations (Taylor et al., 1999).

# Conclusion

We have attempted to indicate that professional development is a necessary but not sufficient condition for literacy reform programs in urban settings. Our interpretation of the literature suggests that resources and creativity must be devoted to applying principles of constructivist learning in communal contexts that promote critical dialogue and support teachers' growth. We acknowledge that this perspective in not synchronous with the current trends. We put forth this perspective with confidence, however. The challenges we confront cannot be overcome by dictatorial, top-down, and draconian mandates; rather, those who are teaching our children and youth must confront them. Policymakers and administrators are responsible for providing the context, opportunities, and leadership needed for the teachers to do their best work.

## REFERENCES

American Institutes of Research. (1999). *An educator's guide to school wide reform.* Washington, DC: Author.

Anders, P., & Evans, K. (1994). Relationship between teachers' beliefs and their instructional practice in reading. In R. Garner & P.A. Alexander (Eds.), *Beliefs about texts and instruction with text* (pp. 137–154). Mahwah, NJ: Erlbaum.

Anders, P., Hoffman, J., & Duffy, G. (2000). Teaching teachers to teach reading: Paradigm shifts, persistent problems, and challenges. In M.L. Kamil, P.B. Mosenthal, P.D. Pearson, & R. Barr (Eds.), *Handbook of reading research* (Vol. 3, pp. 719–742). Mahwah, NJ: Erlbaum.

Anders, P., & Richardson, V. (1991). Research directions: Staff development that empowers teachers' reflection and enhances instruction. *Language Arts, 68*(4), 316–321.

Au, K. (1990). Changes in teacher's views of interactive comprehension instruction. In L.C. Moll (Ed.), *Vygotsky and education: Instructional implications and applications of sociohistorical psychology* (pp. 271–286). New York: Cambridge University Press.

Au, K.H. (1985, April). *Instruction: The implications of research on the Kamehameha approach in developing reading comprehension ability.* Paper presented at the annual meeting of the American Educational Research Association, Chicago, IL.

Bealor, S. (1992). Minority literature book groups for teachers. *Reading in Virginia, 17*, 17–21.

Bean, T., & Zulich, J. (1992). Teaching students to learn from text: Preservice content teachers' changing view of their role through the window of their student-professor dialogue journals. In J. Zutell & S. McCormick (Eds.), *Literacy theory and research: Analyses from multiple paradigms* (39th yearbook of the national reading conference, pp. 171–178). Chicago: National Reading Conference.

Berman, P., & McLaughlin, M.W. (1975). *Federal programs supporting educational change: A model of educational change* (Vol. 5, Executive Summary, R-1589/4-HEW). Santa Monica, CA: RAND.

Berman, P., & McLaughlin, M.W. (1976). Implementation of educational innovations. *Educational Forum, 40*(3), 344–370.

Bos, C., & Anders, P. (1994). The study of student change. In V. Richardson (Ed.), *Teacher change and the staff development process: A case in reading instruction* (pp. 181–198). New York: Teachers College Press.

Brophy, J., & Good, T. (1986). Teacher behavior and student achievement. In M.C. Wittrock (Ed.), *Handbook of research on teaching* (3rd ed., pp. 328–375). New York: Macmillan.

Bruer, J. (1994). Classroom problems, school culture, and cognitive research. In K. McGilly (Ed.), *Classroom lessons: Integrating cognitive theory and classroom research* (pp. 273–290). Cambridge, MA: MIT Press.

Carter, K., & Richardson, V. (1989) A curriculum for an initial-year-of-teaching program. *The Elementary School Journal*, *89*(4), 405–419.

Cazden, C. (2001). *Classroom discourse: The language of teaching and learning* (2nd ed.). Portsmouth, NH: Heinemann.

Conyers, J.G., Ewy, B., & Vass, L. (1999). Developing a common language and spirit. In M. Scherer (Ed.), *A better beginning: Supporting and mentoring new teachers* (124–132). Alexandria, VA: Association for Supervision and Curriculum Development.

Feiman-Nemser, S., Carver, C., Schwille, S., & Yusko, B. (1999). Beyond support: Taking new teachers seriously as learners. In M. Scherer (Ed.), *A better beginning: Supporting and mentoring new teachers* (pp. 3–12). Alexandria, VA: Association for Supervision and Curriculum Development.

Feiman-Nemser, S., & Parker, M.B. (1993). A comparison of two U.S. programs for beginning teachers. *International Journal of Educational Research*, *19*(8), 699–718.

Fenstermacher, G.D. (1994). The knower and the known: The nature of knowledge in research on teaching. In L. Darling-Hammond (Ed.), *Review of research in education* (Vol. 20, pp. 1–54) Washington, DC: American Educational Research Association.

Fisher, C., Beliner, D., Filby, N., Marliave, R., Cahen, L., & Dishaw, M. (1980). Teaching behaviors, academic learning time, and student achievement: An overview. In C. Denham & A. Lieberman (Eds.), *Time to learn* (pp. 227–228).

Washington, DC: National Institute of Education.

Floden, R. (2001). Research on effects of teaching: A continuing model for research on teaching. In V. Richardson (Ed.), *Handbook of research on teaching* (4th ed., pp. 3–16). Washington, DC: American Educational Research Association.

Flood, J., Lapp, D., Ranck-Buhr, W., & Moore, J. (1995). What happens when teachers get together to talk about books? Gaining a multicultural perspective from literature. *The Reading Teacher*, *48*, 720–723.

Gage, N.L. (Ed.). (1975). *NIE conference on studies in teaching: Panel 6, teaching as clinical information processing*. East Lansing MI: National Center for Research on Teaching Learning. (ERIC Document Reproduction Service No. ED111807)

Gage, N.L. (1978). *The scientific basis of the art of teaching*. New York: Teachers College Press.

Garet, M.S., Porter, A.C., Desimone, L., Birman, B.F., & Yoon, K.S. (2001). What makes professional development effective? Results from a national sample of teachers. *American Educational Research Journal*, *38*(4), 915–945.

Good, T.L., & Grouws, D.A. (1979). The Missouri mathematics effectiveness project: An experimental study of fourth-grade classrooms. *Journal of Educational Psychology*, *71*(3), 355–362.

Griffin, G.A. (Ed.). (2002). *Rethinking standards through teacher preparation partnerships*. Albany: State University of New York Press.

Grossman, P. (2000). Memo to U.S. Department of Education: Thoughts on evaluation of partnerships grants program. Washington, DC: U.S. Department of Education.

Grossman, P., Valencia, S., Thompson, C., Martin, S., Place, N., & Evans, K. (2001). Transitions into teaching: Learning to teach writing in teacher education and beyond. In C.M. Roller (Ed.), *Learning to teach reading: Setting the research agenda* (pp. 80–99). Newark, DE: International Reading Association.

Grossman, P., Wineburg, S., & Woolworth, S. (2001). Toward a theory of teacher community. *Teachers College Record, 103*(6), 942–1012.

Hare, D., & Heap, J.L. (2001). *Effective teacher recruitment and retention strategies in the Midwest: Who is making use of them?* Naperville, IL: North Central Regional Educational Laboratory.

Hoffman, J., & Roller, C.M. (2001). The IRA excellence in reading teacher preparation commission's report: Current practices in reading teacher education at the undergraduate level in the United States. In C.M. Roller (Ed.), *Learning to teach reading: Setting the research agenda* (pp. 32–79). Newark, DE: International Reading Association.

Humphrey, D., Adelman, N., Esch, C., Riehl, L., Shields, P., & Tiffany, J. (2000). *Preparing and supporting new teachers: A literature review.* Menlo Park, CA: SRI International.

Ingersoll, R.M. (2001). Teacher turnover and teacher shortages: An organizational analysis. *American Educational Research Journal, 38*(3), 499–534.

Joyce, B.R., & Showers, B. (1981). Transfer of training: The contribution of coaching. *Journal of Education, 163*(2), 163–172.

Kennedy, M. (1998, April). *The relevance of content in inservice teacher education.* Paper presented at the annual meeting of the American Educational Research Association, San Diego, CA.

Ladson-Billings, G. (2000). Fighting for our lives: Preparing teachers to teach African-American students. *Journal of Teacher Education, 51*(3), 206–214.

Ladson-Billings, G. (2001). *To Canaan: Crossing over to Canaan: The journey of new teachers in diverse classrooms.* San Francisco: Jossey-Bass.

Le Fevre, D., & Richardson, V. (2002). Staff development in early reading intervention programs. *Teaching and Teacher Education, 18*(4), 483–500.

Lewis, M.S. (1996). *Supply and demand of teachers of color.* East Lansing, MI: National Center for Research on Teaching Learning. (ERIC Document Reproduction Service No. ED390875)

Little, J.W. (1989). District policy choices and teachers' professional development opportunities. *Educational Evaluation and Policy Analysis, 11*(2), 165–179.

Little, J.W. (1990a). The mentor phenomenon and the social organization of teaching. In C.B. Cazden (Ed.), *Review of research in education, 1990* (pp. 297–351). Washington, DC: American Educational Research Association.

Little, J.W. (1990b). The persistence of privacy: Autonomy and initiative in teachers' professional development. *Teachers College Record, 91*, 509–536.

Little, J.W. (2002). Locating learning in teachers' communities of practice: Opening up problems of analysis in records of everyday work. *Teaching and Teacher Education, 18*(8), 917–946.

Maloch, B., Flint, A.S., Eldridge, D., Harmon, J., Loven, R., Fine, J., et al. (2003). Understandings, beliefs, and reported decision making of first-year teachers from different reading teacher preparation programs. *The Elementary School Journal, 103*(5), 431-457.

Matlin, M.L., & Short, K.G. (1996). Study groups: Inviting teachers to learn together. In K.F. Whitmore & Y.M. Goodman (Eds.), *Whole language voices in teacher education* (pp. 85–92). York, ME: Stenhouse.

Mosenthal, J. (1987). Learning from discussion: Requirements and constraints on classroom instruction in reading comprehension strategies. In J.E. Readence & R.S. Baldwin (Eds.), *Research in literacy: Merging perspectives* (36th yearbook of the National Reading Conference, pp. 169–176). Chicago: National Reading Conference.

National Center for Research on Teaching and Learning. (2000). *NCRTL explores learning from mentors: A study update.* Retrieved August 2, 2004, from http://www.educ.msu.edu/alumnoi/newed/ne66c3~5.htm

Odell, S.J., & Huling, L. (2000). *Quality mentoring for novice teachers.* Indianapolis, IN: Kappa Delta Pi.

Ortiz, M. (2001). *The literacy related beliefs and practices of three primary bilingual teachers*. Tucson: The University of Arizona.

Palincsar, A.S., Magnusson, S.J., Marano, N., Ford, D., & Brown, N. (1998). Designing a community of practice: Principles and practices of the GIsML community. *Teaching and Teacher Education, 14*(1), 5–19.

Peck, S. (2003). "I do have this right. You can't strip that from me": Valuing teachers' knowledge during literacy instructional change. In D.L. Schallert, C.M. Fairbanks, J. Worthy, B. Maloch, & J.V. Hoffman (Eds.), *Fifty-first yearbook of the national reading conference* (pp. 344–356). Oak Creek, WI: The National Reading Conference.

Placier, P., & Hamilton, M.L. (1994). Schools as contexts: A complex relationship. In V. Richardson (Ed.), *Teacher change and the staff development process: A case in reading instruction* (pp. 135–159). New York: Teachers College Press.

Raphael, T., Florio-Ruane, S., & George, M. (2001). *Book club plus: A conceptual framework to organize literacy instruction* (CIERA Report No. 3-015). Ann Arbor, MI: Center for the Improvement of Elementary Reading Achievement, School of Education, University of Michigan.

Raymond, M., Fletcher, S., & Luque, J. (2002). *Teach for America: An evaluation of teacher differences and student outcomes in Houston, Texas*. Palo Alto, CA: Center for Research on Education Outcomes, Stanford University.

Reiman, A.J., & Theis-Sprinthall, L. (1997). *Mentoring and supervision for teacher development*. Boston: Allyn & Bacon.

Richardson, V. (Ed.). (1994a). *Teacher change and the staff development process: A case in reading instruction*. New York: Teachers College Press.

Richardson, V. (1994b). Teacher inquiry as staff development. In H. Sockett & S. Hollingsworth (Eds.), *Teacher research and educational reform* (93rd yearbook of the National Society for the Study of Education: Part I, pp. 186–203). Chicago: University of Chicago Press.

Richardson, V. (2003). Constructivist pedagogy. *Teachers College Record, 105*(9), 1623–1640.

Richardson, V. (2003, January). The dilemmas of professional development. *Phi Delta Kappan*, 401–406.

Richardson, V., & Placier, P. (2001). Teachers change. In V. Richardson (Ed.), *Handbook of research on teaching* (4th ed., pp. 905–947). Washington, DC: American Educational Research Association.

Shaver, J. (1987). Implications from research: What should be taught in social studies. In V. Richardson-Koehler (Ed.), *Educators' handbook: A research perspective*. White Plains, NY: Longman.

Shulman, J.H., & Colbert, J.A. (1988). *The intern teacher casebook*. San Francisco: WestEd.

Shulman, L.S. (1974). The psychology of school subjects: A premature obituary? *Journal of Research in Science Teaching, 11*(4), 319–339.

Smylie, M.A. (1988). The enhancement function of staff development: Organizational and psychological antecedents to individual teacher change. *American Educational Research Journal, 25*(1), 1–30.

Smylie, M.A. (1989). Teachers' views of the effectiveness of sources of learning to teach. *The Elementary School Journal, 89*(5), 543–558.

Stallings, J., Needels, M., & Stayrook, N. (1980). *How to change the process of teaching basic reading skills in secondary schools: Phase II and Phase III* (Final report, Rev. materials). Menlo Park, CA: SRI International.

Stansbury, K. (2000). *Lifelines to the classroom: Designing support for beginning teachers*. San Francisco: WestEd.

Taylor, B., Pearson, P.D., Clark, K., & Walpole, S. (1999). *Beating the odds in teaching all children to read* (CIERA Report No. 2-006). Ann Arbor, MI: Center for the Improvement of Early Reading Achievement, University of Michigan.

Tushnet, N., Briggs, D., Elliott, J., Exch, C., Haviland, D., Humphrey, D.C., et al. (n.d.). *Final report of the independent evaluation of the beginning teacher support and assessment program.* San Francisco: WestEd.

Wilson, S., & Berne, J. (1999). Teacher learning and the acquisition of professional knowledge: An examination of research on contemporary professional development. In A. Iran-Nejad & P.D. Pearson (Eds.), *Review of research in education* (No. 24, pp. 173–209). Washington, DC: American Educational Research Association.

Wilson, S.M., Floden, R.E., & Ferrini-Mundy, J. (2002). Teacher preparation research: An insider's view from the outside. *Journal of Teacher Education, 53*(3), 190–204.

Wood, C. (1999). How can new teachers become the best? In M. Scherer (Ed.), *A better beginning: Supporting and mentoring new teachers* (pp. 120–123). Alexandria, VA: Association for Supervision and Curriculum Development.

Worthy, J., & Patterson, B. (2001). "I can't wait to see Carlos!" Preservice teachers, situated learning, and personal relationships with students. *Journal of Literacy Research, 33*(2), 303–344.

# CHAPTER 14

# The Importance of Professional Development to Unlock the Potential of Students in Urban Settings: A Response to Virginia Richardson and Patricia Anders

*Eric J. Cooper and Yvette Jackson*

> I suppose that it is a truth too well attested to you, to need a proof here, that we are a race of beings...who have long been looked upon...as scarcely capable of mental endowments.... I apprehend you will embrace every opportunity to eradicate that train of absurd and false ideas and opinions, which so generally prevail with respect to us; and that your sentiments are concurrent with mine...that we were all afforded, without partiality, the same sensations and endowed with the same facilities. —Benjamin Banneker (as cited in Zinn, 2003, p. 89)

Benjamin Banneker's quote was captured in a letter to one of America's founding fathers, Thomas Jefferson. These attitudes continue to this day to reflect American and worldwide beliefs about race, and the ability of black Americans in particular, to succeed in academic pursuits (Zinn, 2003). This belief, driven by stereotypical threats to African American students by often unknowing educators, results in African American underachievement. A result of low expectations is students who may become traumatized and internalize through a self-fulfilling prophecy that indeed they are not capable of a high level of academic achievement (Cooper, 2004).

In responding to Richardson and Anders, we share the perspective of black Americans. Growing up in the United States, we have personally experienced the structural and institutional racism that pervades our culture. We can feel the pain and the hurt that many students of color feel when marginalized by having limited opportunities and resources for learning. We work in school districts around the country where underachievement is the norm, where *urban* euphemistically refers to low-performing students of color, where 73% of the teachers identify themselves as white or racially and culturally different from their students—sometimes leading to misunderstanding about student capacity to learn (Mahiri, 1998, 2004).

Richardson and Anders begin their chapter with a deep understanding that the teacher remains the single most important school-based factor related to student achievement. This central notion is consistent with a large body of research (Cooper, 2004; Darling-Hammond, 2000; Levine & Cooper, 1991; Sanders & Rivers, 1996). The authors by extension clearly recognize the role that professional development plays in the school reform equation—namely, that education reform is dependent on professional development of teachers and principals—but with the caveat that, by itself, professional development is insufficient for widespread change resulting in improvements for all students.

Richardson and Anders also recognize that there are broad differences among professional development programs. These differences range from those referred to as "drive-by," "single-shot," and "fly-by" workshops to those that are more sustained and that adhere to "research-based" interventions. Emanating from the latter is an implied pedagogy that is "grounded in constructivist learning theory" rather than one that favors direct instruction and formulaic approaches as a goal, to an approach in which teachers are guided beyond scripted instruction to a much richer and more complex approach to teaching and learning. Whether the reader agrees with this assumption, however, is not the sole concern of the authors. Their primary thrust is to illuminate effective elements of professional development. To reiterate Richardson and Anders, these elements include

- mutual agreement among participants,
- supportive administration,
- adequate funds,
- buy-in from participants,
- encouragement of collegiality toward learning communities,
- a focus on subject-matter content rather than generic teaching methods, and
- involvement of an outside facilitator and staff developer.

The authors go on to cite general categories that can help those interested in deepening and strengthening professional development in their schools and districts. We believe that Richardson and Anders provide a compelling chapter on professional development and its importance. Those who are engaged in school and systemic reform would do well to heed their guidance in developing an effective and sustained implementation program.

In the National Urban Alliance for Effective Education (NUA), we work with a primary interest in accelerating learning for those urban students whose family and life circumstances cause them to be dependent on the school for learning. We are cognizant of the national achievement gap between "school dependent" nonwhite children and youth who live in poverty and those who are white and live in wealthier circumstances. In this work we experience firsthand with district-based partners the national tragedy of underachieving urban students, and the tragic gap that exists between their potential and their performance (Cooper, 2004). Though the "gap" also exists between middle-class nonwhite and white and Asian students, the data on students who struggle with poverty are the most alarming (e.g., dropout rates, incarceration, joblessness) (Cooper, 2004).

Considering the components of professional development for application to urban education cited by Richardson and Anders, it is imperative that we first come to understand the causes of the achievement gap. The most prevalent are (1) lack of good preschool experience (early childhood research suggests that children who are to succeed in the K–12 experience require 3,000 to 4,000 hours of "good" preschool; see Adams, 1996); (2) the lack of political will by stakeholders to close the gap (Hilliard, 1991); (3) a lack of belief in the capacity of children to learn (Delpit, 1995; Kohn, 1998); (4) a belief that intelligence is innate and fixed and a conclusion that the educational disparity is a fact of nature (Singham, 1998); (5) the existence of a cultural gap between teachers and children of color that causes missed opportunities for learning (Delpit, 1995); and (6) negative peer pressure exerted by nonwhites on nonwhites about acting "white" or too smart (Ogbu, 2003; Thernstrom & Thernstrom, 2003). All but one of the reasons for the achievement gap make some sense (see point 4), and the nature of the problem cited, in turn, suggests courses of action. Sadly, however, the courses of action often proposed to address the achievement gap avoid suggestions for sustained professional development of teachers as advocated by Richardson and Anders and instead favor ones that take students out of the mainstream and into dead-end educational pathways—for example, use of boot camps, a focus on low-level instructional scripts versus ones that stress high standards and expectation, special education for those who act out and who were not nurtured during their early schooling, and minimum competency schools to help the masses meet basic education standards (which may succeed at this goal but do not significantly facilitate access to higher education) (Bowen & Bok, 1998).

There are many success stories about dramatic achievement for children of color cited in individual schools throughout the United States (Council of Great City Schools, 2003; Hughes, 1995; Sanders & Rivers, 1996; Sizemore, Brossard, & Harrigan, 1983). The simple truth is this: Many schools always have and continue to reach traditionally underperforming students, raising their performance to levels beyond average and even to excellence (Haycock, 1998). Yet many continue to argue, in the face of the evidence of dramatic school achievement for children who live in poverty, that either nature or community culture, or still will—all resistant to or unreachable by educators—are the root and reasons for low achievement. We believe that an often-cited quote of Ronald Edmonds (1982) provides the answer: "We can whenever and whereof we choose, successfully teach all children, whose education is of importance to us." We believe, like Edmonds, that it is a matter of adult community and institutional will, committed to an irrefutable belief in the capacity of all students to learn at the highest levels.

The challenge is how we as a nation not only support success in the individual schools reported here but also in entire school districts (Kahle, 1997; Resnick & Hall, 1998). We know of no other intervention that holds broad-based promise to reach this goal than that proposed by Richardson and Anders in their chapter, that is, professional development that sustains instructional transformation and that both leads to and is supported by districtwide policies and practices (see also "Hey, Governors," 2003; Seattle Public Schools, 2003). All educational innovations, such as charter schools, parent intervention workshops, small schools, professional development, packaged literacy programs, and early childhood initiatives, rely ultimately on the teachers and administrators who shoulder the responsibility for educating urban schoolchildren and youth. To reach the goal of competence in districtwide policies and practices, however, will require at times painful decisions related to how schools are staffed, who is held responsible and accountable for change, "how performance is recognized and rewarded, how ineffective employees are removed, how services like information management and human resources operate, and how money is spent" (Hess, 2004, pp. 11-12).

The NUA is a group of educational activists who work hard to animate the principles and realize the promise of the elements described by

Richardson and Anders, as well as those that research suggests may lead to systemic improvement. The NUA Professional Development Model (NUAPDM) is based on the recognition that if all students are to meet high standards in mastering challenging material and instruction, teachers must understand the importance of "addressing the prior knowledge; the learning context; the connection among culture, language, and cognition; and the motivational patterns of all students, and must use the best instructional strategies for developing students' higher order skills and understanding" (NUA, 1999, p. 1).

On entering a school district that has requested its assistance, the NUA employs interventions that first study and then address obstacles to effective instruction, including systemic transformation from the classroom to the boardroom, from the business community to the statehouse. Using an instructional assessment or audit, NUA consultants first study how teachers, the school, and system focus on instruction and provide engaged academic time for students. The assessment also includes information about how stakeholders engage or disengage with the school community. This is predicated on the assumption that schools are a reflection of the purposes, values, and aims of the community. The assessment establishes the setting and rationale for the program reflected in the NUAPDM. The NUAPDM is designed to improve students' comprehension and literacy. After agreements on parameters and purposes of the initiative, consultants in an NUA project go into schools to demonstrate lessons in the application of higher order cognitive strategies in reading, writing, math, science, or other skill or subject areas, and then coach each teacher to use these strategies in their classrooms. In addition, the consultants help teachers to assess their instructional arrangements and to develop and implement plans for improving these arrangements. All of this is done with an eye on building local capacity for sustained change. The larger professional development framework within which an agreed on multischool and district-based initiative proceeds includes five sets of first-year activities that are sequenced and carried out as follows (NUA, 1999). (The seminars are more broadly outlined than the others because of space limitations.)

## The Framework

NUA professional development is based on the recognition that if all students are to meet high standards in mastering challenging content and skills, educators must understand the importance of addressing the prior knowledge; the learning context; the cultural, linguistic, and cognitive abilities; and the motivational patterns of all students, and must use the best instructional strategies for developing students' higher order skills and understanding.

## Seminars

A minimum of five large, all-day, cross-school seminars are held throughout the school year. A minimum of one third of each school's staff is recommended to attend the seminars to ensure successful schoolwide implementation of the strategies. It is required that the same teachers attend the sessions in yearly cohorts. Each cognitive strategy presented is modeled in large- and small-group sessions; is applied to real-life problems and content that appear in both narrative and expository material; stresses the importance of content knowledge in the enabling of higher order thinking and the skills of reading, writing, and mathematics; is linked to activities involving communication (writing and speaking) in curriculum areas; is presented in the context of cognitive research; and is considered with implications for teaching and learning, curriculum development, and assessment.

The rationale is given for each strategy introduced, consultants model its use, and then participants are given time to practice it during the seminars or in their own classrooms. A strong metacognitive and affective component is part of each seminar, especially during the first year of the program. NUA consultants are particularly sensitive to instructional issues related to ethnic and racial bias; gender bias; inclusion and different kinds of learners; attention to multiple intelligences; and English as a second language, English-language learner, and limited English proficient students.

## The Demonstration Lesson

Consultants visit the participants' schools to demonstrate to teachers how to apply the strategies presented in the large-group seminars in classroom instruction. Each NUA consultant demonstrates accelerated learning strategies that use the materials that the teachers are using with their students. School-based participants observe the demonstration lessons in designated classrooms.

## Consultant Site Visit

On many occasions consultants visit the schools to conduct activities that help participants with individual or schoolwide implementation issues, and that give participants with individual or schoolwide implementation issues opportunities to deal with knowledge, attitudes, and expectations and their own biases related to gender, race, ethnicity, and the teaching of higher-level thinking. This reflection attends directly to a root cause of the achievement gap discussed earlier—the will to succeed.

## Leadership Training

The literature is replete with studies that recognize the impact of principal support on instructional change. Principal support also is helpful in evaluating and extending appropriate modeling of instructional interventions. Recognizing this, the NUA works with participating principals to help them develop into instructional leaders.

## Community Advocacy

For schools to change, the community must engage in ways that make and sustain opportunities for transformation. It takes focused effort to, for example, change beliefs of parents and educational professionals about the learning potential of their children and students. It takes courage to develop sensitivity to the nascent conflicts about what parents want for their own children and what they want for "other people's children." The goal is to help the community recognize that if the citizens continue to place their personal and perceived interests of their own racial, ethnic, or socioeconomic group above the common interests of all of the residents, then the outcome may result in a political and policy crisis that may lead to social conflicts—potentially damaging to the overall health of the community. One such strategy is to help community stakeholders understand the direct relationship between school effectiveness and property values. Most successful neighborhoods understand it, but political leaders often overlook it and engage in "school bashing" that does not improve the schools or support the tax base. NUA advocates practical investments in sustainable change that includes addressing issues of governance, accountability, structural change required such as school size, and administrative and organizational arrangements that may facilitate or frustrate necessary changes.

# Realizing Potential

As Richardson and Anders have done so well in their chapter, identifying the combination of educational interactions that can unlock the immense potential that exists in classrooms of urban students requires an irrefutable belief in their potential, the desire to try all means to tap it, and the confidence and competence to connect to the students through what we all value most—personal identity. When our perceptions and expectations expand to recognize the power of culture and language in the learning process, we can explore the endless opportunities for creating the bridges that confident and competent teachers and students provide. These bridges allow students to see connections and relationships between their world and the world we are trying to open to them through education interventions. If we are to "teach to change the world," then we most certainly have to "teach students how to read the world" (Mahiri, 2004). For many urban students, educators often have to provide the motivation and interventions that enable and allow them the opportunity to pursue their dreams of success. What is required is a call to action—reinforcing for all educators the responsibilities they take on when working in urban school systems. They must accept those responsibilities. The whole community must support them—not with comfort no matter what the results, but with convictions, resources, and mutual accountability.

The poem that follows was written by an African American 10th-grade student at Arlington High School, Indianapolis, Indiana, who was taught by a white language arts teacher how to read the world. He came into her class underperforming several years below grade-level standards. Many of his previous teachers did not believe in his capacity to learn sufficiently to enter a college or university of his choice. He is presently a junior at a four-year college in the midwestern United States.

My Stream of Consciousness

You think that I don't know that you think
I got an F because I'm lazy and indifferent.
But maybe I'm just underchallenged and underappreciated.
Deep down I am begging you to teach me
To learn and create—not just to memorize and regurgitate.
I'm asking you to help me find my own truth.
I'm asking you to help me find my own beauty.
We need a miracle in public education
One for every kid who subconsciously wants
To be pushed to the edge/taken to the most extreme limits.
I want you to make my brain work in a hundred different ways every day.
I'm asking you to make my head ache with knowledge—spin with ideas.
I want you to make my mind my most powerful asset.

—Siem Tesfaslase

# REFERENCES

Adams, M.J. (1990). *Beginning to read: Thinking and learning about print.* Cambridge, MA: MIT Press.

Bowen, W.G., & Bok, D. (1998). *The shape of the river: Long-term consequences of considering race in college and university admissions.* Princeton, NJ: Princeton University Press.

Cooper, E.J. (2004). The pursuit of equity and excellence in educational opportunity. In D. Lapp, C. Collins-Block, E.J. Cooper, J. Flood, N. Roser, & V. Tinajero (Eds.), *Teaching all the children: Strategies for developing literacy in an urban setting* (pp. 12-30). New York: Guilford.

Council of Great City Schools. (2003). *Beating the odds: A city-by-city analysis of student performance and achievement gaps on state assessments: Results from the 2001–2002 school year.* Washington, DC: Author. Retrieved October 15, 2004, from http://www.cgcs.org/pdfs/bto3.pdf

Darling-Hammond, L. (2000). Teacher quality and student achievement: A review of state policy evidence. *Educational Policy Analysis Archives, 8*(1). Retrieved October 15, 2004, from http://epaa.asu.edu/epaa/v8n1

Delpit, L.D. (1995). *Other people's children: Cultural conflict in the classroom.* New York: New Press.

Edmonds, R. (1982). Programs of school improvement: An overview. *Educational Leadership, 40*(3), 4-12.

Haycock, K. (1998). *Thinking K–16* (Vol. 3, No. 2). Washington, DC: Education Trust.

Hess, F. (2004). *Common sense school reform.* New York: Palgrave Macmillan.

Hey, governors, learn what our city schools do that works [Editorial]. (2003, August 17). *Indianapolis Star News,* p. A25. Retrieved October 15, 2004, from http://www.nuatc.org/articles/pdf/indystar17aug03.pdf

Hilliard, A.G., III. (1991). Do we have the will to educate all children? *Educational Leadership, 49,* 31-36.

Hughes, M.S. (1995). *Achieving despite diversity: Why are some schools successful in spite of the obstacles they face? A study of effective and less effective elementary schools in West Virginia using quantitative and qualitative measures.* Charleston: West Virginia Education Fund.

Kahle, J.B. (1997). Systemic reform: Challenges and changes. *Science Educator, 6,* 1-6.

Kohn, A. (1998). Only for *my* kid: How privileged parents undermine school reform. *Phi Delta Kappan, 79,* 569-577. Retrieved October 15, 2004, from http://www.alfiekohn.org/teaching/ofmk.htm

Levine, D.L., & Cooper, E.J. (1991). The change process and its implications in teaching thinking. In L. Idol & B. Jones (Eds.), *Educational values and cognitive instruction: Implications for reform* (pp. 387-410). Hillsdale, NJ: Erlbaum.

Mahiri, J. (1998). *Shooting for excellence: African American and youth culture in new century schools.* New York: Teachers College Press.

Mahiri, J. (2004). *What they don't learn in school: Literacy in the lives of urban youth.* New York: Peter Lang.

National Urban Alliance. (1999). *Briefing notebook.* New York: Columbia University Teachers College.

Ogbu, J. (2003). *Black American students in an affluent suburb: A study of academic disengagement.* Mahwah, NJ: Erlbaum.

Resnick, L.B., & Hall, M.W. (1998). Learning organizations for sustainable education reform. *Daedalus, 127,* 89-118.

Sanders, W.L., & Rivers, J.C. (1996). *Cumulative and residual effects of teaching on future students: Value-added research and assessment.* Knoxville: University of Tennessee.

Seattle Public Schools. (2003). *Eliminating the achievement gap—A report to the community.* Seattle, WA: Author. Retrieved October 15, 2004, from http://www.seattleschools.org/area/eag/rep_comm.pdf

Singham, M. (1998, September). The canary in the mine: The achievement gap between black and white students. *Phi Delta Kappan, 80,* 8-15.

Sizemore, B., Brossard, C., & Harrigan, B. (1983). *An abashing anomaly: The high-achieving predominately black elementary schools.* Pittsburgh, PA: University of Pittsburgh Press.

Thernstrom, A., & Thernstrom, S. (2003). *No excuses: Closing the racial gap in learning.* New York: Simon & Schuster.

Zinn, H. (2003). *A people's history of the United States: 1492–present.* New York: HarperCollins.

CHAPTER 15

# Culture and Language: Bidialectical Issues in Literacy

*Carol D. Lee*

anguage is the primary medium of communication for humans. It is also the primary symbol system through which we as humans reason (C. Taylor, 1985; Turner, 1996). Sociolinguists make the case that as human beings we create and sustain interpersonal relationships and position social realities, in part, through face-to-face interactions through language (Bakhtin, 1981; Cook-Gumperz, 1986; Fairclough, 1992; Gee, 1991). In different historical epochs, new technologies have reconfigured how person-to-person interactions take place—writing letters, talking on the phone (some that allow speakers to see one another as they talk), communicating through synchronous and asynchronous time over the Internet, video conferencing, and so forth (Alvermann & Hagood, 2000; Eisenstein, 1979; New London Group, 1996; Scribner, 1997). As Gee (2000) notes, "social and institutional order is the product of moment-by-moment intricacies of social and verbal interaction that produce and reproduce that order" (p. 195).

Literacy may be defined as reasoning through language, both oral and text based. Literate practices take place in many contexts, with different norms for participation (Barton, 1994; Barton & Hamilton, 1998; Gasden & Wagner, 1995; Heath, 1983; McLaughlin, 1989; Moss, 1994b; Resnick & Resnick, 1977; Ward, 1971). There are subject matter literacies with highly specialized norms for argumentation, text analysis, and the kinds of problems that are deemed relevant. There are literate practices outside school and professional communities. Examples include literate practices within urban gang communities (Conquergood, 1997), hip hop communities (Rose, 1994), technology-rich communities of practice (Internet communication, computer games, Web design; see Gee, 2000), and religious communities (such as doctrina in some Latino Catholic churches; Baquedano-Lopez, 2001). Each of these communities values specialized ways of using language that serve as indices of membership (Bakhtin, 1986; Gee, 2000/2001; Gilyard, 1991; Goodwin, 1991). Literate practices are cultural.

By cultural, I mean these practices have a routine, often intergenerational quality and serve as indices of belief systems and a sense of identity as either a member or peripheral participant in a defined community. These communities may be defined by ethnicity or race, the use of a particular national language or language variety (e.g., varieties of Spanish or Africanized Englishes such as African American English [AAE]), religion, profession, discipline, or interests. This chapter will focus specifically on relationships among speaking one of the many dialects of American English, engagement in literate practices, and opportunities to learn particular ways of reading and writing in schools.

Societies have different attitudes about language variation. In many societies, speaking multiple national languages is encouraged. That is not the case in the United States (Ferguson & Heath, 1981). Hymes (1981) observes, "it may sometimes seem that there are only two kinds of language in the United States, good English and bad" (p. v). However, even in countries that value multiple national languages, there may also be attitudes toward dialects within a national language that reflect social hierarchies based on race, ethnicity, or class. In the United States, there are very naive attitudes about the range of variation in the dialects of spoken English. Referring to the range of national languages and dialects of English spoken in the United States, Hymes (1981) says, "the United States is a country rich in many things, but poor in knowledge of itself with regard to language" (p. v). Certain regional dialects are viewed as more prestigious than others. For example, Bostonian English is often viewed as more prestigious than Appalachian English or the features of English that characterize a range of Southern speakers. Dialects may differ with regard to vocabulary ("soda" in New York, "pop" in Chicago), phonology, syntax (e.g., use of copula or habitual be and use of double negative in AAE; use of a-prefixing in Appalachian English, as in "And we's a-gonna chop the coon out if it was in there, I's a kinda halfway thought maybe it just treed a possum or something"; see Wolfram & Christian, 1976, p. 181), as well as ways of using language in particular contexts (use of "sir" or "ma'am" in the South; or engagement in playful forms of ritual insult among speakers of African American Vernacular English [AAVE]; see Wolfram, 1981; Wolfram, Adger, & Christian, 1999). Some dialects include hybrids of several national languages (such as Tex-Mex) or dialects within the same language, such as Puerto Rican English. Other variations include Creoles such as the Gullah or Geechee language of the South Carolina low country (Wolfram et al., 1999). (A Creole is a language that began as a pidgin, with restricted uses, among people who did not share a common language, but over time gained more broad usage as the systematic native language of a community.) The point is that there is tremendous variation in dialects of English, and there are many complex issues involved in understanding how they are taken up in language arts instruction. It is interesting, however, that in a country like China, which has many dialects of Chinese (Mandarin, Cantonese, Pekingese), each of which is mutually unintelligible (Ball & Farr, 2003), such variation in national dialects does not appear to interfere with students' abilities to learn to read and write. All students, other than those who speak Mandarin, must essentially learn what is tantamount to a new language when they enter school and are learning to read. It is equally interesting that internationally the United States ranks lower than many other industrialized countries in the degree to which SES predicts academic achievement.

There are many folk theories about language variation, including dialect variation, that are both implicitly and explicitly articulated within U.S. society. Because teachers (elementary and high school) have so little training about language, it is not surprising that teachers are likely to share these common folk theories. I will briefly discuss each of these folk theories because they have implications for the teaching of the English language arts (see also Brock, Boyd, & Moore, 2003).

1. *Some dialects are linguistically superior and more complex than others.* Noted sociolinguist Walt Wolfram (1981) states, "Language scholars take as axiomatic that the speech variety acquired by a given ethnic group has no relation to the physical or mental characteristics of that group" (p. 55). Among the classic studies that document the linguistic complexity of a so-called nonstandard dialect, AAVE, are Labov's *Language in the Inner City* (1972) and Smitherman's *Talkin and Testifying* (1977). These and a host of other studies document the systematic and contextual nature of phonology, syntax, vocabulary, genres, and social registers in AAVE (Baugh, 1983; Mitchell-Kernan, 1981; Mufwene, Rickford, Bailey, & Baugh, 1998). For a review of the structure and pragmatics of U.S. English dialects, see Wolfram et al. (1999) and Wolfram and Schilling-Estes (1998).

2. *There are mainstream and nonmainstream dialects, and never the twain shall meet.* The notion of mainstream language is a social construction. As such, it is subject to negotiation and change over time. There are at least three arenas in which so-called mainstream and nonmainstream dialects are taken up in hybrid practices. In advertising and popular media, vocabulary, syntactic forms, and prosodic patterns of AAE are strategically

employed to sell ideas. In youth culture, AAE holds a dominating influence over language use (Smitherman, 1973). This was also evident in the blues, in rhythm and blues, and in current hip hop. The popularity of white rapper Eminem is a clear current example. In canonical literature, the language of everyday experience is often captured in service of literary ends. As Alice Walker (1988) describes the protagonist of her Pulitzer Prize–winning novel, *The Color Purple*,

> Celie speaks in the voice and uses the language of my step-grandmother, Rachel, an old black woman I loved. Did she not exist; or in my memories of her, must I give her the proper English of, say, Nancy Reagan?
>
> And I say, yes, she did exist, and I can prove it to you, using the only thing she, a poor woman, left me to remember her by—the sound of her voice. Her unique pattern of speech. Celie is created out of language. In *The Color Purple*, you see Celie because you "see" her voice. To suppress her voice is to complete the murder of her. And this, to my mind, is an attack upon the ancestors, which is, in fact war against ourselves. (pp. 63–64)

Writers such as Paul Laurence Dunbar, Sterling Brown, Zora Neale Hurston, Langston Hughes, Alice Walker, Amiri Baraka, Haki Madhubuti, Sonia Sanchez, and August Wilson routinely incorporate and sculpt AAVE forms in their works (Jones, 1991). In each of these arenas, a nonstandard dialect assumes a privileged and marked position in communication.

3. *So-called nonmainstream dialects interfere with students' abilities to read and write well.* During the 1960s and 1970s, many ethnic and racial groups, particularly those living in poverty (characterized not only by phenotypic features but also language, particularly vernacular, use) were defined as "culturally deprived." Reading instruction programs such as DISTAR were used to overcome presumed deficits in language of such students (Bereiter & Engelmann, 1966). Presumed "mainstream" pronunciation and sentence structures were taught through scripted direct instruction. Readers were developed using controlled vocabulary with phonetic spellings to teach emergent reading. Particular features of AAE phonology were presumed to interfere with students' abilities to pronounce words correctly. Orr (1987) argued that AAE interfered with black students' abilities to reason mathematically (see Baugh, 1988, for a critique of Orr). Thus there has been a history of research and interventions based on the assumption that nonmainstream dialects interfere with learning to read (Stotsky, 1999). I will take up this assertion in more detail in a later section of this chapter.

4. *Members of ethnic or regional groups all speak the same dialect.* Studies of language variation consistently document the diversity of language use among members of particular speech communities. Issues related to age, gender, region, education, and income levels influence language use within a given dialect or variety of national language. People are known to code switch, moving back and forth in the use of dialect, register, or national language, depending on the pragmatic demands of the social context. This means, for example, that one cannot assume that all black people speak AAVE or AAE for that matter. (Orlando Taylor makes a distinction between AAE and its vernacular variety.) The same black person may speak AAVE in familial settings, the register or social language of physics at work, and the English of Wider Communication (Smitherman, 2000c) in court or professional settings. Young children have been known to code switch dialect or register in make-believe play in preschool settings. This in-group variation and strategic code switching across ages suggest that schools often underconceptualize the complexity and range of language resources that students (especially black and brown speakers of nonmainstream dialects and national languages other than English) bring to classroom tasks (Morgan, 1993).

5. *Dialects and language varieties remain the same over time.* Norms for appropriateness in language use within a national language and across dialects change over time. Thus what may be considered "correct" grammar in one historical period may be quite different in another. For example, the syntax underlying "It is I" is considered correct in terms of school grammar. However, few Americans use it. Even in classrooms, it is likely if the teacher asks, "Is that you, Jabari?" that Jabari will answer, "It's me," with no reprimand or correction from the teacher. In fact, in most settings, to use the syntax "It is I" will position speakers as those who think they are somehow better than others. Any study of the evolution of English as a language, from its origins in Great Britain to what is now known as World Englishes (Bamgbose, Banjo, & Thomas, 1997; Schneider, 1996) (i.e., Nigerian English, Indian English, Australian English, etc.) makes clear that English, as is the case with any national language, is dynamic. As Wolfram et al. (1999) note,

> multiple negation was an acceptable structure for English in the past. During the Old English and Middle English periods in the history of English, the only way certain negative sentences could be formed was through the use of double negatives.... The change to favoring the use of a single negative in sentences like "They can't do anything" is a relatively recent development. (p. 13)

Changes may come from relationships with other nation states or institutions (such as the influence of the Normans of France and the Latin of the world Catholic church on the evolution of British English) as well as from changes in economics, politics, and the general social order. These same observations can be made about dialects within national languages as well. Lay audiences (including teachers, policymakers, and boards of education) often presume that the structures and phonology of the Standard English taught in schools are somehow a holy grail of correctness that never changes. I believe this is one of the reasons that teachers, parents, and policymakers get so emotional over issues of language policy in schools (e.g., the debate over the decision of the Oakland School Board to include Ebonics in instruction to improve educational outcomes; see Perry & Delpit, 1998; Smitherman, 1981, 1998, 2000a).

6. *The only influence on dialects of English is British English.* In many subtle ways, the United States, perhaps because of its short history in relation to other nations in the world, still seems to view Great Britain as its primary intellectual ancestry. In the early part of the 20th century, there were debates in U.S. universities about the appropriateness of American Literature as a course of study in English departments. To this day, an English major in an American university is likely to have a great deal of exposure to the literature from the British isles, in contrast to other literatures of the World Englishes. In virtually every U.S. high school, students are required to take one year of American Literature as well as one year of British Literature (Applebee, 1993). This subtle preoccupation with Great Britain is one reason that dialects such as Bostonian English or the English of the Eastern New England region are often viewed as superior to other dialects, such as African American Vernacular English (AAVE) and those of the southern regions of the United States. This folk theory regarding American English plays an interesting role in the country's attitude toward AAVE (Holloway, 1990). There is a significant body of research documenting the West African origins of many features of AAVE, including syntax, phonology, prosody, lexicon, and speech genres (Mufwene, 1993; Rickford & Rickford, 1976). In an ironic way, many people of African descent in the United States face a double marker of difference—skin color and language—both reminders of America's sordid history with the African continent.

## Interrogating Assumptions About Language Difference

A commonly held assumption about speakers of nonstandard American English dialects is that the language experiences in their families are not sufficiently rich to prepare them for the demands of reading and writing in school (Bernstein, 1970). This is especially the case for young children entering school (Anderson, Wilson, & Fielding, 1988). This assumption is reflected in the following observation by Wilkinson and Silliman (2000) in the chapter "Classroom Language and Literacy Learning" from the *Handbook of Reading Research, Volume 3*:

> Because prior school experiences are combined with home interactions, some children enter school knowing about how to use language for a variety of "school-like" purposes. They have expectations about classrooms. Because not all students learn the "rules of the game" of mainstream education, some have difficulty knowing how to participate appropriately. They may also have less experience with a variety of literacy functions and forms. Students' participation in school activities, such as reading aloud, question and answer exchanges with teachers, and receiving evaluation of their discourse contributions from teachers, determines their access to learning. The educational failure of some students may be caused in part by differences in the communicative patterns between students and teachers who come from different cultural backgrounds. (p. 340)

In that same handbook, Purcell-Gates (2000) synthesizes the literature on family literacy practices, including the research studies that show positive correlations between particular ways that middle-class families are presumed to use language and achievement in early reading. These family literate practices include "open-ended questions, function/attribute questions, and expansions; respond[ing] appropriately to children's attempts to answer these questions" (Purcell-Gates, 2000, p. 857; Whitehurst et al., 1988). Purcell-Gates makes an important observation about studies during the 1980s linking home environment, IQ, and language development. She notes, "However, findings from study after study documented that SES, when examined as separate from specific home environment factors, was a weak or negative predictor (White, 1982). Rather, investigators identified specific home practices...that varied within SES and that were much more explanatory of academic achievement" (p. 854). This is important because it situates the possible explanatory mechanism in practices rather than groups. Gutiérrez and Rogoff (2003) make a similar argument about the implications for instruction of presumed learning styles among language and ethnic minorities (Irvine & York, 1995). I am not aware of any nationally representative sample that documents the range of home-language practices with young children that are typical of a majority of low-income families or families of a particular speech community or language group. As has been typical of research on the implications of language differences for instruction, findings are based on small sample sizes and then extrapolated to entire populations. In addition, the research typically cited does not address the ways that demands of school-based literacies have changed over time (see Kaestle, Damon-Moore, Stedman, Tinsley, & Trollinger, 1991; Resnick & Resnick, 1977; Scribner, 1997) and what that has meant for home-to-school transitions for low-income and ethnic minority families. Studies by Clark (1984), Hammer (2001), and D. Taylor and Dorsey-Gaines (1988) document very different patterns of language interactions than are typically presented in the research on family literate practices in low-income African American families. These are complex issues, and their complexity is not often addressed in either research or practice. Teale (1986) notes that "virtually all children in a literate society like ours have numerous experiences with written language before they ever get to school" (p. 192). By contrast, in an ethnographic study of a low-income, nonliterate Appalachian family, Purcell-Gates (1995) found that children did not see print as a meaning-making phenomenon. These findings suggest that research is needed to document the range of ways of using language, in this case in terms of dialect variation in American English among families, especially low-income and ethnic minority families, and frameworks for considering the instructional implications of these language patterns.

What I find most problematic about the line of reasoning about home-language deficits as limiting factors in literacy achievement is the implicit assumption that the onus of responsibility is on children and families (Traub, 1999). This is not to deny that children and families bear important responsibilities for children's learning. However, schools are sites of professional expertise (just as hospitals are sites of professional medical expertise). This means, I think, that schools as organizations and teachers as professionals should have sufficient knowledge of the demands of school-based literate practices to adjust the nature of face-to-face interactions in classrooms (Haycock, 1998). They should have knowledge to scaffold support for literacy learning by connecting with the prior knowledge and experiences that students bring (Steffensen, Joag-Dev, & Anderson, 1979). I believe this to be the case even when a class has students with diverse language backgrounds. The personal backgrounds of teachers (in terms of ethnicity, race, language use, or SES) should not be the determining factor of how they teach students, because teaching should be based primarily on professional knowledge rather than personal knowledge (Anders & Evans, 1994; Baron, Tom, & Cooper, 1985; DeMeis & Turner, 1978; Rist, 1970). One classic example of the limits of professional knowledge in helping language minority students to learn school-based literate tasks is the research on sharing time by Michaels (1981) and Cazden (Cazden, Michaels, & Tabor, 1985). I will discuss the details of this work in a later section of this chapter.

Fundamentally, there is nothing in the nature of learning to read and write that requires answering known questions, interpreting as a command what is in one dialect an indirect request in structure but semantically intended as a directive, or answering questions only when asked. There is no reason that students cannot learn to make decontextualized accounts of experience, even when they are used to not mentioning certain details in familial exchanges because of presumed shared knowledge. The demands of translating from contextualized accounts to decontextualized accounts spiral as students progress in learning to write different genres and to construct arguments within different subject matters. I have very smart graduate students who struggle to learn to write in the specialized and highly decontextualized register of the academic research essay.

This attention to the implications of dialect and language differences for instruction has been triggered by the increasing ethnic, racial, and language diversity within the U.S. population. The attention to this demographic data is based on another assumption, namely, that ethnic, racial, and language differences make teaching more difficult. This observation is reflected again in Wilkinson and Silliman (2000):

> As classroom composition changed substantially during the last decade of the 20th century, the focus of research questions changed to reflect: (a) aspects of second language acquisition and their impact on literacy learning...; (b) African American dialect differences and effects of variations on reading, writing, and classroom participation...; and (c) promoting literacy learning in children and youth with atypical language development...including second language learners with atypical language development. (p. 340)

This is another common line of reasoning. It does not address the fact that this has always been a nation of immigrants, giving deference to the original native population who may themselves have immigrated in ancient times to the Americas. Relations among European immigrants were constructed as important differences during the 19th and early decades of the 20th centuries. Some of the same assumptions regarding deficits in family interactions and ways of using language were popular in explaining the achievement gap of immigrant communities at that time (Tyack, 1974). During these same periods, people of African, Asian, Latin American, Pacific Islander, and Native American origin were enrolled in public schools. However, the educational experiences of these ethnic groups (who spoke different national languages as well as different varieties of English) were not the purview of educational research, except to monitor differences in graduation rates but not levels of achievement in reading or writing (see Resnick & Resnick, 1985). The broader context of ignoring the educational experiences of these groups in the early part of the 20th century includes the development of IQ tests as a means of sorting the intellectual capacity of populations based on race, ethnicity, gender, and SES (Gould, 1981; Hernstein & Murray, 1994); and controversies over what kind of education was appropriate for these populations, based on different goals for education (see J. Anderson, 1988; Apple, 1979; Apple & Beyer, 1988; DuBois, 1973; McDermott, 1987; Varenne & McDermott, 1998; Woodson, 1969). This was the same period, for example, in which Native American children were taken from their families on reservations and placed in schools explicitly organized to indoctrinate the children into being Christian and socialized into European American social norms. The point here is that the challenges to schools posed by students who differ from a presumed European American middle-class norm are nothing new and have been endemic to public education in the United States for at least the last several hundred years.

In addition, as stated earlier, it places the onus of responsibility on students to come to school having appropriated particular discourse norms, rather than on teachers and schools to adapt to the discursive resources and world experiences that students bring. These presumed school-based discursive norms bear little relationship to the discursive norms of the disciplines into which students are being apprenticed (see Jones, 1991; Ochs, Jacoby, & Gonzales, 1994). For that reason, there is no a priori requirement that instructional talk be limited to the range of discursive practices that characterize U.S. classrooms (Cazden, John, & Hymes, 1972).

This first prevailing assumption further specifies that sources of the problem are, in part, attributable to differences between oral and written language. It is presumed that children from middle-class homes who speak what is called Standard English are apprenticed into forms of language use that more closely approximate what students will meet in the demands of written forms in learning to read. This logic is captured in the following statement from Purcell-Gates (2000) on family literacy:

> The language one reads when reading books and written texts of different genres is not the same language one speaks or hears. Written language differs in specific and identifiable ways from oral (Chafe & Danielewicz, 1987). Thus developing readers and writers need to learn the different linguistic registers of the written texts they will read and write. Written language differs from oral along a continuum reflecting degree of decontextualization and formality as well as genre-related style. (p. 856)

Purcell-Gates is discussing these issues in relation to emergent literacy and the role of children's discursive interactions with their families (especially as relates to storybook reading as preparation for learning to read in school). However, I take issue with this fundamental claim in the broader context of students' literacy learning. While there is no question that written genres and oral genres are not the same, the range of distinction is quite context and genre dependent. In many genres of canonical literature, especially poetry, the novel, and drama—in some traditions—authors are attempting to capture the nuances and prosody of oral language interactions. Gee (1989) has described the emergent nature of metalinguistic knowledge of a literary story structure, using one of the students from Michaels's (1981) study of sharing time. Gee demonstrates the nascent literary quality of an oral story in a vernacular dialect deemed by the teacher to be ill-formed. In Lee's (1993, 1995a, 1995b, 2000) work, elements of metalinguistic knowledge of African American speakers are explicitly scaffolded to support students' abilities to comprehend complex canonical literary texts. The point is that there are complex issues involved in understanding how students' discursive practices in their families and communities are taken up to support learning to read and to write, and these issues are not sufficiently examined in the research literature or in practice. The problem may not be so much the limitations of language use in the families of children from low-income backgrounds who speak vernacular dialects. Rather, the problem may be with the ability of the research community and teachers to recognize what in these language practices may be generative for literacy learning. I suspect the latter to be the case.

In the following sections of this chapter, I will discuss the research findings, observations of practices, and unresolved issues about the implications of dialect variation among U.S. English speakers in terms of instructional discourse, reading comprehension, and writing instruction. I will illustrate salient issues using AAE as the primary case. I use AAE as the primary case because there has been more educational research on this dialect than any other spoken in the United States. Issues related to AAE illustrate the same positioning and debates around other dialects of American English based on ethnicity, such as Puerto Rican English (Wolfram, 1974; Zentella, 1981), Appalachian English (Wolfram & Christian, 1976), Vietnamese English (Wolfram & Hatfield, 1984), and varieties of American Indian English (Leap, 1993; Wolfram, Christian, Potter, & Leap, 1979), as well as dialects based on region.

## Dialect Variation and Reading Instruction

Most of the theorizing about dialect interference with reading addressed the decoding demands of early reading and focused on children who were speakers of AAVE (Rickford & Rickford, 1995). Reading research has documented the important role of fluency in learning to read and comprehend (Sulzby & Teale, 1991). If readers have to concentrate most of their short-term memory on recognizing or sounding out words, then they do not have the mental attention to simultaneously try to make sense of what they are reading. This core tenet of research on early reading is, however, complex because we also know that semantic knowledge (of topics and often by extension of vocabulary) can also compensate for word recognition problems. There is, however, a delicate balance of how much skill in one area can compensate for lack of skill in the other. Recognizing these nuances is important in evaluating the mixed findings on dialect interference in reading among AAVE speakers.

The argument went something like this. Because certain phonemes were not articulated by AAVE speakers, children would make no distinctions in pronunciation between words like *told* and *toll*, *mist* and *miss*, *four* and *foe*, *pin* and *pen*, *feel* and *fill*; and words like *breath*, *mouth*, and *bath* would be pronounced as though they ended in /f/ (Labov, 1995, p. 47). It was also claimed that certain tense markers in Standard English would not be recognized by AAVE speakers. This line of reasoning is complicated by a number of factors. First, all members of a speech community do not employ typical features of the dialect in all instances where they might be applicable. Thus that AAVE speakers use the /ed/ ending sometimes and not other times suggests that they are at least aware of its meaning. Second, the range of diversity in the use of typical features of a dialect is also influenced by the pragmatic demands of the context of talking (setting, interlocutors, social and power relationships among interlocutors, past experiences with other dialects, and the footing or perspective each interlocutor elects to bring to the exchange). Finally, speakers of vernacular dialects often have a better understanding of the mainstream dialect than vice versa (Wolfram et al., 1999).

Several studies have attempted to test this hypothesis of dialect interference (Baratz, 1969). Stewart (1969) created a set of AAVE dialect primers, but because of negative reactions from teachers and parents who saw the experiment as an attempt to introduce bad language practices, the experiments were never completed. In 1977, Houghton Mifflin produced a reading series that included African American literature and an audio-cassette of an AAVE adult speaker who served to introduce children to the materials. The Bridge program was developed by black psychologists Gary and Charlesetta Simpkins and black educator Grace Holt (Simpkins, Holt, & Simpkins, 1977). The program was tested in 27 classes ranging from grades 7 through 12. Students using Bridge gained an average of 6.2 months for 4 months of instruction, significantly greater than for the control group (Labov, 1995; Simpkins & Simpkins, 1981). The program was not one of artificially written dialect readers and included a focus on cultural socialization as well.

Other studies have documented that direct teaching of the phonology of Standard English did not improve reading achievement (Melmed, 1971; Rentel & Kennedy, 1971 [testing dialect interference with Appalachian dialect speakers]. Another set of studies examined the possible grammatical influence of dialect on reading comprehension. The thinking behind these studies was that the AAVE speaker must essentially translate a Standard English syntactical form into its AAVE counterpart to comprehend it. It was argued that this might not pose a problem at the level of an individual sentence, but the cumulative effect across a reading passage might pose problems. These hypotheses were not borne out by the research (Johnson & Simons, 1973; Sims, 1972). These studies used stories written in AAVE syntax and in Standard English syntax along with measures of oral fluency, recall, and comprehension. Labov (1970) used an experimental design with junior high school AAVE speakers and found that subjects were able to comprehend past tense markers about half of the time.

Others tested vocabulary interference based on cultural differences. Although the research in this area is the most limited, it is one that may be worthy of further study for a number of reasons. First, it is one basis on which to interrogate the claims made about the deficits of children who are members of marginalized ethnic and racial minorities, who speak vernacular dialects, and who will most often live in persistent, intergenerational poverty. That is, because of impoverished verbal interactions within their families and lack of experience with interactive, dialogic storybook reading at home, these children enter school with limited vocabularies and a lack of understanding of syntactic forms that are claimed to exemplify the kinds of texts they will be expected to learn to read in school (see the earlier quote from Purcell-Gates). Second, vocabulary is based on experience, the kinds of activities in which one routinely engages. Thus it is possible to look, in a more objective fashion, at practice (which is observable) rather than simplifying the meaning of patterns of phonology (difficulty distinguishing *pin* and *pen* is not the sole purview of AAVE speakers), syntax (such as subject–verb agreement), and prosody.

The logic of these early studies was to determine whether students' levels of understanding would differ from items based on a white middle-class sample if the experimenter selected vocabulary items that were within the experiences of students, in this case AAVE speakers. Hall and Guthrie

(1980) report the findings of the experiment carried out by Williams and Rivers (1972):

> They found that when the vocabulary on this test was changed so that it re-flected their experiential network, poor black children in the St. Louis pub-lic schools performed at a level comparable to the white middle-class sample on which the test was standardized. (p. 444)

These findings are similar to work on the limitations of traditional IQ tests (Hilliard, 1976; O. Taylor & Lee, 1987). That is, to what extent are findings on IQ tests related to the context and content of the tests rather than the innate ability of those tested. This research, though limited in scope, has implications for the selection of texts in instruction, an area that has been hotly contested in school districts (see McCarthy, 1990). The question may follow, whether using readings that include vocabulary with which children are familiar based on life experiences would make a differ-ence in reading achievement, especially in the early grades. This is not to imply that school should not be a site to expand significantly the range of children's deep knowledge of a wide range of vocabulary and topics. It is simply to suggest that the use of readings with familiar vocabulary may have some place in the development of children's reading capacities. This prem-ise itself is not really under question. But when the criteria for selection of texts involve issues of race and ethnicity, the debate becomes very intense (see Stotsky, 1999).

On these questions of dialect interference, Labov (1995) concluded, "The conclusion of most sociolinguists was that the semantic and structural differences between AAVE and other dialects were not great enough to be the primary causes of reading failure. Dialect differences affected education primarily as symbols of social conflict" (p. 49).

One interesting and perhaps crucial caveat from these studies is the in-fluence of situation, task, and setting on displays of children's talk, and by extension of children's (and others') competencies (Cole, Dore, Hall, & Dowley, 1978). Although designed to reexamine the findings of Williams and Rivers (1972) on the effects of vocabulary content (described earlier in this chapter), a study by Hall, Reder, and Cole (1975) introduces another sig-nificant set of variables into understanding the broader role of context on displays of competence. They designed an experiment to test "the effects of racial group membership and dialect on unstructured and probed recall for comprehension of simple stories" (Hall & Guthrie, 1980, p. 444). Hall and Guthrie (1980) describe the design of the study and its findings:

Thirty-two children, age 4 years 6 months, were the subjects for the experiment. Sixteen were black and an equal number were white. Subgroups of four children within each racial group were randomly assigned to the experimental conditions such that order of exposure to experimenter (black and white) and dialects (Standard English vs. Vernacular Black English) were counterbalanced. They found that whites performed better than blacks in SE; blacks performed better than whites in VBE; blacks tested in VBE were equivalent to whites tested in SE; and whites performed better in SE than in VBE. (p. 445)

Although a small study, its basic premises align with a more comprehensive framework for understanding the circumstances of displays of competence, in this case in the area of reading comprehension. The focus largely on the phonological, syntactic, lexical, and prosodic features of dialects as the explanatory mechanism for school failure in reading reflects a very narrow view of language and language competence. Linguists have consistently made the case that no dialect is inherently superior to another. Some have said that the only difference between a dialect and a language is that a language is backed up by an army. Wolfram et al. (1999) have noted,

there are some isolated dialects on the Southern seaboard, such as Tangier Island and Smith Island in Virginia and Maryland, and Ocracoke and Harkers Island on the Outer Banks of North Carolina, that are probably more difficult to comprehend in natural conversation for speakers of other varieties than African American Vernacular English. (p. 68)

# Dialect Variation Beyond the Morphological and Syntactic Levels

The early work with dialect readers and experiments to test the hypothesis of dialect interference as a cause of reading failure, particularly among African American children and adolescents, focused largely on language at the level of syntax, phonology, and vocabulary. More recent work has taken a very different orientation, looking at speech genres and their relationship to formal written genres.

Sociocultural research on the thinking practices that underlie everyday practices showed that people engage, for example, in mathematical reasoning as they shop (Lave, Murtaugh, & de la Rocha, 1984), in dairy factories as they approximate arrays in packing (Scribner, 1984), as semi-illiterate and illiterate Liberian tailors design patterns (Lave, 1977), or as semi-illiterate and illiterate Brazilian street children manage the tasks of selling candy on the street (Nunes, Schliemann, & Carraher, 1993).

Influenced by this body of research, Lee (1993, 1995a, 1995b, 2000, 2001) analyzed the problem-solving demands of reading literature broadly and of reading particular literary genres. Based on a long-standing body of research on speech genres within AAVE, Lee hypothesized that AAVE speakers produced and interpreted (obviously with different levels of expertise based on age, gender, and experience) metaphors, symbols, irony, satire, and unreliable narrators in oral genres such as signifying. *Signifying* is a form of ritual insult that is common among AAVE speakers (Mitchell-Kernan, 1981). However, in most instances, the strategies used in these everyday speech events are tacit. Lee developed a framework called Cultural Modeling to scaffold students' tacit knowledge developed in everyday settings to support response to literature.

In Cultural Modeling, teachers or curriculum designers select what are called *cultural data sets*. These are texts—in multiple media—from the everyday experiences of students that pose interpretive problems similar to those students will meet in canonical texts. Canonical texts in an instructional unit are organized around generative interpretive problems: symbolism, irony, satire, and use of unreliable narrators. The idea is to design units of instruction to give students extended practice with a particular interpretive problem (Smith & Hillocks, 1988). These problems are considered generative because they apply across traditional notions of genre. If a reader can recognize that a stretch of text should not be interpreted literally, but figuratively, and then reconstruct a warrantable meaning, that reader can attack a Keats poem, a Dostoevsky novel, or an August Wilson play. Units of instruction begin with the introduction of cultural data sets. Such data sets may include stretches of signifying dialogues, rap lyrics, rap videos, film clips, and TV or magazine ads. Discussions of these cultural data sets focus on how students understand the texts. The function of what Lee (1998) calls metacognitive instructional conversations is to apply public strategies that students use tacitly in one context to a new context.

As thinking strategies are made public with culturally familiar texts, students then move to apply those once tacit, now explicit strategies to canonical texts. Lee hypothesizes that reading literature requires several kinds of knowledge. These include strategic knowledge of the kinds of interpretive problems the reader will meet in a text and knowledge of the social codes operating in the text, that is, cultural models of what makes the humans in the literature act as they do. In Cultural Modeling, designers select as initial texts those for which the students are expected to have greater knowledge of the social codes operating in texts. With African American students, for example, this means beginning instruction with African

American canonical texts. Thus, students initially have extensive experiences in applying newly learned strategies in texts to which they bring relevant cultural knowledge. They then move to canonical texts where they now have greater experience in using literary strategies and can apply them to texts that are further removed from their personal experiences. In Cultural Modeling, Lee situates relevant prior cultural knowledge based on observations of students' life experiences and ways of using language, rather than assuming that because students are members of particular racial and ethnic groups, they will all have a particular set of life experiences or models of how the world works (Gutiérrez & Rogoff, 2003). For example, in a unit on symbolism, cultural data sets include "The Mask," a rap song by the Fugees, and "Sax Cantor Riff," a short film by noted African American filmmaker Julie Dash (who made the award-winning film *Daughters of the Dust*) from the HBO series *Subway Stories*. The initial anchoring texts are a short story by John Edgar Wideman, "Damballah" (actually a chapter from his novel *Damballah*), and Toni Morrison's *Beloved*. Texts that follow include chapters from Amy Tan's *The Joy Luck Club* ("Rice Husband" and "Ying, Ying"); William Faulkner's "A Rose for Emily" and "Wash"; Virginia Woolf's "A Haunted House"; poems by Emily Dickinson ("Because I Could Not Stop for Death"); Robert Hayden's "Runnagate, Runnagate"; Frances Harper's "The Slave Mother"; Robert Frost's "The Road Not Taken"; Dylan Thomas's "Do Not Go Gentle Into That Good Night"; and selections from Milton's *Paradise Lost* and Dante's *Inferno*.

In two studies, both in inner-city high schools working with African American students with histories of low achievement as measured by standardized assessments in reading, students, many of whom had reading scores in the bottom quartile, tackled such challenging canonical works. In the first study, in assessments designed to test their close reading of short stories that had not been read in class, students gained statistically significant change in pre to post scores compared with a control group. In the second study, a three-year intervention in an inner-city high school, students demonstrated strong competence in local assessments as well as schoolwide increases in the standardized assessment in reading used by the district.

An important contribution of Cultural Modeling is to conceptualize how to scaffold cultural models and uses of language at the level of speech genres situated in home and community experiences to support complex subject matter learning. Rather than looking for deficits, Cultural Modeling assumes that students bring strengths, and the challenge for teachers, researchers, and curriculum designers is to understand the semiotic potential of these strengths and their relationships to the demands of subject matter learning. Cultural

Modeling further calls for a fundamental reorganization of the English Language Arts curriculum at the high school level (Lee, 2004).

## Dialect Variation and Writing Instruction

In many ways, research on dialect variation and writing instruction is much more comprehensive in both scope and conceptualization than its counterpart in reading (Shaughnessy, 1977). This may be because researchers in written composition often have formal training in sociolinguistics. It may also be because of the proactive work of some professional organizations, such as the College Composition and Communication Conference (CCCC; 1974), an affiliate of the National Council of Teachers of English. CCCC has spearheaded several formal positions on the right of students to their own language (Smitherman, 1999). Several important and comprehensive reviews of the research on written composition and language variation are Ball (2002), Ball and Farr (2003), and Farr (1991). I have liberally drawn from all three in this chapter.

As is the case with reading, dialect influence in written composition may be seen at the level of syntax, vocabulary, overall register, and the structure of genres. In schools, the most common focus for speakers of vernacular dialects is syntax, the teaching of grammar, although, particularly at the higher grades, grammar is becoming taught less and less. Written composition in elementary and high schools is dominated by a focus on the writing process: brainstorming, writing drafts, editing (in many cases with peer feedback), rewriting, and proofing. Although this is the dominant orientation to teaching writing in K–12 schools, it has been critiqued. Delpit (1986, 1988, 1995) has argued that students from low-income communities who are speakers of vernacular dialects need explicit instruction in what she calls "the language of power." She further asserts that such students need to learn explicitly how to translate from their everyday language to academic discourses, situating each as appropriate in different contexts. In the writing process literature, explicit attention to the language of power would likely occur only in what are called minilessons, rather than as a foundational component of instruction. Some have argued that speakers of vernacular dialects need to learn to translate specific phonological and syntactic patterns from their everyday language to the language of academic discourse, because these will be represented in spelling and sentence structure in written composition for school (Patton-Terry, 2004).

Others have critiqued the writing process as taught in schools, suggesting a more complex view of the knowledge that writers need. Hillocks

(1986, 1995) emphasizes the genre-specific nature of knowledge that writers need. The demands of composing an argument are different from a narrative. In addition, the structure of arguments differs based on developmental differences (e.g, young children versus adolescents) as well as by subject matter. The structure of argumentation in physics is different from history or literature. Hillocks argues that students need knowledge of form, as reflected in genres. For each genre, writers develop declarative knowledge (that the form exists, an ability to describe its features), procedural knowledge (how to produce the form in written registers), and conditional knowledge (when to produce the appropriate forms). Based on principles of learning derived from cognitive and the learning sciences (Bransford, Brown, & Cocking, 2000), Hillocks (1975) called for the design of what he calls gateway activities that provide students with concrete experiences that require reflection on declarative, procedural, and conditional knowledge of form. Such gateway activities include working in small groups to describe a sea shell so another student in the group can recognize it, as preparation for decontextualized and elaborate descriptions required for good narrative writing; deducing claims, evidence, and warrants from pictures that carry within them evidence to argue for or against a position (e.g., deducing from the details in a cartoon whether the woman lying at the bottom of the stairs fell or was pushed) (see Hillocks, 1995, for fuller descriptions of gateway activities by genre).

Although Hillocks does not make a case for the special effectiveness of this approach for speakers of vernacular dialects or English-language learners, the framework I believe addresses, in pedagogically specific ways, what Delpit implies when she calls for teachers to make the rules of the language game explicit. Hillocks offers an orientation toward being explicit that is fundamentally different from teaching from models, more open-ended constructivist approaches to the writing process, and from scripted approaches to teach the writing process as a simple series of linear steps. Hillocks has routinely tested this approach and taught preservice teachers to design teaching activities based on the framework in an inner-city elementary school in Chicago.

Lee (Lee, Rosenfeld, Mendenhall, Rivers, & Tynes, 2003) has extended Hillocks's model to address how teachers can scaffold the discursive knowledge that AAVE speakers bring to elementary classrooms to teach narrative composition. Using the Cultural Modeling framework to teach narrative writing, drawing on existing sociolinguistic research (Champion, 1998, 2003; Mitchell-Kernana, 1981; Smitherman, 1977), Lee hypothesized that AAVE-speaking children would be exposed to oral storytelling in their families and extended social networks where features of what Smitherman (1994, 2000b) calls the African American Rhetorical Tradition (AART) would be common. The cultural data sets (or gateway activities, to use Hillocks's term) presented to elicit detailed narrative accounts included pictures that captured representative scenes or scenarios from African American life as experienced in many communities. These included pictures by the famed African American artist Annie Lee (see www. annieleearts.com). For example, in her painting *Six No Uptown*, a group of African American women are sitting around the kitchen table playing Bid Whiz. Lee hypothesized that the students in her study would recognize this scene, could imagine the dialogue of the women, the sound of the cards hitting the table, and the noise and smells of the kitchen. Using as prompts pictures, clips from films with African American characters telling dramatic stories, and presentations by African American storytellers, children in grades 3 and 6 produced written narratives. The narratives were evaluated by a team of researchers for the presence of features of AART and for primary trait scoring (Cooper & Odell, 1999). Findings indicated a high use of AART and high evaluations of quality of narrative writing.

Several long-term research programs have documented ways that features of AAVE are successfully taken up in the writing of elementary and high school students. These studies have focused on what Smitherman (1994, 2000b) calls the AARTs: (a) rhythmic, dramatic, evocative language; (b) reference to color-race-ethnicity (when the topic does not call for it); (c) use of proverbs, aphorisms, and Biblical verses; (d) sermonic tone; (e) direct-address-conversational tone; (f) cultural references; (g) ethnolinguistic idioms; (h) verbal inventiveness, unique nomenclature; (i) cultural values and community consciousness; and (j) field dependency.

Smitherman (1994, 2000a) carried out a longitudinal study of samples of student writing on the National Assessment of Educational Progress (NAEP). This was a follow-up to earlier research she had conducted on the 1969 and 1979 NAEP essays, along with earlier research by Scott (1981). Smitherman investigated several questions: (1) whether there were any differences in the use of AAVE syntax in student writing from the earlier study to the 1984 and 1988/1989 NAEP writing samples; (2) whether there were any relationships between the production of AAVE syntax and an African American discourse style; and (3) whether there were any relationships between the presence of features of the AART and primary trait and holistic scoring. Smitherman found no relationship between AAVE syntax and African American discourse style; the higher the presence of African American discourse style, the higher the rating on both primary trait and holistic scoring; African American students performed better with imaginative narrative writing than expository forms.

Smitherman's findings are powerful for several reasons. First, her design was rigorous. Her sample size was large (867 essays), so that generalizations from it are stronger. There could be no researcher bias in the scoring of the writing samples, because they had already been evaluated by NAEP (Smitherman was using a secondary data set in this study), and scoring for the presence of African American discourse features included interrater reliability checks. Just as Gee (1989) had pointed out in a discourse analysis of a small sample of oral stories from the research on sharing time by Michaels (1981) and Cazden (Cazden et al., 1985), in narrative writing African American discourse features had complex literary value and were associated with a quality of writing that would be expected for much older children. In both cases, features of African American discourse were deemed to improve student writing, not detract from it. Smitherman's research is part of a larger body of research on composition that documents how the linguistic strengths of oral African American discourse can be proactively taken up to improve students' academic writing (Ball, 1992, 1995b; Dyson, 2003; Redd, 1994). This body of work represents a very different orientation to relationships between oral language competencies among speakers of vernacular dialects of English and academic writing than the deficit views that have dominated research on both reading and writing suggest.

Although Smitherman notes the strengths of narrative writing (although not exclusively), Ball has documented preferences in expository structures by African American high school students. Ball (1992, 1995a, 1995b; Ball & Farr, 2003) observed three expository structures used by the African American high school students in her sample. These expository structures were not taught by teachers but were used by students because of their own preferences. These preferred styles include circumlocution, narrative interspersion, and recursion. In narrative interspersion, "the speaker or writer intersperses a narrative within expository text" (Ball, 1992, p. 511). The function of the narrative is to communicate and emphasize the point of the essay. In recursion, "the speaker discusses a topic and then restates it using different words or images" (Ball, 1992, p. 511). Ball illustrates the pattern of recursion with examples from a Martin Luther King, Jr., speech. Among the important findings in Ball's research on African American expository styles is that these features are present in both informal everyday talk, as well as in formal settings of political oratory (such as the Martin Luther King speech) and the argument structures routinely employed by African American ministers. In both the political and the religious settings, these structures are employed both orally and in writing (see Moss, 1994a, 2001). To test the implications of these preferred expository styles, Ball and Cooks (1998) designed an intervention that used Web-based technology to support student writing in both school and community organizations, and that served as a forum for preservice teacher education.

These reported links between oral and written forms provide an interesting arena for intervention design as carried out by Ball and Cooks (1998), Lee (Lee et al., 2003), and Mahiri (1996, 1998). In some respects, one source of inspiration for such design work in teaching written composition is the studies on sharing time by Michaels and Cazden and the follow-up by Gee (1989) and Champion (1998). Sharing time is a routine activity in primary classrooms. Students are asked to bring an object from home and then to tell a story orally about that object. The purpose of the activity is to help children bridge their more contextualized stories of personal experience to the more decontextualized features of academic writing. Michaels and Cazden found that the white middle-class teacher responded differently to the stories told by white children and those told by black children. Michaels argued that the teacher did not understand the underlying structure of the black children's stories and therefore did not know how to scaffold their stories. She posited that the middle-class white children told *topic centered* stories (with a linear sequencing of events and thematic cohesion) and the black children told *topic associative* stories (where events were not necessarily sequenced in a linear fashion and where the point of view shifted to reflect the point of view of the narrator or characters). Gee (1989) countered that the topic associative stories were actually linguistically more complex and literary. Gee's point was to illustrate what an emergent sense of story structure might be (the child whose story he analyzed would probably not recognize his analysis). Gee also implied the need to understand such emergent structures and their potential relationships to more mature structures represented in diverse written genres. I have taken that challenge to heart and used his essential premises to inform the narrative writing intervention described in the opening section on writing in this chapter.

Although the links among Michaels, Cazden, and Gee's analyses have been very informative to how we think about taking up language resources that students bring to school, the attention to the sharing time studies also reflects the dearth of educational research on the range of language competencies among speakers of vernacular dialects. I emphasize here educational research because there has been much work on dialect variation among sociolinguists and researchers studying language acquisition. However, research and practice that address the implications of the findings from linguistics and language acquisition are very few and often simplistic. In education circles, it has been taken as a given that topic associative story-telling was the narrative structure employed by low-income African American children. This reflects a tendency in educational research to take up simplistic explanations for cultural and language diversity and to assume that all members of ethnic, racial, and language groups fit the patterns reflected in the paucity of research on such matters.

By contrast, Hyon and Sulzby (1994) found a wider range of narrative structures in a large sample of African American kindergartens (see also Hicks, 1991). Hyon and Sulzby documented that their sample employed both presumed mainstream and nonmainstream narrative patterns. However, Champion and her colleagues have carried out what is probably the most extensive research on narrative styles among African American children who are speakers of AAVE. Champion has documented a range of narrative structures not identified in the research literature before. Equally important, Champion has documented that the context of eliciting stories makes a difference in the length and complexity of stories children tell (Bloome, Champion, Katz, Morton, & Muldrow, 2001; Champion, 1998, 2003; Champion, Seymour, & Camarata, 1995). As with the earlier discussion of the studies by Cole et al. (1978) and Hall et al. (1975), we find again that context matters for displays of competence. There is certainly research that demonstrates how the specific nature of face to face interactions in classrooms can extend or inhibit students' opportunities to learn (Green & Dixon, 1994). It may also be that the contexts of assessment may also constrain how well students are able to display what they know.

## Instructional Discourse and Dialect Variation

The teaching of reading and writing in schools takes place in the envelope of instructional discourse. We know that social identities and relationships are negotiated and sustained in face-to-face verbal (and nonverbal) interactions. Classroom culture may be defined, in part, by norms for who can talk, about what, and how. What language or language varieties are available as resources for students, how they know what language(s) are privileged, and how students know when and where they can enter are powerful socializing forces for participation in classrooms (Cazden, 1988; Green & Dixon, 1994; Mehan, 1979). What language resources are available in instruction is complicated. There are questions not only about dialects, registers, and national languages, but also about what it means to learn the social languages of the academic disciplines. There are also important developmental considerations around these issues as well.

Research has documented how teachers make qualitative judgments about students' potential and social positioning both within and outside the classroom based on how the students use language (Cazden, 1988; Cazden et al., 1972; DeMeis & Turner, 1978; Piestrup, 1973; Rist, 1970). Some have argued that learning the language of the academic disciplines (not just appropriate vocabulary and registers but also the modes of argumentation in both oral and written channels) is somewhat like learning a second language. I have argued that the only way a child or adolescent learns to talk and reason like a physicist at home is if both parents are physicists and, over a long period of time, the child has been able to hang out in physics labs. Otherwise, even middle-class speakers of the presumed Standard English have an uphill battle to learn to speak the language of physics. Second-language learning requires many consistent opportunities to hear and interact with native speakers in authentic contexts, to have the space to make errors, especially in learning irregular forms and specialized contexts for use. I argue here that all students, especially speakers of vernacular dialects, also need similar opportunities to learn the language of the disciplines. The process of learning from errors in second-language acquisition almost always involves using competence in the first language as a scaffold to understand the structure and pragmatics of the second language. I make the case here that the same is true not only of bilingual learners but also of bidialectical learners.

One of the classic studies of how vernacular languages can be used to scaffold literacy learning is the work of the KEEP Project (Au, 1980; Tharp & Gallimore, 1988). By creating space for a genre of talk known as "Talk Story" among native Hawaiian speech communities, native Hawaiian children learned to engage books they read and become better readers. Talk Story is a participation structure that provides roles allowing students to engage in multiparty overlapping talk. As the students engaged in this participation structure in discussions outside of school, teachers were able to scaffold how the students could use this participation structure to become more actively involved in making sense of stories they read. In a similar vein, the problems in the sharing time research cited earlier were due, in part, to teachers' lack of understanding of discourse practices of students outside of school. Moll and his colleagues in the Funds of Knowledge Project have provided a powerful model for how teachers can gain a greater understanding of what Moll calls funds of knowledge embedded in community-based practices (Moll & Greenberg, 1990). This includes knowledge of how families and communities use language.

Lee's (1997, 2001) work in Cultural Modeling documents the use of African American discourse norms as a basis for instructional conversations. In the literature classes, when these African American students, speakers of AAVE, were most deeply engaged in solving interpretive problems in canonical works of literature, they engaged in multiparty overlapping talk, call and response, tonal semantics, and dramatic use of gestures. Lee (Lee & Majors, 2000) found positive relationships between the quality of literary reasoning and the invocation of these African American discourse features. Other studies by Foster (1987) and Piestrup (1973) make a similar case. The landmark text by Cazden et al. (1972) included what are now classic studies of how norms for instructional talk in classrooms impeded students from effective participation. Among the studies was the Phillips (1983) study of discursive norms on a Navajo reservation. In this study, Anglo teachers interpreted Navajo students' silence as indicators of a lack of understanding. Phillips showed that the students had learned in their community to sit and wait long enough for other interlocutors to completely finish an exchange.

## Conclusions

Language use, especially dialect variation, is always complex and contextual. In terms of racial and ethnic minorities and families living in persistent intergenerational poverty, research on the implications of language competencies in service of the teaching of reading and writing have, on the whole, reasoned from a deficit perspective. I have tried to account in this chapter for another body of research situated from very different assumptions (Cole, Gay, Glick, & Sharp, 1971; Dreeben & Gamoran, 1986). Fundamentally, these are questions that are not sufficiently researched. In part because of the limitations of existing research, the ways that assumptions about dialect variation are taken up in the teaching of literacy in K–12 schools does not take into account the range of affordances and constraints that particular ways of using language make possible. On the basis of these claims, I make the following recommendations for research, practice, and public policy.

- Both preservice and inservice teachers need extensive training about the history of English, dialect variation, and second-language acquisition, and need to understand how what we know about language influences opportunities to learn.

- Teachers need to examine the ways that they move between dialects (and perhaps national languages) as they move across settings, as a way of interrogating in personally meaningful ways the social nature of language use.

- Teachers need to examine the complex array of genres and registers that are part of the repertoire of reading and writing reflected in the subject matters, in ways that are developmentally appropriate.

- Policymakers need to reexamine their support for scripted and low-level teaching of reading and writing, based on long held assumptions about what certain students cannot do, assumptions that are most often marked by how students use language.

- Researchers, test developers, and teacher preparation institutions need to rethink the influences of the context of both teaching and testing on student achievement.

- Professional literacy organizations, such as the International Reading Association, National Council of Teachers of English, and National Reading Conference, need to develop a coordinated campaign (again) to help the public develop a better understanding of language structure, history, and use.

- All of the preceding entities need to wrestle with the ongoing assumptions regarding race and ethnicity that underlie (a) how research studies on language and literacy are often designed and (b) how educational public policy for low-income ethnic and racial minorities restricts the range of ways that children and adolescents may display literate competencies.

## REFERENCES

Alvermann, D.E., & Hagood, M.C. (2000). Critical media literacy: Research, theory, and practice in "new times." *Journal of Educational Research, 93*(3), 193–205.

Anders, P.L., & Evans, K.S. (1994). Relationship between teachers' beliefs and their instructional practice in reading. In R. Garner & P.A. Alexander (Eds.), *Beliefs about texts and instruction with text* (pp. 137–153). Hillsdale, NJ: Erlbaum.

Anderson, J. (1988). *The education of blacks in the south: 1860–1935.* Chapel Hill: University of North Carolina Press.

Anderson, R.C., Wilson, P.T., & Fielding, L.G. (1988). Growth in reading and how children spend their time outside of school. *Reading Research Quarterly, 23,* 285–303.

Apple, M.W. (1979). *Ideology and curriculum.* New York: Routledge.

Apple, M.W., & Beyer, L.E. (Eds.). (1988). *The curriculum: Problems, politics, and possibilities* (2nd ed.). Albany: State University of New York Press.

Applebee, A.N. (1993). *Literature in the secondary school: Studies of curriculum and instruction in the United States* (NCTE Research Report No. 25). Urbana, IL: National Council of Teachers of English.

Au, K.H. (1980). Participation structures in a reading lesson with Hawaiian children: Analysis of a culturally appropriate instructional event. *Anthropology and Education, 11*(2), 91–115.

Bakhtin, M.M. (1981). *The dialogic imagination: Four essays by M.M. Bakhtin* (M. Holquist, Ed.; C. Emerson & M. Holquist, Trans.). Austin: University of Texas Press.

Bakhtin, M.M. (1986). *Speech genres and other late essays* (V.W. McGee, Trans.). Austin: University of Texas Press.

Ball, A.F. (1992). Cultural preferences and the expository writing of African-American adolescents. *Written Communication, 9*(4), 501–532.

Ball, A.F. (1995a). Community based learning in an urban setting as a model for educational reform. *Applied Behavioral Science Review, 3*, 127–146.

Ball, A.F. (1995b). Text design patterns in the writing of urban African-American students: Teaching to the strengths of students in multicultural settings. *Urban Education, 30*, 253–289.

Ball, A.F. (2002). Three decades of research on classroom life: Illuminating the classroom communicative lives of America's at-risk students. In W.G. Secada (Ed.), *Review of research in education* (Vol. 26, pp. 71–112). Washington, DC: American Educational Research Association.

Ball, A., & Cooks, J. (1998, February). *Literacies unleashed through technology: Expanding community-based discourse practices and instilling a passion to write in urban at-risk youth and their teachers.* Paper presented at the annual meeting of the National Council of Teachers of English, Los Angeles, CA.

Ball, A.F., & Farr, M. (2003). Language varieties, culture, and teaching the English language arts. In J. Flood, D. Lapp, J.R. Squire, & J.M. Jensen (Eds.), *Handbook of research on teaching English language arts* (2nd ed., pp. 435–445). Mahwah, NJ: Erlbaum.

Bamgbose, A., Banjo, A., & Thomas, A. (1997). *New Englishes: A West African perspective.* Ibadan, Nigeria: Africa World Press.

Baquedano-Lopez, P. (2001). Narrating community in doctrina classes. *Narrative Inquiry, 10*(2), 429–452.

Baratz, J. (1969). A bidialectical task for determining language proficiency in economically disadvantaged children. *Child Development, 40*(8), 889–901.

Baron, R., Tom, D.Y.H., & Cooper, H.M. (1985). Social class, race and teacher expectations. In J.B. Dusek (Ed.), *Teacher expectations.* Hillsdale, NJ: Erlbaum.

Barton, D. (1994). *Literacy: An introduction to the ecology of written language.* Oxford, UK: Blackwell.

Barton, D., & Hamilton, M. (1998). *Local literacies: Reading and writing in one community.* London: Routledge.

Baugh, J. (1983). *Black street speech: Its history, structure, and survival.* Austin: University of Texas Press.

Baugh, J. (1988). Twice as less, Black English and the performance of Black students in mathematics and science [Book review]. *Harvard Educational Review, 58*, 395–403.

Bereiter, C., & Engelmann, S. (1966). *Teaching disadvantaged children in the preschool.* Englewood Cliffs, NJ: Prentice Hall.

Bernstein, B. (1970). Social class, language, and socialization. In P.P. Giglioli (Ed.), *Language and social context: Selected readings* (pp. 157–178). London: Penguin.

Bloome, D., Champion, T., Katz, L., Morton, M.B., & Muldrow, R. (2000). Spoken and written narrative development: African American preschoolers as storytellers and storymakers. In J.L. Harris, A.G. Kamhi, & K.E. Pollock (Eds.), *Literacy in African American communities* (pp. 45–76). Mahwah, NJ: Erlbaum.

Bransford, J., Brown, A.L., & Cocking, R.R. (2000). *How people learn: Brain, mind, experience, and school.* Washington, DC: National Academy Press.

Brock, C., Boyd, F., & Moore, J. (2003). Variation in language and the use of language across contexts: Implications for literacy learning. In J. Flood, D. Lapp, J.R. Squire, & J.M. Jensen, *Handbook of research on teaching the English language arts* (2nd ed., pp. 446–458). Mahwah, NJ: Erlbaum.

Cazden, C.B. (1988). *Classroom discourse: The language of teaching and learning.* Portsmouth, NH: Heinemann.

Cazden, C.B., John, V.P., & Hymes, D. (Eds.). (1972). *Functions of language in the classroom.* New York: Teachers College Press.

Cazden, C.B., Michaels, S., & Tabors, P. (1985). Spontaneous repairs in sharing time narratives: The intersection of metalinguistic awareness, speech event and narrative style. In S.W. Freedman (Ed.), *The acquisition of written language: Response and revision.* Westport, CT: Ablex.

Chafe, W., & Danielewicz, J. (1987). Properties of spoken and written language. In R. Horowitz & S.J. Samuels (Eds.) *Comprehending oral and written language* (pp. 81–113). New York: Academic Press.

Champion, T. (1998). "Tell me somethin' good": A description of narrative structures among African-American children. *Linguistics and Education, 9*(3), 251–286.

Champion, T. (2003). *Understanding story-telling among African American children: A journey from Africa to America.* Mahwah, NJ: Erlbaum.

Champion, T., Seymour, H., & Camarata, S. (1995). Narrative discourse among African American children. *Journal of Narrative and Life History, 5*(4), 333–352.

Clark, R. (1984). *Family life and school achievement: Why black children succeed or fail.* Chicago: University of Chicago Press.

Cole, M., Dore, J., Hall, W.S., & Dowley, G. (1978). Situation and task in young children's talk. *Discourse Processes, 1*(2), 119–176.

Cole, M., Gay, J., Glick, J.A., & Sharp, D.W. (1971). *The cultural context of learning and thinking: An exploration of experimental anthropology.* New York: Basic Books.

College Composition and Communication Conference. (1974). *Students' rights to their own dialects.* Urbana, IL: Author.

Conquergood, W. (1997). Street literacy. In J. Flood, S.B. Heath, & D. Lapp (Eds.), *Handbook of research on teaching literacy through the communicative and visual arts* (pp. 354–375). New York: Macmillan.

Cook-Gumperz, J. (Ed.). (1986). *The social construction of literacy.* New York: Cambridge University Press.

Cooper, C., & Odell, L. (Eds.). (1999). *Evaluating writing: The role of teachers' knowledge about text, learning, and culture.* Urbana, IL: National Council of Teachers of English.

Delpit, L.D. (1986). Skills and other dilemmas of a progressive Black educator. *Harvard Educational Review, 56*(4), 379–385.

Delpit, L.D. (1988). The silenced dialogue: Power and pedagogy in educating other people's children. *Harvard Educational Review, 58*(3), 280–298.

Delpit, L.D. (1995). *Other people's children: Cultural conflict in the classroom.* New York: Norton.

DeMeis, D.K., & Turner, R.R. (1978). Effects of students' race, physical attractiveness, and dialect on teachers' evaluations. *Contemporary Educational Psychology, 3*(1), 77–86.

Dreeben, R., & Gamoran, A. (1986). Race, instruction and learning. *American Sociological Review, 51*(5), 660–669.

DuBois, W.E.B. (1973). *The education of Black people: Ten critiques 1906–1960.* New York: Monthly Review Press.

Dyson, A.H. (2003). *The brothers and sisters learn to write: Popular literacies in childhood and school cultures.* New York: Teachers College Press.

Eisenstein, E.L. (1979). *The printing press as an agent of change: Communications and cultural transformations in early-modern Europe.* Cambridge, UK: Cambridge University Press.

Fairclough, N. (1992). *Discourse and social change.* Cambridge, UK: Polity Press.

Farr, M. (1991). Dialects, culture and teaching the English language arts. In J. Flood,

J.M. Jensen, D. Lapp, & J.R. Squire (Eds.), *Handbook of research on teaching the English language arts* (pp. 365–371). New York: Macmillan.

Ferguson, C.A., & Heath, S.B. (Eds.). (1981). *Language in the USA*. New York: Cambridge University Press.

Foster, M. (1987). *"It's cookin' now": An ethnographic study of a successful Black teacher in an urban community college.* Unpublished doctoral dissertation, Harvard University, Cambridge, MA.

Gasden, V.L., & Wagner, D.A. (Eds.). (1995). *Literacy among African-American youth: Issues in learning, teaching, and schooling.* Cresskill, NJ: Hampton Press.

Gee, J.P. (1989). The narrativization of experience in the oral style. *Journal of Education, 171*(1), 75–96.

Gee, J.P. (1991). *Social linguistics and literacies: Ideology in discourses.* London: Falmer.

Gee, J.P. (2000). Teenagers in new times: A new literacy studies perspective. *Journal of Adolescent & Adult Literacy, 43*, 412–420.

Gee, J.P. (2000/2001). Identity as an analytic lens for research in education. In W.G. Secada (Ed.), *Review of research in education 2000–2001* (No. 25, pp. 99–126). Washington, DC: American Educational Research Association.

Gilyard, K. (1991). *Voices of the self: A study of language competence.* Detroit, MI: Wayne State University Press.

Goodwin, M.H. (1991). *He-said-she-said: Talk as social organization.* Bloomington: Indiana University Press.

Gould, S.J. (1981). *The mismeasure of man.* New York: Norton.

Green, J., & Dixon, C. (1994). Talking knowledge into being: Discursive and social practices in classrooms. *Linguistics and Education, 5*(3&4), 231–239.

Gutiérrez, K., & Rogoff, B. (2003). Cultural ways of learning: Individual traits or repertoires of practice. *Educational Researcher* (C.D. Lee, Guest Ed.), *32*(5), 19–25.

Hall, W., & Guthrie, L. (1980). On the dialect question and reading. In R. Spiro, B. Bruce, & W. Brewer (Eds.), *Theoretical issues in reading comprehension: Perspectives from cognitive psychology, linguistics, artificial intelligence, and education* (pp. 221–244). Hillsdale, NJ: Erlbaum.

Hall, W.W., Reder, S., & Cole, M. (1975). Story recall in young black and white children: Effects of racial group membership, race of experimenter, and dialect. *Developmental Psychology, 11*(5), 628–634.

Hammer, C.S. (2001). "Come and sit down and let mama read": Book reading interactions between African American mothers and their infants. In J.L. Harris, A.G. Kamhi, & K.E. Pollock (Eds.), *Literacy in African American communities* (pp. 21–44). Mahwah, NJ: Erlbaum.

Haycock, K. (1998). Good teaching matters...a lot. *Magazine of History, 13*(1), 61–63.

Heath, S.B. (1983). *Ways with words: Language, life, and work in communities and classrooms.* New York: Cambridge University Press.

Hernstein, R.J., & Murray, C. (1994). *The bell curve: Intelligence and class structure in American life.* New York: Simon & Schuster.

Hicks, D. (1991). Kinds of narrative: Genre skills among first graders from two communities. In A. McCabe & C. Peterson (Eds.), *Developing narrative structure* (pp. 55–87). Hillsdale, New York: Erlbaum.

Hilliard, A.G. (1976). *Alternatives to IQ testing: An approach to the assessment of gifted minority children* (Final Report to the Special Education Support Unit). Sacramento: California State Department of Education.

Hillocks, G. (1975). *Observing and writing.* Urbana, IL: National Council of Teachers of English.

Hillocks, G. (1986). *Research on written composition: New directions for teaching.* Urbana, IL: National Council of Teachers of English.

Hillocks, G. (1995). *Teaching writing as reflective practice: Integrating theories.* New York: Teachers College Press.

Holloway, J.E. (Ed.). (1990). *Africanisms in American culture.* Bloomington: Indiana University Press.

Hymes, D. (1981). Foreword. In C. Ferguson & S.B. Heath (Eds.), *Language in the USA* (pp. v–ix). New York: Cambridge University Press.

Hyon, S., & Sulzby, E. (1994). African American kindergarteners' spoken narratives: Topic associating and topic centered styles. *Linguistics and Education*, *6*(2), 121–152.

Irvine, J., & York, D.E. (1995). Learning styles and culturally diverse students: A literature review. In J.A. Banks & C.M. Banks (Eds.), *Handbook of research on multicultural education* (pp. 484–497). New York: Gale.

Johnson, K.R., & Simons, H.D. (1973). *Black children's reading of dialect and standard of texts: Final report*. East Lansing, MI: National Center for Research on Teacher Learning. (ERIC Document Reproduction Service No. ED076978)

Jones, G. (1992). *Liberating voices: Oral tradition in African American literature*. New York: Penguin.

Kaestle, C.F., Damon-Moore, H., Stedman, L., Tinsley, K., & Trollinger, W.V. (1991). *Literacy in the United States: Readers and reading since 1880*. New Haven, CT: Yale University Press.

Labov, W. (1970). The logic of nonstandard English. In F. Williams (Ed.), *Language and poverty: Perspectives on a theme*. New York: Academic Press.

Labov, W. (1972). *Language in the inner city: Studies in the Black English vernacular*. Philadelphia: University of Pennsylvania Press.

Labov, W. (1995). Can reading failure be reversed: A linguistic approach to the question. In V.L. Gasden & D.A. Wagner (Eds.), *Literacy among African-American youth: Issues in learning, teaching, and schooling* (pp. 39–68). Cresskill, NJ: Hampton Press.

Lave, J. (1977). Cognitive consequences of traditional apprenticeship training in West Africa. *Anthropology and Education Quarterly*, *8*(3), 177–180.

Lave, J., Murtaugh, M., & de la Rocha, O. (1984). The dialectic of arithmetic in grocery shopping. In B. Rogoff & J. Lave (Eds.), *Everyday cognition: Its develop-*

*ment in social context* (pp. 67–94). Cambridge, MA: Harvard University Press.

Leap, W.L. (1993). *American Indian English*. Salt Lake City: University of Utah Press.

Lee, C.D. (1993). *Signifying as a scaffold for literary interpretation: The pedagogical implications of an African American discourse genre*. Urbana, IL: National Council of Teachers of English.

Lee, C.D. (1995a). A culturally based cognitive apprenticeship: Teaching African American high school students' skills in literary interpretation. *Reading Research Quarterly*, *30*, 608–631.

Lee, C.D. (1995b). Signifying as a scaffold for literary interpretation. *Journal of Black Psychology*, *21*(4), 357–381.

Lee, C.D. (1997). Bridging home and school literacies: A model of culturally responsive teaching. In J. Flood, S.B. Heath, & D. Lapp (Eds.), *Handbook of research on teaching literacy through the communicative and visual arts* (pp. 330–341). New York: Macmillan.

Lee, C.D. (2000). Signifying in the zone of proximal development. In C.D. Lee & P. Smagorinsky (Eds.), *Vygotskian perspectives on literacy research: Constructing meaning through collaborative inquiry* (pp. 191–225). New York: Cambridge University Press.

Lee, C.D. (2001). Is October Brown Chinese: A cultural modeling activity system for underachieving students. *American Educational Research Journal*, *38*(1), 97–142.

Lee, C.D. (2003, April). *Cultural modeling and pedagogical content knowledge of the teacher of literature*. Paper presented at the annual meeting of the American Educational Research Association, Chicago.

Lee, C.D., & Majors, Y. (2000). *Cultural modeling's response to Rogoff's challenge: Understanding apprenticeship, guided participation and participatory appropriation in a culturally responsive, subject matter specific context*. Paper presented at the annual meeting of the American

Educational Research Association, New Orleans, LA.

Lee, C.D., Rosenfeld, E., Mendenhall, R., Rivers, A., & Tynes, B. (2003). Cultural modeling as a frame for narrative analysis. In C. Daiute & C. Lightfoot (Eds.), *Narrative analysis: Studying the development of individuals in society.* Thousand Oaks, CA: Sage Publications.

Mahiri, J. (1996). *African American and youth culture as a bridge to writing development.* Berkeley: National Center for the Study of Writing and Literacy, School of Education, University of California; Washington, DC: U.S. Department of Education, Office of Educational Research and Improvement, Educational Resources Information Center.

Mahiri, J. (1998). *Shooting for excellence: African American and youth culture in new century schools.* New York: National Council of Teachers of English.

McCarthy, C. (1990). Multicultural education, minority identities, textbooks, and the challenge of curriculum reform. *Journal of Education, 172*(2), 118–129.

McDermott, R. (1987). Achieving school failure: An anthropological approach to illiteracy and social stratification. In G.D. Spindler (Ed.), *Education and cultural process* (2nd ed., pp. 173–209). Prospect Heights, IL: Waveland Press.

McLaughlin, D. (1989). The sociolinguistics of Navajo literacy. *Anthropology and Education Quarterly, 20*(4), 275–290.

Mehan, H. (1979). *Learning lessons: Social organization in the classroom.* Cambridge, MA: Harvard University Press.

Melmed, P.A. (1971). *Black English phonology: The question of reading interference.* Ann Arbor, MI: University Microfilms.

Michaels, S. (1981). "Sharing time": Children's narrative styles and differential access to literacy. *Language in Society, 10,* 423–442.

Mitchell-Kernan, C. (1981). Signifying, loud-talking and marking. In A. Dundes (Ed.), *Mother wit from the laughing barrel: Readings in the interpretation of Afro-American folklore* (pp. 310–328). Englewood Cliffs, NJ: Garland.

Moll, L., & Greenberg, J.B. (1990). Creating zones of possibilities: Combining social contexts for instruction. In L.C. Moll (Ed.), *Vygotsky and education: Instructional implications and applications of sociohistorical psychology* (pp. 319–348). New York: Cambridge University Press.

Morgan, M. (1993). The Africanness of counterlanguage among Afro-Americans. In S. Mufwene (Ed.), *Africanisms in Afro-American language varieties.* Athens: University of Georgia Press.

Moss, B. (1994a). Creating a community: Literacy events in African-American churches. In B.J. Moss (Ed.), *Literacy across communities* (pp. 147–178). Cresskill, NJ: Hampton Press.

Moss, B.J. (Ed.). (1994b). *Literacy across communities.* Cresskill, NJ: Hampton Press.

Moss, B.J. (2001). *A community text arises: A literate text and a literary tradition in African-American churches.* Cresskill, NJ: Hampton Press.

Mufwene, S.S. (Ed.). (1993). *Africanisms in Afro-American language varieties.* Athens: The University of Georgia Press.

Mufwene, S.S., Rickford, J., Bailey, G., & Baugh, J. (1998). *African-American English: Structure, history, and use.* New York: Routledge.

New London Group. (1996). A pedagogy of multiliteracies: Designing social futures. *Harvard Educational Review, 66*(1), 60–92.

Nunes, T., Schliemann, A.D., & Carraher, D.W. (1993). *Street mathematics and school mathematics.* New York: Cambridge University Press.

Ochs, E., Jacoby, S., & Gonzales, P. (1994). Interpretive journeys: How physicists talk and travel through graphic space. *Configurations, 2*(1), 151–172.

Orr, E.W. (1987). *Twice as less: Black English and the performance of black students in mathematics and science.* New York: Norton.

Patton-Terry, N. (2004). *African American English, linguistic awareness, and early spelling ability: A cross-sectional, developmental analysis of spelling and linguistic* knowledge in young, typically develop-ing African American English speakers. Unpublished doctoral dissertation, Northwestern University.

Perry, T., & Delpit, L.D. (Eds.). (1998). The real Ebonics debate: Power, language and the education of African-American children. Boston: Beacon Press.

Phillips, S.U. (1983). The invisible culture: Communication in classroom and community on the Warm Springs Indian Reservation. New York: Longman.

Piestrup, A. (1973). Black dialect interference and accommodation of reading instruction in first grade (Monograph No. 4). Berkeley, CA: Language-Behavior Research Laboratory.

Purcell-Gates, V. (1995). Other people's words: The cycle of low literacy. Cambridge, MA: Harvard University Press.

Purcell-Gates, V. (2000). Family literacy. In M.L. Kamil, P.B. Mosenthal, P.D. Pearson, & R. Barr (Eds.), Handbook of reading research (Vol. 3, pp. 853–888). Mahwah, NJ: Erlbaum.

Redd, T. (1992, April). Untapped resources "styling" in Black students' writing for Black audiences. Paper presented at the annual meeting of the American Educational Research Association, San Francisco, CA.

Rentel, V.M., & Kennedy, J.J. (1972). Effects of pattern drill on the phonology, syntax, and reading achievement of rural Appalachian children. American Educational Research Journal, 9(1), 87–100.

Resnick, D.P., & Resnick, L.B. (1977). The nature of literacy: An historical exploration. Harvard Educational Review, 43(3), 370–385.

Resnick, D.P., & Resnick, L.B. (1985). Standards, curriculum, and performance: A historical and comparative perspective. Educational Researcher, 14(4), 5–20.

Rickford, J.R., & Rickford, A.A. (1976). Cut-eye and suck teeth: African words and gestures in new world guise. Journal of American Folklore, 89(353), 194–309.

Rickford, J.R., & Rickford, A.A. (1995). Dialect readers revisited. Linguistics and Education, 7(2), 107–128.

Rist, R. (1970). Student social class and teacher expectations: The self-fulfilling prophecy in ghetto education. Harvard Educational Review, 40(3), 411–451.

Rose, T. (1994). Black noise: Rap music and black culture in contemporary America. Hanover, NH: Wesleyan University Press.

Schneider, E.W. (1996). Focus on the USA: Varieties of English around the world (General series, Vol. 16). Philadelphia: John Benjamins.

Scott, J. (1981). Mixed dialects in the composition classroom. In M. Montgomery & G. Bailey (Eds.), Language variety in the South: Perspectives in black and white. Tuscaloosa: University of Alabama Press.

Scribner, S. (1984). Studying working intelligence. In B. Rogoff, & J. Lave (Eds.), Everyday cognition: Its development in social context (pp. 9–40). Cambridge, MA: Harvard University Press.

Scribner, S. (1997). Literacy in three metaphors. In S. Scribner, E. Tobach, M.B. Parlee, L.M. Martin, & A.S. Kapelman (Eds.), Mind and social practice: Selected writings of Sylvia Scribner (pp. 206–214). New York: Cambridge University Press.

Shaughnessy, M.P. (1977). Errors and expectations: A guide for the teacher of basic writing. New York: Oxford University Press.

Simpkins, G., Holt, G., & Simpkins, C. (1977). Bridge: A cross-culture reading program. Boston: Houghton Mifflin.

Simpkins, G., & Simpkins, C. (1981). Cross-cultural approach to curriculum development. In G. Smitherman (Ed.), Black English and the education of Black children and youth (Proceedings of the National Invitational symposium on the KING decision, pp. 212–240). Detroit: Department of Africana, Wayne State University.

Sims, R. (1972). A psycholinguistic description of miscues created by selected young readers during oral reading of text in black dialect and standard English.

Unpublished doctoral dissertation, Wayne State University, Detroit, MI.

Smith, M., & Hillocks, G. (1988). Sensible sequencing: Developing knowledge about literature text by text. *English Journal, 77*, 44–49.

Smitherman, G. (1973). The power of the rap: The Black idiom and the new Black poetry. *Twentieth Century Literature*, 259–274.

Smitherman, G. (1977). *Talkin and testifyin: The language of Black America*. Boston: Houghton Mifflin.

Smitherman, G. (1981). "What go round come round": King in perspective. *Harvard Educational Review, 51*(1), 40–56.

Smitherman, G. (1994). "The Blacker the berry, the sweeter the juice": African American student writers and the NAEP. In A.H. Dyson & C. Genishi (Eds.), *The need for story: Cultural diversity in classroom and community*. Urbana, IL: National Council of Teachers of English.

Smitherman, G. (2000a). African American student writers in the NAEP, 1969–1988/89 and "The Blacker the berry, the sweeter the juice." In G. Smitherman (Ed.), *Talkin that talk: Language, culture and education in African America* (pp. 163–194). New York: Routledge.

Smitherman, G. (2000b). Ebonics, King, and Oakland: Some folks don't believe fat meat is greasy. In G. Smitherman (Ed.), *Talkin that talk: Language, culture and education in African America* (pp. 150–162). New York: Routledge.

Smitherman, G. (2000c). *Talkin that talk: Language, culture and education in African America*. New York: Routledge.

Steffensen, M.S., Joag-Dev, C., & Anderson, R. (1979). A cross-cultural perspective on reading comprehension. *Reading Research Quarterly, 15*, 10–29.

Stewart, W.A. (1969). On the use of Negro dialect in the teaching of reading. In J. Baratz & R. Shuy (Eds.), *Teaching black children to read*. Washington, DC: Center for Applied Linguistics.

Stotsky, S. (1999). *Losing our language: How multicultural classroom instruction is undermining our children's ability to read, write, and reason*. New York: Free Press.

Sulzby, E., & Teale, W. (1996). Emergent literacy. In R. Barr, M.L. Kamil, P.B. Mosenthal, & P.D. Pearson (Eds.), *Handbook of reading research* (Vol. 2, pp. 727–757). White Plains, NY: Longman.

Taylor, C. (1985). *Human agency and language* (Philosophical papers, Vol. 1). Cambridge, UK: Cambridge University Press.

Taylor, D., & Dorsey-Gaines, C. (1988). *Growing up literate: Learning from inner-city families*. Portsmouth, NH: Heinemann.

Taylor, O., & Lee, D. (1987). Standardized tests and African-American children: Communication and language uses. *Negro Educational Review, 38*(2/3), 67–80.

Teale, W. (1986). Home background and young children's literacy development. In W. Teale & E. Sulzby (Eds.), *Emergent literacy: Writing and reading* (pp. 173–206). Westport, CT: Ablex.

Tharp, R., & Gallimore, R. (1988). *Rousing minds to life: Teaching, learning, and schooling in social context*. New York: Cambridge University Press.

Traub, J. (1999, January 16). What no school can do. *The New York Times Magazine*, pp. 52–56.

Turner, M. (1996). *The literary mind: The origins of thought and language*. New York: Oxford University Press.

Tyack, D.B. (1974). *The one best system: A history of American urban education*. Cambridge, MA: Harvard University Press.

Varenne, H., & McDermott, R. (1998). *Successful failure: The school America builds*. Boulder, CO: Westview.

Walker, A. (1988). Coming in from the cold. *Living by the word* (pp. 54–68). San Diego, CA: Harcourt.

Ward, M.C. (1971). *Them children: A study in language learning*. New York: Holt, Rinehart and Winston.

White, K.R. (1982). The relation between socioeconomic status and academic achievement. *Psychological Bulletin, 91*(3), 461–481.

Whitehurst, G., Falco, F., Lonigan, C., Fischel, J., DeBaryshe, B., Valdez-Menchaca, M., et al. (1988). Accelerating language development through picture book reading. *Developmental Psychology, 24*(4), 552–559.

Wilkinson, L., & Silliman, E.R. (2000). Classroom language and literacy learning. In M.L. Kamil, P.B. Mosenthal, P.D. Pearson, & R. Barr (Eds.), *Handbook of reading research* (Vol. 3, pp. 337–360). Mahwah, NJ: Erlbaum.

Wolfram, W. (1974). *Sociolinguistic aspects of assimilation: Puerto Rican English in New York City.* Washington, DC: Center for Applied Linguistics.

Wolfram, W. (1981). Varieties of American English. In C. Ferguson & S.B. Heath (Eds.), *Language in the USA* (pp. 44–68). New York: Cambridge University Press.

Wolfram, W., Adger, C.T., & Christian, D. (1999). *Dialects in schools and communities.* Mahwah, NJ: Erlbaum.

Wolfram, W., & Christian, D. (1976). *Appalachian speech.* Washington, DC: Center for Applied Linguistics.

Wolfram, W., Christian, D., Potter, L., & Leap, W. (1979). *Variability in the English of two Indian communities and its effects on reading and writing.* Washington, DC: Center for Applied Linguistics.

Wolfram, W., & Hatfield, D. (1984). *The tense marking in second language learning: Patterns of spoken and written English in a Vietnamese community* (NIE Final Report G-83-0035). Washington, DC: Center for Applied Linguistics.

Wolfram, W., & Schilling-Estes, N. (1998). *American English: Dialects and variation.* Oxford, UK: Blackwell.

Woodson, C.G. (1969). *The mis-education of the Negro.* Washington, DC: Associated Publishers.

Zentella, A.C. (1997). *Growing up bilingual: Puerto Rican children in New York.* Oxford, UK: Blackwell.

# CHAPTER 16

# Culture and Language: Bidialectical Issues in Literacy: A Response to Carol Lee

*Arnetha F. Ball*

For the past 10 years, my work has focused on an interdisciplinary investigation of the oral and written literacies of culturally and linguistically diverse populations. I have been particularly interested in writing, writing instruction, and the discourses of education in classrooms and community-based organizations across U.S. and South African national boundaries. This, by necessity, has included an emphasis on the preparation of teachers to work with poor, marginalized, and underachieving students. Carol Lee and I have common research interests in the application of sociocultural and learning theory to issues of language and literacy as they relate to a wide range of students from diverse backgrounds and bidialectal students in particular. Therefore, as an educational linguist, I read Lee's chapter with great interest and enthusiasm.

Lee's chapter focuses on relationships among speaking one of the many dialects of American English, engagement in literate practices, and opportunities to learn particular ways of reading and writing in schools. Lee draws heavily on the work of linguistic scholars, and she concurs with Hymes who, when referring to the range of variation in national languages and dialects of English spoken in the United States, noted that the United States is a country rich in many things, but poor in knowledge of itself with regard to language (Hymes, 1981). This was an accurate observation more than two decades ago, and it remains true today. Lee stresses this point and elaborates on the many complex issues involved in understanding how this is taken up in instructional settings. She provides a rich description of the many folk theories about language and dialect variation that are both implicitly and explicitly articulated within U.S. society. Because elementary and high school teachers often receive little training about language, it is not surprising that teachers are likely to share an array of common, yet misinformed, folk theories. Lee explicates several of these folk theories and their implications for the teaching of English language arts. Over the years, my work has focused on the eradication of these misinformed folk theories through research on the linguistic resources dialect-speaking students bring into the classroom and alternative educational environments (Ball, 1992, 1995a, 1995b, 1995c, 1998; Ball & Farr, 2003; Ball & Heath, 1993). In my efforts to gain a better understanding of factors associated with successful school performance by diverse student populations, I have been influenced by the advice of Baugh, who cautions researchers not to emphasize analyses of students' failure at the expense of their successes.

> The well-known practice of analyzing such failure has contributed little to the long-term interests of black students. They [students] would be better served if researchers devoted as much attention to evaluations of programs in which black students have experienced academic success. (Baugh, 1988, p. 403)

In her description of the existing assumptions about students' language differences, Lee summarizes the research on the home–school language connection and proposes that schools as organizations and teachers as professionals should have sufficient knowledge of the demands of school-based literate practices to adjust classroom interactions and provide literacy learning scaffolds to complement the prior knowledge and experiences that students bring. Lee further discusses the research findings, observations of practices, and unresolved issues about the implications of dialect variation among U.S. English speakers in terms of classroom discourse and literacy instruction. In this discussion, she uses African American speakers as a primary case to illustrate ways that elements of metalinguistic knowledge can be explicitly scaffolded to support students' learning. Lee notes that K–12 schools do not take into account the range of freedoms and constraints that particular ways of using language make possible and concludes by making seven recommendations for research, practice, and policy.

As a way of extending Lee's discussion on language, culture, and bidialectical issues, I focus on two aspects of her chapter that I found particularly interesting as a writing researcher and teacher educator. I will frame my remarks by elaborating on these two important points and conclude my discussion with implications for research, policy, and teacher education. Briefly stated, I will elaborate on (1) Lee's discussion of the valuable research conducted by writing scholars that documents the linguistic resources African American Vernacular English (AAVE) speakers bring into the classroom setting and (2) her discussion of teachers' lack of understanding of the linguistic resources these students use outside of school and how they can be used to enhance the educational experience.

## Writing Research on Language, Culture, and Bidialectalism

A substantial body of sociolinguistic research has been developed to document the linguistic characteristics of dialect speakers in the United States, including AAVE (Ball, 1992; Baugh, 1990, 1992; Edwards, 1992; Fasold, 1972; Kochman, 1972; Labov, 1972a; Poplack & Tagliamonte, 1994, Wolfram, 1969); Puerto Rican English (Wolfram, 1974; Zentella, 1981); Appalachian English (Wolfram & Christian, 1976); varieties of American Indian English (Leap, 1993; Wolfram, Christian, Potter, & Leap, 1979); Vietnamese English (Wolfram & Hatfield, 1984); and others (Amastae & Elias-Olivares, 1982; Ferguson & Heath, 1981; Labov, 1980). This work makes it clear that a wide variety of dialects exist in the United States, and that these varieties are as complex and as regularly patterned as are academic varieties. These researchers confirmed that, although dialect speakers often have different linguistic rules that govern their grammars or use of lexical items, contrary to mainstream folk theories, they do not have linguistic deficits. As Lee points out, the study of the writing of bidialectal speakers spans the past four decades. The goal of much of the educational research on the writing of bidialectal students in traditional and nontraditional classrooms was designed to help us understand how written language unites the social and the cognitive lives of students and to help us gain insights into the events of classrooms that support student achievement and their acquisition of effective communication systems.

The research on language variation and writing has identified particular linguistic features used by bidialectal speakers outside of school that can be observed by teachers in school settings (Ball, 1995a, 1998). Research in this area has identified similar characteristics in the writing of AAVE speakers, Latino and Indian bilinguals, and deaf users of American sign language. A challenge that remains for researchers is the investigation of issues of assessing the writing of students from diverse linguistic backgrounds within the classroom setting. Ball (1998) discusses issues of assessment with culturally and linguistically diverse students and provides examples of instances in which characteristic features of AAVE-speaking students' home language appear in their written text at the phonological, syntactic, semantic, and discourse levels. Ball (1997) discusses how including the voices of teachers from diverse backgrounds can be helpful in improving the writing lives of bidialectal students and broaden debates about the reform of writing instruction.

Ball and Farr (2003) discuss the concept of biloquialism, which calls for the learning of new, academic writing patterns without eliminating the dialect varieties students bring from their home and community settings. This culturally sensitive approach promotes the maintenance of bidialectalism. Advocates of this instructional approach call for the recognition of students' language and linguistic practices as resources. The goal of this kind of instruction is to enable students to switch from one linguistic style or dialect to another, guided by a sense of appropriateness to the context in which the language is used. Much of the research in this area is motivated by the researchers' desire to explore ways to improve educational practice and points to new strategies aimed at reducing educational failure.

Over the past four decades, a great deal of research has focused on the AAVE speakers' writing as it relates to their linguistic code, including investigations of the use of variation among full, contracted, and zero forms of inflected copula and auxiliary be; analyses of suffix /-s/ variation; phonological, syntactic, and semantic features; and the use of narratives by this population. Far less attention, however, has been devoted to investigating the ways AAVE speakers use oral and written expository forms. This omission from the research is perplexing, especially because researchers such as Britton (1975) and Applebee (1981) have reported that expository writing accounts for 63% to 85% of adolescents' writing activity in U.S. and British schools, and because there is a steady increase in the demand for competence in the use of oral and written exposition as students progress through the educational system.

Focusing on African American adolescents' written exposition, Ball (1992) investigated the hypothesis that devices young African Americans use in informal exposition constitute untapped language resources that educators can use in designing language arts curricula. I also proposed that African American adolescents have preferred patterns of expository organizations. After conceptualizing what those patterns might look like, I investigated significant educational implications. Using questionnaires, interviews, and detailed linguistic analyses of expository texts produced by more than 100 elementary and secondary students from diverse backgrounds, I conducted a survey study, preference study, case study, and teacher evaluation study to investigate my hypotheses. The case study revealed that exposition produced by African American adolescents in informal settings reflected a wide range of organizational patterns, although the exposition they produced in academic settings was more restricted in variety of organizational patterns. The preference study revealed that a wide range of students from culturally and linguistically diverse backgrounds indicated similar preferred patterns when producing informal conversational tasks. It also revealed that African American high school students indicated distinct preference patterns from the other groups of students when writing academic expository texts. The teacher evaluation study revealed that students' choice of organizational patterns does have important influences on teacher evaluation. I have also found that when students are made aware of cultural resources and their accompanying thinking strategies through engagement with community and culturally relevant texts, students can apply that once tacit information, which has now been made explicit, to the production of expository texts required in academic settings. A great deal more work is needed in this area to support reconceptualizations of expository instruction in elementary, secondary, and college classrooms. Increasing our knowledge of how bidialectal students use expository texts successfully in informal settings can help us in the design of more successful and more engaging academic curriculum that empowers students and enriches their school experience.

## Enhancing Teachers' Knowledge of Language, Cultural, and Bidialectal Issues

As Lee has pointed out, most teachers lack sufficient knowledge of and appreciation for the linguistic resources bidialectal students bring to the classroom and how those resources can be used to enhance the educational experience (Ball & Mohammad, 2003). Ball's research project, Literacies Unleashed, provides a framework for the design of investigations of the transformative power of reflective, introspective, and critical writing as a tool for facilitating the development of teachers who are well informed about the linguistic resources bidialectal students bring to the classroom and how those resources can be used to enhance classroom experiences. Early in the project, however, we learned that increasing teachers' knowledge about diverse students' language and linguistic practices was important but not sufficient. We learned that if significant changes were to take place in classroom settings, changes would need to occur in teachers' attitudes about their students and their language practices. Therefore, perhaps a more important component of the Literacies Unleashed project is that it provides a framework for investigating the transformative power of reflective, introspective, and critical writing as a tool for facilitating the development of teachers who are committed to using their increased knowledge in strategic ways to enhance the teaching and learning of students from culturally and linguistically diverse backgrounds (Ball, 1999, 2000c, 2005). This research draws on cultural historical activity theory and shows promise of increasing our understanding of the types of activities that need to occur in teacher education programs to facilitate the development of teachers who are committed to working with our nations' increasingly diverse student populations. In this study I hypothesized that using writing as a pedagogical tool can play a critical role in the professional development of teachers who are preparing to teach diverse student populations. As teachers in our teacher education program were exposed to strategically designed activities, their changing perspectives were facilitated by and revealed through their written discourses as they moved beyond the production of seemingly appropriate communication about theory and practice toward an internalization and synthesizing of ideas that led to transformed practices in their experiences as teachers.

Part of a larger program of research that investigates teacher education, policies, and pedagogies that impact the teaching and learning of marginalized students in the United States and South Africa, this study documented how teachers move beyond surface-level engagements with theory toward transformative engagements that led them to take positions of reflective commitment that guided them in their efforts to become more effective teachers of our schools' most vulnerable learners. Structurally, the United States and South Africa are both seeking ways to more effectively educate large numbers of linguistically diverse students. Having experienced similar histories of social, economic, and educational inequalities in the education of marginalized populations, both countries now perceive the state of education for linguistically diverse and economically disadvantaged populations to be in crisis, and both countries have the potential to learn a great deal from each other as they strive to prepare teachers to teach diverse students in a global society.

Drawing heavily from the work of Vygotsky (1934/1978) and Leont'ev (1981) to build a theoretical frame that could help to explain how teachers' professional identities change over time, I hypothesized that change in teachers' developing ideologies concerning their work with dialect speaking students could be facilitated through engagement with carefully designed activities (Ball, 2000b). I also hypothesized that teachers' changing ideologies would be revealed in their oral and written discourses as they considered issues of teaching diverse student populations. To investigate these issues, I collected the oral and written texts of more than 100 U.S. and South African teachers enrolled in my course over a three-year period. The data included the teachers' narrative essays of their own literacy experiences, transcripts of classroom discussions, journal entries, and reflections they wrote in response to carefully selected course readings and course experiences. I proposed that as teachers were exposed to strategically designed readings and activities within a teacher education program, their perspectives on literacy and attitudes toward teaching diverse student populations would be affected in positive ways—and that those changes would be reflected in their changing discourse practices. Findings revealed that changes did, in fact, occur in teachers' ideologies about literacy and about teaching diverse students when they chose to actively engage in our course activity system, which functioned as a mediating mechanism for psychological and cognitive change and development. A critically important part of that activity occurred through engagements with reflective, introspective, and critical writing and through metacognitive-raising discursive conversations about theory and practice, which challenged teachers' preconceived notions about language diversity, students' abilities, and teacher efficacy. This use of writing as a pedagogical tool and metacognitive-raising discursive conversations gave teachers abundant opportunities to struggle with theory and with the realities of implementing those theories through critical written reflections, teacher research projects, and classroom teaching experiences within a supportive, yet challenging, learning context (Ball, 2005).

For decades, educators and linguists have examined the importance of language and its impact on education (Cazden, 2001; Foster, 1987, 1992; Heath, 1983). What these studies have in common are their attention to classroom discourse, speech events, and performative aspects of language and their relationship to teaching and learning. The use of metacognitive-raising discursive conversations in our course was based on this information. A next step that is needed in the research—a topic to which I have recently turned my attention—involves the development of more critical discourse analytic tools and approaches that can assist us in gauging the effectiveness of teacher education programs in preparing teachers to work with diverse student populations. These approaches should concern themselves not only with issues of classroom practices but also with issues of how classroom practices within teacher education programs can facilitate teachers' movement toward positions of reflective commitment to teaching diverse student populations. My intent in conducting this investigation is to help us consider ways that discourse analysis can be used to reflect the effectiveness of our efforts to develop more teachers who are well informed and committed to teaching all students—culturally and linguistically diverse students in particular.

# Implications for Research, Policy, and Teacher Education

Rose (1989) proposes that if schools are to play a significant role in improving writing and literacy skills in the United States for all students, "we'll need a guiding set of principles that do not encourage us to retreat from, but to move us closer to, an understanding of the rich mix of speech and ritual story that is America" (p. 238). This implies the need for the following:

- A broader *theory of literacy and learning* that includes an understanding of cultures and cultural resources that all students bring to the learning environment, including bidialectal students.

- An expanded agenda for *research* that asks how these students adapt the language and literacy resources they already control to a range of writing practices (e.g., doing expository and analytical writing, composing multimedia electronic documents, explaining scientific concepts, arguing persuasively, shaping narrative, and inquiring effectively).

- An expanded *policy* agenda for supporting program development and research designed to investigate issues that facilitate accomplishment of the goals we have discussed.

- An expanded, more inclusive image of literacy education and an emphasis in *teacher professional development* that recognizes the multiple purposes and practices of literacy and the diverse patchwork of learners who now inhabit our schools. This expanded image would require all teacher education programs to offer a minimum of two required courses that focus on (1) the centrality of language, literacy, and culture in teaching and learning and (2) the processes and supports needed to ensure successful reading and writing in content area teaching and learning.

Research confirms that the single most critical variable in students' successful experiences in the classroom is the teacher. Current movements in educational reform have been based on the belief that real change comes only with the support, participation, and leadership of those who will ultimately implement the reform or change. The role of the teacher is therefore central. Unless teachers play a vital role in envisioning, planning, and implementing a reform movement that recognizes the language and linguistic resources of bidialectal students in our classrooms, efforts toward reform in this area are doomed to fail. For reforms to be effective, programs must have teachers that are committed to the reform process and who have the will and the capacity to implement the change. Teachers who seek a transformed pedagogy must challenge themselves to critically reflect on, analyze, and actively begin to change the communication patterns through which literacy is practiced in their classrooms (Ball, 2000a). They must decide for themselves which discourse practices should be included and which should be excluded, and whether the zones of validity and acceptability for uses of language and literacies in their classrooms should be broadened.

At the teacher training level, professional development programs require radical change so that teachers gain an appreciation for the role they must play in allowing bidialectal students' voices to be heard, legitimized, and leveraged within their classroom. A radical shift of priorities in the use of time within teacher professional development programs would eventually have to occur if such perspectives are to take hold among future classroom teachers. Teachers must be educated concerning the selection and allocation of instructional resources, materials, and methodologies that are representative of a wide variety of different ethnic and cultural group experiences. Teachers must be nurtured in the development of professional and extra professional identities that foster a pride in their abilities to teach all students well.

At the classroom level, bidialectal students' preferred modes of expression should be included in the curriculum, not only as a building block for bridging bidialectal students' experiences with academic-based writing but also as a rich resource of knowledge that all students should know as they broaden their abilities to express their ideas in a variety of forms. The inclusion of these resources in the curriculum is a strategy that is in keeping with other educational approaches that have successfully used the cultural resources of their students to enrich the learning experience. Rather than avoid these students' cultural experiences, identities, and interests, successful programs within the academy and within the extra curriculum have consciously sought them out and used them as one of the major sources of the curriculum. We have identified several obstacles to the mastery of good writing skills by bidialectal students. Contrary to popular belief, empirical studies indicate that an interference caused by students' use of their heritage language is not one of those obstacles. Research on teaching writing tells us, in fact, that bidialectal students experience the same difficulties that other students experience. They perform poorly when they are unfamiliar with the expected conventions, when they have not received explicit instruction, when they are taught by underprepared teachers, and when they are being taught by those who believe that bidialectal students are a homogeneous group who are incapable of learning. In particular, they do poorly when they are being taught by those who are seeking a one-size-fits-all solution.

In our most recent publication, Ted Lardner and I (Ball & Lardner, 2005) share an important message with researchers, program administrators, teacher education programs, and teachers concerning innovations that can be implemented with the potential of yielding profound differences in our efforts toward crafting classrooms that unleash literate possibilities, not only for their African American students but also for all of their students. Throughout our book we touch on many important innovations, but we understand that many teachers want to know how to enact the themes we've shared in our examples from community-based organizations and the lives of actual teachers. Many classroom teachers want to know some concrete steps they can take as they embark on the journey toward implementing the transformative changes we propose. As a starting point, what we provide in the final section of our book is a discussion called Playin' The Dozens, in which we present 12 changes teachers can initiate and monitor as they reflect on, analyze, and transform their classrooms and their classroom practices. For those teachers who want to teach culturally and linguistically diverse students in more powerful, more effective, and more sensitive ways but just don't know where or how to begin, these 12 steps can be used as an initial point from which they can begin to implement the themes outlined throughout the book. It is critical, however, that teachers realize that the 12 suggestions we provide are merely a starting a point. The real challenge remains for each individual teacher and for our profession as a whole to move beyond these starting points in generative ways to implement a transformed pedagogy that is well suited for the unique population of culturally and linguistically diverse students they serve. The suggestions we provide elaborate on teachers' need to

1. Readjust their attitudes concerning their culturally and linguistically diverse students and the language resources they bring into the classroom.

2. Confront racial insecurities and prejudices.

3. Hold high expectations and communicate them.

4. Create a space for affect in their classrooms.

5. Create opportunities for students to play multiple roles in the classroom.

6. Integrate performance in the classroom.

7. Develop a knowledge base of the basic discourse patterns of their bidialectal students.

8. Recognize, accept, and incorporate varied oral and written discourse patterns.

9. Reconceptualize the writing conference.

10. Position culturally and linguistically diverse students as informants and interpreters.

11. Reassess approaches to assessment.

12. Seek nurturing professional collaborations that model and support efficacious teaching.

Over the past four decades, our profession has grappled with issues of urban education and the intersection of issues related to race, class, gender, and cultural and linguistic diversity in the learning environment. As a result of this grappling, we are beginning to remove some of the folk theories and myths that exist in our own minds and in the minds of our fellow professionals. The challenge still remains, however, for us to seriously consider how best to move these conversations beyond the pages of our research reports and scholarly journals, to become conversations of central concern to policymakers and "mainstream" scholars, practitioners, and administrators in our field such that the dialogues result in the implementation of changed policies and changed practices within language arts and content area classrooms. It is important that reading and writing research move forward within an interdisciplinary arena of inquiry that takes significant and positive steps toward building a more powerful theoretical framework that

> include[s] more analytic attention to how the complex of sociocultural experiences enter into literacy learning experiences that have roots in social class, ethnicity, language background, family, neighborhood, and gender. Without serious attention to the unfolding of this wider cultural frame in literacy learning, our vision of the whole remains partially obscured. (Dyson & Freedman, 1991, p. 4)

It is important that the research community begin to communicate with teachers and policymakers rather than theorizing among themselves about what should be happening within classrooms. They should also initiate interdisciplinary collaborations with professionals within schools and within community-based organizations to facilitate the design and implementation of effective programs that address the needs of urban bidialectal students.

# REFERENCES

Amastae, J., & Elias-Olivares, L. (Eds.). (1982). *Spanish in the United States: Sociolinguistic aspects.* Cambridge, UK: Cambridge University Press.

Applebee, A.N. (1981). *Writing in the secondary school: English and the content areas* (Research Monograph No. 21). Urbana, IL: National Council of Teachers of English.

Ball, A.F. (1992). Cultural preference and the expository writing of African-American adolescents. *Written Communication, 9*(4), 501–532.

Ball, A.F. (1995a). Community-based learning in urban settings as a model for educational reform. *Applied Behavioral Science Review, 3*(2), 127–146.

Ball, A.F. (1995b). Investigating language, learning, and linguistic competence of African-American children: Torrey revisited. *Linguistics and Education, 7*(1), 23–46.

Ball, A.F. (1995c). Text design patterns in the writing of urban African-American students: Teaching to the strengths of students in multicultural settings. *Urban Education, 30*(3), 253–289.

Ball, A.F. (1997). Expanding the dialogue on culture as a critical component when assessing writing. *Assessing Writing, 4*(2), 169–202.

Ball, A.F. (1998). Evaluating the writing of culturally and linguistically diverse students: The case of the African American English speaker. In C.R. Cooper & L. Odell (Eds.), *Evaluating writing: The role of teachers' knowledge about text, learning, and culture* (2nd ed., pp. 225–248). Urbana, IL: National Council of Teachers of English.

Ball, A.F. (1999). Preservice teachers' perspectives on literacy and its use in urban schools: A Vygotskian perspective on internal activity and teacher change. In C. Lee & P. Smagorinsky (Eds.), *Vygotskian perspectives on literacy research: Constructing meaning through collaborative inquiry* (pp. 314–359). Cambridge, MA: Cambridge University Press.

Ball, A.F. (2000a). Empowering pedagogies that enhance the learning of multicultural students. *Teachers College Record, 102*(6), 1006–1034.

Ball, A.F. (2000b). Preparing teachers for diversity: Lessons learned from the U.S. and South Africa. *Teaching and Teacher Education, 16*(4), 491–509.

Ball, A.F. (2000c). Preservice teachers' perspectives on literacy and its use in urban schools: A Vygotskian perspective on internal activity and teacher change. In C. Lee & P. Smagorinsky (Eds.), *Worlds of meaning: Vygotskian perspectives on literacy research* (pp. 314–359). Cambridge, UK: Cambridge University Press.

Ball, A.F. (2005). *Carriers of the torch: Addressing the global challenge of preparing teachers for diversity.* New York: Teachers College Press.

Ball, A.F., & Farr, M. (2003). Language varieties, culture, and teaching the English language arts. In J. Flood, J.M. Jensen, D. Lapp, & J.R. Squire (Eds.), *Handbook of research on teaching the English language arts* (2nd ed., pp. 435–445). New York: Macmillan.

Ball, A.F., & Heath, S.B. (1993). Dances of identity: Finding an ethnic self in the arts. In S.B. Heath & M.W. McLaughlin (Eds.), *Possible selves: Achievement, ethnicity, and gender for inner-city youth* (pp. 69–93). New York: Teachers College Press.

Ball, A.F., & Lardner, T. (2005). *African American literacies unleashed: Vernacular English and the composition classroom.* Carbondale: Southern Illinois University Press.

Ball, A.F., & Muhammad, R.J. (2003). Language diversity in teacher education and in the classroom. In G. Smitherman & V. Villanueva (Eds.), *Language diversity in the classroom: From intention to practice* (pp. 76–88). Carbondale: Southern Illinois University Press.

Baugh, J. (1988). Review of twice as less: Black English and the performance of Black students in mathematics and science by Eleanor Wilson Orr. *Harvard Educational Review, 58*, 395–403.

Baugh, J. (1990). A survey of the suffix /-s/ analyses in Black English. In J.A. Edmondson, C. Feagin, & P. Mühlhäusler

(Eds.), *Development and diversity: Language variation across time and space* (pp. 297–307). Arlington: University of Texas and Summer Institute of Linguistics.

Baugh, J. (1992). Hypercorrection: Mistakes in production of vernacular African American English as a second dialect. *Language and Education, 6*, 47–61.

Britton, J. (1975). *The development of writing abilities*. London: Macmillan.

Cazden, C.B. (2001). *Classroom discourse: The language of teaching and learning* (2nd ed.). Portsmouth, NH: Heinemann.

Dyson, A.H., & Freedman, S.W. (1991). *Critical challenges for research on writing and literacy: 1990–1995*. Berkeley, CA: Center for the Study of Writing.

Edwards, W.F. (1992). Sociolinguistic behavior in a Detroit inner-city black neighborhood. *Language in Society, 21*(1), 93–115.

Fasold, R. (1972). *Tense marking in Black English*. Washington, DC: Center for Applied Linguistics.

Ferguson, C., & Heath, S.B. (Eds.). (1981). *Language in the USA*. Cambridge, UK: Cambridge University Press.

Foster, M. (1987). *It's cookin now: An ethnographic study of the teaching style of a successful Black teacher in a White community college*. Unpublished doctoral dissertation, Harvard University.

Foster, M. (1992). Now it's really cookin': Sociolinguistics and the African-American community: Implications for literacy. *Theory Into Practice, 31*, 303–311.

Heath, S.B. (1983). *Ways with words: Language, life, and work in communities and classrooms*. Cambridge, UK: Cambridge University Press.

Hymes, D. (1981). *"In vain I tried to tell you": Studies in Native American ethnopoetics*. Philadelphia: University of Pennsylvania Press.

Kochman, T. (Ed.). (1972). *Rappin' and stylin' out: Communication in urban black America*. Urbana: University of Illinois Press.

Labov, W. (1972). *Language in the inner-city: Studies in the Black English vernacular*. Philadelphia: University of Pennsylvania Press.

Labov, W. (Ed.). (1980). *Locating language in time and space*. New York: Academic Press.

Leap, W. (1993). *American Indian English*. Salt Lake City: University of Utah Press.

Leont'ev, A.N. (1981). The problem of activity in psychology. In J. Wertsch (Ed.), *The concept of activity in Soviet psychology* (pp. 37–71). Armonk, New York: Sharpe.

Poplack, S., & Tagliamonte, S. (1994). -S or nothing: marking the plural in the African-American diaspora. *American Speech, 69*, 227–259.

Rose, M. (1989). *Lives on the boundary: The struggles and achievements of America's underprepared*. New York: Free Press.

Vygotsky, L.S. (1978). *Mind in society: The development of higher psychological processes* (M. Cole, V. John-Steiner, S. Scribner, & E. Souberman, Eds. & Trans.). Cambridge, MA: Harvard University Press. (Original work published 1934)

Wolfram, W. (1969). *A sociolinguistic description of Detroit Negro speech*. Washington, DC: Center for Applied Linguistics.

Wolfram, W. (1974). *Sociolinguistic aspects of assimilation: Puerto Rican English in New York City*. Washington, DC: Center for Applied Linguistics.

Wolfram, W., & Christian, D. (1976). *Appalachian speech*. Washington, DC: Center for Applied Linguistics.

Wolfram, W., Christian, D., Potter, L., & Leap, W. (1979). *Variability in the English of two Indian communities and its effects on reading and writing* (Final Rep. No. NIE-G-77-0006). Washington, DC: Center for Applied Linguistics.

Wolfram, W., & Hatfield, D. (1984). *The tense marking in second language learning: Patterns of spoken and written English in a Vietnamese community*. Washington, DC: Center for Applied Linguistics.

Zentella, A.C. (1981). *Hablamos los Dos. We speak both: Growing up bilingual in El Barrio*. Unpublished doctoral dissertation, University of Pennsylvania.

# CHAPTER 17

# The Persistence of Inequality: English-Language Learners and Educational Reform

*Kris D. Gutiérrez*

M y task is to provide a synthesis of research related to literacy education for English Learners (ELs). I have chosen to focus on what recent empirical work suggests about how this increasingly vulnerable student population has fared under new mandates that define what counts as literacy, literacy learning and instruction, and assessment in ways that impede opportunity to learn. Given what we are learning about the effects of new educational policies, it is important to examine what is at stake for ELs if the current trend in literacy education persists.

## Some Context

For a moment I thought that September 11, 2001, might disrupt the prevailing assumptions that would lead us to believe that public education is about providing technical skills for a labor force or that the teaching of literacy learning is a neutral, benign, scientific, and technical issue. I thought that this critical moment would have made evident the need for a more interconnected, thoughtful, and reflective world—one in which a rich literacy toolkit could play a critical role in moving us away from overly simplistic, binary, and uncomplicated analyses of our world and our individual and collective relation to it. I hoped that literacy in the broader sense would be more about using language, reading, and writing as tools for comprehending texts across genres and communities, as tools for entering complex conversations and contemplating conflicting perspectives. I also was hopeful that these troubling and complicated times would present a new imperative around the need for a more critical and equitable education that would begin to level the unequal playing field.

Instead, as a profession, we have become more narrow, insular, and locked into discussions about scientifically based research and methods without addressing the practical logics (Bourdieu, 1980) of such discourses or the pervasive inequities inherent in both old practices and new remedies for the schooling of urban children. And practices that push for forms of critical literacy as educational outcomes have become risky to carry out, if not unpatriotic. New literacy practices for urban children, most of whom are poor and speak a language or register other than standard English, organize literacy instruction that socializes students in under-resourced schools to a new work order (Apple, 2001; Gee, 1999; Gee, Hull, & Lankshear, 1996).

More specific to the focus of this chapter, educational and social policies in the United States are restructuring the instructional terrain in ways that previous policy configurations have not. Most notably, national, state, and local reforms are aligning around narrow beliefs about the fundamental purposes of schooling, language use and citizenship, nationalism, teacher professionalism, and accountability. Further, attempts at the federal level to nationalize curricula and pedagogy and to define and regulate the parameters of educational research and teacher preparation buttress this alignment (Gándara, 2000; Gutiérrez et al., 2002). Specifically, the current educational agenda is oriented toward disrupting and eradicating particular sets of practices, while reviving and bolstering other practices that delimit opportunities to learn, that is, opportunities for full participation in the valued practices of academic and social activity. While some may champion this trend in the coordination of reforms, this chapter will focus on how the current alignment in national, state, and local social and educational policies creates a new institutionalized educational architecture that has deleterious consequences on ELs in both low- and high-performing schools (Gutiérrez, Zavala, Asato, Pacheco, & Olson, 2003). To be clear, the argument advanced here is certainly not against the value of alignment but rather it is an argument that asks for a serious examination of what literacy and social outcomes result from this imposed alignment.

In the new educational activity, commodified instructional packages reinforce reductive or narrow literacy practices that socialize students from nondominant groups (I prefer to use the term *nondominant students* instead of *minority* or *diverse students* because it better describes their social position) to new notions and practices of literacy that make them "look like readers"—the kind of procedural display about which Bloome and his colleagues have written (Bloome, Puro, & Theodorou, 1989)—without providing them the requisite skills afforded more privileged students. Of significance, these literacy and larger educational reforms are creating a new archaeology of knowledge that has material effects on students and their communities (Luke, in press-a, in press-b). What are the practical effects of the new educational terrain on urban students, specifically ELs? To help us gauge the local effects, we need to ask the following questions:

- What are the current schooling conditions for students from nondominant groups, especially ELs?
- How can we create and sustain access to robust and equitable learning communities in the context of a growing constellation of educational reform initiatives and decreased fiscal and human resources?
- How do current educational discourses and practices manage diversity?

To answer these questions in any comprehensive way requires us first to understand how the persistence of inequality can be found, in part, in the layers of social and educational policies, past and present, that shape a school's literacy practices. Their cumulative effect has created the current conditions in which ELs continue to receive a substantially inequitable education in relation to their English-speaking peers, even when those peers are similarly economically disadvantaged.

## English Learners in California: A Case Study

California serves as an appropriate context in which to examine the increasing vulnerability of the United States' fastest growing student population, as ELs constitute one fourth of the state's entire public school population, and one out of every three elementary students is an EL (Rumberger, Callahan, & Gándara, 2003). Few schools in California have no ELs and in many schools more than 25% of the students speak a home language other than English. Nearly 84% of ELs are Spanish dominant, while 89% speak Spanish, Vietnamese, Hmong, or Cantonese (Rumberger & Gándara, 2000).

Rumberger and Gándara (2000, 2004) have documented the current state of education for ELs in California. Today, ELs are significantly more segregated from their peers and have considerably less access to appropriately prepared teachers, materials, facilities, and rigorous coursework, or sufficient instructional time and assistance to meet their academic needs. On the whole, ELs are denied multiple pathways to success because they receive inadequate counseling or academic support. Their educational tracking is facilitated by assessment practices that do not measure learning or adequately assess their learning needs (Yaden, Rueda, Tsai, & Esquinca, in press). Similarly, their teachers are not provided the professional development required to meet their students' needs (Gándara, Rumberger, Maxwell-Jolly, & Callahan, 2003). Clearly, educational inequalities exacerbate the already deplorable conditions of ELs in California, and we should expect U.S. trends to be similar.

Hakuta's (1998) analysis further supports the case that ELs in California are continually denied basic opportunities to learn. He reports that ELs are more likely to be in classrooms with uncredentialed teachers than their English-only peers and are taught by teachers who have little preparation to teach them. Consider the consequence of this trend in light of what we know this student population needs to succeed. As Hakuta (1998) points out,

> [ELs who] start out substantially behind their English-speaking counterparts, must be taught both English language skills (including academic English) and academic content to receive equal educational opportunities on par with their native English-speaking grade-level peers. To achieve this objective of equal access, English Learners must receive instruction from teachers with the specialized knowledge needed to teach English and academic content to second-language learners and must be provided access to specialized instructional materials geared toward those not yet fluent in English. These principles are recognized both as necessary pedagogical practice and by long-standing legal requirements. (p. 1)

*Opportunity to learn* should be a fundamental goal in the schooling of ELs today and should serve as a benchmark for assessing educational outcome. Despite claims in the public media that there is an increase in the reading achievement of ELs, there is growing evidence that the current constellation of local, state, and national reforms further reduces access to meaningful opportunities to learn. Specifically, we learn that

- English-only policies regulate language use among students and teachers and minimize opportunities to use language to learn content knowledge or to make sense of texts or classroom discussions (Hakuta, 1998; Moll & Ruiz, 2002; Rumberger & Gándara, 2004).

- A hastily implemented class-size reduction policy, implemented without the requisite credentialed teachers to meet the new demand of smaller teacher-to-student ratios, increases the likelihood that ELs disproportionately receive instruction from under-prepared teachers (Gándara et al., 2003).

- Standards-based instructional practices, designed to address the achievement gap and disparate practices across California, have become the new scripted program in which the teaching of the standards becomes the object of instruction. The standards are not used to enrich learning for ELs (Baker, Inn, Herman, & Koretz, 2002; Crosland & Gutiérrez, 2003; Darling-Hammond, 2003).

- New reading initiatives organized around prescriptive literacy instruction and reductive views of literacy learning offer an impoverished reading diet to ELs (Moll & Ruiz, 2002).

- Social promotion and retention practices that in general assume a remedial stance to address the achievement gap perpetuate academic tracking for ELs.

- Significant cutbacks in teacher professional development activities are accompanied by a narrowing of teacher credential requirements related to teaching multilingual and multicultural student populations (Darling-Hammond, 2001).

- High-stakes assessment programs orient the content and nature of instruction of low-performing schools (Abedi, 2001).

- A new overarching national educational framework, No Child Left Behind (NCLB), reorganizes the form, content, and delivery of literacy education for poor children, especially ELs across the United States (Abedi & Dietel, 2004; Gutiérrez, 2004; Gutiérrez et al., 2003; Linn, Baker, & Betebenner, 2002).

## Regulating Language and Literacy

Language and literacy policies are at the core of new educational reforms, and English-only policies have helped facilitate their implementation, in spite of what is known about the importance of the primary language in meaningful or deep learning. As colleagues and I have argued elsewhere, English-only policies are ahistorical and the public discourse around English-only reflects this ahistorical understanding of the language policies and practices ELs have experienced throughout U.S. history, or even the past four decades in California (Gutiérrez, Baquedano-Lopez, & Asato, 2001). Before the implementation of bilingual education, English immersion was the standard educational model. In 1974, Lau v. Nichols provided the legal remedy that mandated that ELs receive the same instruction as English-speaking children. As the U.S. Supreme Court argued three decades ago:

> There is no equality of treatment merely by providing students with the same facilities, textbooks, teachers, and curriculum, for students who do not understand English are effectively foreclosed from any meaningful education. (*Lau v. Nichols*, 1974)

Thus, these new polices, put forth as advances, are in fact recycled policies and practices that ignore history and promote inequities (Gutiérrez et al., 2001).

Further, these language policies are not grounded in research about language and literacy development in the first and second language. Of significance, they are based on very narrow notions of the role of language in learning that are antithetical to understandings of the primacy of language in the processes of deep learning.

## Challenging Prevailing Views of Learning

One important step in challenging narrowing notions of language and literacy would be to examine the conceptions of learning and development that undergird prevailing reform initiatives. Cultural–historical theories of learning and development, more commonly known as sociocultural theory, are useful in exposing the limitations of particular views of learning that inform so many reading programs and practices today. For example, a sociocultural view argues that human beings interact with their worlds primarily through mediational means, that is, through cultural artifacts or tools and symbols, including language (Vygotsky, 1978). This principle helps us understand the important mediational role a student's primary language plays in learning and literacy development. Language from a cultural–historical perspective is considered the preeminent tool for learning and human development and is said to mediate individuals' activity in the valued practices of their communities across a lifespan (Cole, 1996; Cole & Engestrom, 1993). What then are the consequences for learning and development for children who are not allowed to use their home language—the most powerful sense-making tool they have—in the service of learning?

Of significance to the teaching of ELs and other students from non-dominant groups, sociocultural views of literacy learning center attention on cultural practices (i.e., valued activities of individuals and their communities with particular features and routines) as fundamental to mediating or assisting literacy development (Gutiérrez & Rogoff, 2003). According to this sociocultural view, we learn more about an individual and community's literacy practices from knowing about the cultural activities, that is, social practices, in which the individual or group participates. By focusing on the cultural activity of various communities and the nature of learning and participation therein, we begin to understand how other participants, tools, and the social ecology of individuals' lives influence literacy learning.

Following this perspective, literacy learning is considered a socially mediated process that cannot be understood apart from its context of development, the forms of mediation (assistance) available, and the nature of participation available across various cultural practices, including classroom literacy practices. Thus, in contrast to conceptions of literacy as the acquisition of a series of discrete skills, a sociocultural view of literacy argues that literacy learning cannot be abstracted from the cultural practices in which they are nested. How learning is organized in classrooms, then, has tremendous influence on what gets learned.

This point is supported by theories of language socialization that suggest that human beings undergo a lifelong process of socialization and are socialized to particular language practices through language itself. Specifically, language socialization is the process whereby novices gain knowledge and skills relevant to membership in a social group through participation in the cultural practices of the community (Ochs, 1988). From a language socialization perspective, language practices and the status of one's language in those practices play a central and dynamic role in the construction of social languages (discourses) and identities. In this way, the literacy practices of the classroom also socialize children to specific language practices and their use.

Similarly, the New Literacy Studies framework (Barton, Hamilton, & Ivanic, 2000; Luke, 1994; Luke & Carrington, 2002) proposes that as children are socialized to particular literacy practices, they are simultaneously socialized into discourses that position them ideologically within the larger social milieu. To what discourses and identities are ELs being socialized in environments that restrict and even prohibit their primary language use?

Although not the specific focus of this chapter, a more complex analysis of the persistence of educational inequity would address the interplay between new language policies and issues of race and ethnicity. Indeed today, language has become a proxy for race, another means of identifying, segregating, and homogenizing a student population to neutralize diversity and facilitate institutional racism and discrimination (Gutiérrez, Asato, Santos, & Gotanda, 2002). As Crosland (2004) argues, educational reform, including language policies, must be understood against a backdrop of "colorblind" or "race-neutral" policies that "define 'racism' as race conscious policies impeding racial harmony" (p. 10). To counter this trend, Crosland argues, equity advocates call for a race-conscious agenda that explicitly confronts the ongoing consequences of institutionalized racism in schools. As we have argued elsewhere, English-only policies are organized responses to the increasing presence of a new, growing language group in the community; these policies are grounded in anti-immigrant sentiments in a time of dwindling human and fiscal resources and perceived loss of power and influence (Gutiérrez et al., 2002).

## Productive Learning Environments

As we have seen in California, voter decisions about English-only policies were made without consideration of the evidence about the benefits of primary language instruction or the use of the primary language to learn in both formal and nonformal learning environments. The focus on learning and the consequences of participating in rich literacy practices gets lost easily in the diversionary debates about English-only and related reading programs. The public has simply conflated their notions of bilingual education with the contribution of the home language to learning. It is important to decouple the political discussions of bilingual education and English-only from what we know about the benefits of primary language in acquiring content knowledge, and learning and participating more productively in schooling activity.

While there are numerous programs that yield productive literacy learning, there is much to be learned from studies of nonformal or out-of-school settings that document how new configurations of the learning environment, forms of participation, and the use of children's complete linguistic toolkit promote learning (Hull & Schultz, 2002; Nicolopolou & Cole, 1993; 1999), identity development (Heath & McLaughlin, 1993), and literacy learning in particular (Gutiérrez, Baquedano-Lopez, Alvarez, & Chiu, 1999; Vásquez, 2003).

In contrast to settings that restrict the use of the students' linguistic repertoire, these environments organize literacy learning around sociocultural principles of learning in ways that privilege and foster hybrid language practices, that is, the strategic use of the students' complete linguistic toolkit in the service of learning. In these learning environments, no single language is privileged and students' repertoires become tools for participating and making meaning in collaborative activity. We have documented how such practices help build successful strategies that draw from local and cultural knowledge as a means to expand students' knowledge of literacy, as well as the sociocultural knowledge of how and when to use this knowledge in academic contexts (Gutiérrez, Baquedano-Lopez, & Tejeda, 1999).

But out-of-school settings need not be the only sites of meaningful learning for ELs. The productive use of the primary language in school settings has been more fully documented by Thomas and Collier (2003), who report the effects of different types of language instructional programs on ELs.

These findings have implications for designing effective literacy instruction for these students. I will highlight a few significant and relevant claims. Given the preponderance of English-only programs, their study found that students immersed in English instruction show large decreases in reading and math achievement by grade 5, when compared to students who received bilingual/ESL services. The largest number of dropouts comes from the English-only group; those remaining in school and who finished grade 11 ranked at the 12th percentile on standardized reading tests. Given that Latinos have the highest dropout rates in the United States, this finding should be of grave concern. Clearly, more research is needed about the relation between the high dropout rates and students' participation in English-only and primary language programs.

At the same time, students participating in dual immersion (or two-immersion) programs continue to outperform students in all other models of language instruction. Consider the following:

> Spanish-speaking immigrant students after 1–2 years of U.S. schooling achieved at a median of the 62nd NCE (71% percentile) in Grades 3–6. These immigrants arrived on or above grade level and maintained above grade level performance in Spanish in the succeeding two years.
>
> In 90-10 Transitional bilingual education classes, native-Spanish speakers reached the 56th to 60th NCE (61st to 68th percentile) for Grades 1–4, and after moving into all-English instruction in Grade 5, they tested at the 51st NCE, still on grade level in Spanish reading.
>
> In reading achievement across the curriculum, native-Spanish speakers outperformed native-English speakers when tested in their native language, for Grades 1–8, regardless of the type of bilingual program Spanish-speaking students received. Native-Spanish speakers remained significantly above grade level at every grade except sixth grade (at the 49th NCTE), reaching the 64th NCTE (74th percentile) in 8th grade. (Thomas & Collier, 2003, p. 8)

These findings are supported by our own studies of 29 high-poverty, higher performing schools in California that retain some form of primary language instruction. (Higher performing was defined as a school with a state academic performance score [API] of at least 5 [10 is high]. These schools also had high concentrations of poverty, mobility, and ELs.) My colleagues and I found that dual immersion schools consistently met or maintained their targeted growth projections (Gutiérrez et al., 2003). In a recent report on the development of biliteracy, researchers found that in general students participating in two-way immersion programs demonstrated impressive levels of performance on reading, writing, and oral language measures in both English and Spanish by the end of fifth grade (Howard, Christian, & Genesee, 2004).

Similarly, as reported in the Thomas and Collier (2003) study, students' achievement in Spanish was impressive. In general, students receiving four to seven years of dual-language schooling outperformed comparable monolingually schooled students, while the highest quality ESL program only closed the achievement gap by half.

Contrary to English-only policies that transition students quickly into English instruction, research indicates that students with no English or limited English abilities do not benefit from short-term primary language instruction programs, as they generally need four years of instruction in the first language (Thomas & Collier, 2003). In contradiction to the rush-to-English practices, oral English proficiency generally takes three to five years to develop, while academic English can take from four to seven years (Hakuta, Butler, & Witt, 2000). These understandings of the literacy development of ELs are critical to the design of effective contexts for learning and appropriate assessment practices, especially in this high-stakes assessment era (Abedi, 2001; Linn et al., 2002). Consider, for example, the tendency for ELs to score lower than their English dominant counterparts when they first exit their primary language programs; this trend changes over time, as they generally catch up by the time they reach middle school and subsequently outperform English-only students in high school (Rueda, 2003).

In light of these results, there should be increased opportunity for students to build their primary language skills. Instead, studies of the effects of recent English-only policies have documented how ELs in many California schools have increasingly fewer opportunities to receive instructional support in their home language or to use their primary language in the service of learning (Gándara et al., 2003; Rumberger & Gándara, 2000, 2004). This is significantly important in that the strongest predictor of second-language achievement is the amount of schooling in the home language (Tabors & Snow, 1994). Our own studies of the effects of educational reform on ELs have documented that English-only instructional practices exacerbate the inequitable learning conditions of an already vulnerable student population by dramatically reducing and complicating opportunities to learn. Such practices essentialize and homogenize students and define them exclusively on the basis of their language status rather than their diverse backgrounds, language skills, interests, and learning needs.

Most notably, English-only policies combine with other educational reforms to create an impoverished literacy curriculum. As the emphasis on test scores and adequate yearly progress increases, we observe a decreased use of the primary language to learn new content and to make instruction comprehensible, even in contexts where the use of the primary language is legal and official. There is a link between this rapid shift in English language practices and high-stakes assessment programs that require testing in English, as well as to dramatic changes in the focus of local and state reading programs. For example, mandated literacy programs that orient instruction to high-stakes tests are designed for native English speakers. What is perhaps more troubling is that the mandated literacy programs promote reductive, that is, narrow notions of literacy, in which productive talk, meaningful and rigorous texts, and joint activity are rarely employed as tools for mediating literacy learning. This narrow focus on the acquisition of basic skills impedes literacy development in both the home or school language and occurs at the exclusion of instruction in critical reading, writing, and analyses of texts across content areas; and there is virtually no instruction in writing, social studies, and science in many classrooms. Overall, the push toward English-only across the curriculum and higher test scores make oral English language fluency and a narrow set of literacy skills the target of instruction (Gutiérrez et al., 2003). Without an emphasis on biliteracy, academic English, and learning, how serious can the effort to narrow the achievement gap be?

# Reading and the English Learner

As Rueda (2003) points out, reading development for ELs is similar to those of monolingual students, all things being equal. As beginning readers, ELs use their developing knowledge of language, their background knowledge, and their understanding of print conventions. However, primary language instruction makes learning to read a more comprehensible activity and would only promote learning. While listening and speaking develop more quickly than reading and writing skills, by grade 3 ELs will develop about 80% of what English-only students know in listening. This developmental perspective helps us understand why English reading and writing skills will often develop less quickly than in native English speakers. However, more parallel achievement levels across both groups after fifth grade emerge (Moll & Ruiz, 2002; Rueda, 2003). And the significant diversity across ELs accounts for the varying trajectories we should expect to see in this student population. As Tabors and Snow (2001) report,

> Second language learning differentially affects literacy development depending on such factors as the age at which second-language learning is initiated, the language in which exposure to print and early literacy instruction is initiated, and the degree of support for first- and second-language learning and literacy development in both the home and school environments. (p. 177)

Despite such evidence, we see the persistence of English-only curricula in prescriptive, tightly monitored reading programs. However, the increasing vulnerability of ELs cannot be attributed solely to English-only practices. Rather, an impoverished reading and literacy curriculum and English-only instruction in combination have become the program du jour and have done little to eliminate or narrow the significant achievement gap between ELs and English-fluent students. The achievement data in Figure 17.1 illustrate that even with an intensive focus on developing oral English language and basic reading skills, over 70% of California's EL student population, grades 2 through 6, cluster at the bottom two quartiles of the reading section of the state-mandated assessment.

Not only has this trend of underachievement remained constant over the past two years, note that the percentage of students falling below the 50th percentile increases as students enter the middle schools years (see Figure 17.2).

While test scores alone hardly capture the educational disparity ELs experience, they do illustrate that the achievement gap between ELs and their English-speaking counterparts, as illustrated in Figure 17.3, has not narrowed; instead, we see the opposite trend for English-fluent students whose scores cluster above the 50th percentile in reading.

## Figure 17.1
## State SAT-9 ELL, 2001

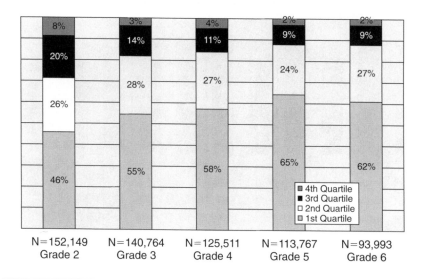

Statistics provided by the California State Department of Education, California Standardized Testing and Reporting (STAR) Program. Retrieved May 1, 2003, from http://data1.cde.ca.gov/dataquest

## Figure 17.2
## SAT-9 ELL Reading Scores, 2001–2002

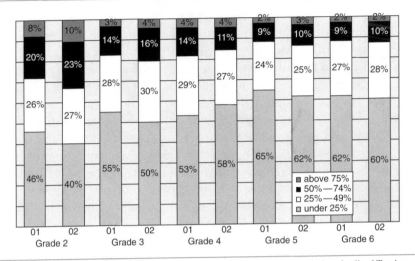

| | above 75% |
|---|---|
| ■ | 50%—74% |
| □ | 25%—49% |
| ▨ | under 25% |

Statistics provided by the California State Department of Education, California Standardized Testing and Reporting (STAR) Program. Retrieved May 1, 2003, from http://data1.cde.ca.gov/dataquest

## Figure 17.3
## SAT-9 Reading EPs, Percentage by Quartiles

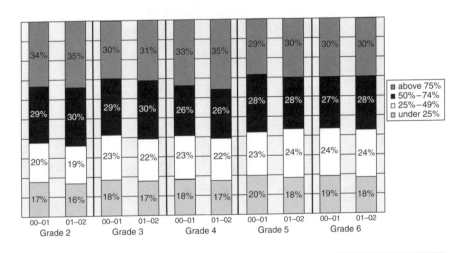

| | above 75% |
|---|---|
| ■ | 50%–74% |
| □ | 25%–49% |
| ▨ | under 25% |

Statistics provided by the California State Department of Education, California Standardized Testing and Reporting (STAR) Program. Retrieved May 1, 2003, from http://data1.cde.ca.gov/dataquest

Of concern, the combined practices of English-only and prescriptive reading programs construct a particular kind of reader—one whose limited literacy repertoire helps ensure limited opportunity across a lifespan. Further, the new reading initiatives, coupled with new mandates of NCLB (2002), will facilitate the construction of what Gee (1999) calls a new level of underclass reader. With NCLB's focus on adequate yearly progress—determined almost exclusively by standardized test performance—and a required participation of 95% of a school's student population in state-mandated assessments, the trend in English-only instruction should persist, even when the children are not yet fluent in academic English (Rueda, in press). The pressure to increase test scores to avoid being labeled a school in need of improvement facilitates the norming or flattening of a very diverse student population and one-size-fits-all interventions to address a perceived uniform set of educational interests and needs.

As with any reform, there are aspects of NCLB that educators, researchers, and policymakers may find useful. The reporting of subgroup performance finally does put ELs on the map, making it easier to identify trends in achievement, as well as discriminatory practices. And these data enable us to observe over time whether these reforms are taking the children anywhere, pedagogically, intellectually, socially, or critically (Darling-Hammond, 1996, 2003).

Although this chapter has focused primarily on data of the schooling experiences of elementary school students, their experiences portend the future of many secondary school students (Valdés & Figueroa, 1994). Thus, to understand how to improve secondary schools and to ensure continued access to higher education, we must assess and intervene early in the schooling experiences of ELs. Opportunity to learn must be understood as both the outcome and consequence of our educational system.

## REFERENCES

Abedi, J. (2001, Summer). *Assessment and accommodations for English learners: Issues and recommendations* (CRESST Policy Brief 4). Los Angeles: National Center for Research on Evaluation, Standards, and Student Testing. Retrieved October 14, 2004, from http://cresst96.cse.ucla.edu/products/newsletters/polbrf4web.pdf

Abedi, J., & Dietel, R. (2004, Winter). *Challenges in the No Child Left Behind Act for English Language Learners* (CRESST Policy Brief 7). Los Angeles: National Center for Research on Evaluation, Standards, and Student Testing. Retrieved October 14, 2004, from http://cresst96.cse.ucla.edu/products/newsletters/policybrief7.pdf

Apple, M.W. (2001). *Educating the "right" way: Markets, standards, God, and inequality.* London: Routledge.

Baker, E.L., Inn, R.L., Herman, J.L., & Koretz, D. (2002, Winter). Standards for educational accountability systems. *The CRESST Line*, pp. 1–4.

Barton, D., Hamilton, M., & Ivanic, R. (Eds.). (2000). *Situated literacies: Reading and writing in context*. London: Routledge.

Bloome, D., Puro, P., & Theodorou, E. (1989). Procedural display and classroom lessons. *Curriculum Inquiry*, *19*, 265–291.

Bourdieu, P. (1980). *The logic of practice*. Stanford, CA: Stanford University Press.

Cole, M. (1996). *Cultural psychology: A once and future discipline*. Cambridge, MA: Belknap Press of Harvard University Press.

Cole, M., & Engestrom, Y. (1993). A cultural-historical approach to distributed cognition. In G. Salomon (Ed.), *Distributed cognition: Psychological and educational considerations* (pp. 1–46). New York: Cambridge University Press.

Crosland, K. (2004, April 13). *Too many students left behind: Race, low performing schools, and the era of colorblind choice*. Paper presented at the annual meeting of the American Educational Research Association, San Diego, CA.

Crosland, K., & Gutiérrez, K. (2003). Standardizing teaching, standardizing teachers: Educational reform and the de-professionalization of teachers in an English-only era. *Educators for Urban Minorities*, *2*(2), 24–40.

Darling-Hammond, L. (1996). Performance-based assessment and educational equity. In E.R. Hollins (Ed.), *Transforming curriculum for a culturally diverse society* (pp. 245–272). Mahwah, NJ: Erlbaum.

Darling-Hammond, L. (2001). Teacher testing and the improvement of practice. *Teaching Education*, *12*(1), 11–34.

Darling-Hammond, L. (2003). Standards and assessments: Where we are and what we need. *Teachers College Record*. Retrieved May 3, 2003, from http://www.tcrecord.org

Gándara, P. (2000). In the aftermath of the storm: English learners in the post-227 era. *Bilingual Research Journal*, *24*, 1–13.

Gándara, P., Rumberger, R., Maxwell-Jolly, J., & Callahan, R. (2003). English learners in California schools: Unequal resources, unequal outcomes. *Education Policy Analysis Archives*, *11*(36), 1–54. Retrieved October 10, 2004, from http://epaa.asu.edu/epaa/v11n36

Gee, J.P. (1999). Reading and the new literacy studies: Reframing the National Academy of Sciences Report on Reading. *Journal of Literacy Research*, *31*, 355–374.

Gee, J.P., Hull, G., & Lankshear, C. (1996). *The New Work Order: Behind the language of the new capitalism*. Boulder, CO: Westview Press.

Gutiérrez, K. (2004). *Rethinking education policy for English learners*. Aspen Institute Congressional Forum, Washington, DC.

Gutiérrez, K., Asato, J., Pacheco, M., Moll, L., Olson, K., Horng, E., et al. (2002). "Sounding American": The consequences of new reforms on English learners. *Reading Research Quarterly*, *37*, 328–343.

Gutiérrez, K., Asato, J., Santos, M., & Gotanda, N. (2002). Backlash pedagogy: Language and culture and the politics of reform. *The Review of Education, Pedagogy, and Cultural Studies*, *24*(4), 335–351.

Gutiérrez, K., Baquedano-Lopez, P., Alvarez, H., & Chiu, M. (1999). Building a culture of collaboration through hybrid language practices. *Theory Into Practice*, *38*(2), 87–93.

Gutiérrez, K., Baquedano-Lopez, P., & Asato, J. (2001). English for the children: The new literacy of the old world order. *Bilingual Review Journal*, *24*(1 & 2), 87–112.

Gutiérrez, K., Baquedano-Lopez, P., & Tejeda, C. (1999). Rethinking diversity: Hybridity and hybrid language practices in the third space. *Mind, Culture, and Activity*, *6*(4), 286–303.

Gutiérrez, K., & Rogoff, B. (2003). Cultural ways of learning: Individual traits or repertoires of practice. *Educational Researcher*, *32*(5), 19–25.

Gutiérrez, K., Zavala, M., Asato, J., Pacheco, M., & Olson, K. (2003). *Nationalizing and institutionalizing reform: The effects of educational policies on teachers and*

*English learners*. Paper presented at the annual meeting of the Linguistic Minority Research Institute, San Diego, CA.

Hakuta, K. (1998, February). *Improving education for all children: Meeting the needs of language minority children*. Paper presented at The Aspen Institute's fifth conference on the Education and Development of American Youth, Washington, DC.

Hakuta, K., Butler, Y.G., & Witt, D. (2000). *How long does it take English Learners to attain proficiency?* (University of California Linguistic Minority Research Institute Policy Report 2000-1). Retrieved October 14, 2004, from http://www.stanford.edu/~hakuta/Docs/HowLong.pdf

Heath, S.B., & McLaughlin, M.W. (Eds.). (1993). *Identity and inner-city youth: Beyond ethnicity and gender*. New York: Teachers College Press.

Howard, E., Christian, D., & Genesee, F. (2004). *The development of bilingualism and biliteracy from grade 3–5: A summary of findings from the CAL/CREDE study of two-way immersion education* (Report No. RR-13). Santa Cruz, CA: Center for Research on Education, Diversity, & Excellence.

Hull, F., & Schultz, K. (Eds.). (2002). *School's out! Bridging out-of-school literacies with classroom practice*. New York: Teachers College Press.

Lau v. Nichols (1974) 414 U.S. 563, 94 S. Ct. 786.

Linn, R.L., Baker, E.L., & Betebenner, D.W. (2002). *Accountability systems: Implications of requirements of the No Child Left Behind Act of 2001* (CSE Technical Report No. 567). Los Angeles, CA: Center for the Study of Evaluation and National Center on Evaluation, Standards, and Student Testing.

Luke, A. (1994). *The social construction of literacy in the classroom*. New York: Macmillan.

Luke, A. (in press-a). Literacy education for a new ethics of global community. *Language Arts*.

Luke, A. (in press-b). Teaching after the market: From commodity to cosmopolitanism. *Teachers College Record*.

Luke, A., & Carrington, V. (2002). Globalisation, literacy, curriculum practice. In R. Fisher, M. Lewis, & G. Brooks (Eds.), *Language and literacy in action* (pp. 231–250). London: Routledge.

Moll, L., & Ruiz, R. (2002). The schooling of Latino students. In M. Suarez-Orozco & M. Paez (Eds.), *Latinos: Remaking America* (pp. 362–374). Berkeley: University of California Press.

Nicolopolou, A., & Cole, M. (1993). The fifth dimension, its play-world, and its institutional contexts: The generation and transmission of shared knowledge in the culture of collaborative learning. In E.A. Forman, N. Minick, & C.A. Stone (Eds.), *Contexts for learning: Sociocultural dynamics in children's development* (pp. 283–314). New York: Oxford University Press.

Nicolopolou, A., & Cole, M. (1999). Literacy and cognition. In D.A. Wagner, L. Venezky, & B.V. Street (Eds.), *Literacy: An international handbook* (pp. 81–86). New York: Garland.

No Child Left Behind Act of 2001, Pub. L., No. 107-110, 115 Stat. 14225 (2002).

Ochs, E. (1988). *Culture and language development: Language acquisition and language socialization in a Samoan village*. Cambridge: Cambridge University Press.

Rueda, R. (2003). Introduction: Children have a right to reading instruction that makes meaningful use of their first language skills. In P.A. Mason & J.S. Schumm (Eds.), *Promising practices for urban reading instruction* (pp. 356–361). Newark, DE: International Reading Association.

Rueda, R. (in press). Student learning and assessment: Setting an agenda. In P. Pedraza & M. Rivera (Eds.), *National Latino/a Education Research Agenda Project*. Mahwah, NJ: Erlbaum.

Rumberger, R., Callahan, R., & Gándara, P. (2003, Fall). *LMRI Newsletter, 13*(1).

Rumberger, R., & Gándara, P. (2000). The schooling of English learners. In G. Hayward & E. Burr (Eds.), *Conditions of*

*Education 2000.* Berkeley: University of California, Policy Analysis for California Education.

Rumberger, R., & Gándara, P. (2004). Seeking equity in the education of California's English learners. *Teachers College Record, 106*(10), 2032–2056.

Tabors, P.O., & Snow, C.E. (1994). English as a second language in pre-school programs. In F. Genesee (Ed.), *Educating second language children* (pp. 103–125). New York: Cambridge University Press.

Tabors, P.O., & Snow, C.E. (2001). Young bilingual children and early literacy development. In S. Neuman & D.K. Dickinson (Eds.), *Handbook of early literacy research* (pp. 159–178). New York: Guilford Press.

Thomas, P.T., & Collier, V.P. (2003). A national study of school effectiveness for language minority students' long-term academic achievement. Santa Cruz, CA: Center for Research on Education, Diversity, & Excellence. Retrieved October 14, 2004, from http://repositories.cdlib.org/crede/rschbrfs/research_brief10

Valdés, G., & Figueroa, R. (1994). *Bilingualism and testing: A special case of bias.* Norwood, NJ: Ablex.

Vásquez, O. (2003). *La Clase Mágica: Imagining optimal possibilities in a bilingual community of learners.* Mahwah, NJ: Erlbaum.

Vygotsky, L.S. (1978). *Mind in society: The development of higher psychological processes.* Cambridge, MA: Harvard University Press.

Yaden, D., Rueda, R., Tsai, T., & Esquinca, A. (in press). Issues in early childhood education for English learners: Assessment, professional training, preschool interventions, and performance in elementary school.

# CHAPTER 18

# Culture, Context, and Diversity: A Perspective on Urban School Reform: A Response to Kris Gutiérrez

*Robert Rueda*

The overall purpose of Kris Gutiérrez's chapter is to take on the rather significant task of considering the implications of shifting educational and social policy context and dizzying number of school reforms for English-language learners. As Gutiérrez notes, in places like California, educational careers are embedded in a federal, state, and local policy context that includes, among other initiatives, English-only instructional policies, class size reduction policies, standards-based instruction, new reading initiatives, social promotion and retention policies, cutbacks in teacher certification or preparation, high-stakes assessment and exit exams, and the No Child Left Behind legislation.

Clearly, the chapter by Gutiérrez is only able to touch selectively on some of the more critical issues related to these policies. The chapter examines four related issues and questions: the state of educational achievement for English-language learners and other nondominant groups, the practical effects of current reforms and policies, ways to create equitable learning communities in the face of shrinking resources, and how current educational practices address issues of diversity. The overarching theme of the chapter as a whole is that inequalities continue to exist (and some would argue are increasing) in a variety of arenas from instruction to access to resources to policy initiatives that differentially affect various groups.

In responding to the chapter, I will first outline some general framing observations. I will then examine some paradoxical features of the major points related to English-language learners and reform found in the discussion by Gutiérrez. Finally, I will discuss in a more general fashion the broader context of school reform initiatives in light of issues of culture and context and consider a useful conceptual model for considering reform and diversity in general.

# General Considerations Related to Diverse Learners and Literacy

## Diversity

Early in the chapter, Gutiérrez notes the familiar demographic changes that characterize large urban school districts. There are some basic points about the issue of diversity that are brought to mind in examining changes in demographic data over the last two to three decades. First, and most obvious, diversity is increasing, and increasing dramatically. Second, diversity characterizes not only states such as California or regions such as the southwest but also urban school districts, states, and regions across the United States. Although diversity may have been thought of in local or regional terms in times past, it is now a national phenomenon.

Second, although student demographics have changed dramatically in many places, the demographics of the teaching force do not reflect such changes. As one example, Los Angeles Unified School district had a total enrollment of 746,852 during the 2002–2003 school year, and only 9.5% of the student body was white. During the 2001–2002 academic year (the most recent year for which data are available), there were 36,822 classified teachers, 48% of whom were white (California Department of Education, 2003). It should be clearly understood that the fact that this disparity exists is presented to note the difference in rate of change between students and teachers in terms of demographics, not to make an argument that demographics should automatically be matched. There may be important social, political, and educationally relevant reasons for considering the implications of these differences, but simple matching as a strategy for overcoming achievement differences in and of itself does not have a great deal of empirical support.

## The Importance of Unpacking Sociocultural Differences

With the increasing demographics found in most public school settings, the educational literature increasingly reflects concerns with sociocultural variables such as race, ethnicity, language, culture, and socioeconomic status (G.G. García, 2003; McLoyd & Ceballo, 1998; Spencer, 1999). A discussion of the unique relationship of each of these factors to educational outcomes is beyond this chapter, but it should be noted that at various times and with varying support, scholars have pointed to each of these as important influences on achievement. The point is raised here not to debate the relative influence of any of these factors but rather to note that these sociocultural factors are not the same and are not interchangeable. The claim is that these factors are not only independently related to achievement, but they are related to each other in complex ways that in turn have complex influences on achievement (Shonkoff & Phillips, 2000). An important reason to point out these relationships is that they are often confounded or used interchangeably in discussions about achievement and reading in particular, for example, comparing groups of students by race or ethnicity and then using this as a proxy for culture. Ethnicity or race is not the same as culture.

## Reading and Literacy

Recent research has shown that beliefs, values, and social and cultural practices are vitally important for children to become literate adults, because adults must be able to use literacy as a tool to coordinate with others, solve problems, and engage in other important activities (Rueda & McIntyre, 2002). Many people on the street and many discussions of reading policy, however, seem to ignore these dimensions for the more straightforward ability to decode text accurately. Moreover, these discussions usually treat literacy as a singular entity and rarely acknowledge the possibility of multiple literacies. As Gutiérrez notes, it is important to distinguish reading from literacy. She suggests the need to differentiate the related but distinct technical skills involved in aspects of reading such as decoding from the broader aspects of literacy (not only cognitive skills but attitudes, beliefs, motivations, and interactional practices) such as using language, comprehending texts across genres and communities, and using text as a tool for thinking critically and reflectively. This distinction is a critical one, because it is possible to be a *reader* and not be *literate*. A short-term and exclusive focus on the low-level mechanical aspects of reading may reduce the opportunities for students to become literate contributors to society later in life.

## Cultural Considerations

While culture is increasingly recognized as important in learning (Lambert & McCombs, 1998), it is often discussed only with reference to students from diverse backgrounds. Stated another way, culture as a construct of importance to learning is most often invoked when the person or activity under question is seen as different from what is expected. However, culture is characteristic of virtually every human activity—it is a part of every teaching and learning encounter in every classroom, even those that are populated by nondominant groups. It is important to recognize that teachers are cultural beings as well. Under ideal circumstances, when these cultural "funds of knowledge," or resources, are recognized, they can be appropriated for instructional purposes in powerful ways (Monzo & Rueda, 2003). The key point in thinking about culture and literacy is that appreciating culture is not the same as appropriating cultural practices and knowledge for instructional purposes. It is precisely for this reason that superficial approaches that focus on dress, foods, and typical customs are doomed to failure. At a minimum, teachers need to recognize that culture is an important mediator of behavior not only for their students but for themselves as well, and culture needs to be considered with instructional goals in mind.

Given these introductory considerations, the following section briefly explores some paradoxical aspects of the issues related to diverse learners and school reform.

# Some Paradoxes Related to ELLs and Reform

For those interested in the reading and literacy development of second-language learners, there are some interesting paradoxes that emerge when considering the points in Gutiérrez's chapter, which I describe next.

## Homogeneity in Diversity

Although diversity is increasing, as noted in Gutiérrez's chapter and earlier in this response, in many places this diversity is in fact relatively much more homogenous than is often thought. For example, there are 55 distinct language groups in the Los Angeles Unified School District represented among the total population of 302,278 English-language learners (California Department of Education, 2003). At first glance, this seems like an extremely diverse setting. However, it turns out that 93.5% of this total group are Spanish speaking. In the district as a whole, the pattern is similar although not extremely so. Although only 9.5% of the total school population are white, suggesting a widely diverse school population, almost three quarters (72%) of the remainder are Hispanic or Latino (California Department of Education, 2003). Therefore it may be that the pattern of diversity is as important as the degree of diversity in a given setting.

The interesting and paradoxical point about this diversity, however, is that in some places, the more diverse some regions become, the more policies are focused on *sameness*. English-only instructional policies, standardized and scripted curriculum, and single-measure accountability assessments all contribute to this push for sameness. The implications for diverse learners are significant.

## The More We Find, the Less We Know: The Knowledge Base on ELLs

At the time I entered the field more than two decades ago, the literature on diverse students and second-language learners was minuscule. This literature has increased significantly, however. It is large enough that there are major syntheses of knowledge that have been completed (August & Hakuta, 1997) and that are currently being undertaken such as the National Literacy Panel on Language Minority Children and Youth funded by the U.S. Department of Education/Institute of Education Sciences. Yet at the same time that the research base on ELLs and diverse learners has increased tremendously, paradoxically we still don't know the answers to some basic questions—there remain significant questions that remain unanswered about how second-language learners become literate adults (G.E. García, 2000).

## Those Who Need It Most Get It Least: The Matthew Effect

As Gutiérrez and several others have noted, the educational experiences of English learners and other students from diverse backgrounds often focus on basic reading skills, while high-achieving and higher SES students often get a curriculum steeped in high-level, complex literate tasks and activities. It is the latter that provide the practice and experience most facilitative of success in navigating the complexities of modern urban life. In short, the paradox is that those who need the best curriculum get the most impoverished one. The "Matthew Effect," first used in reference to low-achieving students, refers to the idea that in reading (as in other areas of life), the rich get richer and the poor get poorer (Stanovich, 1986).

## Group-Based Learning Styles Versus Individual Cultural Practices: The Issue of Unit of Analysis

There is a long tradition in education and reading of focusing on individual students and thinking of the individual as the unit of analysis. This is a perspective that is heavily reflected in both research and instructional practices, likely a result of the pervasive influence of the medical model orientation common in medicine. That is, the literature, especially in earlier decades, often focused on individual cognitions, emotions, attitudes, and other related aspects when looking at reading and literacy, without considering how factors—cultural, sociocultural, and sociopolitical—impact learning and teaching interactions and, ultimately, outcomes. When something is *broken* in terms of reading development and achievement, it is the individual that we still continue to try to fix or remediate.

It is interesting that the longstanding pattern of focusing on the individual is reversed in the case of a common adaptation for "cultural differences," namely, group-based learning styles. This is a common adaptation of instructional practice used to accommodate diverse learners. The basis of this approach is that by virtue of being a member of a particular group, an individual student is assumed to have a preference for a specific learning style that, if accommodated, should lead to improved achievement.

Many authors, including Gutiérrez, have argued that not only are there fundamental conceptual problems with this approach, but also there is not a convincing literature that supports the claim that it boosts achievement (e.g., Gutiérrez & Rogoff, 2003; Stahl, 1999). Although such approaches are intuitively appealing, active approaches to teaching, variety in instructional methods, and high-interest reading materials are much more defensible. The criticism of the learning styles work in the chapter is both timely and needed, in particular the notion that cultural practices are tied to specific activity settings and individuals, not whole groups.

## The Situatedness of Literacy and Schooling

The questions early in Gutiérrez's chapter reinforce the situatedness of both literacy and school as an institution—politically, historically, economically, and so forth. Specifically, these include the following:

- What are the current schooling conditions for students from non-dominant groups, especially ELLs?
- What are the practical effects of the new educational terrain on urban students, specifically ELLs?
- How can we create and sustain access to robust and equitable learning communities in the context of a growing constellation of educational reform initiatives and decreased fiscal and human resources?
- How do current educational discourses and practices manage diversity?

One of the troubling aspects of current reforms is the desire to find the one reform *that works* and then standardize and scale up the reform to larger and larger targets (classrooms, schools, districts, states; see Tyack & Cuban, 1995). Reforms developed and implemented from this perspective assume that the effects of context are negligible and that local considerations will be subsumed under the influence of the effective reform practice or policy. Deviations from prescribed practices are seen as errors in the system to be minimized. Gutiérrez has, with much justification, pointed out the dangers inherent in this perspective for ELLs and other diverse students.

Recently, a competing perspective has been argued, one that incorporates what is known about the dynamic nature of complex social settings such as schools. Datnow, Hubbard, and Mehan (2002) point out that reforms can be approached from the standpoint of a technical, organizational focus, but alternatively, they can be approached as a process of local adaptation. The former encourages a *scale up* without consideration of local contextual features, whereas the latter draws attention to the complex interaction among structural constraints, cultural features, and personal agency as they operate in each cultural (school) setting (Datnow et al., 2002). In essence, specific reforms are "co-constructed," or adapted, by local actors given the unique conditions in that environment. To understand the school reform process, or to begin to think about changing local instructional practice in specific settings, the constellation of these features needs to be assessed and accounted for. It can be argued that in diverse classrooms and schools, taking such factors into account takes on heightened importance. More attention to these factors can provide a useful conceptual model to think about reform as a social process rather than as an implementation issue, taking into account what is known about context on behavior.

## Conclusion

As a general reaction to Gutiérrez's chapter, there are some reasons to be positive. For example, the focus on education is higher than it has ever been. There is an ever-widening body of research on English-language learners. Moreover, wide-ranging legislation such as the No Child Left Behind Act has provided systematic and comprehensive attention to various aspects of schooling. With respect to ELLs, in particular, the legislation does allow for some assessment in primary language and forces the state to identify this group as a separate category on the assessment for accountability purposes. Yet Gutiérrez notes that there are many reasons for concern. The federal legislation, for example, does not have provisions for ELLs who want or need primary language instruction; it does not allow for the purchase of primary language materials; and reclassification to English proficient becomes a more difficult issue.

The push to homogenize instruction for ELLs has also carried over into the domain of research as well. Current debates about federal efforts to restrict the range of acceptable research designs and methodologies suggest that the overall effect may be to reduce needed work on issues of culture and language that may not lend themselves to investigation by methods more suited to clinical trials of well-defined treatments in controlled settings. It is clear that many challenges lie ahead, and continued and multifaceted approaches will be needed to needed to diminish the inequities so clearly pointed out in Gutiérrez's chapter.

## REFERENCES

August, K., & Hakuta, K. (Eds.). (1997). *Improving schooling for language-minority children: A research agenda.* Washington, DC: National Academy Press.

California Department of Education, Educational Demographics Unit. (2003). *Enrollment in California public schools by district and ethnic group, 2003–2003.* Retrieved April 9, 2003, from http://data1.cde.ca.gov/dataquest

Datnow, A., Hubbard, L., & Mehan, H. (2002). *Extending educational reform: From one school to many.* New York: Routledge.

García, G.E. (2000). Bilingual children's reading. In M.L Kamil, P.B. Mosenthal, P.D. Pearson, & R. Barr (Eds.), *Handbook of reading research* (Vol. 3, pp. 813–834). Mahwah, NJ: Erlbaum.

García, G.G. (Ed.). (2003). *English learners: Reaching the highest level of English literacy.* Newark, DE: International Reading Association.

Gutiérrez, K.D., & Rogoff, B. (2003). Cultural ways of learning: Individual traits or repertoires of practice. *Educational Researcher, 32*(5), 19–25.

Lambert, N.M., & McCombs, B.L. (Eds.). (1998). *How students learn: Reforming schools through learner-centered education.* Washington, DC: American Psychological Association.

McLoyd, V.C., & Ceballo, R. (1998). Conceptualizing and assessing economic context: Issues in the study of race and child development. In V.C. McLoyd & L. Steinberg (Eds.), *Studying minority adolescents: Conceptual, methodological, and theoretical issues* (pp. 251–278). Mahwah, NJ: Erlbaum.

Monzo, L., & Rueda, R. (2003). Shaping education through diverse funds of knowledge: A look at one Latina paraeducator's lived experiences, beliefs, and teaching practice. *Anthropology and Education Quarterly, 34*(1), 72–95.

Rueda, R., & McIntyre, E. (2002). Toward universal literacy. In S. Stringfield & D. Land (Eds.), *Educating at-risk students* (One hundred-first yearbook of the National Society for the Study of Education, pp. 189–209). Chicago: University of Chicago Press.

Shonkoff, J.P., & Phillips, D.A. (2000). *From neurons to neighborhoods: The science of early childhood development.* Washington, DC: National Academy Press.

Spencer, M.B. (1999). Social and cultural influences on school adjustment: The application of an identity-focused cultural ecological perspective. *Educational Psychologist, 34*, 43–57.

Stahl, S.S. (1999). Different strokes for different folks. *American Educator*, 1–5.

Stanovich, K.E. (1986). Matthew effects in reading: Some consequences of individual differences in the acquisition of literacy. *Reading Research Quarterly*, *21*, 360–407.

Tyack, D., & Cuban, L. (1995). *Tinkering toward utopia: A century of public school reform*. Cambridge, MA: Harvard University Press.

# CHAPTER 19

# Overrepresentation of Culturally and Linguistically Diverse Students in Special Education in Urban Schools: A Research Synthesis

*Cheryl A. Utley, Festus E. Obiakor,*
*and Elizabeth B. Kozleski*

W ith the authorization of the Individuals With Disabilities Education Act of 1997, culturally and linguistically diverse (CLD) children were reassured that they would receive a free, appropriate education in inclusive classroom settings. In the 21st century, we are witnessing the continuing dilemma of CLD students being overrepresented in special education classrooms (Council for Exceptional Children, 2002). It is particularly in urban school districts that the overrepresentation of CLD students in special education is problematic, particularly for those students in high-incidence categories of mild mental retardation (MMR), learning disabilities (LD), and emotionally disturbed (ED) (Artiles, 2003; Donovan & Cross, 2002; Ferguson, Kozleski, & Smith, 2001). Earlier, MacMillan and Reschly (1998) examined Office of Civil Rights (OCR) data for three years (1978, 1986, 1990) on the percentage of white, black, and Hispanic students who qualified for special education services in the categories of MMR, severe learning disabilities (SLD), and seriously emotionally disturbed (SED). These authors reported increase(s) in the (1) total percentage of children served in the combined three program categories for all three ethnic groups over the 12-year period, (2) percentages for all three ethnic groups primarily attributable to the increase in the percent of each ethnic group classified as SLD, and (3) percentages of Hispanic students served in individual and combined categories as compared to percentages of black and white students in both the 1986 and 1990 surveys.

The report *Minority Students in Special and Gifted Education* (Donovan & Cross, 2002) noted that

> when children come to school from disadvantaged backgrounds, as a disproportionate number of students from minority backgrounds do, high-quality instruction that carefully puts the prerequisites for learning in place, combined with effective classroom management that minimizes chaos, can put students on a path to academic success. (Executive Summary, p. 5)

The National Academy of Sciences (NAS) committee recommended that the current approach to special education must be reconsidered and described the current knowledge base as follows:

- Among the most frequent reasons for referral to special education are reading difficulties and behavior problems.

- In recent years, interventions appropriate for the general education classroom to improve reading instruction and classroom management have been demonstrated to reduce the number of children who fail at reading or are later identified with behavior disorders.

- There are currently no mechanisms in place to guarantee that students will be exposed to state-of-the-art reading instruction or classroom management before they are identified as having a "within-child" problem.

- Referral for the high-incidence categories of special education currently requires student failure. However, screening mechanisms exist for early identification of children at risk for later reading and behavior problems. And the effectiveness of early intervention in both areas has been demonstrated to be considerably greater than the effectiveness of later, postfailure interventions. (Executive Summary, pp. 5–6)

Evidence supports that important differences do exist among the student background characteristics, school experiences, and academic outcomes of urban and other students, and that these differences represent more than can be attributed to differences in the school concentration of low-income students (U.S. Department of Education, 1996). In the review of state and district assessment data, the document titled *Beating the Odds III: A City-By-City Analysis of Student Performance and Achievement Gaps on State Assessments* (Council of the Great City Schools, 2003) reported the following results on reading goals:

- Reading achievement in urban schools is beginning to improve, with gaps in this subject area narrowing.

- Urban school achievement in reading remains below national averages.

- Students in urban schools tend to be African American, Hispanic, or Asian American; come from low-income families and come from non-English-speaking homes. (n.p.)

Current research on the achievement gap between black and white students in urban schools has shown that low academic achievement coupled with poor instruction in teaching basic reading skills past the primary grades are two challenges facing education. Substantiating this noteworthy fact is the Prospects study by Puma, Karweit, Price, Ricciutti, Thompson, and Vaden-Kiernan (1997). These authors reported that

> the mean weighted reading comprehension score for students in the fall semester of first grade in the Prospects national sample was at the 50th percentile. By contrast, for students in schools in which more than 75 percent of all students received free or reduced-price lunches (a measure of high poverty), the mean score for students in the fall semester of first grade was at approximately the 44th percentile. By the spring of third grade, this difference had expanded significantly. Children living in high-poverty areas tended to fall further and further behind, regardless of their initial reading skill level. (Snow, Burns, & Griffin, 1998, p. 98)

This body of research suggests that CLD students in high-poverty areas are vulnerable to falling further and further behind in reading achievement, especially in urban schools where highly individualized instruction from specifically trained reading specialists is nonexistent.

The primary purpose of this chapter is to provide an overview of the literature on the overrepresentation of CLD students in special education, specifically in the learning disabilities (LD) category. We focus on this category for two reasons. First, this category represents the largest segment of the population with disabilities in the United States (over 50%). Second, consistent with the focus of this volume on reading issues in urban schools, most students with LD exhibit difficulties in reading, and most of the CLD students with LD are educated in urban schools. Our review begins with a discussion of conceptual issues in the category of LD impacting the overrepresentation issue. A review of the overrepresentation of CLD follows this discussion. A secondary purpose is to examine the empirical knowledge base on reading intervention research conducted with CLD students with disabilities in urban schools. We suggest integrating sociocultural frameworks into traditional special education research paradigms. Last, recommendations supporting the need for policy, research, and practice will be addressed.

## Issues and Trends: Overrepresentation of CLD Students in Special Education

Hardman, Drew, and Egan (1999) described the field of LD as controversial, confused, and polarized because it represents the largest single service delivery program for children with disabilities in the United States. They agreed that "in the past, many children now identified as having SLD would have been labeled as remedial readers, remedial learners, or emotionally disturbed or even mentally retarded, if they received any special attention or additional instructional support at all" (p. 173). Many professionals agree that the controversial issues about this specific disability category are rooted in variations of the definition and identification procedures.

The field of LD is one aspect of special education in which issues of definition, identification, appropriate assessment, and instructional practices continue to be heavily debated. For example, research published over the past 10 years suggests that the category of LD has changed its definition and identification parameters to incorporate a significant number of students with low intelligence and students who are underachievers or low achievers. Furthermore, the federal definition of LD does not specify criteria or guidelines for distinguishing the disability category of LD from other disability categories, nor does it stipulate that students with LD cannot demonstrate deficits related to other categories of disability. Distinguishing the child with true LD from the underachiever and low achiever has become very challenging. Kavale (2002) noted that

> Disparities among states were not uncommon and led to the conclusion that the variation in LD diagnostic categories across states is significantly related to distinctions in diagnostic practice in addition to disease prevalence. The primary confounding among high-incidence mild disabilities appears to be between LD and mental retardation (MR). Even though discrepancy remains the primary criterion for LD identification, it seems to be ignored in actual practice. Studies have identified large percentages of students with learning disabilities with lower range intelligence quotient (IQ) scores in the low to low-average range. (p. 3)

Consequently, leaders in the field have proposed that there are generalized characteristics that are representative of many individuals identified as having a mild intellectual, learning, or behavioral disability (Henley,

Ramsey, & Algozzine, 1993; Kavale & Forness, 1998; MacMillan & Reschly, 1997). Kavale and Forness previously described the school population of students with LD:

> The LD category has thus become a catch-all classification with little substantive foundation. Research demonstrating a decline in IQ scores and the increasing recognition of social/emotional deficits among students with LD reveals a fundamental change in the nature of LD caused by incorporating students who would previously have been designated mentally retarded (MR) or emotionally/behaviorally disordered (E/BD). Thus, LD covers not only students experiencing specific academic difficulties but also those who possess learning problems with an overlay of lowered intellectual ability or mild behavior problems. When combined with this perception that LD is a "better," less stigmatizing, and more acceptable classification, the desire for LD, rather than MR or E/BD, designation becomes irresistible and the political climate appears quite willing to accommodate this desire. (1998, p. 250)

The operationalization of the exclusionary clause inherent in the definition of LD has been very difficult because assessment methods distinguishing characteristics describing the categories of MR, E/BD, and medically based conditions have been vague with very little information available. In addition, the use of assessment methods for differentiating children from different cultural backgrounds who have been raised in poor and low socioeconomic status (SES) environments and students who are low achieving continues to be problematic. Criteria for assessing individuals with LD must be clear, observable, measurable, and accepted by professionals in the field. It is believed that the performance of CLD students with LD will mirror the performance of CLD students who do not have disabilities. This belief is not based on data, and there is scant information on the performance of CLD students who are LD (Thurlow, Nelson, Teelucksingh, & Draper, 2001).

In general education and special education programs, CLD students are at risk of misidentification, misassessment, misclassification, misplacement, and misinstruction because they learn differently (Obiakor, 2003; Obiakor et al., 2002). The traditional psychological assessment practices of collecting, describing, and disseminating student information about CLD learners for decision making fail to address the relationship between intraindividual and interindividual differences and disproportionate representation. These traditional approaches to assessment have created bias in labels and categories for CLD students, tend to fail to address their unique abilities, and wrongfully interpret test scores about their capabilities. If general and special educators do not make allowances for individual differences in assessment and instructional practices for CLD students, then the disproportionate representation of CLD students in special education will remain a reality and continue to be unchallenged. In the words of Meyer and Patton (2001),

> Two elements have emerged as keys to understanding the nexus of race, disability, and overrepresentation. There is a disconnect between the race, culture, and class of teachers in most schools on one hand, and the culture, race, and SES [socioeconomic status] of learners they serve on the other. This disconnect is associated with underachievement which contributes significantly to the disproportionate representation of these learners in special education. (p. 6)

# Issues and Theories of Overrepresentation

A thorough understanding of the phenomenon of overrepresentation involves a very complex combination of theories (Artiles, 2003; Artiles & Trent, 1994; Donovan & Cross, 2002; Gottlieb, Gottlieb, & Wishner, 1994; Hebbeler & Wagner, 2001; Heller, Holtzman, & Messick, 1982; Meyer & Patton, 2001; Reschly & Ward, 1991; U.S. Department of Education, 1998; Utley & Obiakor, 2001). According to the National Association of School Psychologists (NASP), the overrepresentation issue implicates the entire special education process as being unfair to students: the quality of instruction prior to referral, the decision to refer, the assessment, placement in special education programs, and the quality of instruction that occurs in that program. Problematic circumstances include the invalid assessment and placement in programs for students with LD where educational progress may be hindered because of teachers' lowered expectations and goals, opportunities for success are restricted, and low-quality instruction exists. Office of Civil Rights investigations have disclosed school discriminatory practices, such as (1) extensive prereferral interventions in school districts with predominantly Caucasian students as compared with schools with predominantly African American students, (2) a greater emphasis on students' behavioral problems as opposed to academic reasons, (3) a greater reliance on IQ tests in the evaluation of CLD, and (4) a disproportionate number of CLD students labeled as learning disabled and placed in restrictive classroom settings.

## *Methods of Identification*

For more than 30 years, the overrepresentation of CLD children in special education programs has sparked controversy (Artiles & Trent, 1994; Gottlieb et al., 1994; Harry, 1992; Meyer & Patton, 2001; Oswald, Coutinho, Best, & Singh, 1999; Patton, Polloway, & Smith, 2000). Recently, the National Research Council (Donovan & Cross, 2002) examined the Office of Civil Rights (1999) placement data and Office of Special Education Programs (OSEP) Child Count data on the enrollment of students in special education programs broken down by racial/ethnic group. In the federal reporting of data by race/ethnicity, the following five groups were identified: (1) American Indian/Alaskan Natives, (2) Asian/Pacific Islander, (3) Hispanics, (4) Blacks, and (5) non-Hispanic Whites. As a means of understanding the overrepresentation of CLD students with LD, two different types of indices have been used to compare placement rates for different racial/ethnic groups: (1) the risk index (RI) and (2) odds ratio (see Table 19.1).

The RI identifies the percentage of all students of a given racial/ethnic group in a given disability category. The RI is calculated by dividing the number of students in a given racial/ethnic group served in a given disability category (e.g., LD) by the total enrollment for that racial/ethnic group in the school population. The 1998 OCR data revealed risk indices for all

## Table 19.1
## Indices of Placement for Learning Disabilities by Race: 1998 OCR and OSEP Data

| Student Race | Risk Index | | Odds Ratio Index | |
|---|---|---|---|---|
| | OCR | OSEP | OCR | OSEP |
| American Indian/ Alaskan Native | 7.45 | 7.30 | 1.24 | 1.20 |
| Asian/Pacific Islander | 2.23 | 2.25 | 0.37 | 0.37 |
| Black | 6.49 | 6.58 | 1.08 | 1.08 |
| Hispanic | 6.44 | 6.81 | 1.07 | 1.12 |
| White | 6.02 | 6.08 | | |
| Total | 6.02 | 6.07 | | |

From Donovan, M.S., & Cross, C.T. (Eds.) (2002), *Minority students in special and gifted education.* Washington, DC: National Academies Press. Copyright © 2002 by the National Academy of Sciences. Reprinted with permission.

OCR placement and membership dates are taken from the Fall 1998 Elementary and Secondary School Civil Rights Compliance Report, National Projections. OSEP data are taken from the 1998–1999 Child Count, and the indices were calculated using estimated K–12 total enrollment data from the U.S. Department of Education, National Center for Education Statistics, Common Core of Data, School Universe Study, 1998–1999, compiled by Mark Glander, National Education Data Resource Center.

racial/ethnic groups that were higher for LD than those found for MR. The NRC (2002) report stated that "Asian/Pacific Islander have placement rates of 2.23 percent. Rates for all other racial/ethnic groups exceed 6 percent, and for American Indian/Alaskan Natives, the rate reached 7.45 percent" (p. 47).

The second index, odds ratio, provides a comparative index of risk and is calculated by dividing the risk index on one racial/ethnic group by the risk index of another racial/ethnic group. In the OCR and OSEP databases, the odds ratios are reported relative to white students. If the risk index is identical for a particular minority group and white students, the odds ratio will equal 1.0. Odds ratios greater than 1.0 indicate that minority group students are at a greater risk of identification, whereas odds ratios of less than 1.0 indicate that they are less at risk. Using the 1998 OCR placement rates, the LD odds ratio for American Indian/Alaskan Natives is 1.24, showing that they have a 24% greater likelihood of being assigned to the LD category than white students. Odds ratios for Asian/Pacific Islander are low (0.37). For both black and Hispanic students, the odds ratios are close to 1.0.

## Trends in Overrepresentation of African American Learners

The majority of reports of special education placement have focused on the seriousness of African American students with disabilities. Data from the *Twenty-Second Annual Report to Congress on the Implementation of the Individuals With Disabilities Education Act* (U.S. Department of Education, 2000) have provided the following statistics:

- African American youth ages 6 through 21 account for 14.8% of the general population. Yet they account for 20.2% of the special education population.
- In 10 of the 13 disability categories, the percentage of African American students equals or exceeds the resident population percentage.
- The representation of African American students in the categories of mental retardation and developmental disabilities is more than twice their national population estimates.

## Trends in the Overrepresentation of English-Language Learners

There are a limited number of studies using extant databases to examine variations in English-learner placement by disability category, grade level, and type of language instruction provided by schools (Finn, 1982). More recently, Artiles, Rueda, Salazar, and Higareda (2000) studied 11 urban school districts in California that have high proportions of English learners, high Latino enrollments, and high poverty levels. The variables studied were student demographics, achievement, English proficiency, and program placement data. Odds ratios were calculated for ELLs and English-proficient students in the categories of mental retardation (MR) and language and speech impairment (LAS). District aggregated data revealed the following variations in placement patterns:

- English-learner representation at the district level is not a problem. ELLs are not overrepresented in grades K–4; however, the problem emerges in grade 5 and consistently increases through secondary special education programs. The percentage of English learners placed in special education that is above the overrepresentation threshold in grades 6–12 ranges from 19% to 26%.

- By disability category, English-learner representation in elementary grades is not a problem; however, they are overrepresented in the MR and LAS categories in secondary grades.

- By special education placement, English learners are more likely to be placed in special education than are English-proficient students. At the secondary level, the placement of English learners compared to English-proficient learners in the MR category is dramatic.

General and special education research has placed considerable emphasis on developing a systematic and rigorous body of knowledge about effective instruction principles and strategies to facilitate learning outcomes in CLD students with and without disabilities. To further understand the complexities of the overrepresentation issue in special education, we must (1) review the empirical research base on instructional practices conducted with CLD students with and without disabilities and (2) focus on strengthening the link between "good" research and effective instructional practice in order to move beyond the discourse on overrepresentation in general and special education. Unfortunately, one of the conclusions reported in *Improving Schooling for Language-Minority Children* (August & Hakuta, 1997) acknowledges that the

> knowledge base of effective education for English-language learners was focused on issues of language and studies were fraught with methodological limitations. It was recommended that more research be conducted that examines the effects of specific instructional practices, academic and social

learning opportunities, and effective teacher practices on the academic
learning outcomes of English-language learners. (p. 191)

We believe that by examining previously published empirical research
reviews that researchers and teachers will be able to create a vision of "what
works" to teach, encourage, and motivate CLD students in urban schools.

# Previously Published Empirical Research Reviews

Two different types of reviews of published articles in refereed journals
have been conducted to examine the knowledge base of special education for
CLD students (Artiles, Trent, & Kuan, 1997; Bos & Fletcher, 1997; Gersten
& Baker, 2000): (1) a methodological research review and analysis of published articles in refereed journals covering a selected period of time and (2)
a meta-analysis of research studies that provides a quantitative summary of
findings across a body of research. The results of individual studies are con-
verted to a standardized metric or effect size (Cooper & Hedges, 1994). Both
types of analyses of research studies use specific criteria to accept or reject
articles for review.

## *Special Education Research*

Artiles et al. (1997) conducted an analysis of 22 years of studies published
in selected refereed journals (1972–1994). The journals selected for the
analysis were *The Journal of Learning Disabilities*, *Learning Disability
Quarterly*, *The Journal of Special Education*, and *Exceptional Children*.
Publications were included in the database if they met the following three
criteria: (1) Articles were data based (either primary or secondary data),
with quantitative, qualitative, or mixed designs. Therefore, essays, literature reviews, rejoinders, editorials, and other manuscripts that treated ethnic minority issues solely from a conceptual perspective were not analyzed.
(2) The study sample included ethnic minority people (i.e., students and
their families) such as African American, Latino, Asian American, and
Native American. These ethnic groups were selected because they represent the largest ethnic minority groups in the United States. (3) If the study
included more than one ethnic group, the data must have been analyzed
by ethnic groups.

The authors reviewed a total of 2,378 empirical articles published in
refereed journals. Using the aforementioned criteria, 58 empirical articles

on ethnic minority studies were analyzed. The proportion of empirical articles published did not exceed the predicted range of 6%–8%. The majority of empirical articles on ethnic minority studies focused on (1) assessment bias ($n$ = 20), (2) sensory-perceptual functioning ($n$ = 8), (3) placement issues (e.g., overrepresentation of CLD in special education), and (4) social functioning of students ($n$ = 6). Other topics identified but with smaller representation (i.e., less than 10%) included family issues, language and speech issues, personality and attitudes issues, evaluation issues and academic achievement issues.

In the second study, Bos and Fletcher (1997) examined empirical research articles on CLD studies that took a sociocultural perspective in the design and reporting of intervention research in general education classrooms. Major categories of the sociocultural framework include (1) student variables, (2) community and family context, (3) district and school context, and (4) classroom context. Student and community/family context variables were expanded to include language and language proficiency, cultural characteristics, information about the acculturation process, and robust measures of socioeconomic status. The district/school and classroom context categories included traditionally used variables in research (e.g., size, location, level, educational philosophy, number of students, students' characteristics, teacher characteristics). The authors reviewed five journals, *Exceptional Children*, *Journal of Learning Disabilities*, *Learning Disabilities Research and Practice*, *Learning Disability Quarterly*, and *Remedial and Special Education* from 1990 to 1995. This search yielded 26 articles that were categorized as descriptive ($n$ = 16) or intervention studies ($n$ = 10). In analyzing the data-based studies, focusing on the teacher characteristics and the use of culturally relevant pedagogy, the authors reported the following:

1. Information about teachers (i.e., types and numbers of teachers, ethnicity, number of years of teaching experience, teacher preparation, grade level taught, and content area) were regularly reported. There was no information regarding the cultural or linguistic background of teachers beyond ethnicity and race or teachers' educational philosophy or beliefs about inclusion.

2. The studies focused on instructional accommodations for students with disabilities in general education classrooms. Students and teachers judged various instructional strategies and grouping patterns as to their effectiveness and feasibility, and classrooms described how teachers were using instructional strategies either

before or after interventions. Grouping patterns (e.g., cooperative learning, peer tutoring and support, ability grouping) were reported; monitoring student learning and providing feedback, as well as communicating with students on a personal level and getting to know students as individuals, were integrated into the interventions.

3. Culturally relevant pedagogical strategies (e.g., adjusting the pacing, simplifying directions, adjusting the instructional level, using advance organizers and study guides, increasing the time or reducing assignments) were less frequently reported. A number of characteristics (e.g., communicating with parents and parent involvement, integrating family and community culture or student background knowledge into the instruction, incorporating conversations into instruction in which students have opportunities to talk about the cognitive processes they are learning to use) were rarely used during instruction. Information regarding the content of the curriculum and its representation to cultural diversity and classroom discourse was notably absent in this research.

## *Exploratory Meta-Analysis of English-Language Learners*

Gersten and Baker (2000) conducted a multivocal research synthesis examining the current state of the knowledge base on the effectiveness of specific instructional practices for English-language learners. The critical question addressed was, What do we really know about effective teaching practices for English-language learners in the elementary and middle school grades? These authors used exploratory meta-analysis (Cooper & Hedges, 1994) and qualitative synthesis (Ogawa & Malen, 1991) techniques to analyze studies of instructional interventions. Based on three data sources (i.e., experimental, descriptive, professional work groups), eight intervention studies and 15 studies on classroom instruction were reviewed. The criteria for studies in the meta-analysis included (1) an objective measure of student performance evaluating intervention effectiveness, (2) a comparison group, (3) the reporting of sufficient data for computing effect size, and (4) the random assignment of students to a treatment condition. According to these authors, the data indicated that

> when the independent variable(s) in a study was well defined and/or implementation was carefully assessed or monitored, the median effect sizes were

higher than they were when the nature of the instructional interventions were more loosely defined (0.31 vs. 0.18). In three of the eight studies, students were randomly assigned to treatment conditions. When random assignment was used, the effect sizes were smaller than when quasi-experimental designs were used (0.31 vs. 0.47). (p. 50)

The results of the 15 descriptive studies using observational techniques showed that (1) oral language used by English-language learners in classrooms was consistently low; (2) students had limited opportunities to respond to higher-order thinking questions or engage in problem-solving activities; (3) instructional techniques produced lower levels of student engagement; (4) whole-class instruction was used exclusively; and (5) low-cognitive tasks (such as copying) and the surface features of language learning were stressed. Last, the professional work group identified specific instructional principles and strategies that integrate English-language development and content area. In conclusion, Gersten and Baker (2000) remarked that

> well-designed and executed studies are needed to uncover the causal links between features of instruction and learning outcomes. Yet during the period from 1985 to 1996, we found a mere eight studies that utilized a valid experimental or quasi-experimental design to explore the impact of instructional strategies on student learning for English-language learners in Grades K–8. (pp. 57–58)

More important, these authors noted that these studies varied widely in terms of the age of the participants (kindergarten in Goldenberg, Reese, and Gallimore, 1992, to middle school in Henderson & Landesman, 1995), intervention length (30 days in Cardelle-Elawar, 1990, to 1 year plus in Henderson & Landesman, 1995, and Saunders, O'Brien, Lennon, & McLean, 1998), and content focus (e.g., reading and language).

## Current Reading Research Studies

Empirically supported interventions for CLD students with disabilities were conducted by searching major relevant journals (1995–2000): *Education and Treatment of Children*, *Exceptional Children*, *Learning Disabilities Research & Practice*, *Learning Disability Quarterly*, and *Education and Training in Mental Retardation and Developmental Disabilities*. The following criteria were used to analyze studies:

- Articles were data based (either primary or secondary data), with quantitative, qualitative, mixed, and single-subject designs. We selected studies that used experimental and quasi-experimental designs that clearly measured effects of instructional variables on ethnic CLD students' academic outcomes. These studies investigated variables in the content areas of reading, spelling, and writing. We excluded empirical studies implementing intervention approaches (e.g., behavior management) designed to improve intelligence, students' attitudes, social behaviors (e.g., acceptance, communication skills), acting out, and disruptive behaviors.

- Articles included empirical studies of African American, Hispanic, Asian/Pacific Islander, and Native American learners with disabilities in grades K–12. In our review, we excluded empirical studies of Canadian and foreign-born students with exceptionalities.

- In our review, we excluded English-language learners with disabilities. This was based on the conclusions of the recent exploratory meta-analysis of English-language learners by Gersten and Baker (2000).

This review examined 17 empirical investigations (see Table 19.2), including three quasi-experimental, four experimental-control group designs, seven single-subject designs, and three case studies. Seventeen studies reported subjects' grade levels in the elementary ($n = 9$), middle ($n = 6$), and high school ($n = 2$) grades. The majority of empirical studies did not report mean chronological ages in years and months of participants in the study. Empirical studies were conducted in six content areas of literacy instruction, reading comprehension, and language. Each study ($n = 17$) reported measures of fidelity to assess the quality of implementation of interventions. All the intervention approaches were implemented to improve the academic outcomes of CLD students with disabilities in content area subject matter in general and special education classrooms. Intervention approaches were implemented across all grade levels with students at risk for school failure, low-achieving students, and students with disabilities (e.g., LD, MMR, and speech or language impairment). Intervention approaches included small-group literacy instruction (e.g., phonemic awareness, letter–sound correspondence, repeated reading), peer-assisted instruction (e.g., classwide peer tutoring and peer-assisted learning strategies), reciprocal teaching, scripted advance organizers, writing strategies, and self-regulated strategies (e.g., scaffolding). These instructional approaches are not unique to special education teachers. General education teachers received training in these procedures through their teacher preparation and professional development programs.

Table 19.2
Description of Intervention Studies

| Reference | Participants | Culturally Diverse Students | No. of Students | Age/Grade Level | Type of Empirical Design | Content/Instructional Approaches |
|---|---|---|---|---|---|---|
| O'Connor, Notari Syverson, & Vadasy (1996) | Students with LD, BD, & MMR | African American (65% of K class); Caucasian ($n = 25\%$ of K class); Other ($n = 10\%$ of K class); urban school district | 107 | Kindergarten | Experimental-Control | *Content: Early Literacy* 1. Word and syllable awareness 2. Rhyming 3. First sound isolation 4. Onset-rime level blending |
| Mathes, Grek, Howard, Babyak, & Allen (1999) | Students at risk for LD | African American ($n = 2$); Caucasian ($n = 1$); middle-class urban area | 3 | First grade | Case Study | Peer-Assisted Learning Strategies (PALS): (1) letter sounds, (2) hearing sounds, (3) sounding out, (4) sentences and stories, (5) lesson sheet design, (6) story sharing; (7) pretend read, (8) read aloud, (9) story retell |
| Jackson, Paratore, Chard, & Garnick (1999) | Students at risk for reading failure; significant language deficits; Students identified for special education placement | Native Spanish speakers ($n = 9$); Native English speakers ($n = 2$); urban | 11 | Second grade | Case Study | Small-group literacy instruction using repeated reading of manageable text (e.g., Reading the Readable Story, Learning About Words, and Rereading Familiar Books) |

| Reference | Participants | Culturally Diverse Students | No. of Students | Age/Grade Level | Type of Empirical Design | Content/Instructional Approaches |
|---|---|---|---|---|---|---|
| Dickson & Bursuck (1999) | Students at risk for reading failure; LD; BD, Speech | African American (*n* = 1); Hispanic (*n* = 2); Caucasian (*n* = 69); lower to middle class | 72 | First grade | Quasi-Experimental | *Content: Early Literacy* (1) Phonemic awareness for reading-modified; (2) spelling through phonics-modified; (3) Wilson Reading System (e.g., letter-sound correspondence, spelling, reading phonetically controlled words) |
| Ezell, Hunsicker, & Quinque (1997) | Normal-achieving | African American (*n* = 24); Caucasian (*n* = 24); urban area | 48 | Fourth grade | Experimental-Control Group Design | *Content: Reading Comprehension* Peer-assisted and teacher-assisted strategies |
| Vadasy, Jenkins, Antil, Wayne, & O'Connor (1997) | High risk for reading disability | High Ethnic and Racial Diversity; 40% and 50% were eligible for free and reduced lunch | 35 | First grade | Experimental-Control Group Study | *Content: Reading Instruction* After-school tutoring lessons: (1) instruction in letter names and sounds, (2) sound categorization, (3) rhyming exercises, (4) onset-rime segmentation task, (5) phonogram exercise using magnetic letter board, (6) spelling words, (7) writing activity, (8) reading storybooks |

*(continued)*

Table 19.2 *(continued)*
Description of Intervention Studies

| Reference | Participants | Culturally Diverse Students | No. of Students | Age/Grade Level | Type of Empirical Design | Content/Instructional Approaches |
|-----------|--------------|----------------------------|-----------------|-----------------|--------------------------|----------------------------------|
| Espin & Foegen (1996) | Mild disabilities (LD or BD) ($n$ = 13); Students were 2 or more years below grade level | Caucasian (50%); African American (44%); Native American (3%); Hispanic (1%); Asian American (1%); urban area | 184 | Mean Chronological Age = 13.25 years; Sixth, Seventh, and Eighth grades | Quasi-Experimental | *Content: Comprehension, Acquisition, and Retention in Reading Comprehension* General outcome measurement procedures |
| Mortweet, Utley, Walker, Dawson, Delquadri, Reddy, Greenwood, Hamilton, & Ledford (1999) | Mild Mental Retardation | African American ($n$ = 5); Caucasian ($n$ = 3); urban area | 8 | Chronological age = 8 years; Second and Third grades | Single-Subject Design (e.g., withdrawal treatment design) | *Content: Spelling* Classwide peer tutoring and teacher-based instruction |
| Schloss, Kobza, & Alper (1997) | Moderate Mental Retardation | African American ($n$ = 2); Caucasian ($n$ = 4); midwest community of 80,000 persons | 6 | Mean Chronological Age = 15 years 7 months; Junior High School and High School | Single-Subject Design (e.g., multiple baseline across subject pairs criteria) | *Content: Math* Peer tutoring using the next dollar strategy |

| Reference | Participants | Culturally Diverse Students | No. of Students | Age/Grade Level | Type of Empirical Design | Content/Instructional Approaches |
|---|---|---|---|---|---|---|
| Morin & Miller (1998) | Mental Retardation | African American (*n* = 2); Caucasian (*n* = 1) | 3 | Chronological age range = 15–16 years; Seventh grade | Single-Subject Design (e.g., multiple baseline design across individuals) | *Content: Math* Concrete-representational-abstract (CRA) sequence; Modeling; guided practice scaffolding) |
| De La Paz & Graham (1997) | Students with LD | African American (*n* = 2); Caucasian (*n* = 1; suburban areas | 3 | Mean Chronological Age = 11 years; Fifth grade | Single-Subject Design (e.g., multiple probe design across subjects) | *Content: Writing* Self-Regulated Strategy Development Model (text structure, knowledge, scaffolding) |
| De La Paz (1999) | Students with LD; low-, average-, and high-achieving students | African American (*n* = 2); Caucasian (*n* = 20); 23% on free and reduced lunch | 22 | Chronological Age Range: 12 years, 7 mos.–14 years, 1 mo.; Seventh–Eighth grades | Single-Subject Design (e.g., multiple probe design) | Self-Regulated Strategy Development Model (e.g., text structure knowledge, scaffolding) |
| Lewis, Graves, Ashton, & Kieley (1998) | Students with LD Normal-achieving students | Hispanic (*n* = 24.1%); Caucasian (*n* = 63.9%) students with LD; Hispanic (*n* = 20.9%); Caucasian (*n* = 60.9% normal-achieving students) | 264 | Mean Chronological Age: 12 years 3 mos.; Sixth grade | Experimental-Control Group | *Content: Writing* The Writing Center program; Teaching writing as a process and direct instruction in writing strategies; Text entry strategy via Mavis Bacon Teaches Typing |

*(continued)*

Table 19.2 (continued)
Description of Intervention Studies

| Reference | Participants | Culturally Diverse Students | No. of Students | Age/Grade Level | Type of Empirical Design | Content/Instructional Approaches |
|---|---|---|---|---|---|---|
| Sexton, Harris, & Graham (1998) | Students with LD | African American ($n = 5$); Caucasian ($n = 1$); suburban area | 6 | Chronological Age Range = 10 years, 5 mos.–12 years, 3 months; Fifth and Sixth grades | Single-Subject multiple baseline across subjects design) | Self-Regulated Strategy Development |
| Troia, Graham, & Harris (1999) | Students with LD | African American ($n = 1$); Caucasian ($n = 2$); low socioeconomic status | 3 | Chronological Age Range: 10 years, 5 mos.–11 years, 9 mos.; Fifth grade | Single-Subject Design (e.g., multiple baseline across subjects design) | Self-Regulated Strategy Development |
| MacArthur, Schwartz, Graham, Molloy, & Harris (1996) | Students with LD | African American ($n = 1$); Caucasian ($n = 7$); Arab American ($n = 1$); suburban area | 9 | Fourth grade | Case Study | Content: Writing Self-Regulated Strategy Development |
| Boyle & Weishaar (1997) | Students with LD | African American ($n = 1$); Caucasian ($n = 37$); Hispanic ($n = 1$); Low-Middle-High SES Levels | 39 | Tenth–Twelfth grades | Quasi-Experimental Study | Content: Reading Comprehension Student-generated and expert-generated cognitive organizers |

Gersten, Baker, and Lloyd (2000) discussed critical issues related to conducting high-quality intervention research using experimental and quasi-experimental group designs. Quoting from the Research Committee of the Council for Learning Disabilities (Rosenberg et al., 1994), these authors noted that

> available descriptions of individuals with disabilities in research reports are vague and inconsistent. Inadequate descriptions of participants make it difficult at best, and sometimes impossible, to evaluate research findings or to replicate studies. These problems are particularly acute for studies involving students with LD because of the complexity and variability of definitions to determine their eligibility for special education. The committee recommended that the following variables be used for describing students with disabilities: (a) gender, (b) age, (c) race or ethnicity, (d) level of English language development, (e) socioeconomic status, (f) achievement levels on standardized tests, and (g) intellectual status of the participants. In research with small sample sizes (fewer than 10 participants), a more thorough description is warranted. (p. 10)

## Sampling Considerations

In describing quality group designs, Gersten et al. (2000) remarked that

> intervention studies with special populations yield nonsignificant results because there are too few participants in each group.... When researchers approach new areas where no such data exist, the old aphorism "20 is plenty" (i.e., 20 students per condition is adequate) remains reasonable advice. Rarely will sample sizes of 12 to 15 be adequate unless the anticipated effects are extraordinarily strong. (p. 9)

The results of this review are consistent with the findings of the empirical literature on CLD and English-language learners conducted by Artiles et al. (1997) and Gersten and Baker (2000). First, there was variation in the sample sizes in reviewed experimental-control group studies. The sample sizes of small- and large-scale studies ranged from 35 to 264 participants. Second, a number of studies reported grade levels of the participants and not chronological ages. Third, regarding the ethnicity of the participants, the majority of studies did not describe the race of the participants. There was only one study that used a broad and global description of the racial makeup of the sample size. In addition, authors did not report an absolute number for the racial makeup of participants. Rather, percentages were used to identify the number of CLD participants in the study, particularly studies that were part of a larger study. Of the 17 empirical studies, four studies were focused on more than one ethnic group (e.g., African American, Hispanic, Arab American). The majority of empirical studies compared one ethnic group (e.g., African American, Hispanic) to Caucasian students. Fourth, because of the small sample sizes in empirical studies, results were not analyzed by race. Consequently, the findings of intervention research studies cannot be generalized to larger populations.

To deal with issues of identification, assessment, and intervention for CLD students, there must be a significant paradigm shift in how we perceive intraindividual and interindividual differences of these students. There is compelling evidence that (1) language differences may impede the students' academic and social competence, (2) CLD students are misclassified as LD, and (3) teachers may have lower expectations for CLD students. Based on these problems, we believe that a narrowly defined paradigm of how CLD students learn and should be taught must be broadened to include socio-cultural frameworks. How can we transform the teaching–learning process to improve reading achievement of CLD students with and without LD in urban schools? Many general and special educators know very little about the cultural traits, behaviors, values, and attitudes different CLD students bring to the classroom and how they affect the ways students act out and interact with peers and adults in instructional situations. In response to the growing concerns about CLD learners in special education, we propose to integrate sociocultural frameworks into reading intervention research.

## Integrating Sociocultural Frameworks in Reading Intervention Research

The social construction of LD has been a topic of great debate by scholars (e.g., Kavale & Forness, 1998; Lyon, 1996). As mentioned earlier, scholars espousing the philosophy that the field of LD originated from a medical model focused on the neurobiological and organic bases of learning problems, whereas other researchers asserted that LD is a construct of society and that its etiology and history directly correlate with the changing standards in education as a result of societal beliefs (Sleeter, 1986). Kavale and Forness noted that the process of identifying children with LD is primarily a function of ideology that is "shaped by the social forces in the environment" (p. 254). To promote change in the system of classifying individuals with LD, researchers and educators need to understand how society, culture, and language influence education and the learning process.

Recently, Keogh, Gallimore, and Weisner (1997) suggested that researchers and educators examine a sociocultural perspective on LD to understand learning problems within multicultural groups. They further remarked that without a "sociocultural perspective it is impossible to separate the learning competencies and problems of individual children from the contexts in which they live and function" (p. 107). Garcia, Wilkinson, and Ortiz (1995) explained that "difficulties experienced by educators in distinguishing cultural or linguistic differences from disabilities can be partially explained by their unfamiliarity with cultural, linguistic, and other influences on student learning, attitudes, and behavior" (p. 631). Other researchers (e.g., Cole & Means, 1981; Gindis, 1995; Rogoff & Chavajay, 1995; Wertsch, 1991) have observed that sociocultural activities and how people think, remember, reason, and express their ideas influence the intellectual and social development of children. Also, in non-Western cultures, learning is affected by neurological and biological factors in addition to sociocultural contexts in which children live. As a result, the development of LD in children is inherently related to children's sociocultural experiences and biological and organic factors. Therefore, an examination of a sociocultural perspective has implications for defining the construct of LD and the assessment and intervention research conducted with CLD students.

In today's society and school-based settings, reading achievement and performance on standardized assessments are highly valued. If educational performance is used as an index of learning, then *one* critical component of defining LD is the normative performance of individuals in reading achievement. However, in non-Western countries where intelligence test scores or performance on cognitive ability tests have little relevance to survival in society, educational competencies related to literacy are not emphasized and relevant to being productive members in society. In examining a sociocultural perspective, Keogh et al. (1997) questioned many assumptions about the concepts of ethnicity and culture in defining and classifying individuals with LD. These issues are focused on (1) using ethnicity as a marker variable for culture in the classification of persons as learning disabled; (2) defining cultural characteristics of multicultural groups with precision and accuracy; (3) identifying characteristics of subgroups and of individuals within specific ethnic and cultural groups; and (4) distinguishing ethnicity and culture by acknowledging variations in three different ways: among ethnically defined groups, within ethnically defined groups, and among individuals within ethnic and cultural groups. In differentiating aspects of culture and ethnicity, Longstreet (1978) and Byrd (1995) outlined five areas that must be taken into consideration: (1) intellectual modes (e.g., ethnic influence and emphasis on the development of intellectual abilities and approaches to learning), (2) verbal communication (e.g., categories describing oral language, verbal communications, and sociability), (3) nonverbal communication (e.g., gestures and body language, personal space, and touching), (4) orientation modes (e.g., body and spatial orientations, and attention modes), and (5) social value patterns.

As researchers and educators become aware of the influence of the role of sociocultural factors on children's learning, they must conceptually and empirically validate the concepts of ethnicity and culture. Massey (1996) stated that the "study of language development cannot be separated from the study of the cultural dictates of the community that the language user is a part of. As important, the relation between primary language, the cultural experiences that shape the use of that language, and success with later societal demands (e.g., school) cannot be ignored" (p. 290). Smith (1998) noted that "many children who are multiculturally and linguistically diverse enter school with sociolinguistic conventions that are mismatched with the content and structure of the school curriculum, thereby causing confusion and misunderstanding" (p. 106). Unfortunately, the cultural mismatch between the school's expectations and students' cultural, linguistic, and socioeconomic backgrounds has resulted in serious problems in teacher attitudes, assessment, and classification.

In summary, we believe that there is a cultural foundation to literacy. Foertsch (1998) described children's cultural background as an important factor that influences how children learn to read. He noted that "the match between cultural expectations for literacy and school expectations for literacy is crucial to the successful acquisition of reading. Children's experiences with literacy vary from culture to culture" (p. 1). For example, storytelling is highly valued over the use of printed materials. In addition, research suggests that the types and forms of literacy practiced in some families—especially low-income, ethnic and cultural minority, and immigrant families—are largely incongruent with the literacy encountered in schools (Tharpe, 1996). This line of research identifies families in literate ways defined by culture.

General and special educators who want to draw on students' prior experiences and make connections to classroom literacy will want to explore the culture-based literacy norms of their students in addition to the elements of literacy proficiency (e.g., phonological awareness, vocabulary and prior knowledge, knowledge of discourse structures, knowledge of literacy styles, and awareness of purposes for reading).

This next section examines the building blocks for literacy instruction for CLD learners with and without exceptionalities. We focus on culturally responsive literacy programs and key principles of this conceptual framework related to improvements in the literacy learning of CLD students with and without disabilities. This entails expanding traditional, packaged literacy programs to incorporate elements of a social constructivist perspective.

# Culturally Responsive Literacy Programs

Culturally responsive literacy programs, as defined by Gay (2000), are based on "cultural knowledge, prior experiences, frames of reference, and performance styles of ethnically diverse students to make learning encounters more relevant and effective for them" (p. 29). She further noted that culturally responsive literacy programs

1. Acknowledge the legitimacy of the cultural heritages of different ethnic groups, both as legacies that affect students' dispositions, attitudes, and approaches to learning and as worthy content to be taught in the formal curriculum. The curriculum content is inclusive, meaning it reflects the cultural, ethnic, and gender diversity of society and the world.

2. Build bridges of meaningfulness between home and school experiences as well as between academic abstractions and lived sociocultural realities.

3. Use a wide variety of instructional strategies that are connected to different learning styles.

4. Teach students to know and praise their own and each other's cultural heritages. School programs and instructional practices draw from and integrate community and family language and culture.

5. Incorporate multicultural information, resources, and materials in all the subjects and skills routinely taught in schools.

For traditional literacy programs to become culturally responsive, the curriculum must incorporate a social constructivist perspective. According to Au (1998),

> A mainstream constructivist orientation tends to assume that similarities among students override differences related to ethnicity, primary language, and social class.... There is the tendency to propose general principles applicable to all students, although individual differences may be considered.... A diverse constructivist perspective assumes that general principles

must be examined and refined so that their specific application to local contexts involving particular groups of children can be understood. Investigations include the possible influences of ethnicity, primary language, and social class on students' responses to particular literacy learning activities and the reshaping of these activities to improve students' opportunities to learn. (pp. 307–308)

General and special educators must expand their vision of reading strategies and concepts in school so that school definitions of reading are transformed. Scribner (1997) explained that "reading is situated in readers' sociocultural contexts, which in turn implies reading research be located in the realm of literacy and its practice, where mind and society meet" (p. 190). Artiles (2002) reiterated this perspective suggesting that future research

ought to examine goal-directed reading performance in a wider range of productive literacy practices so that we can begin to map out similarities and differences in the underlying processes involved in people's everyday literacy practices. This will help us understand, for example, how a student's lack of ability in school literacy tasks, as documented by traditional approaches, does not necessarily preclude the student's ability to perform other literacy practices in and out of school contexts. (p. 694)

Au (1998) has proposed seven core principles in the social constructivist framework:

1. *Goal of instruction.* The school literacy learning of students will be improved as educators establish students' ownership of literacy as the overarching goal of the language arts curriculum.

2. *Role of home language.* The school literacy learning of students must recognize the importance of students' home languages and come to see biliteracy as an academic outcome.

3. *Instructional materials.* The school literacy learning of students will improve as educators use materials that present diverse cultures in an authentic manner, especially through the works of authors of diverse backgrounds.

4. *Classroom management and interaction with students.* The school literacy learning of students will improve as educators become culturally responsive in their management of classrooms and interactions with students. This perspective suggests that innovations to classroom management and interaction with students may need to be adjusted on the basis of differences in students' cultures.

5. *Relationship to the community.* The school literacy learning of students will be improved if educators make stronger ties to the community.

6. *Instructional materials.* The school literacy of students will be improved as educators provide students with both authentic literacy activities and a considerable amount of instruction in the specific literacy skills.

7. *Assessment.* The school literacy learning of students will be improved when educators use forms of assessment that eliminate or reduce sources of bias (e.g., prior knowledge, language, and question type).

# Recommendations for Future Directions: Research and Practice

To understand and recommend approaches to developing reading instruction that accommodate the various sociocultural histories and experiences of students, the research community needs to uncover approaches to teaching reading that work with specific populations of students. In doing this work, researchers must be careful to describe the students with whom they work, carefully noting the learning and sociocultural variations among students both initially and as changes occur that can be attributed to specific literacy approaches.

Eligibility for special education should occur as a result of careful teaching and analysis of student learning. Rather than waiting for students to fail, special education policy should encourage multidisciplinary teams of classroom, literacy, and special educators to work together to develop effective reading approaches for students struggling to read. Identifying CLD students as LD requires a complex understanding of the relationship among learning, culture, language, and ethnicity. Until researchers can unpack these complex intricacies, it is critical that students who are struggling readers and writers receive the support and teaching they need to be able to read to learn. In this way, the professional knowledge of special and general educators, combined with that of literacy specialists, can contribute to building a new generation of robust and successful readers and writers.

### Acknowledgment

The authors acknowledge the support of the National Center for Culturally Responsive Educational Systems (NCCRES) under grant #H326E020003 awarded by the Office of Special Education Programs, U.S. Department of Education.

# REFERENCES

Artiles, A.J. (2002). Culture in learning: The next frontier in reading difficulties research. In R. Bradley, L. Danielson, & D.P. Hallahan (Eds.), *Identification of learning disabilities: Research to policy* (pp. 693–701). Mahwah, NJ: Erlbaum.

Artiles, A.J. (2003). Special education's changing identity: Paradoxes and dilemmas in views of culture and space. *Harvard Educational Review, 73*(2), 164–202.

Artiles, A.J., Rueda, R., Salazar, J., & Higareda, J. (2000). English-language learner representation in special education in California urban school districts. In D.J. Losen & G. Orfield (Eds.), *Racial inequality in special education* (pp. 117–136). Cambridge, MA: Harvard University Press.

Artiles, A.J., & Trent, S.C. (1994). Overrepresentation of minority students in special education: A continuing debate. *Journal of Special Education, 27*, 410–437.

Artiles, A.J., Trent, S.C., & Kuan, L. (1997). Learning disabilities empirical research on ethnic minority students: An analysis of 22 years of studies published in selected refereed journals. *Learning Disabilities Research & Practice, 12*(2), 82–91.

Au, K.H. (1998). Social constructivism and the school literacy learning of students of diverse backgrounds. *Journal of Literacy Research, 30*(2), 297–319.

August, D., & Hakuta, K. (1997). *Improving schooling for language-minority children: A research agenda.* Washington, DC: National Academies Press.

Bos, C.S., & Fletcher, T.V. (1997). Sociocultural considerations in learning disabilities inclusion research: Knowledge gaps and future directions. *Learning Disabilities Research & Practice, 12*(2), 92–99.

Boyle, J.R., & Weishaar, M.K. (1997). The effects of expert-generated versus student-generated cognitive organizers on the reading comprehension of students with learning disabilities. *Learning Disabilities Research & Practice, 12*(4), 228–235.

Byrd, H.B. (1995). Curricular and pedagogical procedures for African American learners with academic and cognitive disabilities. In B.A. Ford, F.E. Obiakor, & J.M. Patton (Eds.), *Effective education of African American learners: New perspectives* (pp. 123–150). Austin, TX: Pro-Ed.

Cole, M., & Means, B. (1981). *Comparative studies of how people think: An introduction.* Cambridge, MA: Harvard University Press.

Cooper, H., & Hedges, L.V. (1994). *The handbook of research synthesis.* New York: Russell Sage Foundation.

Council for Exceptional Children. (2002). *Addressing overrepresentation of African American students in special education: The prereferral intervention process.* Arlington, VA: Author.

Council of the Great City Schools. (March, 2003). *Beating the odds III: A city-by-city analysis of student performance and achievement gaps on state assessments* [Executive summary]. Retrieved October 14, 2004, from http://www.cgcs.org/reports/beat%5Fthe%5Foddsiii.html

De La Paz, S. (1999). Self-regulated strategy instruction in regular education settings: Improving outcomes for students with and without learning disabilities. *Learning Disabilities Research & Practice, 14*(2), 92–106.

De La Paz, S., & Graham, S. (1997). Strategy instruction in planning: Effects on the writing performance and behavior of students with learning difficulties. *Exceptional Children, 63*(2), 167–181.

Dickson, S.V., & Bursuck, W.D. (1999). Implementing a model for preventing reading failure: A report from the field. *Learning Disabilities Research & Practice, 14*(4), 191–202.

Donovan, M.S., & Cross, C.T. (Eds.). (2002). *Minority students in special and gifted education.* Washington, DC: National Academies Press.

Espin, C.A., & Foegen, A. (1996). Validity of general measures for predicting secondary students' performance on content area tasks. *Exceptional Children*, *62*(6), 497–514.

Ezell, H.K., Hunsicker, S.A., Quinque, M.M. (1997). Comparison of two strategies for teaching reading comprehension skills. *Education and Treatment of Children*, *20*(4), 365–382.

Ferguson, D., Kozleski, E., & Smith, A. (2001). *On...transformed, inclusive schools: A framework to guide fundamental change in urban schools*. Denver, CO: National Institute for Urban School Improvement.

Finn, J. (1982). Patterns in special education placement as revealed by the OCR surveys. In K.A. Heller, W.H. Holtzman, & S. Messick (Eds.), *Placing children in special education: A strategy for equity* (pp. 322–381). Washington, DC: National Academy Press.

Foertsch, M. (1998). *A study of reading practices, instruction, and achievement in District 31 schools*. Oak Brook, IL: North Central Regional Education Laboratory. Available: http://ncrel.org/sdrs/areas/31abs.htm

Garcia, S.B., Wilkinson, C.Y., & Ortiz, A.A. (1995). Enhancing achievement for language minority students: Classroom, school, and family contexts. *Education and Urban Society*, *27*(4), 441–462.

Gay, G. (2000). *Culturally responsive teaching: Theory, research, and practice*. New York: Teachers College Press.

Gersten, R., & Baker, S. (2000). The professional knowledge base on instructional practices that support cognitive growth for English-language learners. In R. Gersten, E.P. Schiller, & S. Vaughn (Eds.), *Contemporary special education research: Syntheses of the knowledge base on critical instructional issues* (pp. 31–80). Mahwah, NJ: Erlbaum.

Gersten, R., Baker, S., & Lloyd, J.W. (2000). Designing high-quality research in special education: Group experimental designs. *The Journal of Special Education*, *34*(1), 2–18.

Gindis, B. (1995). The social implication of disability: Vygotsky's paradigm for special education. *Educational Psychologist*, *30*(2), 77–81.

Goldenberg, C., Reese, L., & Gallimore, R. (1992). Effects of literacy materials from school on Latino children's home experiences and early reading achievement. *American Journal of Education*, *100*(4), 497–536.

Gottlieb, J., Gottlieb, B., & Wishner, J. (1994). Special education in urban America: It's not justifiable for many. *The Journal of Special Education*, *27*, 453–465.

Hardman, M.L., Drew, C.J., & Egan, M.W. (1999). *Human exceptionality: Society, school, and family* (6th ed.). Boston: Allyn & Bacon.

Harry, B. (1992). Making sense of disability: Low-income, Puerto-Rican parents' theories of the problem. *Exceptional Children*, *61*, 364–377.

Hebbleler, K., & Wagner, M. (2001). *Representation of minorities and children of poverty among those receiving early intervention and special education services: Findings from two national longitudinal studies*. Menlo Park, CA: Stanford Research Institute.

Heller, K.A., Holtzman, W.H., & Messick, S. (1982). *Placing children in special education: A strategy for equity*. Washington, DC: National Research Council.

Henderson, R.W., & Landesman, E.W. (1995). Effects of thematically integrated mathematics instruction on students of Mexican descent. *Journal of Educational Research*, *88*(5), 290–300.

Henley, M., Ramsey, R.S., & Algozzine, R. (1993). *Characteristics of and strategies for teaching students with mild disabilities*. Boston: Allyn & Bacon.

Jackson, J.B., & Paratore, J.R. (1999). An early intervention supporting the literacy learning of children experiencing substantial difficulty. *Learning Disabilities Research & Practice*, *14*(4), 254–267.

Kavale, K.A. (2002, August). *Discrepancy models in the identification of learning disability*. Paper presented at the Learning Disabilities Summit Meeting, Washington, DC.

Kavale, K.A., & Forness, S.R. (1998). The politics of learning disabilities. *Learning Disability Quarterly*, *21*(4), 245–275.

Keogh, B.K., Gallimore, R., & Weisner, T. (1997). A sociocultural perspective on learning and learning disabilities. *Learning Disabilities Research and Practice, 12*(2), 107–113.

Lewis, R.B., Graves, A.W., Ashton, T.M., & Kieley, C.L. (1998). Word processing tools for students with learning disabilities: A comparison of strategies to increase text entry speed. *Learning Disabilities Research & Practice, 13*(2), 95–108.

Longstreet, W.S. (1978). *Aspects of ethnicity: Understanding differences in pluralistic classrooms.* New York: Teachers College Press.

Lyon, G.R. (1996). Learning disabilities. *The Future of Children: Special Education for Students with Disabilities, 6*(1), 54–76.

MacArthur, C.A., Schwartz, S.S., Graham, S., Molloy, D., & Harris, K. (1996). Integration of strategy instruction into a whole language classroom: A case study. *Learning Disabilities Research & Practice, 11*(3), 168–176.

MacMillan, D.L., & Reschly, D.J. (1997). Issues of definition and classification. In W.E. MacLean, Jr. (Ed.), *Ellis' handbook of mental deficiency, psychological theory, and research* (3rd ed., pp. 47–74). Mahwah, NJ: Erlbaum.

MacMillan, D.L., & Reschly, D.J. (1998). Overrepresentation of minority students: The case for greater specificity or reconsideration of the variables examined. *The Journal of Special Education, 32*(1), 15–24.

Massey, A. (1996). Cultural influences on language: Implications for assessing African American children. In A.G. Kamhi, K.E. Pollack, & J.L. Harris (Eds.), *Communication development and disorders in African American children: Research, assessment, and intervention* (pp. 285–306). Baltimore: Brookes.

Mathes, P.G., Grek, L.M., Howard, J.K., Babyak, A.E., & Allen, S.H. (1999). Peer-assisted learning strategies for first-grade readers: A tool for preventing early reading failure. *Learning Disabilities Research & Practice, 14*(1), 50–60.

Meyer, G., & Patton, J.M. (2001). *On the nexus of race, disability, and overrepresentation. What do we know? Where do we go?* Washington, DC: Office of Special Education Programs.

Morin, V.A., & Miller, S.P. (1998). Teaching multiplication to middle school students with mental retardation. *Education and Treatment of Children, 21*(1), 22–36.

Mortweet, S., Utley, C.A., Walker, D., Dawson, H., Delquadri, J., Reddy, S.S., et al. (1999). Classwide peer tutoring: Teaching students with mild mental retardation in inclusive classrooms. *Exceptional Children, 65*(4), 524–536.

National Center for Education Statistics. (1998). *National educational longitudinal study.* Ann Arbor, MI: Interuniversity Consortium for Political and Social Research.

Obiakor, F.E. (2003). *The eight-step multicultural approach: Learning and teaching with a smile.* Dubuque, IA: Kendall Hunt.

Obiakor, F.E., Algozzine, B., Thurlow, M., Gwalla-OGisi, N., Enwefa, S., Enwefa, R., et al. (2002). *Addressing the issue of disproportionate representation: Identification and assessment of culturally diverse students with emotional or behavioral disorders.* Arlington, VA: Council for Children with Behavioral Disorders.

O'Connor, R.E., Notari-Syverson, A., & Vadasy, P.F. (1996). Ladders to literacy: The effects of teacher led phonological activities for kindergarten children with and without disabilities. *Exceptional Children, 63*(1), 117–130.

Ogawa, R.T., & Malen, B. (1991). Towards rigor in reviews of multivocal literatures: Applying the exploratory case study method. *Review of Educational Research, 61*(3), 265–286.

Oswald, D.P., Coutinho, M.J., Best, A.M., & Singh, N.N. (1999). Ethnic representation in special education: The influence of school-related economic, and demographic variables. *Journal of Special Education, 32*(4), 194–206.

Patton, J., Polloway, E., & Smith, T.E.C. (2000). Educating students with mild mental retardation. In M.L. Wehmeyer & J.R. Patton (Eds.), *Mental retardation in the 21st century* (pp. 71–89). Austin, TX: Pro-Ed.

Puma, M., Karweit, N., Price, C., Ricciutti, A., Thompson, W., & Vaden-Kiernan, V. (1997). *Prospects: Final report on student outcomes.* Washington, DC: U.S. Department of Education, Planning, and Evaluation Services.

Reschly, D.J., & Ward, S.M. (1991). Use of adaptive measures and overrepresentation of Black students in programs for students with mental retardation. *American Journal on Mental Retardation, 96,* 257–268.

Rogoff, B., & Chavajay, P. (1995). What's become of research on the cultural bases of cognitive development? *American Psychologist, 50,* 859–877.

Rosenberg, M.S., Bott, D., Majsterek, D., Chiang, B., Simmons, D., Gartland, D., et al. (1994). Minimum standards for the description of participants in learning disabilities research. *Remedial and Special Education, 15*(1), 56–59.

Saunders, W., O'Brien, G., Lennon, D., & McLean, J. (1998). Making the transition to English literacy successful: Effective strategies for studying literature with transition students. In R. Gersten & R. Jiménez (Eds.), *Effective strategies for teaching language minority students* (pp. 99–132). Belmont, CA: Wadsworth.

Schloss, P.J., Kobza, S.A., & Alper, S. (1997). The use of peer tutoring for the acquisition of functional math skills among students with moderate retardation. *Education and Treatment of Children, 20*(2), 189–208.

Scribner, S. (1997). The practice of literacy: Where mind and society meet. In E. Tobach, R.J. Falmagne, M.B. Parlee, L.M.W. Martin, & A.S. Kapelman (Eds.), *Mind and social practice: Selected writings of Sylvia Scribner* (pp. 190–205). New York: Cambridge University Press.

Sexton, M., Harris, K.R., & Graham, S. (1998). Self-regulated strategy development and the writing process: Effects on essay writing and attributions. *Exceptional Children, 64*(3), 295–311.

Sleeter, C.E. (1986). Learning disabilities: The social construction of a special edu-

cation category. *Exceptional Children, 53*(1), 46–54.

Smith, C.R. (1998). *Learning disabilities: The interaction of learner, task, and setting.* Boston: Allyn & Bacon.

Snow, C., Burns, M.S., & Griffin, P. (1998). *Preventing reading difficulties in young children.* Washington, DC: National Academy Press.

Tharpe, G. (1996). Cognitive and affective assessment of African American students: Perspectives of a school psychologist. In N. Gregg, R.S. Curtis, & S.F. Schmidt (Eds.), *African American adolescents and adults with learning disabilities: An overview of assessment issues* (pp. 3–14). Athens: University of Georgia.

Thurlow, M.L., Nelson, J.R., Teelucksingh, E., & Draper, I. (2001). Multiculturalism and disability in a results-based educational system: Hazards and hopes for today's schools. In C.A. Utley & F.E. Obiakor (Eds.), *Special education, multicultural education, and school reform: components of quality education for learners with mild disabilities* (pp. 155–172). Springfield, IL: Charles C. Thomas.

Troia, G.A., Graham, & Harris, K. (1999). Teaching students with learning disabilities to mindfully plan when writing. *Exceptional Children, 65*(2), 235–252.

Vadasy, P.F., Jenkins, J.R., Antil, L.R., Wayne, S.K., & O'Connor, R.E. (1997). Community-based early reading intervention for at-risk first graders. *Learning Disabilities Research & Practice, 12*(1), 29–39.

U.S. Department of Education. (1996). *To assure the free appropriate public education of all children with disabilities* (18th annual report to Congress on the implementation of the Individuals With Disabilities Act). Washington, DC: U.S. Government Printing Office.

U.S. Department of Education. (1998). *Elementary and secondary school civil rights compliance report.* Washington, DC: Author.

U.S. Department of Education. (2000). To assure the free appropriate public education of all children with disabilities (22nd annual report to Congress on the implementation of the Individuals With Disabilities Act). Washington, DC: U.S. Government Printing Office.

Utley, C.A., & Obiakor, F.E. (2001). *Special education, multicultural education, and school reform: Components of quality education for learners with mild disabilities.* Springfield, IL: Charles C. Thomas.

Wertsch, J.V. (1991). *Voices of the mind: A sociocultural approach to mediated action.* Cambridge, MA: Harvard University Press.

# CHAPTER 20

# A Loss of Equity, Excellence, and Expectations Through Overrepresentation of Culturally and Linguistically Diverse Students in Special Education: A Response to Cheryl Utley, Festus Obiakor, and Elizabeth Kozleski

*Victoria J. Risko*

> We "must understand that difference does not signify deficit...disadvantaged [or disability]." (Edwards & Dandridge, 2000, p. 255)

The overrepresentation of culturally and linguistically diverse students in special education, discussed more fully by Utley, Obiakor, and Kozleski in their chapter, signals the inability of U.S. schools to respond to students' individual differences and the loss of ideals that are fundamental to a just and democratic education for all students. There are few goals for U.S. schools that are more important than the provision of educational opportunities that are equitable and excellent and hold high expectations for every student. These goals, however, are more complicated to achieve and controversial than they may seem. In fact, the goals of achieving equity and excellence and holding high expectations for all to succeed academically may defy self-evident solutions—especially if those solutions don't challenge the tradition and authority of assessment and teaching practices currently in place.

This chapter is organized around three themes. One focuses on a brief synopsis of the persistence of a problem that has been documented for decades despite policy designed to mitigate its existence. The second theme focuses on the potential power of a comprehensive approach to resolving a problem that is multifaceted. The third theme relates to recommendations for research, instruction, and policy. The main thesis of this chapter is centered on the importance of distinguishing cultural and linguistic differences from disability and educational implications that can be derived from such a distinction.

# A Persistent Problem

Despite numerous reports of overrepresentation of culturally and linguistically diverse students in special education programs, the problem persists. In 1968, Lloyd Dunn, a special educator, warned that resegregation of minorities would occur if we did not provide appropriate safeguards to ensure fair assessments of students' diverse experiences, knowledge, and language prior to special education placements. Unfortunately, this warning has gone unheeded.

As reported by Utley, Obiakor, and Kozleski, researchers have examined data reported by schools and documented disproportionate special education placements of African American students, especially males (e.g., Artiles & Trent, 1994; Chinn & Hughes, 1987; Harry & Anderson, 1994; Heller, Holtzman, & Messick, 1982; MacMillan & Reschly, 1998; Zhang & Katsivannis, 2002), native Americans (Zhang & Katsivannis, 2002), and Latino students (McLaughlin, Artiles, & Pullin, 2001; Zhang & Katsivannis, 2002). In addition, researchers (e.g., Artiles & Trent, 1994; Oswald, Coutinho, Best, & Singh, 1999) have traced a link between levels of school poverty (most often located in urban areas) and disability placement.

Typically, these researchers analyze and cross-reference data reported in three federal government publications (i.e., reports from the U.S. Department of Education, Office of Civil Rights; the National Center for Education Statistics; and the U.S. Census Bureau). In 1974, the Office of Civil Rights (OCR) became the official government office to analyze and report trends of overrepresentation. In 1998, the OCR reported for the first time disability data by race and ethnicity, which made it feasible for researchers and educators to trace more precisely placement patterns within districts, states, and geographic regions, and document placement variations across geographic regions.

## Policies Initiated to Mitigate the Problem

This history of a documented problem is not without efforts from U.S. legislators to resolve it. The passage of the Elementary and Secondary

Education Act in 1965, with funding for Title I programs, was initiated to close achievement gaps by placing reading specialists in high-poverty schools and requiring schools to report yearly assessment data to account for how the schools met their state's performance standards. Similar requirements for assessments and accountability now exist with the Individuals with Disabilities Education Act (IDEA). This act (initiated in 1966, and originally named the Education for All Handicapped Children Act) became authorized as IDEA in 1975 to ensure that all students with disabilities would receive appropriate education. Concern about the overrepresentation issue was the catalyst for IDEA amendments that were passed by the U.S. Congress in 1997 and upheld in 2003.

Unfortunately, the IDEA has never been funded at its full capacity. And the use of a prereferral process, viewed as a mechanism to screen students adequately and prevent unfair placements of minority students in special education, has never reached its potential. Coupling insufficient resources and inadequate assessment procedures during the prereferral process renders IDEA legislation ineffective for stemming the overrepresentation problem (e.g., Donovan & Cross, 2002).

In January 2002, the U.S. Congress passed the No Child Left Behind legislation that provides Reading First and Early Reading First funding opportunities for schools that teach students (prekindergarten through third grade) who live in poverty and have low scores on national tests of reading and writing. The history of educational funding was repeated once again; funding was inadequate at the federal and state levels (Mathis, 2003).

There are predictions that the problem of overrepresentation may become even greater in the 21st century, given the projections of more immigrants and diversity in U.S. schools. Artiles, Trent, and Palmer (2004), for example, referring to data reported by the U.S. Census Bureau (1999) and the U.S. Department of Education (2000), projected that by 2010 approximately 50% of school-age children will be students of color, including native, migrant, and immigrant children. It is very likely that our failure to have a plan and corresponding resources for an educational response to such diversity will result in what Slattery (1995) describes as a "debilitating crisis" for the United States (p. xvii).

# Diverse Cultural Practices and Language Require Multiple Educational Pathways

Providing instruction that is responsive to individual differences is a goal central to principles of democratic education. Attempts to accomplish this goal (e.g., with reduced class size, increased time for voluntary reading and individual conferences, student-led literature discussion groups, data-based instructional decisions) during the last decades of the 20th century hold promise when combined with other factors such as teacher quality and appropriate instructional materials. Unfortunately, in the past we have followed a tradition of what Bartolome (1994) refers to as a "methods fetish"—the goal to find the "best" method corresponding to particular mainstream ideologies. This goal represents a mindset that favors a "one size fits all" approach to instruction instead of a predisposition for developing fuller, more complex understandings of how multiple factors contribute to academic learning in successful classrooms.

Learning and curriculum theorists as diverse as Arendt (1958), Counts (1932), Dewey (1916), Giroux (1988), and Siegel and Fernandez (2000) remind us that practices leading to inequality and injustice (e.g., practices that result in overrepresentation practices) require attention to not only educational practices (i.e., what to do differently) but also societal views (i.e., how we think about equitable educational opportunities) that must be challenged if we are to establish schools that function based on democratic principles. As posed by Henry Giroux (1988), we need to decide "whether schools [should] uncritically serve and reproduce the existing society or challenge the social order in order to develop and advance its democratic imperatives" (p. 243).

The overrepresentation problem, a social practice that has been reproduced for decades, will not change until we break with the tradition and authority of practices that limit a comprehensive view of academic learning. Similarly, Utley, Obiakor, and Kozleski call for a shift from a disability paradigm to a paradigm that acknowledges the importance of children's ethnicity and culture on learning. And because reading is often the presenting problem for student referrals, we need a broader view of what counts as a literate individual. At the heart of such comprehensive reform efforts is the need to acknowledge the complicated intersection of culture, language, and experiences and its affect on academic performance and participation.

Such a step forward propels us to draw away from beliefs that equate difference in out-of-school experiences or school performance with disadvantage or disability. Students with diverse cultural and language backgrounds bring a wealth of information learned from their own experiences, including possible nontraditional experiences with reading and writing outside of school. Examples of nontraditional literacy experiences documented by researchers include a rich storytelling heritage (Nieto, 1997), the reading of all documents that come to the family home and writing of all correspondence when a mother is unable to read or write (McClain, 2000), and the translation of English materials for Spanish-speaking parents (Trueba, 1984). Every student comes to school with experiences, language, and information that for some students align more closely with the school curriculum than for other students. It is not the culturally and language diverse students who are deficit, but the curriculum that fails to capitalize on the students' background and make connections to the learning goals.

There are least three assumptions associated with current educational practices that may impede progress in providing culturally responsive and appropriate instruction. First, there is the widespread use of "fixed" timelines (e.g., by the end of third grade, during the first six weeks of school) for achieving academic goals and state standards. Such timelines assume that all children are learning at the same pace, a problem for most children (Eisner, 2003), but particularly biased against students who may need more time to acquire academic language (e.g., English-language learners may learn conversational English in two years but require five to seven years to become fluent in the academic language of English) (Solano-Flores & Trumbull, 2003) and information that they did not learn prior to school.

Second, Au (2000) and others note fundamental flaws with the concept "achievement gap." Au explains that the practice of comparing students based on norm-referenced test scores will always place minority students at a disadvantage, "because of the assumption that the distribution of scores must follow the normal curve" (p. 845). She argues that the tests used for such comparisons are typically narrow in scope, test skills in isolation, and do not account for the multiple literacy skills students have acquired in out-of-school (home and community) activities.

Third, the increasing emphasis on the five reading components highlighted by the National Reading Panel (National Institute of Child Health and Human Development [NICHD], 2000) brings with it assumptions about the privilege of these components (and associated teaching of these skills) over other literacy skills students may bring with them (e.g., use of a first language to support search for word meanings) and adherence to traditional skill sequences that may be biased against the use of students' out-of school or first-language knowledge (e.g., storytelling knowledge, as described earlier, and knowledge of letter sounds already acquired in their first language; see Labov, 2003). In addition, the current assumption associated widely with the No Child Left Behind legislation that children should first "learn to read" (with an initial emphasis on phonics, word recognition, and fluency) *before* they "read to learn" (with a transition in upper primary grades to more emphasis on vocabulary learning and higher levels of comprehension) suggests a stage theory that has not been supported with scientific evidence. This *stage* notion of literacy learning is insensitive to reading and writing processes (e.g., language cues support word recognition, and word recognition is enhanced with comprehension) that occur simultaneously, and it ignores the learning from life's experiences and language exchanges that help even young children acquire "reading to learn" skills and strategies (e.g., storytelling) before formal reading instruction begins (Freeman & Freeman, 1999). Taking a comprehensive and cultural view of literacy development is vital to educational reform, or "far from advancing the academic achievement of marginalized groups, these mainstream definitions of literacy will serve only to legitimate and exacerbate current inequities" (Jiménez, 2003, p. 122).

# Multiple Pathways—A Beginning

A comprehensive effort to overcome overrepresentation practices requires a deliberate commitment to advancing social and economic policies that affect the well-being of families, providing equitable distribution of resources to schools, and changing current assessment and instructional practices.

## Social and Economic Policies

Gee's (1999) recommendation for a return to social programs directed toward the reduction of poverty has direct implications for goals of equity and excellence in education. The association between lower school performance (that can lead to placement in special programs) and the socioeconomic conditions of schools and families cannot be ignored. As described by the National Reading Panel (NICHD, 1998), poor readers are primarily concentrated "in certain ethnic groups and in poor, urban neighborhoods, and rural towns" (p. 98). Gee argues that the performance differences existing between minority and white students that diminished between the late 1960s and early 1980s (Jencks & Phillips, 1998; Neisser, 1998) when the U.S. government funded social programs (e.g., programs targeting improved nutrition, cognitive-oriented early start programs, smaller class sizes, affirmative action) rose again when these programs were dismantled during the later 1980s and 1990s.

Similarly, funding and resource allocations affect school quality. Darling-Hammond (1995) concluded that urban schools actually receive less money for their programs, have limited access to high-quality teachers and teaching, and, too frequently, offer a reductionist approach (e.g., reduced instructional time, limited curricular resources, and emphasis on basic skills) to curriculum development. Conversely, affluent schools have more highly qualified teachers, small class sizes, and enriched curriculum opportunities, such as college preparatory courses and current materials and resources. The panel selected to serve on the National Research Council (Donovan & Cross, 2002) to study minority representation in special education noted these inequities and advocated for a higher level of per-pupil expenditures and the provision of increased revenue to urban schools to attract highly qualified teachers and provide high-quality, individualized instruction (prior to special education placement).

In his analysis of how funds are allocated at the state and local level, Wong (1994) concluded that even though the official U.S. federal policy is to promote equity nationwide in instructional effectiveness, state and local leaders typically reallocate their education budgets to equalize "situations" instead of directing the funds to students who are not achieving. For example, Wong found that most state and local funds (the largest sources of monies that support public education) were allocated to equalize "interdistrict" disparities (e.g., providing equal numbers of textbooks, ensuring equity of instructional time per subject across districts) instead of providing instructional resources that would impact directly on student learning.

## *Testing Practices*

Providing assessments that are not racially or culturally discriminatory is complicated; test bias is an issue that remains unresolved (Russo & Talbert-Johnson, 1997; Solano-Flores & Trumbull, 2003). The use of nationwide testing practices, such as the National Assessment of Educational Progress (NAEP) and other standardized, norm-referenced tests, is problematic. Contrary to claims that these tests are scientific and objective, test items are contrived, skills and knowledge are tested in isolation, and content selection is arbitrary and representative of the "values, culture, and experience of the [white, male, middle-class] authors" (Gipps, 1999, pp. 360–361).

To create equitable testing conditions, skills and knowledge should be tested within contexts that are authentic to students' learning activities and sufficiently rich to enable meaningful connections to prior knowledge and (both in school and out-of-school) experiences. Tests should provide a sufficient number of items to be able to "generalize about a student's knowledge in a given domain" (Solano-Flores & Trumbull, 2003, p. 8) and account for language as a source of measurement error. Completing a microanalysis of test items, Solano-Flores and Trumbull (2003) concluded that standardized, norm-referenced tests are invalid and biased against second-language learners. Tests translated to students' first language, they argued, did not provide accurate or meaningful semantic and syntactic representations of the first language. In addition, they concluded that testing in only one language does not account for the academic concepts students are learning in their second language; thus, they recommended testing second-language learners in both languages (not simultaneously) with authentic assessments to account more fairly for the information they have acquired.

To mitigate overrepresentation issues, we need assessments that will help teachers differentiate performance that is influenced by cultural and language experiences from performance that is affected by disability. Performance-based measures hold promise as tools for evaluating knowledge and skills within authentic learning contexts. They are most useful when they are diagnostic, provide multiple opportunities for data collection (recognizing that students' cultural and language knowledge are not static but constantly changing as they appropriate new customs, ideas, and language information), and include students' self-evaluations. Such assessments, if implemented in optimal ways, have the potential to represent students' learning across multiple settings (school, home, and community) and applications (Au, 2000; Street, 1996); examine how students read and understand text ideas and apply knowledge to new examples and different contexts and domains (Langer, 2001); and take many different forms, such as portfolios, student–teacher conferences, or sociodramatic play (Riojas-Cortez, 2001). To be effective, however, teachers will need support in the development and interpretation of assessments that are situated within authentic learning activities (McGill-Franzen, Ward, Goatley, & Machado, 2002) and the use of data to plan for meaningful instruction.

## Designing Instruction

Responsive and appropriate instruction for culturally and linguistically diverse students, consistent with constructivist and social cultural theories, builds on students' prior knowledge and experiences (instead of assuming that such experiences are deficient). To plan for culturally responsive and appropriate instruction, we can draw from lessons learned from research conducted in classrooms and schools that "defy the odds" within urban settings and with diverse learners (Au, 2000; Au & Kawakami, 1994; Fisher, Obidah, Pelton, & Campana, chapter 5 this volume; Langer, 2001; Moll, 2003; Taylor, Pearson, Clark, & Walpole, 1999).

Effective teachers use multiple strategies to support students' active learning and deep processing of information. These include teacher facilitation of rich dialogic conversations that involve students learning from each other (Langer, 2001) within literature circles and book-club formats; multiple grouping arrangements with flexible assignments and student choice (Lapp & Flood, chapter 9 this volume); multiple ways to participate in large-group and small-group activities, including apprenticed partnerships with peers and teachers to allow for observation and gradual development of expertise; access to texts on different levels (easy to more difficult texts) and written in more than one language; and encouragement of participation in two languages and use of hybrid languages during the process of making sense of a new language and to facilitate the transfer of linguistic information from the first to second language (Labov, 2003; Manyak, 2000).

Recently, Moll (2003) described his work in a bilingual school in Arizona where students learn literacy in Spanish for the first few years (even those students who come to school with English as their first language) and then gradually learn English and literacy in English. He describes learning trajectories (as measured by achievement tests) that go forward and backward and stay steady for a while before achieving literacy proficiency in both languages. He attributes the success of the program to educational sovereignty (power and agency for decision making is shared by the school and the community), highly qualified teachers, the fact that Spanish is protected and given status, instruction that represents community values and culture, after-school programs that provide opportunities for teacher-study groups, and close observation of students' literacy development. Culture is the mediating variable for learning; instructional events are organized around cultural activities or cultural heritage and contributions of community members.

**Referral Process.** Referral is viewed, typically, by classroom teachers as a call for specialized assessments and individualized instruction for students who are not achieving in their classrooms. Rather than instituting models of early assessment that lead to differentiated and appropriate instruction within classrooms, U.S. schools usually apply the "wait to fail" principle (Donovan & Cross, 2002, p. 6) that leads to referral that is followed by a "wait and see" period (and continued loss of appropriate instruction) to determine the outcome of the specialized testing.

An alternative model would provide a prereferral mechanism where students are evaluated on assessments that are developmentally and contextually appropriate (using a variety of tests, including the performance-based measures as described earlier), and adjusted instruction is provided in the classroom. Such a plan is consistent with recommendations of the National Research Council (Donovan & Cross, 2002) focusing on minority placements in special education and the recommendation of a task force that was formed by the International Reading Association to study the issue of overrepresentation of minorities in special education settings. In a position statement, the International Reading Association (2003) recommends early attention to students who may not be achieving in traditional literacy programs; the provision of culturally relevant assessment and teaching strategies in the regular classroom; and the collaboration among classroom teachers, literacy specialists, and special educators to design exemplary literacy instruction that is responsive to each student's cultural experiences, prior knowledge, and linguistic development. Researchers associated with the International Reading Association estimate that special education placements could be reduced up to 20% with the implementation of this plan.

## Building the Pool of Qualified Teachers

Numerous educators fear that teachers are ill-prepared for teaching in urban classrooms and teaching students with diverse cultural and linguistic backgrounds. In addition, current efforts to establish alternate teacher certification programs (apart from teacher education programs located in colleges and universities) may create a new wave of teachers who have even less experience teaching in poverty areas and diverse student populations.

Teachers in many schools do not represent the culture, race, and SES levels of their students. And this lack of shared history may contribute to lower expectations and misconceptions about students' differences. People of color represent approximately 16% of public school population (with much higher percentages reported in urban schools and geographic regions with a high proportion of immigrants or diverse populations) but only 8% of public school teachers overall and 4% of teacher educators (King, 1993; Russo & Talbert-Johnson, 1997).

Attempts to provide directions for teacher education and professional development programs have led to calls for preparing teachers who are "ethnosensitive" (e.g., Farr, 1991). *Ethnosensitivity* is described as the ability to examine carefully students' language, experiential development, and interests associated with reading and writing opportunities; obtain information about their students' experiences by listening to them in multiple settings, watching their engagement in reading and writing activities, and visiting students out of school to learn about their interests and experiences; use this assessment information to choose classroom texts and reading and writing activities that build on their students' home culture and language; develop reading and writing activities that have a purpose for the students and focus on higher-order thinking (rather than a concentration of lower-order skills as observed by Fitzgerald, 1995); and provide multiple opportunities to write for different purposes and read texts of different genre (Au & Kawakami, 1994; Farr, 1991; Fitzgerald, 1995). In addition, effective teachers hold high expectations for their students' success and recognize that participation in literacy acts (e.g., storytelling, question asking, question answering) may vary greatly across and within different cultural groups (Au, 2000).

Having identified characteristics of effective culturally relevant practices, we have some empirical evidence that teachers from cultures different from the students they teach can learn to teach in ways that are consistent with these descriptors of effective practice and be successful (Au & Kawakami, 1994; Ladson-Billings, 1994). Yet this research is limited to a small group of investigators.

## Meeting the Challenges: Implications for Research, Teacher Education and Professional Development, and Policy

To resolve a problem as complex as overrepresentation of culturally and linguistically diverse students in special education requires a multifaceted and comprehensive plan. Even though "literacy attainment for all" is a priority for legislators, educators, and other U.S. citizens, there are insufficient funding sources and research efforts to attain this goal. The problem of overrepresentation for educators is not unlike problems associated with health care and the nation's economy, wherein huge sums of monies are allocated to target a comprehensive study of systems of factors. Attempts to resolve this education problem will require sufficient funding to address multiple conditions (e.g., poverty, teacher preparation) contributing to the problem. Accordingly, these recommendations for policy and research focus on several factors with the goal of advancing efforts on all simultaneously.

Educational policy and funding should

- Increase funding of a comprehensive set of social programs targeting conditions of poverty.
- Increase funding to support the full funding of IDEA and NCLB legislation.

- Include in IDEA funding monies allocated for prereferral programs and support of high-quality instruction located in the regular classroom.

- Distribute funds and resources equitably to all schools—with additional funds allocated to urban schools to mitigate current inequities—for professional development programs, recruiting highly qualified teachers (including teachers of color), and for local control and development of instructional programs that provide alternative pathways to achieving educational goals.

- Broaden policy guidelines linked to specific methods and timelines for achieving state standards and educational goals, with specific attention to the acknowledgment that principles of effective practice should be adapted to local circumstances.

Research should focus on

- The nature of difficulties experienced by educators in distinguishing cultural or linguistic differences from disabilities and how to best prepare teachers who might be unfamiliar or insensitive to differences created by cultural, linguistic, and other influences on student learning, attitudes, and behavior.

- Multiple perspectives and research designs to identify situated characteristics of effective practices for culturally and language diverse students—practices that are mutually synergistic and responsive to multiple cultural, language, and engagement factors affecting literacy development.

- The study of instructional decisions effective teachers make that could lead to broader visions of assessment and instruction.

- The careful study and delineation of culture, language, and literacy activity as variable within and across groups—developing assessment and instructional models that are sensitive to and privilege multiple cultures and multiple literacies.

## REFERENCES

Arendt, H. (1958). *The human condition.* Chicago: University of Chicago Press.

Artiles, A.J., & Trent, S.C. (1994). Overrepresentation of minority students in special education: A continuing debate. *The Journal of Special Education, 27*(4), 410–437.

Artiles, A.J., Trent, S.C., & Palmer, J.D. (2004). Culturally diverse students in spe-

cial education: Legacies and prospects. In J.A. Banks & C.A. McGee Banks (Eds.), *Handbook of research on multicultural education* (2nd ed., pp. 716–735). San Francisco: Jossey-Bass.

Au, K. (2000). A multicultural perspective on policies for improving literacy achievement: Equity and excellence. In M.L. Kamil, P.B. Mosenthal, P.D.

Pearson, & R. Barr (Eds.), *Handbook of reading research* (Vol. 3, pp. 835–851). Mahwah, NJ: Erlbaum.

Au, K., & Kawakami, A.J. (1994). Cultural congruence in instruction. In E.R. Hollins, J.E. King, & W. Hayman (Eds.), *Teaching diverse populations. Formulating a knowledge base* (pp. 5–23). Albany: State University of New York Press.

Bartolome, L. (1994). Beyond the methods fetish: Toward a humanizing pedagogy. *Harvard Educational Review, 64*(2), 173–194.

Chinn, P.C., & Hughes, S. (1987). Representation of minority students in special education classes. *Remedial and Special Education, 8*(4), 41–46.

Counts, G.S. (1932). *Dare the schools build a new social order?* New York: John Day.

Darling-Hammond, L. (1995). Inequality and access to knowledge. In J.A. Banks & C.A.M. Banks (Eds.), *Handbook of research on multicultural education* (pp. 465–483). New York: Macmillan.

Dewey, J. (1916). *Democracy and education: An introduction to the philosophy of education.* New York: Macmillan.

Donovan, M.S., & Cross, C.T. (Eds.). (2002). *Minority students in special and gifted education.* Washington, DC: National Academy Press.

Dunn, L. (1968). Special education for the mildly retarded: Is much of it justifiable? *Exceptional Children, 35,* 5–22.

Edwards, P.A., & Dandridge, J.C. (2000). Developing collaboration with culturally diverse parents. In V.J. Risko & K. Bromley (Eds.), *Collaboration for diverse learners: Viewpoints and practices* (pp. 251–272). Newark, DE: International Reading Association.

Eisner, E.W. (2003). Questionable assumptions about schooling. *Phi Delta Kappan, 84*(9), 648–657.

Farr, M. (1991). Dialects, culture, and teaching the English language arts. In J. Flood, J.M. Jensen, D. Lapp, & J.R. Squire (Eds.), *Handbook of research on teaching the English language arts* (pp. 3654–3671). New York: Macmillan.

Fitzgerald, J. (1995). English as-a-second-language reading instruction in the United States: A research review. *Journal of Reading Behavior, 27,* 115–152.

Freeman, D., & Freeman, Y.S. (1999). The California Reading Initiative: A formula for failure for bilingual students? *Language Arts, 76*(3), 241–248.

Gee, J.P. (1999). Critical issues: Reading and the new literacy studies: Reframing the National Academy of Sciences report on reading. *Journal of Literacy Research, 31*(3), 355–374.

Gipps, C. (1999). Socio-cultural aspects of assessment. In A. Iran-Nejad & P.D. Pearson, (Eds.) *Review of Research in Education, 24,* 355–392. Washington, DC: American Educational Research Association.

Giroux, H. (1988). *Schooling and the struggle of public life: Critical pedagogy in the modern age.* Minneapolis: University of Minnesota Press.

Harry, B., & Anderson, M. (1994). African American males in special education: A critique of the process. *The Journal of Negro Education, 63*(4), 602–619.

Heller, K.A., Holtzman, W.H., & Messick, S. (Eds.). (1982). *Placing children in special education: A strategy for equity.* Washington, DC: National Academy Press.

International Reading Association. (2003). *The role of reading instruction in addressing the overrepresentation of minority children in special education in the United States: A position statement of the International Reading Association.* Newark, DE: Author.

Jencks, C., & Phillips, M. (Eds.). (1998). *The Black–White test score gap.* Washington, DC: Brookings Institution.

Jiménez, R.T. (2003). Literacy and Latino students in the United States: Some considerations, questions, and new directions. *Reading Research Quarterly, 38,* 122–128.

King, S.H. (1993). The limited presence of African-American teachers. *Review of Educational Research, 63*(2), 115–149.

Labov, W. (2003). When ordinary children fail to read. *Reading Research Quarterly*, *38*, 128–131.

Ladson-Billings, G. (1995). Multicultural teacher education. In C.A.M. Banks & J.A. Banks (Eds.), *Handbook of research on multicultural education* (pp. 747–759). New York: Macmillan.

Langer, J. (2001). Beating the odds: Teaching middle and high school students to read and write well. *American Educational Research Journal*, *38*(4), 837–880.

MacMillan, D.L., & Reschly, D.J. (1998). Overrepresentation of minority students: The case for greater specificity or reconsideration of the variables examined. *Journal of Special Education*, *32*(1), 15–24.

Manyak, P. (2000). Borderlands literacy in a primary-grade immersion class. In T. Shanahan & F.V. Rodriguez-Brown (Eds.), *Forty-ninth yearbook of the National Reading Conference* (pp. 91–108). Chicago: National Reading Conference.

Mathis, W.J. (2003). No Child Left Behind: Costs and benefits. *Phi Delta Kappan*, *84*(9), 679–686.

McClain, V.P. (2000). Lisa and her Mom: Finding success in reading the word/world. *Language Arts*, *78*(1), 21–28.

McGill-Franzen, A., Ward, N., Goatley, V., & Machado, V. (2002). Teachers' use of new standards, frameworks, and assessments: Local cases of NYS elementary grade teachers. *Reading Research and Instruction*, *41*(2), 127–148.

McLaughlin, M.J., Artiles, A.J., & Pullin, D. (2001). Challenges for the transformation of special education in the 21st century: Rethinking school culture in school reform. *Journal of Special Education Leadership*, *14*(2), 51–62.

Moll, L.C. (2003, February). *Biliteracy development in "marked" children: Sociocultural considerations*. Presentation given at Vanderbilt University, Nashville, TN.

National Institute of Child Health and Human Development. (2000). *Report of the National Reading Panel. Teaching children to read: An evidence-based assessment of the scientific research literature on reading and its implications for reading instruction* (NIH Publication No. 00-4769). Washington, DC: U.S. Government Printing Office.

Neisser, U. (Ed.). (1998). *The rising curve: Long-term gains in IQ and related measures*. Washington, DC: American Psychological Association.

Nieto, S. (1997). We have stories to tell: Puerto Ricans in children's books. In V.J. Harris (Ed.), *Using multi-ethnic literature in the K–8 classroom* (pp. 59–94). Norwood, MA: Christopher-Gordon.

Oswald, D.P., Coutinho. M.J., Best, A.M., & Singh, N.N. (1999). Ethnic representation in special education: The influence of school-related economic and demographic variables. *The Journal of Special Education*, *32*(4), 194–206.

Riojas-Cortez, M. (2001). Preschoolers' funds of knowledge displayed through sociodramatic play episodes in a bilingual classroom. *Early Childhood Education Journal*, *29*(1), 35–40.

Russo, C.J., & Talbert-Johnson, C. (1997). The overrepresentation of African American children in special education: The resegregation of educational programming? *Education and Urban Society*, *29*(2), 136–148.

Siegel, M., & Fernandez, S.L. (2000). Critical approaches. In M.L. Kamil, P.B. Mosenthal, P.D. Pearson, & R. Barr (Eds.), *Handbook of reading research* (Vol. 3, pp. 141–151). Mahwah, NJ: Erlbaum.

Slattery, P. (1995). *Curriculum development in the postmodern era*. New York: Garland.

Solano-Flores, G., & Trumbull, E. (2003). Examining language in context: The need for new research and practice paradigm in the testing of English-language learners. *Educational Researcher*, *32*(2), 3–13.

Street, B. (1996). *Social literacies: Critical approaches to literacy development, ethnography, and education*. New York: Longman.

Taylor, B., Pearson, P.D., Clark, K., & Walpole. S. (1999). *Beating the odds in teaching all children to read* (CIERA Report No. 2-006). Ann Arbor, MI: University of Michigan, Center for the Improvement of Early Reading Achievement.

Trueba, H.T. (1984). The forms, functions, and values of literacy: Reading for survival in a barrio as a student. *Journal for the National Association for Bilingual Education*, *9*(1), 21-39.

U.S. Census Bureau. (1999). *Poverty in the United States*. Washington, DC: U.S. Census Bureau.

U.S. Department of Education. (2000). *National Center for Education Statistics: Statistics in Brief*. Washington, DC: Author.

Wong, K.K. (1994). Governance structure, resource allocation, and equity policy. In L. Darling-Hammond (Ed.), *Review of research in education* (Vol. 20, pp. 257–289). Washington, DC: American Educational Research Association.

Zhang, D., & Katsivannis, A. (2002). Minority representation in special education: A persistent challenge. *Remedial and Special Education*, *23*(3), 180–187.

# Political and Organizational Contexts of Literacy Development in Urban Schools: Local and State Concerns

To complete our picture of urban literacy development, we invited authors whose expertise is more oriented toward political and organizational features of urban schools. Chapter 21 by Douglas B. Reeves presents research about a systemic reform implemented in several urban high schools. Reeves's contribution is provocative for many reasons, as pointed out in Donna Ogle's response in chapter 22. While Ogle and Reeves present different explanations for the success of the schools in which Reeves has worked, they agree on one point: The research is clear that "variables in teaching, curriculum, and leadership are profoundly important. In fact, these variables, which teachers and leaders can control, are more influential over student achievement than are the intractable variables of poverty, culture, and language."

Charles Taylor Kerchner attempts to bring coherence and unity to school reform. In chapter 23, he uses the metaphor of the writing process to critique efforts to reform urban schools. Timothy V. Rasinski responds in chapter 24, asking if we should "close the book" on school reform. These two chapters provide a stimulating and creative metaphor for thinking about the complexities and issues inherent in school reform.

To conclude this volume, Virginia Roach takes on the challenges of describing state policy and its impact on urban reading programs in chapter 25, and Cathy M. Roller responds in chapter 26. Roach masterfully summarizes the history of the influence of state policies on reading programs. In turn, Roller reinterprets and extends the historical background to today's challenges and demands of the Reading First and No Child Left Behind legislation. These two chapters are an apt conclusion to this volume, bringing home the immediate challenges of responding to the multiple complex issues represented in chapters 1–24.

# CHAPTER 21

# High Performance in High-Poverty Schools: 90/90/90 and Beyond

*Douglas B. Reeves*

This chapter provides a review of research in high-poverty schools that have also demonstrated high academic performance. I originally coined the term "90/90/90" in 1995 based on observations in Milwaukee, Wisconsin, where schools had been identified with the following characteristics: 90% or more of the students were eligible for free and reduced lunch, 90% of more of the students were members of ethnic minority groups, and 90% of more of the students met the district or state academic standards in reading or another area (Reeves, 2000). Since that time, the term has been broadly applied to describe successful academic performance in schools with significant numbers of poor and minority students. Although the term has been used and the techniques have been frequently replicated, the suggestion that effective teaching practices can mitigate the impact of poverty remains controversial. After a review of the original research and subsequent replication of it, I consider some of these controversies in light of the continuing evidence that, although economic deprivation clearly affects student achievement, demographic characteristics do not determine academic performance. The evidence that follows makes clear that inappropriate commercial use of the term 90/90/90 is not supported by the research and should be challenged. There is no such thing as a proprietary 90/90/90 system, nor are the methods employed by successful high-poverty schools the copyrighted property of any consultant, conference, or author. The practices are mundane, inexpensive, and, most important, replicable. Finally, this chapter includes new research that suggests that consistent application of the 90/90/90 techniques holds promise for improving student achievement and closing the equity gap in schools of any demographic description.

## The Original 90/90/90 Research

Research conducted at the Center for Performance Assessment on the 90/90/90 schools has been particularly instructive in the evaluation of the use of standards and assessment (see Reeves, 2004). The research includes four years of test data (1995 through 1998) with students in a variety of school settings, from elementary through high school. Center analysis considered data from more than 130,000 students in 228 buildings. The school locations included inner-city urban schools, suburban schools, and rural schools. The student populations ranged from schools whose populations were overwhelmingly poor and/or minority to schools that were largely Anglo and/or economically advantaged.

One reason that the research in these schools was so productive is that the districts maintained careful records on actual instructional practices and strategies. This allowed researchers to investigate associations between instructional strategies and academic achievement results. It is important to acknowledge, however, that these results are only associative in nature. I make no claim that a single instructional intervention can be said to *cause* a particular achievement result. What I can say with a high degree of confidence, however, is that there are some consistent associations between some classroom strategies (for example, performance assessments that require writing) and student achievement in a wide variety of tests and subjects. One final note: I make absolutely no claim that the schools in the study were the beneficiaries of any proprietary program or model of instruction.

The research literature in every field from pharmaceuticals to education contains too many studies that purport to show the effectiveness of treatments that the authors of the research have used. My role in this investigation is that of journalist and researcher, not of architect of any program or intervention. Hence, I do not claim any credit for improved academic achievement that rightfully belongs to the students, teachers, and administrators in the study.

## Characteristics of 90/90/90 Schools

The 90/90/90 schools have the following characteristics:

- More than 90% of the students are eligible for free and reduced lunch, a commonly used indicator of low-income families.
- More than 90% of the students are from ethnic minorities.
- More than 90% of the students met or achieved high academic standards, according to independently conducted tests of academic achievement.

The educational practices in these schools are worthy of notice for several reasons. First, many people assume that there is an inextricable

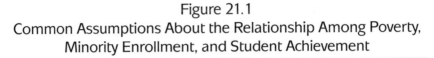

Figure 21.1
Common Assumptions About the Relationship Among Poverty,
Minority Enrollment, and Student Achievement

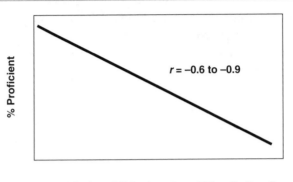

relationship among poverty, ethnicity, and academic achievement. The graph in Figure 21.1 expresses the commonly held belief that poverty and ethnic minority enrollment are inextricably linked to lower levels of student achievement. In this chart, the prevailing hypothesis leaves no room for students in the upper right-hand corner of the graph—that is, schools that have high academic achievement coincident with high poverty and high minority enrollments. This is consistent with national observations dating back to the 1960s, in which demographic characteristics were regarded as the dominant variables influencing student achievement. In fact, the actual data from the December 1998 Comprehensive Accountability Report of the Milwaukee Public Schools shows a different story. In individual schools, there are striking numbers of students who are poor and who are members of ethnic minorities who are also academically proficient. Throughout the entire system of more than 100,000 students, the relationship between poverty and student achievement is not the postulated –0.6 to –0.9, but rather –0.2. Although the impact of poverty clearly has not been eliminated, the prevailing hypothesis that poverty and ethnic minority status are invariably linked to low student achievement does not conform to the data.

## Common Characteristics of High-Achievement Schools

Our research on the 90/90/90 schools included both site visits and analyses of accountability data. The site visits allowed us to conduct a categorical analysis of instructional practices. In the same manner that the authors of *In Search of Excellence* (Peters & Waterman, 1982) identified the common practices of excellent organizations, we sought to identify the extent to which there was a common set of behaviors exhibited by the leaders and teachers in schools with high achievement, high minority enrollment, and high poverty levels. As a result, we found five characteristics that were common to all 90/90/90 schools. These characteristics were

- a focus on academic achievement
- clear curriculum choices
- frequent assessment of student progress and multiple opportunities for improvement
- an emphasis on nonfiction writing
- collaborative scoring of student work

## Focus on Academic Achievement

After visiting all the 90/90/90 schools, we noticed profound differences between the assessment and instructional practices of these schools and those of low-achieving schools. First, and most important, the 90/90/90 schools had a laser-like focus on student achievement. The most casual observer could not walk down a hallway without seeing charts, graphs, and tables that displayed student achievement information, as well as data about the continuous improvement students had made. The data were on display not only in principals' offices but also throughout the schools. In addition, we saw school trophy cases full of exemplary academic work, including clear, concise essays, wonderful science projects, terrific social studies papers, and outstanding mathematics papers. In short, the 90/90/90 schools made it clear to the most casual observer that academic performance was highly prized.

The focus on achievement in these schools included a particular emphasis on improvement. The comprehensive accountability system in use by these schools forced every school to identify five areas in which they measured improvement. Although the school could choose the goal from a menu, the common requirement was to focus on a few indicators of improvement in contrast to the typical school improvement plan that contains a large number of unfocused efforts to improve. The focus on improvement is especially important in an environment where many students come to school with academic skills that are substantially below grade level. The consistent message of charts showing weekly improvement from the fall through the spring was, "It's not how you start here that matters, but how you finish." Improvements of more than one grade level in a single year were common, and teachers and administrators paid particular attention to students whose deficiencies in reading and writing would have a profound impact on their success in other subjects. Some students spent as much as three hours a day in literacy interventions designed to get students to desired achievement levels. There did not appear to be any consistency with regard to the intervention programs in use by these schools. Some used Success for All, others used Reading Recovery, while others used the Efficacy Model. Others had no specified program at all but, using their own teaching staff, consistently applied focused intervention for students in need.

## Curriculum Choices

Such a focus on achievement inevitably leads to curriculum choices, spending more time on the core subjects of reading, writing, and mathematics and less time on other subjects. It is possible, for example, that many of the teachers in these schools did not "cover the curriculum" in the strict sense of checking off objectives from a wide variety of curricular areas. They chose—wisely, we believe—to emphasize the core skills of reading, writing, and mathematics to improve student opportunities for success in a wide variety of other academic endeavors later. It is interesting to note parenthetically that, despite their disproportionate emphasis on language arts and mathematics, these schools also significantly outperformed their peer schools on science tests as well. This makes an important point that eludes those who remain committed to a coverage model: Tests of science, social studies, study skills, and virtually every other subject area are, in fact, tests of reading and writing.

## Frequent Assessment of Student Progress With Multiple Opportunities for Improvement

Many of the high-poverty schools included students whose skills were significantly below grade level in academic achievement as they entered the school. The consistent message of the 90/90/90 schools is that the penalty for poor performance is not a low grade, followed by a forced march to the next unit. Rather, student performance that is less than proficient is followed by multiple opportunities to improve performance. Most of these schools conducted weekly assessments of student progress.

It is important to note that these assessments were not district or state tests but instead assessments constructed and administered by classroom teachers. The consequence of students performing badly was not an admonishment to "wait until next year" but rather the promise that "you can do better next week."

A frequent challenge to this practice is that students should learn to "get it right the first time." The flaw in such a statement is the implied assumption that the traditional one-shot assessment is successful in leading students to get it right the first time. In fact, when students know that there are no additional opportunities to succeed, they frequently take teacher feedback on their performance and stuff it into desks, backpacks, and wastebaskets. Students in this scenario are happy with a D and unmotivated by an F. After all, there is nothing that they can do about deficient performance anyway. In a classroom assessment scenario in which there are multiple opportunities to improve, however, the consequence for poor performance is not a bad grade and discouragement, but more work, improved performance, and respect for teacher feedback. In this respect, the use of teacher evaluation based on assessment scoring guides looked much more like active coaching after which improvement was required and much less like final evaluation from which there was no reprieve.

## Written Responses in Performance Assessments

By far, the most common characteristic of the 90/90/90 schools was their emphasis on requiring written responses in performance assessments. Although many schools with similar demographic characteristics employed frequent assessment techniques, many of the less successful schools chose to emphasize oral student responses rather than written responses. The use of written responses appears to help teachers obtain better diagnostic information about students, and it certainly helps students demonstrate the thinking process that they employed to find a correct (or even an incorrect) response to an academic challenge. Only with a written response from students can teachers create the strategies necessary to improve performance for both teacher and learner.

In virtually every school we evaluated, student scores on creative writing were significantly higher than informative and narrative writing scores. As a result, teachers in the successful 90/90/90 schools placed a very high emphasis on informative writing. They typically used a single scoring rubric to evaluate student writing and applied this scoring guide to every piece of written work.

Whether the student was writing a book report, lab report, social studies report, analysis of a sporting event, description of a piece of music, or a comparison of artists, the message was the same: This is the standard for good writing, and there are no compromises on these expectations for quality.

The benefits of such an emphasis on writing appear to be twofold. First, students process information in a much clearer way when they are required to write an answer. They "write to think" and thus gain the opportunity to clarify their own thought processes. Second, teachers have the opportunity to gain rich and complex diagnostic information about why students respond to an academic challenge the way that they do. In contrast to the binary feedback (right/wrong) provided by most assessments and worksheets, the use of performance assessments that require written responses allows the teacher to diagnose obstacles to student learning. By assessing student writing, teachers can discern whether the challenges faced by a student are the result of vocabulary issues, misunderstood directions, reasoning errors, or a host of other causes that are rarely revealed by typical tests.

The association between writing and performance in other academic disciplines was striking, which gets to the heart of the curriculum choices that teachers must make. At the elementary level, for example, teachers were faced with a formidable set of curriculum standards in both science and writing. Many of the most successful schools reported that they had to sacrifice time allocated to every other curriculum area except reading, writing, and mathematics. Nevertheless, more than 80% of the 135 elementary schools in the study improved in science scores in 1998, as compared with 1997. The Pearson correlation between writing improvement and science improvement is striking: 0.74—a large correlation in virtually any area of social science research. This correlation took place without any changes in the science curriculum and few apparent modifications in teaching methods. I would offer the same caution as provided earlier in the chapter that correlation is not causation. Nevertheless, when two variables appear to behave in such a similar way, it is difficult to escape the conclusion that an emphasis on writing improvement has a significant impact on student test scores in other disciplines, including science.

## External Scoring

Another striking characteristic of the 90/90/90 schools was frequent external scoring of assessments. Although many schools continue to rely on the idiosyncratic judgment of individual teachers for a definition of *proficiency*, the high-achieving schools made it clear that no accident of geography or classroom assignment would determine expectations for students. Rather, these schools developed common assessment practices and reinforced those common practices through regular exchanges of student papers. One teacher would exchange papers with another teacher; principals would exchange papers with another school; and in one of the most powerful research findings, principals would take personal responsibility for evaluating student work.

When teachers exchange papers, it is imperative that they have a uniform basis on which to evaluate student work. The degree of agreement among teachers in their use of performance assessment scoring can be measured by interrater reliability. *Reliability*, when the term is applied to traditional tests, is a measure of consistency. In the case of measuring consistency in scoring, it is simply the percentage of teachers who score an identical piece of student work the same way. If, for example, 10 teachers evaluate a piece of student work, and 8 believe that the work is proficient, and 2 believe that it is only progressing, then there is an 80% reliability rating for that test. This degree of reliability—80%—is the target at which teachers should aim as they jointly evaluate student work. It is very unusual (but not unheard of) for that level of agreement to be achieved the first time that teachers jointly score student work. More frequently, there are disagreements among teachers on the evaluation of student work. These disagreements usually stem from one of two causes. First, teachers often use implicit scoring criteria that are not part of the official scoring guide. Examples of implicit criteria include such statements as "he should have written in cursive," or "she knew that she should have included that character in her essay." Although these expectations may have been reasonable to these teachers, those criteria did not appear in the scoring guide. It is therefore little wonder that other teachers, who did not share those implicit expectations, failed to mark students down for these failings.

The second cause of teacher disagreement is the lack of clear specifications in the scoring guide itself. Too frequently a disagreement among evaluators leads to an argument rather than to an exploration of how agreement can be achieved through a revision of the scoring guide. "If we change the definition of proficient from this to that, perhaps we could agree on how to mark this paper." Words such as these are the basis of a far more meaningful discussion than, "Of course it's proficient! Don't you see?"

## Long-Term Sustainable Results Without Proprietary Programs

One of the most powerful findings of the 90/90/90 study is the continuous nature of the success of these schools, even as the poverty of students attending these schools remains intractable. Several of the schools described later have consistently appeared on the 90/90/90 list, even as students change from year to year, as the effects of poverty grow more onerous, and as parents participating in welfare reform programs are less likely to be at home before and after school. Moreover, these schools are achieving success without proprietary programs. Let there be no doubt: My role in this research is as researcher and reporter. None of the 90/90/90 schools used a specific program or any other proprietary model to achieve their success. On the contrary, I observed effective teachers and administrators using strikingly similar techniques without the assistance of externally imposed methods of instruction. The techniques used by these schools are replicable, but there is certainly not a need for schools to purchase special textbooks, curriculum materials, or secret information to achieve the level of success enjoyed by these schools.

## Nonproprietary Instructional Practices

In an era in which school leaders appear to engage in a perpetual quest for the magic bullet of educational success, it is noteworthy that none of the 90/90/90 schools relied exclusively on a proprietary program to achieve their success. Instead, these schools used consistent practices in instruction and assessment, with support from local teachers. For those who believe that education remains an interactive process that cannot and should not be "teacher-proofed," these research findings are encouraging. The other edge of this particular razor is that we cannot depend on proprietary systems to save us. It is the collective work of teachers, students, parents, and leaders that will ultimately lead us out of the present malaise. Every one of the 90/90/90 schools had academic content standards, but so do many ineffective schools. The distinguishing characteristic of the 90/90/90 schools was not merely that they had standards, but rather how the standards were implemented, monitored, and assessed.

## Data From the 90/90/90 Studies

A current list of some of the 90/90/90 schools from Milwaukee, Wisconsin, is provided by the school system in their comprehensive accountability report. Since the publication of the first list in 1998, the number of schools qualifying for the designation has more than tripled. The data were independently verified by Schmoker (2001) in direct interviews with Milwaukee administrators. These schools have graciously hosted hundreds of visitors in the past few years as their successes have become more widely recognized.

Researchers and educators should always be willing to share their sources of information and welcome the reviews of colleagues in the field. However, I cannot help but note how profoundly disturbing it is to me that I am frequently requested—demanded is not too strong a term—to produce the names and locations of these schools. In fact, these schools have received significant public attention through the *Video Journal of Education* (Linton Professional Development Corporation, 1998a, 1998b).

Research should, of course, be subject to verification and scrutiny. Nevertheless, I cannot avoid noticing that in my many years of conducting, writing, and reviewing educational research, I have never seen such a demand for "names, dates, and places" accompanying the allegation that children who are poor and children of ethnic minority groups perform badly on tests. When *The Bell Curve* (Herrnstein & Murray, 1994) was published with the widely accepted assertion that children who are black and poor perform badly on academic achievement tests, I cannot recall a single instance of demands for the names of students who were subjects of the studies cited. When we have demonstrated that poor and black children perform well, we are inundated with demands for verification. These demands speak volumes about the expectations of children based on their appearance and economic status.

After the original accountability report documenting the 90/90/90 schools, the Milwaukee Public Schools issued subsequent accountability reports. The findings from these reports are striking. In brief, these findings include the following:

- Techniques used by the 90/90/90 schools are persistent. The students are still poor, and their economic opportunities have not improved. Nevertheless, more than 90% of the students in these schools continue to meet or exceed state standards.

- Techniques used by the 90/90/90 schools are replicable. The first time the district tracked these schools, only seven 90/90/90 schools were identified. In the most recent report, 13 schools meet the criteria for this distinguished label.

- Techniques used by the 90/90/90 schools are consistent. These schools are not lurching from one fad to another. Although they differ in some respects with regard to implementation, they are consistent with regard to the following areas of emphasis:

    Writing—students write frequently in a variety of subjects.

    Performance Assessment—the predominant method of assessment is performance assessment. This does not mean that these schools never use multiple-choice items. However, it is performance assessment in several different disciplines that local observers have associated with student progress.

Collaboration—teachers routinely collaborate, using real student work as the focus of their discussion.

Focus—teachers in these schools do not try to "do it all" but are highly focused on learning.

## Additional Information on Success in Challenging School Environments

Over the years, I have continued to hear doubts and challenges about the ability of poor students to perform well. Indeed, the charge is frequently leveled that comprehensive accountability systems are disadvantageous for poor schools. In fact, systematic research from comprehensive accountability systems allows us to document and celebrate the success of students in these schools. Two additional sources of research on this subject come from strikingly different sources. Samuel Casey Carter, author of the *No Excuses: Lessons From 21 High-Performing, High-Poverty Schools* (2001), provides a conservative viewpoint. (The details of these cases are available www.heritage.org.) A politically liberal viewpoint is often associated with Haycock and the Education Trust (Haycock, 1999; Jerald, 2001). Their landmark research on student success in high-poverty schools makes a striking case that these schools are not isolated anecdotes. Indeed, the fundamental finding from the Education Trust studies is that however important demographic variables may appear in their association with student achievement, teaching quality is the most dominant factor in determining student success. It turns out, of course, that teaching quality and subject matter certification are much more likely to occur in economically advantaged schools. The case made by Haycock and others at the Education Trust is clear: The key variable is not poverty, but teaching quality. Although poverty and other demographic variables may be important, they are not determinative in predicting student success. The detailed research from Education Trust, including an interactive program allowing the user to specify the characteristics of a school and find specific data on comparable high-performing schools throughout the United States, is available at www.edtrust.org.

The consensus of the evidence from very different perspectives is clear: Effective teaching and leadership make a difference. The lessons of the 90/90/90 schools as well as the lessons of other studies provide convincing evidence that accountability systems, properly designed, can provide a wealth of information for those desiring to find the keys to improved achievement for all students.

## Using the 90/90/90 Practices to Improve Achievement and Close the Equity Gap

Researchers and practitioners must always confront the gap between theory and reality, between anecdote and evidence. "Sure it worked there," the skeptics say, "but our kids are different." The ultimate test of the 90/90/90 research is whether it is sustainable and replicable. Simpson (2003) provides compelling evidence that the practices of the 90/90/90 schools can be applied in a diverse urban environment with similar results:

> Like the city, Norfolk Public Schools, the first public school system in Virginia, has seen its fortunes go up and down. It's an urban district that serves a diverse population: 67% of students are black and 28% are white. More than 65% of students qualify for free and reduced-price lunches.... 100% of our schools met the state benchmarks in writing in all grades tested. 100% of our high schools met the state benchmarks in chemistry. 100% of our middle schools are fully accredited in earth science. 100% of our middle and high schools showed positive trends in reading, literature, and research. Also, our schools reduced the achievement gap between white and black students in third, fifth and eighth grades, with both groups continuing to improve. They decreased disciplinary actions by 15 percent, the number of long-term suspensions by 14 percent, and the number of expulsions by 66 percent.
>
> In addition, we have two 90/90/90 schools. These are schools with more than 90% of students eligible for free and reduced-price lunch, more than 90% are minority students, and more than 90% of students met high academic standards on the state's Standards of Learning tests. (pp. 43–44)

At the beginning of the 2002–2003 school year, I examined the accountability reports of each of the schools in Norfolk, Virginia, and conducted numerous site visits and interviews. In particular, I wondered if the buildings that experienced gains of 20% or more in their academic achievement in language arts, mathematics, science, and social studies were significantly different from their counterparts in other schools. The schools with the greatest gains were not similar demographically, as they included high-poverty and low-poverty student populations. The financial support, staffing patterns, union agreements, and central office support were similar for all schools. Therefore, neither the demographic variables of students nor the external variables of funding and labor agreements could explain the extraordinary differences between the schools. The keys to improved academic achievement are professional practices of teachers and leaders, not the economic, ethnic, or linguistic characteristics of the students. The Norfolk accountability system revealed striking similarities to other research on the characteristics of successful schools. Although surely there are many other traits shared by effective organizations of all types, the Norfolk Accountability System provided an insight into measurable indicators that were linked to the largest gains in student achievement. These characteristics also make clear that successful accountability is not the exclusive domain of the Department of Accountability in the central office, but rather it is a responsibility shared throughout the system on many levels. The observations made on the basis of this inquiry are strikingly similar to observations I have made in other school systems over the course of several years. The following paragraphs highlight the nine characteristics that distinguished the schools with the greatest academic gains.

## The Impact of Collaboration

First, the schools devoted time for teacher collaboration. This was not merely an exercise in idle discussion or an attempt to get along in a friendly and collegial fashion. Rather, collaboration meetings were focused on an examination of student work and a collective determination of what the word *proficiency* really means. At first, teachers identified wide variations in their opinions and were alarmed to see how differently they evaluated the same piece of student work. The most effective schools made time for collaboration very frequently and in some cases did this every day. Where does the time come from for effective collaboration? None of these schools had extra money in the budget or more hours in the day. Rather, they used the time that they already had with an intentional focus on collaborative scoring of student work. For example, the principals made their faculty meetings announcement-free zones. Rather than drone through a laundry list of announcements (with inevitable comments and controversies), their rule was that the transmission of information would always be in writing. This allowed time formerly devoted to faculty meeting announcements to be dedicated to collaboration. The principals were literally on the same side of the table as their faculty members, with faculty members who were experienced in collaborative scoring taking turns facilitating faculty meetings. The other source of time for collaboration was professional development meetings. Rather than presentations by outside staff developers, a significant degree of the professional development time was allocated to collaborative scoring. These educators knew that collaboration is hard work. Moreover, they understood that it is a skill acquired over time. Hence these remarkably effective schools did not have a collaboration day or a collaboration workshop but rather made the collaborative scoring of student work a part of their regular routine.

## The Value of Feedback

Second, the schools with significant improvements provided significantly more frequent feedback to students than is typically the case with a report card. Emulating their most successful colleagues in music and physical education, teachers provided feedback in real time. They knew that a basketball coach does not provide tips on an effective jump shot nine weeks after a missed shot, nor does a great music teacher note the improper position of the violinist's left hand weeks after noticing the mistake, but rather coaches and musicians provide precise and immediate feedback. In some cases, teachers took a triage approach, providing successful and self-directed students with traditional report cards, while providing students who were struggling with weekly reports on their progress. Their approach to feedback was consistent with Marzano and his colleagues (Marzano, Pickering, & Pollock, 2001) whose meta-analysis of research on student achievement revealed that feedback had a profound impact on student achievement, provided that the feedback was timely, accurate, and specific. The emphasis that these teachers placed on accuracy in feedback was remarkable. Unlike the positive distortion that clouds so much classroom feedback (Foersterling & Morgenstern, 2002), teachers with large gains were committed to feedback that was consistently accurate, with student performance compared to unambiguous expectations.

## The Impact of Time

Third, the schools with large gains made dramatic changes in their schedule. Although they had the same budget, state requirements, teachers' union contract, and other restrictions as other schools in the system, the schools with large gains made remarkable schedule changes. At the elementary level, they routinely devoted three hours each day to literacy, with two hours of reading and one hour of writing. At the secondary level, they routinely provided double periods of English and mathematics. This was not a shell game in which they used the block schedule to double up some times but cut back on English and math in other times, but rather it represented a genuine increase in instructional hours of math and English. The essential nature of instructional time is hardly a new idea, yet in an astonishing number of schools, the schedule is revered more than the Pledge of Allegiance,

Constitution, and Magna Carta combined. To break the mold in student achievement, these schools discovered, they had to break the schedule. It is interesting that this commitment to time for literacy instruction occurred in a state in which social studies and science content examinations were required. These teachers and principals did not change the schedule to overemphasize literacy because they disregarded science and social studies, but rather because they knew that literacy was essential for success in every content area.

## Action Research and Midcourse Corrections

Fourth, teachers engaged in successful action research and midcourse corrections. In many of the schools with the greatest gains, the school accountability plans were not static documents set in concrete before the beginning of the school year but were dynamic and flexible guides. They asked the central office for permission to change goals and strategies that were not effective and start new ones that held promise, even during the school year. Moreover, these faculties and leaders learned from one another. An illustration of their commitment to the application of action research is the use of word walls at the secondary level. Because both the school improvement data and the instructional techniques associated with those improvements are transparent in a system of holistic accountability, the teachers who had achieved great things with students were subject to being questioned by colleagues throughout the system about their success. In earlier years, when elementary educators reported significant improvements in vocabulary, and reading comprehension results were associated with the implementation of word walls, the secondary science and social studies educators decided to adopt the idea. They created walls with words containing essential science and social studies vocabulary, sometimes associated with vivid visual images, and used those vocabulary words throughout the year. In other examples of effective action research, teachers replicated one another's writing rubrics, interdisciplinary assessments, and student motivation practices.

## Aligning Teacher Assignments With Teacher Preparation

Fifth, principals made decisive moves in teacher assignments. Some writers have argued that when test scores go down, the entire school should be reconstituted, and the entire faculty dismissed. In my observations, however, principals have made impressive gains by reassigning teachers to different grades within the same school. Consider what has happened to the curriculum—particularly in the fourth, fifth, and sixth grades—over the past decade. There has been an enormous growth in the complexity of the curriculum, particularly in math and science, with an accompanying set of assumptions about the undergraduate curriculum of the teachers responsible for those grades. Those assumptions have sometimes been wildly inappropriate. When the fourth-grade curriculum requires an understanding of algebra and scientific inquiry, but the teacher's undergraduate preparation does not include those subjects, this is a challenge that will not be solved with a one-day staff development course in academic standards. The teachers whose undergraduate backgrounds fail to match the standards are not bad people, nor are they unprofessional educators. Rather, their preparation is better suited to a different grade level. Effective leaders know that they should seek not to fix the person but rather find a job (and accompanying set of standards) that best meets the teacher's abilities and backgrounds. By making decisive moves in teacher assignments, these principals saved the careers of some teachers and dramatically improved the achievement of their students.

## Constructive Data Analysis

Sixth, successful schools included an intensive focus on student data from multiple sources, and specifically focused on cohort data. They were less interested in comparing last year's fourth-grade class to this year's fourth-grade class (which contains, in most instances, different children) and more interested in comparing the same student to the same student. Their most important questions were not, "Is this year's class different from last year's class?" but rather "What percentage of a group of students is proficient now compared to a year ago?" "What percentage of our students have gained one or more grade levels in reading when we compare their scores today to their scores a year ago?" "Of those students who were not proficient a year ago, what percentage are now proficient?" "Of those students who were proficient a year ago, what percentage are now advanced?"

In brief, these teachers compared the students to themselves rather than to other groups of students. This analysis allowed them to focus their teacher strategies on the needs of their students and not on generic improvement methods.

## Common Assessments

Seventh, the schools with the greatest improvements in student achievement consistently used common assessment. This is a dangerous recommendation to consider in an era in which the most frequently heard complaint across the educational landscape is that students are overtested.

To be sure, many students are overtested, but they are underassessed. The distinction between testing and assessment must be clear. Testing implies an end-of-year, summative, evaluative process in which students submit to a test and the results—typically many months later—are used by newspapers and policymakers to render a judgment about education. By the time the results are published, they are ancient history in the eyes of the student and teacher. Contrast this to the best practice in assessment, in which students are required to complete a task and then very soon—within minutes, hours, or days—they receive feedback that is designed to improve their perform-ance. Effective assessment is what great music educators and coaches rou-tinely provide to their students. Moreover, great educators use assessment data to make real-time decisions and restructure their teaching accordingly. The track coach, for example, does not use the previous year's data to make decisions about assembling relay teams or selecting students to compete for the state finals. Rather, the most recent data available are far more im-portant than the final results from the previous year. Similarly, the data from last quarter on a school-based assessment are far more helpful than the data from last year's test. Common assessments also provide a degree of consis-tency in teacher expectations that is essential if fairness is our fundamental value. Although individual teachers must have discretion on a day-to-day and hour-to-hour basis to teach, reteach, and otherwise meet the needs of individual students, they do not have the discretion to presume that their students "just can't do it." The use of a common assessment for each major discipline allows for a combination of daily discretion and independence by teachers, while preserving a schoolwide commitment to equity and consis-tency of expectations.

## The Value of Every Adult in the System

Eighth, these remarkably successful schools employed the resources of every adult in the system. In holistic accountability systems, we can explore the extent to which professional development is distributed among all adults in the system. In a few remarkable cases, for example, there is profound re-spect for every employee, including bus drivers and cafeteria workers. The respect for these employees is evidenced by their inclusion in professional development opportunities in classroom management and student behav-ior. Leaders recognized that the students' day does not really begin in the classroom, but on the bus or perhaps during free breakfast. By committing their systems to consistency in the education and behavior of adults, these leaders ensure that every adult leader, from the bus driver to the food service employee to the classroom teacher, is regarded as a significant adult leader in the eyes of students. The language concerning student behavior, sanctions, and rewards is consistent, and the results are impressive. Concomitant with gains in student achievement, these schools witnessed dramatic improvements in student behavior, including a reduction of bus misbehavior and disciplinary incidents outside the classroom.

Holistic accountability (Reeves, 2001) reviews allow a consideration of other extraordinary performances, including those by school nurses, library and media center specialists, school secretaries, custodians, counselors, psychologists, security guards, and many other unsung heroes whose exceptional efforts are disregarded in the typical accountability report. Although holistic accountability does not provide a cookie-cutter approach to school success, it does reveal the remarkable impact of every adult in the system on student achievement.

## Cross-Disciplinary Integration

Ninth, there is explicit involvement of the subjects that are frequently and systematically disregarded in traditional accountability systems—music, art, physical education, world languages, technology, career education, consumer and family education, and many other variations on the these themes. Analysis of holistic accountability data reveals that the involvement of these seemingly peripheral subjects in academic achievement is neither serendipitous nor insignificant. Rather, there is a deliberate strategy of involvement in these subjects in the improvement of academic results for all students. A few examples will serve to illustrate the point. Teachers meet together to review student achievement data at a deep level, including the subscale scores. The discussion is not that "math scores are low" but rather than "the subscales reveal that we need to work in particular in fractions, ratio, and measurement." This leads the music teachers to develop activities in which musical rhythms reveal the relationship of whole notes, half notes, and quarter notes. Art teachers work on perspective and other representational art that make explicit use of scale. Physical education teachers allow students to choose to run either a millimeter or a kilometer, and when they make the wrong choice, it is a lesson most students remember well.

In a striking example of collaboration in Norfolk, the teachers in music, art, and physical education collaborated to teach a social studies unit about African studies and the nation of Mali, the ancestral home of many of the students' ancestors. Using dance, literature, vocabulary, geography, history, song, and other engaging activities that crossed disciplinary boundaries, the teachers took the Mali unit out of the shadows of the final week of school and infused it throughout the school year. It is hardly an accident that these students also displayed astonishing improvements in their performance on state social studies tests.

## Other Urban Success Stories

Norfolk is hardly an isolated example of success in urban school systems. In Indianapolis, Indiana, the Wayne Township Metropolitan School Corporation is among many that have demonstrated that academic improvement is compatible with high percentages of minority and poor students in the student body. In St. Louis, Missouri, Chris Wright and her colleagues have led successful initiatives in both the Riverview Gardens and Hazelwood school districts. Now, under the leadership of John Oldani and Dennis Dorsey of the Cooperating School Districts of St. Louis County, these techniques are having an impact throughout the St. Louis area. In Los Angeles County and Orange County, California, urban, suburban, and rural school systems are collaborating to create significant gains in student achievement.

The Wayne Township results are particularly interesting, because they represent not only an example of successful accountability but also the ability of a complex urban school system to replicate the success of other systems. The Wayne Township experience demonstrates that holistic accountability is not merely the result of idiosyncratic case studies but rather the result of systematic replication of best practices from within and outside a school system. The demographic characteristics of Wayne Township might be those of any urban system, with 26 different languages spoken by the students, free and reduced-price lunch enrollment as high as 80% in some schools, and minority enrollment increasing in a number of schools to the point that a majority of students are from minority ethnic backgrounds in some buildings. What is unusual, however, is the relentless focus of this school system on collaboration, academic standards, and nonfiction writing at every level. In particular, the years from 1999 through 2003 represent an extraordinary effort to augment the state's accountability system with a district-based holistic accountability system. In addition to the state tests, the district administers pre- and posttests for every student in the fall and spring of each academic year. For the year ending in June 2002, every single school made significant gains in mathematics and language arts. In addition, the schools with the highest poverty levels made the greatest gains, perhaps because those schools displayed the most intensive focus on changing schedules, instructional practices, building-level assessment, and leadership. It was therefore no surprise that when the state tests were administered in fall 2002, every building displayed significant growth, but those buildings with the highest poverty levels displayed the greatest growth in academic achievement. These gains exceeded 20% in the case of several schools within the district.

Without a constructive accountability system, these results might be passed off as the temporary reaction to test preparation resulting from pressure from state authorities. The facts contradict such a presumption. Every school in Wayne Township tracked specific practices in leadership and teaching. In the case of those schools with the greatest gains, there were common assessments on a monthly or quarterly basis. In addition, faculty meetings and staff development sessions were routinely devoted to collaborative scoring of student work. Each of the schools had common scoring rubrics so that there were consistent descriptions of what the word *proficient* means in practice. Following the lead of the district, each school embraced the use of *power standards* so that teachers were able to focus on a few of the most important standards rather than every single standard established by the state. This is among the most important observations of this holistic accountability study: Higher test scores resulted not from mindless test prep and frantic coverage of every standard but rather from the thoughtful application of the most important standards to creative and engaging teaching strategies.

It is noteworthy that the schools that had the greatest gains did not eliminate special area courses, such as music, art, physical education, and technology. Rather, these courses were explicitly a part of the academic preparation of every student. In schools with the highest gains, every teacher in the special areas was given the standards in mathematics and language arts in which students needed the greatest amount of help. Each of these teachers incorporated some of those language arts and math standards into their daily lessons.

Finally, the principal was personally involved in the evaluation of student work. The building leader regularly met with students and parents to discuss student achievement in specific terms. Moreover, the principals personally administered common assessments every month in language arts and math. By giving up faculty meetings, the principal helped to provide additional time for collaborative scoring of student work. The principal also encouraged every teacher to display proficient and exemplary student work in a highly visible manner. The result of these displays was that every student, parent, and teacher had a clear and consistent understanding of what the schoolwide scoring rubrics meant in practice.

## The Impact of Holistic Accountability on Equity

Figure 21.1 (refer to page 364) shows the typical negative relationship between poverty and student achievement. The more likely a school is to have high percentages of poor and minority students, the less likely the school is to have a high proportion of the students achieve academic proficiency. The line extending from the upper left to the lower right shows that as the percentage of students in poverty (as defined by those eligible for free or reduced lunch) increases, the achievement (as measured by test scores) decreases. This relationship is not perfectly negative (–1.0), but it is substantial in most national research, ranging from –0.6 to –0.9. The prevailing assertion in more than four decades of research on the topic is that variables such as student poverty account for 90% or more of the variation in student test scores (Marzano, 2003). If we stop at Figure 21.1, then these prevailing assertions will carry the day. The accountability evidence, however, suggests that there are specific teaching, leadership, and curriculum strategies that will mitigate the impact of poverty.

As impressive as the improvements in academic achievement were in Wayne Township, the gains in equity were nothing short of extraordinary, as shown in Figures 21.2 through 21.5, which indicate that the negative relationship between student poverty and student achievement is not a certainty. Although the grade 6 language arts scores are disappointingly negative (–0.35), in both grades 3 and 6, the relationships between poverty and achievement are far lower than is the case nationally, and in three of four examples, the relationships are almost flat. In other words, this school system has demonstrated that the relationship between poverty and student achievement can be negligible.

## Equity Need Not Be a Dream

The Wayne Township experience demonstrates that equity need not be a dream. Every single building in the district—elementary through high school—achieved one of the following two equity indicators: (1) The difference between students eligible for free and reduced-price lunch and the average was less than 10%, which is another way of saying that (2) the difference between the largest minority group of students and the average was less than 10%. These data points are totally consistent with the improvements in equity in Milwaukee, Freeport, Riverview Gardens (St. Louis metropolitan area), and others. Although no one disputes that poverty, linguistic differences, and culture can be important variables influencing student achievement, the research is clear that variables in teaching,

Figure 21.2
Relationship Between Poverty
and Third-Grade Language Arts Achievement

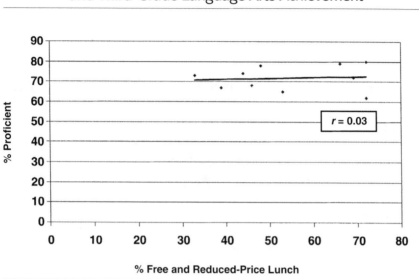

% Free and Reduced-Price Lunch

Figure 21.3
Relationship Between Poverty and Third-Grade Mathematics

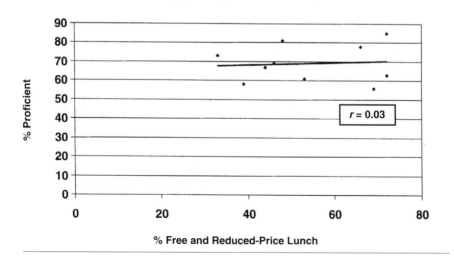

% Free and Reduced-Price Lunch

curriculum, and leadership are profoundly important. In fact, these variables, which teachers and leaders can control, are more influential over student achievement than are the intractable variables of poverty, culture, and language.

### Figure 21.4
### Relationship Between Poverty and Sixth-Grade Language Arts

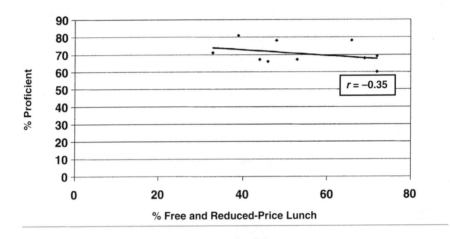

### Figure 21.5
### Relationship Between Poverty and Sixth-Grade Mathematics

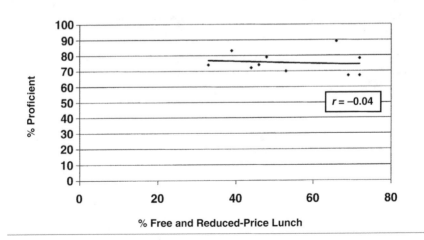

# Critics, Cynics, and Urban Education Success

We must take a few minutes to address the inevitable critics who appear to be constitutionally unable to believe that a success story in urban education exists. Whenever I share results such as those in Norfolk, Wayne Township, Milwaukee, Riverview Gardens, Freeport, or other successful urban schools, critics inevitably roll their eyes and allege that this surely must be a flash in the pan, the product of a frenzy of test preparation rather than sustainable reform. Others have claimed that the results must be caused by the exclusion of underperforming children on test day. Still other critics claim that the students and teachers must be engaged in a massive cheating conspiracy. Others take issue with the methodology of the research, particularly if careful research controls (such as mobility and attendance) are used. The presence of those controls inflates achievement, the critics charge. After all, the studies reflect students who actually attend school. Of course, the absence of those controls would lead to charges of sloppy research. Either way, the critics find a way to ignore the continuing pile of research, of which my studies represent only a few pebbles. Marzano (2003) has assembled the most impressive evidence, using meta-analytic techniques, which indicate importance of teaching, curriculum, and leadership relative to poverty and ethnic identity. Demographic characteristics are relevant, but the preponderance of the evidence indicates that these characteristics are not destiny when it comes to academic achievement. The following is a brief consideration of challenges that I have heard made to the 90/90/90 research:

*The only measure of success in this study is test scores, and there are better ways to assess student achievement.* Test scores are a way, but by no means the only way, to assess student achievement. It is interesting that one of hallmarks of the 90/90/90 schools was an unwillingness to tolerate annual state or district tests as the sole measurements of achievement. These schools consistently elevate the importance of classroom-based, teacher-made tests that are collaboratively scored and used to provide immediate feedback to both students and teachers. From a research and policy perspective, however, it is necessary to have some consistent data to understand student achievement. Although accountability should indeed be a holistic endeavor with multiple assessments of achievement, common tests of literacy and mathematics are a useful way to evaluate student achievement over time. Finally, the best accountability systems, including the one used in the original 90/90/90 research, included a balance of state, district, and school-based measures. Moreover, it included a narrative report from each school, providing a balance of qualitative observation and quantitative data.

*The excessive time devoted to reading means less time for science and social studies.* This is true. Schools in the study were required by state law to take science and social studies tests, yet they made a deliberate trade-off to devote more time to reading comprehension and nonfiction writing, even if it meant that they had fewer hours of social studies instruction. This trade-off was wise for two reasons. First, their scores in social studies and science did not decline, but increased. One can speculate that it might have had something to do with the improved ability of students to read the questions on the social studies and science tests. Second, our interviews of social studies and science teachers at the secondary level revealed their nearly unanimous conviction that the key to greater success in those disciplines at the secondary level was not more social studies and science instruction in elementary school, but students who could enter secondary school able to read on grade level. A substantial body of research (Foersterling & Morgenstern, 2002; Klentschy, Garrison, & Amaral, 2000) supports the teachers in this conviction.

*The controls for attendance and mobility provide a positive bias for 90/90/90 schools.* This is not true. The accountability system provided "two-column" reporting for students to display the impact of mobility and attendance. In one column, the report shows the results for all students, and in the next column it shows the results for those students who were continuously enrolled during the school year. For attendance, the "all student" number was separated from the results for those students who attended school at least 90% of the time. These controls were made for all schools, not just the 90/90/90 schools. Therefore, a parallel comparison was made to high-poverty, high-minority schools for students with good attendance and continuous enrollment but who did not have the success of students in the 90/90/90 schools. This is just good research design. In pharmaceutical research, we compare patients who receive the medicine (the experimental group) to those who receive a placebo (the control group). The research is only useful if those in the experimental group really take their medicine. If we are studying the impact of certain strategies in curriculum, teaching, and educational leadership, our research is of questionable value if we analyze the effects on students who were not present for the curriculum, teaching, and leadership strategies. Finally, it is noteworthy that the schools that had high mobility (as defined by more than 80% of students taking the spring test not enrolled in September) and also high achievement had strikingly similar characteristics to the 90/90/90 schools, with an emphasis on writing and collaboration.

*The 90/90/90 schools used expensive programs, such as Success for All.* This is not true. Some schools used Success for All, and others did not.

This makes emphatically clear that the brand name alone of a literacy program is not the predictor of success, but rather that the professional practices employed by teachers and leaders in the building predicted success. In fact, some Success for All schools had high results, but others had poor results. It was the replicable professional practices, not particular programs, that were associated with student success.

*The effects are transient and dependent on a particularly effective principal and faculty.* This is not true. The effects are sustainable, with some schools maintaining this designation through different principals and high faculty turnover. The effects are replicable with schools in other places (where there is also high turnover and teacher inexperience, particularly in high-poverty schools). In the words of one teacher in the original study, "Nobody volunteered to come to this school." Nevertheless, their collaboration, focus, and professional practices delivered results.

## Conclusion

Perhaps the most compelling argument against any research about success in high-poverty schools is the observation that there are cases where teachers are doing all the right things, and yet student achievement remains low. There are no magic potions to deliver improved student achievement. The best that researchers and policymakers can do is to examine the preponderance of the evidence and draw appropriate conclusions. When a jury is presented with the evidence in a court case, it rarely has a perfect data set with unquestionable research. Rather, the jury confronts conflicting information, including information with errors, uncertainties, and differing interpretations. From this mix, we ask 12 people of good will and common sense to draw an appropriate conclusion based on the preponderance of the evidence. The 90/90/90 research and the other evidence offered in this article fall far short of perfection. They do, however, contribute to the larger body of evidence that, in its totality, suggests useful strategies for high-poverty schools. Moreover, in any research project, we must recognize that perfection is not an option. Rather, we can only choose among the errors that we commit and attempt to minimize the risk of our errors. From a research perspective, we must choose between the risk of confirming a hypothesis that is not true and the risk of failing to confirm a hypothesis that is true. In the case of the professional practices recommended in this chapter, we also have two potential errors. The first error is the replication of these practices, including an increase in our commitment to literacy, nonfiction writing, and collaboration, and the subsequent discovery that the students really did not need all of that extra work after all. What is the risk of this strategy? Excessively literate students? Teachers who collaborate too much? The other error is the failure to act while we search for perfection or persist in a state of disbelief. Risks attendant with such delay will be debilitating for another generation of students. I do not claim that the 90/90/90 research and its many counterparts in the literature are perfect. I only suggest that the risks of this research being wrong are minimal. If the research is correct and ignored, however, the risks are serious.

## REFERENCES

Carter, S.C. (2001). *No excuses: Lessons from 21 high-performing, high-poverty schools.* Washington, DC: The Heritage Foundation.

Foersterling, F., & Morgenstern, M. (2002). Accuracy of self-assessment and task performance: Does it pay to know the truth? *Journal of Educational Psychology,* 94(3), 576–585

Haycock, K., and others (Eds.). (1999). *Dispelling the myth: High-poverty schools exceeding expectations.* Washington, DC: The Education Trust.

Herrnstein, R., & Murray, C. (1994). *The bell curve: Intelligence and class structure in American life.* New York: Free Press.

Jerald, C. (2001). *Dispelling the myth, revisited: Preliminary findings from a nationwide analysis of high-performing schools..* Washington, DC: The Education Trust.

Klentschy, M., Garrison, L., & Amaral, O. (2000). *Valle Imperial Project in Science (VIPS): Four-Year Comparison of Student Achievement Data, 1995-1999* (VIPS, National Science Foundation Grant No. ESI-9731274). Calexico, CA: The Educational Research Institute San Diego State University.

Linton Professional Development Corporation. (1998a). Assessments and scoring guides based on standards (*Video Journal of Education* No. 803). Linton Productions, Inc.

Linton Professional Development Corporation. (1998b). Standards that work: Helping teachers understand standards (*Video Journal of Education* No. 802). Linton Productions, Inc.

Marzano, R.J. (2003). *What works in school: Translating research into action.* Alexandria, VA: Association for Supervision and Curriculum Development.

Marzano, R.J., Pickering, D., & Pollock, J.E. (2001). *Classroom instruction that works: Research-based strategies for increasing student achievement.* Alexandria, VA: Association for Supervision and Curriculum Development

Peters, T.J., & Waterman, R.H. (1982). *In search of excellence: Lessons from America's best-run companies.* New York: Warner Books.

Reeves, D.B. (2000). *Accountability in action: A blueprint for learning organizations.* Denver, CO: Advanced Learning Press.

Reeves, D.B. (2001). *Holistic accountability: Serving students, schools, and community.* Thousand Oaks, CA: Corwin.

Reeves, D.B. (2004). *Accountability in action: A blueprint for learning organizations* (2nd ed.). Denver, CO: Advanced Learning Press.

Schmoker, M. (2001). *The results fieldbook: Practical strategies from dramatically improved schools.* Alexandria, VA: Association for Supervision and Curriculum Development.

Simpson, J.O. (2003, January). Beating the odds. *American School Board Journal,* 190(1), 43–44, 47.

# CHAPTER 22

# The Seduction of Simple Solutions: A Response to Douglas Reeves

*Donna Ogle*

The 90/90/90 schools described in Douglas Reeves's chapter certainly provide evidence that a high level of student poverty does not ensure academic failure. By highlighting schools that have beaten the odds, Reeves points the way to overcoming the impact of poverty and urban environments. As a result of both district evaluations and his consulting with districts on ways to use data and standards to improve school instructional effectiveness, he has identified what he labels as a few "mundane, inexpensive, and, most important, replicable" practices that make the difference. These include linking ongoing assessments with instruction, collaborative scoring of student work, an emphasis on nonfiction writing, a focus on academic achievement, and clear curriculum choices—with more time on the core subjects of reading, writing, and mathematics. These findings provide supports for U.S. educators and literacy educators in particular and pose a clear challenge to us to put more effort into creating schools where all children have a more equal opportunity to achieve.

Reeves's identification of measurable goals, adherence to standards, and regular monitoring of students' growth as fundamental to urban school success provides added support for our own synthesis of the research on what is needed for all students to be successful (see *Making a Difference Means Making It Different*, International Reading Association [IRA], 2000). The strong similarities among the urban school districts described in Reeves's chapter make our effort here even more important; we know that a shared, intensive, and intelligent focus on learning can improve achievement. Rather than having an abundance of competing programs operating within the school (the "Christmas tree" effect), the urban schools that are making a difference are focused on literacy and math and carefully monitor student and teacher efforts. Their seriousness and sustained focus produce results.

As a way of extending the reflection on what Reeves has presented, I focus on two aspects of his chapter that I, as a reading educator working in urban schools, found particularly thought-provoking. By raising a few questions, we can explore the connections between Reeves's work and our development of policies for reading instruction in the schools. The first area I explore relates to Reeves's finding that the use of writing assessment is the most powerful way to focus teachers on individual student progress. Why is writing the focus and not reading development? The second deals with his identification of the variables that make a difference in school achievement. Although there is a difference in those first mentioned in relation to the Milwaukee schools and a more extensive set of nine characteristics derived from the Norfolk, Virginia, schools, they still may underestimate the larger contextual conditions that contribute to the successes these schools and others experience. Are these characteristics sufficient to create schools where high levels of literacy are realized?

## Finding the Windows to Students' Literacy Development

Reeves makes a strong case for the value of instructional assessment as a foundation for school achievement. His data from the school districts that are experiencing success indicate the impact of measurable goals and regular monitoring of students growth.

We know about and find confirmed in these studies the importance of carefully monitoring students' progress in learning to read and in knowing students' patterns of strengths and weaknesses (Allington & Cunningham, 1996; Barr & Dreeben, 1991; Fountas & Pinnell, 1996). Reeves's work adds emphasis to the importance of helping urban teachers develop their abilities to carefully diagnose and monitor students' growth in learning and make instructional decisions based on their students' development and interests.

However, despite the importance of reading development to all student learning, it is a focus on *writing* assessment that he has found in both Milwaukee and Wayne Township, Indiana, to be the basis for teachers' shared attention. No mention is made of reading assessments. Why is this? What does this mean for our field? Why does writing work well for shared thinking about instruction? Is it, as Allington and Cunningham (1996) explain, "Because writing results in a visible, external product, assessing and evaluating children's writing development seems easier than monitoring their reading development" (p. 132)? Should we be thinking more deeply of ways to help teachers make reading more visible and more "discussable"?

Do we have assessments like retellings and think-alouds that can be shared across teachers to stimulate collaborative discussions about student learning and lead to instructional planning?

As reading educators, we struggle to help teachers find assessments of reading development that are clear and easy to administer. The experience we have in Illinois reinforces Reeves's finding. Illinois school districts have regularly focused attention on the writing test of the Illinois Standards-Based Assessment Test (ISAT) rather than the reading test. They bring in experts to train teachers in ways to improve writing scores. And often they experience success. Although there is a relationship between reading and writing that is important, the kinds of writing tasks that are included on several state high-stakes tests do not necessarily map onto the kinds of writing–reading experiences that enhance students' thinking and learning. For example, in Illinois the writing test has been very influenced by coaching. The formula represented by the "hamburger"—an opening paragraph, two or three elaboration paragraphs, and a closing paragraph—has become the structure within which students can perform well. The content and individuality of expression do not add much to the score differences. Therefore, the structural aspects of particular patterns of writing are evaluated directly, but quality and coherence of ideas are not. When the Illinois State Board of Education developed a website for performance samples that would illustrate the state standards, it had a hard time finding examples of students' reading progress that could be easily shared. If we take seriously the importance of having "products" that can generate shared conversations about students' growth and identify instructional needs, we may do well to intensify our own efforts in making such assessments more accessible and providing supports to districts in that effort.

For example, my colleagues Rebecca Barr and Camille Blachowicz have developed a classroom-based early literacy screening for Illinois called the ISEL—the Illinois Screening of Early Literacy. It contains seven sections that tap the basic skills kindergarten and first-grade children need to develop as readers—alphabet recognition, story listening, phonemic awareness, letter sounds, developmental spelling, word recognition, and passage reading. Each section is easy to administer and provides the kinds of data classroom teachers want to plan their instruction. In addition, teachers are given Watch Scores that indicate the level of performance needed for successful development of literacy based on what the large norming group of students in Illinois achieved. This tool provides a clear database that can be discussed in team and grade-level meetings. And as we implement this process with teachers in our ARDDP (Advanced Reading Development

Demonstration Project) schools, we are experiencing the difficulty of changing the teachers' orientation so that the use of these data becomes part of their thinking as they plan instruction. Developing a diagnostic sense can be achieved with reading assessment data, and it takes a strong, sustained professional development effort.

Reeves raises an important point about the use of student data in planning and implementing fast-paced, appropriate instruction. Are we focused enough on building the kinds of ongoing reading assessment monitoring tools urban teachers need? What assessments of reading work most effectively for teachers individually and collaboratively? Can we better help schools implement the fifth IRA reading right, "Children have a right to reading assessment that identifies their strengths as well as their needs and involves them in making decisions about their own learning" (IRA, 2000, p. 7)?

## Focus But Not Oversimplify

As we explore the complex of issues surrounding literacy development in urban poverty settings, it is important to keep that larger contextual frame in mind as we look at schools that have been successful. What did it take to produce these 90/90/90 schools? Is it as simple as Reeves seems to imply? Clearly, we have evidence that schools and teachers can and are making a difference. Reeves writes about mundane, inexpensive, and replicable practices—not commercial programs that make a difference. What an important finding! Teachers and administrators, not programs, create high levels of literacy achievement. However, as I read the opening section of the chapter, I was uncomfortable because it seemed to imply that achieving 90/90/90 was easy. (In other studies of successful schools, the criteria are generally lower than 90% student success.) The steps are simple, but they are not easy. Nor, in most cases, are they sufficient. Without some attention to the larger context, some readers of these reports may find cause to too easily reprimand other schools where achievement is less exemplary and to set about improving schools in a too simplistic manner. (As one former state superintendent of Illinois put it to me, "What is the low-lying fruit that I can pluck to turn around our schools?") Achieving a culture where teachers collaborate and set goals for each student based on performance data is a *tremendous* achievement. Focusing on a few key components is essential, *and* establishing the larger context for those components to function well is also critical.

I emphasize the importance of not making these achievements seem too easily attainable from the research on successful high-poverty schools

(Success for All—Success for Some; NSDC Exemplary Schools; Golden Spike Schools in Illinois—none were middle or high schools) and from years of work with schools and districts that have wanted similar results. For example, our current University–Chicago Public Schools literacy project is a partnership made possible through the Chicago Community Trust. We are teaming with teacher leaders in nine Chicago schools all with high levels of poverty and over 90% minority students. The project designed around assessment of early literacy as the foundation for instructional change in literacy also makes clear that these performance assessment practices are not easily implemented—and that other factors also influence their efficacy.

I am making the point that we must be cautious in providing simple lists—and implying that these simple solutions are simple to implement. The recent study of "outlier" schools in Illinois by our former State Superintendent of Schools Glenn "Max" McGee identified a more varied list of conditions in the successful high-poverty, high-performing (66% meet state standards) schools. His report indicates over and over again not only the commonalities among the schools, including leadership and quality teachers, but also a variety of other conditions leading to their success. Given the nature of other reports, like McGee's, that also identify characteristics of successful urban schools, we need to reflect on Reeves's data and his conclusions in light of these other identified variables. Let me elaborate on just a few of these added factors.

## District-Level Conditions Are Important

For example, in Milwaukee, the showcase district that is making some remarkable improvements, the process has been underway for several years. The building level achievements are part of a larger district culture. The whole district is involved in student achievement. In fact, the mission statement of the Milwaukee Public Schools is "Milwaukee Public Schools will be the first urban school district where all students reach high standards" (Schmoker, 2001).

At many levels the district focused resources and commitment to this goal. Included were the following:

- Student performance data were analyzed systematically and collectively at every school—to set measurable achievement goals.
- Personnel were creatively reassigned to enable the district's most effective teachers and special education staff to help low-achieving readers.

- Students were grouped strategically to allow more small-group instruction for the lowest-achieving students.
- Schools remained open in the evenings for tutoring sessions—from 6:00 p.m. to 9:00 p.m.—to accommodate student schedules.
- Grant funds found to provide tutoring services for 1,500 students in the first year and up to 20,000 students in successive years. The extra help enabled many of these students to improve their achievement.
- Summer school and tutoring services provided in neighborhood schools resulted in a marked increase in attendance. (Schmoker, 2001, p. 38)

The characteristics that Reeves outlines for the individual 90/90/90 schools are better interpreted when seen in the context of the broader district culture and support system. And despite the district's strong support, it is taking time for schools to reach the high standard that some have achieved. The example of Norfolk, Virginia, also underscores the importance of a district-supported and focused change context. As we consider the district as an important context for successful schools, we may ask the question, Why are so few of the successful schools and districts in our largest urban cities? Milwaukee and Norfolk are by far the largest of the success stories. Does this have some significance as we think of efforts needed to improve schools in New York, Chicago, and Los Angeles? Does the context of these districts influence schools in some less supportive ways?

## Student and Family Support and Involvement Are Also Critical

Milwaukee schools not only, have teachers working closely with data on student development, but they have resources provided to help them get added resource help for students most in need—through added special teachers, reading coaches, and evening tutoring. A major focus within the district now is neighborhood schools—another unstated factor that encourages parent involvement in the schools and permits children to have access to more school-based resources.

The experiences of the KIPP (Knowledge Is Power Project) middle schools begun by Mike Feinberg and David Levin also illustrate that schools that are overcoming the odds and producing high levels of student achievement. To accelerate the learning of the urban disadvantaged students, KIPP schools insist on more time—longer school days—up to 10 hours, alternate Saturday classes, and summer school. Teachers carry cell phones so they can be reached around the clock if students need help. They also know that the principal is key to the success of the school and so have initiated a special principal preparation program.

It is interesting that when Rod Paige summarized KIPP's success, he said teachers have succeeded because they focus on "high expectations, rigorous standards, accountability and results" (Alliance for Excellent Education, 2002, n.p.). These factors are definitely part of the mix, but as in Milwaukee, there are other supporting conditions like *time* for instruction, closely aligned principals and teachers, and the choice of who attends the school—factors that are not mentioned in Reeves's chapter yet are essential elements contributing to the success of the project schools.

## Professional Development Opportunities for Teachers Comprise Another Key Area in the Success of These Programs

Teachers do not learn to use assessment data well and adjust instruction to individual student needs without significant and ongoing professional development. Milwaukee has a strong teacher professional development commitment and, up to winter 2003 (with the U.S. national financial crisis affecting schools), had implemented a program of literacy coaches in the schools.

Reeves certainly agrees that quality teachers are essential to school success. As he concludes, "the research is clear that variables in teaching, curriculum, and leadership are profoundly important. In fact, these variables, which teachers and leaders can control, are more influential over student achievement than are the intractable variables of poverty, culture, and language."

When Reeves and Rod Paige fail to mention some of these added conditions and support systems, it is not inconceivable that eager school boards or community leaders might expect that teachers in individual schools could make the high-achievement gains without looking deeper at the context and conditions that allow teachers to implement performance-focused instruction. It is from being asked too often by superintendents for simple, easy solutions that I want leaders and researchers to insist on the intensive and sustained effort that produces the outstanding gains documented by Reeves and others. Reeves clearly demonstrates that good performance-oriented assessment and aligned teaching are central practices in schools that eliminate the effects of poverty. Can we afford to focus on them without also attending to other important contextual supports in the district, and in parents' and students' involvement?

## Some Next Steps

While trying to broaden the lens around Reeves's work, I want to empha-size another area from his work that deserves more attention as we con-sider policy issues related to urban schools—the quality of and support for teachers. Reeves certainly emphasizes that quality teachers are essential to school success. This area of teacher and school quality is one that we as lit-eracy researchers and educators can influence most directly. The third chil-dren's right in *Making a Difference Means Making It Different* (IRA, 2000) states that "Children have a right to well-prepared teachers who keep their skills up to date through effective professional development" (p. 5). Under the No Child Left Behind Act, schools are required to have highly qualified teachers in all classrooms. State after state is finding this requirement too hard to meet. Yet, we know that quality teachers make the difference for children—not commercial programs or even particular reading assess-ments. Given the declining numbers of well-educated and high-quality teachers coming into many urban settings today, we need to examine the ways we can create scaffolds for their learning about the essential compo-nents of reading, developing sensitivity to individual student differences and the ability to create instructional plans for differentiated instruction.

How can we more effectively reach the teachers and schools that most need high-quality professional development support? Can we turnkey this work in a way similar to the Milwaukee schools by developing a group of lo-cal staff leaders who can continue the effort? Reeves work underscores the importance of finding solutions that are not dependent on particular indi-viduals. The teachers most in need of ongoing high-quality professional de-velopment are in our urban school districts. Reading educators and researchers within IRA have a real challenge to provide quality professional development support where it is most needed—making knowledge and in-structional practices available to urban teachers and administrators who want to succeed in creating classrooms of readers and writers. Can we bridge the cultural and contextual divisions?

The solutions to improving school achievement—to more 90/90/90 schools—may be simple, and that is the good news. Implementing them is not easy; that is our challenge and the reason for us to continue examining schools and districts that are successful in raising levels of literacy and learn-ing. Will our literacy policies and programs respond to the conditions of urban America? Do we have tools to assess reading development that can be easily used in urban schools? Can we help schools define the essentials and use time and energy wisely? What is our relationship to schools that need sustained, focused staff development in literacy? Do we want to celebrate *our* successes in supporting 90/90/90 schools and districts?

## REFERENCES

Alliance for Excellent Education. (2002, November 4). *Straight A's: Public education policy and progress, 2*(20). Retrieved October 12, 2004, from http://www.all4ed.org/publications/StraightAs/Volume2No20.html

Allington, R.L., & Cunningham, P.M. (1996). *Schools that work: Where all children read and write.* New York: HarperCollins.

Barr, R., & Dreeben, R. (1991). Grouping students for reading instruction. In R. Barr, M.L. Kamil, P.B. Mosenthal, & P.D. Pearson (Eds.), *Handbook of reading instruction* (Vol. 2, pp. 885–910). White Plains, NY: Longman.

Fountas, I., & Pinnell, G.S. (1996). *Guided reading: Good first teaching for all children.* Portsmouth, NH: Heinemann.

International Reading Association (IRA). (2000). *Making a difference means making it different: Honoring children's rights to excellent reading instruction.* Newark, DE: Author.

Schmoker, M. (2001). *The results fieldbook: Practical strategies from dramatically improved schools.* Alexandria, VA: Association for Supervision and Curriculum Development.

CHAPTER 23

# A Rhetoric for School Reform

*Charles Taylor Kerchner*

C hanging school systems is a bit like putting words on paper. Change may appear to be random, the organizational equivalent of stream of consciousness or improvisation. Change may be impossible to implement, the organizational equivalent of writer's block. Or change may appear as the rarest of literary jewels, a well-crafted essay, where parts link and logic, style, and passion dance together. Like essay writers, organizations make mistakes. They often do not understand the assignment. Their ideas are not always cogent. Or they mess up the mechanics.

It is not surprising, therefore, that change efforts over the last 20 years have been disappointing to many. In 1983, the National Commission on Excellence in Education, in its report *A Nation at Risk: The Imperative for Educational Reform* (1983), grabbed national attention with a bold rhetorical stroke by comparing the problems of the U.S. education system to invasions by foreign powers. Hundreds of state and federal initiatives took root, and education reform has stayed on the public policy agenda ever since, thus confounding public policy scholars used to the short-term attention given any issue. State legislatures mandated standards, accountability, testing, and increased attention to teacher training. Various bodies produced comprehensive school design programs, such as America's Choice and Success for All. Foundations provided large grants for urban school reform. Charter schools multiplied despite the opposition of the educational establishment. Twenty years later, analysts and critics still point to the slowness of change, the paucity of student achievement gains, the recalcitrance of the education establishment (see Koret Task Force, 2003, for critical commentary on this point). But the problem is not so much recalcitrance as it is system design. As Deming noted years ago, if people are working hard and things are not getting better, the problem must lie with the system rather than the people (Mann, 1987). School reforms appear disjointed and improvisational, or as one school reformer put it: much singing and little opera (Kerchner, Abbott, Ganley, & Menefee-Libey, 2000). Schools have failed to develop a rhetoric of reform.

Urban school systems look messy and complex, but the set of problems they have to solve is not unlike those teachers face in classrooms every day. Most of the elements of big organizations are also reproduced in small ones (Caplow, 1983). Both classrooms and school districts need to be in control and moving forward at the same time. In one of the classic books on organizations, Lawrence and Lorsch (1967) describe the essential problem of organizations as steering between structures that are so loose that things fly apart and those that are so tight that the place grinds to a halt. Rosenholtz (1989) struck a similar theme in differentiating between stuck and moving schools. The tendency toward bureaucratic mire or organizational anarchy is well represented in the literature on contemporary public schools, and when school systems fail to steer the course, students do not learn, or at least not as much as they should. Holding classrooms, schools, or districts together while making them move is part of normal operations, but changing organizations as they continue to work is another task altogether.

Organizational change involves unfreezing the organization. It is simultaneously radical and conservative, incremental and pattern breaking. Schools were expected to re-create themselves along new organizational models, even as they continued to operate. In several school districts we studied, educators used the same words to describe what they were doing. "It's like building the plane as it's rolling down the runway," they said (Kerchner & Caufman, 1993):

> Like a plane taxiing down the runway, these schools were expected to take off with a full load of students and carry them to a predetermined location. But they were expected to provide a different type of flight with fewer bumps, better movies, and first-class service throughout. The schools we visited were expected to be "new and improved" in the commercial argot. Yet all the daily functions and conventional operations continued. Classes were held, bells sounded for successive periods, fights broke out in hallways, grade cards were issued, students were subjected to discipline and suspension—all the rituals and folkways associated with school continued to be acted out. (p. 6)

The same was true with school districts. Almost all existing structures remained: school boards, superintendents, central offices, thousands of laws, rules, compliance mandates, civil rights expectations, labor relations agreements, and political realities. School change was an essay written on already full sheets of paper, more revision than exposition. Why then is change such a large problem? I argue that the problem largely arises in three critical errors. First, whereas the proponents of school reform think of change as an imperative, school administrators and teachers often take the assignment as optional. Second, both those who design reforms and those who implement them fail to think in full paragraphs, and the logic between initiating reform and getting results is muddied. Third, all involved fail to understand the grammar of schooling, longstanding historical and cultural rules that make certain kinds of change possible and others very difficult.

## Treating the Assignment as Optional

No classroom event cuts closer to the utilitarian bone than the question from the back of the room, emanating from a student stretched so prone that only the raised hand is visible: "Teacher, is this going to be on the test?" Away fly the beauty, passion, engagement, and inspiration that the teacher thought were planned into the lesson. To the front comes the essential question: "Do we have to do this stuff?"

In school districts, as in classrooms, the answer is often "no." The history of education reform teaches that most reform attempts live short and unhappy lives. Some vanish without a trace. Others become examples of how schools change reform rather than the other way around.

Since *A Nation at Risk*, there have been four distinct waves of reform. In the first wave, governors and state legislatures sought to fix education through intensification. In the words of one California legislator, they sought to "make the little buggers work harder" (Tyack & Cuban, 1995, p. 59). As it turned out, it wasn't just the little ones that were to be working harder. More rigorous academic standards for students also brought on higher professional standards for teachers, a more rigorous curriculum, longer school days, more highly qualified teachers, and more homework (Passow, 1990). A second wave of reform focused on school-level changes such as restructuring, site-based management, teacher empowerment, and professionalism (Kirst, 1990). The third wave advocated "systematic school reform," the notion that a cluster of activities was needed together (Smith & O'Day, 1991). The assumption was that by changing the conditions surrounding teaching, teaching itself would change, and student achievement would increase (Olson & Rothman, 1993).

The fourth wave of reform, which has become U.S. national policy since 2000, is to intensify and attach consequences to testing. Rather than structurally change schools or districts and hope for change, the technique switched to intensively testing students, making results public, and attaching test results to consequences for students and schools. The fourth wave of reform came to resemble the first: make people work harder. It also attaches a variety of rewards and sanctions: "naming and shaming" poorly performing schools by making test scores public, creating intervention teams to coach and prod underperforming schools, district or state takeovers that replace the school leadership, and allowing students to leave "failing" schools for better public or private classrooms.

All four waves of reform have been intensely political, and commentators attach blame for the perceived failures of reform to the major political actors in the system. Superintendents are pictured as temporary nomads with often-superficial knowledge of the districts they lead. School boards are pictured as inept, narrowly political, and fractious. Teacher unions receive the most approbation from policy and editorial commentators, and they are frequently labeled as intransigent and self-interested. All four of these statements are facile stereotypes, but the reality appears somewhat more benign.

Although the tenure of urban superintendents has increased in the last few years, it still hovers around three years, far shorter than the time necessary to substantively restructure a school district. During their tenure, superintendents generally work at a relentless pace at what commentator John Merrow (2000) called "the toughest job in America." Their job is to initiate reform, and school boards generally give them substantial leeway in doing so. But, the rapid turnover among superintendents leads to an equally fast turnover in educational initiatives called "policy churn" (Hess, 1999). Rapid turnover at the top leaves principals and teachers skeptical about reforms. Teachers and principals "often resent becoming agents of someone else's career advancement. Fearing that rapid and visible change imposed by a new superintendent may lead to inchoate programs and wasted energy, teachers and others often become cynical and resist superintendents' enthusiastic plans to reform them and their schools" (Johnson, 1996, p. 92). In fact, superintendents often paint themselves into corners based on their personal ambition, or they find that the knowledge of organizations they thought that they had was, in fact, localized knowledge and influence from their former superintendency. More than a few superintendents have been unable to replicate the reforms they had created in one city when they moved to another.

School boards, often pictured as fractious and destructive, have actually supported most change. Hess (1999), who studied a stratified sample of 57 urban school districts, found boards "tend to cohesively endorse reform proposals" (p. 60). Even boards that were publicly fractious tended to unite behind the superintendent's reform initiatives. Hess tells of the deeply split Duval County, Florida, board, which voted 4–3 when deciding whether to bring in a facilitator to help them form more of a team environment. But the board agreed on reform, and on Hess's cohesion instrument scored 8.3 out of 10 in support. Hess argues that boards support reform because the public expects it and challenges board members who fail to support reform. In urban districts board members are often politically ambitious; in half the districts in the Hess study a member ran for higher office. Many more thought seriously about it. Failure to take reform seriously causes efforts, often supported by business and civic leadership, to purge the reluctant board members, as happened in Atlanta, St. Louis, and Los Angeles, among other cities (see Hess, 1999, pp. 68–70; Kerchner et al., 2000). However, supporting the initiation of reform and supporting its implementation involve different politics. Initiating reforms is an act of *unitary* politics: general support of a big idea (Mansbridge, 1990; Peterson, 1976; Reich, 1988). Implementation of reforms involves *pluralist* politics, the jockeying for positions, supporting particular interest groups, bargaining, compromise, and frictional conflict.

Teacher union officials are often depicted as recalcitrant about reform. Indeed, there is a delicious irony in the fact that teachers unions, which organized in opposition to the authority system of public education, should be the fiercest defender of the system against alternative ways of delivering schooling. However, for the most part union leaders are reflecting their members' views. Unlike many policy activists, most teachers do not believe that public education is facing a large institutional change or that schooling needs to change in major ways. I am told that polls done by the unions themselves show that teachers want help with problems of student achievement, but that they do not particularly associate their unions with this function. Teachers who work at charter schools seem disassociated with the union and public education altogether (Koppich, Holmes, & Plecki, 1998). After reading my book on union reform, a 30-year veteran teacher wrote, "I do not want to pay union dues to an organization that does anything but help me in defense, income, benefits. Do you understand?" (personal communication, April 4, 2002).

Just as one can observe and enumerate examples of union organizing around educational quality and student achievement, any observer would be forced to note that teacher union organizing outside of its industrial origins has not spread rapidly (Kerchner & Koppich, 1993; Kerchner, Koppich, & Weeres, 1997). Both U.S. national unions exhibit tentativeness about how departures from industrial unionism should proceed. In the late 1980s, the American Federation of Teachers (AFT) promoted site-based management and school decentralization as the keystones of organizational reform, only to abandon the effort in favor of a strong emphasis on standards and adoption of a limited number of coherent reform strategies. The National Education Association's (NEA's) New Unionism was supposed to ignite a bubbling pot of locally initiated reforms, but the evidence from the first years illustrates the difficulties of moving forward. In sum, union reform appears to have little of the momentum that characterized the growth of collective bargaining in the 1960s and 1970s. Without a driving force behind it, such as statutory change, the new unionism is likely to remain not only new, but novel (Koppich & Kerchner, 2003).

The Los Angeles Educational Alliance for Reform Now (LEARN), a 1990s reform program, provides an instructive example. In many ways, LEARN was a textbook example of how to initiate reform. It drew from the best of contemporary ideas for organizing the school district around decentralization and autonomy linked to accountability. Built on ideas from the teacher union president, it created a seemingly unbeatable political coalition that supported measures that had been synthesized from effective efforts at reform from that era. LEARN's initiation garnered 7–0 school board support, endorsement from the superintendent, and widespread civic and political backing. It seemed the perfect plan, but as we shall see, the implementation faltered (Kerchner et al., 2000).

For teachers, LEARN was literally an optional assignment. The voting rules to become a LEARN school required that 75% of the faculty agree. The idea was to avoid disingenuousness or compliance issues by not forcing schools into the program and to gradually spread the program throughout the district. There was wisdom in this idea, but making the assignment optional meant that there were parts of the city where there were involved elementary schools and nonparticipating high schools. Pockets of overt resistance grew at some high schools, and these were associated with schism in United Teachers of Los Angeles between the supporters of the then president Helen Burnstein, who supported LEARN, and the former president Wayne Johnson, who did not.

LEARN also became an optional assignment at the central office. Because of strong civic and business community support, resistance was not overt, but successive superintendents became less committed to the program. LEARN schools also stood out as odd or different among the schools in a cluster of schools, and within two years of the program's inception, schools in the program were removed from the administrative control of their geographic clusters and began to report directly to the LEARN office. The reorganization effectively isolated the reforming schools from those who were not. In 1999, the program officially came to an end. Participating schools were given plaques and banners declaring them to be LEARN schools, and some schools still proudly call themselves such. But as a reform that would single-handedly reorganize the district, LEARN was defeated.

# Not Writing in Complete Paragraphs

Just as teachers of writing are trained to look for logical linkages between sentences, organizational analysts learn to look for whether one element of change is being propelled by another. For example, one might find intensive professional development, leading to changes in teaching strategies, which produce higher achievement measures, which in turn increase student enthusiasm and teacher senses of efficacy, and which increase the demand for greater engagement in one's own professional development. Each part of the circle of action reinforces the next. Thinking in these terms becomes the basic building block in systems thinking (Senge, 1990). Although the idea is a straightforward one, constructing a reinforcing loop is often a difficult exercise, even as a thought experiment.

Consider for a moment what could go wrong in the implementation of a new reading program. The district purchases a new program and associated texts from a vendor. The program comes with teacher aids and a professional development package. District personnel receive training from the vendor's staff, including lots of advice about how to simultaneously provide "professional development" and to make the program "teacher-proof." Now, think about what happens in the implementation process. Sometimes the texts and other materials do not arrive in the school, a victim of budget cutbacks or delivery delays. As one new teacher said, "They want me to teach this stuff, but they don't give me the stuff to teach" (Kauffman, Johnson, Kardos, Liu, & Peske, 2000, p. 1). Sometimes the staff development goes badly, and then teachers rebel and call in their union representatives to complain. People actively organize *against* the new program. Sometimes key administrators leave. Sometimes the new program produces *lower* test scores in the first year or two of implementation, something that Fullan and Stiegelbauer (1991) call "implementation dip." A lot can go wrong.

The California Learning Assessment System (CLAS) development began in the late 1980s. In addition to tightly linking assessment to curriculum frameworks, CLAS was designed to be a more thorough performance examination. It had longer writing assignments presented in problem-solving situations, and it was holistically scored as opposed to checking right or wrong answers.

CLAS was an almost perfect example of professionally driven reform. Hundreds of teachers and some of the best-known subject-matter specialists and testing and measurement experts in the United States were involved in creating the test (Chrispeel, 1997). It would be fair to characterize CLAS as containing much of the leading-edge thinking among educators about what children should know and how schools can tell whether they know it.

CLAS was administered twice. In 1994 its budgetary reauthorization was vetoed by Governor Pete Wilson (SB 1273). What had started as an example of professional competence and design ended as an example of the tension between technical precision and political common sense. (For a summary of the political process, see PACE, 1995). CLAS had always been controversial. Religious groups complained that the writing prompts asked students to reflect on their home lives and on moral dilemmas that should not be the province of the public schools. Others objected to the holistic scoring techniques and the lack of "objective" scores. The controversy intensified after the first round of test administration in 1993. Some schools, including some from the wealthiest areas in the state, that had fared well on previous assessments did poorly on the new test. *The Los Angeles Times* published an investigation critical of the sampling procedures, one that claimed that some 11,000 sampling errors produced results that invalidated any cross-school or cross-district comparisons (Wilgoren, 1994). Conservative foundations filed suit against the test. And finally, the California Teacher's Association denounced the test and particularly its administration by the California Department of Education. The Department's advocacy function was also somewhat weakened during this period. Superintendent Bill Honig, the architect of many of the previous decade's reforms, resigned from office, leaving the superintendency in the hands of an acting administrator.

Regardless of the politics, the effect of the CLAS test veto was to leave the school reform effort in Los Angeles (as well as the rest of the state) without an anchor assessment, particularly one that worked at the individual level. To be sure, there are still other indicators available, but neither LEARN nor the school district had invested in a comprehensive indicator system that would connect changes in classroom practice and school organization with measured cognitive assessment or any other forms of student output. Some LEARN schools became proficient at tracking their progress, but this characteristic did not become widespread.

In organizational change, as in writing, one thing should lead to another. But that is not always the case. Organizations, and not just public schools, often engage in incomplete cycles of decision making. Decisions to do things are not always followed with actions (March, 1981). Preferences about what to do are not stable (Arrow, 1974). School boards, for example, are notorious for oscillating between command-and-control superintendents and those bent on decentralization. The curriculum swings between recitation and engagement, phonics and whole language. Failure to think and act in terms of one thing influencing another leads to improvisational reforms or spinning wheels, in which there is much action but not necessarily much progress (Hess, 1999; Kerchner et al., 2000).

For most of the past century, those who study organizations have thought about and analyzed organizations as social systems. This body of work has produced important analytical capacity, such as systems analysis, formal modeling, and practical kinds of artificial intelligence such as the Internet search engines and personal digital assistants. The social systems approach also makes it possible to draw some rough-and-ready design principles from what we know about organization behavior. These are usable by any teacher or practitioner as a way of examining organizational change in the same way one would grade an essay.

## How Long Is the Causal Chain?

The more inclusive a reform, the harder it is to get change started and to keep it going. Advocates of shared decision making, distributive leadership, or other forms of breaking down hierarchy argue that participation yields psychological commitment (buy in) to the reform once it begins. But simply making the decisional process complex frequently stops forward motion. In a study of community redevelopment programs in Oakland, California, Pressman and Wildavsky (1973) illustrate the devastating effect of requiring successive decisions. Suppose there were a reform that everyone liked; in fact, there was a near-certain, 9 out of 10 probability that the school board, union, school site council, finance committee, curriculum council, principals' association, district advisory committee, and superintendent would all approve. If each had to approve in order, there would be less than a 50–50 chance that the project would get off the ground. (The compound probability: $.9 \times .9 \times .9 \times .9 \times .9 \times .9 \times .9 = .48$.) Of course, most projects are not nearly so uncontroversial, and thus the probability that they will be implemented is much lower. Long decisional chains also lead to what Malen, Ogawa, and Kranz (1989) have called "process paralysis"—fatigue and inaction brought on by seemingly endless meetings and decisions about seemingly trivial matters.

## How Big Is the Zone of Wishful Thinking?

Almost all school reforms contain a "zone of wishful thinking," a series of necessary actions not under control of the reformers. As Hill and Celio (1998) examined the major urban reform models in *Fixing Urban Schools*, they found that all of them—including the contracting-out model they advocated—required that "several key actors must develop capabilities and patterns of action that they do not have now" (pp. 17–18). The contracting model assumes highly independent schools competing for students. In order for contracting-out to work, enough private contractors would have to show up to operate schools, organizations that had not previously run public schools would have to learn how to do so effectively, there would have to be an adequate supply of teachers, parents must be able to exercise choice wisely, and public authorities must be able to determine the value added from each school.

As Hill and Celio note, there is no reason that their contracting model cannot travel through the zone of wishful thinking. "But they required actions and capabilities that are extremely rare today" (p. 19). Other reform ideas face similar hazards:

> Two other proposals, charter schools and education vouchers, have similar blue zones [of wishful thinking]. Both assume, for example, a massive response of new suppliers wanting to run schools, an adequate supply of teachers who will be willing and able to cope with the demands of working in an environment of competition and strict performance accountability, and public authorities who learn how to protect students against low-quality schools or inequitable admissions processes without interfering with schools' ability to pursue coherent instructional programs. The voucher proposal also makes an assumption that contracting and charter proposals do not: that entrepreneurs will spontaneously offer good schools in poverty areas where teaching can be difficult and parents are less demanding. (Hill & Celio, 1998, p. 19)

Among public school critics, Hill and Celio are virtually alone in describing their own proposals with such candor. Yet, candor is necessary for success, but it is seldom present. Many reforms become politicized and their proponents and detractors become sufficiently convinced of the *correctness* of their positions that problems of implementation are never fully addressed. Commercial vendors provide a curriculum that has an apparent pathway to success, but the implementation often leaves students behind and teachers increasingly frustrated because the official plan makes no provision for failure. Teachers are simply told to press on.

## Can You See the Future From Here?

Novels need a plot, essays advance a logical argument, narratives recount a story, and school reform needs a plan to "connect the dots," as teachers frequently put it. Just as Hill and Celio (1998) constructed a causal sequence for the reforms they examined, school reformers need a carefully thought out map through the hazards of change. They seldom get one. Principals and teachers are much more likely to receive mandates than maps marking the main roads and showing possible alternatives and detours.

The plot outline or storyboard of school change can either be accomplished from the beginning or from the end, forward or backward. Implementation can be laid out as a series of steps from legislation or reform adoption to the classroom. Good implementation planning does this. But a more informative process may start with the assumption that implementation begins at the bottom of the organization rather than the top (Elmore, 1983). Instead of imagining a law or school district policy, one would think first about how teachers and students would have to work differently to accomplish the goals in mind. If the object were to raise standardized test scores, for example, then what is it that students would do differently than they do now? What combination of tasks would lead a first-grade English-language learner to know more at the end of the year than is now the case? Examining these steps requires schools to come to grips with an embedded theory of learning. It's one thing to *adopt* a program in standards-based instruction, for example. It is quite another to know that standards-based instruction changes a class by devoting more time to word attack, reading out loud, writing and revising, or whatever other activity is contemplated. Once it is understood what a student will do differently, one can then talk about what teachers need to do differently. Are there specific skills that teachers need that they don't have now? Are there organizational routines that need to be changed, for example, the process and timing of interventions that bring speech or special education specialists into the classrooms? Once these questions are answered, it is possible to ask what school principals, superintendents, and public policy should do.

Indicators of success provide another way to see into the future. Indicator systems have become a staple of social statistics. Communities use indicators to keep track of progress toward robust and stable neighborhoods. Firms use them to benchmark quality. Schools are beginning to use them as a way to integrate organizational functioning and student achievement (Bryk, 1998).

The idea of educational indicators, which had its origins in the early 1900s, gained contemporary currency with a federal panel on school outcomes and was articulated by Bryk and Hermanson (1993) in a much-cited article in *Review of Educational Research*. Simply put, their idea is that there should be a way to connect the large public school scorecards—test scores and the like—with the more authentic indicators of success that teachers rely on to inform their practices, such as engagement in work, recent evidence of breakthroughs, peak performance versus coasting along. For many students, simply a record of a week's unbroken attendance, turning in of homework, and paying attention in class may well be considered a milestone.

Unfortunately, most classroom artifacts remain unconnected to the work of the school and unconnected to what the public knows about the school. Public data are almost always derived from statistical summaries of test scores, attendance, graduation rates, and other measures produced by the state or the school district. These are almost always disconnected from the work of the school, and thus a school with unsatisfactory test scores is often unsure about what it does or does not do to cause those scores. The test scores are simply artifacts—usually from *last* year's class—that the school district uses to admonish the school. As a result, schools have a tendency to attribute or blame test scores on external factors, such a poverty, transience, or social state: *those* students or families.

As an alternative, Bryk and Hermanson suggest a pyramid of interconnected data from all levels in the school organization. A simplified version appears in Figure 23.1.

Data about achievement exist at three levels—public, school, and classroom—but without organizational connectors, the data from one level seldom inform the others. The most obvious ways these connections can be made is through systematic disaggregation of gross public indicators into small school, team, or classroom levels, where test scores are associated with

## Figure 23.1
## Indicators and Feedback Loops for Student Achievement

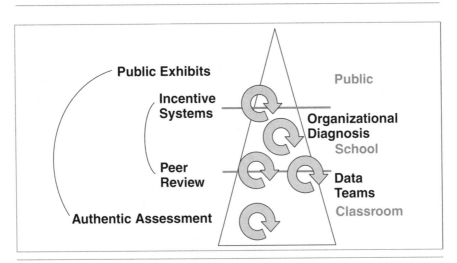

individual students in ways that allow teachers to have discussions about them. At the same time, an indicator system can consciously make classroom data more public. Figure 23.1 shows a number of organizational feedback loops that connect the hierarchical levels. For example, teacher tests and student exhibits can become part of the public examination of achievement data, allowing parents to see what high-standard work looks like and allowing the school and district to compare the expected standards with the work that students are actually assigned and complete. School data teams can examine disaggregated data, drawing attention to particular students and their needs. Schools can use forms of organizational diagnosis to analyze how the work routines of teachers and administrators facilitate or block information flows within a school or district. All these make a complete school reform plan easier.

Just as a complete paragraph needs a series of logically connected thoughts, a complete school reform plan needs connected action. Action becomes difficult when a long series of approvals is necessary; even appealing reforms can fail to win the necessary consent. Educational reforms often engage in wishful thinking by requiring resources that the reformers cannot control. And often they don't have a way to see the future clearly or a means of reacting to contingencies when they arise.

## Violating the Grammar Rules

Like the teachers of English with poised red pencils, schools and school systems have grammar rules. Whereas linguistic grammar covertly organizes meaning in communication and dictates what is (and what is not) a syntactically correct sentence, the "grammar of schooling" determines what the public constitutes to be a "real school" (Tyack & Cuban, 1995, p. 107). Schools that depart from this collective understanding—such as those that do not issue report cards or those that do not group children according to age—draw attention. They are labeled *alternative*, *nontraditional*, or *progressive*, all terms of denigration. Over the last 80 years, relatively little has changed in the way schools divide the curriculum into subjects, divide students into individual classrooms, and award grades and credits as evidence of learning.

Just as there is a grammar to schools, there is also a grammar to public school systems. This grammar includes those defining features of U.S. public school system: "direct operation of schools by elected school boards, compliance-based accountability, civil service employment for teachers, mandatory assignment of students to schools and control of funds by central district bureaucracies" (Hill, Pierce, & Guthrie, 1997, p. vii).

Variations from the norm are deemed perverse or abnormal because educators and public have come to assume that the grammar embodies the necessary features of a proper school. The established institutional forms prescribed by the grammar are cemented into place and further legitimized "by everyday custom in schools and by outside forces, both legal mandates and cultural beliefs, until they are barely noticed" (p. 86). Similar to how native speakers effortlessly absorb, instinctively understand, and unwittingly accept their tongue's linguistic structure, most educators have naturally adopted the grammar of schools, and accordingly, they rarely explicitly acknowledge, discuss, or question the way they think about schools and how they operate. This grammar provides the foundation for what Senge (1990) would call our "mental models" of schools—those "deeply ingrained assumptions, generalizations, or even pictures or images that influence how we understand [schools] and how we take action" (p. 8).

School restructuring reforms nearly always violate the institutional grammar. Efforts at changing governance structures in large urban districts tend to erode over time. In the late 1960s, New York City decentralized governance by dividing the city into smaller school districts, each with a school board and a powerful local superintendent. The districts still exist, but their powers have been substantially curtailed. In the late 1980s, Chicago radically decentralized school governance, creating elected councils for each school with the power to hire and fire the principal and with substantial autonomy over curricular decisions. Within four years of the outset of this experiment in "democratic localism," the schools were radically recentralized, even though the local boards continue to exist (Bryk, 1998). At the turn of the 21st century, Los Angeles decentralized school governance into semiautonomous local school districts. This was the fourth administrative decentralization effort in a decade, but this one was intended to pave the way for a possible legal breakup of the district into smaller units. Within months, elements of recentralization began to reappear. A districtwide reading program and testing program were adopted, and almost all the fiscal and regulatory requirements remained in place.

Historically, pedagogical reform efforts have met similar effects. The efforts of educators to fail in reforming high schools have been a longstanding puzzlement. One of the boldest and best-studied efforts took place in the 1930s and 1940s when 29 high schools began an experiment in revamping the curriculum around progressive education ideals. More than 200 colleges and universities were persuaded to admit students from these high schools, which had either discarded or modified the Carnegie Unit as a means of accounting for adequate preparation for college. As recorded in the historically famous Eight Year Study, the experiment worked. Students did as well in college as those who studied in more traditional ways, and they were more active in campus political, artistic, and social life (Tyack & Cuban, 1995). One would think that the results would have justified more curricular experimentation. The opposite was true. By 1950 the participants in the study themselves agreed that the reforms had atrophied. Core courses and the Carnegie Unit reappeared, and "students write fewer articles in English and social science but they are better spellers" (Tyack & Cuban, 1995, p. 100).

The political opposition to progressive educators in the 1940s and 1950s grew in ways not unlike the opposition to whole language instruction today: "The more militant progressives became increasingly like true believers in a particular version of the faith and increasingly isolated from public scrutiny and discourse" (Elmore, 1996, p. 11). Isolation breeds attack from traditionalists and arrogance among the advocates.

Reforms are also vulnerable to shallow adoption. They tend to lose their intellectual edge as they spread and to drift into clichés or buzzwords. Progressive education became a parody of itself capable of being portrayed as watered-down content, life adjustment, and self-expression instead of learning (Cremin, 1962). In the same way, it is relatively easy for a school to adopt a packaged program or curriculum in literature, for example, and thus claim to be *doing* literacy. The act of adoption substitutes for thorough implementation.

Substantive reforms thus remain localized and relatively isolated. Often practitioners like it that way. Several years ago a colleague and I wrote a descriptive analysis of Humanitas, a strikingly successful interdisciplinary program in the Los Angeles Unified School District (Kerchner & Donaldson, 1989). Years later I asked one of the participants about the program and its growth. He replied, "We're trying to fly this thing under the radar; if the district gets hold of it and mandates its use, they'll make our work impossible." Isolated examples of what *could be* tend not to be brought to scale.

In the 1960s, a particularly coherent and powerful set of reforms sought to change the grammar of high schools. The National Science Foundation, in a series of initiatives, sought to make physics, chemistry, and biology less textbook-oriented and more the object of discovery and experimentation. The idea progressed through bringing strong teachers together with interested scientists to write new courses of study that made studying science more like *doing* science. The object was not so much learning facts but understanding the scientific concepts and methods of inquiry. The experiment covered many schools. Aspects of it continue, but the results were evaluated as "broad but shallow" (Elmore, 1996, p. 13).

With the benefit of hindsight, it is easy to see that the curriculum development projects failed to understand the extent to which their efforts violated the grammar of schooling. It was assumed a clearly superior curriculum would be self-validating and would spread of its own accord, not through the complex process of changing texts, teacher training, and school operations.

> In the few instances where the advocates for the curriculum development projects appeared to be on the verge of discovering a way to change practice on a large scale...they failed to discern the significance of what they were doing because they saw themselves as developers of new ideas about teaching and not as institution-changing actors. (Elmore, 1996, p. 14)

At the same time, foundations began to support "high schools of tomorrow" through what became known at the Model Schools Project. The high schools project violated several grammar rules. Instead of a set schedule, days and weeks were designed around a "flexible modular schedule" in which some classes ran for long periods, and others did not meet at all during a day or week. Courses were variable in length, too, with minicourses to capture topics of current interest. Teachers worked in teams, and classrooms became resource centers. Rather than marching "platoon style" from classroom to classroom, students would move between educational spaces at different times, and when they had nonclass time they were free to congregate in areas of campus set aside as social centers, or in some cases leave school altogether.

They met fierce resistance. Conservative parents called the schools "zoos" and blamed low achievement on the new scheduling and teaching practice. Principals found that schools were hard to control, and that teachers' practices hadn't changed as much as they thought. Parents in Portland, Oregon, resisted changes in the high schools there (Tyack & Cuban, 1995). In Claremont, California, and in a host of other innovative schools, the principal left shortly after the program began (Hoffman, 1991). In Cleveland Heights, Ohio, the program fell victim to administrative turnovers, racial conflict, and a teacher union determination to kill the plan as a "clever management trap" (Tittle, 1995, p. 236). As Tyack and Cuban note, "A bold yet fragile challenge to the grammar of schooling, the 'High Schools of Tomorrow' of the 1960s and early 1970s ebbed as 'back to basics' and 'excellence' became mottoes of the next wave of reform" (1995, p. 107).

# A Work in Progress: Revise and Resubmit

The essay on school reform is still incomplete. It lacks both plot and conclusion, but there are some lessons that can be drawn from the last two decades.

First, when the assignment is optional, many educators opt out. A theory of change based on gradual acceptance of innovations fails to explain what happens in public education. New ideas don't spread like wildfire through urban school districts. The gradual adoption idea, widely used in marketing commercial products and in economic development projects, suggests that change projects first accommodate the eager early adopters, move to scale with second and third waves, and don't worry too much about the laggards. School reform programs generally have little trouble recruiting early adopters, but then resistance sets in. Gradual change becomes too gradual, superintendents leave, funders lose interest, and the innovation, now termed *failed*, is replaced with a new one. As a result, governments and school districts retain their longstanding fondness for mandates. School districts find that it is easier to gain at least the appearance of change by ordering the implementation of a new program, idea, or curriculum, than by waiting for teachers and principals to adopt an innovation on their own. Mandates are quicker. They operate within the tenure of a contemporary superintendent.

Second, when change is mandated, teachers and principals become passengers rather than drivers of the school reform bus. They don't have a road map; and often they don't care. Their job, as it is made abundantly clear to them, is to comply, not to think through how one thing logically links with another. Districts assume that with a little staff development that teachers will *get it*. Implementation programs move on to a new topic next year, with the assumption that teachers have fully integrated the last topic into their classrooms. As a result, the artifacts of change are often present without the substance. A visitor to a classroom can be assured the teacher inside is *doing* standards-based instruction because Standard 3.1.7 is clearly posted in the room, but little else is happening, and the change literally does not make sense to the teacher doing the work.

A mental model of change, the idea about how one thing links to another, is essential if school reform is to avoid being stuck while trying to change. To the extent that the teachers and students doing the work don't understand what to do and how to improvise when things do not work as planned, school change is reduced to following rules. It is easier to follow rules than it is to create reinforcing loops of change within a school or within a classroom. But without the self-knowledge of what it takes to move a school or district it is almost impossible to build lasting change that systemically deepens over time.

Third, when the planned change violates the grammar of schooling the system rejects it. As a result, it is much easier to reform around the periphery of a school system than to change its core. It is easier, for example, to create a parent center or to hire a community outreach worker than to integrate parents and families into the regular learning experience in a classroom. The constant introduction of new programs at the edges of a school gives the illusion of change, when often there is little. Introducing new programs creates great busyness in a school, and busyness is often taken as a proxy for progress.

Failure of school change to get at the core of things leads school reform to a divide. There are two visions about how change occurs in schools. One is an apocalyptic vision of "break the mold" school designers and the anti-institutional advocates of market solutions. The other is the *Tinkering Toward Utopia* vision of gradual change within an existing institutional framework (Tyack & Cuban, 1995). School reform over the last 20 years in particular has proceeded largely by promising the former but delivering the latter. The reform mode most generally used by the test and accountability advocates in this new millennium is to stay within the existing grammar and work toward gradual improvement. In terms of school organization, their plan is literally back to the basics.

The school reform radicals are radical mostly about school governance rather than school operations. They believe that by introducing multiple operators of schools, all with transparent accountability, schools will rapidly improve. But there is little in the new governance ideas to suggest that the new schools will be radically different from the ones we know now: individual classrooms, graded schools, progression between levels based on Carnegie Units or other markers. In fact, the experience with public and private school operators in other countries suggests that private operators often appeal to parents by being more traditional and less pedagogically innovative than their public counterparts.

If that is the case, then the rhetoric of real change becomes one of systematically creating organizations that learn from their own experience. History is, indeed, a teacher.

Success is not built on success; it's built on learning from failure.

## Acknowledgment

I would like to thank Weijiang Zhang for assistance in writing this chapter.

# REFERENCES

Arrow, K.J. (1974). *The limits of organizations*. New York: Norton.

Bryk, A.S. (1998). *Charting Chicago school reform: Democratic localism as a lever for change*. Boulder, CO: Westview.

Bryk, A.S., & Hermanson, K.L. (1993). Educational indicator systems: Observations on their structure, interpretation and use. In L. Darling-Hammond (Ed.), *Review of research in education* (Vol. 19, pp. 405–450). Washington, DC: American Educational Research Association.

Caplow, T. (1983). *Managing an organization* (2nd ed.). New York: Holt, Rinehart and Winston.

Chrispeel, J.H. (1997). Educational policy implementation in shifting political climate: The California experience. *American Educational Research Journal, 34*(3), 453–481.

Cremin, L.A. (1962). *The transformation of the school: Progressivism in American education, 1876–1957*. New York: Knopf.

Elmore, R.F. (1983). Complexity and control: What legislators and administrators can do about implementing public policy. In L.S. Shulman & G. Sykes (Eds.), *Handbook of teaching and policy* (pp. 342–369). New York: Longman.

Elmore, R.F. (1996). Getting to scale with good educational practice. *Harvard Educational Review, 66*(1), 1–26.

Fullan, M.G., & Stiegelbauer, S. (1991). *The new meaning of educational change*. New York: Teachers College Press.

Hess, F.M. (1999). *Spinning wheels: The politics of urban school reform*. Washington, DC: Brookings Institution Press.

Hill, P.T., & Celio, M.B. (1998). *Fixing urban schools*. Washington, DC: Brookings Institution Press.

Hill, P.T., Pierce, L.C., & Guthrie, J.W. (1997). *Reinventing public education: How contracting can transform America's schools*. Chicago: University of Chicago Press.

Hoffman, P.W. (1991). *A historical case study of the Claremont High School flexible modular scheduling innovation,*

*1963–1981*. Unpublished doctoral dissertation, Claremont Graduate School, Claremont, California.

Johnson, S.M. (1996). *Leading to change: The challenge of the new superintendency*. San Francisco: Jossey-Bass.

Kauffman, D., Johnson, S.M., Kardos, S.M., Liu, E., & Peske, H.G. (2000, April). *"Lost at sea": New teachers' experiences with curriculum and assessment*. Paper presented at the annual meeting of the American Educational Research Association, New Orleans, LA.

Kerchner, C.T., Abbott, J., Ganley, D., & Menefee-Libey, D. (2000). *The impact of the Los Angeles metropolitan project on public education reform*. Claremont, CA: Claremont Graduate University.

Kerchner, C.T., & Caufman, K.D. (1993). Building the airplane while it's rolling down the runway. In C.T. Kerchner & J.E. Koppich (Eds.), *A union of professionals: Labor relations and educational reform* (pp. 1–24). New York: Teachers College Press.

Kerchner, C.T., & Donaldson, C. (1989). Autonomous work groups and curriculum reform. In J.M. Rosow & R. Zager (Eds.), *Allies in educational reform: How teachers, unions, and administrators can join forces for better schools* (pp. 275–293). San Francisco: Jossey-Bass.

Kerchner, C.T., & Koppich, J.E. (1993). *A union of professionals: Labor relations and educational reform*. New York: Teachers College Press.

Kerchner, C.T., Koppich, J.E., & Weeres, J.G. (1997). *United mind workers: Unions and teaching in the knowledge society*. San Francisco: Jossey-Bass.

Kirst, M. (1990). The crash of the first wave. In S.B. Bacharach (Ed.), *Education reform: Making sense of it all* (pp. 20–29). Boston: Allyn & Bacon.

Koppich, J.E., Holmes, P., & Plecki, M.L. (1998). *New rules, new roles? The professional work lives of charter school teachers*. Washington, DC: National Education Association.

Koppich, J.E., & Kerchner, C.T. (2003, February 12). Negotiating what matters most: Rethinking teacher collective bargaining. *Education Week*, *56*, 41.

Koret Task Force. (2003). Schools and our future. *Education Next*, *3*(2), 9–16.

Lawrence, P.R., & Lorsch, J.W. (1967). *Organization and environment: Managing differentiation and integration.* Boston: Division of Research, Graduate School of Business Administration, Harvard University.

Malen, B., Ogawa, R.T., & Kranz, J. (1989). *An analysis of site based management as an education reform strategy.* Department of Educational Administration, University of Utah.

Mann, N.R. (1987). *The keys to excellence: The Deming philosophy.* Los Angeles: Prestwick.

Mansbridge, J.J. (Ed.). (1990). *Beyond self-interest.* Chicago: University of Chicago Press.

March, J.G. (1981). Decision making perspective: Decisions in organizations and theories of choice. In A.H. Van de Ven & W.F. Joyce (Eds.), *Perspectives on organizational design and behavior* (pp. 205–244). New York: Wiley.

Merrow, J. (2000, April). *The toughest job in America: Public broadcast service.* Retrieved April 7, 2003, from http://www.pbs.orgmerrow/tv/tough/video.html

National Commission on Excellence in Education. (1983). *A nation at risk: The imperative for educational reform* (A report to the Secretary of Education, 226006 ed.). Washington, DC: U.S. Department of Education.

Olson, L., & Rothman, R. (1993, April 21). Roadmap to reform [Quality Counts series]. *Education Week*, 13–17.

PACE. (1995). *Conditions of education in California 1994–95.* Berkeley: Policy Analysis for California Education.

Passow, H. (1990). How it happened, wave by wave. In S.B. Bacharach (Ed.), *Education reform: Making sense of it all* (pp. 10–19). Boston: Allyn & Bacon.

Peterson, P.E. (1976). *School politics, Chicago style.* Chicago: University of Chicago Press.

Pressman, J., & Wildavsky, A. (1973). *Implementation: How great expectations in Washington are dashed in Oakland or, why it's amazing that federal programs work at all, this being a saga by two sympathetic observers who seek to build morals on a foundation of ruined hopes.* Berkeley: University of California Press.

Reich, R. (Ed.). (1988). *The power of public ideas.* Cambridge, MA: Ballinger.

Rosenholtz, S.J. (1989). *Teachers' workplace: The social organization of schools.* White Plains, NY: Longman.

Senge, P.M. (1990). *The fifth discipline: The art and practice of the learning organization.* New York: Doubleday.

Smith, M., & O'Day, J. (1991). Systemic school reform. In S.H. Fuhrman & B. Malen (Eds.), *The politics of curriculum and testing* (pp. 233–267). London: Falmer.

Tittle, D. (1995). *Welcome to Heights High: The crippling politics of restructuring America's public schools.* Columbus: Ohio State University Press.

Tyack, D., & Cuban, L. (1995). *Tinkering toward Utopia: A century of public school reform.* Cambridge, MA: Harvard University Press.

Wilgoren, J., & O'Reilly, R. (1994, April 10). Scoring of school tests found to be inaccurate. *Los Angeles Times*, p. A1.

CHAPTER 24

# Should We Close the Book on School Reform? A Response to Charles Taylor Kerchner

*Timothy V. Rasinski*

n his chapter, Charles Taylor Kerchner cleverly chooses a literary metaphor—rhetoric—"Changing school systems is a bit like putting words on paper." Kerchner uses this rhetorical metaphor to explain three major impediments to systemic and successful school reform. In like manner, I will try to use Kerchner's metaphor to respond to his chapter and suggest possible approaches for overcoming the impediments that he has identified.

## Just Another Optional Assignment

Writing, like many subjects in school, is viewed as an activity that students will engage in only if they know it is required or will show up on an examination. Similarly, Kerchner argues, school personnel and others often recognize that school reform efforts have a short half-life and usually die of a lack of interest and inertia. Changing politics and administrators often leads to changing visions of schools and changing initiatives for school reforms. Like students uninterested in doing more than they have to, school personnel reason that the reform effort will not last long and, therefore, do little to support it. Indeed, the lack of interest and commitment becomes a self-fulfilling prophecy. The school reform effort does die.

Let's take a look at why students choose to take so lightly certain assignments and opportunities for learning. Students quickly learn that they are not going to be held accountable for all assignments. When students learn that a particular fact is not going to be tested or an assignment is not going to be graded, many choose not to invest themselves in the assignment. The assignment has no apparent or intrinsic value for them, and they are not held accountable for the learning.

I see the same thing happen occasionally when I am asked to do a professional development session (usually for secondary teachers) from areas other than English. As soon as the principal leaves the session, the level of interest and participation among some teachers drops precipitously. Often it is marked by the appearance of the sports section of newspapers. These teachers see little relevance in a session on teaching students to read, and the only authority figure who can hold them accountable has removed himself or herself from the room. Unless I get these teachers reinvolved in the session quickly, they are likely to remain distant and may actually undermine the entire session actively or passively.

Perhaps a sense of gamesmanship applies to school reform. Why is it that school personnel and others choose not to invest themselves in a particular reform effort? Borrowing from the school metaphor, then, I would guess that they see the effort as having little value for them, and they recognize that in the long run they will not be held accountable for implementing the reform.

The answer to this dilemma is perhaps twofold. First, teachers and other stakeholders need to be convinced of the value of the school reform effort. They need evidence that it works or has the potential to work, and they need to see that the effort has benefits for them and for their students. In many cases, reform efforts are imposed on teachers with minimal effort to help them understand the rationale for the reform of the evidence to support its implementation.

Second, teachers and stakeholders need to be held accountable for their participation in the effort. Just as students are more likely to invest themselves in a learning activity if they know that it will be part of Friday's test, teachers and others are more likely to become active participants in the process if they realize they will be held accountable according to some standard.

In the recently passed literacy legislation at the national level, No Child Left Behind and Reading First, schools, principals, and teachers will be held accountable for student progress—students will be expected to make "adequate yearly progress" in order for teachers to count their efforts as successful. If they know that their participation in the school reform effort (i.e., the Reading First program) will most likely lead to their success, they will more than likely commit themselves actively to that effort.

Alternatively, a different metaphor may better explain what Kerchner calls an "optional assignment." Perhaps a better phrase to describe this impediment to reform would be "ever-changing assignments." Kerchner describes the situation as one reform following another before the previous reform initiative can even been completed, let alone bear fruit. He observes,

"The rapid turnover among superintendents leads to an equally fast turnover in educational initiatives called 'policy churn' (Hess, 1999). Rapid turnover at the top leaves principals and teachers skeptical about reforms."

When writing instructions and assignments constantly change from one area of focus to another—one day the class works on persuasive essays, the next poetry, and a few days later it is business letters—students may become overwhelmed by the task(s) and choose to opt out of them. At the very least, students may become skeptical of what they are learning and the teacher's ability to teach. Students do not develop a sense of mastery or closure for any of the types of writing studies. Their lack of a sense of accomplishment and closure may cause many students to treat the various assignments in a very superficial manner or not at all.

The answer to this impediment, suggested by the metaphor, should be clear to identify, yet may be challenging to implement. One of the major findings of the writing reform efforts of the 1970s and 1980s was the recognition that writing takes time. Writers develop their writing by working on a piece over a period of days, weeks, and months, not hours. In a similar fashion, then, those responsible for reform efforts must recognize that reform efforts must be given time to develop and flourish. A reform plan must be so clearly detailed and supported by the school administrations that it will survive any one superintendency.

In my quarter century or so in literacy education, I have seen the pendulum swing from prescriptive curricula to back-to-basics, to whole language, and now to our current emphasis on the five essential elements of reading: phonemic awareness, phonics, fluency, vocabulary development, and comprehension (National Institute of Child Health and Human Development, 2000). In April 2003 I received word from colleagues that in a recent budget proposal the Ohio legislature has chosen to remove funding for the state's regional professional development centers (RPDCs). If passed, the RPDCs may, among other things, have to cancel summer literacy institutes they had already planned and advertised for 10,000-plus teachers in the state. California has gone from basal-oriented programs to a literature initiative and then to a strong phonics orientation in less than two decades. Clearly, at the national, state, local, and building levels, we are too quick to move from one reform effort to the next. Teachers and principals equate these efforts with fads and, after being burned in the past, choose not to fully invest themselves in the new ones coming down the pike.

I am unable to detail the mechanics of developing reform plans that will truly be long term. But it seems to me that features such as research-based planning, clarity of the plan and its execution, beginning small and broadening if warranted, progress monitoring, and accountability for those involved are essential to any such reform effort. Moreover, the phrase now often associated with President George W. Bush seems relevant—"stay on message."

## Incomplete Paragraphs

The second obstacle to school reform, according to Kerchner, can be characterized as writing incoherently or writing in incomplete paragraphs. Those of us in literacy education know that one of the toughest tasks to teach students is writing coherent summaries. Too often students create summaries that do not contain important information, contain too much irrelevant information, or are not logically organized.

This lack of logical coherence and consistency apparently is also missing in many school reform efforts. According to Kerchner, "Organizations, and not just public schools, often engage in incomplete cycles of decision making. Decisions to do things are not always followed with actions.... The curriculum swings between recitation and engagement, phonics and whole language." Kerchner notes that this sort of process often results in plenty of action but not much in the way of results.

So let us extend Kerchner's metaphor to ask how teachers solve the problem of students writing incomplete and incoherent paragraphs and essays. Perhaps the first approach is a matter of scale. Rather than initially working with students on overly extensive and complex texts to summarize, teachers will more often choose texts that are short, simple, and transparent in their organization and identification of key points. Students will be asked to work on such texts before moving on to gradually more sophisticated ones.

In a similar manner, then, this solution may suggest that school reform efforts need to begin on a smaller scale and with more clearly defined sets of objectives. Instead of dealing with the state or a school system, perhaps initial reform efforts should be directed at individual schools with a specific goal in mind, say, increasing student performance in reading in the primary grades or increasing parent involvement beyond grade 1. Players within the individual school can handle such readily defined and accomplishable tasks, while others from the school district office or outside agency may study how the school has attained its goal.

From simple goals in small settings, broader goals can be established in larger settings such as school pairs or clusters. The smaller projects become models for ever larger and more complex projects. Just as students eventually are able to summarize succinctly and coherently more complex texts, a gradual increase in complexity and geography in school reform efforts will lead to projects that are logically planned and implemented.

Returning to the writing metaphor, authors of books do not typically write all chapters at the same time, and they do not normally write various elements of a chapter simultaneously. More typically, chapters of a book and segments of a chapter are identified and developed one at a time in a linear fashion. Authors often write from a general plan or outline they have developed in advance.

In a similar vein, school reform efforts need to be very well developed and implemented in their appropriate sequence. Trying to do too much at one time or everything at the same time is simply a recipe for chaos. In one of our local school systems, a new reading program was chosen for implementation. However, it was chosen so late in the school year that the actual materials were not delivered to individual schools until well into the following school year. In another school, the literacy reform effort was aimed at increasing student reading at home. However, the school library had been neglected for years, and most teachers had very small classroom libraries; as a result, students had few materials to take home to read. In both cases, the reform efforts were doomed before they ever began—not because of a lack of enthusiasm and commitment from the teachers, but because of a lack of attention to planning.

## Violating the Grammar Rules

Continuing with his literary metaphor, Kerchner calls his final impediment to school reform "violating the rules of grammar." Grammar rules or conventions were developed to make communication easier. On the one hand, if everyone understands and follows the rules of grammar, spelling, and other mechanical aspects of writing, the communication between writer and reader will be facilitated. On the other hand, too great attention on grammar can hinder writing. Students who are not good spellers or who are not yet strong in some of the surface-level aspects of written composition can often be paralyzed in their writing. Teachers who demand strict adherence to the rules of grammar may cause students to see their ideas as not worth the effort of putting them on paper.

For schools, rules or conventions (i.e., consolidated schools, report cards for parents, traditional summer vacations, students segregated by grades) were developed to make schools run more smoothly and efficiently.

Kerchner argues, however, that many school reform efforts violate the existing grammar rules or conventions about how schools ought to work and are thus doomed to failure by those who insist that the conventions must be followed. He comments,

- "School restructuring reforms nearly always violate the institutional grammar."
- "Variations from the norm are deemed perverse or abnormal because educators and public have come to assume that the grammar embodies the necessary features of a proper school."
- "Efforts at changing governance structures in large urban districts tend to erode over time."

Kerchner similarly notes that curriculum reform efforts that deviate too greatly from convention suffer similar fates.

Although grammar rules, in general, are meant to facilitate language transactions, we must also recognize that they are not immutable—they can be changed. One only needs to look at evolution of the *Style Manual of the American Psychological Association*, now in its fifth edition, to see how conventions for research report writing have changed over time. At one time, for example, research reports were largely written in third-person passive voice. Now, many journal editors encourage authors to write in a more conversational manner—first-person, active voice.

Perhaps one answer, then, to the grammar problem in school reform efforts is to change the style manual. Those responsible for governing education need to provide clear guidance to curriculum reformers about the extent to which grammar rules or conventions may be violated or changed and communicate this message to all stakeholders—parents, teachers, principals, and the general public. Conversely, those responsible for educational governance need to specify and publicize the parameters of educational reform efforts so that educational reformers can indeed develop and implement plans that adhere to the current conventions.

Reading First and No Child Left Behind could be thought of as attempts to develop a new style manual for educational reform in primary-grade literacy education. To that extent, we may wish to applaud these efforts. However, there are fears in the field that that the new grammar rules established by this recent legislation may be enforced with the same degree of attention to conformity as the teacher with a red pen and on the lookout for grammar violations in student essays.

Perhaps what is most needed is a greater understanding in the field about the nature of conventions—that they have a purpose, but that they can be altered. Many of our most renowned authors regularly and purposefully violate grammar rules (e.g., not using uppercase letters when they are normally called for; using run-on sentences in a stream-of-consciousness style). Their work is still accepted and highly regarded. The same sort of toleration for breaking conventions and rules, perhaps, needs to be applied to school reform efforts.

## What's Needed—Old Answers or New Metaphors?

I realize that my so-called answers to the impediments identified by Kerchner may be easy to describe but difficult to implement. It may be, for example, easy to say that a greater tolerance for reform efforts that do not conform to our conventional sense of schools is needed. But achieving a greater level of tolerance among all stakeholders is a complex and perplexing task. Moreover, my responses to Kerchner's impediments may not be the correct answers at all. There may be other, more appropriate and effective responses to be found.

What I find particularly intriguing about Kerchner's chapter is his employment of a metaphor as the focal point for his discussion. Metaphors provide us with tools for creative problem solving (Schon, 1979), for analyzing and synthesizing (Sticht, 1979), and for developing new knowledge and understandings from existing domains of knowledge (Petrie, 1979). Kerchner's use of a writing metaphor to describe impediments to educational reform provided me, a person somewhat familiar with writing and writing instruction, with a novel framework for thinking about educational reform and possible responses to the impediments he describes.

Changing how schools work is a serious problem that has, to a large extent, as noted by Kerchner, resisted our best attempts at reform. Perhaps we need to think outside the box in conceptualizing possible solutions to the problems confronting school reform. Perhaps we need to seek just the right metaphor that sends us in the right direction for making urban schools work best for children and their communities. Have there been other institutions or processes that have experienced success in their efforts to change? Perhaps employing these as the metaphors or models for school reform will lead to the sustained and successful efforts that we seek.

# REFERENCES

Hess, F.M. (1999). *Spinning wheels: The politics of urban school reform.* Washington, DC: Brookings Institution Press.

Petrie, H.G. (1979). Metaphor and learning. In A. Ortony (Ed.), *Metaphor and thought* (pp. 438–461). Cambridge, UK: Cambridge University Press.

Schon, D.A. (1979). Generative metaphor: A perspective on problem-setting in social policy. In A. Ortony (Ed.), *Metaphor and thought* (pp. 254–283). Cambridge, UK: Cambridge University Press.

Sticht, T.G. (1979). Educational uses of metaphor. In A. Ortony (Ed.), *Metaphor and thought* (pp. 486–498). Cambridge, UK: Cambridge University Press.

# CHAPTER 25

# State Policy and Its Impact on Urban Reading Programs

*Virginia Roach*

U.S. founding fathers established the provision of education as a state responsibility. States, in turn, recognized local districts and towns as the primary providers of actual educational services. Although the U.S. system of education is commonly viewed as highly decentralized (Rentner, 1999), states have always maintained a significant role in establishing the foundational policies of the system. This includes policies related to teacher education and licensure, program and graduation requirements, and, of course, education funding. Urban school districts, like all districts in a state, are impacted by state education policies. The "reading wars" of the 1990s, coupled with the increasing role of state education policy throughout that decade, influenced district reading programs. However, the demographic characteristics of urban districts, the often strained relationship between state and urban district officials, and, more recently, the changing nature of state policy as a result of the federal No Child Left Behind (NCLB) Act, place unique demands on urban districts and their reading programs. In this chapter, I first explore the nature of state education policy and state reading policy over the past 15 years. Next, I review the new policy landscape, given the federal NCLB Act and its impact on state reading policy. The relations between many state and urban districts are then discussed, as is the impact of state (and federal) reading policy on urban districts. I conclude with implications for state and district policy in the new federal–state policy milieu.

## State Policy and the Role of State Policymakers

Education is primarily a state responsibility. Although officials in every state are quick to point out their strong culture of "local control," constitutionally, each state has the responsibility for education of its citizenry (National Association of State Boards of Education [NASBE], 1996). This responsibility has been consistently exercised by state policymakers. Although the specific policy roles, processes, and tools have varied somewhat over the years, the primary building blocks of state policy remain remarkably consistent.

The role of education policymakers across the states is viewed with a surprising degree of unanimity. Whether policymakers are legislators, members of a state board of education, governors, members of the judiciary, agency officials or nongovernmental task force members, they are generally viewed as having five major responsibilities (Education Commission of the States, 1991; McDonnell, McLaughlin, & Morison, 1997; National Commission on Governing America's Schools, 1999):

1. Establishing a vision for education in the state through the creation of expectations and standards.

2. Reviewing existing state education policies to ensure alignment and consistency.

3. Debating options for policy adjustment and new policy strategies through engagement with the public as well as public discourse.

4. Making actual policy adjustments and changes—both in terms of the actual policies themselves and the level at which those policies are funded.

5. Monitoring and evaluating the impact of policy decisions through reporting and accountability mechanisms at both the state and local levels.

To carry out these basic functions, state policymakers use a variety of policy tools. These include the formal, commonly referenced tools such as legislation, executive orders, state board of education and agency rules and regulations, agency guidelines, and budget proposals. Enacted laws, rules, regulations, and guidelines generally carry the force of law. Other tools that are used, but not commonly thought of, include education agreements and contracts entered into between two public agencies or a public and private agency, judicial decisions, task force and commission reports, and agency work plans. Contracts and agency agreements, as well as judicial decisions, carry the force of law. However, task force and commission reports can be just as powerful in directing public policy by creating a vision, debating a policy option, setting forth a new strategy, or analyzing the results of a policy course thus far. Such commission reports can often result in changes in law or other formal policy instruments (MacRae & Wilde, 1979; Palumbo, 1994).

How these policy tools are combined and used form the policy processes deployed by a state. Common processes used include mandates, inducements, and reporting and accountability mechanisms. Mandates evoke a compliance response. District, school, or individual officials have either conformed to the mandate, or they have not. The policy literature views mandates with dubious efficacy. Mandates are most successful when the policy goal is clear and unambiguous, and when the object of the mandate has an expectation that noncompliance will result in some sort of negative sanction or penalty (Firestone, 1989). Compliance is typically seen as a minimum standard. Faced with compliance requirements, the regulated often expend the least energy possible to meet that standard. Inducements, however, provide *incentives* for local education officials to conform to a particular type of behavior. Inducements typically come in the form of payments for experimentation and recognition for performance. Inducements are opportunistic in nature and typically do not require a radical departure from current practice or policy because they are, by definition, only applied to a limited pool of the regulated (Firestone, 1989; Palumbo, 1994).

Reporting and accountability mechanisms have increased in use and altered with the standards-based reforms of the late 1980s through the 1990s. Historically, states gathered data on the inputs to the educational process, such as the number of books in school libraries and the square footage allocation per student in a school. Other information gathered and reported included district planning documents and program descriptions that provided evidence that certain programs—either state or federally funded—were serving the target population. These data have been (and are) reported through accreditation processes, program compliance and certification processes, and the school improvement reviews (Roach, Dailey, & Goertz, 1997).

Reporting and accountability mechanisms have been the focus of a great deal of reform language—and some change—over the past decade. States now deploy statewide compilations of school and/or district performance data with which to compare achievement across educational units or across time within the same unit. Many states have these comparisons readily available electronically through a state-sponsored webpage on the Internet. This has elevated the "stakes" of reporting by making the general public much more aware of the actual performance of local schools (Roach et al., 1997). Along with the format, the *content* of what is being reported has changed. Student outcome data—scores on standardized tests in reading, writing, and mathematics—are the most common student outcomes reported across the states (Meyer, Orlofsky, Skinner, & Spicer, 2002), with all states now required to report such data in mathematics and reading as a result of NCLB.

The policy processes discussed thus far are generally seen as top-down (Smith & O'Day, 1993). The watershed report *A Nation at Risk: The Imperative for Educational Reform* (National Commission on Excellence in Education, 1983) spawned greater public attention to education and subsequent wave after wave of educational reform. Initial top-down responses to *A Nation at Risk* were to increase state graduation requirements and the licensure requirements for teachers. Then, in response to the disappointing results of these top-down policies, bottom-up policy reforms were enacted in the 1980s. In the late 1980s and early 1990s, the process of "site-based management," coupled with the availability of waivers to state policies perceived as impeding educational programming at the local level, were used as bottom-up reforms. These bottom-up reforms posited that policy and practice should be defined as closely to the classroom as possible (Consortium for Policy Research in Education, 1996; Fisher, Pumpian, & Roach, 1999).

The reviewed policy processes have not been entirely successful in shaping local education policy and practice. As early as the late 1970s, researchers documented the compromised implementation of mandates (Elmore, 1980; Mann, 1978). Furthermore, inducements have been shown to be both limiting in their impact (Firestone, 1989) and prone to distract schools from their mission and focus (Raber & Roach, 1998). A blunt instrument, state policy has often been seen as setting a minimal standard but not supple enough to guide the complex task of teaching and learning (Manzo, 1998; Wohlstetter & Malloy, 2001). Those district and school officials who had the will and capacity to reform have used the "hook" of state policy to further their own policy goals and interests (Firestone, 1989; Fisher et al., 1999; Fuhrman, Clune, & Elmore, 1988). Newer policy approaches have not been entirely successful, either. Site-based management relies on building- and classroom-level knowledge and expertise and a trust that educators will hold the same interests and goals as families, communities, and the policymakers they elect to represent them. Unfortunately, this is not always the case (Raber & Roach, 1998). Site-based management, in some instances, meant resegregating schools or retrenching from best practices because of the lack of vision and capacity at the school level.

Fifteen years ago, with the advent of standards-based reform, new types of policies were enacted to enhance the likely success of state policy goals, while providing flexibility at the local level. Standards-based reforms provided top-down vision and required local accountability for student outcomes. Local districts, in turn, were given greater flexibility in how to configure programs and curriculum to help students achieve these outcomes

(Raber & Roach, 1998). Contrary to many policy initiatives in the past, this reform was not program-specific but rather spanned programs to encompass the teaching and learning process more generally (Fuhrman et al., 1988). Mandates were rewritten to focus on *outcomes*, not the mandated *processes* of earlier years. Although processes were drafted to be less directive, the responsibility for outcomes was devolved to the local district and building level. Through standards-based reform, state policymakers were asked to review their primary roles and to focus on each: to create a vision for education through the standards for student performance they created; to assure alignment by making reform systemic in nature; to provide greater flexibility in program implementation with the guarantee of greater accountability for student success; and to deploy new policy options such as district takeovers, school reconstitutions, and choice options for students for accountability purposes (Smith & O'Day, 1993).

By setting standards for what students should know and be able to do, standards-based reform ostensibly focuses the whole education enterprise back onto the teaching and learning process. Curriculum content and performance standards place new degrees of importance on what is being taught—and who learns—in schools. It is important to note that standards-based reform also reasserts the role of the state in education policy. Indeed, states "increasingly have flexed their policy muscle" throughout the period (Fuhrman et al., 1988).

Standards-based reform has been the predominant policy paradigm operating across the states since the mid-1990s. By 2001, every state except Iowa had adopted standards in core subject areas. Every state had at least one assessment to measure school or student performance, and all but three states either had or were planning a report card to hold schools accountable for student performance (Meyer et al., 2002).

## State Reading Policy Throughout the 1990s

Understanding the role of state policymakers and the tools and processes they deploy to implement their policies is a critical part of understanding the impact of state policy on reading programs. As noted earlier, one of the key roles of state policymakers is to debate options and make policy adjustments based on those options. Reading has been a chief topic of debate over the past 15 years. At the core of the debate are competing philosophies about the best way to teach reading. Researchers, university experts, and practitioners have lined up on either side of the whole language versus phonics debate. Yet, commentators note, the underlying text to much of this "war" is competing educational philosophies about direct instruction versus constructivist learning—a decidedly older philosophical discussion among educators (Coles, 1998; Nager & Shapiro, 2000; Wohlstetter & Malloy, 2001). The professional debate among reading experts about the relative merits of whole language versus phonics instruction has been visible and political and has used state policymakers as protagonists and pawns on either side of the issue (Coles, 1998; Manzo, 1998; Sandham, 1999).

Unfortunately, the reading wars were professionally debated at the same time state policymakers were becoming more active. Between 1990 and 1998, over 100 legislative bills related to reading were introduced in state houses across the United States, 67 of them between 1996 and 1998 (Manzo, 1998). By 2000, 46 states had some law in place regarding classroom reading instruction. These cluster in four overarching categories: teacher training, intervention efforts, classroom practices, and professional development (Jacobs, 2002).

Protracted policy debates tend to polarize positions (Allison, 1971), and the reading dispute is no exception. Throughout the 1990s, reading bills became more prescriptive, emphasizing specific instructional approaches (St. John et al., 2000). Policy informants persuaded policymakers to support either whole language or phonics rather than taking a policy position based on a review of all the available research. Of the states with reading legislation, 36% have statutes describing specific instructional strategies or methods related to phonics instruction (Jacobs, 2002).

The resultant impact of these policy changes on districts is debatable. On one hand, state funds targeted toward phonics versus whole language instruction has angered local officials who claim that state lawmakers are "trying to control what goes on in the classroom" without taking into consideration the complexity of classroom instruction (Manzo, 1998). On the other hand, researchers have noted "although the ideology about reading changed frequently over the last century, instructional practice and curriculum have been slow to follow" (Wohlstetter & Malloy, 2001). And, in a study comparing state statutes to state scores on the National Assessment of Educational Progress (NAEP), "no significant difference could be found among NAEP scores when compared to categories of state reading statutes" (Jacobs, 2002, p. 62).

At question is the degree of culpability of the state policymakers through the reading wars. "[S]ome reading experts say that lawmakers have been too quick to use the research to promote their own agendas," while other commentators have noted that "[lawmakers] have a tendency to look for simple solutions to very complex problems" (Manzo, 1998, n.p.). Yet, as laypeople, few policymakers come to office holding views related to their fundamental philosophy toward education and conceptions of curriculum. That is left to professional experts to mold through public hearings, task forces, and investigations—the processes that policymakers use to engage the public in discourse and gather data for policy decisions. And, given the tools at their disposal, complex solutions may not be readily available. Allington and Woodside-Jiron (as cited in St. John et al., 2000) contend that the reading research itself "promotes political agendas."

## Recent Developments in State Reading Policy

There have been two significant developments in state reading policy in the past five years. First, educators and policymakers have called a truce in the phonics versus whole language battle. Second, a new federal mandate largely defines the types of reading programs to be supported by federal and, by association, state funds.

After the decade of state reading policy turmoil, a truce was called by policymakers, practitioners, and researchers. In 1998, Department of Education Secretary Richard Riley called for an end to the "reading wars" (Riley, 1998). The Learning First Alliance, National Reading Panel, and other high-visibility groups recommended a middle ground in instructional approaches. The Alliance, for example,

> calls on educators, policy makers, and others to adopt practices that are consistent with available research on how to teach reading effectively. This research calls for explicit, systematic instruction in phonemic awareness and phonics along with early and continued exposure to rich literature and writing opportunities. (Learning First Alliance, 1998, p. 4)

Recent research syntheses "stress two main elements of literacy reform: word identification and comprehension" (Wohlstetter & Malloy, 2001, p. 47). Indeed, a key theme emerging from the regional hearings of the National Reading Panel, convened by the National Institute of Child Health and Human Development (NICHD; 2000), was "the need to develop a clear understanding of how best to integrate different reading approaches to enhance the effectiveness of instruction for all students" (p. 2).

Since the time this truce was put forward, state policymakers have been facing one of the most sweeping legislative reforms imposed on education since the passage of the original Elementary and Secondary Education Act in 1965 (Rentner, 1999). The NCLB Act is fundamentally a federal assessment-based accountability mechanism. According to a U.S.

Department of Education press release, NCLB is based on four key elements: accountability for results, control and flexibility for states and communities, concentrating resources on proven education methods, and choices for parents (Kozberg, 2002).

This law is highly prescriptive with respect to the nature of assessment, accountability, curriculum (through testing), and content (through calibration of state assessments with the National Assessment of Educational Progress). The prescriptive nature of the law casts state policymakers more as brokers between a highly directive federal policy that provides the vision, strategies, and evaluation standards, on the one hand, and the local districts, on the other, that will be evaluated.

Section three of NCLB contains the parameters for the Reading First program. According to Rentner et al. (2003), Reading First "will award $5 billion over the next six years to states and school districts for programs to teach reading using scientifically based methods" (p. 102). Scientifically based methods for purposes of the Reading First program include four main elements related to empirical methodology, data analyses, reliability and validity, and peer review (Rentner et al., 2003).

State officials reported concern over the constraining nature of the scientifically based research requirements. Just as district officials have complained about the prescriptive, political nature of state reading policies over the past decade, state officials are now concerned about the prescriptive and political nature of the federal requirement for scientifically based programs. As noted by Rentner et al. (2003), "Particular controversy has arisen about whether the Administration intends to impose strict phonics-based teaching methods on the schools by approving or denying federal funding through the Reading First program and perhaps others" (p. 113).

As implemented in the states, these philosophical concerns could have a devastating impact on urban reading programs. Although reference to scientifically based research is threaded throughout NCLB, that stipulation is defined differently for the Reading First program than it is for other portions of the NCLB, including Title I programs.

Title I funds are for students who are not achieving at grade level and who are eligible for supplemental services by virtue of their poverty status. Title I programs are primarily found in urban districts, given their high concentration of poor students, and represent a major source of funding for reading programs in those districts. The Reading First definition of scientifically based research applies only to that program and is "less rigorous" than the definition for Title I (Rentner et al., 2003). In a recent survey, state Title I officials reported using the Reading First definition for Title I because it *is* less rigorous or because they have not received specific guidance for a definition of scientifically based research for Title I programs (p. 110). At the local level, districts run the risk of being found out of compliance in their Title I programs if they apply state guidance on scientifically based research based on the Reading First definition. Hence, urban districts could be disproportionately impacted by the state interpretations of the new law.

A survey conducted by the Center on Education Policy on the second year's implementation of NCLB showed that districts are relying heavily on state guidance to determine whether their programs meet the definition of scientifically based (Rentner et al., 2004). Given that state-level respondents perceived the Reading First provisions as strictly enforced, hopefully the margin for noncompliance has been minimized. A protracted application approval process, due to close scrutiny of the state applications, meant that many states did not receive their grants for up to 18 months after the funds were available, with districts just receiving Reading First funding in late 2003.

## Relationship of the State to Urban Districts

Understanding the impact of state reading policy trends on urban reading programs also requires understanding the typical relationship between state and urban policymakers and officials.

Unfortunately, relations between officials at the state level and large, urban districts are typically not as smooth as they are between officials at the state level and suburban districts. There are several reasons for this. First, large, urban districts typically represent problems in the eyes of state policymakers. Although cities represent large concentrations of population, they also represent concentrations of societal ills such as poverty, crime, and unemployment. Although the *rates* of these events may not be any more frequent than in other, less densely populated areas of the state, the absolute numbers of children, families, and incidents may be much greater in urban areas (National Coalition for an Urban Children's Agenda, 1990).

Second, many state education officials do not have experience working in large, urban districts. As a result, their ability to provide technical assistance to these districts may be limited. With no assistance, state interaction may seem punitive and focused on compliance. Large districts may feel like easy targets, making them less willing to take advantage of state inducements. This scenario further feeds into a compliance-monitoring relationship that is generally distrustful from district to state (Fisher et al., 1999).

In many states there is a suburban backlash to the cities, often fueled by racial tensions, creating an "us versus them" mentality (Kozal, 1991). Although large city delegations can be quite powerful in state legislatures (Fisher et al., 1999), the balance of power has shifted in many states to suburban communities. This has resulted in legislative action targeted at big city schools in recent years. Such action has removed school boards (Harrisburg, Pennsylvania), removed superintendents (St. Louis, Missouri), and created state oversight panels (Philadelphia, Pennsylvania), all with the explicit message that the district cannot govern itself.

Finally, historical policy arrangements may actually set up competing policy structures and approaches to issues. For example, in New York State, licensure is expressly a state function. However, the state established that a few urban districts—New York City among them—were allowed to license teachers themselves. This process of district licensure established parallel structures that can be at odds with the state goals.

Large, urban districts may have competing policy goals with the state. Urban districts often create a negative image for state policymakers that is then reinforced by state takeovers and reduced state funding. Even in those instances where there is not hostility from state officials toward an urban district, the capacity of the state officials to provide technical assistance to urban districts may be very limited. For the reasons cited in this section, the relationship between states and large, urban districts has not always been positive.

# Putting It All Together: The Impact of State Policy on Urban Reading Programs

State policymakers have fundamental roles that they fulfill, regardless of the specific "wave" or policy reform in which they are engaged. Furthermore, while state policymakers have become increasingly active over the past two decades, they continue to apply their craft with, essentially, the same set of tools and processes. These tools and processes are necessarily blunt, simple, and relatively inflexible. State policy tools and processes are well suited to political manipulation by researchers, subject matter experts, and ideologues of all stripes. Against this general policy backdrop rests the reading wars and the latest debate about scientifically based research. Added to this mix is the strained relationship between many large, urban districts and state officials. Through this framework it seems inevitable that district policies and programs will collide with state intentions. At the least, this confluence of factors will place unique demands on urban districts.

Research has shown that reading difficulties disproportionately impact urban students (Wohlstetter & Malloy, 2001). This is because the characteristics that are associated with reading difficulty—low socioeconomic status, family poverty, and low income level of the community—are all more prevalent in urban areas. Not surprisingly, urban districts are often the target of reading reform. Furthermore, given their size, they are relatively easy targets for state or federal monitoring efforts. Such was the case with New York City in a 2003 controversy over the districtwide reading curriculum.

As part of the reorganization of the New York City schools, the chancellor, appointed by the mayor, recommended a common core curriculum in reading. No sooner had the choice of reading curriculum been announced than word came from federal officials that the program would probably not pass the scientifically based method requirement of NCLB (Goodnough, 2003b). This immediately pitted the authority of the federal government, as mediated through the New York State Department of Education, against the authority of the mayor, who had gained control over the city schools in 2002 through New York State legislative action (Gewertz, 2002). Just as with the reading wars at the state and federal level, this public action drew supporters to both sides—the mayor versus the federal government. As a result of the criticism of federal and state officials, the mayor eventually supplemented the original proposed program with another program agreeable to state and federal reviewers (Goodnough, 2003a, 2003b).

What are the implications of this? How do policymakers and local officials ensure that the current discussion over NCLB and reading policy produces a better likelihood for student reading success, rather than repeating the failures of the reading wars or past policy approaches states have employed? The primary roles of policymakers prove instructive in providing guidance. State policymakers should consider the following:

*Develop clear, consistent criteria for scientifically based research across all facets of the No Child Left Behind Act.* All districts, but urban districts in particular, are vulnerable to being found out of compliance with NCLB if state officials merely use the definition for scientifically based research delineated in the Reading First portion of the act. Given that urban districts rely so heavily on Title I funds as well as Reading First, Comprehensive School Reform, and the Title II State Program to Improve Teacher Quality funds, accurate guidance is essential from the state. The McKenzie Group (1999) reported that "Title I is both a financial 'lifeboat' and a catalyst for systemic reform, providing districts with much needed financial resources and with incentives for developing standards-based accountability systems" (p. 3). To lose these resources through noncompliance could be devastating to an urban district. State policymakers have a key role in assuring alignment and consistency in guidance across the portions of the Act, even if that alignment is not forthcoming from the federal government.

*Set a vision for state reading policy that is comprehensive and takes into consideration both phonemic awareness and comprehension through the use of rich texts, full of complex meaning.* In addition to the vision, state policy needs to be flexible enough to allow local districts and schools to build their reading programs, based on the school and community context. In a recent study of state-funded, research-based reading reforms in urban districts, St. John et al. (2000) found that "the process of intervening to improve early literacy instruction in urban schools is more complex than is implied in the notion of adopting any single intervention method, or any combination of intervention methods, as the answer" (p. 23). State policymakers should set the vision, but allow local educators to develop the specific program that will meet the needs of their students. As noted by Wohlstetter and Malloy (2001), "effective schools spent large amounts of instructional time on reading. Certainly, it would be important for schools to have the authority to control the amount of instructional time spent on reading" (p. 54).

*Foster communication and trust among the public and levels of government.* One of the key roles of state policymakers is to engage the public in discourse about education. So, too, policymakers must engage educators and local officials in discourse about their work. In the McKenzie Group (1999) study of 13 urban districts, in which 10 were found to have increases in their "highest poverty schools meeting the district or state proficiency standard in either mathematics or reading," local officials reported the need for "collaborative relationships with stakeholders as key to success" (pp. 1, 3).

*Ensure adequate funding.* As stated at the beginning of this chapter, a key role of state policymakers is to assure that policies are adequately funded. Although state officials bristle at the request by urban leaders for more financial support for education, the fact remains that there are more highly concentrated needs in urban districts than in other areas of the state (National Coalition for an Urban Children's Agenda, 1990). Additional funding is required if urban districts are to meet new mandates in reading and implement the types of reading reforms called for in NCLB, the report of the National Reading Panel, and recommendations of other groups. As reported by St. John et al. (2000), there is "strong evidence to support the idea that categorical funding for early reading interventions can improve educational outcomes in urban schools" (p. 27).

*Focus state support on building the professional knowledge and skills of educators to teach reading to every student.* Massell (1998) notes in her study of standards-based reforms that meeting the new challenges of this reform "will take substantial new training and professional development" (p. 2). Furthermore, the McKenzie Group (1999) reported that urban superintendents saw professional development of their teachers as one of the top priorities in improving student achievement. However, professional development needs to be curriculum-specific to render increased school performance and student achievement. States can support teacher professional knowledge and skill development by "involving educators in curriculum, assessment and other policy activities, setting professional development standards, and brokering information for districts, school and teachers" (Massell, 1998, p. 3).

State policymakers have played a vigorous role in delineating urban reading policy in the past 15 years. Ironically, their actions now under the new NCLB federal law may have more significant impact on teacher practice and resource availability than all the legislation passed during the height of the reading wars. State policymakers can support urban reading programs by ensuring policy alignment and consistency; delineating a vision for reading achievement that provides flexibility in classroom instruction; and developing adequate financial support for curriculum, materials, and professional development for teachers.

## REFERENCES

Allison, G. (1971). *Essence of decision: Explaining the Cuban missile crisis.* Boston: Little, Brown.

Coles, G. (1998, November 25). No end to the reading wars. *Education Week.* Retrieved March 10, 2003, from http://www.edweek.org/ew/ew_printstory.cfm?slug=14coles.h18

Consortium for Policy Research in Education. (1996). *Public policy and school reform. A research summary.* Philadelphia: University of Pennsylvania.

Education Commission of the States. (1991). *Exploring policy options to restructure education.* Denver, CO: Author.

Elmore, R. (1980). *Complexity and control: What legislators and administrators can do about implementing public policy.* Washington, DC: U.S. Department of Education.

Firestone, W.A. (1989). Using Reform: Conceptualizing district initiative. *Educational Evaluation and Policy Analysis, 11*(2), 151–164.

Fisher, D., Pumpian, I., & Roach, V. (1999). *California case study on the promotion of large scale change and inclusive practices.* Chicago: Erikson Institute.

Fuhrman, S., Clune, W., & Elmore, R. (1988). Research on education reform. Lessons on the implementation of policy.

*Teachers College Record*, *90*(2), 237–257.

Gewertz, C. (2002, June 19). N.Y.C. mayor gains control over schools. *Education Week*. Retrieved March 12, 2003, from http://www.edweek.org/ew/ew_printstory .cfm?slug=41nyc.h21

Goodnough, A. (2003a, April 5). More intensive reading program is added for struggling pupils [Electronic version]. *The New York Times*. Retrieved September 9, 2004, from http://iamvoyager.com/ news/pr_4_5_03.jsp

Goodnough, A. (2003b, February 26). Schools chancellor stands by his choice of reading program. *The New York Times*, p. B2.

Jacobs, L.C. (2002). Legislating literacy: An analysis of state statutes affecting reading instruction in United States public schools. *Dissertation Abstracts International*, *63*(5), 1769A.

Kozal, J. (1991). *Savage inequalities: Children in America's schools*. New York: Crown Press.

Kozberg, L. (2002, January 8). *Paige joins President Bush for signing of historic No Child Left Behind Act of 2001* [Press release]. Retrieved September 5, 2004, from http://www.ed.gov/news/press releases/2002/01/01082002.html

Learning First Alliance. (1998). *Every child reading: An action plan of the Learning First Alliance*. Washington, DC: Author.

MacRae, D., & Wilde, J. (1979). *Policy analysis for public decisions*. North Scituate, MA: Duxbury Press.

Mann, D. (Ed.). (1978). *Making change happen?* New York: Teachers College Press.

Manzo, K.K. (1998, April 29). More states moving to make phonics the law. *Education Week*. Retrieved March 10, 2003, from http://www.edweek.org/ew/ ew_printstory.cfm?slug=33read.h17

Massell, D. (1998). *State strategies for building local capacity: Addressing the needs of standards-based reform* (CPRE Policy Briefs). Philadelphia: Consortium for Policy Research in Education.

McDonnell, L.M., McLaughlin, M.J., & Morison, P. (Eds.). (1997). *Educating one and all: Students with disabilities and*

*standards-based reform*. Washington, DC: National Academy Press.

McKenzie Group. (1999). *Student achievement and reform trends in 13 urban districts*. Washington, DC: Author.

Meyer, L., Orlofsky, G.F., Skinner, R.A., & Spicer, S. (2002). The state of the state. *Education Week*, *21*, 17.

Nager, N., & Shapiro, E.K. (Eds.). (2000). *Revisiting a progressive pedagogy: The developmental-interaction approach*. Albany: State University of New York Press.

National Association of State Boards of Education (NASBE). (1996). *A motion to reconsider: Education governance at a crossroads* (Report of the NASBE Study Group on Education Governance). Alexandria, VA: Author.

National Coalition for an Urban Children's Agenda. (1990). *Implementing the children's agenda*. Alexandria, VA: National Association of State Boards of Education.

National Commission on Excellence in Education. (1983). *A nation at risk: The imperative for educational reform*. Washington, DC: U.S. Department of Education.

National Commission on Governing America's Schools. (1999). *Governing America's schools: Changing the rules*. Denver, CO: Education Commission of the States.

National Institute of Child Health and Human Development. (2000). *Report of the national reading panel. Teaching children to read: An evidence-based assessment of the scientific research literature on reading and its implications for reading instruction* (NIH Publication No. 00-4769). Washington, DC: U.S. Government Printing Office.

Palumbo, D. (1994). *Public policy in America: Government in action* (2nd ed.). Fort Worth, TX: Harcourt.

Raber, S., & Roach, V. (1998). *The push and pull of standards-based reform: How does it affect local school districts and students with disabilities?* Alexandria, VA: National Association of State Boards of Education.

Rentner, D.S. (1999). *A brief history of the federal role in education.* Washington, DC: Center on Education Policy.

Rentner, D.S., Chudowsky, N., Fagan, T., Gayler, K., Hamilton, M., Jennings, J., et al. (2003). *From the capital to the classroom: State and federal efforts to implement the No Child Left Behind Act.* Washington, DC: Center on Education Policy.

Rentner, D.S., Kober, N., Chudowsky, N., Fagan, T., Hamilton, M., Joftus, S., et al. (2004). *From the capital to the classroom: Year 2 of the No Child Left Behind Act.* Washington, DC: Center on Education Policy.

Riley, R.W. (1998, September 18). Remarks as prepared for delivery by U.S. Secretary of Education Richard W. Riley. Retrieved September 5, 2004, from http://www.ed.gov/inits/readingsummit/readsum.html

Roach, V., Dailey, D., & Goertz, M. (1997). *State accountability systems and students with disabilities.* Alexandria, VA: National Association of State Boards of Education.

Sandham, J.L. (1999, May 26). Partisan politics lend new twist to state debates. *Education Week.* Retrieved March 10, 2003, from http://www.edweek.org/ew/ew_printstory.cfm?slug=39legis.h18

Smith, M., & O'Day, J. (1993). Systemic reform and educational opportunity. In S. Fuhrman (Ed.), *Designing coherent policy. Improving the system* (pp. 250–312). San Francisco: Jossey-Bass.

St. John, E.P., Manset, G., Chung, C., Simmons, A.B, Musoba, G.D., Manoil, K., et al. (2000). *Research-based reading reforms. The impact of state-funded interventions on educational outcomes in urban elementary schools.* Bloomington: Indiana Education Policy Center, Indiana University.

Wohlstetter, P.A., & Malloy, C.L. (2001). Organizing for literacy achievement: Using school governance to improve classroom practice. *Education and Urban Society, 34*(1), 42–65.

# CHAPTER 26

# Delivering Strong Urban Reading Programs in the Current Policy Environment: Reinvent, Circumvent, or Just Plain Vent? A Response to Virginia Roach

*Cathy M. Roller*

Virginia Roach's chapter provides an analysis and history of the influences of state policies on reading programs that is quite helpful. It details the policy tools and processes that state policymakers have available to them and also highlights the changing role of state policymakers in the current political environment so heavily influenced by the No Child Left Behind (NCLB) Act of 2001. There are two aspects of the chapter that I will focus on. First is the conclusion: "A blunt instrument, state policy has often been seen as setting a minimal standard and not supple enough to guide the complex task of teaching and learning." Second are the challenges related to scientifically based reading research and scientifically based research as defined in NCLB. After responding to these issues, I will report on actions the International Reading Association (IRA) has taken in relation to Reading First and suggest some options for urban educators.

## Working With Blunt Instruments

As Roach notes, if education policies, particularly those related to reading instruction, are to accomplish their goals, they must in the end change what happens in classrooms. However, traditional policy processes have not been entirely successful in shaping local education policy and particularly local practices. She notes that there are research data showing that the implementation of mandates is often compromised, that inducements are both limiting and prone to distract schools from their mission and focus, and that accountability and reporting mechanisms often have failed to impact classroom instruction and children's achievement. The analogy of state policy processes to blunt instruments is an apt one.

What would it take to sharpen our tools? A much more extensive knowledge of how teachers deliver instruction and adapt it to individual students during ongoing instruction, and a much better understanding of the relationship of policy goals to that ongoing instruction, are needed. Perhaps one of the most threatening aspects of Reading First is that its developers had a very extensive knowledge of how teachers deliver instruction, and the goal of their policy was closely related to that understanding. The goal was sharply conceived, and the technology exists, in particular commercial products, to achieve the policy goal. For example, consider the definition of the essential components of reading in Reading First and its implied goal of improving early reading instruction by using explicit and systematic instruction.

> Essential Components of Reading Instruction
>
> (3) Essential Components of Reading Instruction: The term "essential components of reading instruction" means explicit and systematic instruction in—
>
> (A) phonemic awareness;
>
> (B) phonics;
>
> (C) vocabulary development;
>
> (D) reading fluency, including oral reading skills; and
>
> (E) reading comprehension strategies.

The call for explicit and systematic instruction has been interpreted by many as *direct instruction*. Commercial products using direct instruction technology certainly meet the definition in the law, and the influence of the University of Oregon's website on the implementation of Reading First confirms that the policy goal—that is, to improve reading achievement by using explicit and systematic instruction—can be directly linked to direct instruction at University of Oregon. The fact that explicit and systematic instruction is not restricted to direct instruction, and that there are other commercial products and district-developed curricula that are explicit and systematic without relying on direct instruction formats, seems often to be lost in the hysteria surrounding Reading First. The issue here is that the policy tool developed by the U.S. federal government, NCLB and Reading First, is much sharper than we have experienced in the recent past, and many state officials feel as if they are being cut.

The advantage of direct instruction in this policy environment is that it has a very complete vision of classroom instruction that is focused specifically on ongoing instruction in the classroom, and it has the technology through commercial and nonprofit sources to deliver it. The careful scripts known as "teaching procedures" appear to leave little to the teacher's discretion, and the materials easily meet the requirements of the law. Much of the controversy surrounding the Reading First implementation is a reaction to the apparently sharp edges of the tools built into the law.

However, NCLB in no way requires the use of direct instruction practices. The language of the law is "explicit and systematic." Good instruction is always systematic and sometimes explicit—particularly explicit when students are failing to learn the strategies and content of the curriculum. The task is to demonstrate that particular materials, practices, and teaching procedures are systematic and also to demonstrate how they are explicit. Although the Reading First tool is sharp, it lacks the specificity to cut if educators know how to position materials and teaching practices as explicit and systematic.

# Based on Scientifically Based Reading Instruction

A second thorny issue posed by Reading First is scientifically based reading research (SBRR) and scientifically based research (SBR). The law requires recipients to use practices supported by SBRR in the case of Reading First, and SBR in the case of the remainder of the NCLB. The requirements have caused great consternation among implementers. What is it? How can I recognize it? How do I know if something is supported by it? In the case of Reading First, the Department of Education's answer has been to refer to the National Reading Panel report (National Institute of Child Health and Human Development, 2000), indicating that instructional practices identified in the report as being supported by scientifically based reading research are acceptable for the implementation of Reading First. However, the report simply does not address many crucial elements of reading instruction, and although the use of the report has provided some definition, considerable confusion still remains.

One reason for the confusion is that NCLB includes two definitions of related research. The first is SBRR in the Reading First section of the act:

> (6) Scientifically Based Reading Research—The term "scientifically based reading research" means research that—

(A) applies rigorous, systematic, and objective procedures to obtain valid knowledge relevant to reading development, reading instruction, and reading difficulties; and

(B) includes research that—

(i) employs systematic, empirical methods that draw on observation or experiment;

(ii) involves rigorous data analyses that are adequate to test the stated hypotheses and justify the general conclusions drawn;

(iii) relies on measurements or observational methods that provide valid data across evaluators and observers and across multiple measurements and observations; and

(iv) has been accepted by a peer-reviewed journal or approved by a panel of independent experts through a comparably rigorous, objective, and scientific review. (No Child Left Behind Act of 2001, Sec. 1208)

## The second, SBR, which applies to the remainder of the act is

(37) Scientifically Based Research—The term "scientifically based research"—

(A) means research that involves the application of rigorous, systematic, and objective procedures to obtain reliable and valid knowledge relevant to education activities and programs; and

(B) includes research that—

(i) employs systematic, empirical methods that draw on observation or experiment;

(ii) involves rigorous data analyses that are adequate to test the stated hypotheses and justify the general conclusions drawn;

(iii) relies on measurements or observational methods that provide reliable and valid data across evaluators and observers, across multiple measurements and observations, and across studies by the same or different investigators;

(iv) is evaluated using experimental or quasi-experimental designs in which individuals, entities, programs, or activities are assigned to different conditions and with appropriate controls to evaluate the effects of the condition of interest, with a preference for random-assignment experiments, or other designs to the extent that those designs contain within-condition or across-condition controls;

(v) ensures that experimental studies are presented in sufficient detail and clarity to allow for replication or, at a minimum, offer the opportunity to build systematically on their findings; and

(vi) has been accepted by a peer-reviewed journal or approved by a panel of independent experts through a comparably rigorous, objective, and scientific review. (No Child Left Behind Act of 2001, Sec. 9101)

Note that while both definitions agree, scientifically based research "(i) employs systematic, empirical methods that draw on observation or experiment;" the fourth roman numeral in the second definition specifically includes research that is evaluated by experimental and quasi-experimental designs. Most lay readers are confused by the two definitions, and some think that SBR is restricted to experimental and quasi-experimental research. Clearly this is not the case because the first numeral in each of the definitions includes research that draws from either observation or experiment. These two definitions are very blunt instruments indeed, and they leave much room for ambiguity. Hence the consistent calls from the states for clarification of the meaning of SBR and SBRR. The intent of the law, to encourage research-based practices, is relatively clear. The implementation of the law with respect to scientifically based research is opaque. Many states are worried about compliance and frustrated about what is acceptable and unacceptable for the use of Reading First and Title I funds.

## What Is the International Reading Association Doing?

Given the lack of clarity in the law, IRA has taken several actions. First, we have prepared a summary of the National Reading Panel report (IRA, 2000) that enumerates key findings and refers the reader to the page of the full report where those findings are discussed. It is essential that participants in Reading First activities know the content of the report because it is frequently misinterpreted and on occasion purposely misinterpreted. Second, we have developed a position statement to provide clarification about evidence-based reading instruction, *What Is Evidence-Based Reading Instruction? A Position Statement of the International Reading Association* (2002b). Third, we have published a book, *Evidence-Based Reading Instruction: Putting the National Reading Panel Report Into Practice* (2002a), which is a collection of articles from *The Reading Teacher* and *Reading Research Quarterly* organized around the five essential components outlined in the report: phonemic awareness, phonics, fluency, vocabulary, and comprehension. The book is useful because it translates the abstract language of the NRP report into concrete practices that are consistent with the findings of the report. Fourth, we have trained a national cadre of professional developers to deliver workshops related to Reading First. (For more information about these trainers and the workshops, write to kbaughman@reading.org.)

Another IRA book, *What Research Has to Say About Reading Instruction*, Third Edition (Farstrup & Samuels, 2002), includes a chapter by Timothy Shanahan (2002) that is helpful in thinking about the issues of evidence-based reading instruction. He suggests that we use three terms to refer to research support for instructional practices: *research-related*, *research-based*, and *research-proven*. Programs including the five essential components from Reading First would qualify as research-related because they incorporate practices identified through the research of others. Research-based programs, such Anne Marie Palincsar's reciprocal teaching or Pressley's transactional strategies, would qualify as research-based because they were developed by conducting a program of research. Research-proven would mean that the particular program has been tested and proven effective with students similar to the students with which the program will be used. To my knowledge, there are still no programs that meet this level of evidence. Although the intent of NCLB—to encourage use of materials and instructional practices based on scientifically based research—is laudatory, the intent is way ahead of the existing capacity in the field, and we will continue to sort through the voluminous research studies to make reasoned professional judgments about what practices are supported by research.

## So What Do Urban Districts Do About Reading Instruction?

Although Reading First is a somewhat sharper policy tool than urban educators have encountered in the past, the cutting edge is still blunt. That means there are ambiguities in the law. I would argue that any stakeholder has at least one of three choices when confronting any policy: They can vent, they can circumvent, or they can reinvent. All three of these choices are viable and appropriate for a variety of stakeholders in a variety of situations.

*Venting.* Particularly in the cases where policy exacerbates difficulties and causes major disruptions, venting is appropriate, and most stakeholders do vent at one time or another. However, venting as described here is more than just blowing off steam. It is strong and aggressive opposition to proposed policies. In general, vociferous opposition does not accomplish a lot because it does not propose specific changes and alternative policies. The basic message is "this is bad—get rid of it." Venting is important because it is sometimes the only option available for those who disagree with policymakers. It is particularly suited to individuals and small homogenous groups of stakeholders who clearly share the opinion that nothing in the policy is good, and it must be eliminated. It is also a crucial option for a democracy because it gives voice to groups who often do not have access to power. It also helps policymakers gauge the range of existing views and opinions. Urban school districts may occasionally be in a position where venting is the only available option, and they generally can get access to the press and media for a hearing in the public eye.

*Circumventing.* Urban school districts, however, are more likely to be in the position of circumventing. At one point in her chapter, Roach notes, "Those district and school officials who had the will and capacity to reform have used the 'hook' of state policy to further their own policy goals and interests." In a sense she is suggesting that some urban educators are skilled at circumventing. They are capable of looking at the strengths, weaknesses, and ambiguities of the law and implementation and creating instruction that will achieve the goal of improved reading performance—a goal that is shared by Reading First. Urban districts can offer good, effective instruction within the framework of Reading First, and I would argue that urban districts need to do everything they can to make sure that whatever is implemented in the Reading First initiative is excellent reading instruction. In the case of Reading First, this means understanding exactly what is in the law, understanding how that intersects with each district's own policy goals and interests, and interpreting any ambiguities in ways that advance the goal of reducing the achievement gap. The resources developed by IRA are aimed at those who are struggling to implement Reading First well.

*Reinventing.* Reinventing requires more knowledge resources and energy, but it means developing alternative policy agendas that are more consistent with goals and interests of the urban district. This role requires resources and a significant power base. It is more likely to be undertaken by coalitions and associations of like-minded stakeholders. Until IRA and other interested stakeholders get out in front and develop strong policy initiatives that lead to improved instruction, higher reading achievement, and a closing of the achievement gap, we will constantly be in the position of reacting to ambiguous policy initiatives instead of proposing and championing them.

## REFERENCES

Farstrup, A.E., & Samuels, S.J. (2002). *What research has to say about reading instruction* (3rd ed.). Newark, DE: International Reading Association.

International Reading Association. (2000). *International Reading Association's summary of the (U.S.) National Reading Panel report "Teaching children to read."* Retrieved April 2, 2003, from www.reading.org/advocacy/nrp/chapter2.html

International Reading Association. (2002a). *Evidence-based reading instruction:*

*Putting the National Reading Panel report into practice.* Newark, DE: Author.

International Reading Association. (2002b). *What is evidence-based reading instruction? A position statement of the International Reading Association.* Newark, DE: Author.

National Institute of Child Health and Human Development. (2000). *Report of the National Reading Panel. Teaching children to read: An evidence-based assessment of the scientific research literature on reading and its implications for reading instruction* (NIH Publication No. 00-4769). Washington, DC: U.S. Government Printing Office.

No Child Left Behind Act of 2001, Pub. L. No. 107–110, 115 Stat. 1425 (2002). Retrieved October 12, 2004, from http://thomas.loc.gov

Shanahan, T. (2002). What reading research says: The promises and limitations of applying research to reading education. In A.E. Farstrup & S.J. Samuels (Eds.), *What research has to say about reading instruction* (3rd ed., pp. 8–24). Newark, DE: International Reading Association.

# Author Index

# Subject Index

Note: Page numbers followed by *f* indicate figures; those followed by *t* indicate tables.

## A

AAE. *See* African American English
AART. *See* African American Rhetorical Tradition
AAVE. *See* African American Vernacular English
ACCOUNTABILITY: and effects of poverty, 11-13, 30-31; No Child Left Behind Act on, 419, 432-433; recommendations for, 32; and school reform, 418-419; state policies on, 428
ACHIEVEMENT: of adolescents, family involvement and, 118-120; assumptions about, 364, 364*f*; in high-poverty schools, 362-397; indicators and feedback loops for, 408-409, 409*f*; 90/90/90 schools and, 365-366; poverty and, 3-34. *See also* gap
ACTION RESEARCH: in 90/90/90 schools, 375-376
ADAMS, HAL, 102-103
ADDAMS, JANE, 54
ADD (ATTENTION-DEFICIT DISORDER), 40
ADI. *See* assessment, diagnosis, and instruction
ADOLESCENCE: term, 195
ADOLESCENT LITERACY: as construct, 203-204; term, 194
ADOLESCENTS: family involvement and, 118-120; literacy instruction and, 187-204
ADVANCED READING DEVELOPMENT DEMONSTRATION PROJECT (ARDDP), 391-392
AFRICAN AMERICAN ENGLISH (AAE), 242, 244-245, 251
AFRICAN AMERICAN RHETORICAL TRADITION (AART), 260
AFRICAN AMERICAN STUDENTS: national versus urban, 4*f*-5*f*; overrepresentation in special education, 321; performance of, 7*f*; placement for learning disabilities, 320*t*; school violence and, 70; testing policies and, 12; and violence, 72-73
AFRICAN AMERICAN VERNACULAR ENGLISH (AAVE), 153, 192, 242-246, 251-263, 265; dialectal readers in, 183; teacher

background knowledge on, 181-182; and writing, 277-279
AFTER-SCHOOL PROGRAMS: and effects of poverty, 17-18
AMERICAN ASSOCIATION OF SUICIDOLOGY, 79
AMERICAN BAR ASSOCIATION COMMISSION ON DOMESTIC VIOLENCE, 75
AMERICAN FEDERATION OF TEACHERS, 402
ARDDP. *See* Advanced Reading Development Demonstration Project
ARGUMENTATIVE DISCUSSION, 193
ASIAN STUDENTS: placement for learning disabilities, 320*t*
ASSESSMENT: 90/90/90 schools and, 366-369, 377-378. *See also* testing policies
ASSESSMENT, DIAGNOSIS, AND INSTRUCTION (ADI), 166-169
ASTHMA, 37-38
ATTENTION-DEFICIT DISORDER (ADD), 40
AUTHORS IN TRAINING, 135

## B

BACKGROUND KNOWLEDGE: for teachers, 181-182
BANNEKER, BENJAMIN, 231
BARBARA BUSH FOUNDATION FOR FAMILY LITERACY, 66
BEAR (BE EXCITED ABOUT READING), 137
BEHAVIORAL DISORDERS, 39-40
BELIEFS: of teachers, and professional development, 215-216
BIDIALECTICALISM: and literacy, 241-287; teacher preparation on, 279-281; and writing, 277-279
BLOCKERS, 63
BOOK CLUBS: for professional development, 212
BOOKS TO GO, 136-137
BOOK SWAP, 134-135
BOOK TALKS, 137
BOOSTERS, 63
BREAKFAST PROGRAMS, 39
BRIDGE PROGRAM, 252-253
BRIDGES TO LITERACY, 134